Inside Windows® Debugging

Tarik Soulami

Published with the authorization of Microsoft Corporation by:
O'Reilly Media, Inc.
1005 Gravenstein Highway North
Sebastopol, California 95472

ISBN: 978-0-7356-6278-0

1 2 3 4 5 6 7 8 9 LSI 6 5 4 3 2 1

Printed and bound in the United States of America.

Microsoft Press books are available through booksellers and distributors worldwide. If you need support related to this book, email Microsoft Press Book Support at mspinput@microsoft.com. Please tell us what you think of this book at http://www.microsoft.com/learning/booksurvey.

Acquisitions Editor: Russell Jones
Developmental Editor: Russell Jones
Production Editor: Melanie Yarbrough
Editorial Production: Waypoint Press
Technical Reviewer: John Mueller
Copyeditor: Roger LeBlanc
Indexer: Christina Yeager
Cover Design: Twist Creative • Seattle
Cover Composition: Karen Montgomery
Illustrator: Steve Sagman

Contents at a Glance

Contents

PART III OBSERVING AND ANALYZING SOFTWARE BEHAVIOR

Chapter 13 Common Tracing Scenarios 457

Chapter 14 WinDbg User-Mode Debugging Quick Start 505

Foreword

Like many others, I am a firm believer in using tools to expand our understanding of how systems really work. In fact, I began my career as a performance tools developer. My boss at that time had many simple sayings; among them was one of my favorites, "Our team is only as good as our people and our people are only as good as our tools." As a manager, I've made it a priority to ensure we dedicate many of our top engineers to tools development and I have always encouraged using tools to teach and grow engineers.

Teaching books such as Tarik's are meant to help improve the productivity, understanding, and confidence of others. Being an individual who has had both a lifelong passion for tools and learning, as well as someone who has spent more than a decade and a half working in Windows, it is an honor and a pleasure for me to write the foreword to Tarik's insightful book.

For decades, the Windows team has worked tirelessly to improve the core capabilities of the platform and to make it more suitable for increasingly diverse hardware configurations and software stacks. This hard work has paid off; Windows today is the preeminent platform for developers, consumers, and businesses across the globe. With more than 1 billion PCs and customers, Windows is both the market-leading server and client computing platform. Variants of Windows run on small form-factor mobile devices, within embedded intelligent systems, on uniform and non-uniform (NUMA) memory architectures, on the XBOX gaming console, and on single CPU systems as well as those with hundreds of processors. Windows runs in clustered configurations with failover capabilities and sits atop hypervisors and Virtual Machines. And of course, Windows is in the cloud.

Enormous platform success and diversity can be accompanied by an equally enormous and diverse set of technical challenges. Thousands of engineers at Microsoft, and tens to hundreds of thousands outside of Microsoft, are involved in building, debugging, and troubleshooting a multitude of diverse configurations and solutions. To understand issues in a vastly diverse problem space, foundational tools, techniques, and concepts are essential.

To that end, Tarik has done an excellent job in detailing how a set of key foundational Windows tools work. In detailing these tools, Tarik succeeds in expanding the reader's awareness of key operating system concepts, architectures, strengths, and limitations. With the concepts understood and the tools mastered, readers can expect to be able to tackle all types of performance and debugging challenges. I believe Tarik's book will become a staple for a broad set of individuals, from novices to experts.

Michael Fortin, Ph.D.
Distinguished Engineer, Windows Fundamentals
Microsoft Corporation

Introduction

One exciting aspect of software programming is that there are usually many ways to accomplish the same goal. Unfortunately, this also presents software engineers with unique challenges when trying to make the best design or implementation choice for each situation. Experience plays a major role, and the learning process is often progressive as one learns to avoid past mistakes. Sadly, though, experience is often a variable concept. I have met several software engineers who, after spending a very long time working on an area, still lacked a basic understanding of how it *really* worked beyond the repetitive day-to-day tasks they grew accustomed to. I have also met others who have perfected their craft in a field after only a few years of working experience.

This book introduces a few techniques for methodically approaching software development problems primarily using the two "Swiss Army knives" of expert Microsoft Windows developers—namely, the Windows debuggers (WinDbg) and the Windows Performance Toolkit (Xperf). By focusing on *why* features and components work the way they do in the system rather than simply on *how* they work or *what* they do, this book tries to accelerate the process of learning by experience and to minimize the number of mistakes made when approaching new problems. An important part of the process is learning to compare and contrast with known solutions to existing ones.

Software engineering is still inherently a practical science. (Some might even argue it's an art rather than a science.) While there is certainly no substitute for real experience, the topic can definitely be approached with the same methodical persistence that works so well for other scientific disciplines. In fact, this approach works even better in software engineering because all behaviors can be explained rationally. After all, it is all just code—whether it's your own code or code written by others that you end up consuming in your software—and code can always be traced and understood.

Although this book deals with several architectural pillars of the Windows operating system as part of its debugging and tracing experiments, my main goal in writing it is less about covering those details and more about encouraging and developing this critical mindset. I hope to demonstrate how this approach can be used for solving a few interesting problems as part of this book, and that you continue to systematically apply debugging and tracing as you expand your learning beyond the topics directly covered here.

This book is not really about teaching native or managed code programming, either, although you'll find several good coding examples in the companion source code. Because it takes an inside-out look at how to explore the system using debugging and tracing tools, this book will probably appeal more to software engineers with the desire to understand system internals rather than those with a need to quickly learn how to make use of a specific technology. However, I believe the approach and mindset it aspires to inculcate are applicable regardless of the technology or level of expertise. In fact, contrary to what many think, the higher the level of technology involved, the harder it becomes to grasp what goes on behind the scenes and the more expertise is needed in order to investigate failures when things inevitably go awry and require debugging skills to save the day. In pure C, for example, a call to *malloc* is just that: a function call. In C++, a call to the *new* keyword is emitted by the compiler as a call to the *new* operator function to allocate memory for the object, followed by code to construct the object (again, emitted by the compiler to possibly initialize a virtual pointer and invoke the constructors of the base classes, construct member data objects, and finally invoke the user-provided constructor code for the target leaf class). In C# (.NET), things get even more involved, because a one-line call to the *new* keyword might involve compiling new code at runtime, performing security checks by the .NET execution engine, loading the modules where the target type is defined, tracking the object reference for later garbage collection, and so on.

Who Should Read This Book

This book is aimed at software engineers who desire to take their game to the next level, so to speak, and perfect their mastery of Windows as a development platform through the use of debugging and tracing tools.

Assumptions

Readers should have basic familiarity with the C/C++ and C# programming languages. A basic knowledge of the Win32 and .NET platforms is helpful, but not strictly required, because this book makes every effort to introduce basic concepts before expanding into more advanced topics.

Organization of This Book

This book is divided into three parts:

- Part 1, "A Bit of Background," provides a brief overview of Windows development frameworks and the layers in the operating system that support them. This basic knowledge is important to have when trying to make sense of the data surfaced by debugging and tracing tools.

- Part 2, "Debugging for Fun and Profit," covers the architectural foundations of debuggers in the Windows operating system. It also presents a number of extensible strategies that will help you make the most of the Windows debuggers. In addition, this part also shows how to use the WinDbg debugger to better understand system internals by analyzing the important interactions between your code and the operating system.
- Part 3, "Observing and Analyzing Software Behavior," continues this theme. It presents the Event Tracing for Windows (ETW) technology and illustrates how to leverage it in debugging and profiling investigations.
- Finally, you'll find two short appendices at the end of the book that recap the most common debugging tasks and how to accomplish them using WinDbg.

The table of contents will help you locate chapters and sections quickly. In addition, each chapter starts with a list of the main points covered in the chapter, and concludes with a summary section. You can also download the source code for all the experiments and examples shown throughout the book.

Conventions in This Book

This book presents information using conventions (listed in the following table) designed to make the information readable and easy to follow:

Convention	Meaning
Sidebars	Boxed sidebars feature additional bits of information that might be helpful for a given subject.
Notes	Notes provide useful observations related to the content discussed in the main text.
Inline Code	Inline code—that is, code that appears within a paragraph—is shown in *italic* font.
Code Blocks	Code blocks are shown in a different font to help you distinguish code from text easily. Important statements appear in bold font to help you focus on those aspects of the code.
Debugger Listings	Debugger listings are shown in a different font, and important commands are bolded to highlight them. The listings are also often prefixed with the output from the standard *vertarget* debugger command, which displays the OS version and CPU architecture where the experiment was conducted.
Function Names	Function names are sometimes referenced using their WinDbg symbolic names. For example, *kernel32!CreateFileW* refers to the CreateFileW Win32 API ("W" for the Unicode flavor) exported by the *kernel32.dll* module.

System Requirements

You will need the following hardware and software to follow the experiments and code samples in this book:

- **Operating System** Windows Vista or later. Windows 7 (or Windows Server 2008 R2) is highly recommended.
- **Hardware** Any computer that supports the Windows 7 operating system (OS) requirements. Except for the live kernel debugging experiments, a second computer to serve as a host kernel-mode debugger machine is typically required for kernel debugging.

Note The target and host don't really need to be separate physical machines. A common kernel debugging configuration—detailed in Chapter 2, "Getting Started"—is to run the target machine where you conduct the experiments as a Windows 7 virtual OS on a Windows Server 2008 R2 physical host computer, and run the kernel debugger in the host OS.

- **Hard disk** 1 GB of free hard-disk space to download and save the Windows Software Development Kit (SDK) and Driver Development Kit (DDK) ISO images. 40 MB of free hard-disk space to download and compile the companion source code. An additional 3 GB is required for installing Microsoft Visual Studio 2010.
- **Software** The following tools are used in the debugging and tracing examples shown throughout this book:
  - Version 7.1 of the Windows 7 SDK, which can be downloaded from the Microsoft Download Center at *http://www.microsoft.com/download/en/details.aspx?id=8442*. Both the Windows Debuggers (WinDbg) and Windows Performance Toolkit (Xperf) are part of this SDK.
  - The Application Verifier tool, which can also be downloaded from the Microsoft Download Center at *http://www.microsoft.com/download/en/details.aspx?id=20028*.
  - The System Internals suite of developer tools, which can be downloaded from *http://technet.microsoft.com/en-us/sysinternals/bb842062*.
  - Visual Studio 2010, any edition (excluding the free, stripped-down Express edition). The Visual Studio Ultimate edition is preferred because some advanced features, such as static code analysis and performance profil-

ing, are not supported in other editions. The 90-day, free trial version of Visual Studio offered by Microsoft, which can be downloaded at *http://www.microsoft.com/download/en/details.aspx?id=12187*, should suffice.

- The Windows 7 Driver Development Kit (DDK) is used to compile the companion source code and can also be downloaded from the Microsoft Download Center at *http://www.microsoft.com/download/en/details.aspx?id=11800*.

Code Samples

Most of the chapters in this book include experiments and examples that let you interactively try out new material introduced in the main text. The programs used in these experiments can be downloaded from the following page:

http://go.microsoft.com/FWLink/?Linkid=245713

Follow the instructions to download the Inside_Windows_Debugging_Samples.zip file.

Installing the Code Samples

Follow these steps to install the code samples on your computer so that you can use them with the experiments and examples provided in this book:

1. Unzip the Inside_Windows_Debugging_Samples.zip file that you downloaded from the book's website into a folder named *Book*\Code.

Warning Do not use directory names with spaces in the path hierarchy that you choose to download the samples to. The DDK build environment, which will be described shortly in the "Compiling the Code Samples" section, will fail to compile the source code if you do. It is recommended that you use *\Book\Code* as the root of the source code because this is the assumed location used when referencing the programs in the main text. The samples in the companion source code are organized by chapter, so there should be a folder for every chapter under this root path location.

2. If prompted, review the displayed end user license agreement. If you accept the terms, select the accept option, and then click Next.

Running the Code Samples

The code samples are organized by chapter and are referenced in the book main text by their respective directory path locations to help you find them easily.

Local Administrator rights are required by some sample programs. In Windows Vista and later, a command prompt must be launched as elevated in order to have full administrative privileges even when the user account is a member of the local built-in Administrators security group. To do so in Windows 7, for example, you need to right-click the Command Prompt menu item in the Windows Start menu, and select Run As Administrator, as shown in the following screen shot:

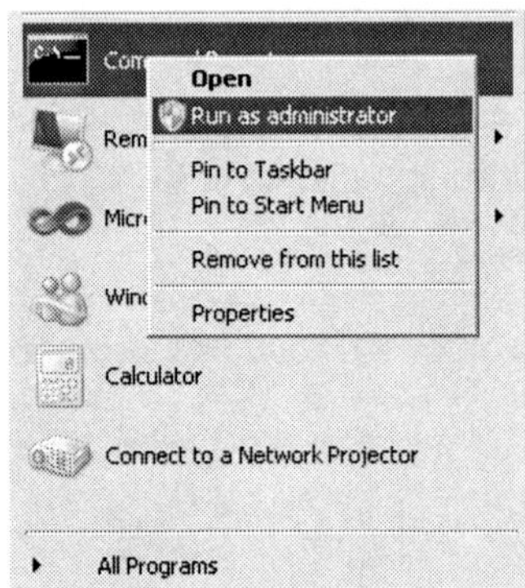

Compiling the Code Samples

The supporting programs used in the experiments presented in the book main text fall into three categories:

- **C++ samples** The binaries for these programs are deliberately omitted from the downloadable ZIP file. When you compile these code samples locally, WinDbg locates their symbols and source code files automatically. So the experiments presented in the early chapters of this book will "just work" in this configuration, without needing to specify the source and symbol locations explicitly in WinDbg. The steps to compile all the native C++ code samples at once are included later in this section.

- **C# (.NET) samples** For convenience, the compiled .NET programs are included in the downloadable ZIP file. You can use them as-is and you won't lose much, given WinDbg doesn't support source-level .NET debugging, but you can also follow the instructions included in the following section to recompile them if you prefer.

- **JavaScript and Visual Basic samples** These scripts are interpreted by the corresponding scripting engines and do not require compilation.

Compiling the .NET Code Samples

Compiling the .NET code samples from the companion source code requires version 4.0 of the Microsoft .NET Framework or later. Though this version isn't installed by default on Windows 7, .NET Framework 4.0 gets installed by many other dependent programs, such as Visual Studio 2010. You can also download and install a standalone version from the Microsoft download center at *http://www.microsoft.com/download/en/details.aspx?id=17851*.

Each C# code sample from the companion source code will have a helper compilation script under the same directory. This script uses the .NET 4.0 C# compiler directly and is easy to invoke, as illustrated in the following command:

```
C:\book\code\chapter_04\LoadException>compile.bat
```

If this script fails to find the C# compiler, you should verify that you've installed .NET 4.0 in the default directory location where this script expects it to exist. If .NET 4.0 exists but was installed to a different location on your system, you need to modify the script and provide that path instead.

Compiling the C/C++ Code Samples

You can compile the C/C++ code samples from the companion source code using the Windows 7 Driver Development Kit (DDK) build tools. The following steps detail this process. I strongly recommend that you complete these steps before you start reading, because you'll need the code samples to follow the experiments shown later in this book.

1. Download the Windows 7 DDK ISO image from the Microsoft Download Center at *http://www.microsoft.com/download/en/details.aspx?id=11800*, and save it to your local hard drive. Set plenty of time aside for this download if you have a slow Internet connection; the DDK ISO file is over 600 MB in size.

2. After the download is complete, mount the saved ISO file into a drive letter. There are several free tools for mounting ISO images on Windows. Virtual Clone Drive, which you can find on the Internet, is good freeware that works well both on Windows Vista and Windows 7. With that freeware installed, you should be able to right-click the ISO file and mount it, as shown in the following screen shot:

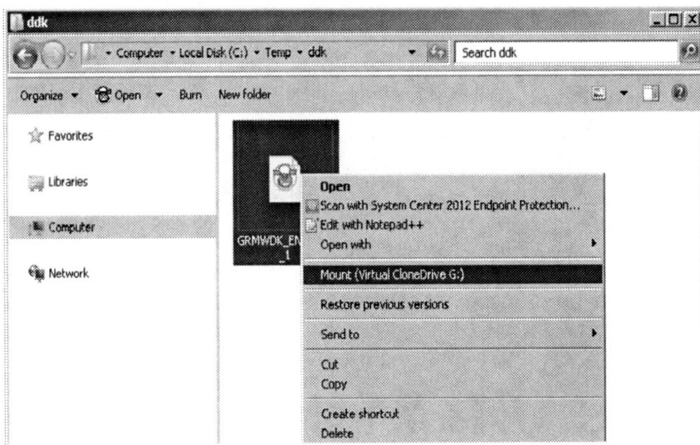

3. Double-click the newly mounted drive to kick off the DDK setup program, as shown here:

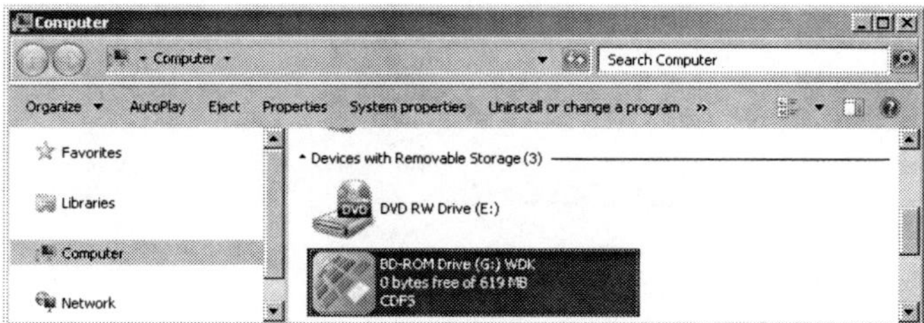

4. Select the Full Development Environment components from the DDK.

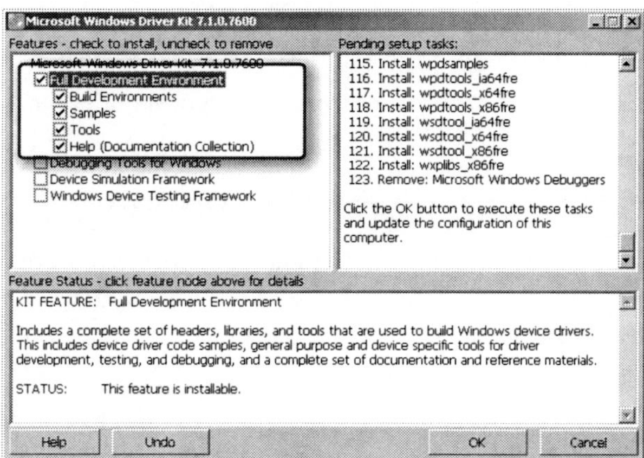

5. Then Install the components to the C:\DDK\7600.16835.1 directory, as shown in the following screen shot. This step will take several minutes to complete.

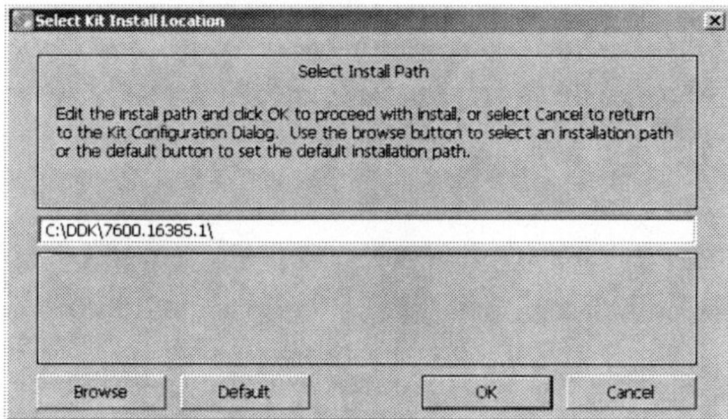

6. You can now unmount the DDK drive by right-clicking the mounted drive letter and selecting the Unmount menu action. This concludes this one-time installation of the Windows DDK build tools.

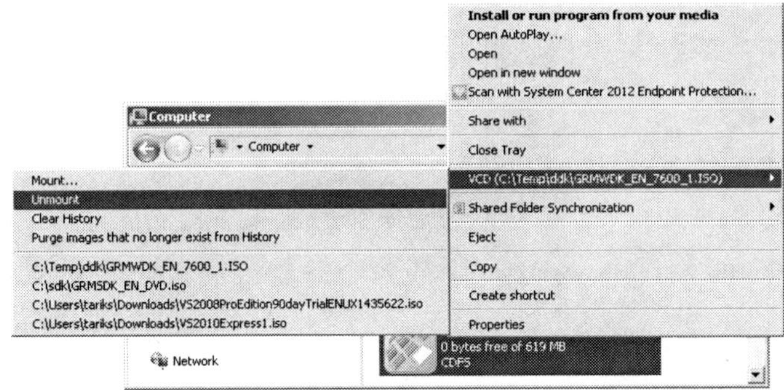

7. To build *x86* binaries, first start a command prompt window and type the following command:

```
C:\DDK\7600.16385.1>bin\setenv.bat c:\DDK\7600.16385.1
```

8. You can then build all the native code samples at once. Simply navigate to the root directory that you extracted the companion source code to and issue the following command. It should take only a minute or so to build all the C/C++ code from the companion source code:

```
C:\book\code>bcz
```

Acknowledgments

I am indebted to Vance Morrison for reviewing my rough drafts. Vance has been a role model for me since I joined Microsoft, and his critical insight was tremendously helpful in improving the quality of my writing. I only hope that I came close to his high standards.

I'd also like to thank Silviu Calinoiu and Shawn Farkas for their detailed review of my draft chapters. Their attention to detail and precise feedback was tremendously helpful.

Kalin Toshev provided valuable technical feedback during the formative stages of this book, and his unwavering dedication to test-driven software development really inspired me to write this book. This book owes a lot to him.

Ajay Bhave, Cristian Levcovici, and Rico Mariani provided several ideas for improving the material covered in this book. This book certainly wouldn't be the same without their help and guidance.

Special thanks to Michael Fortin for writing the foreword, and to all my colleagues in the Windows fundamentals team for their support during the writing of this book.

Finally, I have to acknowledge my family, who play an important part in my life. I would like to dedicate this book to my parents for providing me with the opportunity to reach for my dreams and always being there when I needed them. Your love and support mean the world to me.

Errata & Book Support

We've made every effort to ensure the accuracy of this book and its companion content. Any errors that have been reported since this book was published are listed on our Microsoft Press site at oreilly.com:

http://go.microsoft.com/FWLink/?Linkid=245712

If you find an error that is not already listed, you can report it to us through the same page.

If you need additional support, email Microsoft Press Book Support at *mspinput@microsoft.com.*

Please note that product support for Microsoft software is not offered through the addresses above.

We Want to Hear from You

At Microsoft Press, your satisfaction is our top priority, and your feedback our most valuable asset. Please tell us what you think of this book at:

http://www.microsoft.com/learning/booksurvey

The survey is short, and we read every one of your comments and ideas. Thanks in advance for your input!

Stay in Touch

Let's keep the conversation going! We're on Twitter: *http://twitter.com/MicrosoftPress*

PART 1

A Bit of Background

One of my esteemed mentors at Microsoft once told me the following story. He came back home one night to be greeted by a dismayed look on his wife's face. Her cherished wedding ring had just vanished down the bathroom sink drain and she was completely stumped. For all she knew, the wedding ring might very well have been in the ocean by the time they were having that conversation. To her, anything beyond the drain plug was a black box. My mentor, using the slight advantage of plumbing knowledge he had over his wife, knew about those nifty structures called "sink traps," which are usually J-shaped pipes located just beneath the sink. These are intended to "trap" a little bit of water and prevent sewer gas from flowing out of the drain pipes into the living space. But in addition, the traps also conveniently capture objects and keep them from going down the drain immediately. As it turned out, the ring was indeed in the sink trap, and he was able to retrieve it relatively easily.

The reason my mentor told me this story was to illustrate a close parallel in the world of software engineering: If you treat the APIs and frameworks you use in your code as pure black boxes, you might be able to get by for a little while, but you are certainly bound to experience some pretty anxious moments when you need to investigate failures that fall just outside of your own code, even if the solution—just like in the lost ring analogy—is right under your nose.

The first part of this book explores how your programs interact with the Microsoft Windows operating system (in a loose sense) and demonstrates why it's useful to have at least a cursory understanding of both those interactions and of the role of each subsystem. It also examines some important development frameworks shipped by Microsoft, and analyzes their positions relative to each other and to the operating system (OS) developer interfaces. It then concludes by introducing the Windows Software Development Kit (SDK) tools and, more specifically, the Swiss Army knives of expert Windows developers—namely, the Windows debugger (WinDbg) and the Windows Performance Toolkit (Xperf). This knowledge will serve as a perfect segue to the rest of the book, where you'll use debugging and tracing to write better software for the Windows operating system.

CHAPTER 1

Software Development in Windows

In this chapter

Windows Evolution

Though this book focuses primarily on the post-Vista era of Windows, it's useful to look back at the history of Windows releases, because the roots of several building blocks of the underlying architecture can be traced all the way back to the Windows NT (an abbreviation for "New Technology") operating system. Windows NT was first designed and developed by Microsoft in the late '80s, and continued to evolve until its kernel finally became the core of all client and server versions of the Windows operating system.

Windows Release History

Windows XP marked a major milestone in the history of Windows releases by providing a unified code base for both the business (server) and consumer (client) releases of Windows. Though Windows XP was a client release (its server variant was Windows Server 2003), it technically succeeded both Windows 95/98/ME (a lineage of consumer operating systems that find their roots in the MS-DOS and Windows 3.1 operating systems) and Windows NT 4/Windows 2000, combining for the first time the power of the Windows NT operating system kernel and its robust architecture with many of the features that had made Windows 95 and Windows 98 instant hits with consumers and developers alike (friendly user design, aesthetic graphical interface, plug and play model, rich Win32 and DirectX API sets, and so on).

Though both the server and client releases of Windows now share the same kernel, they still differ in many of their features and components. (For example, only the server releases of Windows support multiple concurrent remote desktop user sessions.) Since the release of Windows XP in 2001, Windows Server has followed a release cycle that can be loosely mapped to corresponding Windows client releases. Windows Server 2003, for instance, shares many of the new kernel and API features that were added in Windows XP. Similarly, Windows Server 2008 R2 represents the server variant of Windows 7, which was released in late 2009. (Don't confuse this with Windows Server 2008, which is the server variant of Windows Vista.)

Figure 1-1 illustrates the evolution of the Windows family of operating systems, with their approximate release dates relative to each other.

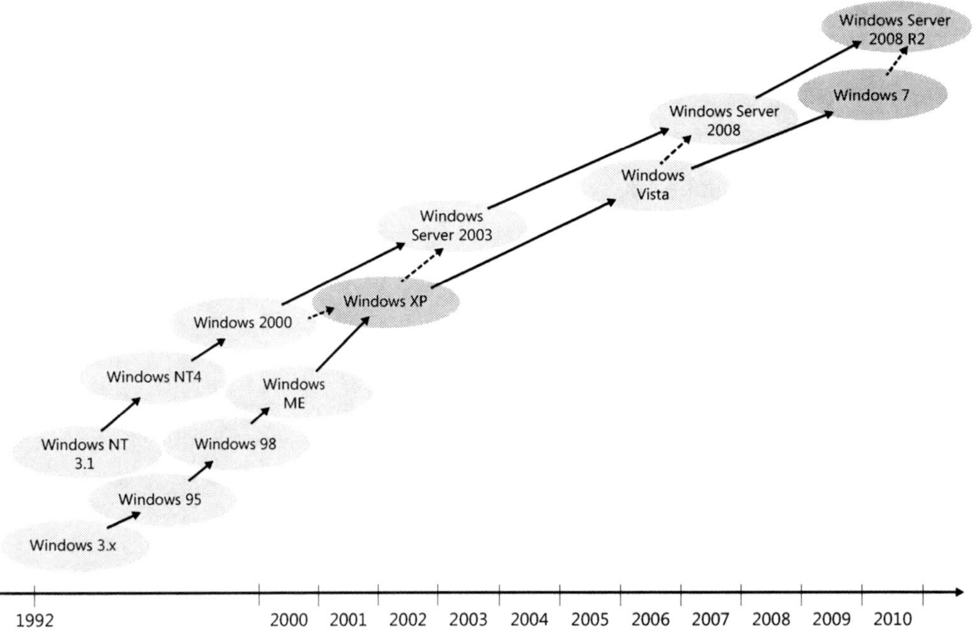

FIGURE 1-1 Timeline of major client and server releases of the Windows operating system since the early 90s.

Supported CPU Architectures

Windows was ported to many CPU architectures in the past. For example, Windows NT supported Alpha and MIPS processors until Windows NT 4. Windows NT 3.51 also had support for Power PC (another RISC family of processors that is used in many embedded devices, including, for example, Microsoft Xbox 360). However, Windows later narrowed its support to three CPU architectures: *x86* (a 32-bit family of processors, whose instruction set was designed by Intel), *x64* (also known as AMD-64, in reference to the fact this architecture was first introduced by AMD, though Intel also now releases processors implementing this instruction set), and *ia64* (another 64-bit instruction set designed by Intel in collaboration with Hewlett-Packard).

Microsoft shipped the first *ia64* version of Windows XP in late 2001 and followed it with an *x64* version in 2005. Microsoft later dropped support for *ia64* on client editions, including Windows XP. The *x86*, *x64*, and *ia64* architectures supported in Windows Server 2003 and Windows XP are exactly those that were also supported when Windows Server 2008 R2 and Windows 7 shipped at the end of 2009, though *x86* and *x64* are clearly the more widely used Windows architectures nowadays. Note, however, that Windows Server no longer supports *x86*; it now supports only 64-bit architectures. Also, Microsoft announced early in 2011 that its upcoming release of the Windows operating system will be capable of running on *ARM* (in addition to the *x86* and *x64* platforms), a RISC instruction set that's widely used in embedded utilities, smartphones, and tablet (slate) devices thanks in large part to its efficient use of battery power.

Understanding the underlying CPU architecture of the Windows installation you are working on is very important during debugging and tracing because you often need to use native tools that correspond to your CPU architecture. In addition, sometimes you will also need to understand the disassembly of the code you are analyzing in the debugger, which is different for each CPU. This is one reason many debugger listings in this book also show the underlying CPU architecture that they were captured on so that you can easily conduct any further disassembly inspection you decide to do on the right target platform. In the following listing, for example, the *vertarget* command shows a Windows 7 AMD64 (*x64*) operating system. You'll see more about this command and others in the next chapter, so don't worry about how to issue it for now.

```
lkd> $ Multi-processor (2 processors or cores) Windows 7 x64 system
lkd> vertarget
Windows 7 Kernel Version 7600 MP (2 procs) Free x64
Built by: 7600.16385.amd64fre.win7_rtm.090713-1255
```

Given the widespread use of *x86* and *x64*, and because you can also execute *x86* programs on *x64* machines, the majority of experiments in this book are conducted using the *x86* architecture so that you can follow them the way they're described in this book regardless of your target architecture. Though *x86* has been the constant platform of choice for Windows since its early days in the '80s, 64-bit processors continue to gain in popularity even among home computers and laptops, which now often carry *x64* versions of Windows 7.

Windows Build Flavors

The *vertarget* debugger command output shown in the previous section referred to the Windows version on the target machine as a "free" (also known as *retail*) build. This flavor is the only one ever shipped to end users by Microsoft for any of the supported processor architectures. There is, however, another flavor called a "checked" (also known as *debug*) build, which MSDN subscribers can obtain from Microsoft if they want to test the software they build with this flavor of the Windows operating system. It's important to realize that checked flavors are mostly meant to help driver developers; they don't derive their name at all from being "tested"—or otherwise "checked"—more thoroughly than the free flavors.

If you recall, the Introduction of this book recommended using the Driver Development Kit (DDK) build environment if you wanted to recompile the companion C++ sample code. As was explained then, you can also specify the build flavor you want to target (the default being *x86* free in the Windows 7 DDK) when starting a DDK build environment. This is, in fact, also how the checked flavor of Windows is built internally at Microsoft because the same build environment made available in the DDK is also used by Windows developers to compile the Windows source code. For example, the following command starts a DDK build environment where your source code is compiled into *x64* binaries using the checked (*chk*) build flavor. This essentially turns off a few compiler optimizations and defines debug build macros (such as the DBG preprocessor variable) that turn on "debug" sections of the code, including assertions (such as the NT_ASSERT macro).

```
C:\DDK\7600.16385.1>bin\setenv.bat c:\DDK\7600.16385.1 chk x64
```

Naturally, you don't really need a checked build of Windows to run your checked binaries, and the main difference between your "free" and "checked" binaries is that the assertions you put in your code will occur only in the "checked" flavor. The benefit of the checked flavor of Windows itself is that it also contains many additional assertions in the system code that can point out implementation problems in your code, which is usually useful if you are developing a driver. The drawback to that Windows flavor, of course, is that it runs much slower than the free flavor and also that you must run it with a kernel debugger attached at all times so that you can ignore assertions when they're hit; otherwise, those assertions might go unhandled and cause the machine to crash and reboot if they are raised in code that runs in kernel mode.

Windows Servicing Terminology

Each major Windows release is usually preceded by a few public milestones that provide customers with a preview of the features included in that release. Those prerelease milestones are usually called *Alpha*, *Beta1*, *Beta2*, and *RC* or release candidate, in this chronological order, though several Windows releases have either skipped some of these milestones or named them differently. These prerelease milestones also present an opportunity for Microsoft to engage with customers and collect their feedback before Windows is officially "released to manufacturing," a milestone referred to as *RTM*.

You will again recognize the major version of Windows in the build information displayed by the *vertarget* command that accompanies many of the debugger listings presented in this book. For example, the following listing shows that the target machine is running Windows 7 RTM and that July 13, 2009 (identified by the "090713" substring in the following output) is the date this particular Windows build was produced at Microsoft.

```
lkd> vertarget
Windows 7 Kernel Version 7600 MP (2 procs) Free x64
Built by: 7600.16385.amd64fre.win7_rtm.090713-1255
```

In addition to the major client and server releases for each Windows operating system, Microsoft also ships several servicing updates in between those releases that get automatically delivered via the Windows Update pipeline and usually come in one of the following forms:

- **Service packs** These releases usually occur a few years apart after RTM and compile the smaller updates made in between (and, on occasion, new features requested by customers) into a single package that can be applied at once by both consumers and businesses. They are often referred to using the "SP" abbreviation, followed by the service pack number. For example, SP1 is the first service pack after RTM, SP2 is the second, and so on.

  Service packs are considered major releases and are subjected to the same rigorous release process that accompanies RTM releases. In fact, many Windows service packs also have one or more release candidate (RC) milestones before they're officially released to the public. The number of service packs for a major Windows release is often determined by customer demand and also the amount of changes accumulated since the last service pack. Windows NT4, for example, had six service packs, while Windows Vista had three.

- **GDR updates** GDR (General Distribution Release) updates are issued to address bugs with broad impact or security implications. The frequency varies by need, but these updates are usually released every few weeks. These fixes are also rolled up into the following service pack release.

  For example, the following output indicates that the target debugging machine is running a version of Windows 7 SP1. Notice also that the version of *kernel32.dll* that's installed on this machine comes from a GDR update subsequent to the initial Windows 7 SP1 release.

  ```
  0:000> vertarget
  Windows 7 Version 7601 (Service Pack 1) MP (2 procs) Free x86 compatible
  kernel32.dll version: 6.1.7601.17651 (win7sp1_gdr.110715-1504)
  ```

Windows Architecture

The fundamental design of the Windows operating system, with an executive that runs in kernel mode and a complementary set of user-mode system support processes (*smss.exe*, *csrss.exe*, *winlogon.exe*, and so on) to help manage additional system facilities, has for the most part remained unchanged since the inception of the Windows NT operating system back in the late '80s. Each new version of Windows naturally brings about a number of new components and APIs, but understanding how they fit in the architectural stack often starts with knowing how they interact with these core components of the operating system.

Kernel Mode vs. User Mode

Kernel mode is an execution mode in the processor that grants access to all system memory (including user-mode memory) and unrestricted use of all CPU instructions. This CPU mode is what enables the Windows operating system to prevent *user-mode* applications from causing system instability by accessing protected memory or I/O ports.

Application software usually runs in user mode and is allowed to execute code in kernel mode only via a controlled mechanism called a *system call.* When the application wants to call a system service exposed by code in the OS that runs in kernel mode, it issues a special CPU instruction to switch the calling thread to kernel mode. When the service call completes its execution in kernel mode, the operating system switches the thread context back to user mode, and the calling application is able to continue its execution in user mode.

Third-party vendors can get their code to run directly in kernel mode by implementing and installing signed *drivers*. Note that Windows is a monolithic system in the sense that the OS kernel and drivers share the same address space, so any code executing in kernel mode gets the same unrestricted access to memory and hardware that the core of the Windows operating system would have. In fact, several parts of the operating system (the NT file system, the TCP/IP networking stack, and so on) are also implemented as drivers rather than being provided by the kernel binary itself.

The Windows operating system uses the following layering structure for its kernel-mode operations:

- **Kernel** Implements core low-level OS services such as thread scheduling, multiprocessor synchronization, and interrupt/exception dispatching. The kernel also contains a set of routines that are used by the executive to expose higher-level semantics to user-mode applications.
- **Executive** Also hosted by the same "kernel" module in Windows (NTOSKRNL), and performs base services such as process/thread management and I/O dispatching. The executive exposes documented functions that can be called from kernel-mode components (such as drivers). It also exposes functions that are callable from user mode, known as *system services*. The typical entry point to these executive system services in user mode is the *ntdll.dll* module. (This is the module that has the system call CPU instruction!) During these system service calls, the executive allows user-mode processes to reference the objects (process, thread, event, and so on) it implements via indirect abstractions called object *handles,* which the executive keeps track of using a per-process handle table.
- **Hardware Abstraction Layer** The HAL (*hal.dll*) is a loadable kernel-mode module that isolates the kernel, executive, and drivers from hardware-specific differences. This layer sits at the very bottom of kernel layers and handles key hardware differences so that higher-level components (such as third-party device drivers) can be written in a platform-agnostic way.
- **Windows and Graphics Subsystem** The Win32 UI and graphics services are implemented by an extension to the kernel (*win32k.sys* module) and expose system services for UI applications. The typical entry point to these services in user mode is the *user32.dll* module.

Figure 1-2 illustrates this high-level architecture.

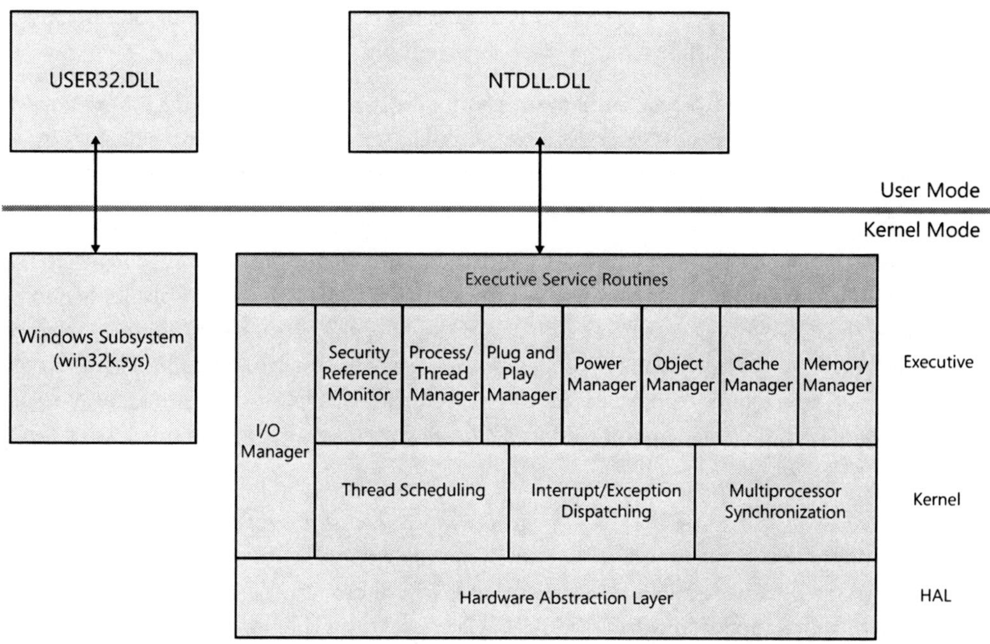

FIGURE 1-2 Kernel-mode layers and services in the Windows operating system.

User-Mode System Processes

Several core facilities (logon, logoff, user authentication, and so on) of the Windows operating system are primarily implemented in user mode rather than in kernel mode. A fixed set of user-mode system processes exists to complement the OS functionality exposed from kernel mode. Here are a few important processes that fall in this category:

- ***Smss.exe*** User sessions in Windows represent resource and security boundaries and offer a virtualized view of the keyboard, mouse, and physical display to support concurrent user logons on the same OS. The state that backs these sessions is tracked in a kernel-mode virtual memory space usually referred to as the *session space*. In user mode, the session manager subsystem process (*smss.exe*) is used to start and manage these user sessions.

  A "leader" *smss.exe* instance that's not associated with any sessions gets created as part of the Windows boot process. This leader *smss.exe* creates a transient copy of itself for each new session, which then starts the *winlogon.exe* and *csrss.exe* instances corresponding to that user session. Although having the leader session manager use copies of itself to initialize new sessions doesn't provide any practical advantages on client systems, having multiple *smss.exe* copies running concurrently can provide faster logon of multiple users on Windows Server systems acting as Terminal Servers.

- ***Winlogon.exe*** The Windows logon process is responsible for managing user logon and logoff. In particular, this process starts the logon UI process that displays the logon screen when the user presses the Ctrl+Alt+Del keyboard combination and also creates the processes responsible for displaying the familiar Windows desktop after the user is authenticated. Each session has its own instance of the *winlogon.exe* process.

- ***Csrss.exe*** The client/server runtime subsystem process is responsible for the user-mode portion of the Win32 subsystem (*win32k.sys* being the kernel-mode portion) and also was used to host the UI message loop of console applications prior to Windows 7. Each user session has its own instance of this process.

- ***Lsass.exe*** The local security authority subsystem process is used by *winlogon.exe* to authenticate user accounts during the logon sequence. After successful authentication, LSASS generates a security access token object representing the user's security rights, which are then used to create the new explorer process for the user session. New child processes created from that shell then inherit their access tokens from the initial explorer process security token. There is only one single instance of this process, which runs in the noninteractive session (known as session 0).

- ***Services.exe*** This system process is called the *NT service control manager* (SCM for short) and runs in session 0 (noninteractive session). It's responsible for starting a special category of user-mode processes called *Windows services*. These processes are generally used by the OS or third-party applications to carry out background tasks that do not require user interaction. Examples of Windows services include the spooler print service (*spooler*); the task scheduler service (*schedule*); the COM activation services, also known as the COM SCM (*RpcSs* and *DComLaunch*); and the Windows time service (*w32time*).

  These processes can choose to run with the highest level of user-mode privileges in Windows (*LocalSystem* account), so they are often used to perform privileged tasks on behalf of user-mode applications. Also, because these special processes are always started and stopped by the SCM process, they can be started on demand and are guaranteed to have at most one active instance running at any time.

All of the aforementioned system-support processes run under the *LocalSystem* account, which is the highest privileged account in Windows. Processes that run with this special account identity are said to be a part of the trusted computing base (TCB) because once user code is able to run with that level of privilege, it is also able to bypass any checks by the security subsystem in the OS.

User-Mode Application Processes

Every user-mode process (except for the leader *smss.exe* process mentioned earlier) is associated with a user session. These user-mode processes are boundaries for a memory address space. As far as scheduling in Windows is concerned, however, the most fundamental scheduling units remain the threads of execution and processes are merely containers for those threads. It's also important to realize that user-mode processes (more specifically, the threads they host) also often run plenty of code in kernel mode. Although your application code might indeed run in user mode, it's often the case that it also calls into system services (through API layers that call down to NTDLL or USER32 for the system call transitions) that end up transitioning to kernel mode on your behalf. This is why it makes sense to always think of your software (whether it's user-mode software or kernel drivers) as an extension of the Windows operating system and also that you understand how it interacts with the "services" provided by the OS.

Processes, in turn, can be placed in containers called *job objects*. These executive objects can be very useful to manage a group of processes as a single unit. Unlike threads and processes, job objects are often overlooked when studying the Windows architecture despite their unique advantages and the useful semantics they provide. Figure 1-3 illustrates the relationship between these fundamental objects.

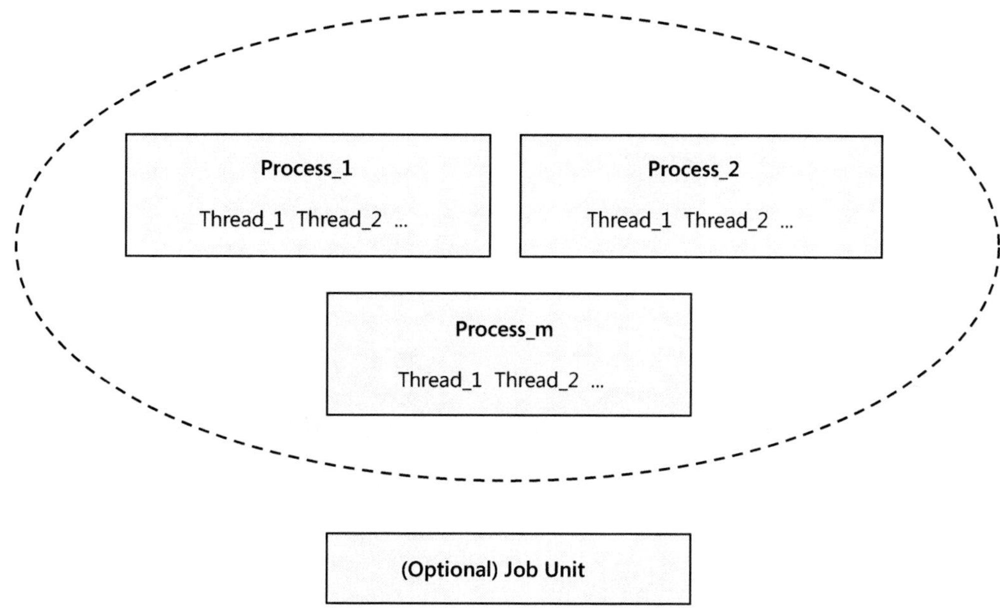

FIGURE 1-3 Threads, processes, and jobs in Windows.

Job objects can be used to provide common execution settings for a set of processes and, among other things, to control the resources used by member processes (such as the amount of memory consumed by the job and the processors used for its execution) or their UI capabilities.

One particularly useful feature of job objects is that they can be configured to terminate their processes when their user-mode job handle is closed (either using an explicit *kernel32!CloseHandle* API call, or implicitly when the kernel runs down the handles in the process handle table when the process kernel object is destroyed). To provide a practical illustration, the following C++ program shows how to take advantage of the job-object construct exposed by the Windows executive in a C++ user-mode application to start a child ("worker") process and synchronize its lifetime with that of its parent process. This is often useful in the case of worker processes whose sole purpose is to serve requests in the context of their parent process, in which case it becomes critical not to "leak" those worker instances should the parent process die unexpectedly. (The reverse is more straightforward because the parent process can easily monitor when the child dies by simply waiting on the worker process handle to become signaled using the *kernel32!WaitForSingleObject* Win32 API.)

To follow this experiment, remember to refer back to the Introduction of this book, which contains step-by-step instructions for how to build the companion source code.

```
//
// C:\book\code\chapter_01\WorkerProcess>main.cpp
//
class CMainApp
{
public:
    static
    HRESULT
    MainHR()
    {
        HANDLE hProcess, hPrimaryThread;
        CHandle shProcess, shPrimaryThread;
        CHandle shWorkerJob;
        DWORD dwExitCode;
        JOBOBJECT_EXTENDED_LIMIT_INFORMATION exLimitInfo = {0};
        CStringW shCommandLine = L"notepad.exe";

        ChkProlog();

        //
        // Create the job object, set its processes to terminate on
        // handle close (similar to an explicit call to TerminateJobObject),
        // and then add the current process to the job.
        //
        shWorkerJob.Attach(CreateJobObject(NULL, NULL));
        ChkWin32(shWorkerJob);

        exLimitInfo.BasicLimitInformation.LimitFlags =
            JOB_OBJECT_LIMIT_KILL_ON_JOB_CLOSE;
        ChkWin32(SetInformationJobObject(
            shWorkerJob,
            JobObjectExtendedLimitInformation,
            &exLimitInfo,
            sizeof(exLimitInfo)));

        ChkWin32(AssignProcessToJobObject(
            shWorkerJob,
            ::GetCurrentProcess()));

        //
        // Now launch the new child process (job membership is inherited by default)
        //
        wprintf(L"Launching child process (notepad.exe) ...\n");
        ChkHr(LaunchProcess(
            shCommandLine.GetBuffer(),
            0,
            &hProcess,
            &hPrimaryThread));
```

```
            shProcess.Attach(hProcess);
            shPrimaryThread.Attach(hPrimaryThread);

            //
            // Wait for the worker process to exit
            //
            switch (WaitForSingleObject(shProcess, INFINITE))
            {
                case WAIT_OBJECT_0:
                    ChkWin32(::GetExitCodeProcess(shProcess, &dwExitCode));
                    wprintf(L"Child process exited with exit code %d.\n", dwExitCode);
                    break;
                default:
                    ChkReturn(E_FAIL);
            }

            ChkNoCleanup();
        }
    };
```

One key observation here is that the parent process is assigned to the new job object before the new child process is created, which allows the worker process to automatically inherit this job membership. This means in particular that there is no time window in which the new process would exist without being a part of the job object. If you kill the parent process (using the Ctrl+C signal, for example), you will notice that the worker process (*notepad.exe* in this case) is also terminated at the same time, which was precisely the desired behavior.

```
C:\book\code\chapter_01\WorkerProcess>objfre_win7_x86\i386\workerprocess.exe
Launching child process (notepad.exe) ...
^C
```

Low-Level Windows Communication Mechanisms

With code executing in kernel and user modes, and also inside the boundaries of per-process address spaces in user mode, the Windows operating system supports several mechanisms for allowing components to communicate with each other.

Calling Kernel-Mode Code from User Mode

The most basic way to call kernel-mode code from user-mode components is the *system call* mechanism mentioned earlier in this chapter. This mechanism relies on native support in the CPU to implement the transition in a controlled and secure manner.

One inherent drawback to the system call mechanism is that it relies on a hard-coded table of well-known executive service routines to dispatch the request from the client code in user mode to its intended target service routine in kernel mode. This doesn't extend well to kernel extensions implemented in the form of drivers, however. For those cases, another mechanism—called *I/O control commands* (*IOCTL*)—is supported by Windows to enable user-mode code to communicate with kernel-mode drivers. This is done through the generic *kernel32!DeviceIoControl* API, which takes the user-defined IOCTL identifier as one of its parameters and also a handle to the device object to which to dispatch the request. The transition to kernel mode is still performed in the NTDLL layer (*ntdll!NtDeviceIoControlFile*) and internally also uses the system call mechanism. So, you can think of the IOCTL method as a higher-level user/kernel communication protocol built on top of the raw system call services provided by the OS and CPU.

Internally, I/O control commands are processed by the I/O manager component of the Windows executive, which builds what is called an *I/O request packet* (*IRP* for short) that it then routes to the device object requested by the caller from user mode. IRP processing in the Windows executive uses a layered model where devices have an associated driver stack that handles their requests. When an IRP is sent to a top-level device object, it travels through its device stack starting at the top, passing through each driver in the corresponding device stack and giving it a chance to either process or ignore the command. In fact, IRPs are also used in kernel mode to send commands to other drivers so that the same IRP model is used for interdriver communication in the kernel. Figure 1-4 depicts this architecture.

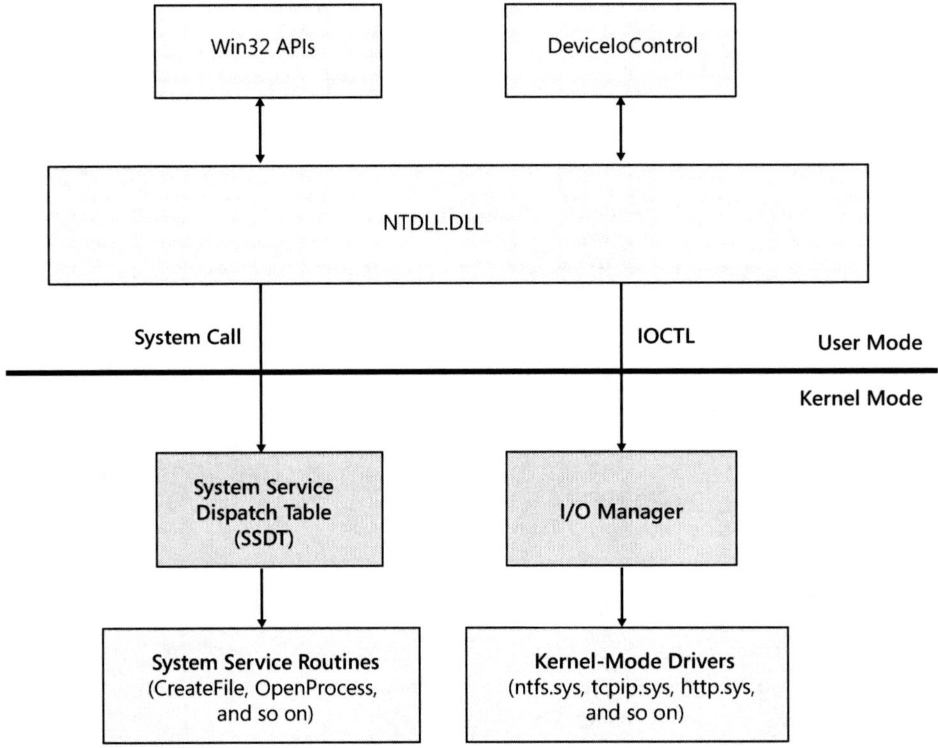

FIGURE 1-4 User-mode to kernel-mode communication mechanisms.

Calling User-Mode Code from Kernel Mode

Code that runs in kernel mode has unrestricted access to the entire virtual address space (both the user and kernel portions), so kernel mode in theory could invoke any code running in user mode. However, doing so requires first picking a thread to run the code in, transitioning the CPU mode back to user mode, and setting up the user-mode context of the thread to reflect the call parameters. Fortunately, however, only the system code written by Microsoft really needs to communicate with random threads in user mode. The drivers you write, on the other hand, need to call back to user mode only in the context of a device IOCTL initiated by a user-mode thread, so they do not need a more generic kernel-mode to user-mode communication mechanism.

A standard way for the system to execute code in the context of a given user-mode thread is to send an asynchronous procedure call (APC) to that thread. For example, this is exactly how thread suspension works in Windows: the kernel simply sends an APC to the target thread and asks it to execute a function to wait on its internal thread semaphore object, causing it to become suspended. APCs are also used by the system in many other scenarios, such as in I/O completion and thread pool callback routines, just to cite a couple.

Interprocess Communication

Another way for communicating between user-mode processes and code in kernel mode, as well as between user-mode processes themselves, is to use the advanced local procedure call (ALPC) mechanism. ALPC was introduced in the Windows Vista timeframe and is a big revision of the LPC mechanism, a feature that provided in many ways the bloodline of low-level intercomponent communication in Windows since its early releases.

ALPC is based on a simple idea: a server process first opens a kernel port object to receive messages. Clients can then connect to the port if allowed by the server owning the port and start sending messages to the server. They are also able to wait until the server has fetched and processed the message from the internal queue that's associated with the ALPC port object.

In the case of user/user ALPC, this provides a basic low-level interprocess communication channel. In the case of kernel/user ALPC channels, this essentially provides another (indirect) way for user-mode applications to call code in kernel mode (whether it's in a driver or in the kernel module itself) and vice versa. An example of this communication is the channel that's established between the *lsass.exe* user-mode system process and the security reference monitor (SRM) executive component in kernel mode, which is used, for example, to send audit messages from the executive to *lsass.exe*. Figure 1-5 illustrates this architecture.

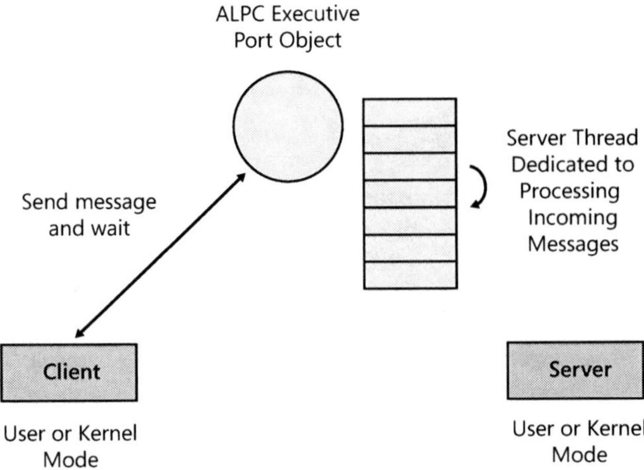

FIGURE 1-5 ALPC communication in Windows.

ALPC-style communication is used extensively in the operating system itself, most notably as it pertains to this book to implement the low-level communication protocol that native user-mode debuggers employ to receive various debug events from the process they debug. ALPC is also used as a building block in higher-level communication protocols such as local RPC, which in turn is used as the transport protocol in the COM model to implement interprocess method invocations with proper parameter marshaling.

Windows Developer Interface

Developers can extend the services that ship with the Windows operating system by building extensions in the way of kernel drivers or standalone user-mode Windows applications. This section examines some of the key layers and APIs that make building these extensions possible.

Developer Documentation Resources

Microsoft documents several APIs that developers can use when building their applications. The difference between these published interfaces and the internal (private) implementation details of the platform is that Microsoft has committed over the past two decades to building an ecosystem in which the public interfaces are carried forward with new releases of Windows, affording application developers the confidence that the applications they build today will continue to work on future OS versions. It's fair to say that this engineering discipline is one of the reasons Windows has been so successful with developers and end users alike.

Microsoft documents all of the interfaces and APIs it publishes on the Microsoft Developer Network (MSDN) website at *http://www.microsoft.com/msdn*. When writing your software, you should use only officially supported public APIs so that your software doesn't break when new versions of the operating system are released by Microsoft. Undocumented APIs can often disappear or get renamed, even in service pack releases of the same OS version, so you should never target them in your software unless you are prepared to deal with the wrath of your customers when your software ominously stops working after a new Windows update is installed. That's not to say you shouldn't be interested in internal implementation details, of course. In fact, this book proves that knowing some of those details is often important when debugging your programs and can help you analyze their behaviors more proficiently, which in turns also helps you write better and more reliable software in the long run.

In addition to documenting the public APIs written by Microsoft for developers, the MSDN website also contains a wealth of articles describing features or areas at a higher level. In particular, it hosts a special category of articles, called *Knowledge Base articles* (KB articles for short) that are published by Microsoft's customer support team to document workarounds for known issues. Generally speaking, the MSDN website should be your first stop when looking up the documented behavior of the APIs you use in your code or when trying to learn how to use a new feature in the OS.

WDM, KMDF, and UMDF

Developers can run their code with kernel-mode privileges and extend the functionality of the OS by implementing a kernel-mode driver. Though the vast majority of developers will never need to write a kernel driver, it's still useful to understand the layered plug-in models used by Windows to support these kernel extensions because this knowledge sometimes can help you make sense of kernel call stacks during kernel-mode debugging investigations.

Driver extensions are often needed to handle communication with hardware devices that aren't already supported because—as mentioned earlier—user-mode code isn't allowed to access I/O ports directly. In addition, drivers are sometimes used to implement or extend system features. For example, many tools in the SysInternals suite—including the process monitor tool, which installs a filter driver to monitor access to system resources—internally install drivers when they're executed to implement their functionality.

There are many ways to write drivers, but the main model used to implement them in Windows is the Windows Driver Model (WDM). Because this model asks a lot from driver developers in terms of handling all the interactions with the I/O manager and the rest of the operating system and often results in a lot of duplicated boilerplate code that has to be implemented by all driver developers, the kernel-mode driver framework (KMDF) was introduced to simplify the task of writing kernel-mode drivers. Keep in mind, however, that KMDF doesn't replace WDM; rather, it's a framework that helps you more easily write drivers that comply with WDM's requirements. Generally speaking, you should write your drivers using KMDF unless you find a good reason not to do so, such as when you need to write non-WDM drivers. This is the case, for instance, for network, SCSI, or video drivers, which have their own world, so to speak, and require you to write what is called a "miniport" driver to plug into their respective port drivers.

A subset of hardware drivers also can be executed completely in user mode (though without direct access to kernel memory space or I/O ports). These drivers can be developed using another framework shipped by Microsoft called the user-mode driver framework, or UMDF. For more details on the different driver models and their architectures, you can find a wealth of resources on the MSDN website at *http://msdn.microsoft.com*. The OSR website at *http://www.osronline.com* is also worth a visit if you ever need to write or debug drivers in Windows.

The NTDLL and USER32 Layers

As mentioned earlier in this chapter, the NTDLL and USER32 layers contain the entry points to the executive service routines and kernel-mode portion of the Win32 subsystem (*win32k.sys*), respectively.

There are hundreds of executive service stubs in the NTDLL module (*ntdll!NtSetEvent*, *ntdll!NtReadFile*, and many others). The majority of these service stubs are undocumented in the MSDN, but a few stub entry points were deemed generally useful to third-party system software and are documented. The NTDLL.DLL system module also hosts several low-level OS features, such as the module loader (*ntdll!Ldr** routines), the Win32 subsystem process communication functions (*ntdll!Csr** routines), and several run-time library functions (*ntdll!Rtl** routines) that expose features such as the Windows heap manager and Win32 critical section implementations.

The NTDLL module is used by many other DLLs in the Win32 API to transition into kernel mode and call executive service routines. Similarly, the USER32 DLL is also used by the Windows graphics architectural stack (DirectX, GDI32, and so on) as the gateway to transition into kernel mode so that it can communicate with the graphics processing unit (GPU) hardware.

The Win32 API Layer

The Win32 API layer is probably the most important layer to learn for developers who are new to Windows because it's the official public interface to the services exposed by the operating system. All of the Win32 API functions are documented in the MSDN, along with their expected parameters and potential return codes. Even if you are writing your software using a higher-level development framework or API set, as most of us do these days, being aware of the capabilities exposed at this layer will help you get a much better feel for a framework's advantages and limitations relative to other choices, as well as the raw capabilities exposed by the Win32 API and Windows executive.

The Win32 API layer covers a large set of functionality, going from basic services like creating threads/processes or drawing shapes on the screen to higher-level areas such as cryptography. The most basic services at the bottom of the Win32 API's architectural stack are exposed in the *kernel32.dll* module. Other widely used Win32 DLL modules are *advapi32.dll* (general utility functions), *user32.dll* (Windows and user object functions), and *gdi32.dll* (graphics functions). In Windows 7, the Win32 DLL modules are now layered so that lower-level base functions aren't allowed to call up to higher-level modules in the hierarchical stack. This layering engineering discipline helps prevent circular dependencies between modules and also minimizes the performance impact of bringing a new DLL dependency from the Win32 API set into your process address space. This is why you will see that many of the public APIs exported in the *kernel32.dll* module now simply forward their calls to the implementation defined in the lower-level *kernelbase.dll* DLL module, which is useful to know when trying to set system breakpoints in the debugger. This layered hierarchy is demonstrated in Figure 1-6.

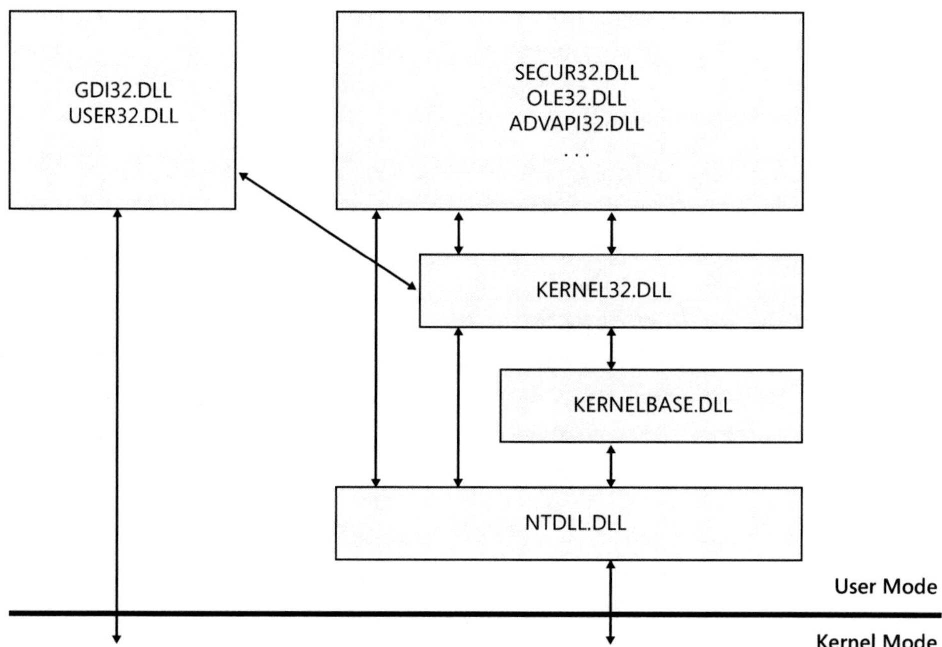

FIGURE 1-6 Low-level Win32 DLL modules.

The COM Layer

The Component Object Model (COM) was introduced by Microsoft in the mid-90s as a user-mode framework to enable developers to write reusable object-oriented components in different programming languages. If you are new to COM, the best resource to use to get started and gain an understanding of its model is the "Component Object Model Specification" document, which you can still find online. Though this is an old (circa 1995) and relatively long document, it provides a great overview of the COM binary specification, and much of what it describes still holds true to this day.

Over time, the use of the term "COM" grew to cover a number of different but related technologies, including the following:

- The object model itself, which the label "COM" was technically designed to describe at first. Key parts of this object model are the standard *IUnknown* and *IClassFactory* interfaces, the idea of separation of class interfaces (the public contract) from the internal COM class implementation, and the ability to query a server object for an implementation of the contracts that it supports (*IUnknown::QueryInterface*). This model, in its pure form, is one of the most elegant contributions by Microsoft to the developer ecosystem, and it has had a deep impact that still reverberates to this day in the form of various derivative technologies based on that model.
- The interprocess communication protocol and registration that allows components to communicate with each other without the client application having to know where the server component lives. This enables COM clients to transparently use servers implemented

locally in-process (DLLs) or out-of-process (EXEs), as well as servers that are hosted on a remote computer. The distinction between COM and Distributed COM (DCOM, or COM across machines) is often only theoretical, and most of the internal building blocks are shared between the two technologies.

- The protocol specifications built on top of the COM object model to enable hosts to communicate with objects written in multiple languages. This includes the OLE Automation and ActiveX technologies, in particular.

COM in the Windows Operating System

COM is omnipresent in the Windows operating system. Although the Microsoft .NET Framework has largely superseded COM as the technology of choice for Windows application-level development, COM has had a lasting impact on the Windows development landscape, and it's far from a dead technology as it continues to be the foundation for many components (for example, the Windows shell UI uses COM extensively) and even some of the newest technologies in the Windows development landscape. Even on a Windows installation with no other additional applications, you will still find thousands of COM class identifiers (CLSID for short) describing existing COM classes (servers) in the COM registry catalog, as shown in Figure 1-7.

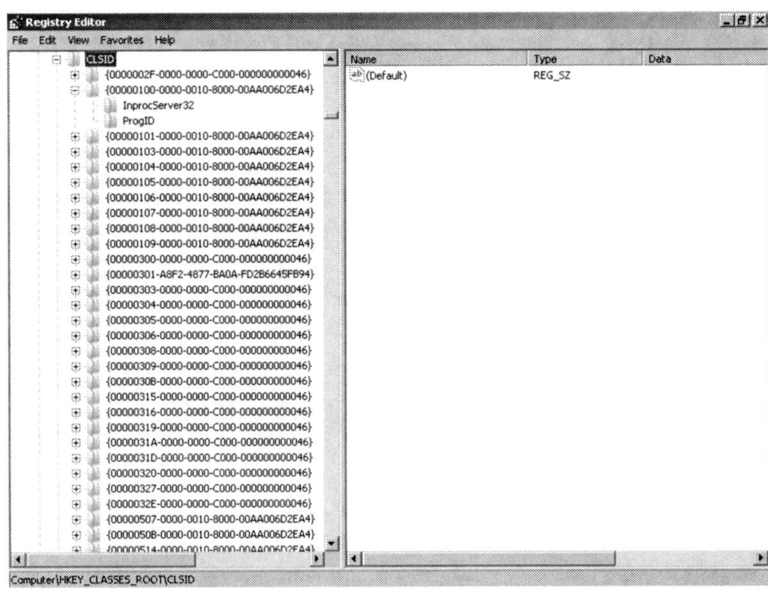

FIGURE 1-7 COM CLSID hive in the Windows registry.

More recently, the new model unveiled by Microsoft for developing touch-capable, Windows runtime (WinRT) applications in its upcoming version of Windows also uses COM for its core binary compatibility layer. In many ways, COM remains required knowledge if you really want to master the intricacies of Windows as a development platform. In addition, its design patterns and programming model have an educational value of their own. Even if you are never going to write a COM object (server), the programs and scripts you write often use existing COM objects, either explicitly or indirectly via API calls. So, knowing how COM works is particularly useful in debugging situations that involve such calls.

COM developers usually interact primarily with language-level features and tools when writing or consuming COM servers. However, debugging COM failures also requires knowledge of how the system implements the COM specification. In that sense, there are a few different aspects to the COM landscape that can all come into play during COM debugging investigations:

- **The COM "Library"** This is essentially Microsoft's system implementation of the COM binary specification. The COM library consists primarily of the COM run-time code and Win32 APIs (*CoInitialize*, *CoCreateInstance*, and others) that ship as part of the *ole32.dll* system module. This run-time code also uses support provided by two Windows services collectively referred to as the *COM service control manager* (*COM SCM*). These services are the *RpcSs* service, which runs with *NetworkService* privileges, and the *DComLaunch* service, which runs with *LocalSystem* privileges.
- **COM language tools** These are the source-level compilers and tools to support COM's binary specification. This includes the interface definition language (IDL) compiler (MIDL), which allows COM classes and interfaces to be consumed inside C/C++ programs, and the binary type library importer and exporter tools, which enable cross-language interoperability in COM. Note that these tools do not ship with the OS, but come as part of developer tools such as the Windows SDK.
- **COM frameworks** These are frameworks that make it easier for developers to write COM components that conform to the COM binary specification. An example is the Microsoft C++ Active Template Library (ATL).

Writing COM Servers

The COM specification places several requirements on developers writing COM objects and their hosting modules. Writing a COM object in C++ entails, at the very least, declaring its published interfaces in an IDL file and implementing the standard *IUnknown* COM interface that allows reference counting of the object and enables clients to negotiate contracts with the server. A class factory object—a COM-style support object that implements the *IClassFactory* COM interface but doesn't need to be published to the registry—must also be written for each CLSID to create its object instances.

On top of all of this, the developer is also required to implement the hosting module (DLL or EXE) so that it also conforms to all the other requirements of the COM specification. For example, in the case of a DLL module, a C-style function (*DllGetClassObject*) that returns a pointer to the class factory of CLSIDs hosted by the module must be exported for use by the COM library. For an executable module, the COM library can't simply call an exported function, so *ole32!CoRegisterClassObjects* must be called by the server executable itself when it starts up in order to publish its hosted COM class factories and make COM aware of them. Yet another requirement for DLL COM modules is to implement reference counting of their active objects and export a C-style function (*DllCanUnloadNow*) so that the COM library knows when it's safe to unload the module in question.

Microsoft realized that this is a lot to ask of C++ COM developers and introduced the Active Template Library (ATL) to help simplify writing COM server modules and objects in the C++ language. Although the majority of C++ COM developers in Windows use ATL to implement their COM servers, keep in mind that you can also write COM objects and their hosting modules without it (if you feel inclined to do so). In fact, ATL ships with the source code of its template classes, so you can study those implementation headers and see how ATL implements its functionality on top of the COM services provided by the COM library in the operating system. As you'll see after looking at that source code, ATL takes care of much of the heavy lifting and boilerplate code for writing COM servers so that you don't have to. This allows you to focus on writing the code that implements your business logic without much of the burden imposed by the necessary COM model plumbing.

Managing Module Lifetimes in COM Servers

To give you a practical scenario so that you get a better feel for the type of features ATL provides, consider the problem of managing the lifetime of COM servers. As mentioned earlier, COM servers implement reference counting to determine when their hosting server module (DLL or EXE) can be unloaded safely. In the COM ATL library, for example, every time a new COM object is created within a COM module (*CAtlDllModule*), a global (per-module) integer variable counting the number of live objects implemented by that module is incremented by one. This special reference count is often referred to as the COM module's *lock count*. When the last reference to the object is released, the lock count is decremented by one. In addition, a client is also allowed to put a lock on the server (that is, increment its global lock count by one) by calling the *LockServer* method of the *IClassFactory* standard COM interface (implemented by the *CComClassFactory* class in ATL).

In the case of DLL COM servers, this essentially provides a simple implementation to ref-count the COM module so that when its *DllCanUnloadNow* function is called, the module is able to see the number of outstanding client references it has (the lock count) and, when that number drops to zero, report to the COM library that it's free to unload the DLL if it wants to. A host process is able to force this cleanup at any time by calling the *ole32!CoFreeUnusedLibraries* COM runtime function, which internally invokes the exported *DllCanUnloadNow* functions from all in-process DLL COM server modules loaded in the client process and unloads the modules that return TRUE.

The lock count is also used by COM EXE servers. In the case of ATL, for example, COM EXE modules (*CAtlExeModule*) use an extra thread that periodically checks their lock count and shuts the process down after a certain period of inactivity after its lock count drops to zero. You can see this logic in the ATL implementation headers, as in the *MonitorShutdown* callback shown in the following listing.

```
//
// c:\ddk\7600.16385.1\inc\atl71>atlbase.h
//
void MonitorShutdown() throw()
{
```

```
    while (1)
    {
        ::WaitForSingleObject(m_hEventShutdown, INFINITE);
        DWORD dwWait = 0;
        do       {
            m_bActivity = false;
            dwWait = ::WaitForSingleObject(m_hEventShutdown, m_dwTimeOut);
        } while (dwWait == WAIT_OBJECT_0);

        if (!m_bActivity && m_nLockCnt == 0)
        {
            ::CoSuspendClassObjects();
            if (m_nLockCnt == 0)
                break;
        }
    }
    ::CloseHandle(m_hEventShutdown);
    ::PostThreadMessage(m_dwMainThreadID, WM_QUIT, 0, 0);
}
```

Note that COM as an OS component and platform leaves implementing this module reference counting scheme up to the developer writing the COM server. Fortunately, however, the good folks at Microsoft who wrote the ATL framework took care of this on behalf of all the Windows developers writing COM servers using that framework.

Consuming COM Objects

Communication between COM clients and servers is a two-step process:

- **COM activation** This is the first step in the communication, where the COM library locates the class factory of the requested CLSID. This is done by first consulting the COM registry catalog to find the module that hosts the implementation of the COM server. The COM client code initiates this step with a call to either the *ole32!CoCreateInstance* or *ole32!CoGetClassObject* Win32 API call. Note that *ole32!CoCreateInstance* is simply a convenient wrapper that first calls *ole32!CoGetClassObject* to obtain the class factory, and then invokes the *IClassFactory::CreateInstance* method implemented by that class factory object to finally create a new instance of the target COM server.

- **Method invocations** After the COM activation step retrieves a proxy or direct pointer to the COM class object, the client can then query the interfaces exposed by the object and directly invoke the exposed methods.

A key point to understand when consuming COM objects in your code is the potential involvement of the COM SCM behind the scenes to instantiate the hosting module for the COM object and its corresponding class factory during the COM activation step. This is done because COM clients sometimes need to activate out-of-process servers in different contexts, such as when the COM server object needs to run in processes with higher privileges or in different user sessions, which requires the participation of a broker process that runs with higher privileges (the *DComLaunch* service). Another reason is that the *RpcSs* Windows service also handles cross-machine COM activation requests (the DCOM case) and implements the communication channel in a way that's completely transparent to both COM clients and servers. It's especially important to understand this involvement during debugging investigations of COM activation failures. Once the COM activation sequence retrieves the requested class factory, however, the COM client is then able to directly invoke COM methods published by the server class without any involvement on the part of the COM SCM. Figure 1-8 summarizes these steps and the key components involved during the COM activation sequence.

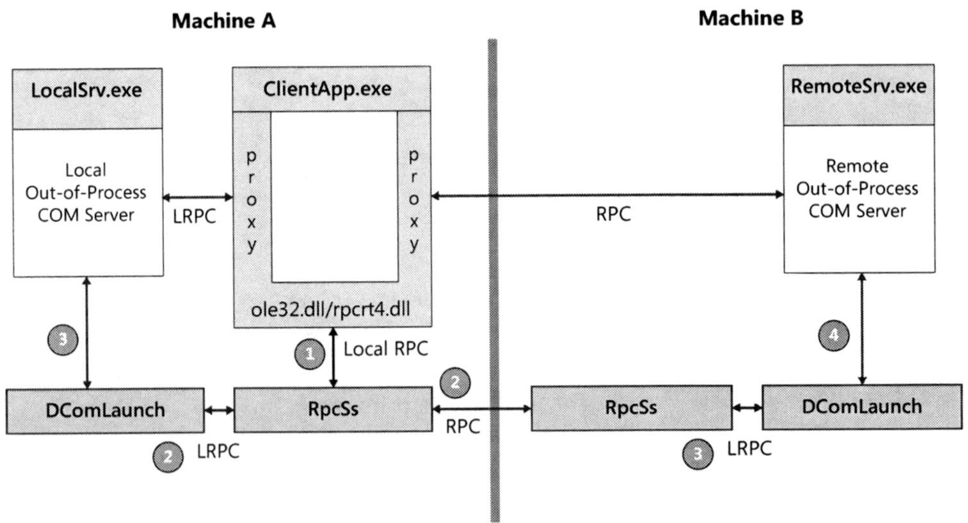

FIGURE 1-8 COM activation components.

The nice thing about the COM model, as mentioned earlier in this section, is that the client doesn't need to know where the COM server implementation lives, or even the language (C++, Microsoft Visual Basic, Delphi, or other) in which it was written (provided it has access to a type library or a direct virtual table layout that describes the COM types it wants to consume). The only thing that the client needs to know is the CLSID of the COM object (a GUID), after which it can query for the supported interfaces and invoke the desired methods. COM in the OS provides all the necessary "glue" for the client/server communication, provided the COM server was written to conform to the COM model. In particular, COM supports accessing the following COM server types using the same consistent programmatic model:

- **In-process COM servers** The hosting DLL module is loaded into the client process address space, and the object is invoked through a pointer returned by the COM activation sequence. This pointer can be either a direct virtual pointer or sometimes a proxy, depending on whether the COM runtime needs to be invoked to provide additional safeguards (such as thread safety) before invoking the methods of the COM server.
- **Local/remote out-of-process COM servers** For local out-of-process COM servers, local RPC is used as the underlying interprocess communication protocol, with ALPC as the actual low-level foundation. For remote COM servers (DCOM), the RPC communication protocol is used

for the intermachine communication. In both cases, the proxy memory pointer that is returned to the client application from the COM activation sequence takes care of everything that's required to accomplish COM's promise of transparent remoting. Figure 1-9 illustrates this aspect.

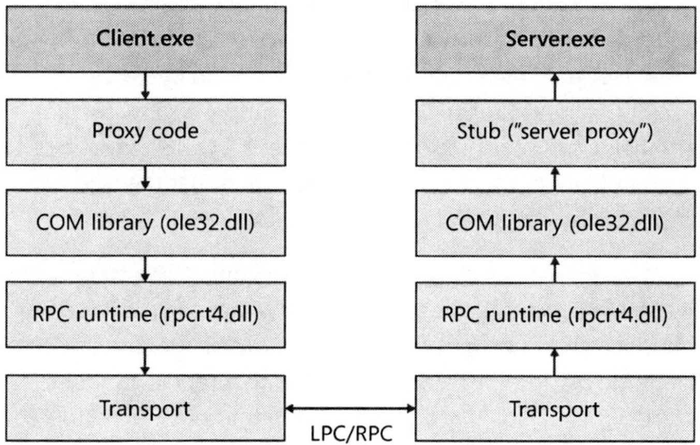

FIGURE 1-9 Out-of-process COM method invocations.

The CLR (.NET) Layer

Like COM, the .NET Framework is also a user-mode, object-oriented platform that enables developers to write their programs in their language of choice (C#, Microsoft Visual Basic .NET, C++/CLI, or other). However, .NET takes another leap and has those programs run under the control of an execution engine environment that provides additional useful features, such as type safety and automatic memory management using garbage collection. This execution engine environment is called the *Common Language Runtime* (*CLR*) and is in many ways the core of the .NET platform. Understanding this layer is often helpful when debugging applications built on top of the various .NET class libraries and technologies (ASP.NET, WCF, WinForms, WPF, Silverlight, and so on).

The CLR runtime is implemented as a set of native DLLs that get loaded into the address space of every .NET executable, though the core execution engine DLL decides when to load the other DLL dependencies. Because of their reliance on this execution environment, .NET modules (also called *assemblies*) are said to be *managed*, as opposed to the unmanaged native modules that execute in the regular user-mode environment. The same user-mode process can host both managed and unmanaged modules interoperating with each other, as will be explained shortly in this section.

Programs in .NET are not compiled directly into native assembly code, but rather into a platform-agnostic language called the *Microsoft .NET Intermediate Language* (usually referred to as MSIL, or simply IL). This IL is then lazily (methods are compiled on first use) turned into assembly instructions by a component of the execution engine called the *Just-in-Time .NET compiler*, or *JIT*.

.NET Side-by-Side Versioning

One of the issues that plagued software development in Windows prior to the introduction of the .NET Framework was the fact that new DLL versions sometimes introduced new behaviors, breaking existing software often through no fault of the application developer. There was no standard way to strongly bind applications to the version of the DLLs that they were tested against before they got released. This is known as the "DLL hell" issue. COM made the situation better by at least ensuring binary compatibility: instead of C-style exported DLL functions simply disappearing or altering their signatures from underneath their consumers (resulting in crashes!), COM servers were able to clearly version their interfaces, allowing COM clients to query the interfaces that they were tested against and providing the safety of this extra level of indirection.

The .NET Framework takes the idea of strong binding and versioning one step further by ensuring that .NET programs are always run against the version of the CLR that they were compiled to target or, alternatively, the version specified in the application's configuration file. So, new versions of the .NET Framework are installed side by side with older ones instead of replacing them. The exception to this is a small shim DLL called *mscoree.dll* that's installed to the *system32* directory (on 64-bit Windows; a 32-bit version is also installed to the *SysWow64* directory) and that always matches the newest .NET Framework version present on the machine. This works because newer versions of *mscoree.dll* are backward compatible with previous versions of the CLR. For example, if both .NET versions 4.0 and 2.0 are installed on the machine, the *mscoree.dll* module in the *system32* directory will be the one that was installed with the CLR 4.0 release.

.NET Executable Programs Load Sequence

The IL assemblies produced by the various .NET compilers also follow the standard Windows PE (Portable Executable) format and are just special-case native images from the perspective of the OS loader, except they have a marker in their PE header to indicate they are managed code binaries that should be handled by the .NET CLR. When the Windows module loader code in *ntdll.dll* detects the existence of a CLR header in the executable PE image it is about to launch, control is immediately transferred to the native CLR entry point (*mscoree!_CorExeMain*), which then takes care of finding and invoking the managed IL entry point in the image.

Note To support earlier OS versions (more specifically, Windows 98/ME and earlier service packs of Windows 2000 and Windows XP), which were not aware of the CLR header because the .NET Framework hadn't shipped at the time those operating systems were released, managed PE images also had to have a regular native entry point consisting of a very thin stub (*jmp* instruction) that simply invokes the CLR's main entry point method (*mscoree!_CorExeMain*). Fortunately, the Windows releases supported by .NET are now natively capable of loading managed code modules, and this stub is no longer strictly required.

Note that the OS module loader doesn't really know which version of the CLR should be loaded for the managed image. This is the role of the *mscoree.dll* native shim DLL, which determines the correct version of the CLR to load. For CLR v2 programs, for example, the execution engine DLL loaded by *mscoree.dll* is *mscorwks.dll*, while for CLR v4 the execution engine implementation resides inside the *clr.dll* module. Once the CLR execution engine DLL for the target version is loaded, it pretty much takes control and becomes responsible for the runtime execution environment, ensuring type safety and automatic memory management (garbage collection), invoking the JIT compiler to convert IL into native assembly code on-demand, performing security checks, hosting the native implementation for several key threading and run-time services, and so on. The CLR is also responsible for loading the managed assemblies hosting the object types referenced by the application's IL, including the core library that implements some of the most basic managed types (*mscorlib.dll* .NET assembly). Figure 1-10 illustrates these steps.

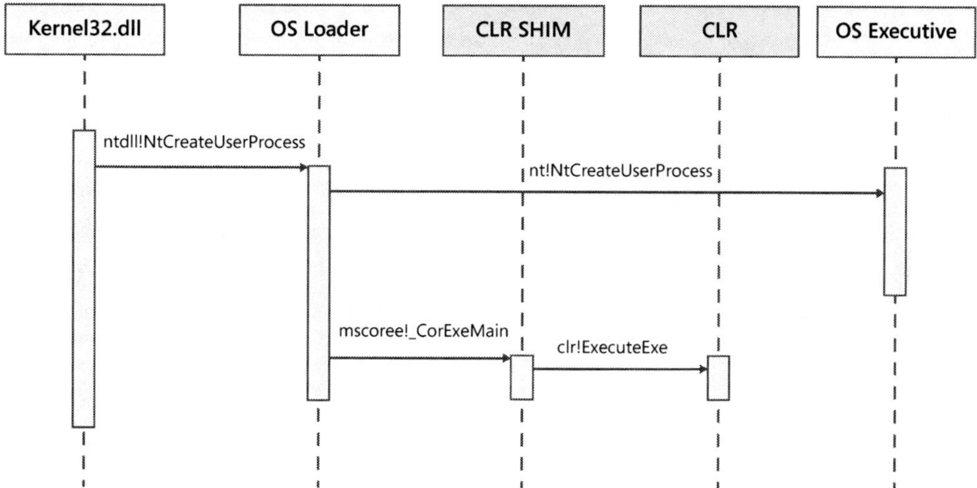

FIGURE 1-10 Loading steps for .NET executable programs.

Interoperability Between Managed and Native Code

When the first version of the .NET Framework was introduced back in early 2002, it had to be able to consume existing native code (both C-style Win32 APIs and COM objects) to ensure that the transition to managed code programming was seamless for Windows developers. Interoperability between managed and unmanaged code is possible fortunately, thanks in large part to two CLR mechanisms: *P/Invoke* and *COM Interop*. P/Invoke (the *DllImport* .NET method attribute) is used to invoke C-style unmanaged APIs such as those from the Win32 API set, and COM Interop (the *ComImport* .NET class attribute) can be used to invoke any existing classic COM object implemented in unmanaged code.

Managed/native code interoperability presents a few technical challenges, however. The biggest challenge is that the garbage collection scheme that the CLR uses for automatic memory management requires it to manage objects in the managed heap so that it is able to periodically clear defunct (nonrooted) objects, and also so that it can reduce heap fragmentation when dead objects are collected. However, when transitioning to run native code as part of the same process address space, it's often necessary to share managed memory with the native call (in the form of function parameters, for instance). Because the CLR garbage collector is free to move these managed objects around when it decides to perform a garbage collection, and because the garbage collector is completely unaware of the operations that the native code might attempt, it could end up moving the shared managed objects around, causing the native code to access invalid memory. The CLR execution engine takes care of these technical intricacies by marshaling function parameters and pinning managed objects in memory during the managed to unmanaged transitions.

Conversely, you can also consume code that you develop using .NET from your native applications using the COM Interop facilities provided by the CLR. The C/C++ native code is able to consume the types published by a .NET assembly (by means of the *ComVisible* .NET attribute) using their type library, in the same fashion that native COM languages are able to consume types from different languages. The .NET Framework ships with a tool called *regasm.exe*, which can be used to easily generate type libraries for the COM types in a .NET assembly. The .NET Framework and Windows SDKs also include a development tool, called *tlbexp.exe*, that's able to do the same thing.

The CLR shim DLL (*mscoree.dll*) again plays a key role in this reverse COM Interop scenario because it's the first native entry point to the CLR during the COM activation. This shim then loads the right CLR execution engine version, which then loads the managed COM types as they get invoked by the native code. This extends the functionality provided by the COM library in the OS without it having to know about the intricacies of managed code. During the COM activation sequence that the native application initiates, the COM library ends up invoking the standard *DllGetClassObject* method exported from *mscoree.dll*. If you used *regasm.exe* to generate the type library for the C# COM types, *mscoree.dll* also would've been added to the registry as the *InProcServer32* for all the managed COM classes hosted by the .NET DLL assembly. The CLR shim DLL then forwards the call to the CLR execution engine, which takes care of implementing the class factory and standard native COM interfaces on behalf of the managed COM types.

Microsoft Developer Tools

Microsoft typically releases supporting tools (compilers, libraries, and the like) for developers to write code that targets its technologies. These releases are referred to as *development kits*. For example, there is a software development kit (SDK) for developers of Windows Phone applications, a .NET SDK that contains tools to write and sign code for the .NET Framework, an Xbox development kit (XDK) for game developers, and so on. Many of these development kits, including the .NET and Windows Phone SDKs, are available as free downloads from the Microsoft Download Center at *http://www.microsoft.com/downloads*.

The Windows team at Microsoft also ships two important software development kits that include many of the tools presented in this book: more specifically, the Windows Driver Development Kit

(DDK), which contains the build environment used to compile all the native C++ code samples in the book's companion source code, and the Windows Software Development Kit, which contains the Windows debuggers and Windows Performance Toolkit. Both of these development kits are free and available for download from the Microsoft Download Center.

The Windows DDK (WDK)

Each release of Windows is accompanied by a driver development kit targeted for use by Windows driver developers, which contains the headers, libraries, and tools needed for building drivers, as well as several code samples for writing WDM, KMDF, and UMDF drivers.

One of the most useful features included with this kit is a full-blown build and development environment that can be used not only for driver development but for any kind of C/C++ development. It includes C/C++ compilers and many other native development frameworks, including the STL (Standard C++ Template Library) and ATL (Active Template Library for building COM servers) template libraries and their respective implementation headers.

The native C++ code samples from the companion source code use a small portion of ATL that provides support for smart pointers and basic string and collection operations (arrays, hash tables, and so on). Although ATL also comes with the Microsoft Visual Studio suite, the build environment of the DDK was chosen for this book's companion source code so that readers without Visual Studio can follow the case studies and experiments presented in this book.

The Windows SDK

Another important development kit shipped to support new Windows releases is the Windows SDK. Microsoft sometimes ships more than one SDK version per major Windows release: for example, versions 7.0 and 7.1 of the SDK target Windows 7 developers, with version 7.1 bringing many improvements to some of the key tools covered in this book.

The Windows SDK contains useful documentation and samples for building applications on Windows, as well as the public (official) header files and import libraries that are required for compiling your native Windows applications. In addition, the Windows SDK also contains two of the main debugging and tracing tools covered in this book—namely, the Windows debuggers package and Windows Performance Toolkit.

Step-by-step instructions for how to acquire and install those SDK tools will be provided when they're introduced in the following parts of this book so that they're closer to where you will end up needing them.

Summary

This chapter introduced some common terminology and also served as a very short and, admittedly, fast-paced introduction to important layers (Kernel, Executive, NTDLL, Win32, COM/.NET) in the Windows architecture and software development landscape. The following points are also worth remembering as you read the rest of this book:

- Server and client Windows releases share a common kernel and follow a relatively similar release schedule, so it's important to know the client variant of each server release and vice versa. When this book states that a certain kernel feature is added in Windows 7, for example, it's also implied that the Windows Server 2008 R2 kernel has the same capability.
- The CPU architecture of your OS (*x86* or *x64*) is always important to know when performing debugging and tracing experiments.
- When studying a new API set or platform feature, you should try to piece together an architectural diagram in your mind and understand where that new feature fits relative to the existing OS layers and development frameworks. This comes in handy when you later need to debug or trace the code in your software that uses the feature in question.
- When analyzing development frameworks and whether to use them in building your software, you should also try to understand how they are implemented on top of the built-in OS services and what additional functionality they provide. This should help you make an informed choice as to what frameworks fit your scenario best and whether taking the dependency is worth the productivity benefits you would gain.

Many of the concepts discussed in this chapter will be revisited in practical debugging and tracing situations. If you are like me, you will find that these topics start hitting a lot closer to home, so to speak, once you get into the habit of using debugging and tracing to confirm your understanding of the theoretical background. So, don't hesitate to come back and consult this chapter again as you run the debugging and tracing explorations proposed in this book. You might want to double-check some of the theory that has been covered here.

PART 2

Debugging for Fun and Profit

Debuggers are an essential weapon in the arsenal of software developers and are useful in every step of the development process—not only after bugs surface. In a typical test-driven development methodology, software developers start prototyping small units of code that can be unit-tested independently, simultaneously using a debugger to step through the unit tests and exercise all the code branches before finally putting those small building blocks together to build more complex solutions.

Chapter 2, "Getting Started," introduces debugger usage using a variety of practical debugging experiments rather than a laundry listing of available debugger commands. If you don't completely understand a particular debugger experiment, don't get discouraged; instead, continue reading the rest of the chapters. You'll find that the usage patterns are often illustrated by multiple examples and experiments. Be sure to also read the Appendixes for a short glossary of important concepts and commands.

Chapter 3, "How Windows Debuggers Work," offers an inside study of the basic debugger mechanisms and how the operating system makes them possible. Chapter 4, "Postmortem Debugging," follows with an in-depth look at two more fundamental topics: Just-in-Time (JIT) and dump debugging. This part of the book also offers a practical look at ways to prevent and debug common problems. Chapter 6, "Code Analysis Tools," shows how static and runtime code analysis can help catch bugs early during the development cycle. Chapter 8, "Common Debugging Scenarios, Part 1," and Chapter 9, "Common Debugging Scenarios, Part 2," cover several common code defects related to the reliability, security, and concurrency facets of your software. They also detail generic debugging techniques you can apply to debug and rid your code of those costly bugs.

Debuggers are also a great tool for diving into the interactions between your code and the operating system. To use the debuggers in this manner, however, you must first add a few tricks to your repertoire. If you're already comfortable with using the Windows debuggers, make sure you at least read Chapter 5, "Beyond the Basics," and Chapter 7, "Expert Debugging Tricks," for important background information. You should then read Chapter 10, "Debugging System Internals," which demonstrates this particular use of the debuggers. As you begin applying this approach consistently, you'll be able to use the debuggers to take your game to the next level in terms of your mastery of Microsoft Windows as a development platform.

CHAPTER 2

Getting Started

In this chapter

This chapter introduces the Microsoft debugging tools most commonly used in Windows software development, namely, the Windows debuggers (WinDbg) and the Microsoft Visual Studio debugger, though the coverage is centered on WinDbg. The chapter also outlines steps for setting up your environment so that you can follow the debugging experiments conducted throughout the rest of the book.

The chapter contains a quick introduction to user-mode debugging with WinDbg. Although you might prefer the Visual Studio environment when debugging the applications you write and compile on the same development environment, the Windows debuggers can be more convenient when conducting debugging investigations in live production environments or when you also need to step into code you didn't write yourself, such as third-party applications for which you don't have the source code or the components that ship with the Windows operating system itself.

A section that covers kernel-mode debugging concludes this chapter. Keep in mind that kernel-mode debugging isn't useful only for kernel or driver developers. Fortunately, most of us will never need to write kernel-mode software, and the vast majority of the examples and experiments in this book are aimed at developers of user-mode applications. That being said, kernel-mode debugging can sometimes be a better option even when debugging the behavior of user-mode applications, especially when you need to examine more than one process as part of your investigation. In a way, you can think of kernel-mode debugging as a debugging environment with systemwide scope. The fact that it also gives you access to kernel-mode memory is an added bonus, of course.

Introducing the Debugging Tools

This section will show you how to install the Windows debuggers toolset, as well as one of the free trial editions of the Microsoft Visual Studio suite. Because the bulk of this part is devoted to the Windows debuggers, you can follow most of the experiments using the Windows debuggers package only, so you can delay downloading Visual Studio until you encounter an experiment that requires it. This is especially helpful if you have a slow Internet connection because the Visual Studio download is fairly large.

Acquiring the Windows Debuggers Package

The Windows debuggers are free. They used to be available as a standalone installer (MSI) but are now bundled with the Windows 7 Software Development Kit (SDK). As a result, installing the right version of the debuggers is a topic that deserves detailed coverage.

Installing the Windows Debuggers

1. Download the Windows 7 SDK, and save it to your local hard drive. You need version 7.1 (labeled "Microsoft Windows SDK for Windows 7 and .NET Framework 4"), which you can obtain at *http://www.microsoft.com/download/en/details.aspx?id=8442*. There are ISO files for each of the CPU architectures that Windows 7 supports (x86, ia64, and x64), but you need to download only one of them because all three ISO images carry the debugger MSI installers from every supported CPU architecture. If you have a slow Internet connection, you'll need to set plenty of time aside for this download, given the file is more than 500 MB in size.

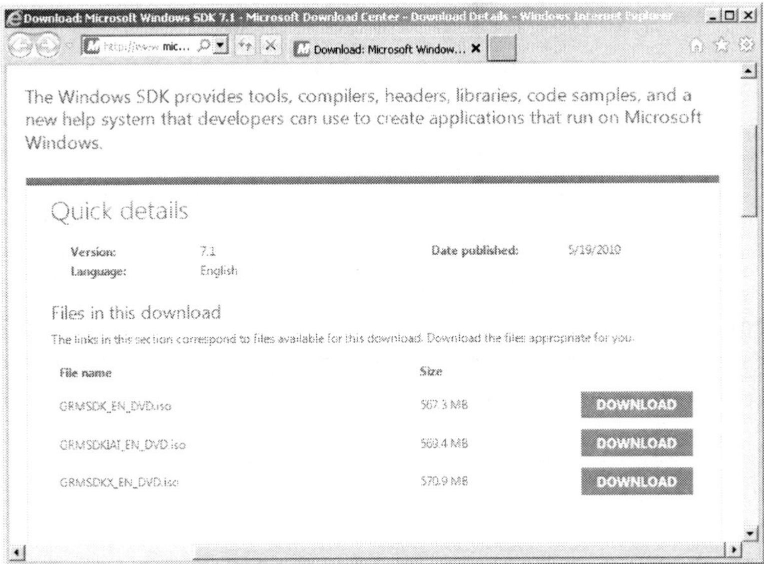

2. After the download is complete, mount the saved SDK ISO file into a drive letter. You can use the Virtual Clone Drive freeware that you used back in the Introduction to mount the Driver Development Kit (DDK) ISO file and configure the environment used for building the C/C++ code samples from the companion source code. When that freeware is installed, you should be able to right-click the downloaded SDK ISO file and mount it, as shown in the following screen shot:

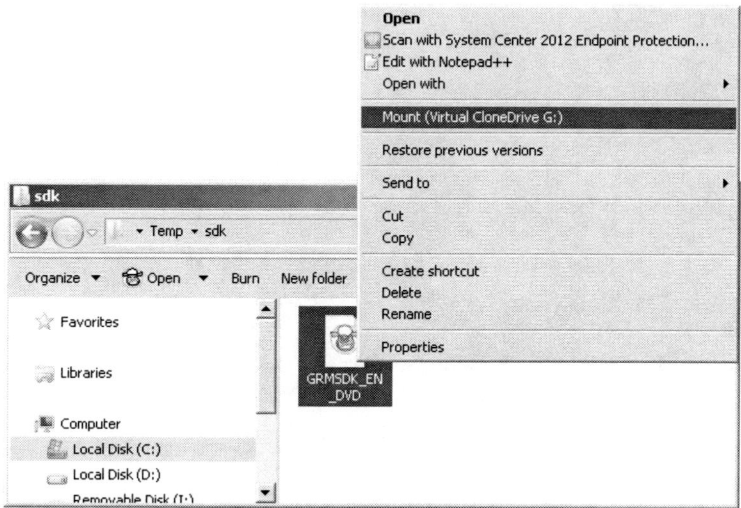

3. Right-click the newly mounted drive letter, and open its root directory. Do not double-click the drive letter because that will start the default action, which is to install the full Windows 7 SDK.

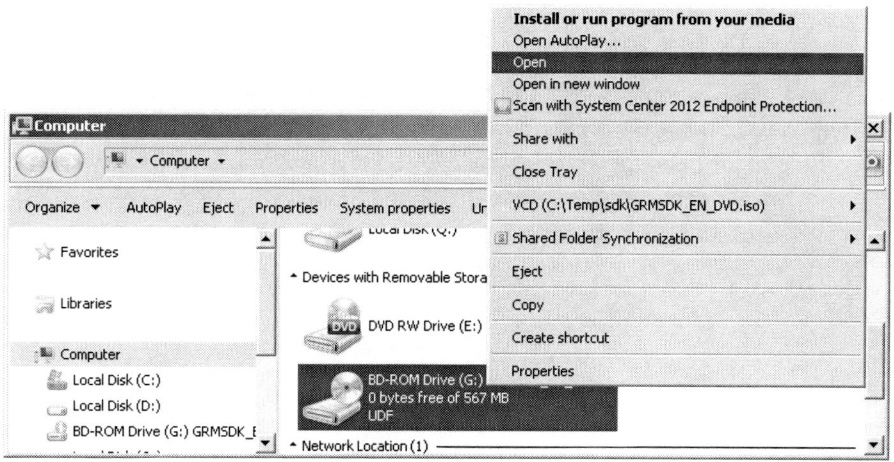

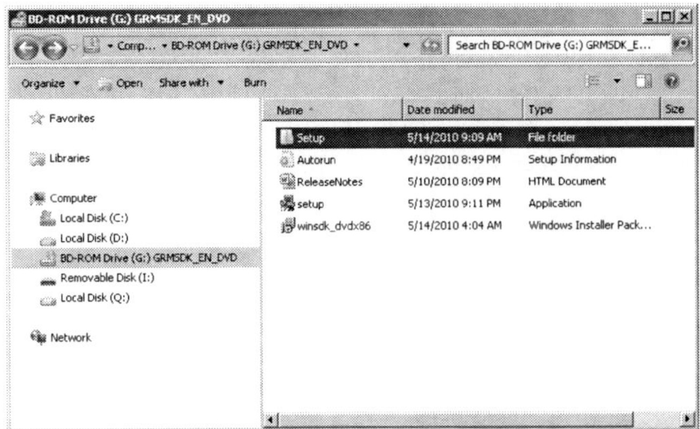

4. Under the Setup subdirectory, you'll find the Windows debuggers from all three supported CPU architectures.

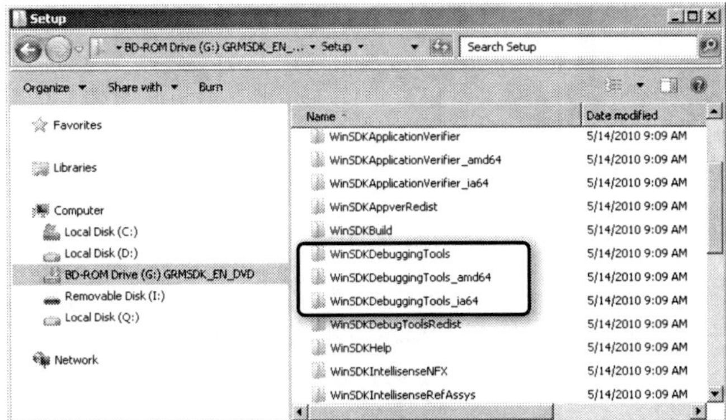

5. Install the *x86* version of the debuggers from the WinSDKDebuggingTools directory, regardless of whether your Windows version is 32-bit or 64-bit. You'll need it to follow the user-mode experiments from this chapter because they all use *x86* code samples that work both on 32-bit and 64-bit Windows. Also, install the *x64* version side by side with the *x86* version of the debuggers if you have a 64-bit machine. You'll need this version to run the kernel-mode debugging experiments, which require the version of the WinDbg debugger that's native to your platform.

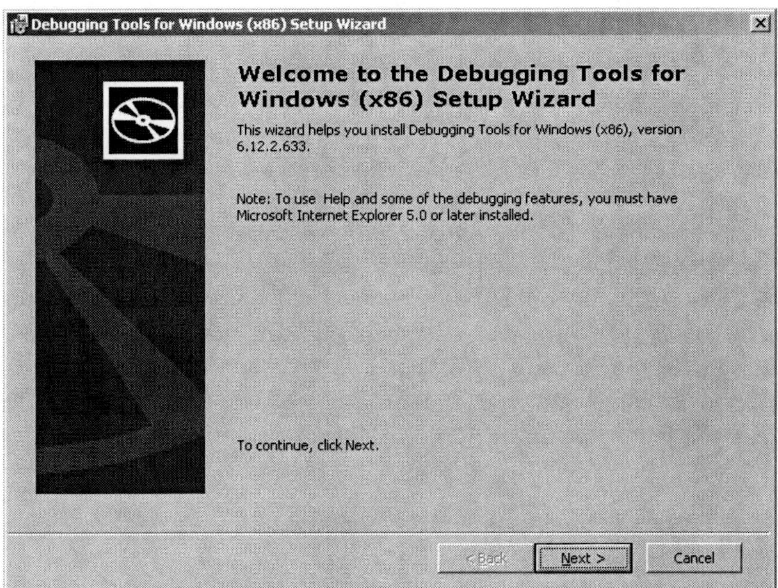

The debugger MSI setups should take only a few seconds to complete and install the architecture-specific *windbg.exe* debugger binary under the Program Files folder (by default). The package also contains other command-line debuggers, such as the *cdb.exe* and *ntsd.exe* user-mode debuggers and the *kd.exe* kernel-mode debugger. Several useful utilities are also included, such as the *tlist.exe* tool used to list running user-mode processes on the machine and the *kill.exe* tool, which can be used to forcibly terminate a running process on the system.

```
C:\Program Files\Debugging Tools for Windows (x86)>dir /b *.exe
...
cdb.exe
convertstore.exe
...
kd.exe
kill.exe
list.exe
...
tlist.exe
umdh.exe
usbview.exe
vmdemux.exe
windbg.exe
```

6. Now that WinDbg is installed to its target location, you can unmount the SDK drive letter. Although it's no longer needed for using the WinDbg debugger at this point, *be sure to keep the SDK ISO file for future use*. You'll need it again when it is time to install the Windows Performance Toolkit (Xperf) in the next part of this book.

Acquiring the Visual Studio Debugger

As mentioned earlier, you can skip this section if you already have a full version of Visual Studio 2010 installed on your machine, or if you have a slow Internet connection and would rather wait until you encounter a debugging experiment that requires Visual Studio because of the size of the Visual Studio trial edition download.

Unlike the Windows debuggers, Visual Studio is a commercial suite that requires a license from Microsoft for all editions except for a free, stripped-down edition called the Visual Studio Express edition. However, you can also follow the code experiments in this book that use Visual Studio using the free, 90-day trial of the Ultimate edition. Although the Visual Studio Express edition is also a free alternative to the full Visual Studio suite, this stripped-down edition is missing important debugging features. My recommendation is to use the 90-day trial of the full suite to follow the Visual Studio debugging experiments in this book.

Installing Visual Studio 2010 Ultimate (Trial Version)

There are two ways you can acquire the Visual Studio 2010 Ultimate trial edition. In either case, be aware that this is a 3-GB download, so it can be a rather lengthy process on a slow Internet connection.

- Use the web setup installer offered on the Microsoft Download Center website at the following URL: *http://www.microsoft.com/download/en/details.aspx?id=12752*. Or use the process described in the next step.
- Download the Visual Studio 2010 Ultimate trial edition ISO image from *http://www.microsoft.com/download/en/details.aspx?id=12187*, and then install it locally.

Comparing the WinDbg and Visual Studio Debuggers

One unfortunate limitation of WinDbg when compared to Visual Studio in the case of .NET applications is that it doesn't currently support source-level, managed-code debugging. In addition to .NET debugging, Visual Studio also supports native code debugging, as well as the concept of mixed-mode debugging (debugging managed and unmanaged code in the same process simultaneously). Moreover, the Visual Studio debugger also supports a wide range of programming languages, including native C/C++, managed-code languages (C#, Microsoft Visual Basic .NET, and so on) as well as script languages (VBScript/JScript). Table 2-1 summarizes some of the high-level capabilities in the WinDbg and Visual Studio debuggers.

TABLE 2-1 Side-by-Side Comparison of Microsoft Debuggers

	WinDbg	Visual Studio 2010
Graphical user interface	✔	✔
Kernel-mode debugging	✔	✖
User-mode debugging	✔	✔

	WinDbg	Visual Studio 2010
Managed-code debugging	✔ (without source-level debugging support, though)	✔
SQL debugging	✖	✔
Script debugging	✖	✔

Another way to compare the two debuggers is to think of the scenarios where they prove most effective. While the WinDbg debugger excels at debugging investigations in production environments, the Visual Studio debugger is designed to provide an optimal debugging experience during the code development process. Although a reduction of a few seconds in the time it takes to write code and step through it inside the debugger might not seem like a big deal when you start your coding, the best engineers I have worked with always made it a priority to invest time in optimizing this sequence, striving to reduce it to a single click of a button (the F5 shortcut in Visual Studio) no matter how complex the post-build setup might be (copying binaries to a test machine, running DLLs inside their target host process, and so on). Doing so early in project development removes a major barrier to test-driven development, making it more efficient to add and step through new code under the debugger without adding an exorbitant amount of time to the development process. For those reasons, the integrated Visual Studio debugger works best during the development and debugging iterations in test-driven development, with WinDbg coming in support for post-coding debugging investigations.

User-Mode Debugging

This section will show you how to start using WinDbg for basic debugging tasks. It also introduces you to some common debugging commands you'll see throughout the debugging experiments presented in this book.

Debugging Your First Program with WinDbg

You're now ready to start using WinDbg for debugging user-mode applications. One way to see the advantages of this system debugger in action is to use it first in an experiment to step through your own code, and then in another example where you also use it to step into a Win32 API call to see how it's internally implemented.

Debugging Your Own Code

To see how WinDbg can be used to debug a simple C++ program, take the "Hello World!" code sample from the companion source code and compile it for the *x86* platform using a DDK build command window. For more information on how to compile the native C/C++ programs from the companion source code, refer to the procedure described in the Introduction of this book.

This experiment uses the *x86* version of the *windbg.exe* debugger, which you can also use to debug *x86* programs running on 64-bit Windows. You can start the previous C++ program directly under the control of the WinDbg debugger by typing the following command:

```
C:\book\code\chapter_02\HelloWorld>"c:\Program Files\Debugging Tools for Windows
(x86)\windbg.exe" objfre_win7_x86\i386\HelloWorld.exe
```

Note that the text you see in the initial debugger screen might look slightly different from the text in Figure 2-1, though the UI should look very similar.

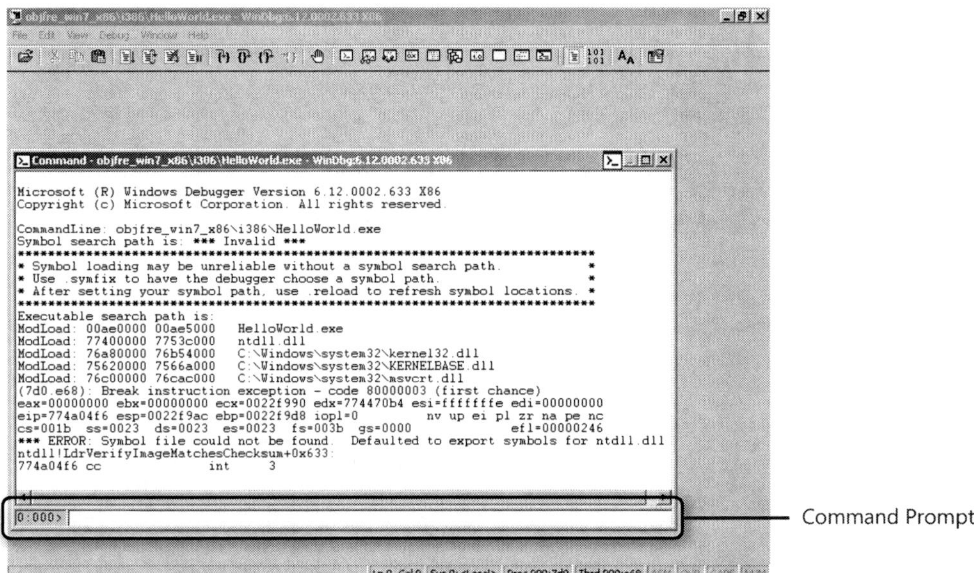

FIGURE 2-1 Compiling and launching the "Hello World!" program under WinDbg.

If you are new to WinDbg, you might be a little lost at first and unsure what to do next when you see this initial debugger UI. When you use Visual Studio, the debugger launches your program and stops at its entry point when you press the F10 shortcut, just the way you would expect if you're interested in stepping into your own code. In WinDbg, however, the program's execution stops much earlier, right after the OS loader code in NTDLL is done initializing the process. This has some advantages, but it forces you to run a few more steps to get further ahead to the program's entry point.

In the WinDbg command window is a text box that starts with the *0:000>* prefix (outlined in Figure 2-1). This is where you type your debugger commands. The easiest way to advance the execution of the program to its entry point is to set a breakpoint in that function using its (case-insensitive) symbolic name and the *bp* command (*bp HelloWorld!wmain*) and then let the program's execution continue using the F5 shortcut (or the *g* command). These steps are demonstrated in the following listing and corresponding Figure 2-2, where the bold text lines represent the input commands that you should enter into the debugger's command window (without the prefix!) and the lines in regular type represent the output from those commands. Lines that start with the dollar sign ($) are used to insert debugger comments to annotate the commands used in the WinDbg listings throughout this book, while lines that start with an ellipsis (...) are used to indicate truncated output from the debugger commands.

```
0:000> vercommand
command line: '"c:\Program Files\Debugging Tools for Windows (x86)\windbg.exe"
objfre_win7_x86\i386\HelloWorld.exe'
0:000> $ set a breakpoint at the program's main function
0:000> bp HelloWorld!wmain
0:000> $ Let the target program continue its execution
0:000> g
...
Breakpoint 0 hit
HelloWorld!wmain:
...
```

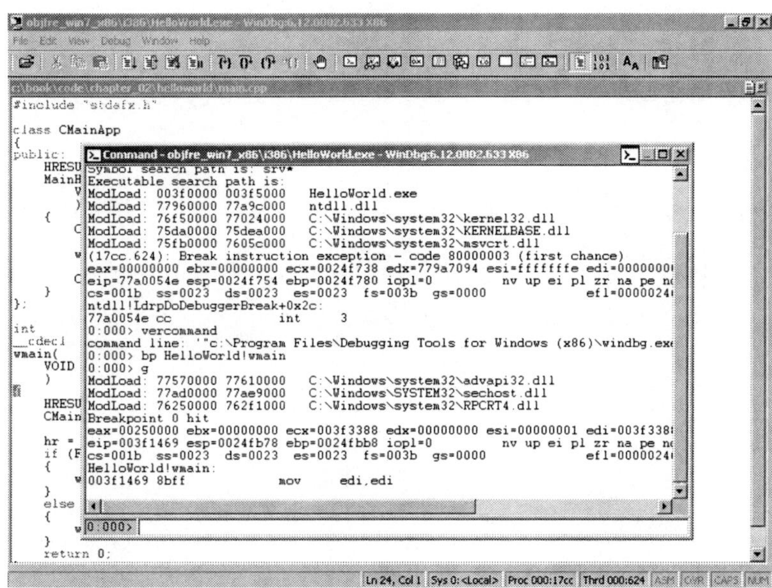

FIGURE 2-2 Breaking at a program's entry point in WinDbg.

Notice how WinDbg automatically loads the source code corresponding to this program when it hits the *wmain* breakpoint. For the debugger to be able to correctly resolve source files, you typically also need to set the source path using the *.srcpath* command or append to the existing source path using the *.srcpath+* command. In this case, it isn't needed because you are debugging code that was compiled on the same machine, and the debugger can automatically locate the source files for your code.

You should now have two windows inside the main WinDbg window area: a command window and a source code window. The next (minor) challenge if you are new to the WinDbg user interface is to settle on a window arrangement that works best for you. A common setup that I use is to dock the command window, which you can easily do by invoking the Dock menu action of the command window, as illustrated in Figure 2-3.

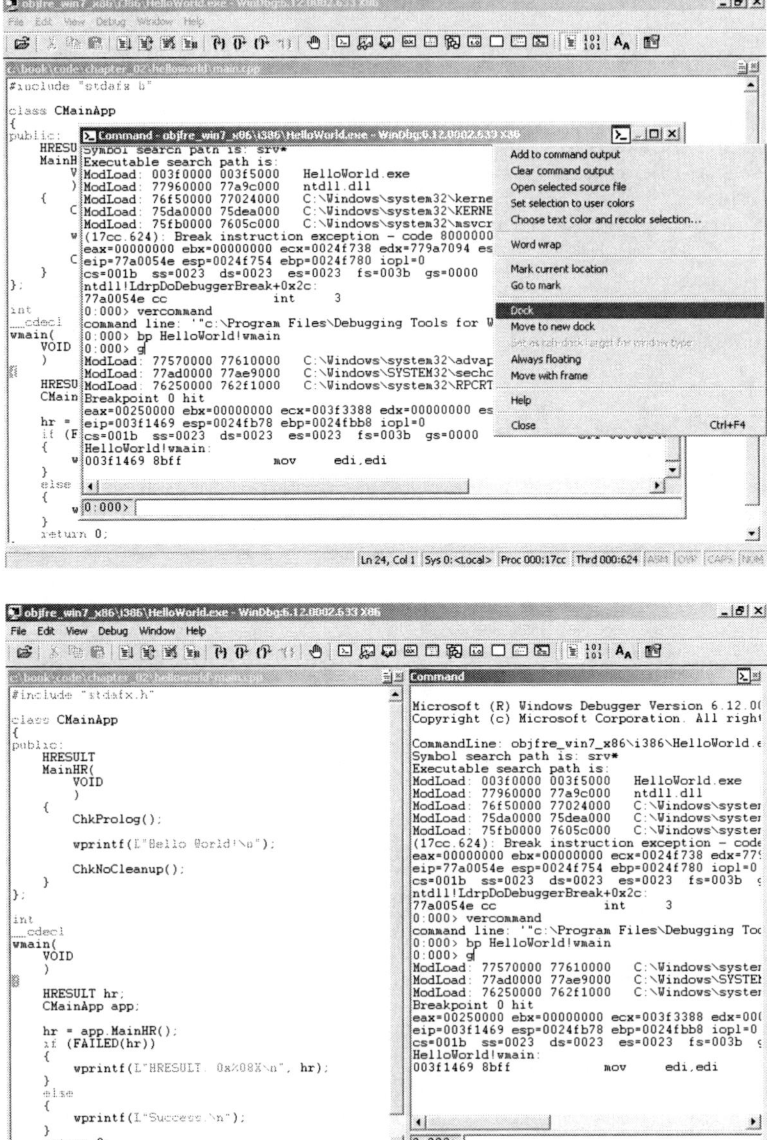

FIGURE 2-3 Docking the command window in WinDbg.

The previous command docks the window to either the left or right side of the screen. Notice how you now have a command prompt where you can type your debugging commands and a source window where you can see the source line that is about to get executed. As in the Visual Studio case, you can also use the F10 shortcut to step over a function call and the F11 shortcut to step into it. You can also add more windows to your view by choosing one of the View menu actions, though you'll find that the command and source windows are sufficient once you become familiar with the direct debugger commands to access each view output. For example, typing **r** in the command window is equivalent to View\Registers and typing **dv** is equivalent to View\Locals. Here is an example:

```
0:000> $ Dump the local variables of the current function
0:000> $  Notice that the compiler optimized the two local variables (hr, app) out
0:000> dv
0:000> $ Display the values of all the CPU registers
0:000> r
eax=00250000 ebx=00000000 ecx=003f3388 edx=00000000 esi=00000001 edi=003f3388
eip=003f1469 esp=0024fb78 ebp=0024fbb8 iopl=0         nv up ei pl zr na pe nc
cs=001b  ss=0023  ds=0023  es=0023  fs=003b  gs=0000             efl=00000246
HelloWorld!wmain:
003f1469 8bff            mov     edi,edi
```

Docking Windows in WinDbg

One of the silly annoyances of the WinDbg user interface is that it occasionally does a poor job of automatically docking new windows, such as the ones you invoke using the View menu. If you get into a state where you would rather just go back to the default window arrangement rather than fight the finicky user interface, you can delete all the saved workspaces for the current process by using the File\Delete Workspaces menu action. If you are unhappy with the window arrangement for all your sessions and not just a single program, you can also manually delete the [HKEY_CURRENT_USER\Software\Microsoft\Windbg\Workspaces] registry key. When you re-start *windbg.exe*, you will be back to a pristine state. Note that this also deletes other workspace data such as saved breakpoints, so be sure you don't mind that before you wipe out your saved workspaces.

You can now terminate the debugging session, which you can do in one of two ways:

- Close the debugger window, or type **q** in the debugger's command prompt. This also terminates the target process at the same time.
- The other way to quit the debugging session is to type **qd** (which stands for "quit and detach") in the debugger's command prompt. This exits the debugger but doesn't kill the target process. In the case of the previous debugging session, the effect is that the target process prints the "Hello World!" message before exiting, when it would've vanished before printing that message had the *q* command been used instead.

```
0:000> $ Terminate the session but let the target process continue running
0:000> qd
```

When asked whether you would like the debugger to save your workspace or not, answer yes or no based on whether you want the debugger to save the debugging session's settings (such as permanent breakpoints or the window arrangement in the UI) for when you start a new debugging session for the same target process.

Debugging System Code

Now that you've seen how to use the WinDbg debugger to step through your own code in a simple scenario, it's time to try it in a situation that involves system code for which you don't have the source code. The ability to seamlessly transition between your own code and the system code that it invokes is one of several features that make WinDbg the debugger of choice for system-level debugging in Windows.

This experiment uses the *notepad.exe* text editor as an example to demonstrate how you can set system breakpoints. In the previous experiment, the program was started directly using the *windbg.exe* command line, but you can also use *windbg.exe* to start debugging a program after it has already been started. This second approach is known as "attaching" a debugger to the program. You can do that easily in the *windbg.exe* user interface by using the F6 shortcut, which brings up a dialog box that allows you to select the user-mode program you would like to attach to.

To follow this experiment as described in this section, you need to use the *x86* versions of both *notepad.exe* and the *windbg.exe* debugger. If you're running on a 64-bit version of Windows, you can use the 32-bit *notepad.exe* from *%windir%\SysWow64* instead of the 64-bit version under *system32*. Once you've started *notepad.exe*, use the F6 shortcut in *windbg.exe* to attach to that new process, which should be near the bottom of the Attach dialog box because new processes tend to be listed at the end of the process list. (The process ID might be different from the one shown in Figure 2-4, naturally.)

```
C:\Program Files\Debugging Tools for Windows (x86)>windbg.exe
```

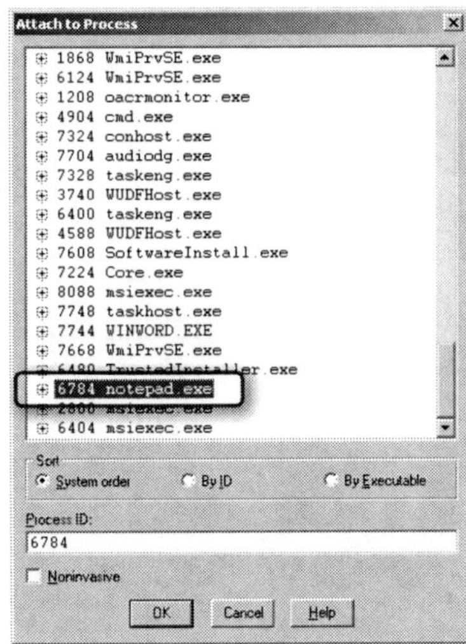

FIGURE 2-4 Attaching to an existing process in WinDbg (using the F6 shortcut).

After clicking OK, you will again be presented with a command window where you can enter debugging commands, just like in the case of the "Hello World!" experiment shown earlier in this chapter. Now that you have *notepad.exe* stopped inside the debugger, you might, for example, want to add a breakpoint so that you can break back into the debugger as you open a new file in the *notepad.exe* UI (using the File\Open dialog box) and see which API is being called to display the new dialog box. To do that, however, you need to point the debugger to *symbol files*. Without proper symbols, you'll be unable to list the function names that are present in the *notepad.exe* module, so you wouldn't be able to find the virtual address of the breakpoint you are seeking. In particular, the useful *windbg.exe "x"* command that lists the available symbols in a loaded module will fail and warn you that symbols for the target module couldn't be located, as illustrated in the following listing.

```
0:001> x notepad!*open*
*** ERROR: Module load completed but symbols could not be loaded for C:\Windows\system32\
notepad.exe
```

In the previous section where *windbg.exe* was used to step through your own code, the symbol file for the main program (*HelloWorld.pdb*) was automatically loaded by WinDbg because it could find it under the same path as the main executable, right where the C++ linker placed it during the build process. In this case, however, the symbol file for *notepad.exe* isn't shipped in Windows. Instead, Microsoft makes the symbols for the products it ships available to developers on what is called a *symbols server*, which is an online repository for all the symbol files from the past public product releases by Microsoft. To set the debugger symbols search path in WinDbg to point to the Microsoft online symbols server, you can use the *.symfix* debugger command and then reload the symbols (*.reload*) for all the loaded modules (including the main *notepad.exe* executable module and the system DLL modules it loads as dependencies).

```
0:001> .symfix
0:001> .reload
Reloading current modules
.............................................................
```

Unfortunately, the *x* command doesn't work with wildcards the very first time; you have to let the target go and break back into the debugger again. (The *x notepad!** command, which lists all the symbols from the module, works without this extra step, but its output will be too large to process efficiently.) So, you should type **g** and use the Debug\Break menu action from the debugger UI to break back after the target runs as a workaround.

```
0:001> $ Use Debug\Break after hitting 'g' to break back again into the debugger
0:001> g
(86c.e18): Break instruction exception - code 80000003 (first chance)
...
ntdll!DbgBreakPoint:
774340f0 cc              int     3
0:001> x notepad!*open*
0011401c notepad!CLSID_FileOpenDialog = <no type information>
00111248 notepad!_imp__OpenClipboard = <no type information>
0011c30c notepad!szOpenCaption = <no type information>
00113f21 notepad!InvokeOpenDialog = <no type information>
00113bcd notepad!ShowOpenSaveDialog = <no type information>
...
```

As you can see in the preceding listing, there is a function whose name (shown in bold text) strongly suggests that it might be called when the File\Open dialog box is invoked, which you can verify by setting a breakpoint and observing that it gets hit every time you open a new file in the *notepad.exe* UI.

```
0:001> bp notepad!ShowOpenSaveDialog
0:001> $ Use File\Open... in the notepad.exe UI after you hit 'g'...
0:001> g
Breakpoint 0 hit
...
notepad!ShowOpenSaveDialog:
```

You can now list the stack trace at the time of this breakpoint by using the *k* debugger command, which is one of the most important debugger commands in WinDbg.

```
0:000> k
ChildEBP RetAddr
0026f564 00113fdb notepad!ShowOpenSaveDialog
0026f590 00113ef0 notepad!InvokeOpenDialog+0xba
0026f608 001117f7 notepad!NPCommand+0x147
0026f624 769cc4e7 notepad!NPWndProc+0x49f
0026f650 769cc5e7 USER32!InternalCallWinProc+0x23
0026f6c8 769ccc19 USER32!UserCallWinProcCheckWow+0x14b
0026f728 769ccc70 USER32!DispatchMessageWorker+0x35e
0026f738 001114d7 USER32!DispatchMessageW+0xf
0026f76c 001116ec notepad!WinMain+0xdd
0026f7fc 76aced6c notepad!_initterm_e+0x1a1
0026f808 774637f5 kernel32!BaseThreadInitThunk+0xe
0026f848 774637c8 ntdll!__RtlUserThreadStart+0x70
0026f860 00000000 ntdll!_RtlUserThreadStart+0x1b
```

Once you type **g** again, you'll see the new File\Open dialog box show up on the screen. If you break back into the debugger while this dialog box is still active (again using the Debug\Break menu action in the WinDbg UI), you'll see that the debugger context is now in a new thread, as indicated by the thread number in the command prompt's prefix (015 in the listing shown here, though the actual thread number you'll see will vary from one run to the next).

```
0:015> $ current thread number is no longer thread #0
```

Using the ~ debugger command, which in the WinDbg user-mode debugger allows you to see all the active threads contained within the process being debugged, you'll notice several new threads in the process.

```
0:015> ~
   0  Id: 86c.1eb0 Suspend: 1 Teb: 7ffdf000 Unfrozen
   1  Id: 86c.124c Suspend: 1 Teb: 7ffde000 Unfrozen
   2  Id: 86c.1a4c Suspend: 1 Teb: 7ffdc000 Unfrozen
...
  14  Id: 86c.1c78 Suspend: 1 Teb: 7ffad000 Unfrozen
. 15  Id: 86c.dcc Suspend: 1 Teb: 7ffac000 Unfrozen
```

The ~ command can also be combined with the *s* suffix to change (switch) the current thread context in the WinDbg user-mode debugger. This allows you to switch the current thread context over to the main UI thread (thread number 0 is the first thread in the process), list its stack trace, and see that the dialog box is now waiting for user input.

```
0:015> $ Switch over to thread #0 (main UI thread)
0:015> ~0s
0:000> k
ChildEBP RetAddr
0026f298 77446a04 ntdll!KiFastSystemCallRet
0026f29c 75626a36 ntdll!ZwWaitForMultipleObjects+0xc
0026f338 76acbd1e KERNELBASE!WaitForMultipleObjectsEx+0x100
0026f380 769c62f9 kernel32!WaitForMultipleObjectsExImplementation+0xe0
0026f3d4 73e31717 USER32!RealMsgWaitForMultipleObjectsEx+0x13c
0026f3f4 73e317b8 DUser!CoreSC::Wait+0x59
0026f41c 73e31757 DUser!CoreSC::WaitMessage+0x54
0026f42c 769c66ed DUser!MphWaitMessageEx+0x2b
0026f448 77446fee USER32!__ClientWaitMessageExMPH+0x1e
0026f464 769c66c9 ntdll!KiUserCallbackDispatcher+0x2e
0026f468 769e382a USER32!NtUserWaitMessage+0xc
0026f49c 769e3b27 USER32!DialogBox2+0x207
0026f4c0 769e3b76 USER32!InternalDialogBox+0xcb
0026f4e0 769e3b9a USER32!DialogBoxIndirectParamAorW+0x37
0026f500 76b8597b USER32!DialogBoxIndirectParamW+0x1b
0026f54c 00113c2f COMDLG32!CFileOpenSave::Show+0x181
0026f564 00113fdb notepad!ShowOpenSaveDialog+0x62
...
0:000> $ You can also use * to list the call stacks of all the other threads in the process
0:000> ~*k
```

You're now done with this first system debugging experiment and can close the debugging session, but you've been able to learn important details about how the File\Open dialog box is implemented in *notepad.exe*. You can see from the functions in the previous call stack that *notepad.exe* internally uses the common controls from the COMDLG32 system DLL, which in turn use the lower-level Win32 APIs in the USER32 system DLL to wait for user input (*USER32!NtUserWaitMessage*). Notice in addition that the user-mode WinDbg debugger is able to list function calls only as far as the system call (*ntdll!KiFastSystemCallRet*) and doesn't display what happens on the other side of the fence (the kernel-mode side of the call), which highlights one important limitation of user-mode debugging. In this particular case, however, it's not very hard to guess what happens on that side, and it's reasonable to assume that the thread gets switched out and waits to be awoken by the new input events that get signaled by the kernel-mode Windows subsystem (*win32k.sys*), as was covered in the previous chapter. You can follow that sequence later in this chapter using a kernel debugging session without having to take this leap of faith.

Listing the Values of Local Variables and Function Parameters

When a breakpoint is hit inside the debugger, typically the first thing you want to do is display the call stack of the current thread to see who invoked the code in question. That's exactly what you just did in the previous experiment when you used the *k* debugger command. The other logical question you probably want to answer next is the values of the local variables and arguments passed to the function when it was called.

Listing Parameters and Locals for Your Own Code

When debugging your own code, the *kP* debugger command, which in addition to displaying the stack trace of the current thread also tries to show the parameters to each function on the call stack, works well in most cases. Whether the values that it displays are actually accurate or not depends on several factors, including whether your code was built free or checked and also the CPU architecture it was compiled for. In the *x86* case, in particular, this should just work. To provide a practical illustration, you can use the job object C++ sample from Chapter 1, "Software Development in Windows." For more details on how to compile the programs included with the companion source code, refer back to the procedure in the Introduction of this book.

After starting the program under WinDbg, set a breakpoint at the process-creation Win32 API (*kernel32!CreateProcessW*) that the program calls to create its worker process, as demonstrated in the following listing.

```
0:000> vercommand
command line: '"c:\Program Files\Debugging Tools for Windows (x86)\windbg.exe"
C:\book\code\chapter_01\WorkerProcess\objfre_win7_x86\i386\workerprocess.exe'
0:000> .symfix
0:000> .reload
0:000> bp kernel32!CreateProcessW
0:000> g
...
Breakpoint 0 hit
kernel32!CreateProcessW:
0:000> kP
ChildEBP RetAddr
0012f9c0 00621c06 kernel32!CreateProcessW
0012fa4c 00621eb6 workerprocess!CMainApp::LaunchProcess(
            wchar_t * pwszCommandLine = 0x00176fa8 "notepad.exe",
            unsigned long dwCreationFlags = 0,
            void ** phProcess = 0x0012faec,
            void ** phPrimaryThread = 0x0012fae4)+0x47
[C:\book\code\chapter_01\workerprocess\main.cpp @ 94]
0012fafc 00621f69 workerprocess!CMainApp::MainHR(void)+0xc1
0012fb08 00622701 workerprocess!wmain(void)+0x5
0012fb4c 7633ed6c workerprocess!__wmainCRTStartup(void)+0x102
...
```

Notice that the *kP* command displays the parameters next to each function in the call stack. If you want to display the local variables of higher functions, you can also use the *kn* flavor of the *k* command, which also displays the frame number of every function in the call stack, and switch to the appropriate frame by using the *.frame* debugger command. The *dv* ("dump local variables") and *dt* ("dump type") commands would then run in the context of that frame and display the values of the local variables for that function, respectively.

```
0:000> kn
 # ChildEBP RetAddr
00 0012f9c0 00621c06 kernel32!CreateProcessW
01 0012fa4c 00621eb6 workerprocess!CMainApp::LaunchProcess+0x47
02 0012fafc 00621f69 workerprocess!CMainApp::MainHR+0xc1
03 0012fb08 00622701 workerprocess!wmain+0x5
```

```
04 0012fb4c 7633ed6c workerprocess!__wmainCRTStartup+0x102
0:000> .frame 1
01 0012fa4c 00621eb6 workerprocess!CMainApp::LaunchProcess+0x47
[C:\book\code\chapter_01\workerprocess\main.cpp @ 94]
0:000> dv
pwszCommandLine = 0x00176fa8 "notepad.exe"
dwCreationFlags = 0
      phProcess = 0x0012faec
phPrimaryThread = 0x0012fae4
             si = struct _STARTUPINFOW
             pi = struct _PROCESS_INFORMATION
0:000> $ dt can be used to display the value of local variables that have complex types
0:000> dt pi
Local var @ 0x12fa3c Type _PROCESS_INFORMATION
   +0x000 hProcess         : (null)
   +0x004 hThread          : (null)
   +0x008 dwProcessId      : 0
   +0x00c dwThreadId       : 0
```

This is all excellent news. However, you'll notice that the *kP* command didn't display the arguments to the *kernel32!CreateProcessW* Win32 function call itself. Moreover, if you try to use the same *dv* command with that Win32 API call frame, you won't be able to dump the local variables, either. This is because the symbols for the operating system (OS) binaries don't contain as much information as the symbol files of your own code. Here is the result:

```
0:000> $ Switch back to frame #0 again (kernel32!CreateProcessW)
0:000> .frame 0
00 0012f9c0 00621c06 kernel32!CreateProcessW
0:000> dv
Unable to enumerate locals, HRESULT 0x80004005
Private symbols (symbols.pri) are required for locals.
```

Listing Parameters and Locals for System Code

Fortunately, you can often work around the lack of support in the OS symbols and still find the locals and arguments to system API calls by following the stack pointer (the *esp* register on *x86*, or the *rsp* register on *x64*) or the saved stack frame pointers on the stack. This section will show you, step by step, how to perform this manual analysis.

As an illustration, you'll apply this technique to find the arguments to the *CreateProcess* Win32 API call, which you weren't otherwise able to get by simply using the *dv* command. Because this section is relatively advanced, don't worry if you find yourself needing to read it more than once before you understand it perfectly. Feel free also to skip it for now and get back to it once you've read the rest of the chapter. However, this technique will be used in several experiments when debugging both user-mode and kernel-mode system code, so you'll eventually need it in your arsenal.

To understand why this technique works, it is important to first remember the conventions used by the C/C++ compilers to emit assembly code for function calls. Most Win32 functions use the *__stdcall* calling convention, where the stack is used to pass parameters from the caller to the callee function and the callee restores the stack pointer. The exception to this is Win32 functions with a variable number of arguments (such as the C runtime *printf* function), which aren't able to use this convention and instead use the *__cdecl* calling convention. They do so because only the caller in that special case knows the number of parameters being passed to the callee and, hence, is able to restore the stack pointer location after the call to the function is done.

In the *__stdcall* calling convention on the *x86* platform, the caller pushes the arguments in reverse order and the return address is saved before control is transferred to the callee. The callee function will then usually also set up what is called a *frame pointer* by saving the stack pointer's location at the time of function entry in a special register (*ebp*), and then reserve space on the stack for local variables. Having a frame pointer allows the compiler to easily access function locals and arguments using their relative offsets from the memory address that's kept in the frame pointer register. Incidentally, this also means it's possible to follow this chain of frame pointers to find the parameters and locals of the functions on the call stack. (See Figure 2-5.)

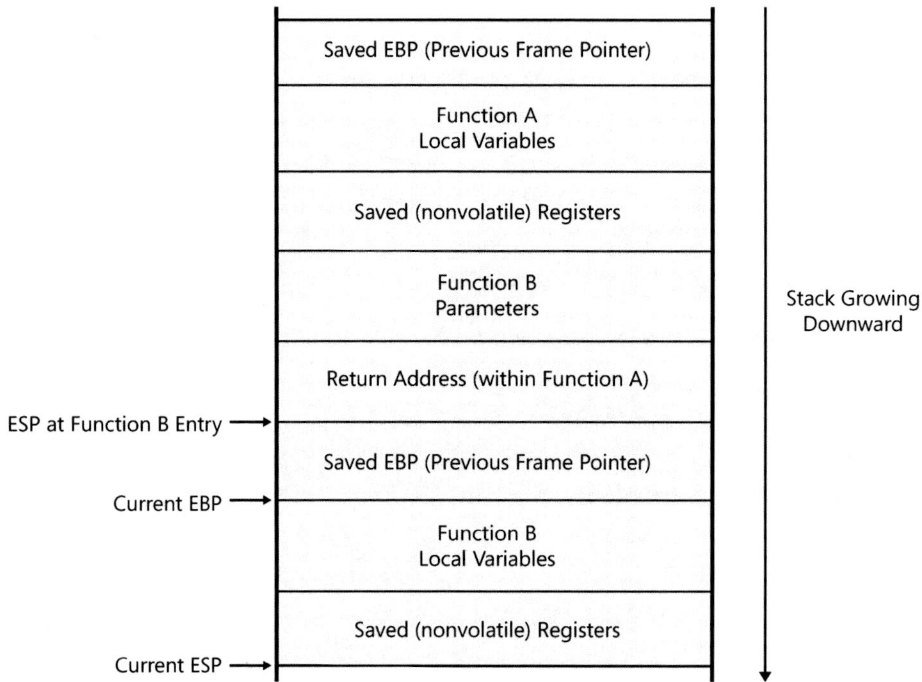

FIGURE 2-5 Stack layout in *__stdcall* calling convention (*x86*).

Now that you understand this background, you are in position to walk the stack and extract the arguments passed to the *CreateProcess* Win32 API call, which like most other Win32 APIs uses the *__stdcall* calling convention. In this case, you own the code that makes the call and already know the parameters you're passing, but this technique would work even if you didn't have that knowledge. As it turns out, the *k* debugger command already walks the stack of the current thread to a certain extent and displays the saved frame pointers for each frame on the call stack in the first column labeled *ChildEBP*.

```
0:000> k
ChildEBP RetAddr
0012f9c0 00621c06 kernel32!CreateProcessW
0012fa4c 00621eb6 workerprocess!CMainApp::LaunchProcess+0x47
0012fafc 00621f69 workerprocess!CMainApp::MainHR+0xc1
0012fb08 00622701 workerprocess!wmain+0x5
0012fb4c 7633ed6c workerprocess!__wmainCRTStartup+0x102
```

At the time of the breakpoint, the *ebp* register hasn't been updated to point to the current function's frame. Notice that the current value of the *ebp* register still contains the frame pointer of the caller function, which you can match with the output of the *k* command from the previous listing. Naturally, the actual values you'll see when you run this experiment on your machine will be different, but you should be able to match them just as described in this section.

```
0:000> r
eax=0012f9f8 ebx=00000000 ecx=00000000 edx=00000000 esi=00000000 edi=0012fa4c
eip=762f204d esp=0012f9c4 ebp=0012fa4c ...
```

If you use the *u* ("unassemble") command at this point to list the next disassembly that's about to get executed, as demonstrated in the following listing where the "." alias is used to conveniently reference the current address stored in the instruction pointer register (*eip*), you'll see that the following three instructions push the previous *ebp* value on the stack (moving *esp* one slot down) and then move the value of the stack pointer (*esp*) to the *ebp* register, establishing the new frame pointer in the process.

```
0:000> u .
kernel32!CreateProcessW:
762f204d 8bff            mov     edi,edi
762f204f 55              push    ebp
762f2050 8bec            mov     ebp,esp
...
```

Once you execute those three instructions using the F11 shortcut or, equivalently, the *t* debugger command, you'll finally get *ebp* holding the current frame pointer as was displayed by the *k* command at the time of the breakpoint. This is demonstrated in the following listing. Note in particular that the debugger was smart enough to perform this simple computation ahead of time and show you the eventual (correct) frame pointer when you used the *k* command even before this prolog was executed.

```
0:000> t
0:000> t
0:000> t
0:000> r ebp
ebp=0012f9c0
```

The value of *ebp* now corresponds exactly to the state depicted in Figure 2-5. You can now use the *dd* command, which dumps memory as a sequence of DWORD (4-byte) values, to display the values right after the memory location that the *ebp* register value points to. The memory slots will represent, in this order, the saved *ebp* (previous frame pointer) and the return address; then in reverse order, it will represent the arguments (shown in bold text in the following debugger listing) passed to the *CreateProcess* Win32 API call (the *__stdcall* convention).

```
0:000> dd 0012f9c0
0012f9c0  0012fa4c 00621c06 00000000 00176fa8
0012f9d0  00000000 00000000 00000000 00000000
0012f9e0  00000000 00000000 0012f9f8 0012fa3c
...
```

In the *CreateProcessW* API documentation on the MSDN website, you'll see that it takes 10 parameters and that the second one is the command-line string to be started by the API call. You can now use the *du* ("dump as a Unicode string") debugger command with the value you obtained earlier from the *dd* command (again, a value that will be different from one run to the next) to view the contents of the memory referenced with that pointer value, as shown here.

```
0:000> du 00176fa8
00176fa8  "notepad.exe"
```

Notice how you were able to use this technique to retrieve the parameters without having to depend on the debugger's *kP* command, which wasn't able to display them for the system API call frame anyway. This step finally concludes this system debugging experiment.

```
0:000> $ Quit the debugging session
0:000> q
```

You can also use this same technique to find the local variables for the other functions on the call stack, not just the first one. You can do this as long as those locals were saved on the stack and you know the order in which they appear and their respective types. However, you would then need to look at the memory that comes before the saved frame pointer rather than the memory right after it.

Note, finally, that this useful technique can be complicated, unfortunately, by the use of other calling conventions—such as the *__fastcall* convention, where arguments might be saved in registers instead of on the stack, which makes it harder to walk the stack backward looking for argument values. This is also the case for binaries compiled for *x64* because the first four function parameters, again, are usually saved in registers rather than on the stack in that case.

Source-Level Debugging in WinDbg

When stepping over or into a line of code in *windbg.exe*, the debugger determines the current debugging mode ("source" or "assembly") and tries to correctly determine how many assembly instructions it should skip before breaking back in again. This is convenient with source-level debugging because it gives the impression of tracing through lines of code. In some cases, however, it can be useful to switch over to assembly-mode stepping even when you're debugging your own code. An example is when trying to step through the assembly expansion of C/C++ pre-processor macros. In *windbg.exe*, you can cancel selection of the Source Mode option in the Debug menu, or similarly use the *"l"* debugger command to quickly toggle between these two (assembly vs. source) debugging modes, as illustrated in the following debugging session.

```
0:000> vercommand
command line: '"c:\Program Files\Debugging Tools for Windows (x86)\windbg.exe"
c:\book\code\chapter_02\HelloWorld\objfre_win7_x86\i386\HelloWorld.exe'
0:000> bp HelloWorld!wmain
```

```
0:000> g
...
Breakpoint 0 hit
0:000> $ The debugger is currently in source-level debugging mode
0:000> l-
Source options are 1:
     1/t - Step/trace by source line
0:000> $ Switch to assembly mode. F10 now only executes one assembly instruction
0:000> l-t
Source options are 0:
    None
0:000> $ F10 shortcut
0:000> p
eax=00090000 ebx=00000000 ecx=00293388 edx=00000000 esi=00000001 edi=00293388
eip=0029146b esp=0008ff04 ebp=0008ff44 iopl=0         nv up ei pl zr na pe nc
cs=001b  ss=0023  ds=0023  es=0023  fs=003b  gs=0000             efl=00000246
HelloWorld!wmain+0x2:
0029146b 55              push    ebp
```

In fact, the "*l*" debugger command is more generic than the Debug\Source Mode WinDbg UI menu action because it supports three more modes (*l*, *s*, and *o*) in addition to the source mode (*t*), as illustrated in the following debugger listing.

```
0:000> $ Re-enable source mode (no assembly lines shown at debugger prompt)
0:000> l+*
Source options are ffffffff:
     1/t - Step/trace by source line
     2/l - List source line at prompt
     4/s - List source code at prompt
     8/o - Only show source code at prompt
0:000> $ F10 shortcut
0:000> p
>   28:      hr = app.MainHR();
0:000> $ Go back to assembly mode again
0:000> l-*
Source options are 0:
    None
0:000> $ Continue debugging, if needed, and then quit the debugging session
0:000> q
```

Symbol Files, Servers, and Local Caches

When building a C/C++ image, the linker generates a file with a *.pdb* (program database) file extension that contains the symbols of the image. Though older tools also kept some debugging information in the image itself or sometimes in a *.dbg* symbol file, most new compiler/linker versions from Microsoft now generate all debugging information in a standalone *.pdb* file. The .NET Microsoft Intermediate Language (MSIL) binaries can also have associated PDB symbol files, but their role in that case is mostly limited to source-level debugging support.

Public vs. Private Symbols

The PDB symbol files contain critical information to enable debugging, such as the mappings between function names and their corresponding memory addresses, the types declared in the image, and also source-line information. You should always generate and archive PDB symbols when building your software, especially for your final released version. That does not mean you need to ship those private symbols with your product, but having them archived for each released version of your software will allow you to debug any issues that your customer base might encounter in the future. Microsoft religiously follows this engineering practice for all of its released products.

By default, the symbol files generated by the C/C++ linker contain a lot of information, probably more than most software vendors feel comfortable exposing externally. So, a post-build processing step (using a tool such as the *binplace.exe* utility) is usually applied to strip private symbol information out of the PDB files and produce what is called *public symbols*. These stripped-down symbols cannot be used for source-level debugging because they don't contain source file or line number information. They also don't include information to help display function parameters, local variable information, or the type information for local variables. Nevertheless, they still contain enough information to enable key debugging scenarios. In fact, you've already successfully used the Microsoft public symbol files in the experiments shown earlier in this chapter where you were able to debug the code in the OS.

Microsoft Symbols Server

Microsoft has made available the public symbols of Windows binaries so that developers can use them to understand the interactions between their code and the services, features, and APIs exposed as part of the operating system. This book uses the public symbols for the Windows operating system throughout. These OS symbols are very useful when trying to understand system components, because they contain the mappings between the symbolic names of every function in the binary and the corresponding virtual memory addresses, in addition to the names of global and static variables.

Note Even though the Microsoft public symbols do not include any type information, an exception to this rule is a few types in the *ntdll.dll* and *nt* (kernel binary) modules. To enable public debugger extension commands—such as the *!heap* extension—to work even when slight changes to the underlying data structures are made (for example, in service pack releases), type information for a few types used in these public extensions is actually left in the public symbol files. These special types (*ntdll!_PEB*, *nt!_EPROCESS*, *nt!_ETHREAD*, *nt!_KTHREAD*, and others) and their fields can be viewed using the *dt* ("dump type") debugger command in WinDbg, just like the rest of the types in your own code.

Microsoft maintains its online repository of public symbols for released products at the nonbrowsable URL *http://msdl.microsoft.com/download/symbols*. Both the Windows and Visual Studio debuggers support looking up symbols on a server based on the version of the binary being debugged. This is a fantastic feature that saves you the trouble of manually looking up the symbols that correspond to the build of the binaries you're using.

Caching Symbols Offline for WinDbg

The Windows debuggers also keep a local cache of the symbols that are downloaded online to speed up symbol lookup when the images are reused in the future. The local path onto which symbols get downloaded is called the *symbols cache* path.

You've already seen the convenient *.symfix* helper debugger command, which sets the symbols search path in the debugger to the Microsoft public symbols server so that you don't need to memorize the *http://msdl.microsoft.com/download/symbols* URL.

```
0:000> vercommand
command-line: '"c:\Program Files\Debugging Tools for Windows (x86)\windbg.exe"
c:\Windows\system32\notepad.exe'
0:000> .symfix
0:000> $ Notice that the debugger symbols path now points to the Microsoft public server
0:000> .sympath
Symbol search path is: srv*
Expanded Symbol search path is: cache*c:\Program Files\Debugging Tools for Windows (x86)\
sym;SRV*http://msdl.microsoft.com/download/symbols
```

When using the *.symfix* command, the debugger, by default, picks the *sym* subfolder of the debugger installation directory to be the symbols cache path, but it's usually a good idea (though not absolutely necessary) to change the default symbols path set by the *.symfix* command to a path that is not restricted to administrative accounts, as illustrated in the following debugger listing. In the *.sympath* command, you can specify an explicit cache path by inserting it between the * signs after the SRV prefix, as shown here.

```
0:000> $ Change the local symbols path (path in between the * signs)
0:000> .sympath SRV*c:\LocalSymbolCache*http://msdl.microsoft.com/download/symbols
0:000> $ Reload symbols for all the loaded modules
0:000> .reload
0:000> $ List all the loaded modules in the process
0:000> lm
start    end        module name
00180000 001b0000   notepad    (deferred)
...
```

As you can see in the output from the *lm* command, which lists all the loaded modules in the target process, WinDbg delays loading the symbol files until it really needs to. However, it is sometimes useful to force the debugger to immediately locate the symbols to determine whether the symbols for a particular module are present on the symbols search path. The */f* option of the *.reload* debugger command can be used for this purpose. This option can take an optional module name or otherwise be used to force reloading symbols for all of the loaded modules.

```
0:000> $ Force the debugger to locate the PDB file corresponding to notepad.exe
0:000> .reload /f notepad.exe
0:000> lm
start    end        module name
00c80000 00cb0000   notepad    (pdb symbols) c:\LocalSymbolCache\notepad.pdb\
E325F5195AE94FAEB58D25C9DF8C0CFD2\notepad.pdb
...
0:000> $ Now force the debugger to locate PDB files for all loaded modules
```

```
0:000> .reload /f
Reloading current modules....................
0:000> $ Continue debugging, if needed, and then quit the debugging session
0:000> q
```

You also can use the standalone *symchk.exe* utility—which comes as part of the Windows debuggers—to download symbols from an Internet symbols server onto a local path and build a cache that can be used to speed up symbol access times. This can be useful if you plan to use the machine in disconnected mode and know that you might not have access to the Internet in the future to download the symbols on demand.

The following command can be used, for instance, to pre-download the symbols for all the system binaries under the *system32* directory from the Microsoft public symbols server and place them under the C:\LocalSymbolCache directory. Be warned, however, that pre-populating this local cache for all the binaries under the *system32* directory can take a long time to complete (even on a fast Internet connection) and also ends up downloading symbols for binaries you might never use. For example, this command resulted in a local symbols cache folder that was larger than 1 GB on my Windows 7 test machine, so be sure you don't mind that before you decide to eagerly cache all the Windows symbols locally.

```
C:\Program Files\Debugging Tools for Windows (x86)>symchk.exe /r c:\Windows\system32 /s
srv*C:\LocalSymbolCache*http://msdl.microsoft.com/download/symbols
...
SYMCHK: PASSED + IGNORED files = 14833
```

Troubleshooting Symbol Resolution Issues in WinDbg

One common problem you will undoubtedly run into during your debugging is mismatched symbols—either because a matching PDB symbol file could not be found on the debugger symbols search path or because none could be matched with the current version of the binary. A command you will find useful when dealing with this problem is the *!sym noisy* command, which adds extra logging to the debugger window so that you know exactly how the debugger engine tried to retrieve the PDB files. When you no longer need this verbose logging, you can type **!sym quiet** to go back to the normal (quiet) mode again, as illustrated in the following debugger listing.

```
0:000> vercommand
command-line: '"c:\Program Files\Debugging Tools for Windows (x86)\windbg.exe"
c:\Windows\system32\notepad.exe'
0:000> $ Turn on verbose symbol lookup
0:000> !sym noisy
noisy mode - symbol prompts on
0:000> .symfix
0:000> .reload
Reloading current modules...................
DBGHELP: ntdll - public symbols
        c:\Program Files\Debugging Tools for Windows (x86)\sym\ntdll.pdb\120028FA453F4CD5A6A404
EC37396A582\ntdll.pdb
0:000> $ Return to quiet mode and continue debugging...
0:000> !sym quiet
0:000> $ Quit the debugging session
0:000> q
```

Name Decoration Considerations

C++ supports having multiple overloads of the same function name that differ only by their argument types. When emitting symbols for multiple overloads, the C/C++ linker *decorates* the symbol names to eliminate the ambiguity by encoding the argument order and their types into the function's symbolic name. Symbol decoration is essentially the C/C++ linker's way of differentiating functions that have different calling conventions or overloads with the same name but different signatures.

Fortunately, the *x* command's support for wildcard characters makes name decoration considerations an issue you likely will never have to deal with in WinDbg. You can always use the *x* command first to list all the overloads of a function (by its simple name) and then use the hexadecimal address of the function you would like to target to set breakpoints in the debugger. With private symbols (your own code), the *x* command actually also displays the parameter type information alongside the symbol name, so it is easy for you to pick the right overload. This is why WinDbg's default mode always displays the undecorated symbol names.

Other debuggers, such as Visual Studio, aren't so kind and require you to use the decorated symbol name when setting system breakpoints. In WinDbg, the *.symopt* command can be used if you want to display the unambiguous decorated symbol names. For example, you can use this command and see that the decorated name for the .NET 4.0 execution engine DLL's entry point is *clr!_DllMain@12*. The *–z* debugger command-line option used here to load the DLL module and inspect its symbols is interesting in its own right, and it's the same option used for loading crash dumps in postmortem debugging—a topic that'll be covered later in this part of the book.

```
"C:\Program Files\Debugging Tools for Windows (x86)\windbg.exe"
-z C:\Windows\Microsoft.NET\Framework\v4.0.30319\clr.dll
...
0:000> .symfix
0:000> .reload
0:000> $ Notice the SYMOPT_UNDNAME (undecorated name) option is set by default
0:000> .symopt
Symbol options are 0x30237:
  0x00000001 - SYMOPT_CASE_INSENSITIVE
  0x00000002 - SYMOPT_UNDNAME
  0x00000004 - SYMOPT_DEFERRED_LOADS
  0x00000010 - SYMOPT_LOAD_LINES
  0x00000020 - SYMOPT_OMAP_FIND_NEAREST
  0x00000200 - SYMOPT_FAIL_CRITICAL_ERRORS
  0x00010000 - SYMOPT_AUTO_PUBLICS
  0x00020000 - SYMOPT_NO_IMAGE_SEARCH
0:000> $ Notice the x command displays non-decorated symbol names
0:000> x clr!*dllmain*
...
6b9bdbd8 clr!DllMain = <no type information>
0:000> $ Disable the SYMOPT_UNDNAME flag now...
0:000> .symopt- 2
Symbol options are 0x30235:
  0x00000001 - SYMOPT_CASE_INSENSITIVE
  0x00000004 - SYMOPT_DEFERRED_LOADS
  0x00000010 - SYMOPT_LOAD_LINES
  0x00000020 - SYMOPT_OMAP_FIND_NEAREST
  0x00000200 - SYMOPT_FAIL_CRITICAL_ERRORS
```

```
  0x00010000 - SYMOPT_AUTO_PUBLICS
  0x00020000 - SYMOPT_NO_IMAGE_SEARCH
0:000> $ Notice the x command now displays the fully decorated names
0:000> x clr!*dllmain*
...
6b9bdbd8 clr!_DllMain@12 = <no type information>
0:000> $ Switch back to the original mode
0:000> .symopt+ 2
0:000> $ Quit the debugger now...
0:000> q
```

Note that the Visual Studio debugger expects C/C++ function symbol names to be in their decorated (unambiguous) form, even when there is no ambiguity involved and there are no overloads. You should keep this in mind when trying to set native breakpoints in Visual Studio at functions for which you do not have source code because, in that case, you need to enter the breakpoints manually. In the Visual Studio debugger, for example, you set a breakpoint at *clr!_DllMain@12* and not at *clr!DllMain* if you want to stop at the DLL entry point of the *clr.dll* module!

Getting Help for WinDbg Commands

The WinDbg debugger comes with an integrated Help file you can invoke by using the F1 shortcut in the UI. This Help file is shown in Figure 2-6 and contains basic documentation for the various debugger commands as well as general content that covers a few common debugging techniques.

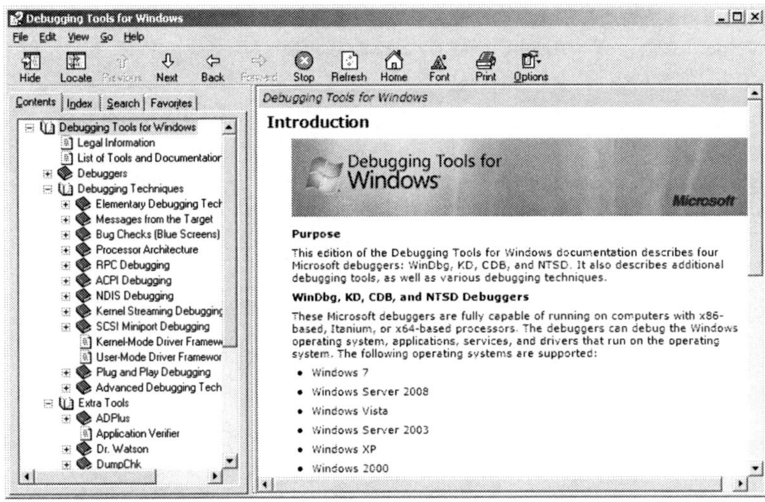

FIGURE 2-6 WinDbg Help file.

You can also use the *.hh* command to get direct help for a particular debugger command—for example, *.hh .symfix* starts the help directly at the page describing the *.symfix* command. This chapter won't exhaustively cover all the available debugger commands because you'll be using many of them in practical situations throughout this book, which is a far more effective approach to memorizing their usage pattern. You can also consult Appendix A, "WinDbg User-Mode Debugging Quick Start," for a short rundown of the most common debugging tasks and the commands to accomplish them.

It is important, however, to understand the three main categories of commands in the WinDbg debugger:

- **Regular built-in commands**, such as *k* (display call stack of the current thread), *r* (display register values), and *dd* (dump memory as a set of DWORD values). These commands are used to debug the target process.
- **Dot commands**, such as *.tlist* (list the running user-mode processes on the debugger machine) and *.restart* (restart the target process). These commands are used to control the debugger. You can use the *.help* debugger command to obtain a list of available "dot" commands.

```
0:000> .help
...
   .srcfix [<path extra>] - fix source search path
   .srcpath [<dir>[;...]] - set source search path
   .srcpath+ [<dir>[;...]] - append source search path
   .symfix [<localsym>] - fix symbol search path
   .sympath [<dir>[;...]] - set symbol search path
   .sympath+ [<dir>[;...]] - append symbol search path
...
   .tlist - list running processes
...
0:000> $ Extra help for a specific dot command
0:000> .hh .tlist
```

- **Extension ("bang") commands**, such as *!gle* (display the last error saved in the thread environment block), *!token* (display the security access token of the current thread), and *!handle* (display information about a user-mode handle). These commands are implemented by debugger extensions, which are used to extend the native debugger functionality. You can use the *.chain* debugger command to view the loaded extension DLLs that are enabled by default, and then use the *!extension_name.help* command to view the commands supported by each of them. Additional extension DLLs can be loaded by using the *.load* command. An example of such an extension is the *sos.dll* managed-code debugger extension, which will be covered in more detail in the next chapter.

```
0:000> .chain
Extension DLL chain:
    dbghelp: image 6.12.0002.633, API 6.1.6, built Mon Feb 01 12:08:26 2010
        [path: c:\Program Files\Debugging Tools for Windows (x86)\dbghelp.dll]
    ext: image 6.12.0002.633, API 1.0.0, built Mon Feb 01 12:08:31 2010
        [path: c:\Program Files\Debugging Tools for Windows (x86)\winext\ext.dll]
    exts: image 6.12.0002.633, API 1.0.0, built Mon Feb 01 12:08:24 2010
        [path: c:\Program Files\Debugging Tools for Windows (x86)\WINXP\exts.dll]
    uext: image 6.12.0002.633, API 1.0.0, built Mon Feb 01 12:08:23 2010
        [path: c:\Program Files\Debugging Tools for Windows (x86)\winext\uext.dll]
```

```
    ntsdexts: image 6.1.7650.0, API 1.0.0, built Mon Feb 01 12:08:08 2010
        [path: c:\Program Files\Debugging Tools for Windows (x86)\WINXP\ntsdexts.dll]
0:000> $ Commands exposed by the exts.dll extension
0:000> !exts.help
acl <address> [flags]          - Displays the ACL
token [-n|-?] <handle|addr>    - Displays TOKEN
...
0:000> $ Extra help for a specific extension command
0:000> .hh !acl
```

Kernel-Mode Debugging

Kernel-mode debugging (KD) is obviously needed when debugging kernel-mode code because the user-mode debuggers do not allow you to see kernel-mode memory. However, the kernel debugger is more than just a debugger for kernel code and can also be used as a systemwide debugger for user-mode processes. You'll see several scenarios in this book where the usage of a kernel-mode debugger to analyze user-mode system components proves better suited to the task at hand than a user-mode debugger, particularly because kernel debugging gives you the ability to naturally observe interactions between multiple components or processes in the system. For example, debugging a Windows Management Instrumentation (WMI) failure might require stepping into several processes, such as the WMI service (the *winmgmt* Windows service, hosted in a *svchost.exe* host process instance running with *LocalSystem* privileges), the WMI host process (*wmiprvse.exe*), or the RPC runtime in the client process. In such cases, it can be more convenient to use a kernel-mode debugger, especially until you become familiar with the interactions between the components involved. Once you know the components involved and decide to zoom in on one of them, you can then use a user-mode debugger so that you don't have to worry about what other processes in the system are doing while you focus on a particular process.

Table 2-2 summarizes some of the capabilities supported in user-mode and kernel-mode debugging and how these two types of debugging complement each other.

TABLE 2-2 Capabilities of User-Mode and Kernel-Mode Debuggers in Windows

	User-Mode Debugger	Kernel-Mode Debugger
Scope	Limited to the process being debugged and its child processes	All processes on the target machine
Stack traces	User-mode frames only	User-mode and kernel-mode frames
Kernel-mode memory and executive objects	No direct access. Interactions with kernel objects are done solely through handles and the *ntdll.dll* layer.	Full access
User-mode memory	Can access all memory in the process. Memory that has been paged-out will be paged-in on demand by the kernel.	Can access only memory that has been paged-in at the time of the kernel debugger break

Unfortunately, one of the main impediments to kernel-mode debugging is that its initial setup generally requires an additional machine to run the debugger on. A second machine is needed because kernel-mode debugging allows debugging of the entire system (including any user-mode debuggers!). As such, an external frame of reference is needed to perform this low-level debugging. In addition, except when the connection is virtualized, a physical cable is also needed to connect the two machines.

This section will show you how to set up a basic kernel-mode debugging environment so that you can maximize your learning from this book. Once you get past this initial setup hurdle, you'll see that kernel-mode debugging isn't inherently harder than user-mode debugging, contrary to what many developers tend to believe.

Your First (Live) Kernel Debugging Session

Before walking you through the steps to set up a true kernel-mode debugging environment, I would be remiss if I didn't cover a much simpler kernel debugging alternative that does not require a second machine. More specifically, manipulating kernel-mode memory (reading and editing global variable values, listing running processes, and so on) can be done directly on the same machine by using *live kernel debugging*.

The "debuggee" machine in a kernel-mode debugging session is usually called the *target machine*, while the machine where the (kernel) debugger resides is called the *host debugger machine*. In the case of live kernel debugging, the host and target machines are the same.

You can follow many of the experiments in this book using live kernel debugging, though a key limitation is that you won't be able to perform more invasive debugging tasks using this method, such as setting code breakpoints. Despite that limitation, the first foray into kernel-mode debugging in this book will start with a live kernel debugging session. This will also provide a practical introduction to some of the basic kernel-mode debugger commands.

The first thing you need to do is configure the target machine to allow kernel-mode debugging. The easiest way to do so is to use the *msconfig.exe* tool that ships in the box with Windows. This is a one-time setup that requires a reboot before the new configuration takes effect.

Enabling Kernel-Mode Debugging for a (Target) Machine

1. Start *msconfig.exe*. The tool will conveniently auto-elevate if you're running as an administrator or ask for an administrator password if you run it as a regular user.

2. On the Boot tab, click the Advanced Options button. In the new dialog box, select the Debug check box and leave the other options unchanged because they won't matter here, at least not in this first live kernel debugging experiment.

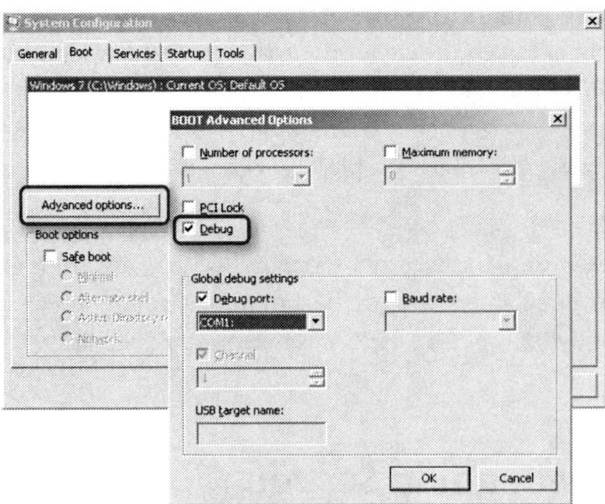

3. Restart the machine when prompted to do so after you click OK.

Because enabling support for kernel-mode debugging in the Windows kernel requires a reboot, it's usually a good idea to perform this step once as part of the original setup of every one of your test machines—just in case you need to attach a kernel debugger to them in the future. The OS will start generating debug events only after a kernel debugger is actually detected, so this first step won't affect the target's execution until you explicitly attach a host debugger to it.

Note The *msconfig.exe* tool can also be run in safe mode. Safe mode is an OS boot option that allows you to start a minimal operating system and rectify configuration mistakes or crashing bugs that might be preventing you from booting successfully into the desktop. This is done by pressing the F8 shortcut when restarting Windows, which brings up a boot menu that allows you to select booting into safe mode. This same boot menu also has a choice that allows you to directly enable kernel debugging on the machine, but that option is less flexible than *msconfig.exe* because it does not allow you to set the properties of the kernel debugging connection. (The connection baud rate is fixed at 19,200, and the highest enumerated serial port is always used. So, COM2 is used when you have two serial ports, for instance.)

Once kernel debugging is enabled for the target machine and you've restarted it at least once, you will be ready to use the live kernel debugging option in WinDbg.

Starting a Live Kernel-Mode Debugging Session

1. To start a new live kernel debugging session, you need to invoke *windbg.exe* from an elevated administrative command prompt. If you simply start *windbg.exe* from the Windows Explorer UI, it won't prompt you for elevation and, subsequently, you'll get an error message when trying to start the live debugging session. For a reminder of how to start an elevated command prompt, refer back to the Introduction of this book.

2. You also need to use the *native flavor* of *windbg.exe* for live kernel-mode debugging, so you won't be able to use the *x86* version of the debugger for live kernel debugging of an *x64* Windows machine. This is why the installation procedure at the start of this chapter recommended that you install both the *x86* and *x64* debugger MSIs, side by side, if you were running on 64-bit Windows.

3. In the new elevated *windbg.exe* instance, start a live kernel debugging session by using the File\Kernel Debug action menu or the Ctrl+K shortcut, and then click the Local tab, as illustrated in the following screen shot:

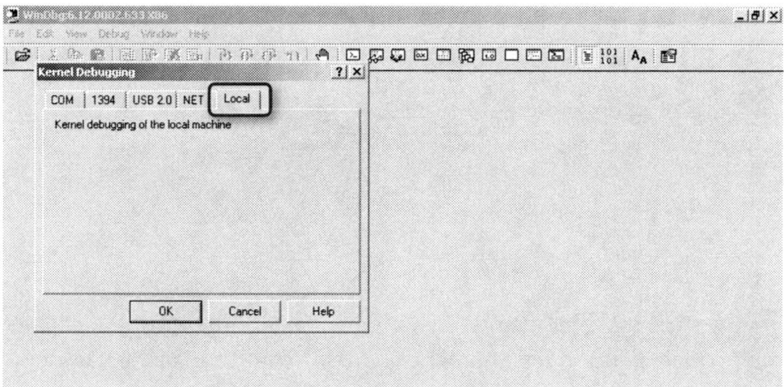

4. When you click OK, you are presented with the familiar WinDbg command prompt, which in the case of live kernel debugging starts with the *lkd>* prefix. You should again set the debugger symbols search path to point to the Microsoft public symbols server by using the same *.symfix/.reload* commands that were used earlier in WinDbg user-mode debugging. Several other WinDbg commands (*k*, *r*, *dd*, and so on) are applicable to both user-mode and kernel-mode debugging, but there are also additional KD-specific commands, of course.

```
lkd> .symfix
lkd> .reload
Loading Kernel Symbols.................................
Loading User Symbols
Loading unloaded module list...............
```

To demonstrate the power of live kernel debugging, you'll use it to run the same *notepad.exe* system debugging experiment that was used earlier in this chapter to introduce WinDbg user-mode debugging commands, except now you will be able to inspect the kernel-mode side of system calls.

While the *windbg.exe* live kernel debugging session is still running, start a new *notepad.exe* instance on the same machine and invoke the File\Open dialog box, as shown in Figure 2-7.

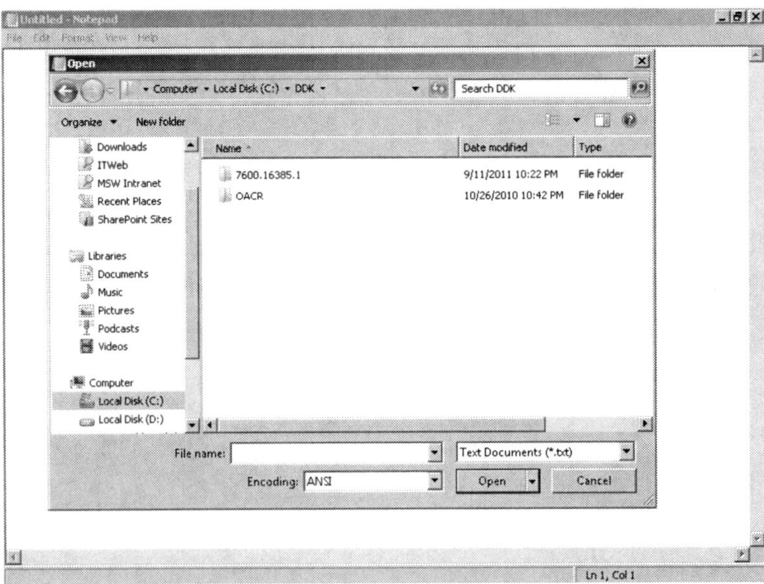

FIGURE 2-7 File\Open dialog box in *notepad.exe*.

Remember that the stack trace for the first thread (the main UI thread) in the *notepad.exe* process, which you were able to see earlier in this chapter using the *k* command in the user-mode debugger, stopped at the system call boundary (*ntdll.dll* layer). Using live kernel debugging, you can now see the other side of the fence!

You can use the *!process* kernel debugger extension command to find the address of the *notepad.exe* executive process object and also that of its first thread object. For more details on these two fundamental kernel debugging commands, be sure to also consult Appendix B, "WinDbg Kernel-Mode Debugging Quick Start," which has a detailed explanation of the two commands and their different options. Note that the addresses you'll see in your debugging session will be different from those shown in this listing. For example, you should take the process address you get from the first command (shown in bold text in the following listing) and use it with the following command. Also, some of the output from the commands was truncated for better readability.

```
lkd> $ Look up all instances of notepad.exe on the system
lkd> !process 0 0 notepad.exe
PROCESS 84f80268  SessionId: 1  Cid: 14d0    Peb: 7ffdf000  ParentCid: 0f34
    DirBase: 7d8abc40  ObjectTable: b13104f0  HandleCount:  56.
        Image: notepad.exe
lkd> $ Display the process instance information and the threads that it contains
```

```
lkd> !process 84f80268 2
...
        THREAD a35bf030  Cid 14d0.1384  Teb: 7ffde000 Win32Thread: ffa33318 WAIT: (UserRequest)
UserMode Non-Alertable
            8500b6a8  SynchronizationEvent
            84c941a8  SynchronizationEvent
        THREAD 89d29268  Cid 14d0.0560  Teb: 7ffdd000 Win32Thread: ffa2d008 WAIT: (UserRequest)
UserMode Non-Alertable
            9f1f07d8  SynchronizationEvent
            84bf2530  SynchronizationEvent
...
```

You can now use the *!thread* extension command to dump the stack trace of the first thread in the process (the main UI thread) using the address of the thread object that you just obtained in the previous step. However, there is a catch! By default, you'll see only the kernel-mode stack of the thread. So, you are able to see the kernel side of the stack but not the user side of the stack that you were able to see earlier in this chapter when using user-mode debugging.

```
lkd> !thread 0xa35bf030
THREAD a35bf030  Cid 14d0.1384  Teb: 7ffde000 Win32Thread: ffa33318 WAIT: (UserRequest) UserMode
Non-Alertable
    8500b6a8  SynchronizationEvent
    84c941a8  SynchronizationEvent
ChildEBP RetAddr  Args to Child
9872c760 82ab865d a35bf030 82b67f08 82b64d20 nt!KiSwapContext+0x26 (FPO: [Uses EBP] [0,0,4])
9872c798 82ab74b7 84c941a8 a35bf030 a35bf12c nt!KiSwapThread+0x266
9872c7c0 82ab3484 a35bf030 a35bf0f0 00000000 nt!KiCommitThreadWait+0x1df
9872c93c 82c63828 00000002 9872ca74 00000001 nt!KeWaitForMultipleObjects+0x535
9872cbc8 82c63595 00000002 9872cbfc 00000001 nt!ObpWaitForMultipleObjects+0x262
9872cd18 82a781fa 00000002 001ef5c4 00000001 nt!NtWaitForMultipleObjects+0xcd
9872cd18 779570b4 00000002 001ef5c4 00000001 nt!KiFastCallEntry+0x12a
001ef610 00000000 00000000 00000000 00000000 ntdll!KiFastSystemCallRet (FPO: [0,0,0])
```

Fortunately, you can get the best of both worlds and force the kernel debugger to load the user-mode stack symbols by using the *.process /r* (which stands for "reload symbols") command. You're now finally able to see the complete stack trace of this thread. You can also use the *!object* kernel debugger extension command to view the event objects that it is waiting on (which you also obtain from the output of the *!thread* command), as demonstrated in the following listing.

```
lkd> .process /r /p 0x84f80268
Implicit process is now 84f80268
Loading User Symbols
...............................................................
lkd> !thread 0xa35bf030
THREAD a35bf030  Cid 14d0.1384  Teb: 7ffde000 Win32Thread: ffa33318 WAIT: (UserRequest) UserMode
Non-Alertable
    8500b6a8  SynchronizationEvent
    84c941a8  SynchronizationEvent
...
Owning Process            84f80268       Image:         notepad.exe
...
ChildEBP RetAddr  Args to Child
98b2c760 82ab865d a35bf030 82b67f08 82b64d20 nt!KiSwapContext+0x26
98b2c798 82ab74b7 84c941a8 a35bf030 a35bf12c nt!KiSwapThread+0x266
```

```
98b2c7c0 82ab3484 a35bf030 a35bf0f0 00000000 nt!KiCommitThreadWait+0x1df
98b2c93c 82c63828 00000002 98b2ca74 00000001 nt!KeWaitForMultipleObjects+0x535
98b2cbc8 82c63595 00000002 98b2cbfc 00000001 nt!ObpWaitForMultipleObjects+0x262
98b2cd18 82a781fa 00000002 001ef5c4 00000001 nt!NtWaitForMultipleObjects+0xcd
98b2cd18 779570b4 00000002 001ef5c4 00000001 nt!KiFastCallEntry+0x12a
001ef570 77956a04 75c76a36 00000002 001ef5c4 ntdll!KiFastSystemCallRet
001ef574 75c76a36 00000002 001ef5c4 00000001 ntdll!ZwWaitForMultipleObjects+0xc
001ef610 7778bd1e 001ef5c4 001ef638 00000000 KERNELBASE!WaitForMultipleObjectsEx+0x100
001ef658 776862f9 00000002 7ffdf000 00000000 kernel32!WaitForMultipleObjectsExImplementation+0
xe0
001ef6ac 73b81717 00000034 001ef6e0 ffffffff USER32!RealMsgWaitForMultipleObjectsEx+0x13c
001ef6cc 73b817b8 000024ff ffffffff 00000000 DUser!CoreSC::Wait+0x59
001ef6f4 73b81757 000024ff 00000000 001ef720 DUser!CoreSC::WaitMessage+0x54
001ef704 776866ed 000024ff 00000000 00000001 DUser!MphWaitMessageEx+0x2b
001ef720 77956fee 001ef738 00000008 001ef990 USER32!__ClientWaitMessageExMPH+0x1e
001ef73c 776866c9 776a382a 000703c6 00000000 ntdll!KiUserCallbackDispatcher+0x2e
001ef740 776a382a 000703c6 00000000 00000001 USER32!NtUserWaitMessage+0xc
001ef774 776a3b27 00080358 000703c6 00000000 USER32!DialogBox2+0x207
001ef798 776a3b76 77280000 003c5670 000703c6 USER32!InternalDialogBox+0xcb
001ef7b8 776a3b9a 77280000 003c5670 000703c6 USER32!DialogBoxIndirectParamAorW+0x37
001ef7d8 7728597b 77280000 003c5670 000703c6 USER32!DialogBoxIndirectParamW+0x1b
001ef824 009a3c2f 003c5670 000703c6 00000000 COMDLG32!CFileOpenSave::Show+0x181
001ef83c 009a3fdb 000703c6 003c5034 00001808 notepad!ShowOpenSaveDialog+0x62
...
lkd> !object 8500b6a8
Object: 8500b6a8  Type: (84ab5e38) Event
    ObjectHeader: 8500b690 (new version)
    HandleCount: 1  PointerCount: 2
```

Note The kernel-mode side of the thread's call stack references functions from a module named *nt*. The WinDbg debugger automatically renames the first module (the kernel module) to *nt* so that you can reference functions in the kernel using the *nt!FunctionName* notation, rather than having to worry about which module actually contains the loaded kernel code: *ntoskrnl.exe* or *ntkrnlpa.exe* for single-processor machines, and *ntkrnlmp.exe* or *ntkrpamp.exe* for multiprocessor machines. You can find the actual kernel binary that's used on your machine by using the *lm* debugger command, which can also take an extra module name argument (the *m* option):

```
lkd> $ Display module information (lm) in verbose mode (v) for the nt module
lkd> lmv m nt
start    end        module name
82c04000 83016000   nt          (pdb symbols)          c:\Program Files\Debugging Tools for
Windows (x86)\sym\ntkrpamp.pdb\2A68384474C44E648D1A1A25FBF1E5D52\ntkrpamp.pdb
    Loaded symbol image file: ntkrpamp.exe...
    FileDescription:  NT Kernel & System
...
```

All kernel modules had to have a short 8.3 name back in the old DOS days, hence the creative names chosen for each kernel flavor module. Being able to reference the kernel module using the *nt* alias in the debugger keeps you from having to figure out the actual name of the kernel binary used on the machine.

Though live kernel debugging can be useful as a noninvasive kernel debugging approach when you aren't able to connect a second host debugger machine, it doesn't allow you to set active breakpoints. This is an unfortunate, though expected limitation because the machine could deadlock and require a hard reboot if you were allowed to set active breakpoints in critical system code paths from within the target machine itself. (This is because those code paths might be required to run in order to service the debugger process that is supposed to handle the breakpoint!)

```
lkd> $ Setting active code breakpoints is not supported during live kernel debugging.
lkd> bp
     ^ Operation not supported by current debuggee error in 'bp'
lkd> $ Can't actively control the target, either. The target isn't frozen to begin with.
lkd> g
     ^ No runnable debuggees error in 'g'
lkd> $ Terminate this live kernel debugging session now...
lkd> q
```

In the previous experiment, for example, this limitation means that though you were able to find the event objects that the thread was waiting on, you won't be able to set a breakpoint and observe when they become signaled so that you can find out the thread and component that are ultimately responsible for unblocking the wait. For this type of more invasive debugging, you need to set up a complete kernel debugging environment with a dedicated host debugger machine, which is the topic of the next section.

Setting Up a Kernel-Mode Debugging Environment Using Physical Machines

To set up a true kernel-mode debugging environment, you need two machines. One machine (the target) needs to be enabled for kernel debugging using *msconfig.exe*, as detailed in the previous section. The other machine (the host debugger) needs to have the Windows debuggers installed. Note that the two machines don't have to be running the same version of the Windows operating system, nor do they need to be from the same processor family or architecture. Also, unless the target machine is run as a virtual OS within the host debugger machine—a useful configuration that will be the subject of a separate section later in this chapter—you also need a cable to physically connect the two machines.

KD Cabling Options

Though the *windbg.exe* Kernel Debugging dialog box (Ctrl+K) has a network tab option (the NET tab) that seems to indicate it's possible to connect the target and host machines via a network connection, kernel debugging over the network isn't supported in Windows 7 and earlier. In September 2011, Microsoft demonstrated kernel debugging over an Ethernet network cable during its Windows Developer Preview Conference that took place in Anaheim, California—a most welcome addition that's sure to make kernel debugging even more accessible in the next version of Windows. That feature isn't available in Windows 7, however, which leaves three cabling options you can choose from to enable kernel debugging communication between the host and target machines:

- **COM serial cable** This is the most basic configuration and has been supported since the very early releases of Windows. The 9-pin, straight-through COM serial cables are cheap (typically, costing only a few U.S. dollars) and are also easy to set up. However, a serial connection can have a baud rate (bits per second) of only up to 115,200, which means it can be particularly slow when transferring large amounts of memory, such as when saving a full kernel memory dump. In addition, most laptop models today no longer have serial ports. This cabling option will not work in those cases.

- **USB 2.0 debug cable** Support for this communication channel was added in Windows Vista. Though I've seen this option work relatively well, I recommend that you leave it as your last resort, when you've already exhausted all the other options and found that they wouldn't work for the hardware that you have. I say that for a couple of reasons. First, USB 2.0 kernel debugging requires a dedicated type of cable that has a special device embedded in the middle of the cable. Regular host-to-host USB cables won't work, and the special debug cables are rather expensive, costing up to 100 U.S. dollars. That's a steep price to pay for a kernel-debugging connection cable. Second, USB 2.0 kernel debugging is rather tedious to set up. For example, you need to find the first USB port and connect the cable to it because it's the only port that works for USB 2.0 KD connections. Because there is no automated way to know which USB port is this first port, this approach often is a frustrating trial-and-error setup process. The Windows debuggers package includes a tool, called *usbview.exe*, that you can use to find out whether you picked the correct port or not, but it's still a trial-and-error exercise.

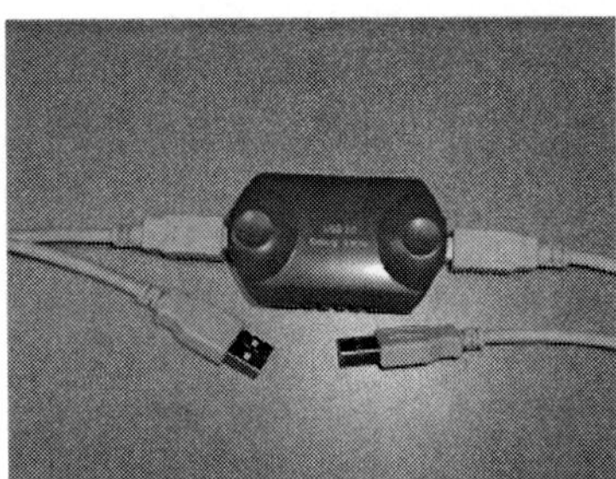

- **1394 (FireWire) cable** This is the best physical cabling option available on Windows 7. It has been supported since the Windows XP release and is much faster than COM serial cabling in KD communications. Though laptop manufacturers sometimes omit exposing 1394 IEEE ports to save manufacturing costs, many Windows 7 machines have them; they're usually next to the USB ports, marked as "1394" or with a distinctive symbol that includes a circle and three sets of bars spreading away from it. FireWire cables are also cheap and easy to find in any retail computer hardware store or online. For the step-by-step guide in the rest of this section, I will use a FireWire cable that I bought for a retail price of less than 5 U.S. dollars. Be sure, however, to check the type of 1394 port you have on your machine so that you don't buy a cable that doesn't fit the ports exposed in your host/target machines. Laptop computers usually have 4-pin (small) 1394 ports, while desktop computers typically have 6-pin (large) 1394 ports (shown in the following illustration). In my case, I purchased a 4-pin/4-pin FireWire cable to use for connecting two laptops running Windows 7. If the target is a laptop and the host is a desktop machine or vice versa, you might need a 4-pin/6-pin cable, which is also easy to find and inexpensive.

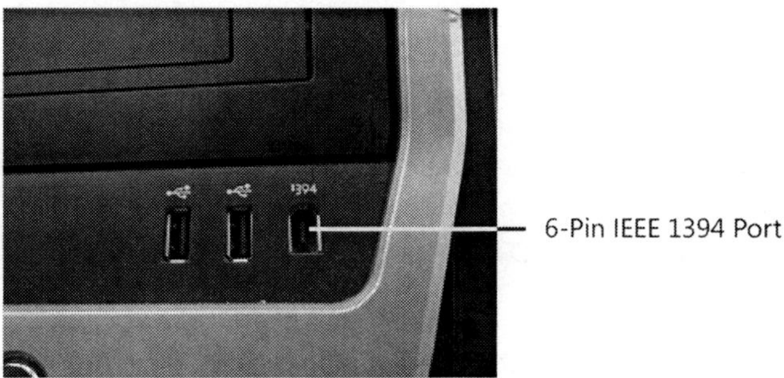

Step-by-Step Guide to Enabling KD over 1394 Ports

Once you've acquired the necessary cable, enabling kernel-mode debugging over 1394 is relatively simple (assuming your machines also have exported 1394 ports you can use with the connecting cable). The following procedure walks you through the steps required to do so.

Starting a Kernel-Mode Debugging Session over 1394

1. When you enabled live kernel debugging earlier in this chapter, you left the kernel debugging port in the *msconfig* advanced boot option dialog box at its default value, which usually is COM1 (meaning the first serial COM port on the machine). Now you need to set that value

to *1394*. Pick a value of *1* for the channel (which is just a numeric identifier used by the host debugger when connecting to the target), as demonstrated in the following screen shot:

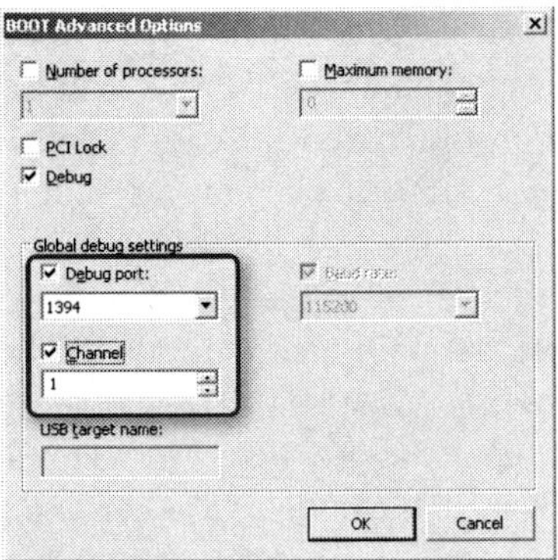

2. After clicking OK, reboot the machine to commit the changes.

3. After the reboot, connect a host debugger machine to your target by hooking the 1394 cable to the appropriate 1394 ports on both machines.

4. You don't need to make any further changes on the target side of the KD connection at this point. On the host machine, start an elevated administrative command prompt, and run *windbg.exe* from that command window. You must start the host debugger with full administrative privileges—at least in this first KD run—because the debugger will try to install a driver, which would fail otherwise.

5. Use the Ctrl+K shortcut to bring up the Kernel Debugging dialog box in the WinDbg UI, just as you did in the live kernel debugging experiment. Click the 1394 tab, and change the value of the Channel text box to *1* so that you match the value that was set in *msconfig.exe* on the target machine during step 1 of this procedure.

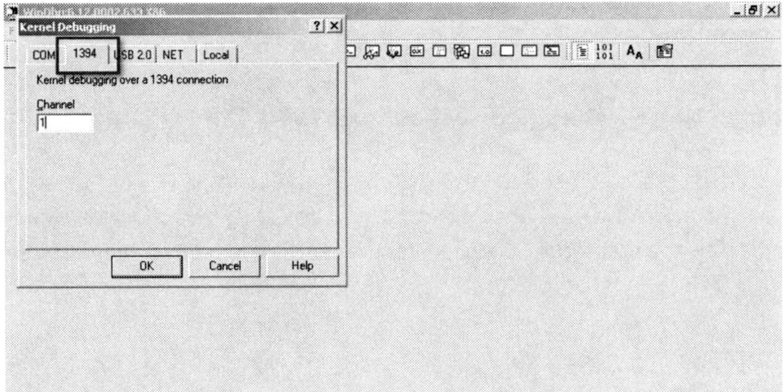

6. You should now see the following text displayed in the WinDbg command window. If you get an error instead of this text, double-check steps 3 and 4 in this procedure and make sure the cable is properly hooked to the 1394 ports, and also that you started WinDbg from an elevated administrative command prompt.

```
Using 1394 for debugging
Checking 1394 debug driver version.
Could not find C:\Windows\system32\drivers\1394kdbg.sys.
Attempting 1394 debug driver installation now.
Driver installation successful.
Retrying 1394 channel open.
Opened \\.\DBG1394_INSTANCE01
Timer Resolution set to 1000 usec.
Waiting to reconnect...
```

7. Notice the bold lines in the preceding output, indicating that the first time you try to use 1394 debugging on the host debugger machine, a new driver is automatically installed by WinDbg to handle the 1394 KD communication. This needs to happen only once and can sometimes take up to a minute or so, so don't get alarmed if the debugger seems stuck for a while after you click Install.

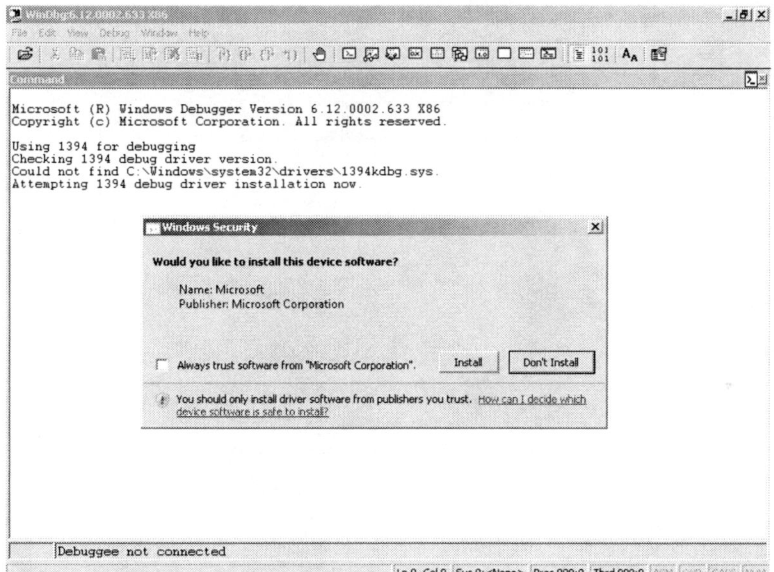

8. You can now use the Debug\Break menu action (or the Ctrl+Break shortcut) to request a break-in into the host kernel debugger. If your kernel debugging connection is working properly, you should see the following debugger output in the main window:

```
*******************************************************************************
*   You are seeing this message because you pressed either                    *
*       CTRL+C (if you run kd.exe) or,                                        *
*       CTRL+BREAK (if you run WinDBG),                                       *
*                                                                             *
*                   THIS IS NOT A BUG OR A SYSTEM CRASH                       *
*                                                                             *
* If you did not intend to break into the debugger, press the "g" key, then   *
* press the "Enter" key now.  This message might immediately reappear.  If it *
* does, press "g" and "Enter" again.                                          *
*******************************************************************************
1: kd> .symfix
1: kd> .reload
```

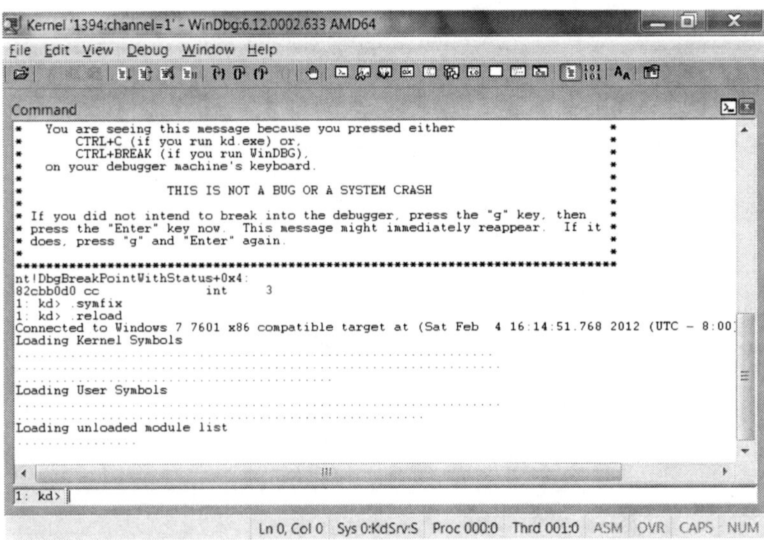

Seeing the previous message after issuing the Debug\Break menu action is the litmus test for whether you have a working KD connection or not. If you are seeing that message, congratulations—you've just completed a successful setup of your first full KD environment!

The target machine also should be frozen (try to move the mouse, for example, and see that it's unresponsive) and will be unblocked only after you issue the *g* debugger command in the host debugger command window. So, don't dismiss the host debugger instance until you first let the target machine free and allow it to continue executing using the *g* command.

```
0: kd> $ Make sure to let the target machine "go" before dismissing the host debugger
0: kd> g
```

If you fail to type **g** before exiting the host debugger, the target machine will remain frozen, but you can still recover from this situation. All you have to do is start a new WinDbg instance, connect to the target again as a host kernel debugger, and issue the *g* command before you terminate the new kernel debugging session.

Notice also the kernel debugger command prefix (*1: kd*>), where *1* indicates the second CPU on this multiprocessor target machine, instead of the live kernel debugger prefix (*lkd*>) or the usual thread number prefix (*0:000*>) that gets displayed in the case of a user-mode debugging session. In the debugger listings you'll find throughout this book, you can easily recognize the type of debugging session from the listing using this clue.

Setting Up a Kernel-Mode Debugging Environment Using Virtual Machines

As mentioned earlier, one of the main barriers preventing software engineers from experimenting and harnessing the full power of kernel-mode debugging is sometimes the simple fact that it requires two machines: a host machine and a target machine. This makes it difficult to use in a home setting, for example, when only a single machine might be available.

Fortunately, even though kernel-mode debugging relies on two machines, the machines do not have to be physical machines. In fact, my favorite kernel-mode debugging environment is one where the target (test) machines are run as virtual machines on my main development computer. Most virtualization solutions today (VMWare, Microsoft Hyper-V, and others) support emulating the serial COM port using named pipes for communicating between the parent and virtual machines, which eliminates the need to connect the host and target machines using a physical serial cable (or any other cable, for that matter). I cannot overemphasize how convenient this is, especially when you want to use kernel-mode debugging for more than one test machine.

The Microsoft Hypervisor Technology

If you can afford to acquire a copy of Windows Server 2008 R2, I recommend that you license your main work machine to use this version of Windows. In addition to several other benefits of Windows Server, this release also supports the hypervisor-based virtualization technology called *Hyper-V*, as long as your machine also meets its hardware requirements—most notably, having a capable CPU model (such as all the Intel Xeon processors). Microsoft also recently confirmed that Hyper-V would be available on the 64-bit Client version of its upcoming Windows release—more great news for developers looking to harness the power of kernel-mode debugging in the next version of Windows.

Microsoft's hypervisor technology relies on the new virtualization extensions in the AMD-V (sometimes referred to by its former codename, Pacifica) and Intel-VT line of processors to implement CPU virtualization and the hypervisor functionality. So, your machine needs to have an *x64* CPU from one of those families of processors to be able to use the Hyper-V technology. When the Hyper-V server role is installed, the hypervisor boot driver (*hvboot.sys*) is enabled, and during the next boot sequence it assumes the responsibility of loading the hypervisor corresponding to the host machine CPU type (*hvax64.exe* for AMD-V and *hvix64.exe* for Intel-VT). The original Windows Server 2008 R2 OS is then made the primary partition, and new virtual machines for supported OS versions can then be installed as child partitions on top of the hypervisor. Each guest OS has its own view of a virtualized CPU thanks to the virtualization extensions instruction set, which is why Hyper-V is often categorized as a hardware-assisted virtualization technology, as opposed to other virtualization technologies implementing CPU virtualization in software.

Configuring Kernel Debugging over a Virtualized COM Port

As of the writing of this book, the latest service packs for Windows XP, Windows Server 2003, Windows Vista, Windows Server 2008, Windows 7, and Windows Server 2008 R2 can all be installed as child partitions (virtual machines). Figure 2-8 shows a configuration with two virtual machines running inside a physical Windows Server 2008 R2 computer.

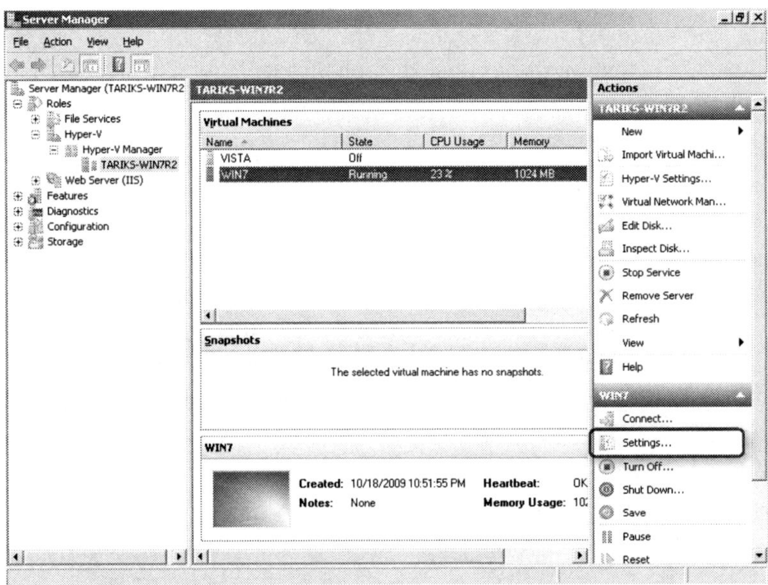

FIGURE 2-8 Hyper-V server role UI in Windows Server 2008 R2.

Starting a Kernel-Mode Debugging Session over a Virtualized COM Port

1. Enable kernel-mode debugging for the virtual machine as previously described in this chapter. Use the default COM1 debug port configuration in *msconfig.exe*.

2. Use the Settings option of the virtual machine in the Hyper-V configuration UI to emulate the COM1 serial port using a named pipe. A reboot of the virtual OS is required for this new configuration to take effect.

Pipe name used in the host kernel debugger

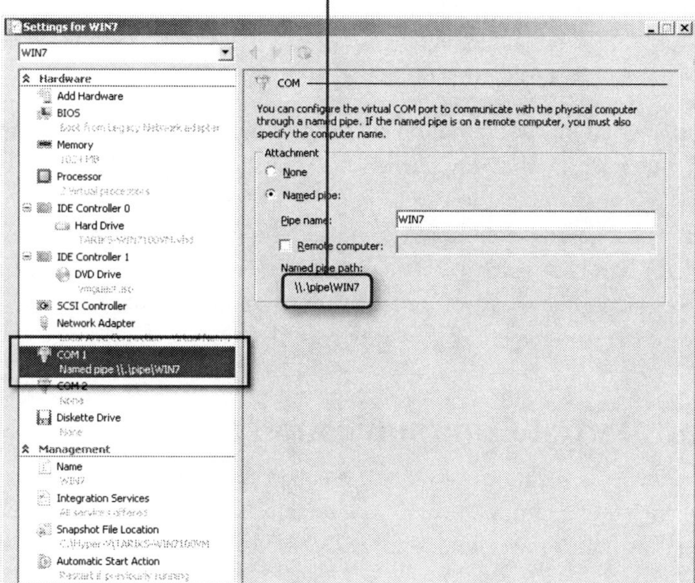

3. Start the host debugger on the primary OS. Use the usual Ctrl+K shortcut to select your kernel debugging transport. Click the COM tab, and select the Pipe check box. In the Port text box, type the pipe name that was displayed in the previous Hyper-V Settings dialog box.

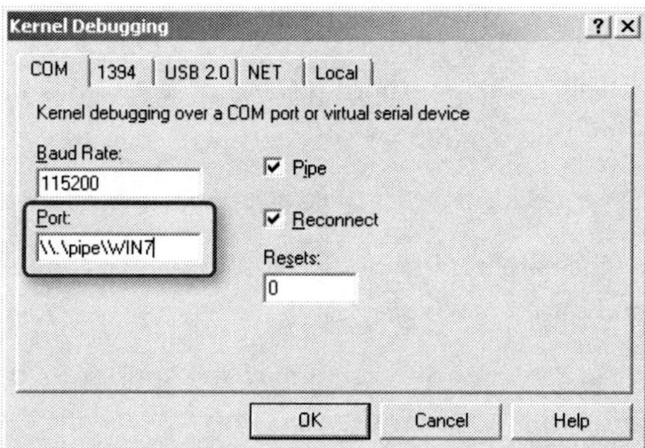

If you have more than one virtual machine, you can start multiple *windbg.exe* instances concurrently on the host OS and debug multiple virtual machines (VMs) simultaneously.

Benefits of Testing Using Virtual Machines

One of the nice side effects of using virtual machines as the target machines in a kernel-mode debugging session is that it is easy to reboot or shut down those instances when they become stuck because of intrusive debugging experiments. This can be very convenient, especially if you are working remotely and do not have physical access to the host and target machines. For example, if you are connecting to the host (development) machine using a Remote Desktop connection, you won't lose access if a virtual machine (target test machine) unexpectedly experiences a kernel bug check. Even in such an extreme condition, you can restart the virtual target test machine easily from within the development (typically, more stable) host machine. All you need to do is maintain the Remote Desktop connection to the host debugger machine.

Yet another great feature of many virtualization solutions is their ability to save *snapshots* and quickly restore the VM state back to what it was when the snapshot was taken. In the case of the Microsoft Hyper-V solution, for example, this can be easily achieved by using the Action\Snapshot menu action. This is often useful when debugging complex scenarios because it allows you to go back in time if you hit an unexpected failure (for instance, if you were in the process of testing a device driver and introduced a crashing bug) or if you simply want to set new breakpoints to trace different code paths without having to rerun the entire scenario from scratch.

Diagnosing Host/Target Communication Issues

There are many reasons why you might not be able to break in successfully when trying to attach a host kernel debugger instance to a target machine. The telltale sign of this situation is when you get stuck with the following message in the debugger as you attempt to break in:

```
Waiting for pipe \\.\pipe\WIM7
Waiting to reconnect...
```

In the preceding case, the problem is that I mistyped the name of the virtual pipe used in the host/target communication. Here are a few additional steps you can follow to diagnose these conditions:

- Ensure the target machine has been previously configured using *msconfig.exe* and that its current boot options reflect the correct cabling settings (COM, IEEE 1394, and so on) that you're trying to use for the kernel-mode debugging session.
- Make sure that you've rebooted the machine at least once after you applied those settings.
- If you are using physical cables for the communication, make sure they're connected properly to the correct ports on the host and target machines.
- If you are using a physical COM serial cable for the communication, make sure the baud rate in the kernel-debugger attach options (accessed by pressing Ctrl+K in *windbg.exe*) matches the KD debug boot settings you set on the target machine using *msconfig.exe*.
- If you are using a named pipe to simulate COM serial port communication while debugging a virtual target machine, make sure the name of the pipe you specify when you attach the kernel debugger (by pressing Ctrl+K in *windbg.exe*) is accurate and matches the one that was set in the VM settings.

The kernel debugger also supports a useful tracing mode that causes the packets sent by the host debugger to the target to be logged to the debugger screen. This can be useful if you get into a situation where the target machine stops responding or if the cable connection between the host and target seems to be broken. This tracing mode can be switched on or off by using the Ctrl+Alt+D shortcut in *windbg.exe*.

Understanding the KD Break-in Sequence

Now you'll see a quick overview of how the "break-in" sequence in kernel-mode debugging works internally. An understanding of this process comes in handy when things go awry while you're trying to start a kernel debugging session and get stuck with the ominous "Waiting to reconnect" message.

When kernel debugging is enabled on the target machine using *msconfig.exe* and the machine is rebooted, the OS boot loader detects the debug options for the machine during the following boot and loads the appropriate KD transport extension module: *kdcom.dll* when using a COM serial port cable, *kd1394.dll* for an IEEE 1394 cable, or *kdusb.dll* for a USB 2.0 debug cable. This happens very early during the boot sequence, around the same time that the OS loader also loads the Hardware Abstraction Layer (*hal.dll*) and the kernel image itself.

When KD debugging is enabled, the Windows kernel on the target machine continuously polls for break-in messages from the host debugger. This can be observed in the stack trace you see immediately after each break-in, where the *nt!KdCheckForDebugBreak* frame (shown in bold text in the following listing) represents the internal kernel routine performing the check for the host debugger break-in signal. When such a request is detected, the target OS suspends all the processors on the machine before entering the debugger break-in state. Note that any functions below *nt!KeUpdateSystemTimeAssist* in the stack trace shown in the following listing are immaterial because the clock Interrupt Service Routine (ISR) runs at a high Interrupt Request Level (IRQL) and therefore interrupts any stacks that might happen to be running at that time.

```
*******************************************************************************
*   You are seeing this message because you pressed either                   *
*       CTRL+C (if you run kd.exe) or,                                       *
*       CTRL+BREAK (if you run WinDBG),                                      *
*******************************************************************************
0: kd> .symfix
0: kd> .reload
0: kd> k
ChildEBP RetAddr
975bbb98 8267538f nt!RtlpBreakWithStatusInstruction
975bbba0 82675361 nt!KdCheckForDebugBreak+0x22
975bbbd0 826751ef nt!KeUpdateRunTime+0x164
975bbc28 8267a577 nt!KeUpdateSystemTime+0x613
975bbc28 826910a3 nt!KeUpdateSystemTimeAssist+0x13
974fbb90 8282ef07 hal!HalpRequestIpiSpecifyVector+0x80
974fbba4 828d2d59 hal!HalRequestIpi+0x17
974fbbb8 828d2b2e nt!KiIpiSend+0x31
974fbc34 828d365d nt!KiDeferredReadyThread+0x7e2
...
0: kd> !irql
Debugger saved IRQL for processor 0x0 -- 28 (CLOCK2_LEVEL)
```

Figure 2-9 illustrates this continuous polling loop between the host and target machines during kernel-mode debugging sessions.

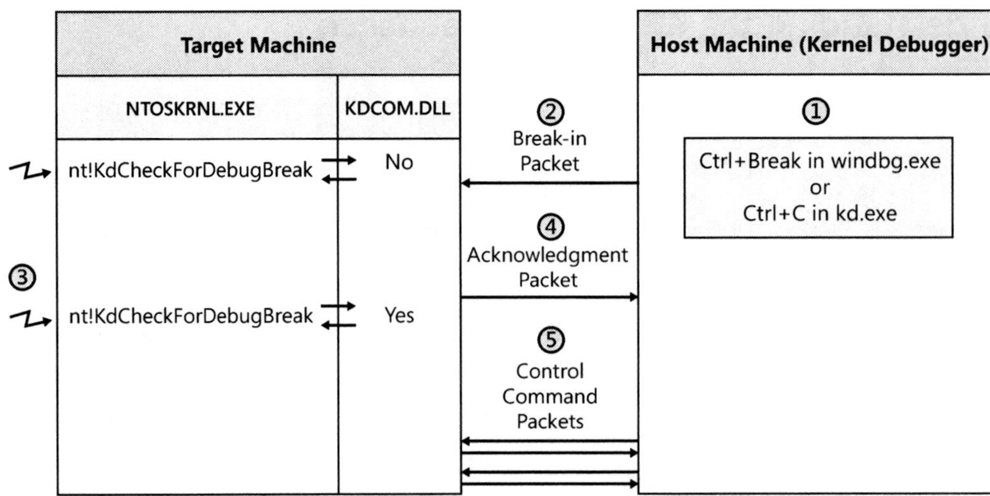

FIGURE 2-9 Communication between host and target machines (kernel-mode debugging).

One interesting corollary of the packet-based transport protocol used in kernel-mode debugging is that an *x86* host debugger will automatically detect the system architecture of the OS installed on the target machine, and it can debug both *x86* or *x64* target machines. In the case of user-mode debugging, by contrast, you cannot use an *x86* debugger to debug an *x64* binary. (The reverse is always possible. In other words, an *x64* debugger installed on an *x64* Windows machine can debug *x64* as well as *x86* binaries running in WOW64 mode.)

Controlling the Target in the Kernel Debugger

As mentioned when live kernel debugging was covered earlier in this chapter, one of the main limitations of that approach is that you can't perform invasive debugging operations such as setting an active breakpoint. In the case of the *notepad.exe* experiment that was used to introduce system debugging both in the case of user-mode and live kernel-mode debugging, you were able to see the full stack trace of a thread (both the kernel and user sides) by using live kernel debugging but still weren't able to figure out when and where the events that the thread was waiting on were going to be signaled.

Now that you have a full kernel-debugging environment, you can finally answer that question without having to guess. To do so, start by running a new *notepad.exe* instance on the target machine and invoke its File\Open dialog box, which is shown in Figure 2-10.

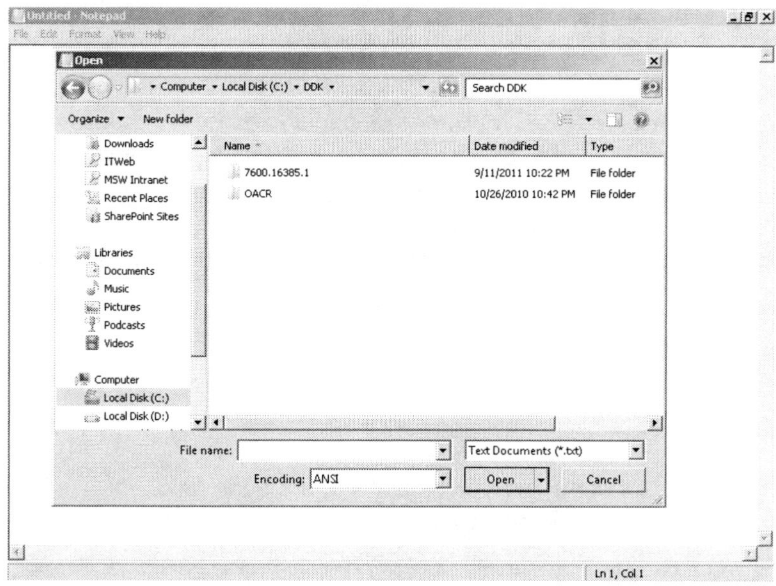

FIGURE 2-10 State of *notepad.exe* process instance on the target machine before breaking in.

While the File\Open dialog box is still active on the desktop of the target OS, issue a break-in request inside the host kernel debugger using the Debug\Break menu action. Once again, you can find the stack trace of the main UI thread in *notepad.exe* and also the addresses of the events that it's waiting on by applying the same steps you used earlier during live kernel debugging.

```
0: kd> .symfix
0: kd> .reload
0: kd> !process 0 0 notepad.exe
PROCESS 85f52a70  SessionId: 1  Cid: 17e0    Peb: 7ffd3000  ParentCid: 063c
    Image: notepad.exe
0: kd> .process /r /p 85f52a70
0: kd> !process 85f52a70 2
PROCESS 85f52a70  SessionId: 1  Cid: 17e0    Peb: 7ffd3000  ParentCid: 063c
    Image: notepad.exe
        THREAD 87322c10  Cid 17e0.04fc  Teb: 7ffdf000 Win32Thread: fe91a188
...
0: kd> !thread 87322c10
THREAD 87322c10  Cid 17e0.04fc  Teb: 7ffdf000 Win32Thread: fe91a188 WAIT: (UserRequest) UserMode
Non-Alertable
    8670e460  SynchronizationEvent
    859470f0  SynchronizationEvent
ChildEBP RetAddr  Args to Child
9a823760 8287e65d 87322c10 8292df08 8292ad20 nt!KiSwapContext+0x26
9a823798 8287d4b7 859470f0 87322c10 87322d0c nt!KiSwapThread+0x266
9a8237c0 82879484 87322c10 87322cd0 00000000 nt!KiCommitThreadWait+0x1df
9a82393c 82a29828 00000002 9a823a74 00000001 nt!KeWaitForMultipleObjects+0x535
9a823bc8 82a29595 00000002 9a823bfc 00000001 nt!ObpWaitForMultipleObjects+0x262
9a823d18 8283e1fa 00000002 0015fa50 00000001 nt!NtWaitForMultipleObjects+0xcd
...
```

```
0015fc88 006c3c2f 04a70da8 00070270 00000000 COMDLG32!CFileOpenSave::Show+0x181
0015fca0 006c3fdb 00070270 0209eb04 00001808 notepad!ShowOpenSaveDialog+0x62
...
```

So far, nothing here is new compared to the live kernel-debugging experiment shown earlier. However, now you can also set a breakpoint to figure out when the events that the main UI thread is waiting on get signaled, as you'll shortly see. Using the address of the event object from the previous listing, you can see that it's currently in the nonsignaled state. Notice the use of the *–r* option of the *dt* ("dump type") command, which allows you to ask the debugger to dump the fields in the target object recursively.

```
0: kd> dt -r nt!_KEVENT 859470f0
   +0x000 Header           : _DISPATCHER_HEADER
      +0x000 Type             : 0x1 ''  ...
      +0x004 SignalState      : 0n0     ...
```

You can use a data breakpoint to monitor every write access to the *Signal* field, which gets set to *1* when the event object gets signaled. Data breakpoints (set using the *ba* command) are slightly different from the regular code breakpoints (set using the *bp* command). You'll see more about them later in Chapter 5, "Beyond the Basics." All you need to know to understand this particular experiment is that data breakpoints provide a way to break whenever an address in memory is executed, read from, or written into by the processor ("break on access").

```
0: kd> ba w4 859470f0+4
0: kd> g
Breakpoint 0 hit
1: kd> k
ChildEBP RetAddr
8a460b44 9534682a nt!KeSetEvent+0x7d
8a460b60 9533bd4e win32k!SetWakeBit+0xfa
8a460b8c 9533bae0 win32k!_PostMessageExtended+0x1aa
8a460ba8 9532f297 win32k!_PostMessage+0x18
8a460bc8 952c5dba win32k!_PostMessageCheckIL+0x6b
8a460c50 952c90fd win32k!xxxSendBSMtoDesktop+0x254
8a460c94 952d11ca win32k!xxxSendMessageBSM+0x7f
8a460cfc 952ce5f2 win32k!xxxUserPowerEventCalloutWorker+0x1c2
8a460d18 95352a65 win32k!xxxUserPowerCalloutWorker+0x2d
8a460d28 8283e1fa win32k!NtUserCallNoParam+0x1b
8a460d28 76f270b4 nt!KiFastCallEntry+0x12a
0049fc30 750a19e4 ntdll!KiFastSystemCallRet
...
```

Notice how the event object is indeed signaled by *win32k.sys*. This shouldn't come as a surprise given what you know from the previous part in this book about *win32k.sys* being the kernel-mode side of the Windows GUI subsystem, where input events start their lives and get dispatched to the UI threads on the interactive desktop. Now that you know how this event is signaled, you should disable the data breakpoint you set earlier using the *bd* debugger command so that the target machine continues its execution without continuously breaking back in to the host debugger:

```
0: kd> bd 0
0: kd> g
```

Setting Code Breakpoints in the Kernel Debugger

Setting code breakpoints (using the *bp* command) in the kernel-mode debugger works very much the same way as in the user-mode debugging case, but there is a twist! Because the breakpoint memory addresses are always interpreted relative to the current process context on the target machine at the time of the debugger break-in, first you need to switch to the target process before you can set breakpoints relative to that process. This wasn't a concern when you set code breakpoints in the user-mode debugger because the context in that case is always that of the debuggee process.

Setting Code Breakpoints in User-Mode Memory

The kernel debugger has global scope, so when you break in, it is very likely that the current process won't be the one you are interested in. More often than not when the machine is in the idle state, the process in question will be the system (NT kernel) "process."

```
0: kd> !process -1 0
PROCESS 85652b78  SessionId: none  Cid: 0004    Peb: 00000000  ParentCid: 0000
    DirBase: 00185000  ObjectTable: 89201ca0  HandleCount: 673.
    Image: System
```

To set code breakpoints inside the *notepad.exe* process from the previous experiment, for instance, you first need to transition over to that process. You do that by using the */i* ("i" for invasive context switch) option of *.process* and typing **g**. The debugger then breaks right back, but this time the current active process is *notepad.exe*. This sequence is demonstrated in the following listing.

```
0: kd> !process 0 0 notepad.exe
PROCESS 85f52a70  SessionId: 1  Cid: 17e0    Peb: 7ffd3000  ParentCid: 063c
    Image: notepad.exe
0: kd> .process /i 85f52a70
You need to continue execution (press 'g' <enter>) for the context
to be switched. When the debugger breaks in again, you will be in
the new process context.
0: kd> g
Break instruction exception - code 80000003 (first chance)
nt!RtlpBreakWithStatusInstruction:
8287b0d0 cc              int     3
1: kd> !process -1 0
PROCESS 85f52a70  SessionId: 1  Cid: 17e0    Peb: 7ffd3000  ParentCid: 063c
    Image: notepad.exe
```

Now that you are in the right process context, you can set the code breakpoint using the *bp* command. For example, the following listing reloads the symbols for user-mode stacks in the current process (*notepad.exe*) and then adds a test breakpoint in user-mode code that should be hit every time the main GUI window message loop of that process receives a UI event. Because this breakpoint will also be hit in other GUI processes on the target machine, the */p* kernel debugger option of the *bp* command is used to further restrict its scope to the *notepad.exe* process only.

```
1: kd> .reload /user
Loading User Symbols.............................
1: kd> x user32!*getmessage*
77076703          USER32!GetMessagePos = <no type information>
```

```
7705cde8          USER32!GetMessageW = <no type information>
7705650b          USER32!NtUserRealInternalGetMessage = <no type information>
...
1: kd> bp /p 85f52a70 USER32!GetMessageW
1: kd> g
Breakpoint 0 hit
USER32!GetMessageW:
1: kd> !process -1 0
PROCESS 85f52a70  SessionId: 1  Cid: 17e0    Peb: 7ffd3000  ParentCid: 063c
    Image: notepad.exe
```

This breakpoint should be hit a lot—in fact, every time the *notepad.exe* UI receives a new GUI message on the target machine. So, make sure you clear it now that you're done with this experiment.

```
1: kd> bc *
1: kd> g
```

Setting Code Breakpoints in Kernel-Mode Memory

Because kernel-mode memory is the same regardless of the active process context, you can set breakpoints in kernel functions without having to first perform an invasive process context switch in the kernel debugger. In that sense, setting code breakpoints in kernel memory is also a simple one-step process, similar to setting code breakpoints in the user-mode debugger.

The following listing, for instance, shows how to set a system breakpoint that would be hit every time a process tries to open a registry key. Notice that there was no need to switch the process context to a particular user-mode process first. You just set the global kernel-mode memory breakpoint, and it will be hit regardless of the process that triggers this system call.

```
0: kd> x nt!Nt*Key
...
82a69f67          nt!NtEnumerateValueKey = <no type information>
82a4c6e8          nt!NtOpenKey = <no type information>
82a67b01          nt!NtEnumerateKey = <no type information>
82a0b4a3          nt!NtSetValueKey = <no type information>
82a4cd54          nt!NtQueryKey = <no type information>
829ec987          nt!NtDeleteKey = <no type information>
82a9cdfb          nt!NtRenameKey = <no type information>
...
0: kd> bp nt!NtOpenKey
0: kd> g
Breakpoint 0 hit
0: kd> !process -1 0
PROCESS 856a88a8  SessionId: 0  Cid: 0d54    Peb: 7ffdf000  ParentCid: 02e0
    Image: WmiPrvSE.exe
0: kd> g
Breakpoint 0 hit
0: kd> !process -1 0
PROCESS 86cead40  SessionId: 0  Cid: 0458    Peb: 7ffdd000  ParentCid: 0250
    Image: svchost.exe
0: kd> .reload /user
0: kd> k
ChildEBP RetAddr
a1e6fd20 8285d1fa nt!NtOpenKey
```

```
a1e6fd20 776a70b4 nt!KiFastCallEntry+0x12a
0b83fd14 776a5d14 ntdll!KiFastSystemCallRet
0b83fd18 75c1dd39 ntdll!ZwOpenKey+0xc
0b83fd44 75c0b3cc kernel32!LocalOpenLocalMachine+0x38
0b83fd68 75c1d067 kernel32!MapPredefinedHandleInternal+0xa3
0b83fdc8 75c1cf92 kernel32!RegOpenKeyExInternalW+0x110
0b83fde8 6bb51511 kernel32!RegOpenKeyExW+0x21
...
0: kd> bl
 0 e 82a4c6e8     0001 (0001) nt!NtOpenKey
0: kd> $ Disable the breakpoint at the end of your experiment
0: kd> bd 0
0: kd> g
```

Getting Help for WinDbg Kernel Debugging Commands

Just as in the case of user-mode debugging, the F1 shortcut (or *.hh* command) can be used to find help information for the various kernel-mode debugging commands. You should also consult Appendix B, "WinDbg Kernel-Mode Debugging Quick Start," for a short glossary of the most common kernel-debugging tasks and the commands used to accomplish them. The Windows debuggers package also includes a document (*kernel_debugging_tutorial.doc*) that describes kernel-mode debugging in some level of detail, so you might want to peruse some of that information as well.

If you're completely new to kernel debugging, keep in mind that future chapters include several practical scenarios involving WinDbg kernel-mode debugging that will make some of the concepts more concrete and approachable. You might also want to wait until you need to try those experiments before you consult this more advanced documentation. By doing so, you would know better the subset of kernel debugging information that would help you the most in your personal debugging tasks.

Summary

In this chapter, you learned several important aspects of user-mode and kernel-mode debugging in Windows and also executed a few practical experiments. With that important first hands-on experience under your belt, the following key points are also worth a recap:

- Visual Studio is a great integrated environment that allows seamless debugging of the code added as part of the routine debugging iterations typically used during test-driven development. It's also the Windows debugger of choice for source-level .NET and script debugging.
- The Windows debuggers are great at deep investigations in production environments or on test machines where the binaries are installed without the corresponding source code. They're also particularly adept at handling transitions between your code and the system APIs it calls when you are interested in studying those interactions.
- Kernel-mode debugging isn't only for driver or kernel developers. The reason this book stresses that method as a complement to user-mode debugging is because it's a great

system-level debugging tool that can also be used as a global debugger for user-mode processes, which is especially useful when studying system internals or debugging scenarios that involve more than one user-mode process.

- Live kernel debugging is a sufficient option for viewing and manipulating kernel memory. It does not require a second machine, so it's also very easy to set up. However, live KD does not allow you to set active breakpoints or perform other invasive kernel-debugging tasks.
- True kernel-mode debugging can be done by either using a virtual machine or using a connection cable and a second host debugger machine. The available cabling options in Windows 7 are to use 1394 (FireWire), COM serial cables, or USB 2.0 cables—in this particular order of preference—based on the ports supported by your machines. If you're able to set up a virtual machine KD environment and avoid cables altogether, that's worth pursuing both for the simplicity of the KD setup and the other testing advantages (snapshots, resets, and so on) that virtualization solutions offer.
- Though user-mode and live kernel-mode debugging are used as the primary options in the debugging experiments presented in this book, a few case studies will need to rely on true kernel-mode debugging. It's important that you prepare an environment that allows you to follow those experiments. If you haven't yet completed setting up a kernel-mode debugger (either using a physical machine or a virtual target machine), now is a good time to go back and follow the step-by-step instructions provided in this chapter and get that environment working before you move ahead to other chapters.

The next chapter will go deeper into these topics and show you how debuggers work in Windows. It will cover some basic mechanisms of debuggers so that you can better understand what you can accomplish with each debugging option.

CHAPTER 3

How Windows Debuggers Work

In this chapter

This chapter explains how different types of debuggers work in Microsoft Windows. If you know these architectural foundations, many debugger concepts and behaviors suddenly start making sense. For example, this chapter explains why certain debugger commands and features work only in user-mode or kernel-mode debugging. You'll also dive into the architecture of managed-code debugging and discover why .NET source-level debugging isn't currently supported by the Windows debuggers.

Following that discussion, you'll learn how the architecture of script debugging relates to that of .NET debugging. With HTML5 and JavaScript becoming more prevalent development technologies for rich client user interfaces, script debugging is likely to garner even more attention from Windows developers in the future. This chapter concludes with a section that explains remote debugging and the key concepts that drive its architecture.

User-Mode Debugging

A user-mode debugger gives you the ability to inspect the memory of the target program you're trying to debug, as well as the ability to control its execution. In particular, you want to be able to set breakpoints and step through the target code, one instruction or one source line at a time. These basic requirements drive the design of the native user-mode debugging architecture in Windows.

Architecture Overview

To support controlling the target in user-mode debugging, the Windows operating system (OS) has an architecture based on the following principles:

- When important debug events, such as new module loads and exceptions, occur in the context of a process that's being debugged by a user-mode debugger, the OS generates message notifications on behalf of the target and sends them to the debugger process, giving the debugger program a chance to either handle or ignore those notifications. During each notification, the target process blocks and waits until the debugger is done responding to it before it resumes its execution.
- For this architecture to work, the native debugger process must also implement its end of the handshake, so to speak, and have a dedicated thread to receive and respond to the debug events generated by the target process.
- The interprocess communication between the two user-mode programs is based on a debug port kernel object (owned by the target process), where the target queues up its debug event notifications and waits on the debugger to process them.

This generic interprocess communication model is sufficient to handle all the requirements for controlling the target in a user-mode debugging session, providing the debugger with the capability to respond to code breakpoints or single-step events, as illustrated in Figure 3-1.

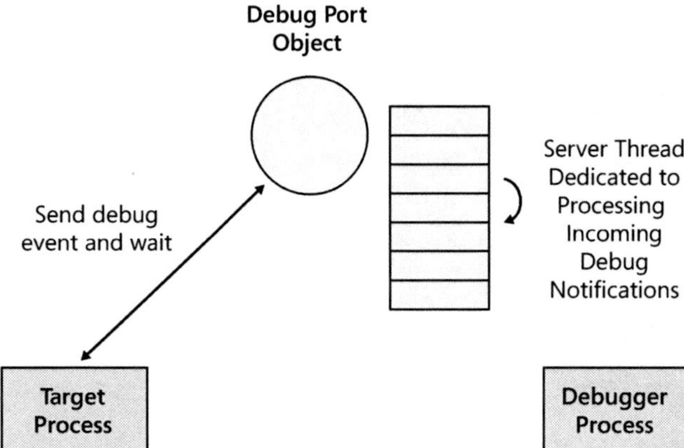

FIGURE 3-1 Native user-mode debugging architecture in Windows.

The other high-level requirement of user-mode debugging is for the debugger to be able to inspect and modify the virtual address space of the target process. This is necessary, for example, to be able to insert code breakpoints or walk the stacks and list the call frames in the threads of execution contained within the target process.

Windows provides facilities exposed at the Win32 API layer to satisfy these requirements, allowing any user-mode process to read and write to the memory of another process—as long as it has sufficient privileges to do so. This system-brokered access is why you can debug only your own processes unless you're an administrator running in an elevated User Acount Control (UAC) context with full administrative privileges (which include, in particular, the special *SeDebugPrivilege*). If you do have those privileges, you can debug processes from any other user on the system—including *LocalSystem* processes.

Win32 Debugging APIs

Debugger programs can implement their functionality and follow the conceptual model described in the previous section by using published APIs in the operating system. Table 3-1 summarizes the main Win32 functions used in Windows user-mode debuggers to achieve their requirements.

TABLE 3-1 Win32 API Support for User-Mode Windows Debuggers

Requirement	Win32 API Function	WinDbg Command(s)
Start a target process directly under the control of a user-mode debugger.	*CreateProcess*, with *dwCreationFlags*: ■ DEBUG_PROCESS ■ DEBUG_ONLY_THIS_PROCESS	Ctrl+E UI shortcut or windbg.exe target.exe
Dynamically attach a user-mode debugger to an existing process.	*OpenProcess*, with at least the following *dwDesiredAccess* flags: ■ PROCESS_VM_READ ■ PROCESS_VM_WRITE ■ PROCESS_VM_OPERATION *DebugActiveProcess*, with the handle obtained in the previous step	F6 UI shortcut or windbg.exe –pn target.exe or windbg.exe –p [PID]
Stop debugging the target process, but without terminating it.	*DebugActiveProcessStop*	*qd* ("quit and detach")
Break into the debugger to inspect the target.	*DebugBreakProcess*	Ctrl+Break UI shortcut or Debug\Break menu action
Wait for new debug events.	*WaitForDebugEvent*	N/A
Continue the target's execution after a received debug event is processed.	*ContinueDebugEvent*	N/A
Inspect and edit the virtual address space of the target process.	*ReadProcessMemory* *WriteProcessMemory*	Dump memory (*dd*, *db*, and so on) Edit memory (*ed*, *eb*, and so on) Insert code breakpoints (*bp*) Dump a thread's stack trace (*k*, *kP*, *kn*, and so on)

With these Win32 APIs, a user-mode debugger can write the code in the thread that it uses to process the debug events it receives from the target using a loop like the one shown in the following listing (pseudo-code).

```
//
// Main User-Mode Debugger Loop
//
CreateProcess("target.exe",..., DEBUG_PROCESS, ...);
while (1)
```

```
{
    WaitForDebugEvent(&event, ...);
    switch (event)
    {
        case ModuleLoad:
            Handle/Ignore;
            break;
        case TerminateProcess:
            Handle/Ignore;
            break;
        case Exception (code breakpoint, single step, etc...):
            Handle/Ignore;
            break;
    }
    ContinueDebugEvent(...);
}
```

When the debugger loop calls the *WaitForDebugEvent* Win32 API to check whether a new debug event arrived, the call internally transitions to kernel mode to fetch the event from the queue of the debug port object of the target process (the *DebugPort* field of the *nt!_EPROCESS* executive object). If the queue is found to be empty, the call blocks and waits for a new debug event to be posted to the port object. After the event is processed by the debugger, the *ContinueDebugEvent* Win32 API is called to let the target process continue its execution.

Debug Events and Exceptions

The OS generates several types of debug events when a process is being debugged. For instance, an event is generated for every module load, allowing the user-mode debugger to know when a new DLL is mapped into the address space of the target process. Similarly, an event is also raised when a new child process is created by the target process, enabling the user-mode debugging session to also handle the debug events from child processes if it wants to do so.

Debug events are similarly generated when any exceptions are raised in the context of the target process. As you'll shortly see, code breakpoints and single-stepping are both internally implemented by forcing an exception to be raised in the context of the target application, which means that those events can also be handled by the user-mode debugger just like any other debug events. To better understand this type of debug event, a quick overview of exception handling in Windows is in order.

.NET, C++, and SEH Exceptions

Two categories of exceptions exist in Windows: language-level or framework-level exceptions, such as the C++ or .NET exceptions, and OS-level exceptions, also known as *Structured Exception Handling* (SEH) exceptions. Both Microsoft Visual C++ and the .NET Common Language Runtime (CLR) use SEH exceptions internally to implement support for their specific application-level, exception-handling mechanisms.

SEH exceptions, in turn, can be separated into two categories: hardware exceptions are raised in response to a processor interrupt (invalid memory access, integer divide-by-zero, and so on), and software exceptions are triggered by an explicit call to the *RaiseException* Win32 API. Hardware exceptions are particularly important to the functionality of user-mode debuggers in Windows because they're also used to implement breakpoints and in single-stepping the target, two fundamental features of any debugger.

At the Visual C/C++ language level, the *throw* keyword used to throw C++ exceptions is translated by the compiler into a call implemented in the C runtime library, which ultimately invokes the *RaiseException* API. In addition, three keywords (*__try*, *__except*, and *__finally*) are also defined to allow you to take advantage of SEH exceptions and structure (hence the SEH name) your code so that you can establish code blocks to handle or ignore the SEH exceptions that get raised from within that code block. Despite this Visual C++ language support, it's important to realize that SEH is a Windows operating system concept and that you can use it with any language, as long as the compiler has support for it.

Unlike C++ exceptions, which can be raised with any type, SEH exceptions deal with only one type: *unsigned int*. Each SEH exception, whether triggered in hardware or software, is identified in Windows using an integer identifier—the *exception code*—that indicates the type of fault that triggered the exception (divide-by-zero, access violation, and so on). You can find many of the exception codes defined by the OS in the *winnt.h* Software Development Kit (SDK) header file. In addition, applications are also free to define their own custom exception codes, which is precisely what the C++ and .NET runtimes do for their exceptions.

Table 3-2 lists a few common exception codes that you'll see frequently during your debugging investigations.

TABLE 3-2 Common Windows SEH Exceptions and Their Status Codes

Exception Code	Description
STATUS_ACCESS_VIOLATION (0xC0000005)	Invalid memory access
STATUS_INTEGER_DIVIDE_BY_ZERO (0xC0000094)	Arithmetic divide-by-zero operation
STATUS_INTEGER_OVERFLOW (0xC0000095)	Arithmetic integer overflow
STATUS_STACK_OVERFLOW (0xC00000FD)	Stack overflow (running out of stack space)
STATUS_BREAKPOINT (0x80000003)	Raised in response to the debug break CPU interrupt (interrupt #3 on *x86* and *x64*)
STATUS_SINGLE_STEP (0x80000004)	Raised in response to the single-step CPU interrupt (interrupt #1 on *x86* and *x64*)

SEH Exception Handling in the User-Mode Debugger

When an exception occurs in a process that's being debugged, the user-mode debugger gets notified by the OS exception dispatching code in *ntdll.dll* before any user exception handlers defined in the target process are given a chance to respond to the exception. If the debugger chooses not to handle this *first-chance* exception notification, the exception dispatching sequence proceeds further and the target thread is then given a chance to handle the exception if it wants to do so. If the SEH exception is not handled by the thread in the target process, the debugger is then sent another debug event, called a *second-chance* notification, to inform it that an unhandled exception occurred in the target process.

Figure 3-2 summarizes this OS exception dispatching sequence, specifically when a user-mode debugger is connected to the target process.

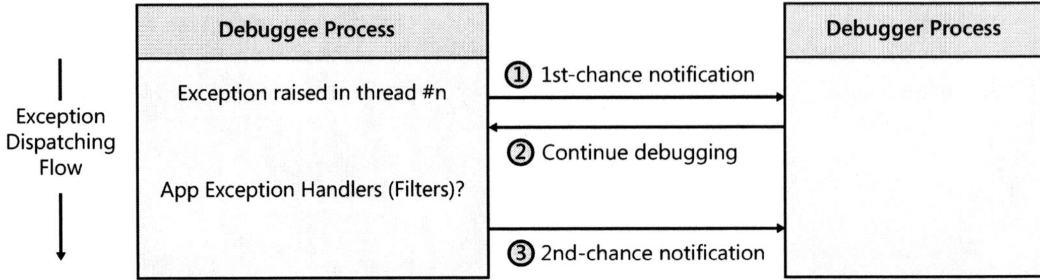

FIGURE 3-2 SEH exceptions and debug event notifications.

First-chance notifications are a good place for the user-mode debugger to handle exceptions that should be invisible to the code in the target process, including code breakpoints, single-step debug events, and the break-in signal. The sections that follow describe these important mechanisms in more detail.

Unlike first-chance notifications, which for user exceptions are simply logged to the debugger command window by default, the user-mode debugger always stops the target in response to a second-chance exception notification. Unhandled exceptions are always reason for concern because they lead to the demise of the target process when no debuggers are attached, which is why the user-mode debugger breaks in when they occur so that you can investigate them. You can see this sequence in action using the following program from the companion source code, which simply throws a C++ exception with a string type. For more details on how to compile the companion source code, refer to the procedure described in the Introduction of this book.

```
//
// C:\book\code\chapter_03\BasicException>main.cpp
//
int
__cdecl
wmain()
{
    throw "This program raised an error";
    return 0;
}
```

When you run this program under the WinDbg user-mode debugger, you see the debugger receive two notifications from the target: the first-chance notification is logged to the debugger command window, while the second-chance notification causes the debugger to break in, as illustrated in the following debugger listing. Notice also how the *throw* keyword used to raise C++ exceptions ends up getting translated into a call to the C runtime library (the *msvcrt!_CxxThrowException* function call in the following listing), which ultimately invokes the *RaiseException* Win32 API to raise an SEH exception with the custom C++ exception code.

```
0:000> vercommand
command line: '"c:\Program Files\Debugging Tools for Windows (x86)\windbg.exe"
c:\book\code\chapter_03\BasicException\objfre_win7_x86\i386\BasicException.exe'
0:000> .symfix
0:000> .reload
0:000> g
(aa8.1fc0): C++ EH exception - code e06d7363 (first chance)
(aa8.1fc0): C++ EH exception - code e06d7363 (!!! second chance !!!)
...
KERNELBASE!RaiseException+0x58:
75dad36f c9              leave
0:000> k
ChildEBP RetAddr
000ffb60 75fd359c KERNELBASE!RaiseException+0x58
000ffb98 00cb1204 msvcrt!_CxxThrowException+0x48
000ffbac 00cb136d BasicException!wmain+0x1b
[c:\book\code\chapter_03\basicexception\main.cpp @ 7]
000ffbf0 76f9ed6c BasicException!__wmainCRTStartup+0x102
000ffbfc 779c377b kernel32!BaseThreadInitThunk+0xe
000ffc3c 779c374e ntdll!__RtlUserThreadStart+0x70
000ffc54 00000000 ntdll!_RtlUserThreadStart+0x1b
0:000> $ Quit the debugging session
0:000> q
```

The Break-in Sequence

User-mode debuggers can intervene at any point in time and freeze the execution of their target process so that it can be inspected by the user—an operation referred to as *breaking into* the debugger. This is achieved by using the *DebugBreakProcess* API, which internally injects a remote thread into the address space of the target process. This "break-in" thread executes a debug break CPU interrupt instruction (*int 3*). In response to this interrupt, an SEH exception is raised by the OS in the context of the break-in thread. As shown in the previous section, this sends the user-mode debugger process a first-chance notification, allowing it to handle this special debug break exception (code *0x80000003*, or STATUS_BREAKPOINT) and finally break in by suspending all the threads in the target process.

This is why the current thread context in the user-mode debugger after a break-in operation will be in this special thread, which isn't a thread you'll recognize as "yours" if you're debugging your own target process. To see this break-in thread in action, start a new instance of *notepad.exe* under the WinDbg user-mode debugger, as shown in the following listing. If you're running this experiment on 64-bit Windows, you can execute it again exactly as shown here by using the 32-bit version of *notepad.exe* located under the *%windir%\SysWow64* directory on *x64* Windows.

```
0:000> vercommand
command line: '"c:\Program Files\Debugging Tools for Windows (x86)\windbg.exe"  notepad.exe'
0:000> .symfix
0:000> .reload
Reloading current modules........................
0:000> ~
   0  Id: 1d90.1678 Suspend: 1 Teb: 7ffde000 Unfrozen
0:000> g
```

Using the Debug\Break menu action, break back into the debugger. You'll see that the current thread context is no longer thread #0 (the main UI thread in *notepad.exe*) but rather a new thread. As you can infer from the function name (*ntdll!DbgUiRemoteBreakin*) on the call stack that you obtain by using the *k* command, this is the remote thread that was injected by the debugger into the target address space in response to the break-in request.

```
(1938.1fb0): Break instruction exception - code 80000003 (first chance)
...
ntdll!DbgBreakPoint:
7799410c cc              int     3
0:001> ~
   0  Id: 1d90.1678 Suspend: 1 Teb: 7ffde000 Unfrozen
.  1  Id: 1d90.17f0 Suspend: 1 Teb: 7ffdd000 Unfrozen
0:001> k
ChildEBP RetAddr
00a4fecc 779ef161 ntdll!DbgBreakPoint
00a4fefc 75e9ed6c ntdll!DbgUiRemoteBreakin+0x3c
00a4ff08 779b37f5 kernel32!BaseThreadInitThunk+0xe
00a4ff48 779b37c8 ntdll!__RtlUserThreadStart+0x70
00a4ff60 00000000 ntdll!_RtlUserThreadStart+0x1b
```

In addition, using the *uf* debugger command to disassemble the current function shows that this thread was executing an *int 3* CPU interrupt instruction just before the debugger got sent the first-chance notification for the debug break exception.

```
0:001> uf .
ntdll!DbgBreakPoint:
7799410c cc              int     3
7799410d c3              ret
```

To see the actual threads in the target process, you can use the *~*k* command to list the call stacks for every thread in the target. You can also use the *s* command to change ("switch") the current thread context in the debugger to one of those threads, as illustrated in the following listing.

```
0:001> $ Switch over to thread #0 in the target
0:001> ~0s
```

```
0:000> k
ChildEBP RetAddr
0019f8e8 760fcde0 ntdll!KiFastSystemCallRet
0019f8ec 760fce13 USER32!NtUserGetMessage+0xc
0019f908 0085148a USER32!GetMessageW+0x33
0019f948 008516ec notepad!WinMain+0xe6
0019f9d8 76f9ed6c notepad!_initterm_e+0x1a1
0019f9e4 779c377b kernel32!BaseThreadInitThunk+0xe
0019fa24 779c374e ntdll!__RtlUserThreadStart+0x70
0019fa3c 00000000 ntdll!_RtlUserThreadStart+0x1b
0:001> $ Terminate this debugging session...
0:001> q
```

Setting Code Breakpoints

Code breakpoints are also implemented using the *int 3* instruction. Unlike the break-in case, where the debug break instruction is executed in the context of the remote break-in thread, code breakpoints are implemented by directly overwriting the target memory location where the code breakpoint was requested by the user.

The debugger program keeps track of the initial instructions for each code breakpoint so that it can substitute them in place of the debug break instruction when the breakpoints are hit, and before the user is able to inspect the target inside the debugger. This way, the fact that *int 3* instructions are inserted into the target process to implement code breakpoints is completely hidden from the user debugging the program, as it should be.

This scheme sounds straightforward, but there is a catch: how is the debugger able to insert the *int 3* instruction before the execution of the target process is resumed (using the *g* command) after a breakpoint hit? Surely, the debugger can't simply insert the debug break instruction before the target's execution is resumed because the next instruction to execute is supposed to be the original one from the target and not the *int 3* instruction. The way the debugger solves this dilemma is the same way it is able to support single-stepping, which is by using the TF ("trap flag") bit of the EFLAGS register on *x86* and *x64* processors to force the target thread to execute one instruction at a time. This single-step flag causes the CPU to issue an interrupt (*int 1*) after every instruction it executes. This allows the thread of the breakpoint to execute the original target instruction before the debugger is immediately given a chance to handle the new single-step SEH exception—which it does by restoring the debug break instruction again, as well as by resetting the TF flag so that the CPU single-step mode is disabled again.

Observing Code Breakpoint Insertion in WinDbg

To conclude this section, you'll try a fun experiment in which you'll debug the user-mode WinDbg debugger! Armed with the background information from this section and the familiarity with using WinDbg commands that you've gained so far, you have all the tools to confirm what WinDbg does when a new code breakpoint is added by the user without having to take my word for it.

To start this experiment, run *notepad.exe* under *windbg.exe*. This experiment once again uses the *x86* flavor of *notepad.exe* and *windbg.exe*, but the concepts are identical on *x64* Windows.

```
0:000> vercommand
command line: '"c:\Program Files\Debugging Tools for Windows (x86)\windbg.exe"  notepad.exe'
0:000> .symfix
0:000> .reload
```

Set a breakpoint at *USER32!GetMessageW*, which is a function that you know is going to be hit in response to any user interaction with the *notepad.exe* user interface. Figure 3-3 represents this first debugging session.

```
0:000> bp user32!GetMessageW
```

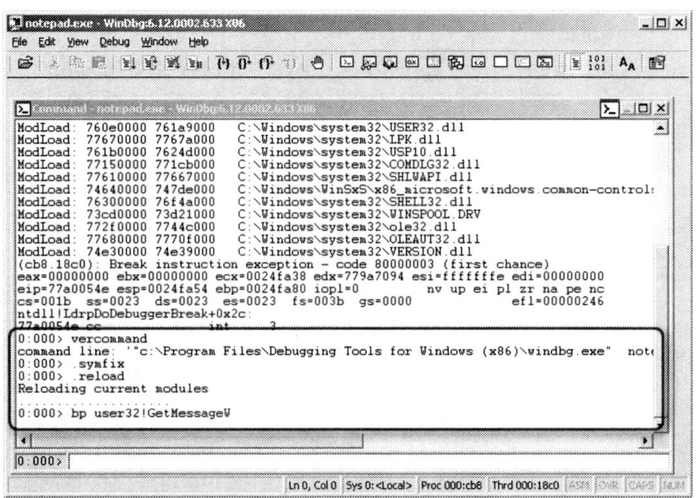

FIGURE 3-3 First WinDbg debugger instance.

Before you use the *g* command to let the target *notepad.exe* continue its execution, start a new *windbg.exe* debugger instance with the same security context as the first one. From this new instance, attach to the first *windbg.exe* process using the F6 shortcut, as illustrated in Figure 3-4. This allows you to follow what happens after you unblock the execution of the *notepad.exe* process from the first debugger instance.

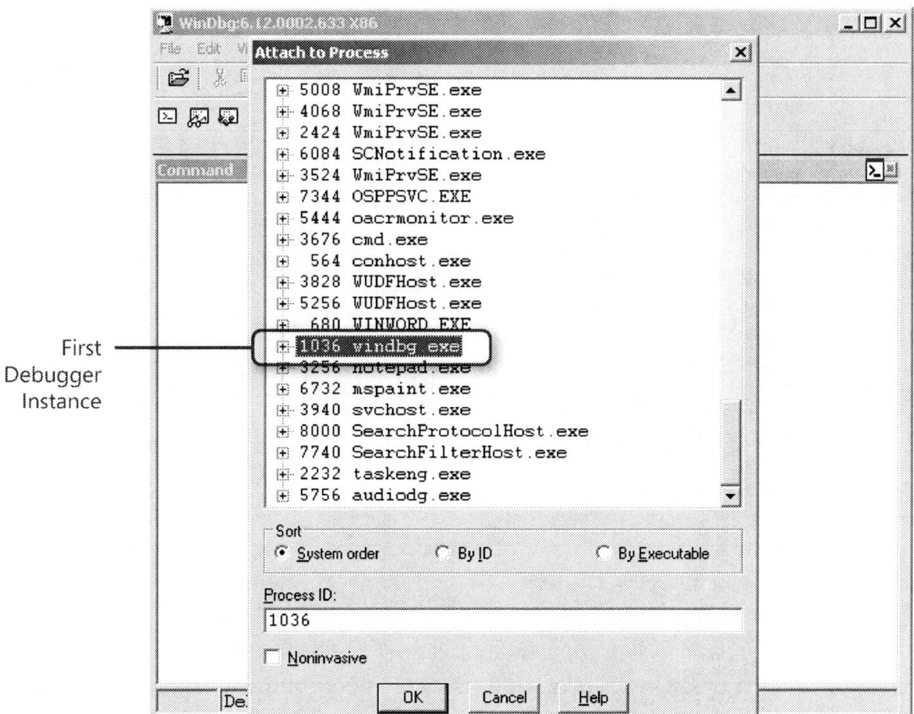

FIGURE 3-4 Debugging the debugger: the second WinDbg debugger instance.

In this new WinDbg instance, set a breakpoint at the *kernel32!WriteProcessMemory* API. As mentioned earlier in this chapter, this is the Win32 API used by user-mode debuggers to edit the virtual memory of their target processes.

```
0:002> $ Second WinDbg Session
0:002> .symfix
0:002> .reload
0:002> x kernel32!*writeprocessmemory*
75e51928 kernel32!_imp__WriteProcessMemory = <no type information>
75e520e3 kernel32!WriteProcessMemory = <no type information>
75eb959f kernel32!WriteProcessMemoryStub = <no type information>
0:002> bp kernel32!WriteProcessMemory
0:002> g
```

Now that you have this breakpoint in place, go back to the first *windbg.exe* instance and run the *g* command to let *notepad.exe* continue its execution.

```
0:000> $ First WinDbg Session
0:000> g
```

Notice that you immediately get a breakpoint hit inside the second *windbg.exe* instance, which is consistent with what you already learned in this chapter, because the first debugger tries to insert an *int 3* instruction into the *notepad.exe* process address space (corresponding to the *USER32!GetMessageW* breakpoint you added earlier).

```
Breakpoint 0 hit
kernel32!WriteProcessMemory:
...
0:001> $ Second WinDbg Session
0:001> k
ChildEBP RetAddr
0092edf4 58b84448 kernel32!WriteProcessMemory
0092ee2c 58adb384 dbgeng!BaseX86MachineInfo::InsertBreakpointInstruction+0x128
0092ee7c 58ad38ee dbgeng!LiveUserTargetInfo::InsertCodeBreakpoint+0x64
0092eeb8 58ad62f7 dbgeng!CodeBreakpoint::Insert+0xae
0092f764 58b67719 dbgeng!InsertBreakpoints+0x8c7
0092f7e8 58b66678 dbgeng!PrepareForExecution+0x5d9
0092f7fc 58afa539 dbgeng!PrepareForWait+0x28
0092f840 58afaa60 dbgeng!RawWaitForEvent+0x19
0092f858 00ebb6cf dbgeng!DebugClient::WaitForEvent+0xb0
0092f874 75e9ed6c windbg!EngineLoop+0x13f
0092f880 779b37f5 kernel32!BaseThreadInitThunk+0xe
0092f8c0 779b37c8 ntdll!__RtlUserThreadStart+0x70
0092f8d8 00000000 ntdll!_RtlUserThreadStart+0x1b
```

You can also check the arguments to the *WriteProcessMemory* API in the previous call stack by applying the technique described in Chapter 2, "Getting Started," where the stack pointer and saved frame pointer values were used to get the arguments to each call from the stack of the current thread. Remember that in the *__stdcall* calling convention, the stack pointer register value points to the return address at the time of the breakpoint, followed by the arguments to the function call. This means that the second DWORD value in the following listing represents the first parameter to the Win32 API call. The values you'll see will be different, but you can apply the same steps described here to derive the function arguments to this API call:

```
0:001> $ Second WinDbg Session
0:001> dd esp
0092edd4  58ce14a2 00000120 7630cde8 58d1b5d8
0092ede4  00000001 0092edf0 00000000 0092ee2c
...
```

In the documentation for the *WriteProcessMemory* Win32 API on the MSDN website at *http://msdn.microsoft.com/*, you'll see that it takes five parameters.

```
BOOL
WINAPI
WriteProcessMemory(
    __in HANDLE hProcess,
    __in LPVOID lpBaseAddress,
    __in_bcount(nSize) LPCVOID lpBuffer,
    __in SIZE_T nSize,
    __out_opt SIZE_T * lpNumberOfBytesWritten
    );
```

The first of these parameters is the user-mode handle for the target process object (*hProcess*) that the debugger is trying to write to. You can use the value you obtained from the *dd* command with the *!handle* debugger extension command to confirm that it was indeed the *notepad.exe* process.

The *!handle* command also gives you the process ID (PID) referenced by the handle, which you can confirm is the PID of *notepad.exe* in the Windows task manager UI or, alternatively, by using the convenient *.tlist* debugger command, as demonstrated in the following listing.

```
0:001> $ Second WinDbg Session
0:001> !handle 120 f
Handle 120
  Type              Process
  GrantedAccess     0x12167b:
         ReadControl,Synch
         Terminate,CreateThread,VMOp,VMRead,VMWrite,DupHandle,SetInfo,QueryInfo
  Object Specific Information
    Process Id  5964
    Parent Process  3736
0:001> .tlist notepad*
 0n5964 notepad.exe
```

Next is the address that the debugger is trying to overwrite (*lpBaseAddress*). Using the *u* debugger command to disassemble the code located at that address, you can see that this second argument does indeed point to the *USER32!GetMessageW* API, which was the target location of the requested code breakpoint.

```
0:001> $ Second WinDbg Session
0:001> u 0x7630cde8
USER32!GetMessageW:
7630cde8 8bff            mov     edi,edi
7630cdea 55              push    ebp
7630cdeb 8bec            mov     ebp,esp
7630cded 8b5510          mov     edx,dword ptr [ebp+10h]
...
```

Finally, the third parameter (*lpBuffer*) is a pointer to the buffer that the debugger is trying to insert into this memory location. This is a single-byte buffer (as indicated by the value of the fourth argument, *nSize*, from the previous listing), representing the *int 3* instruction. On both *x86* and *x64*, this instruction is encoded using the single *0xCC* byte, as you can see by using either the *u* ("un-assemble") or *db* ("dump memory as a sequence of bytes") commands:

```
0:001> $ Second WinDbg Session
0:001> u 58d1b5d8
dbgeng!g_X86Int3:
58d1b5d8 cc              int     3
0:001> db 58d1b5d8
58d1b5d8  cc 00 00 00 00 00 00 00-00 00 00 00 00 00 00 00  ................
...
```

If you continue this experiment with the same breakpoints and type **g** again inside the second *windbg.exe* instance, you can similarly analyze the next hit of the *WriteProcessMemory* breakpoint and confirm that the initial byte from the *USER32!GetMessageW* function (*0x8b* in this case) is surreptitiously restored as the *USER32!GetMessageW* breakpoint gets hit, right before the user is able to issue commands in the first debugger UI, as shown in the following listing.

```
0:001> $ Second WinDbg Session
0:001> g
Breakpoint 0 hit
0:001> k
ChildEBP RetAddr
0092f128 58b84542 kernel32!WriteProcessMemory
0092f160 58adb6a9 dbgeng!BaseX86MachineInfo::RemoveBreakpointInstruction+0xa2
0092f1a4 58ad3bcd dbgeng!LiveUserTargetInfo::RemoveCodeBreakpoint+0x59
0092f1ec 58ad6c0a dbgeng!CodeBreakpoint::Remove+0x11d
...
0:001> dd esp
0092f108  58ce14a2 00000120 7630cde8 00680cc4
0092f118  00000001 0092f124 00479ed8 0000000b
...
0:001> db 00680cc4
00680cc4  8b 00 00 00 00 00 00 00-00 00 00 00 00 00 00 00  ................
...
0:001> $ Terminate both debugging sessions now
0:001> q
```

Kernel-Mode Debugging

The high-level requirements for kernel-mode debugging are similar to those of user-mode debugging, including the ability to control the target (break in, single-step, set breakpoints, and so on) and also manipulate its memory address space. The difference in the case of kernel-mode debugging is that the target is the entire system being debugged.

Architecture Overview

Just like in the case of user-mode debugging, the Windows operating system also designed an architecture that answers the system-level needs of kernel debuggers. In the case of user-mode debugging, that support framework is built right into the OS kernel, where the debug port executive object provides the key to the interprocess communication channel between the debugger and target processes. In the case of kernel debugging, the kernel itself is being debugged, so support for the communication channel is built lower in the architectural stack. This is done using Hardware Abstraction Layer (HAL) extensions that implement the low-level transport layer of the communication channel between the host and target machines during kernel debugging.

There are different transport mediums you can use to perform kernel-mode debugging, and each one of them is implemented in its own transport DLL extension. In Windows 7, for example, *kdcom.dll* is used for serial cables, *kd1394.dll* is used for FireWire cables, and *kdusb.dll* is used for USB 2.0 debug cables. These module extensions are loaded by the HAL very early during the boot process, when the target is enabled to support kernel-mode debugging. Because these modules sit very low in the architecture stack, they can't depend on higher-level OS kernel components that might not yet be fully loaded or otherwise turn out to be themselves in the process of being debugged. For that reason, the KD transport extensions are fairly lightweight and interact directly with the hardware at the lowest possible level without taking any extra device driver dependencies, as demonstrated in Figure 3-5.

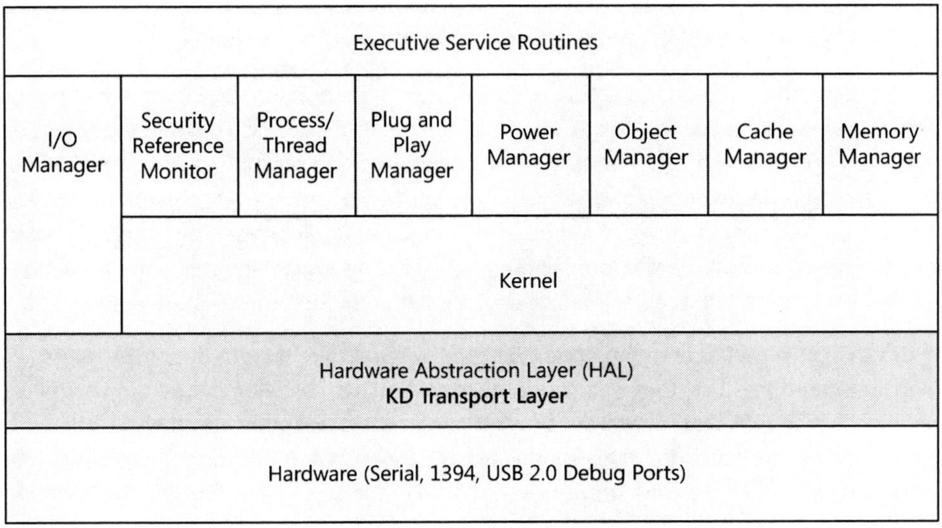

Executive Service Routines

I/O Manager

Security Reference Monitor

Process/ Thread Manager

Plug and Play Manager

Power Manager

Object Manager

Cache Manager

Memory Manager

Kernel

Hardware Abstraction Layer (HAL)

KD Transport Layer

Hardware (Serial, 1394, USB 2.0 Debug Ports)

FIGURE 3-5 KD transport layer in the target OS.

If you disregard for a second how the debugger commands are transmitted from the kernel debugger to the target, the conceptual model for how the kernel on the target processes the commands sent by the kernel-mode debugger is quite similar to how debug events are processed by the user-mode debugger loop:

- The OS kernel periodically asks the transport layer (as part of the clock interrupt service routine) to check for break-in packets from the host debugger. When a new one is found, the kernel enters a break-in loop where it waits for additional commands to be received from the host kernel debugger.
- While the system on the target machine is halted, the break-in loop checks for any new commands sent by the host kernel debugger. This enables the kernel debugger to read register values, inspect or change memory on the target, and perform many other inspection and control commands while the target is still frozen. These send/receive handshakes are repeated until the host kernel debugger decides to leave the break-in state and the target is instructed to exit the debugger break-in mode and continue its normal execution again.
- In addition to explicit break-in requests, the kernel can also enter the break-in loop in response to exceptions that get raised by the target machine, which allows the debugger to intervene and respond to them. This generic handling of exceptions is again used to implement single-stepping and setting code breakpoints inside the target OS during kernel-mode debugging.

Setting Code Breakpoints

Knowing how code breakpoints are implemented during kernel-mode debugging is important so that you can understand situations when you fail to hit breakpoints you insert using the host kernel debugger. There are many similarities between how code breakpoints are internally implemented in user-mode and kernel-mode debugging, but there are also several important differences.

Like in the user-mode debugging case, code breakpoints are also inserted by overwriting the target virtual memory address with the debug break CPU instruction (*int 3*). When the target machine hits the inserted breakpoint, a CPU interrupt is raised and its OS interrupt handler is invoked. Where things diverge between user-mode and kernel-mode debugging is in how the handler dispatches the exception event to the host debugger. In the kernel-mode debugging case, the target OS is halted and enters the break-in send/receive loop, allowing the host debugger to handle the breakpoint by putting the initial byte back in the breakpoint's code location before entering the break-in state.

Another way that kernel debugging code breakpoints are different from their user-mode debugging counterparts is that they might refer to memory that has been paged out to disk on the target machine. In that case, the target simply handles the breakpoint command from the host debugger by registering the code breakpoint as being "owed." When the code page is later loaded into memory, the page fault handler (*nt!MmAccessFault*) in the kernel memory manager intervenes and inserts the breakpoint instruction to the global code page at that time, just as it would have done if the breakpoint had been in a memory location that wasn't paged out at the time of the debugger break-in.

Finally, because the same user-mode virtual memory address can point to different private code depending on the user-mode process context, code breakpoints inserted during kernel debugging are always interpreted relative to the current process context. This is a point that sometimes escapes developers who are new to kernel debugging because it isn't a concern in user-mode debugging. However, this is precisely the reason why you should always invasively switch the process context in the host kernel debugger to the target process before setting breakpoints in user-mode code relative to that process.

Single-Stepping the Target

Single-stepping the target in the host debugger is implemented using the same single-step CPU support and interrupt (*int 1*) that enables you to single-step the target process in a user-mode debugging environment. However, the fact that kernel-mode debuggers have global scope again introduces some interesting side effects you should be aware of so that you are better prepared to deal with them during your kernel-debugging experiments.

The most practical difference you'll see when you try single-stepping the target in a host kernel debugger is that execution sometimes seems to jump to other random code on the system and away from your current thread context. This happens when the thread quantum expires while stepping over a function call and the OS decides to schedule another thread on the processor. When that happens, it seems as if the code you're debugging just jumped to a random location. In reality, what happened is that the old thread got switched out and a new one is now running on the processor.

This usually happens whenever you step over a long function or a Win32 API call that causes the thread to enter a wait state (such as a *Sleep* call). Fortunately, when single-stepping in a host kernel debugger, the target OS not only enables the CPU trace flag but cleverly also finds the next call and inserts an additional debug break instruction at that memory location every time you single-step. This means that by letting the target machine "go" again (using the *g* command) after it seemed you had jumped to an unrelated code location, you break right back at the next call from the original thread (once its wait is satisfied and the thread gets scheduled to run again), which allows you to continue single-stepping the thread you were examining prior to the context switch.

Switching the Current Process Context

There are two ways to resolve symbols for the user-mode stacks of a process on the target machine of a kernel-debugging session. The first way, which you already used in Chapter 2, is to simply switch the current process view in the host debugger and reload the user-mode symbols for that process. This method's main advantage is that it also works in live kernel-mode debugging, where it proves useful when you need to observe multiple user-mode processes during a debugger break-in. In the following live kernel-debugging session, the *.process* command is used with the */r* ("reload user-mode symbols") and */p* ("target process") options to illustrate this important approach. Make sure you start a new *notepad.exe* instance and that you use the values in bold text when you execute these commands because your values are likely to be different from the ones shown in this listing.

```
lkd> !process 0 0 notepad.exe
PROCESS 874fa030  SessionId: 1  Cid: 14ac    Peb: 7ffdf000  ParentCid: 1348
    Image: notepad.exe
lkd> .process /r /p 874fa030
Implicit process is now 874fa030
Loading User Symbols........................
lkd> !process 874fa030 7
PROCESS 874fa030  SessionId: 1  Cid: 14ac    Peb: 7ffdf000  ParentCid: 1348
    Image: notepad.exe
        THREAD 86f6fd48  Cid 14ac.2020  Teb: 7ffde000 Win32Thread: ffb91dd8 WAIT ...
            85685be8  SynchronizationEvent
        ChildEBP RetAddr  Args to Child
        9a99fb10 8287e65d 86f6fd48 807c9308 807c6120 nt!KiSwapContext+0x26
        9a99fb48 8287d4b7 86f6fe08 86f6fd48 85685be8 nt!KiSwapThread+0x266
        9a99fb70 828770cf 86f6fd48 86f6fe08 00000000 nt!KiCommitThreadWait+0x1df
        9a99fbe8 9534959a 85685be8 0000000d 00000001 nt!KeWaitForSingleObject+0x393
        9a99fc44 953493a7 000025ff 00000000 00000001 win32k!xxxRealSleepThread+0x1d7
        9a99fc60 95346414 000025ff 00000000 00000001 win32k!xxxSleepThread+0x2d
        9a99fcb8 95349966 9a99fce8 000025ff 00000000 win32k!xxxRealInternalGetMessage+0x4b2
        9a99fd1c 8283e1fa 000afb80 00000000 00000000 win32k!NtUserGetMessage+0x3f
        9a99fd1c 76f270b4 000afb80 00000000 00000000 nt!KiFastCallEntry+0x12a
        000afb3c 7705cde0 7705ce13 000afb80 00000000 ntdll!KiFastSystemCallRet
        000afb40 7705ce13 000afb80 00000000 00000000 USER32!NtUserGetMessage+0xc
        000afb5c 0055148a 000afb80 00000000 00000000 USER32!GetMessageW+0x33
        000afb9c 005516ec 00550000 00000000 0012237f notepad!WinMain+0xe6
...
```

The second way to switch process views in the host debugger is to perform an *invasive* process context switch on the target machine by using the */i* option of the *.process* command. This method is particularly useful when you need to set breakpoints in user-mode code locations, given they're always interpreted relative to the current process context on the target machine, as you also learned back in Chapter 2. This method requires the target machine to exit the debugger break-in mode and run to complete the request.

After the target is let go by the host debugger, the kernel on that side thaws the frozen processors and exits the break-in loop. Before it does so, however, it also schedules a high-priority work item to transition over to the new process context that was requested by the host debugger.

```
1: kd> !process 0 0 notepad.exe
PROCESS 874fa030  SessionId: 1  Cid: 14ac    Peb: 7ffdf000  ParentCid: 1348
    Image: notepad.exe
1: kd> .process /i 874fa030
You need to continue execution (press 'g' <enter>) for the context
to be switched. When the debugger breaks in again, you will be in
the new process context.
1: kd> g
Break instruction exception - code 80000003 (first chance)
```

The work item that induced the previous debug break runs on a *leased* system thread that runs in the context of the requested process. The host debugger breaks right back in again before any of its threads have a chance to continue executing past where they were at the time of the original break-in. You can also confirm that the current thread context is a kernel thread, and not a thread from the user-mode process itself. Notice that thread is indeed owned by the system (kernel) *process*, which always has a PID value of *4*, as reported by the *Cid* (client thread ID) you get from the *!thread* command.

```
0: kd> !thread
THREAD 856e94c0  Cid 0004.0038  Teb: 00000000 Win32Thread: 00000000 RUNNING on processor 0
ChildEBP RetAddr  Args to Child
8a524c0c 82b30124 00000007 8293b2f0 856e94c0 nt!RtlpBreakWithStatusInstruction
8a524d00 8287da6b 00000000 00000000 856e94c0 nt!ExpDebuggerWorker+0x1fa
8a524d50 82a08fda 00000001 a158a474 00000000 nt!ExpWorkerThread+0x10d
8a524d90 828b11d9 8287d95e 00000001 00000000 nt!PspSystemThreadStartup+0x9e
00000000 00000000 00000000 00000000 00000000 nt!KiThreadStartup+0x19
```

Nevertheless, this system thread is attached to the target process you requested, which you can confirm using the *!process* kernel debugger extension command and *–1* to indicate you would like the current process context displayed.

```
0: kd> !process -1 0
PROCESS 874fa030  SessionId: 1  Cid: 14ac    Peb: 7ffdf000  ParentCid: 1348
    Image: notepad.exe
```

User-mode code breakpoints you enter in this host debugger break-in state will be resolved relative to this process context, exactly as desired.

Managed-Code Debugging

As previously mentioned in Chapter 2, one of the unfortunate limitations of the Windows debuggers is that they don't support source-level debugging of .NET applications. This doesn't mean that you can't use WinDbg to debug managed code; it simply means that you won't have the convenience of source-level debugging, such as single-stepping and source line breakpoints, when doing so. It's as if you were debugging system code without the source code; only it's worse because many important commands that work for native system debugging, such as displaying call stacks using the *k* command, don't even work for managed code. Fortunately, there is at least a workaround in the form of a WinDbg extension called *SOS*, which Microsoft ships with the .NET Framework. This useful extension is covered in more detail later in this section.

Because of this limitation, the Microsoft Visual Studio environment remains the debugger of choice for .NET debugging. To better understand why the Windows debuggers are lacking in this regard, it's useful to first discuss the architecture used by Visual Studio and the .NET Common Language Runtime (CLR) environment to implement their support for managed-code debugging and understand the way they collaborate to present a seamless native/managed debugging experience. Just like other .NET-related discussions in this book, the coverage centers on the architecture in version 4.0 of the .NET Framework.

Architecture Overview

The first challenge when designing an architecture that enables debugging of Microsoft Intermediate Language (MSIL) .NET code is that such code gets translated into machine instructions on the fly by the CLR's Just-in-Time (JIT) compiler. For performance reasons, this run-time code generation is done lazily only after a method is actually invoked. In particular, this means that to insert a code breakpoint, the debugger needs to wait until the code in question is loaded into memory so that it can edit the code in memory and insert the debug break instruction at the appropriate location. The native debug events generated by the OS aren't sufficient by themselves to support this type of MSIL debugging because only the CLR knows when the .NET methods are compiled or how the managed class objects are represented in memory.

For those reasons, the CLR designed an infrastructure for debuggers to inspect and control managed targets with the help of a dedicated thread that runs as part of every .NET process and has intimate knowledge of its internal CLR data structures. This thread is known as the *debugger runtime controller* thread, and it runs in a continuous loop waiting for messages from the debugger process. Even in the break-in state, the managed target process isn't entirely frozen because this thread must still run to service the debugger commands. Any .NET application will have this extra debugger thread even when it isn't being actively debugged with a managed-code debugger. To confirm this fact, you can use the following "Hello World!" C# sample from the companion source code.

```
C:\book\code\chapter_03\HelloWorld>test.exe
Hello World!
Press any key to continue...
```

You can now use the steps described in Chapter 2 to start a live kernel-debugging session and noninvasively observe the threads that the managed process contains when it's active. Notice the presence of the debugger runtime controller thread (the *clr!DebuggerRCThread::ThreadProc* thread routine in the following listing) even though the .NET process isn't being debugged with a user-mode debugger.

```
lkd> .symfix
lkd> .reload
lkd> !process 0 0 test.exe
PROCESS 85520c88  SessionId: 1  Cid: 07b8    Peb: 7ffdf000  ParentCid: 0e5c
    Image: test.exe
lkd> .process /r /p 85520c88
lkd> !process 85520c88 7
PROCESS 85520c88  SessionId: 1  Cid: 07b8    Peb: 7ffdf000  ParentCid: 0e5c
    Image: test.exe
...
    THREAD 9532ed20  Cid 07b8.1e5c  ...
        828d74b0  SynchronizationEvent
        885f5cb8  SynchronizationEvent
        86a0e808  SynchronizationEvent
...
    0116f7fc 5d6bb4d8 00000003 0116f824 00000000 KERNEL32!WaitForMultipleObjects+0x18
    0116f860 5d6bb416 d6ab8654 00000000 00000000 clr!DebuggerRCThread::MainLoop+0xd9
    0116f890 5d6bb351 d6ab8678 00000000 00000000 clr!DebuggerRCThread::ThreadProc+0xca
    0116f8bc 76f9ed6c 00000000 0116f908 779c377b clr!DebuggerRCThread::ThreadProcStatic+0x83
    0116f8c8 779c377b 00000000 6cb23a74 00000000 KERNEL32!BaseThreadInitThunk+0xe
    0116f908 779c374e 5d6bb30c 00000000 00000000 ntdll!__RtlUserThreadStart+0x70
    0116f920 00000000 5d6bb30c 00000000 00000000 ntdll!_RtlUserThreadStart+0x1b
lkd> q
```

Because of its reliance on this helper thread, the managed-code debugging paradigm is often referred to as *in-process* debugging, in contrast to the out-of-process debugging architecture used by native code user-mode debuggers, which requires no active collaboration from the target process. The contract defined by the CLR for managed-code debuggers to interact with the runtime controller thread is represented by a set of COM interfaces implemented in the *mscordbi.dll* .NET Framework DLL. Because this contract is published as a set of COM interfaces, you can write a managed-code debugger in C/C++, and also in any other .NET language, where the COM Interop facilities can be used to consume the CLR debugging objects implemented in this DLL.

The Visual Studio debugger is based on this same CLR debugging infrastructure, which it also uses to implement its support for managed-code debugging. The components used to service the user actions in the debugger are represented, at a high level, in Figure 3-6. The debugger front-end UI processes any commands entered by the user and forwards them to the debugger's back-end engine, which in turn internally uses the CLR debugging COM objects from *mscordbi.dll* to communicate with the runtime controller thread in the managed target process. These COM objects take care of all the internal details related to the private interprocess communication channel between the debugger and target processes.

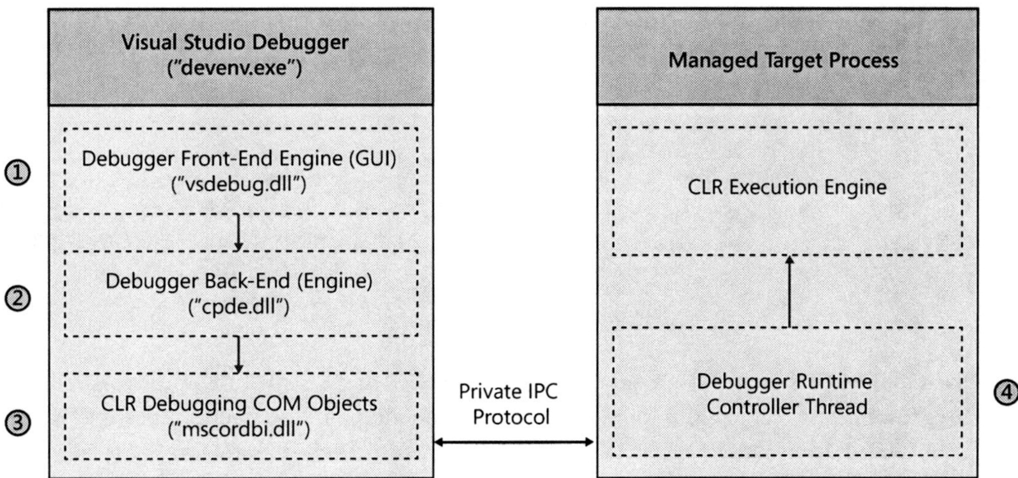

FIGURE 3-6 In-process managed debugging architecture in Visual Studio and the CLR.

This architecture has one big advantage, which is that it insulates the debuggers from the intricate details of the internal CLR execution engine data structures by having a higher-level contract and communication channel between the managed-code debuggers and the CLR debugger controller thread. This means the layouts of those data structures can change without breaking the functionality of those debuggers.

Unfortunately, this architecture also has several drawbacks. First, this model doesn't work for debugging of crash dumps because the target isn't running in that case, so the debuggers can't rely on an active debugger helper thread to perform their actions when debugging a memory crash dump file.

Second, the operating system is unaware that the application is being debugged using this private interprocess communication channel. Up until .NET version 4.0, Visual Studio debugging of managed applications didn't work at all on machines that also had a host kernel debugger attached to them. Because the OS didn't know that the managed process was being debugged, exceptions raised for the purpose of managed debugging were being incorrectly caught by the kernel debugger. The official workaround to this problem was documented in the Knowledge Base (KB) article at *http://support.microsoft.com/kb/303067*, but it's hardly satisfactory because it recommends disabling the kernel debugger entirely. Fortunately, this problem is now fixed in Visual Studio 2010—at least for managed applications compiled for .NET 4.0—because the debugger now also attaches to the target process debug port as a regular native user-mode debugger. However, the in-process managed-debugging architecture is still otherwise being used in that release as the main live, managed-code debugging channel.

Table 3-3 contains a comparative analysis of the in-process and out-of-process debugging architectures.

TABLE 3-3 In-Process and Out-of-Process Managed Debugging Paradigms

	Advantages	**Drawbacks**
In-process debugging	■ Easy access to CLR data structures ■ Faster single-stepping	■ Poor integration with kernel-mode debugging ■ Doesn't work for crash dump debugging
Out-of-process debugging	■ Supports crash dump debugging ■ Natural integration with native debugging ■ No side effects preventing kernel-mode debugging	■ More difficult for the debugger to stay in-sync with the CLR execution engine's data structures

Given the benefits of out-of-process debugging, the CLR and Visual Studio probably will continue to move toward that architecture for managed-code debugging in the future. That trend has already begun in .NET 4.0 and Visual Studio 2010, where the out-of-process architecture is now used to support crash dump debugging of managed processes.

The SOS Windows Debuggers Extension

Many WinDbg commands don't work natively when debugging a .NET target program. For instance, the *k* command cannot display the names of managed functions in a call stack and the *dv* command cannot display the values of local variables from those functions, either. To understand why, remember that MSIL images are compiled on the fly, so the dynamically generated code addresses are completely unknown to the symbols that the Windows debugger relies on to map the addresses to their friendly symbolic names. Even when an MSIL image is precompiled into a native one—a process known as *NGEN'ing* the assembly—the generated native image is actually machine-specific and won't have a corresponding symbol file, either. The .NET Framework DLL assemblies fall into this second category because they are usually NGEN'ed on the machines where they're installed to improve the performance of all the applications that use them.

How SOS Works

To work around the lack of native support for managed-code debugging in the Windows debuggers, the .NET Framework ships the *sos.dll* debugger extension module. This extension was doubly useful in earlier releases of the .NET Framework because it was also the only supported way to perform crash dump debugging of .NET code, given that Visual Studio started supporting out-of-process debugging of managed code only in its 2010 release.

This debugger extension is built as part of the CLR code base, so it has intimate knowledge of the internal layouts of the CLR data structures, allowing it to read the virtual address space of the target process directly and parse the CLR execution engine structures that it needs. These capabilities enable it to support out-of-process managed-code debugging. When using SOS, you'll at least be able to display managed call stacks, set breakpoints in managed code, find the values of local variables, dump the arguments to method calls, and perform most of the inspection and control debugging actions that you can use in native-code debugging—only without the convenience of source-level debugging.

Symbols for .NET modules are used by managed-code debuggers only to enable source-level debugging (source lines, names of local function variables, and so on). Even without symbol files for managed assemblies, you still can do a lot of things you aren't able to do in native-code debugging, where the symbols are absolutely crucial. This is because MSIL images also carry metadata describing the type information for the classes they host, allowing any component with internal knowledge of how to parse that information to use it for displaying function names in a call stack, dump the values of local variables (though without their names), or find the parameters to function calls. This is precisely how the SOS Windows debugger extension enables out-of-process managed-code debugging—even without symbol files or any additional help from the CLR debugger runtime controller thread.

Debugging Your First .NET Program Using SOS

To provide a practical illustration for how to use SOS to debug .NET programs in WinDbg, you'll now use it to debug the following C# program from the companion source code, which you should compile to target CLR version 4.0, as described in the procedure provided in the Introduction of this book.

```
//
// C:\book\code\chapter_03\HelloWorld>main.cs
//
public class Test
{
    public static void Main()
    {
        Console.WriteLine("Hello World!");
        Console.WriteLine("Press any key to continue...");
        Console.ReadLine();
        Console.ReadLine("Exiting...");
    }
}
```

Every version of the CLR has its own copy of the SOS extension DLL that understands its internal data structures and is able to decode them. For this reason, you must always load the version of the extension that comes with the CLR version that's used by the target process you're trying to debug. In addition, the SOS commands work only after the CLR execution engine DLL has been loaded, so you need to wait for its module load event to occur. This happens early during the startup of the .NET target as the CLR shim DLL (*mscoree.dll*) hands the reins over to the CLR execution engine DLL, which is *clr.dll* in the case of CLR version 4 (.NET 4.x), and *mscorwks.dll* in the case of CLR version 2

(.NET 2.x and .NET 3.x). You can get notified of this module load event in the debugger by using the *sxe ld* command, as shown in the following listing.

```
0:000> vercommand
command line: '"c:\Program Files\Debugging Tools for Windows (x86)\windbg.exe"
c:\book\code\chapter_03\HelloWorld\test.exe'
0:000> .symfix
0:000> .reload
0:000> sxe ld clr.dll
0:000> g
ModLoad: 5fad0000 6013e000   C:\Windows\Microsoft.NET\Framework\v4.0.30319\clr.dll
ntdll!KiFastSystemCallRet:
779970b4 c3              ret
0:000> .lastevent
Last event: 1e30.c20: Load module C:\Windows\Microsoft.NET\Framework\v4.0.30319\clr.dll at
5fad0000
```

After the execution engine DLL is loaded, you can load the SOS extension module before any managed code has a chance to run inside the target process. A command you'll find useful when loading the SOS extension DLL is the *.loadby* debugger command. This command works just like the more basic *.load* command, but it looks up the extension module under the same path where its second module parameter was loaded from. By specifying the CLR execution engine DLL module name, you will be sure to load the *sos.dll* extension from the same location so that it matches the precise CLR version of the target. One of the useful SOS commands is the *!eeversion* command, which displays the current version of the CLR in the target process.

```
0:000> .loadby sos clr
0:000> !eeversion
4.0.30319.239 retail
0:000> g
```

The program now waits for user input in the *ReadLine* method. If you break into the debugger at this point by using the Debug\Break menu action, you'll see that the *k* command isn't able to properly display the function names in the managed code frames from the main thread in the .NET process. (Notice the very large offsets in the frames from the *mscorlib_ni* native image of the *mscorlib.dll* .NET Framework assembly, which is indicative of missing or unresolved symbols.) The unmanaged frames are still decoded correctly.

```
0:004> ~0s
0:000> k
ChildEBP RetAddr
0017e998 77996464 ntdll!KiFastSystemCallRet
0017e99c 75ea4b6e ntdll!ZwRequestWaitReplyPort+0xc
0017e9bc 75eb2833 KERNEL32!ConsoleClientCallServer+0x88
0017eab8 75efc978 KERNEL32!ReadConsoleInternal+0x1ac
0017eb40 75ebb974 KERNEL32!ReadConsoleA+0x40
0017eb88 5efc1c8b KERNEL32!ReadFileImplementation+0x75
0017ec08 5f637cc8 mscorlib_ni+0x2c1c8b
0017ec30 5f637f60 mscorlib_ni+0x937cc8
0017ec58 5ef78bfb mscorlib_ni+0x937f60
0017ec74 5ef5560a mscorlib_ni+0x278bfb
0017ec94 5f63e6f5 mscorlib_ni+0x25560a
```

```
0017eca4 5f52a7aa mscorlib_ni+0x93e6f5
0017ecb4 5fad21bb mscorlib_ni+0x82a7aa
0017ecc4 5faf4be2 clr!CallDescrWorker+0x33
0017ed40 5faf4d84 clr!CallDescrWorkerWithHandler+0x8e
0017ee7c 5faf4db9 clr!MethodDesc::CallDescr+0x194
0017ee98 5faf4dd9 clr!MethodDesc::CallTargetWorker+0x21
0017eeb0 5fc273c2 clr!MethodDescCallSite::Call_RetArgSlot+0x1c
0017f014 5fc274d0 clr!ClassLoader::RunMain+0x24c
0017f27c 5fc272e4 clr!Assembly::ExecuteMainMethod+0xc1
0017f760 5fc276d9 clr!SystemDomain::ExecuteMainMethod+0x4ec
0017f7b4 5fc275da clr!ExecuteEXE+0x58
...
```

Fortunately, the *!clrstack* command from the SOS debugger extension allows you to see the managed frames in the thread's call stack.

```
0:000> !clrstack
OS Thread Id: 0xe48 (0)
Child SP IP       Call Site
0017eba8 779970b4 [InlinedCallFrame: 0017eba8]
0017eba4 5efc1c8b DomainNeutralILStubClass.IL_STUB_PInvoke(Microsoft.Win32.SafeHandles.
SafeFileHandle, Byte*, Int32, Int32 ByRef, IntPtr)
0017eba8 5f637cc8 [InlinedCallFrame: 0017eba8] System.IO.__ConsoleStream.ReadFile(Microsoft.
Win32.SafeHandles.SafeFileHandle, Byte*, Int32, Int32 ByRef, IntPtr)
0017ec1c 5f637cc8 System.IO.__ConsoleStream.ReadFileNative(Microsoft.Win32.SafeHandles.
SafeFileHandle, Byte[], Int32, Int32, Int32, Int32 ByRef)
0017ec48 5f637f60 System.IO.__ConsoleStream.Read(Byte[], Int32, Int32)
0017ec68 5ef78bfb System.IO.StreamReader.ReadBuffer()
0017ec7c 5ef5560a System.IO.StreamReader.ReadLine()
0017ec9c 5f63e6f5 System.IO.TextReader+SyncTextReader.ReadLine()
0017ecac 5f52a7aa System.Console.ReadLine()
0017ecb4 0043009f Test.Main() [c:\book\code\chapter_03\HelloWorld\main.cs @ 9]
0017eee4 5fad21bb [GCFrame: 0017eee4]
```

The *mscorlib_ni.dll* module shown in the stack trace output of the *k* command is the NGEN image ("ni") corresponding to the *mscorlib.dll* MSIL image. You can treat these modules just like their MSIL sources for the purpose of SOS debugging. In particular, you can set breakpoints at managed code functions from both MSIL or NGEN images by using the *!bpmd* SOS extension command.

For example, you can set a breakpoint at the *WriteLine* method that would be executed by the next line of source code. This .NET method is defined in the *System.Console* class of the *mscorlib.dll* .NET assembly (or in this case, its *mscorlib_ni.dll* NGEN version). The *!bpmd* command takes the target module name as its first argument (without the extension!) and the fully qualified name of the .NET method as its second argument, as shown in the following listing.

```
0:004> !bpmd mscorlib_ni System.Console.WriteLine
Found 19 methods in module 5ed01000...
MethodDesc = 5ed885a4
Setting breakpoint: bp 5EFAD4FC [System.Console.WriteLine()]
MethodDesc = 5ed885b0
Setting breakpoint: bp 5F52A770 [System.Console.WriteLine(Boolean)]
MethodDesc = 5ed885bc
...
```

```
Adding pending breakpoints...
0:004> g
```

This command adds breakpoints to all overloads of the *WriteLine* method (19 of them in the previous case). If you now press Enter in the active command prompt window from the target process, you'll notice that the debugger hits your breakpoint next.

```
Breakpoint 13 hit
mscorlib_ni+0x2570ac:
5ef570ac 55              push    ebp
```

You can again use the *!clrstack* command to see the current stack trace at the time of this breakpoint. The *–a* option of this command also allows you to view the arguments to the managed frames on the stack.

```
0:000> !clrstack -a
OS Thread Id: 0x18e0 (0)
Child SP IP       Call Site
0018f260 5ef570ac System.Console.WriteLine(System.String)
    PARAMETERS:
        value (<CLR reg>) = 0x01fdb24c
0018f264 004600ab Test.Main()
*** WARNING: Unable to verify checksum for test.exe
 [c:\book\code\chapter_03\HelloWorld\main.cs @ 10]
0018f490 5fad21bb [GCFrame: 0018f490]
```

Notice how this command also displays the address of the .NET string object that was passed to the *WriteLine* method, which you can dump using the *!do* ("dump object") SOS debugger extension command.

```
0:000> !do 0x01fdb24c
Name:        System.String
MethodTable: 5f01f92c
EEClass:     5ed58ba0
Size:        34(0x22) bytes
String:      Exiting...
Fields:
      MT    Field   Offset                 Type VT     Attr    Value Name
5f0228f8  4000103        4         System.Int32  1 instance       10 m_stringLength
5f021d48  4000104        8          System.Char  1 instance       45 m_firstChar
5f01f92c  4000105        8        System.String  0   shared   static Empty
    >> Domain:Value  002a1270:01fd1228 <<
```

Notice that the *!clrstack* command doesn't display the unmanaged functions on the call stack, though it's usually easy to see where the managed calls fit in the overall stack trace by combining the *!clrstack* and the regular *k* back-trace command, which should give you everything you need to know about what code the current thread is currently executing. Note that SOS also has a *!dumpstack* command that attempts to do this merge, but its output can be rather noisy.

The SOS extension also has several other useful commands that you can use to inspect .NET programs, including a variant of the *u* ("un-assemble") command that's also able to decode the addresses of managed function calls in addition to unmanaged addresses. For example, you could use this command to obtain the disassembly of the current function at the time of the breakpoint in the previous case (the *WriteLine* method).

```
0:000> !u .
preJIT generated code
System.Console.WriteLine(System.String)
Begin 5ef570ac, size 1a
>>> 5ef570ac 55              push    ebp
5ef570ad 8bec            mov     ebp,esp
5ef570af 56              push    esi
5ef570b0 8bf1            mov     esi,ecx
5ef570b2 e819000000      call    mscorlib_ni+0x2570d0 (5ef570d0) (System.Console.get_Out(),
mdToken: 060008fd)
...
```

Notice how the regular *u* command, by contrast, doesn't display the friendly name of the function itself or of the call to *get_Out* (a managed method too) that's made inside the same function.

```
0:000> u .
mscorlib_ni+0x2570ac:
5ef570ac 55              push    ebp
5ef570ad 8bec            mov     ebp,esp
5ef570af 56              push    esi
5ef570b0 8bf1            mov     esi,ecx
5ef570b2 e819000000      call    mscorlib_ni+0x2570d0 (5ef570d0)
```

If you would like to experiment with more SOS debugger commands, you can find a listing of those commands and a brief summary of what they do by using the *!help* command in the WinDbg debugger.

```
0:000> !help
-------------------------------------------------------------------------------
SOS is a debugger extension DLL designed to aid in the debugging of managed
programs. Functions are listed by category, then roughly in order of
importance. Shortcut names for popular functions are listed in parenthesis.
Type "!help <functionname>" for detailed info on that function.
...
0:000> $ Terminate this debugging session now...
0:000> q
```

Table 3-4 recaps the basic SOS commands introduced during this experiment.

TABLE 3-4 Basic SOS Extension Commands

Command	Purpose
!eeversion	Display the target CLR (execution engine) version.
!bpmd	Set a breakpoint using a managed .NET method.
!do (or *!dumpobj*)	Dump the fields of a managed object.
!clrstack *!clrstack –a*	Display the managed frames in the current thread's call stack. The optional *–a* option is used to also display the arguments to the functions on the call stack. These values are the extension's best guess, however; so, they're not always accurate.
!u	Display the disassembly of a managed function.

Despite the fact you can achieve a lot of critical debugging tasks using the SOS extension, the managed-code debugging experience in the Windows debuggers still leaves a lot to be desired. The Windows debuggers clearly are not your first choice when debugging the managed code you write yourself, but SOS can still be a good option, especially if you can't get Visual Studio installed on the target machine or if you are debugging without source code—in which case, you don't lose much by using WinDbg anyway.

Script Debugging

Visual Studio also supports source-level debugging of script languages such as VBScript or JScript. This is internally implemented using the same in-process paradigm that managed-code debugging relies on. One of the reasons that the CLR used the in-process debugging model when it was first released to the public in 2002 was that script debugging had been successfully using it for years (since the mid-90s). In both cases, the debugger needs the script host's or the CLR execution engine's collaboration to support source-level debugging of the target process.

Architecture Overview

To understand how script debugging works, it's useful to first explain a few basic concepts about how script languages are executed in Windows. The key to that architecture is the *Active Scripting* specification. This specification was introduced by Microsoft in the 90s and defines a set of COM interfaces to allow script languages that implement them to be hosted in any conforming host application. In Windows, both VBScript and JScript (Microsoft's implementation of JavaScript) are Active Scripting languages whose implementation fully conforms with that specification.

The Active Scripting specification defines a language-processing *engine*, with the Active Scripting *host* using that engine when the script needs to be interpreted. Examples of Active Scripting engines are *vbscript.dll* and *jscript.dll*, which both ship with Windows under the *system32* directory. Examples of Active Scripting hosts include the Internet Information Services (IIS) web server (server-side scripts embedded in ASP or ASP.NET pages), Internet Explorer (client-side script hosting in web pages), and the Windows scripting hosts (*cscript.exe* or *wscript.exe*) that ship with Windows and can be used to host scripts executed from a command prompt. There are also third-party Active Scripting engines to support other script languages, including Perl and Python.

In addition, the Active Scripting specification also defines a contract (a set of COM interfaces, again) for debuggers to take advantage of the host in their operations. An Active Scripting host that supports debugging (that is, implements the required COM interfaces) is called a *smart* host. All recent versions of Internet Explorer, IIS, and the Windows scripting hosts are smart hosts that implement those interfaces, which is at the heart of the magic that enables Visual Studio to debug scripts hosted by any of those processes. A *Process Debug Manager* (PDM) component (*pdm.dll*) is shipped with the Visual Studio debugger to insulate script engines from having to understand the intricacies of script debugging. In many ways, the PDM component serves the same purpose that the CLR runtime debugger controller thread and *mscordbi.dll* serve during managed debugging, as illustrated in Figure 3-7.

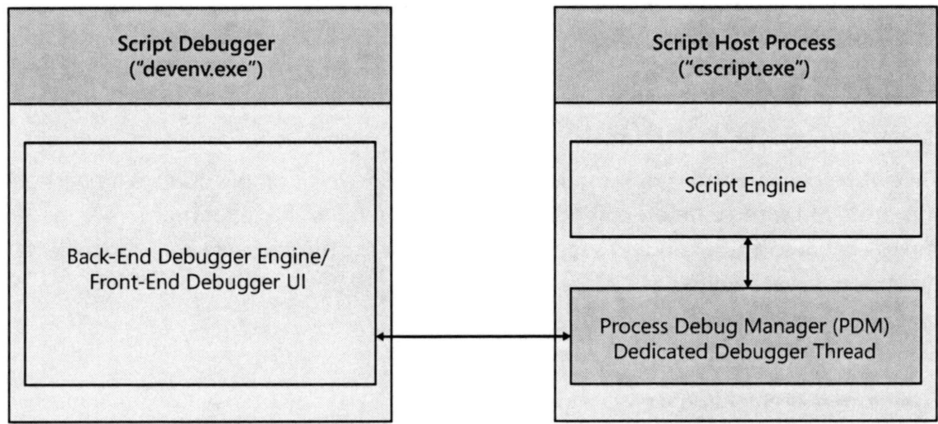

FIGURE 3-7 In-process script debugging architecture.

One way that Active Scripting debugging differs from managed-code debugging is that smart hosts usually do not expose their debugging services by default, whereas in the case of the CLR there is always a debugger thread running in the managed-code process. In Internet Explorer, for instance, you need to first enable script debugging in the host process by clearing the Disable Script Debugging option on the Tools\Internet Options\Advanced tab, as shown in Figure 3-8.

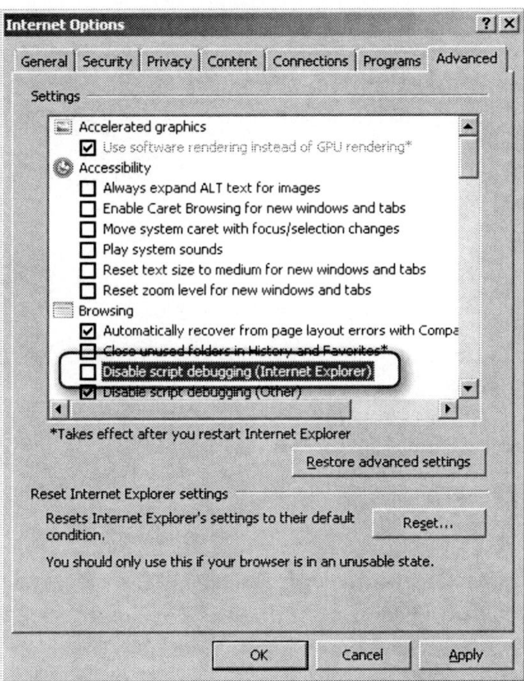

FIGURE 3-8 Enabling Internet Explorer script debugging.

In the same way, you need to explicitly enable debugging of scripts in the Windows scripting hosts (*cscript.exe*/*wscript.exe*) using the *//X* option if you want to also debug the executed scripts. The IIS web server manager also has a UI option for enabling server-side script debugging.

Debugging Scripts in Visual Studio

The following sample script from the companion source code, which simply displays its start time and arguments list to the console before exiting, will serve as a good example for how to use the *//X* option to enable script-debugging support in the *cscript.exe* host process and step through console scripts in Visual Studio.

```
//
// C:\book\code\chapter_03\script>test.js
//
var g_argv = new Array();

//
// store command-line parameters and call the main function
//
for (var i=0; i < WScript.Arguments.length; i++)
{
    g_argv.push(WScript.Arguments(i));
}

WScript.Quit(main(g_argv));

function main(argv)
{
    WScript.Echo("Script started at " + new Date());
    if (g_argv.length > 0)
    {
        WScript.Echo("Arguments: " + g_argv);
    }
}
```

Notice in particular the double slash in the *//X* option in the following command, which *cscript.exe* and *wscript.exe* use to distinguish their own options from the executed script's options.

```
C:\Windows\system32\cscript.exe //X C:\book\code\chapter_03\script\test.js 1 2
Microsoft (R) Windows Script Host Version 5.8
Copyright (C) Microsoft Corporation. All rights reserved.
...
```

When you run the preceding command on a machine with Visual Studio 2010 installed, you'll be presented with a Visual Studio "attach" dialog box similar to the one shown in Figure 3-9. You might get another dialog box to consent to UAC elevation if you invoked the script from an elevated administrative command prompt, given that the Visual Studio debugger also needs to run elevated in that case.

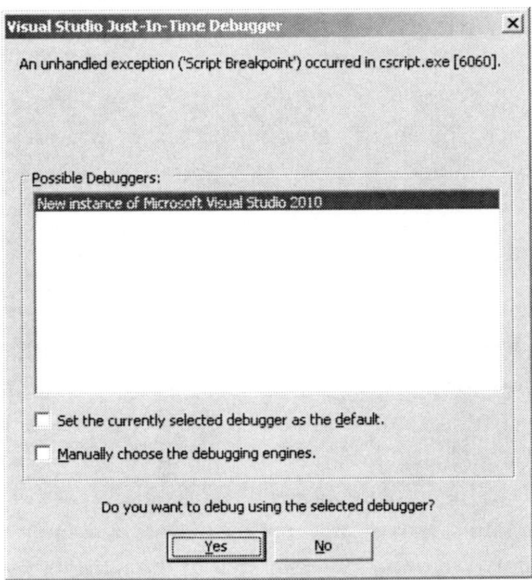

FIGURE 3-9 Attaching to a script using the Visual Studio debugger.

You are then able to use the Visual Studio debugger to step through (using the F10 and F11 shortcuts) the script and debug it (with source-level information!), just as you would with any native-code or managed-code application, as shown in Figure 3-10.

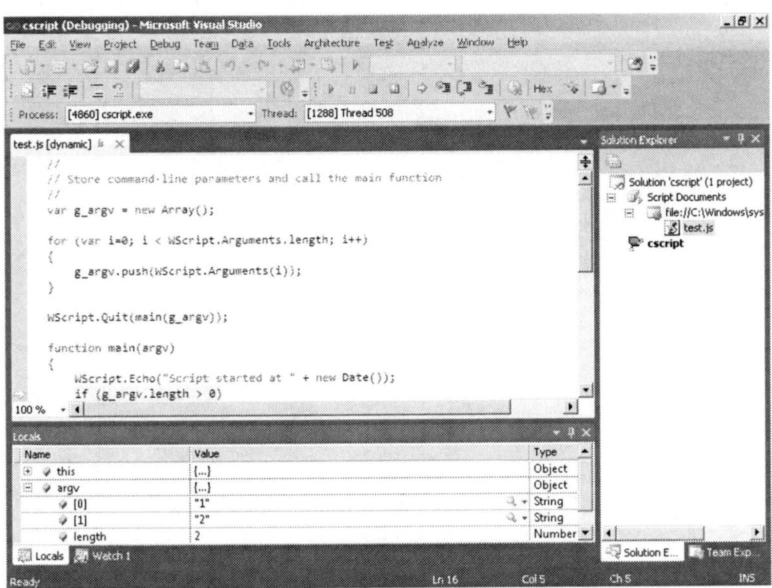

FIGURE 3-10 Source-level script debugging using Visual Studio 2010.

Remote Debugging

Remote debugging is a convenient feature that allows you to control a target remotely using a debugger instance that's running on a different machine on the network. This section provides an inside look at how this feature is implemented by debugger programs in Windows, as well as how you can use it in the case of the WinDbg and Visual Studio debuggers.

Architecture Overview

At a high level, two conceptual models are used to support remote debugging: remote *sessions* and remote *stubs*. In both cases, a process needs to be running on the same machine as the target so that it can carry out the commands that are typed in the remote debugger. In the case of a remote session, the debugger session is entirely on the target machine and the remote debugger instance simply acts as a "dumb" client to send commands to the local debugger instance. In the case of a remote stub, the debugger session is running remotely, with a "stub" broker process running locally on the target machine and acting as a gateway to get information in and out of the target.

Remote sessions are used when collaboration among multiple engineers is needed to investigate a certain failure. In that case, a local debugger instance runs on the repro machine, and developers are then able to start typing commands remotely from their respective machines, take a look at the failure, and even leave comments and see each other's debugging attempts and commands as they get typed in. WinDbg supports this very useful form of remote debugging, which is illustrated in Figure 3-11.

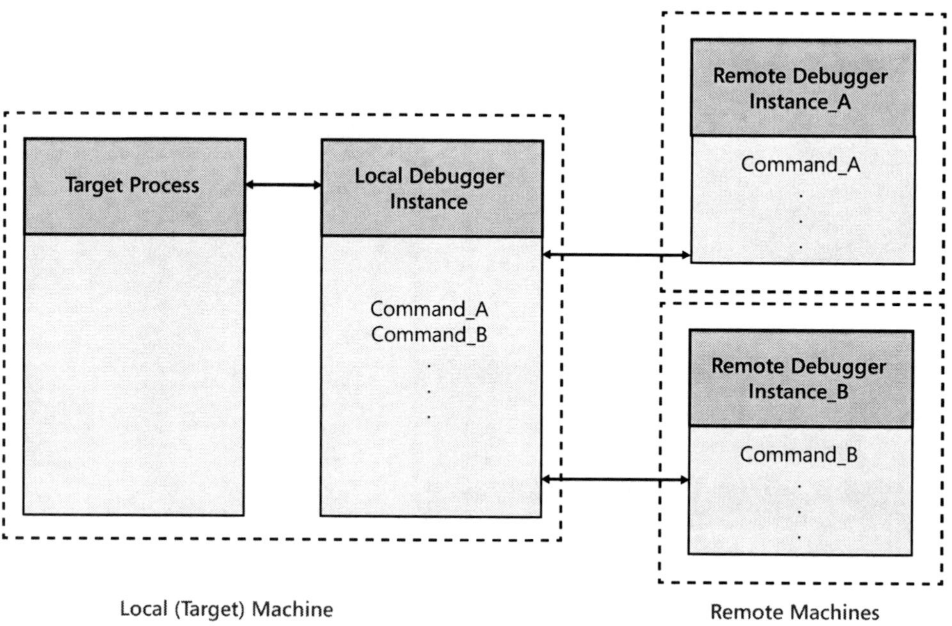

FIGURE 3-11 Remote debugging using remote sessions.

Remote stubs are used when it's important to set up the debugging environment on a remote computer, either because the full debugging environment can't be installed or because the symbols and sources cannot be accessed directly on the target computer. Both the Windows and Visual Studio debuggers support this form of remote debugging, though this architecture is more useful in the case of the Visual Studio debugger. (In fact, remote stubs are the only type of remote debugging that's supported by Visual Studio.) This is because a full Visual Studio debugging environment installation on the target machine is heavy handed, both in terms of the disk space it requires and the time it takes to complete, often making it an inadequate option for production environments. By comparison, the Visual Studio remote-debugging component, which also includes the remote stub process, is more lightweight and can be installed much faster when you need it on the target machine. Figure 3-12 illustrates this second form of remote debugging.

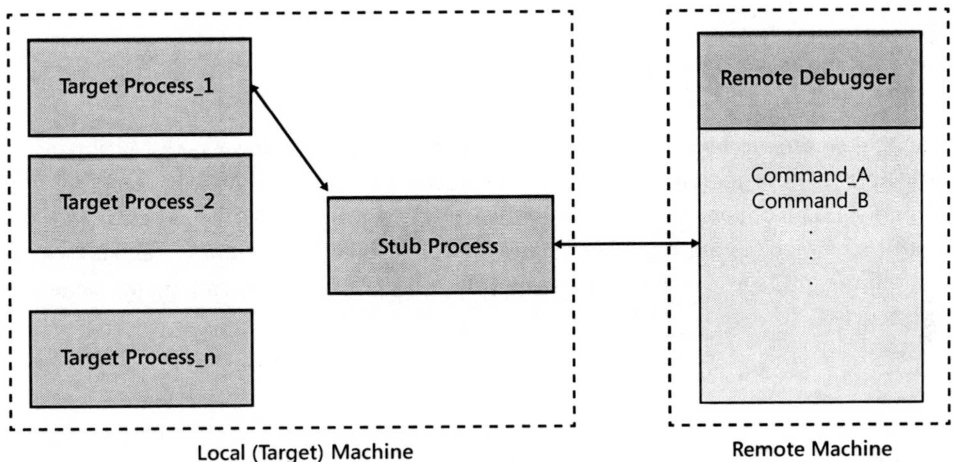

FIGURE 3-12 Remote debugging using remote stubs.

Remote Debugging in WinDbg

As mentioned earlier, WinDbg supports both remote sessions and remote stubs. This section will walk you through the steps for making use of either setup in your remote WinDbg debugging experiments.

Remote Sessions

Starting a WinDbg remote debugging session is straightforward. You use the *.server* debugger command, as illustrated by the following procedure.

Using Remote Sessions in WinDbg

1. From the local WinDbg instance controlling the target process, start a TCP/IP remote session by using the *.server* command, as illustrated in the following listing. This example uses port 4445, but any TCP port that's not currently in use would also work. Using the *.server* command with no arguments reminds you of its syntax.

```
0:000> vercommand
command line: '"c:\Program Files\Debugging Tools for Windows (x86)\windbg.exe"
notepad.exe'
0:000> $ .server without any arguments displays the usage...
0:000> .server
Usage: .server tcp:port=<Socket>  OR  .server npipe:pipe=<PipeName>
0:000> $ Open a remote debugging server session using port 4445
0:000> .server tcp:port=4445
Server started.  Client can connect with any of these command lines
0: <debugger> -remote tcp:Port=4445,Server=TARIKS-LP03
```

2. On the remote machine where you plan to control the target, start a new WinDbg instance (the remote debugger) and connect to the previous TCP port remotely by using the *–remote* command-line option. You can also use the connection string provided in the output from the *.server* command in the preceding listing to remind you of the syntax. Note that the remote and target machines can be the same, so you can also execute this step on the same machine as step 1.

```
windbg.exe -remote tcp:Port=4445,Server=TARIKS-LP03
```

   Notice how any commands you type in the new WinDbg instance's command window (the "remote" debugger) also appear in the first WinDbg instance on the target machine (the "local" debugger). The remote debugger is essentially acting only as a terminal for typing commands that get transferred and, ultimately, processed by the local debugger instance on the target machine.

3. You can terminate the entire debugging session (both the remote and local debugger instances) from the remote machine using the *qq* command. By contrast, the *q* command terminates only the remote instance and leaves the local debugger instance intact.

```
0:000> $ Remote debugger command prompt
0:000> qq
```

In addition to their obvious benefits in remote debugging scenarios, WinDbg remote sessions can be useful even when debugging on the same machine. An example is when you start debugging using one of the command-line Windows debuggers (*cdb.exe* or *ntsd.exe*) and later decide to switch to using WinDbg as a front-end UI to that same session.

Remote Stubs

Commands typed in the remote debugger command window in a remote debugging session are executed as if they were typed on the target machine. In particular, this means that debugger extensions are also loaded into the debugger process on the target machine and that symbols need to be accessible from that machine too. Although remote sessions are by far the more common scenario in WinDbg remote debugging, remote stubs can be used if you don't want to copy the symbols or otherwise make them available over the network so that they're accessible from the target machine.

You can use remote stubs in both user-mode and kernel-mode remote debugging with the Windows debuggers. The *dbgsrv.exe* process, which comes as part of the Windows debuggers package, is used as a stub process in remote user-mode debugging. The *kdsrv.exe* process, also included in the Windows debuggers package, is used in remote kernel-mode debugging.

Just as in the remote session case, you can follow the procedure described here by also running the remote debugger on the target machine, in case you don't have two separate machines.

Using Remote Stubs in WinDbg

1. Open a TCP/IP communication port on the target machine using the *dbgsrv.exe* stub process. This command displays a dialog box when it fails, but it won't show any messages on success.

   ```
   C:\Program Files\Debugging Tools for Windows (x86)\dbgsrv.exe -t tcp:port=4445
   ```

   The *dbgsrv.exe* stub process is running in the background at this point. Using the *netstat.exe* tool that comes with Windows under the *system32* directory, you can display the open network ports on the machine and confirm that this stub process is listening for connections from a remote debugger on TCP port 4445:

   ```
   C:\windows\system32\netstat.exe -a
   Active Connections
     Proto  Local Address          Foreign Address        State
   ...
     TCP    0.0.0.0:4445           TARIKS-LP03:0          LISTENING
   ...
   ```

2. On the remote machine, start a new *windbg.exe* instance and connect to the stub process on the target machine using the File\Connect to a Remote Stub menu action. Leave the Connection String combo box empty, and enter the target machine name in the new Browse

dialog box. WinDbg then automatically enumerates all the open stub sessions on the target machine for you, as demonstrated in the following screen shot:

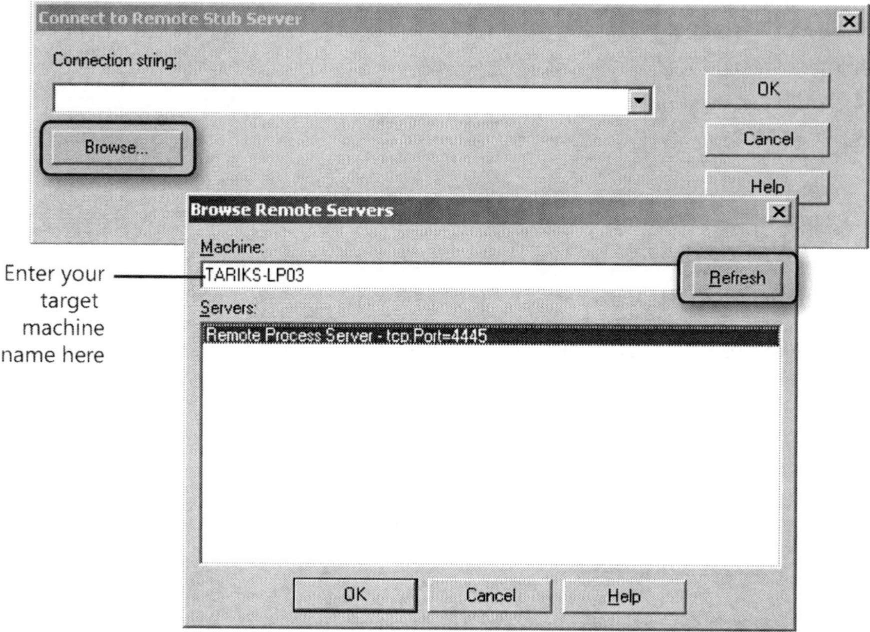

3. After you connect to the remote stub, you can attach to processes running on the target machine by using the familiar File\Attach To A Process menu command (the F6 shortcut). However, this option now shows processes from the target machine, which is exactly what you want in this case. Once attached to a process, you can debug it as if it were running locally, with symbols and debugger extensions located relative to the same remote debugger machine (and not the target machine, as was the case in remote sessions).

4. When you no longer need the remote debugging channel, make sure you terminate the stub process on the target machine so that you release the TCP port it opened earlier for other uses on the machine. You can do that in the Windows task manager UI or by using the *kill.exe* command-line utility from the Windows debuggers package.

```
C:\Program Files\Debugging Tools for Windows (x86)>kill.exe dbgsrv
process dbgsrv.exe (4188) - '' killed
```

This same approach can be used for remote kernel-mode debugging, except you should use the *kdsrv.exe* stub instead of the *dbgsrv.exe* stub. Note that in that case, there are actually three machines involved: the regular target and host kernel debugger machines, and the remote machine you are using to run the debugger instance. The *kdsrv.exe* process is started as a remote stub on the kernel host debugger machine, not the target machine that is being debugged with the kernel debugger. Symbols and extensions are again resolved relative to the remote debugger machine.

Remote Debugging in Visual Studio

Unfortunately, Visual Studio does not support the concept of remote debugging sessions or remote connection strings, which makes it difficult to use it for sharing a debugging session with another developer at the exact point of a particular failure in the way that WinDbg's *.server* command works. Instead, Visual Studio remote debugging uses the remote stub idea, with the *msvsmon.exe* process acting as the remote stub process to which the Visual Studio debugger process (*devenv.exe*) then connects from the remote machine. MSVSMON is also sometimes called the Visual Studio *debug monitor*, highlighting the fact that it controls the execution of the target on the local machine on behalf of the Visual Studio debugger on the remote machine.

The default communication protocol between the remote and the target machines uses Distributed COM (DCOM) with Windows authentication, so you need to configure the user running the debugger with correct security permissions on the target machine. If the account you're using is a domain user, for example, it will need to be an administrator on the target machine or a member of the *Debugger Users* security group created by Visual Studio.

Using Remote Debugging in Visual Studio

1. Start the following C# sample program from the companion source code (and leave it waiting for user input) on the target machine.

```
C:\book\code\chapter_03\HelloWorld>test.exe
Hello World!
Press any key to continue...
```

2. Install the Visual Studio 2010 remote-debugging components on the target machine from *http://www.microsoft.com/download/en/details.aspx?id=475*. This setup installation shouldn't take too long (at least compared to the full Visual Studio installation!) because the download is only a few megabytes large. Cancel the configuration wizard that comes up at the end of the installation.

3. Start the *msvsmon.exe* stub process on the target machine. Use the Tools\Options menu action of MSVSMON to change the server name for the connection, or simply leave the default value unchanged, as shown in the following screen shot.

```
C:\Program Files\Microsoft Visual Studio 10.0\Common7\IDE\Remote Debugger\x86>msvsmon.exe
```

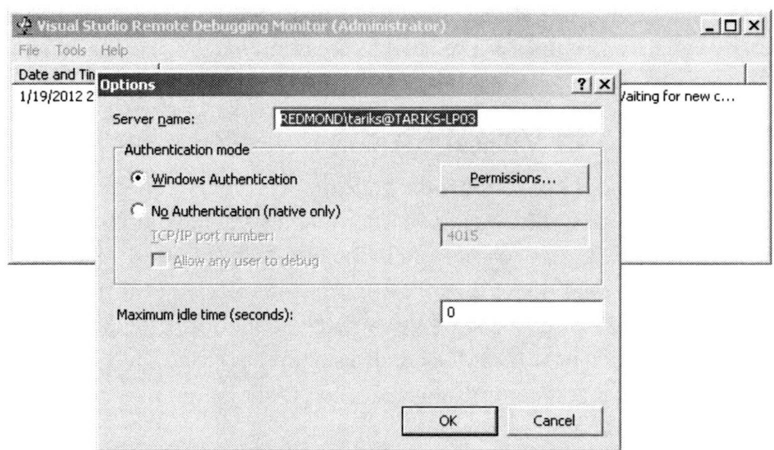

4. On the remote machine, which has the full Visual Studio development environment, use the Tools\Attach To Process menu action to attach to the *test.exe* process remotely. In the Qualifier text box, specify the server name you chose in step 3.

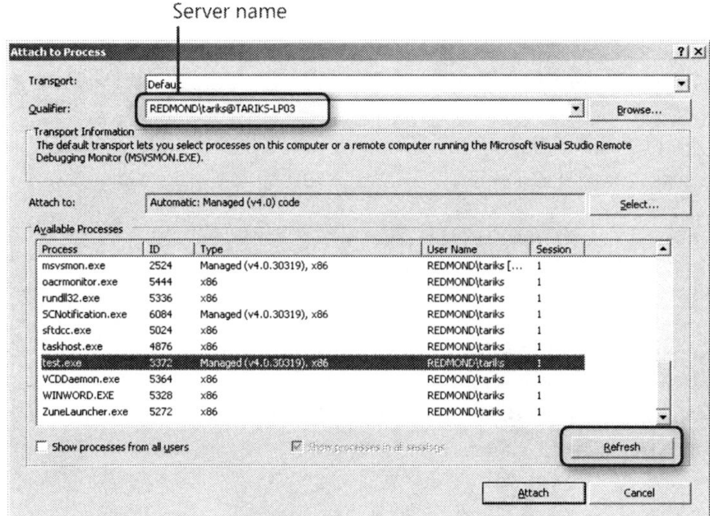

5. If your Windows firewall is enabled (the default behavior), a consent dialog box appears on the target machine. After authorizing the firewall exception, you'll see a list of all the processes that are currently running on the target machine, and you can then attach to the managed *test.exe* process.

You might also see the warning shown in Figure 3-13 as Visual Studio tries to locate the symbols for the managed process. This is because managed-code symbols are resolved relative to the target machine.

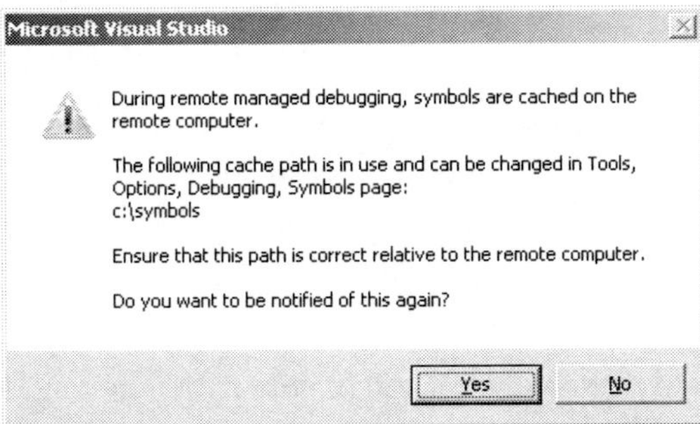

FIGURE 3-13 Managed-code symbols path resolution.

Unlike native code symbols, which are resolved in Visual Studio remote debugging relative to the remote machine (as was the case in the WinDbg stub-based remote debugging case), managed-code symbols are resolved relative to the target machine because of the in-process nature of managed-code debugging. Keep this in mind when you use Visual Studio and you want to perform remote source-level debugging of .NET applications because you need to copy the symbols to the target machine for the debugger to locate them successfully.

Summary

This chapter explained several debugging types and mechanisms in Windows and how they work at the system level. After reading this chapter, the following points should be familiar to you:

- Native user-mode debugging relies on a system-provided architecture that's based on a set of debug events generated by the system on behalf of the target process. These events are sent to a shared debug port object that the OS executive associates with the target process, with a dedicated thread in the debugger process waiting for new events and processing them in that order. This generic framework provides the foundation that user-mode debuggers use to control the target's execution, including setting code breakpoints and single-stepping the target.
- Kernel-mode debugging shares many concepts with user-mode debugging. Because of its global scope, however, a few debugging actions—such as setting code breakpoints and single-stepping the target—are implemented in a slightly different way to accommodate this reality.

- Both script and managed-code debugging use the in-process debugging paradigm, which has a helper thread running in the target process to assist the debugger in its operations. Visual Studio uses this architecture to support both types of debugging.
- The SOS Windows debugger extension can also be used to debug managed code in a completely out-of-process way, though without the convenience of source-level debugging.
- The Windows debuggers support collaborative remote user-mode and kernel-mode debugging using remote sessions. Visual Studio also supports remote debugging, but it uses a different architecture that takes advantage of a remote stub process running on the target machine. The type of remote debugging architecture also affects where symbols and debugger extensions get loaded from, so they each have their practical applications.

Now that you've seen how debuggers can actively debug local and remote targets in Windows, the next chapter will introduce you to another debugging approach when direct live debugging isn't an option. This very important debugging concept is called *postmortem* debugging.

CHAPTER 4

Postmortem Debugging

In this chapter

Software crashes are, sadly, all too common and often occur under unpredictable conditions that make them hard to reproduce, so it would be unfortunate if such crashes left no trace. Fortunately, the Microsoft Windows operating system (OS) has support for automatically capturing partial or full-memory snapshots in response to a crash and saving them to disk for later analysis. These memory *dump* files can then be investigated using debuggers in a passive debugging mode called *postmortem* debugging. Both the Windows debuggers and the Microsoft Visual Studio debugger support this form of analysis, although the Windows debuggers are in many ways superior in this area because of their rich extension model that allows for better analysis of the data structures and memory information that dump files contain.

Instead of leaving only a crash dump behind, the operating system can also be instructed to block an application from exiting when it hits a user-mode crash until a debugger is able to attach to it. This takes advantage of the same underlying infrastructure, but it allows you to perform *live* debugging of the crash. This feature is called *Just-in-Time (JIT) debugging* and is a good place to start this chapter's coverage of postmortem debugging and the OS foundations that make it possible.

Just-in-Time Debugging

JIT debugging has nothing to do with the .NET Just-in-Time (JIT) compiler used to generate native code when executing Microsoft Intermediate Language (MSIL) images. However, they both share the JIT description because they are invoked on the fly. In the particular case of JIT debugging, the debugger *attach* operation is done automatically by the OS when an application encounters an unhandled exception and is about to crash.

Your First JIT Debugging Experiment

To see how JIT debugging works in practice, consider the following C++ sample from the companion source code, which you can compile using the procedure described back in the Introduction of this book. This program has a serious bug (dereferencing a NULL pointer) that causes it to crash with an unhandled access violation Structured Exception Handling (SEH) exception.

```
//
// C:\book\code\chapter_04\NullDereference>main.cpp
//
int
__cdecl
wmain()
{
    BYTE* pMem = NULL;
    pMem[0] = 5;
    wprintf(L"Value at memory address is 0x%x\n", pMem[0]);
    return 0;
}
```

When no JIT debugger is configured on the system, this program simply dies early when it reaches the faulting instruction. To see this in action, run the *ClearJit.bat* batch file provided under the same directory in the companion source code. Clearing the registered JIT debugger requires administrative privileges, so you need to run this batch file from an elevated administrative command prompt. (See the Introduction of this book for a reminder of how to do so.) You'll then see the dialog boxes shown in Figure 4-1 when you execute the previous program and it crashes.

```
C:\book\code\chapter_04\scripts\ClearJit.bat
C:\book\code\chapter_04\NullDereference\objfre_win7_x86\i386\NullDereference.exe
```

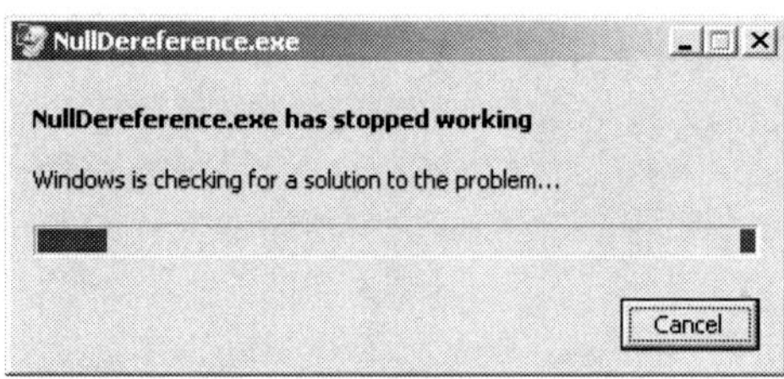

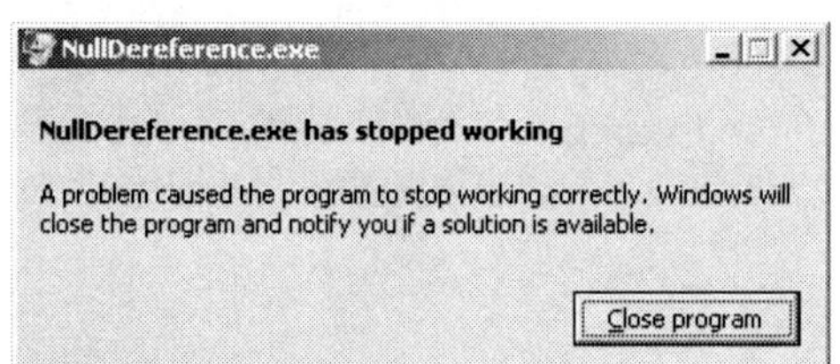

FIGURE 4-1 User-mode program crashes.

In this case, you could run the program again under the control of a user-mode debugger and see where the crash is occurring, given the debugger would stop on second-chance SEH exception notifications. However, this investigation approach might not always be possible, either because the crash is not easy to reproduce or because the scenario involves multiple processes, making it harder to know which one to directly attach a debugger to. Fortunately, you can catch the program in the act, so to speak, and automatically break into an instance of the registered JIT debugger just as the crash is about to occur.

To do so, first set WinDbg as your native JIT debugger on the system, which you can easily do by using the */I* command-line option of *windbg.exe*. This requires administrative privileges, so you need to run this command from an elevated administrative command prompt for this registration step to work successfully. In particular, make sure the dialog box message you see after running this command says that it was successful, as highlighted in Figure 4-2.

```
C:\Program Files\Debugging Tools for Windows (x86)>windbg.exe /I
```

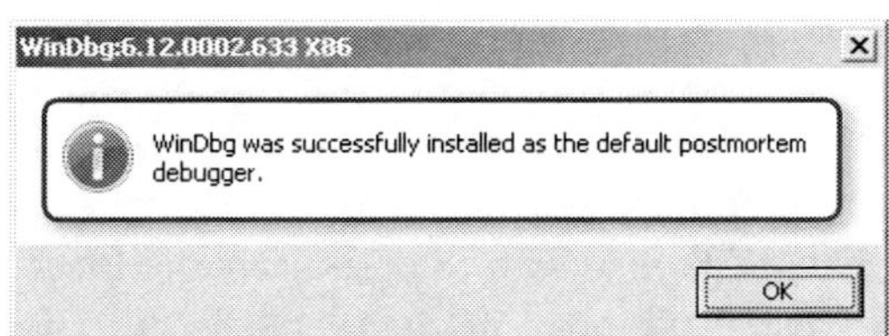

FIGURE 4-2 Setting WinDbg as the default native JIT debugger.

This registration step populates the *AeDebug* registry key shown in Figure 4-3, so another way to verify that the previous command was successful is to check the values in effect under that registry key and make sure they look similar to those in that screen shot.

```
[HKEY_LOCAL_MACHINE\SOFTWARE\Microsoft\Windows NT\CurrentVersion\AeDebug]
```

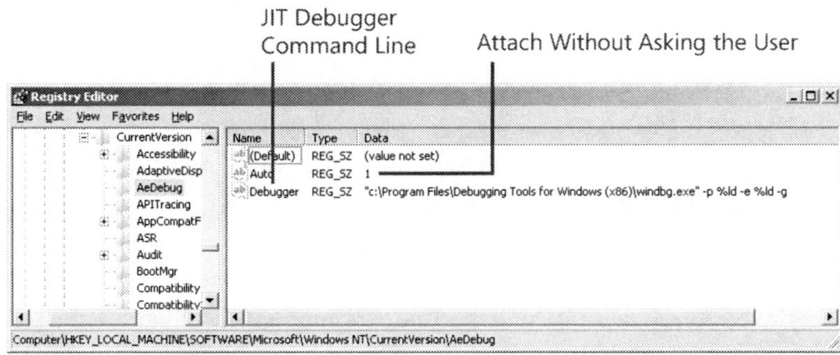

FIGURE 4-3 Registry location of native JIT debugger on the system.

Now that the WinDbg debugger is configured as your default JIT debugger, you can run the crashing scenario again and see that you automatically break into a new WinDbg instance at the exact source/assembly line where the program crashes. Notice in particular that the CPU instruction at the time of the crash was an attempt to move the value *5* to the NULL address stored in the *eax* register. The *k* debugger command also shows the source line of the faulting instruction in this case.

```
(14ec.f80): Access violation - code c0000005 (!!! second chance !!!)
eax=00000000 ebx=00000000 ecx=00222378 edx=00000000 esi=00000001 edi=00222378
eip=002211ee esp=000cfca8 ebp=000cfcf0 iopl=0         nv up ei pl zr na pe nc
cs=001b  ss=0023  ds=0023  es=0023  fs=003b  gs=0000             efl=00010246
NullDereference!wmain+0x9:
002211ee c60005          mov     byte ptr [eax],5           ds:0023:00000000=??
0:000> k
ChildEBP RetAddr
000cfcac 00221364 NullDereference!wmain+0x9
[c:\book\code\chapter_04\nulldereference\main.cpp @ 9]
000cfcf0 7689ed6c NullDereference!__wmainCRTStartup+0x102
000cfcfc 77b637f5 kernel32!BaseThreadInitThunk+0x12
000cfd3c 77b637c8 ntdll!RtlInitializeExceptionChain+0xef
000cfd54 00000000 ntdll!RtlInitializeExceptionChain+0xc2
0:000> $ Conduct any further "live" debugging, then terminate the JIT debugging session
0:000> q
```

Notice that all you had to do to automate catching this bug was register WinDbg as the native JIT debugger on the system (a one-time registration step) and run the scenario that was exhibiting the crash. The OS took care of the rest on your behalf, stopping exactly at the call site of the crash. This is very convenient, especially when you find yourself dealing with complex scenarios that require complicated setup steps and end up starting more than one process before eventually encountering a crash in one of them.

How Just-in-Time Debugging Works

The system components involved during the JIT debugger attach sequence are also the same players responsible for carrying out automatic memory crash-dump generation for user-mode postmortem debugging. Knowing how that magic works internally is also useful when trying to explain how other higher-level forms of JIT debugging such as script and .NET JIT debugging work relative to the native OS JIT debugging capabilities, as you'll see later in this chapter.

One way to break down the JIT debugger attach sequence and analyze it more closely is to change the *Auto* value under the *AeDebug* registry key and set it to *0*. When you use the */I* command-line option to register WinDbg as your default JIT system debugger, that registry string value gets set to *1*, indicating to the OS that the debugger should be automatically attached to the crashing process without asking the user for confirmation. By changing it to *0*, you'll get the confirmation dialog box shown in Figure 4-4 first, when the previous C++ program hits the site of the access violation exception. The companion source code contains a batch file (the *DisableAuto.bat* command in the following steps) to help you change this value for the native view of the registry, as well as the 32-bit view if you happen to be running the experiment on 64-bit Windows:

```
"C:\Program Files\Debugging Tools for Windows (x86)\windbg.exe" /I
C:\book\code\chapter_04\scripts\DisableAuto.bat
C:\book\code\chapter_04\NullDereference\objfre_win7_x86\i386\NullDereference.exe
```

FIGURE 4-4 JIT debugging attach confirmation dialog box with *Auto=0.*

The Close Program button in Figure 4-4 can be used to let the crashing process exit without further debugging, while the Debug button completes the JIT debugging attach sequence by invoking a new instance of the registered JIT debugger and attaching it to the crashing target. For this experiment, however, you should leave this dialog box active for now so that you can take advantage of this interesting checkpoint and inspect the state at this juncture in the overall JIT attach sequence. Because the scenario involves more than one user-mode process in this case and all you intend to do is view the system state at this particular point in time, live kernel debugging again seems like the best choice.

Live kernel debugging should already be enabled on your machine if you worked through Chapter 2, "Getting Started," where you used the *msconfig.exe* tool to configure your machine to support kernel debugging. Remember also that you need to start WinDbg from an elevated administrative command prompt to start a live kernel debugging session. Once you've done so, you can use the *!process* extension command to inspect the state of the crashing process at this point in the JIT attach sequence, as demonstrated in the following listing.

```
lkd> vertarget
Windows 7 Kernel Version 7601 (Service Pack 1) MP (2 procs) Free x86 compatible
Built by: 7601.17640.x86fre.win7sp1_gdr.110622-1506
lkd> .symfix
lkd> .reload
lkd> !process 0 0 nulldereference.exe
PROCESS 861e88c0  SessionId: 1  Cid: 17a8    Peb: 7ffd3000  ParentCid: 11d0
    Image: NullDereference.exe
lkd> .process /r /p 861e88c0
lkd> !process 861e88c0 7
PROCESS 861e88c0  SessionId: 1  Cid: 17a8    Peb: 7ffd3000  ParentCid: 11d0
  Image: NullDereference.exe
     THREAD 85250280  Cid 17a8.0ff8  Teb: 7ffdf000 Win32Thread: 00000000 WAIT:
         866428f8  ProcessObject
         84d268b8  NotificationEvent
     Win32 Start Address NullDereference!wmainCRTStartup (0x00c71495)
     ChildEBP RetAddr  Args to Child
...
     0022f918 768b05ff 00000002 0022f94c 00000000 kernel32!WaitForMultipleObjects+0x18
     0022f984 768b089a 0022fa64 00000001 00000001 kernel32!WerpReportFaultInternal+0x186
     0022f998 768b0848 0022fa64 00000001 0022fa34 kernel32!WerpReportFault+0x70
     0022f9a8 768b07c3 0022fa64 00000001 e31828e5 kernel32!BasepReportFault+0x20
     0022fa34 77b77f1a 00000000 77b1e304 00000000 kernel32!UnhandledExceptionFilter+0x1af
     0022fa3c 77b1e304 00000000 0022fef8 77b51278 ntdll!__RtlUserThreadStart+0x62
     0022fa50 77b1e18c 00000000 00000000 00000000 ntdll!_EH4_CallFilterFunc+0x12
```

```
    0022fa78 77b471b9 fffffffe 0022fee8 0022fb80 ntdll!_except_handler4+0x8e
    0022fa9c 77b4718b 0022fb64 0022fee8 0022fb80 ntdll!ExecuteHandler2+0x26
    0022fac0 77b1f96f 0022fb64 0022fee8 0022fb80 ntdll!ExecuteHandler+0x24
    0022fb4c 77b47017 0022fb64 0022fb80 0022fb64 ntdll!RtlDispatchException+0x127
    0022fb4c 00c711ee 0022fb64 0022fb80 0022fb64 ntdll!KiUserExceptionDispatcher+0xf
    0022fe68 00c71364 00000001 00450e78 004534a8 NullDereference!wmain+0x9
    [c:\book\code\chapter_04\nulldereference\main.cpp @ 9]
...
```

Notice that the faulting thread in the process is in the midst of executing the OS exception-dispatching code from the *ntdll.dll* system module and that it's waiting on a process object. Using the address of that object from the previous listing, you can easily find the identity of that process too.

```
lkd> !process 866428f8 0
PROCESS 866428f8  SessionId: 1  Cid: 1e54    Peb: 7ffde000  ParentCid: 157c
    Image: WerFault.exe
```

This *WerFault.exe* process is, in fact, the owner of the dialog box you previously left active on the desktop as you started this live kernel debugging session. The last *!process* command gave you the process ID (called client ID, or Cid, in the output from the *!process* extension) of this worker process as well as that of its parent. Each user-mode process on the system saves its parent's identifier as part of its executive object when it gets created. However, remember that the parent process could have exited and that the OS might have also recycled its PID, assigning it to another process by this time.

You should be able to use the *!process* extension command once again to look up the parent process by its PID (the *ParentCid* value from the previous listing) and see if it's still active. If it is, you'll see that it's one of the service host instances (*svchost.exe*) that are used by the system to host shared Windows services, as shown in the following listing.

```
lkd> !process 0x157c 1
Searching for Process with Cid == 157c
Cid handle table at a63fd000 with 1249 entries in use

PROCESS 86c71148  SessionId: 0  Cid: 157c Peb: 7ffd6000  ParentCid: 0258
    Image: svchost.exe
...
    Token                             a4a193c0
    ElapsedTime                       00:00:31.456
    UserTime                          00:00:00.000
...
lkd> !token -n a4a193c0
TS Session ID: 0
User: S-1-5-18 (Well Known Group: NT AUTHORITY\SYSTEM)
...
```

The *!token* debugger extension command used in the previous listing also shows that this service process is running with the highest level of security privileges on the system (the built-in *LocalSystem* user account). To find the services hosted inside this *svchost.exe* process instance, you can use the */s* option of the *tlist.exe* tool, which shows only one service in this case, called WerSvc. This name is short for the Windows Error Reporting (WER) service.

```
C:\Program Files\Debugging Tools for Windows (x86)>tlist.exe /s
5500 svchost.exe      Svcs:  WerSvc
```

Another useful observation to make is that the PID of the crashing process is also provided by the system to the new *WerFault.exe* instance so that it can use it during the JIT debugging attach sequence, as shown in the following listing.

```
lkd> $ Replace with the address of WerFault.exe from your experiment...
lkd> .process /r /p 866428f8
lkd> !peb
...
    ImageFile:      'C:\Windows\system32\WerFault.exe'
    CommandLine:    'C:\Windows\system32\WerFault.exe -u -p 6056 -s 32'
...
lkd> .tlist nulldereference.exe
 0n6056 NullDereference.exe
```

The picture is finally complete—you've been able to discover all the components involved during the JIT debugging attach sequence. At this point, you can exit the live debugging session and dismiss the active JIT debugging confirmation dialog box you had left active earlier in this experiment.

```
lkd> q
```

Figure 4-5 summarizes the JIT debugging sequence you were able to dissect in this section, along with the interprocess synchronization that takes place between the faulting process and the WER binaries in the operating system.

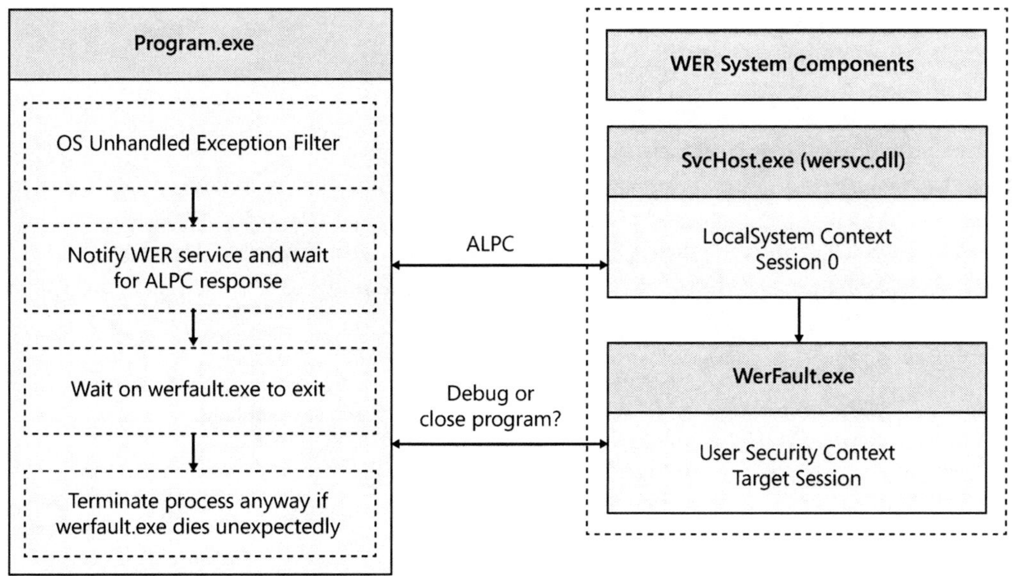

FIGURE 4-5 Native JIT debugger invocation sequence in Windows 7.

Note that in Windows XP, the WER architecture was different and that the native JIT debugger used to be invoked directly by the system's default exception filter code in the faulting process. This presented a few problems, though—in particular, when the faulting thread ran out of stack space—so the JIT debugging architecture in the system was revamped during the Windows Vista timeframe to make it more robust in the face of such conditions by relying on the helper *WerFault.exe* worker process model.

Using Visual Studio as Your JIT Debugger

Just like WinDbg, Visual Studio can also be set as the default native JIT debugger. In addition, it can also be used for JIT debugging of scripts as well as .NET applications, where using it as an alternative to WinDbg also allows you to inspect the source-code information of the crash call site.

Native JIT Debugging

The *AeDebug* registry key scheme that governs JIT debugging at the OS level isn't specific to the Windows debuggers. Visual Studio, in fact, automatically configures itself as the default native, managed, and script JIT debugger as part of its installation process. You can control these settings using the Debug\Options And Settings dialog box from the Visual Studio UI, as shown in Figure 4-6.

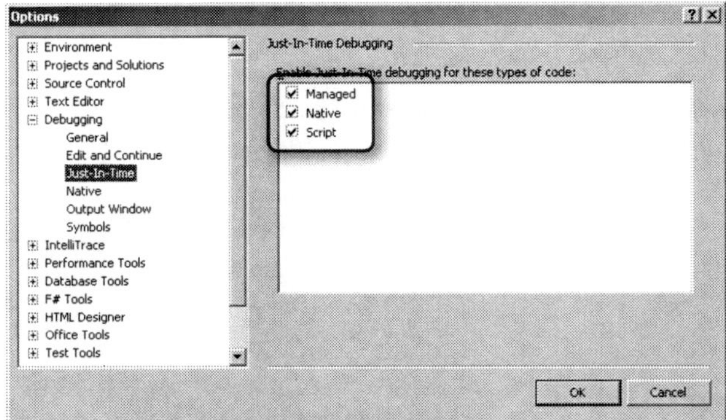

FIGURE 4-6 Configuring JIT debugging options in Visual Studio 2010.

The Native selection in the dialog box sets the *AeDebug* registry key to point to the *VsJitDebugger.exe* proxy process, which handles the JIT debugging attach steps on behalf of the Visual Studio debugger process. When that option is selected in the UI just shown, the values under the *AeDebug* registry key will look similar to those in Figure 4-7.

```
[HKEY_LOCAL_MACHINE\SOFTWARE\Microsoft\Windows NT\CurrentVersion\AeDebug]
```

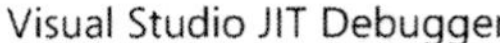

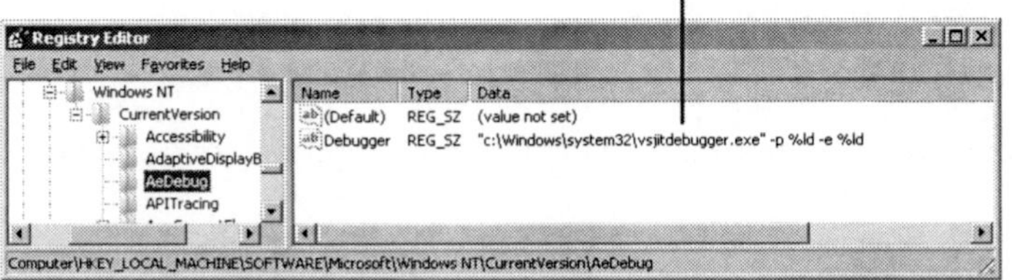

FIGURE 4-7 *AeDebug* registry key with Visual Studio 2010 native JIT debugging.

The Visual Studio debugger will then be invoked whenever any native user-mode process is about to crash, as you can confirm by running the C++ example used earlier to walk through the JIT debugging sequence with WinDbg. After a few confirmation dialog boxes, you can similarly inspect the call site of the crash using Visual Studio, as illustrated in Figure 4-8.

```
C:\book\code\chapter_04\NullDereference\objfre_win7_x86\i386\NullDereference.exe
```

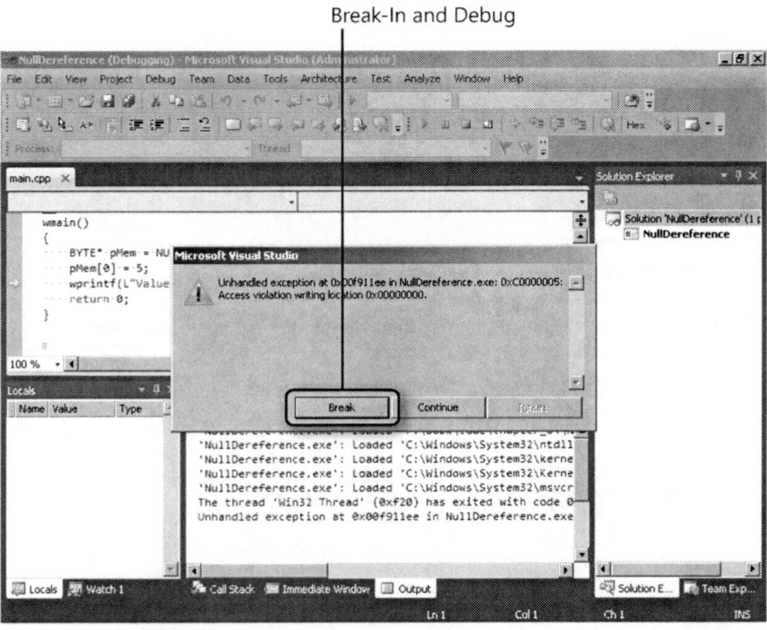

FIGURE 4-8 Visual Studio native JIT debugging.

Managed Code (.NET) JIT Debugging

The JIT debugging story for managed code depends on the version of the Microsoft .NET Framework. In .NET 4.0 programs running on Windows 7, managed JIT debugging is also governed by the same native *AeDebug* OS JIT debugger registry key shown so far in this section. In the case of the Visual Studio debugger, however, the managed JIT debugging option of the Debug\Options And Settings dialog box shown in Figure 4-6 must also be selected. Otherwise, the Visual Studio JIT process will still get invoked by the system, but it would not offer you the option to attach to .NET programs when they crash.

To see managed JIT debugging in action, you can use the following C# program from the companion source code:

```
//
// C:\book\code\chapter_04\ManagedException>NullException.cs
//
public class Test
{
    public static void Main()
    {
        throw new ArgumentNullException();
    }
}
```

Assuming you previously selected the managed-code JIT debugging option from the Debug\Options And Settings dialog box in Visual Studio, you'll see the *VsJitDebugger.exe* process get invoked by WER in response to the unhandled managed-code exception in the previous program. After a few confirmation dialog boxes, you'll again be able to get to the call site of the crash in the Visual Studio debugger, as shown in Figure 4-9.

```
C:\book\code\chapter_04\ManagedException>NullException.exe
Unhandled Exception: System.ArgumentNullException: Value cannot be null.
   at Test.Main() in C:\book\code\chapter_04\ManagedException\NullException.cs:line 7
```

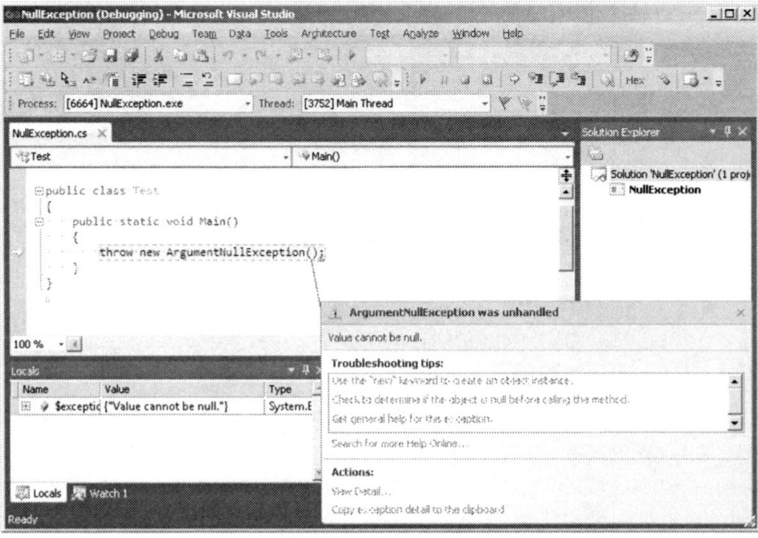

FIGURE 4-9 Visual Studio managed JIT debugging.

Managed JIT debugging worked differently in earlier versions of the .NET Framework because the Common Language Runtime (CLR) execution engine used to override the OS behavior and install its own exception handler to deal with any unhandled managed exceptions raised by .NET processes. This CLR-specific JIT debugger is controlled by the *DbgManagedDebugger* registry value shown in Figure 4-10.

```
[HKEY_LOCAL_MACHINE\SOFTWARE\Microsoft\.NETFramework]
```

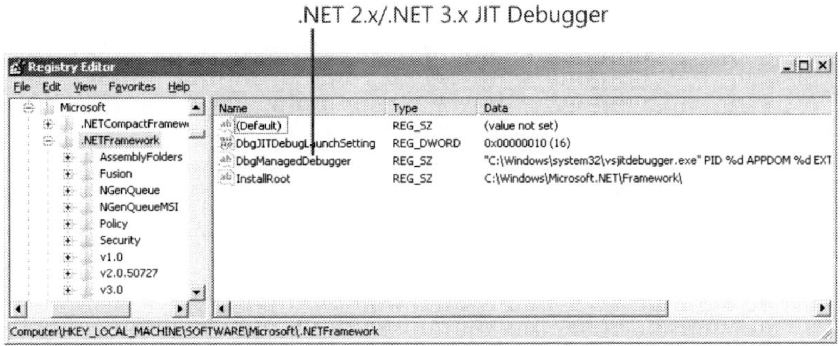

FIGURE 4-10 Legacy CLR JIT debugger registry key.

In addition to registering itself as the default managed JIT debugger in its setup program, Visual Studio 2010 also sets the previous registry key so that any applications compiled against earlier versions of the .NET Framework can also be debugged using the same Visual Studio JIT debugging experience.

Script JIT Debugging

Visual Studio can also be used for script JIT debugging. This is precisely how most forms of script debugging work, including the *//X* command-line option of *cscript.exe* (prefixed with double slash marks to distinguish it from regular options of the script itself) used in the previous chapter when introducing the architecture of script debugging in Windows. The effect of the *//X* option can be broken down into two aspects: First, it enables the Process Debug Manager (PDM) code in the scripting host process so that the debugger is able to communicate with the target host executable when debugging the script. The second thing that the *//X* option does is automatically raise a *debug break* at the beginning of the script's execution. To see this in action, you can use the script from the companion source code, shown next.

```
//
// C:\book\code\chapter_04\scripts>test.js
//

WScript.Quit(main());

function DoWork()
{
    WScript.Echo("Some work...");
}

function DoMoreWork()
{
    WScript.Echo("Some more work.");
}

function main()
{
    DoWork();
    debugger;
    DoMoreWork();
}
```

The early debug break causes Visual Studio to attach to the script as a JIT debugger, as shown in Figure 4-11.

```
C:\book\code\chapter_04\scripts>cscript //X test.js
Microsoft (R) Windows Script Host Version 5.8
Copyright (C) Microsoft Corporation. All rights reserved.
```

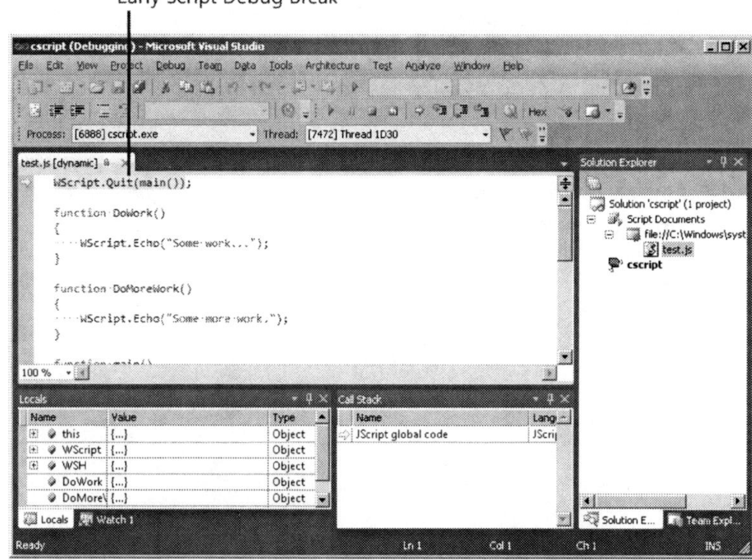

FIGURE 4-11 Visual Studio script JIT debugging (*//X* option).

Note that you can also enable the PDM debugging support in the scripting host process by using the *//D* option (also prefixed with double slash marks), which doesn't break at the beginning of the script the way *//X* does. In the following example, you'll see the JIT debugging attach dialog box appear only in response to the explicit *debugger* JScript statement. (See Figure 4-12.) This is akin to how native and .NET JIT debuggers also get invoked in response to specific run-time events from the target, except the script wouldn't actually die if you decline to debug it.

```
C:\book\code\chapter_04\scripts>cscript //D test.js
Microsoft (R) Windows Script Host Version 5.8
Copyright (C) Microsoft Corporation. All rights reserved.
Some work...
```

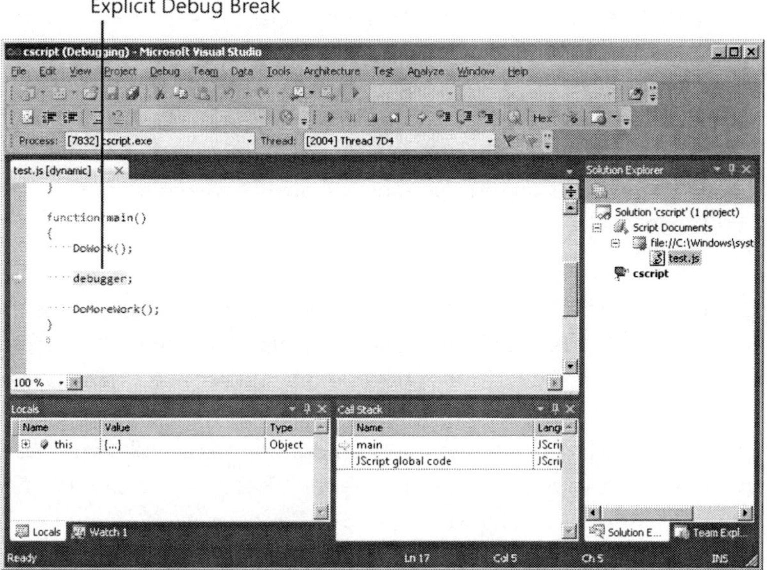

FIGURE 4-12 Visual Studio script JIT debugging (*//D* option).

These script-specific debug breaks aren't raised as regular SEH debug-break exceptions, so they aren't handled by the native OS JIT debugging sequence, either. Instead, they're directly handled by the PDM code on the script host's side, which responds to the debug break by starting the script JIT debugger on demand through out-of-process COM activation. Visual Studio automatically registers the necessary COM classes in the registry during its setup so that its JIT debugger gets loaded during this sequence. The entire transaction that handles the debug break in this case takes place without the WER components in the OS knowing about it because no SEH exceptions are actually generated. So, you can choose to have WinDbg act as your native OS JIT debugger and still use Visual Studio for your script JIT debugging.

Run-Time Assertions and JIT Debugging

Run-time assertions are used to validate assumptions during the execution of an application. Because assertions are usually defined only in checked-build flavors so as not to affect the performance of free builds, they should be used only for confirming internal code invariants and never used as a substitute for proper error handling. The main advantage to using run-time assertions is to cause the code to stop immediately inside a debugger whenever an internal code invariant is broken, when an error code would otherwise bubble up to other functions higher up in the call stack and make it harder to track down the broken invariant.

Most forms of assertion macros end up causing an SEH exception, typically either the *int 3* debug break exception or the new dedicated *int 2c* assertion exception introduced during the Windows Vista release. The advantage of the new assertion instruction is its close integration with the Windows debuggers, which recognize it as an assertion condition, also allowing you to ignore it and continue executing the target (*g*) as if the assertion didn't fire. This is why the new NT_ASSERT macro, which only works on Windows Vista and later, uses the *int 2c* instruction, while the older C run-time assertion macros (_ASSERT or _ASSERTE macros) still use *int 3*. Because these instructions raise an SEH exception, however, they both trigger the native JIT debugging sequence when they get invoked by the target application as broken invariants are detected.

Note Do not confuse run-time assertions with static, compile-time assertions such as the C_ASSERT macro from the *winnt.h* SDK header file. Unlike run-time assertions, compile-time assertions are used to validate assumptions during the compilation process, which is especially useful when using template classes. As the compiler generates new templated code for you, you can employ its ability to validate assumptions during the compilation phase, such as whether a template type is of a given size or whether it has certain traits. The need for a standard compile-time assertion mechanism in the C++ language was recognized in the most recent C++ standard iteration (named C++11) with the introduction of the new *static_assert* keyword, which is also supported in the Microsoft Visual Studio 2010 version of the C++ compiler.

You should keep a few things in mind when deciding what to do when a code invariant is broken and you need to raise a run-time assertion. For example, it's generally a bad idea to show a dialog box. If the UI is displayed inside a Windows service in session 0, for instance, the user won't be able to see it or interact with it. In addition, having assertions show a dialog box can also be a problem for automated testing. The .NET *Debug.Assert* unfortunately suffers from this side effect, so be careful where you use it in your code. The best approach is to limit assertions to calling either *int 3* or *int 2c* and simply let the native JIT debugging architecture in the OS take over. Though not absolutely necessary, it's also a good idea to use inline assertion routines by using compiler intrinsics such as the *__debugbreak* or *__int2c* Visual C++ intrinsics, instead of using wrapper functions such as *kernel32!DebugBreak*. This way, the function raising the assertion will be at the top of the call stack when breaking into the debugger. This is also why the NT_ASSERT macro, for example, uses these intrinsics.

JIT Debugging in Session 0

The native JIT debugger is started in the same user session as the process that's about to crash. For the system and user-provided service processes that run in the noninteractive system session (session 0), in particular, the JIT debugger process from the *AeDebug* registry key also gets started in that same session, meaning that you will not be able to interact with that new debugger instance when it attaches to the target process. You won't get any visual cues to let you know that a crash is actually in progress, either, and you might totally miss the crash if JIT debugging is enabled on the machine.

If you're simply trying to use JIT debugging to investigate a known crash, however, there is good news despite the grim outlook of not being able to interact with the new JIT debugger. Remember from the architectural overview of WER's support for JIT debugging that any user-mode process that's about to crash waits for the new debugger instance specified in the *AeDebug* registry key to attach to it before its execution proceeds forward and the process finally exits. This means that the debugger in the *AeDebug* registry key doesn't really need to attach to the process and, in fact, doesn't even need to be a *true* debugger. If you replace the *Debugger* value under the *AeDebug* key with *cmd.exe*, for instance, you can block the execution of the target at the time of its crash and attach to it as usual by using the F6 shortcut in *windbg.exe* right from your current user session. The crash call site should be there waiting for you when you attach! Be sure, however, to list (*tlist.exe*) and kill (*kill.exe*) any *leaked cmd.exe* instances that get automatically started by WER in session 0 at the end of your experimentation.

Dump Debugging

Memory dump files are vehicles that can be used to save a snapshot state of a process or, sometimes, of the entire system. They can be generated on demand by the OS whenever a crash is about to take place, though they don't always have to be *crash* dumps and you're also able to generate them manually.

Automatic User-Mode, Crash-Dump Generation

A scenario where dump debugging is especially useful is when your code unceremoniously crashes in an end-user environment. In that case, you might not have access to the customer machine for live or JIT debugging. Fortunately, the WER code in the operating system has another very useful debugging hook that allows you to generate crash dump files whenever a crash occurs. This setting can be easily turned on by an end user, and the resulting dump file can then be transmitted to you for further analysis.

The *LocalDumps* Registry Key

The Windows Error Reporting (WER) framework in the OS supports an important registry key that allows you to request automatic crash-dump generation when user-mode processes hit unhandled exceptions. Because there are no tools to configure this key, you'll need to edit the registry manually, though the companion source code contains a script to help automate this task.

For example, the following command, which you'll need to execute from an elevated administrative command prompt, will configure your machine so that crash dumps are automatically captured for each process that crashes as a result of an unhandled exception.

```
C:\book\code\chapter_04\scripts>edit_local_dumps_key.cmd -df c:\dumps -dt 2
```

The first argument to this helper script is the folder location that WER should use when it generates its user-mode crash dumps, and the second argument specifies the type of those dump files. A value of *2* indicates that you would like WER to generate crash dumps with full memory information. Once this command is executed successfully, the *LocalDumps* registry key should look similar to Figure 4-13.

```
[HKEY_LOCAL_MACHINE\SOFTWARE\Microsoft\Windows\Windows Error Reporting\LocalDumps]
```

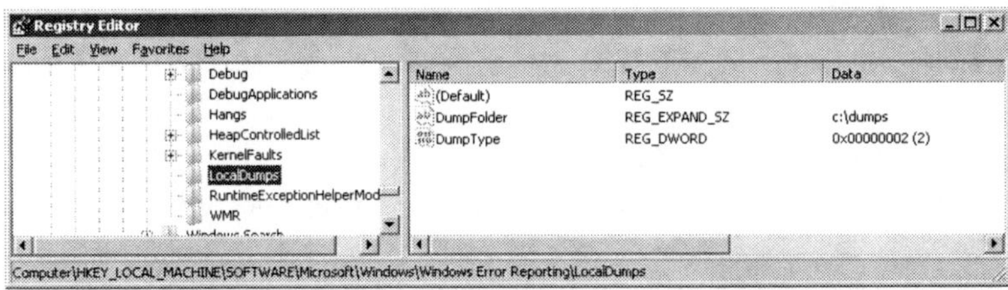

FIGURE 4-13 Automatic user-mode, crash-dump generation using the *LocalDumps* registry key.

I usually leave the previous values as the default configuration on all my machines so that any user-mode crashes get captured and their crash dumps are saved to a well-known directory location on the system. The name of the dump file generated by WER will contain the name of the process that crashed, and the date of the file will tell you when the crash happened too.

Your First Dump Debugging Experiment

This section will show you how to investigate a crash in the startup code path of a test Windows service by using the *LocalDumps* registry key and the support for postmortem dump debugging in the Windows debuggers. The crash scenario used in this experiment is the same access violation example that was used earlier to illustrate native JIT debugging (dereferencing a NULL pointer), except the code here will be running as part of a Windows service in the noninteractive system session (session 0).

```
//
// C:\book\code\chapter_04\ServiceCrash>Main.cpp
//
#define SERVICE_NAME L"ServiceWithCrash"
class CSystemService
{
public:
    static
    VOID
    WINAPI
    ServiceMain(
        __in DWORD dwArgc,
        __in_ecount(dwArgc) LPTSTR* lpszArgv
        )
    {
        ...
        //
        // Do some initialization work before reporting the "running" state
        //
        ChkHr(Initialize());

        //
        // Report running to the Service Control Manager (SCM) process
        //
        g_ServiceStatus.dwCurrentState = SERVICE_RUNNING;
        ChkWin32(SetServiceStatus(
            g_hServiceStatusHandle,
            &g_ServiceStatus
            ));
        ...
    }

private:
    static
    HRESULT
    Initialize(
        VOID
        )
    {
        BYTE* pMem = NULL;

        ChkProlog();

        pMem[0] = 5;
        wprintf(L"Value at memory address is 0x%x\n", pMem[0]);

        ChkNoCleanup();
    }
};
```

Before you can witness the crash, you first need to install this service on your system, which you can do from within your Driver Development Kit (DDK) build environment by running the *setup.bat* batch file from the companion source code. This batch file copies the service binary to the system directory and also registers the new service on the system. It also deletes the *AeDebug* JIT registry key so that native JIT debugging won't interfere with your attempt to automatically collect a memory crash dump for the process. You need to execute this one-time registration step from an elevated administrative DDK build window.

```
C:\book\code\chapter_04\ServiceCrash>build -cCZ
C:\book\code\chapter_04\ServiceCrash>setup.bat
```

Attempting to start the service now will show the following error, which usually indicates that the service process died along the way due to an unhandled SEH exception.

```
C:\book\code\chapter_04\ServiceCrash>net start ServiceWithCrash
The Crashing Bug service is starting.
The Crashing Bug service could not be started.
A system error has occurred.
System error 1067 has occurred.
The process terminated unexpectedly.
```

With the *LocalDumps* registry changes made earlier in this section, you'll see a new dump file appear under the target dump folder location as soon as the crash occurs, as shown in the following command. Note that the name of the dump file contains the Process ID (PID) of the crashing process, so the file name you'll see when you conduct this experiment is likely to be different.

```
C:\book\code\chapter_04\ServiceCrash>dir /b c:\dumps
ServiceWithCrash.exe.4428.dmp
```

You can now load this dump file in WinDbg by using the *–z* command-line option, as shown in the following listing, where you're immediately able to observe the call stack where the crash happened.

```
"C:\Program Files (x86)\Debugging Tools for Windows (x86)\windbg.exe" -z
C:\dumps\ServiceWithCrash.exe.4428.dmp
...
0:003> .symfix
0:003> .reload
0:003> k
ChildEBP RetAddr
0067f12c 74f10bdd ntdll!NtWaitForMultipleObjects+0x15
0067f1c8 7643162d KERNELBASE!WaitForMultipleObjectsEx+0x100
0067f210 76431921 kernel32!WaitForMultipleObjectsExImplementation+0xe0
0067f22c 76459b2d kernel32!WaitForMultipleObjects+0x18
0067f298 76459bca kernel32!WerpReportFaultInternal+0x186
0067f2ac 764598f8 kernel32!WerpReportFault+0x70
0067f2bc 76459875 kernel32!BasepReportFault+0x20
0067f348 772173e7 kernel32!UnhandledExceptionFilter+0x1af
0067f350 772172c4 ntdll!__RtlUserThreadStart+0x62
0067f364 77217161 ntdll!_EH4_CallFilterFunc+0x12
0067f38c 771fb679 ntdll!_except_handler4+0x8e
0067f3b0 771fb64b ntdll!ExecuteHandler2+0x26
0067f460 771b010f ntdll!ExecuteHandler+0x24
0067f460 00211545 ntdll!KiUserExceptionDispatcher+0xf
0067f7b4 002115a7 ServiceWithCrash!CSystemService::Initialize+0x9
[C:\book\code\chapter_04\servicecrash\main.cpp @ 113]
0067f7c4 74f975a8 ServiceWithCrash!CSystemService::ServiceMain+0x48
```

```
[C:\book\code\chapter_04\servicecrash\main.cpp @ 40]
0067f7d8 76433677 sechost!ScSvcctrlThreadA+0x21
0067f7e4 771d9f42 kernel32!BaseThreadInitThunk+0xe
0067f824 771d9f15 ntdll!__RtlUserThreadStart+0x70
0067f83c 00000000 ntdll!_RtlUserThreadStart+0x1b
0:003> q
```

Note that the analysis step in dump debugging can actually be performed on any machine, provided it has access to the proper symbol files. This "capture anywhere/process anywhere" paradigm makes postmortem dump debugging appealing in many debugging situations. In the previous situation, for example, live debugging is less convenient because the service process crashes too early during its execution, making it more difficult to attach a debugger before the process is terminated.

Analyzing Crash Dumps Using the WinDbg Debugger

When you get a crash-dump file, the most urgent concern is usually to figure out what was the immediate cause of the crash. In the case that you just studied, the analysis was easy because you had the source code for the application on the same machine. This is rarely the case because the capture and analysis machines in crash-dump investigations are often different. This section will walk you through the common techniques involved in this critical first step.

Finding SEH Crash Exceptions

When you receive a crash dump file and open it using the *–z* command-line option in WinDbg, your very first step should be to fix the symbols search path in the debugger. This means fixing the search path to include the Microsoft public symbols server and also that of your own symbols.

To quickly find the type of exception that led to the fatal process crash, you can use the useful *.lastevent* debugger command. In the case of the previous service crash dump, for example, the last event reported by this command is an access violation SEH exception, as shown in the following listing.

```
"C:\Program Files (x86)\Debugging Tools for Windows (x86)\windbg.exe" -z
C:\dumps\ServiceWithCrash.exe.4428.dmp
...
0:003> .symfix
0:003> .sympath+ C:\book\code\chapter_04\ServiceCrash\objfre_win7_x86\i386
0:003> .reload
0:003> .srcpath+ C:\book\code
0:003> .lastevent
Last event: d78.133c: Access violation - code c0000005 (first/second chance not available)
```

Although you could analyze crash dump SEH exceptions manually, the best way to start native crash-dump investigations is to use the very useful *!analyze* debugger extension. This command automates (to a certain extent) the process of initial triage of a crash dump; it is also used internally by Microsoft to mine the large number of crash dumps submitted by customers and categorize them into buckets representing similar crash failures. In the case of the previous dump file, for instance, this extension can give you the exact instruction and source line of the bug that led to the process demise, as well as a wealth of other useful information about the crash.

```
0:003> !analyze -v
FAULTING_IP:
ServiceWithCrash!CSystemService::Initialize+1a [c:\book\code\chapter_04\servicecrash\main.cpp @
113]
00211545 c60005          mov     byte ptr [eax],5

EXCEPTION_RECORD:  ffffffff -- (.exr 0xffffffffffffffff)
ExceptionAddress: 00211545 (ServiceWithCrash!CSystemService::Initialize+0x00000009)
ExceptionCode: c0000005 (Access violation)
  ExceptionFlags: 00000000
NumberParameters: 2
   Parameter[0]: 00000001
   Parameter[1]: 00000000
Attempt to write to address 00000000

PROCESS_NAME:  ServiceWithCrash.exe

STACK_TEXT:
0067f7b4 002115a7 00000000 006e96a8 006e96a8 ServiceWithCrash!CSystemService::Initialize+0x9
[c:\book\code\chapter_04\servicecrash\main.cpp @ 113]...

STACK_COMMAND:  ~3s; .ecxr ; kb

FAULTING_SOURCE_CODE:
   108:         BYTE* pMem = NULL;
   109:
   110:         ChkProlog();
   111:
>  112:         pMem[0] = 5;
   113:         wprintf(L"Value at memory address is 0x%x\n", pMem[0]);
   114:
   115:         ChkNoCleanup();
   116:     }
   117:
```

The STACK_COMMAND provided by this extension is particularly interesting. Notice how it gives you steps to get the stack trace at the time of the initial faulting instruction before the SEH exception was dispatched by the OS. The *.ecxr* debugger command listed in those steps deserves further explanation. What that command does is instruct the debugger to restore the register context to what it was when the initial fault that led to the SEH exception took place. When an SEH exception is dispatched, the OS builds an internal structure called an *exception record*. It also conveniently saves the register context at the time of the initial fault in a *context record* structure. The combination of these two important structures is at the heart of how the *!analyze* extension does its magic, but also generally it's how crash-dump analysis of SEH exceptions is made possible by the OS.

```
0:003> dt ntdll!_EXCEPTION_RECORD
   +0x000 ExceptionCode    : Int4B
   +0x004 ExceptionFlags   : Uint4B
   +0x008 ExceptionRecord  : Ptr32 _EXCEPTION_RECORD
   +0x00c ExceptionAddress : Ptr32 Void
   +0x010 NumberParameters : Uint4B
   +0x014 ExceptionInformation : [15] Uint4B
0:003> dt ntdll!_CONTEXT
...
```

```
+0x0a4 Ebx              : Uint4B
+0x0a8 Edx              : Uint4B
+0x0ac Ecx              : Uint4B
+0x0b0 Eax              : Uint4B
+0x0b4 Ebp              : Uint4B
...
```

You can also use the *.ecxr* command directly when you open the dump file. As long as your symbols and sources search paths in the debugger are set up correctly, you should see the debugger automatically open the source file of the crash call site for you when you type that command, just as if you had been performing live analysis and caught the exception early inside the debugger before the process was terminated. (See Figure 4-14.)

```
"C:\Program Files\Debugging Tools for Windows (x86)\windbg.exe" -z
C:\dumps\ServiceWithCrash.exe.4428.dmp
...
0:003> .symfix
0:003> .sympath+ I:\book\code\chapter_04\ServiceCrash\objfre_win7_x86\i386
0:003> .reload
0:003> .srcpath+ I:\book\code\chapter_04\ServiceCrash
0:003> .ecxr
```

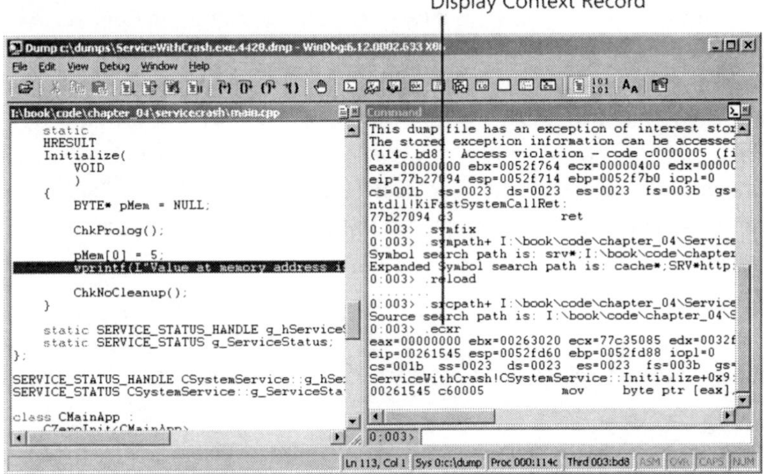

FIGURE 4-14 Switching thread context to the SEH exception context record.

It's unfortunate that the WinDbg debugger doesn't perform this step automatically when you open a crash dump file so that you immediately see the code that crashed rather than the boilerplate, unhandled-exception dispatching stack trace deep inside the WER code in the system.

Finding .NET Crash Exceptions

Managed-code applications typically crash when a .NET exception goes unhandled. Because .NET exceptions are built on top of SEH exceptions, the WER infrastructure for collecting automatic crash dumps can also be used for .NET applications. That being said, the analysis of managed-code crash dumps is quite different because you are usually less interested in the nature of the SEH exception that caused the final crash. What you are really after in the case of .NET crashes is the .NET exception that triggered the process demise.

The most common way of performing this analysis is by using the *SOS* debugger extension that was introduced back in Chapter 3, "How Windows Debuggers Work," though the first problem you'll run into when trying to debug managed-code crash dumps is that you need to find the SOS extension that matches the CLR version used in the crashing process. This extension comes with the .NET Framework, so you might actually need to install the target CLR on the analysis machine if only to get the correct *sos.dll* to use during your postmortem debugging of the crash dump file.

The second problem you might run into when debugging managed crash dumps using the SOS extension is matching the CLR architecture (32-bit or 64-bit) used in the .NET process that crashed. In addition, the debugger you're using during the dump analysis needs to match the architecture of the target CLR and SOS extension DLL. To work around these problems, you can use a 32-bit debugger and SOS extension DLL to analyze dumps of 32-bit .NET processes and a 64-bit debugger and SOS extension DLL to analyze dumps of 64-bit .NET code. These are unfortunate restrictions that you usually don't have to worry about when analyzing native crash dumps but that are important to remember when investigating crash dumps of .NET applications.

Finding the .NET exception that led to the crash is easy once you've loaded the right version of the SOS extension into your WinDbg postmortem debugging session. There is, indeed, a simple SOS command to print that exception information: *!pe* ("print exception"). To illustrate how this works in practice, you can use the following C# example from the companion source code. Because it's common for .NET applications to catch exceptions and throw new ones, this program includes a *nested* exception. You need to know how to deal with this case because you'll often need to find the very first exception that triggered the chain of events leading up to the crash, not simply the last .NET exception that ultimately went unhandled.

```
//
// C:\book\code\chapter_04\LoadException>LoadException.cs
//
public static void Main()
{
    try
    {
        Assembly.Load("MissingAssembly");
    }
    catch (Exception ex)
    {
```

```
        if (ex is FileNotFoundException || ex is ArgumentException)
        {
            throw new ApplicationException("A generic fatal error", ex);
        }
        else
        {
            throw;
        }
    }
}
```

Assuming you still have the same configuration that was used to capture the crash in the service process from the previous experiment—specifically, the *LocalDumps* registry key and no *AeDebug* key—you should see a new dump file appear once this process crashes.

```
C:\book\code\chapter_04\LoadException>LoadException.exe
Unhandled Exception: System.ApplicationException: A generic fatal error
...
C:\book\code\chapter_04\LoadException>dir /b c:\dumps
LoadException.exe.7660.dmp
ServiceWithCrash.exe.4428.dmp
```

By using the *–z* command-line option again to load the new dump file in WinDbg, you're able to quickly determine the unhandled .NET exception by using the *!pe* command, as illustrated in the following listing.

```
"C:\Program Files\Debugging Tools for Windows (x86)\windbg.exe" -z
C:\dumps\LoadException.exe.7660.dmp
0:000> .symfix
0:000> .reload
0:000> !pe
No export pe found
0:000> .loadby sos clr
0:000> !pe
Exception object: 01dbc0bc
Exception type:   System.ApplicationException
Message:          A generic fatal error
InnerException:   System.IO.FileNotFoundException, Use !PrintException 01dbb7d8 to see more.
StackTrace (generated):
    SP       IP       Function
    001DF0DC 004A0139 LoadException!Test.Main()+0xc9
HResult: 80131600
There are nested exceptions on this thread. Run with -nested for details
```

Although this gives you the exception that ultimately led to the crash, you still don't know what operation really caused this program to fail. Notice, however, that the previous exception has an *inner* exception object that the *!pe* command also displays when dumping the *outer* exception. By following the chain of inner exceptions, you should be able to get all the way up to the root cause of this type of .NET crash. In this case, you need to go only one level up to see that the exception was because of a failed attempt to load a nonexisting file. You're also able to see the stack trace for that initial exception and observe that it was raised inside the .NET Framework (*mscorlib.dll*) after you called *Assembly.Load* in your code.

```
0:000> !pe 01dbb7d8
Exception object: 01dbb7d8
Exception type:   System.IO.FileNotFoundException
Message:          Could not load file or assembly 'MissingAssembly' or one of its dependencies.
The system cannot find the file specified.
InnerException:   <none>
StackTrace (generated):
 SP       IP       Function
 001DF0F4 509B3148 mscorlib_ni!System.Reflection.RuntimeAssembly.nLoad...
 001DF120 50A20B4D mscorlib_ni!System.Reflection.RuntimeAssembly.InternalLoadAssemblyName...
 001DF14C 50A20D8D mscorlib_ni!System.Reflection.RuntimeAssembly.InternalLoad...
 001DF170 509BA785 mscorlib_ni!System.Reflection.Assembly.Load...
 001DF17C 004A00B3 LoadException!Test.Main()+0x43
```

Another command that can also be particularly useful during postmortem managed-code debugging with the SOS extension is the *!dso* command, which lists the managed objects on the stack ("dump stack objects"). This command actually provides you with an alternative way to retrieve the .NET exceptions because those objects tend to be at the top of the stack. For example, you can also use the *!dso* command to dump all the .NET objects on the stack and then use the *!do* ("dump .NET object") command to dump the state of each particular exception object in the chain of inner exceptions, as illustrated in the following listing.

```
0:000> !dso
ESP/REG  Object   Name
001DEFA0 01dbc0bc System.ApplicationException
001DEFD8 01dbc0bc System.ApplicationException
001DF01C 01dbc0bc System.ApplicationException
001DF0AC 01dbb438 System.Reflection.AssemblyName
001DF0C0 01dbc0bc System.ApplicationException
001DF17C 01dbc110 System.String    A generic fatal error
001DF180 01dbc0bc System.ApplicationException
001DF184 01dbb7d8 System.IO.FileNotFoundException
...
0:000> !do 01dbc0bc
Name:         System.ApplicationException
Fields: ...
50a9fb8c  4000050       18     System.Exception  0 instance 01dbb7d8 _innerException
0:000> !do 01dbb7d8
Name:         System.IO.FileNotFoundException
Fields:
      MT    Field   Offset                 Type VT     Attr    Value Name
...
50a9f92c  400004e       10        System.String  0 instance 01dbbf0c _message
50a9fb8c  4000050       18     System.Exception  0 instance 00000000 _innerException
...
0:000> !do 01dbbf0c
Name:         System.String
String:       Could not load file or assembly 'MissingAssembly' or one of its dependencies. The
system cannot find the file specified.
...
```

There is yet another way to see the .NET exceptions at the time of the crash, and that's to use the *!threads* command. This command is a close parallel to the ~* native debugger command because both show you a list of the threads in the process, but with the *!threads* command being more .NET-centric in the data that it displays and focusing on only the *managed* threads in the process and their CLR information. In particular, the *!threads* command also gives you the last .NET exceptions that were thrown in each managed thread context (if there were any such exceptions), as demonstrated in the following listing.

```
0:000> .loadby sos clr
0:000> !threads
ThreadCount:      2
UnstartedThread:  0
BackgroundThread: 1
PendingThread:    0
DeadThread:       0
Hosted Runtime:   no
                                   PreEmptive   GC Alloc                Lock
       ID  OSID ThreadOBJ    State GC           Context       Domain    Count APT Exception
   0    1  126c 003dd0a8      a020 Enabled  01cdab68:01cdbfe8 003d6a40     0 MTA System.
ApplicationException (01dbc0bc) (nested exceptions)
   2    2   b3c 003e84d8      b220 Enabled  00000000:00000000 003d6a40     0 MTA (Finalizer)
0:000> !do 01dbc0bc
...
```

Table 4-1 summarizes these SOS extension commands, which you'll find helpful when analyzing unhandled .NET exceptions.

TABLE 4-1 Useful SOS Commands When Analyzing Crash Exceptions in .NET Programs

Command	Description
!pe	Prints details of a .NET exception. The command can be invoked with the address of an exception object or without parameters, in which case it tries to display the last managed exception on the current thread.
!dso *!do*	*!dso* ("dump stack objects") dumps the active .NET object references in the current thread context. When an exception is thrown, the last exception object will be near the top in the output from this command, and the *!do* ("dump object") SOS command can then be used to display the exception details.
!threads	Displays all the managed threads in the process and their information, including any outstanding exceptions in each thread.

Moving Beyond the Immediate Symptom

After you determine the immediate cause of a crash, you usually still need to figure out how the process got there before crashing. Except in the most obvious crashes, this is typically the most challenging part in dump debugging. You need a different mindset than the one you are used to in live debugging investigations.

You can't step through the code or set intermediate breakpoints to help you trace the code path to the crash call site, so you must instead form hypotheses about what might have happened to lead you there. In multithreaded applications, for example, you need to look at more than just the thread that crashed to see what other threads in the process were doing at the same time. You might also need to look at the state of global and static variables using the debugger, and then try to piece together potential scenarios in which those conditions collectively hold true.

Once you've established a plausible theory, it can often be useful to try to replay it inside the debugger—for instance, by forcing global variables to have a certain value in memory or executing threads in a particular order. In complex crashes, this is not always easy to do, but if you are able to reproduce the crash inside the debugger by manipulating the program code flow or data structures in memory, this also gives you the added luxury of being able to test your proposed bug fix once you apply it to your code. This painstaking process is often where great debugging skills and familiarity with both the debuggers and the code base can make all the difference between a futile investigation and a successful one that helps get rid of one more crashing bug from your software.

Analyzing Crash Dumps in Visual Studio

The Visual Studio debugger can also be used to open and analyze dump files. Much of what makes Visual Studio attractive when writing code inside its well-integrated development environment, however, doesn't hold as much appeal during postmortem debugging, where you're usually looking at dump files that were captured on different machines—sometimes even without the corresponding source code. For this reason, WinDbg remains the debugger of choice for postmortem debugging on Windows.

One particular postmortem debugging scenario where you might find Visual Studio preferable, however, is when you're debugging managed crash dumps and want to get source-code information, given that WinDbg doesn't support source-level .NET debugging. This source-level postmortem debugging of .NET code is supported only in Visual Studio 2010, though, and only for code that was built for .NET 4.0 or newer. Earlier versions of Visual Studio supported only *native* debugging of managed crash dumps, and they did that by also using the SOS extension, so they really didn't offer any particular advantage over WinDbg even in this scenario.

To see Visual Studio's new ability to examine .NET 4.0 crash dumps in action, you can try to use it to load the dump that was generated by WER for the nested .NET exception example used earlier in this section. Note that when *devenv.exe* sees a file with a *.dmp* extension on its command line, it assumes that it's a dump file and opens it for postmortem debugging. Figure 4-15 shows the first window you see when debugging a dump file in Visual Studio.

```
"c:\Program Files\Microsoft Visual Studio 10.0\Common7\IDE\devenv.exe"
c:\dumps\LoadException.exe.7660.dmp
```

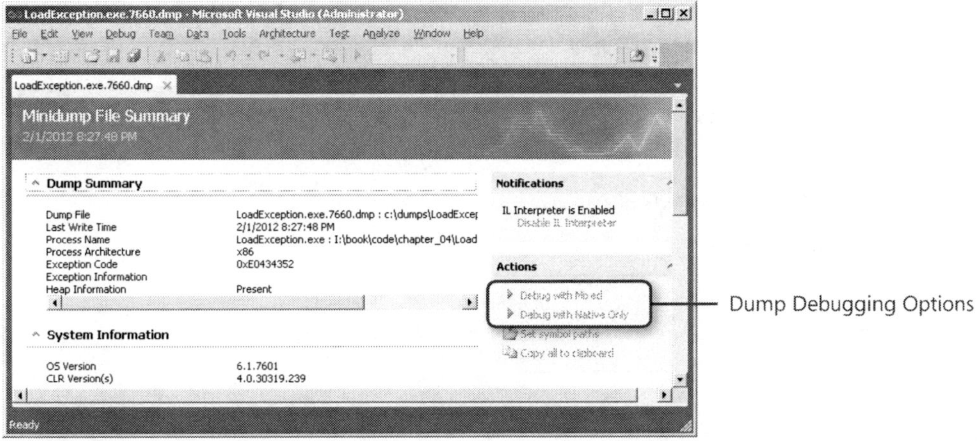

FIGURE 4-15 Source-level managed postmortem debugging in Visual Studio 2010.

Notice that you have the option of performing mixed-mode debugging of the crash dump (debugging both managed and native code in the memory dump at the same time). If this were a crash dump of a .NET 2.0 process, the only option presented to you by Visual Studio would have been the native debugging mode, which requires you to load and use the SOS extension in the Immediate Window of Visual Studio if you also want to inspect the managed code in the dump file.

Manual Dump-File Generation

You can use both the WinDbg and Visual Studio debuggers to generate memory dumps of their live target at any point during a live debugging session. This is convenient when you need to save the state of a bug repro so that you or another person can investigate it later without having to hold the live repro. This is often useful during automated test passes when the repro machines need to get recycled for other test runs.

When generating dump files manually, you need to understand the available dump file types and the subset of information you need to capture to enable successful postmortem debugging of the standalone dump file. There are two types you can use when generating a user-mode memory dump:

- **Full dumps** This type of dump captures the entire memory space of the target process. It also includes the process handle table information so that you can dump open object handles by using the *!handle* extension when analyzing the dump file. If you recall, one of the registry values you had to set when using the *LocalDumps* registry key for automatic crash-dump capture was the dump file type. In the postmortem debugging experiments you conducted so far in this chapter, you set that value to *2*, which told the system to generate full crash dumps.
- **Minidumps** This other type of user-mode dump files gives you better control over the granularity of the data that gets included in the dump file. Contrary to what their names might lead you to believe, minidumps don't necessarily have to be minimal at all because their size can range from very small to very large, depending on the subset of information you choose to include in the minidump. In fact, the largest minidumps are bigger than the full dumps.

To get a better idea of the type of data that goes into a minidump, it's useful to look at the possible flags you can use with the *dbghelp!MiniDumpWriteDump* Win32 API. This API allows you to programmatically save a dump file, and it takes a dump-type parameter that can be a combination of any of the following bit masks.

```
//
// C:\ddk\7600.16385.1\inc\api>imagehlp.h
//
typedef enum _MINIDUMP_TYPE
{
    MiniDumpNormal                          = 0x00000000,
    MiniDumpWithDataSegs                    = 0x00000001,
    MiniDumpWithFullMemory                  = 0x00000002,
    MiniDumpWithHandleData                  = 0x00000004,
    MiniDumpFilterMemory                    = 0x00000008,
    MiniDumpScanMemory                      = 0x00000010,
    MiniDumpWithUnloadedModules             = 0x00000020,
    MiniDumpWithIndirectlyReferencedMemory  = 0x00000040,
    MiniDumpFilterModulePaths               = 0x00000080,
    MiniDumpWithProcessThreadData           = 0x00000100,
    MiniDumpWithPrivateReadWriteMemory      = 0x00000200,
    MiniDumpWithoutOptionalData             = 0x00000400,
    MiniDumpWithFullMemoryInfo              = 0x00000800,
    MiniDumpWithThreadInfo                  = 0x00001000,
    MiniDumpWithCodeSegs                    = 0x00002000,
    MiniDumpWithoutAuxiliaryState           = 0x00004000,
    MiniDumpWithFullAuxiliaryState          = 0x00008000,
    MiniDumpWithPrivateWriteCopyMemory      = 0x00010000,
    MiniDumpIgnoreInaccessibleMemory        = 0x00020000,
    MiniDumpWithTokenInformation            = 0x00040000
} MINIDUMP_TYPE;
```

Notice, for instance, that minidumps can also include data such as thread and process access-token information (the last flag in the enumeration) when this information isn't contained in full dumps. In particular, this means that the *!token* debugger extension command only works in minidumps that had that flag set during their generation.

When generating dump files in WinDbg, you can use the */ma* option of the *.dump* command to generate a minidump with all of the possible bit masks. This is by far the preferred way of generating user-mode dump files, though full dumps are also often an adequate choice. You can use the */o* option to overwrite any previous dump files. It's also usually a good idea to add an optional comment using the */c* option in the dump files you generate by hand so that you can easily differentiate them from each other, as illustrated in the following listing.

```
0:000> .dump /ma /o /c "FileOpen notepad.exe experiment" c:\dumps\ManualDump.dmp
```

When you later open the dump file for postmortem analysis using the *–z* command-line option of WinDbg, the debugger starts by displaying the type of dump file as well as any optional comment that was placed in it, as shown in the following listing.

```
"C:\Program Files\Debugging Tools for Windows (x86)\windbg.exe" -z c:\dumps\ManualDump.dmp
...
```

```
Loading Dump File [c:\dumps\ManualDump.dmp]
User Mini Dump File with Full Memory: Only application data is available

Comment: 'FileOpen notepad.exe experiment'
...
0:000> $ Perform postmortem debugging of the loaded dump, then terminate the session
0:000> q
```

"Time Travel" Debugging

Although dump files can be used to capture a bug repro, they allow you to save only a single memory snapshot. The code paths taken by the application to get there aren't saved, nor are the values of registers and locals over time, so you lose quite a bit of data about the bug repro when you only capture a dump file.

A simple idea that has captured the imagination of software engineers interested in the area of debugging is the ability to collect *traces* that can save a program's function call history and any other important run-time events to disk as it gets executed. At the heart of this idea is being able to intercept program instructions and write a trace handler to save the values of registers, locals, and other important execution environment data to a log file on disk. Much to the delight of debugging enthusiasts in Windows, this powerful technique was included as a first-class feature in Visual Studio 2010 and dubbed *IntelliTrace*.

The MSDN website has plenty of information about this feature, which you can find at the following URL: *http://msdn.microsoft.com/en-us/library/dd264915.aspx*. In a nutshell, though, IntelliTrace allows you to play a scenario inside Visual Studio and save a trace file, which you can then transfer to a different machine and analyze in Visual Studio just like a dump file, except you're able to navigate the trace forward (as if you were doing live debugging) and also go back in time (using the Ctrl+Shift+F11 shortcut in Visual Studio 2010) to see how you got to the call site of the bug. This is why this method of debugging is sometimes referred to as *time travel* or *historical* debugging.

Even though this feature is available only for .NET-managed programs in Visual Studio 2010 (and only when you execute them inside the integrated development environment), it's a harbinger of things to come in the area of debugging and tracing as time-travel debugging ideas become more commonplace in other debuggers and support for more programming languages is added. The possibilities that this approach opens up could revolutionize the way we all think of postmortem debugging in the future.

Kernel-Mode Postmortem Debugging

Most of the concepts you've used so far for user-mode postmortem debugging are also applicable to kernel-mode crashes and postmortem analysis of kernel-mode crash dumps. For example, the *!analyze* debugger extension also works in the kernel debugger, though it would give you the details of the kernel bug check in the case of kernel-mode crashes, as opposed to the SEH exception details when used to analyze crash dumps in the user-mode debugger.

The OS also automatically generates crash dumps when the system halts due to a kernel bug check. If you think about it, this is all the more critical in the case of kernel crashes because you won't be able to block the system from rebooting to look at the crash the way you can analyze user-mode crashes using JIT debugging. This is why, unlike automatic user-mode crash-dump generation, which requires the *LocalDumps* registry key, the system's default behavior is to automatically generate kernel-mode crash dumps and save them under a known location so that you have a chance to analyze them once the machine reboots after a system crash.

These settings can be configured in the system-settings control panel item, where you can use the Startup And Recovery dialog box in the Advanced tab to view the default kernel crash-dump generation settings, as illustrated in Figure 4-16.

```
C:\Windows\System32\SystemPropertiesAdvanced.exe
```

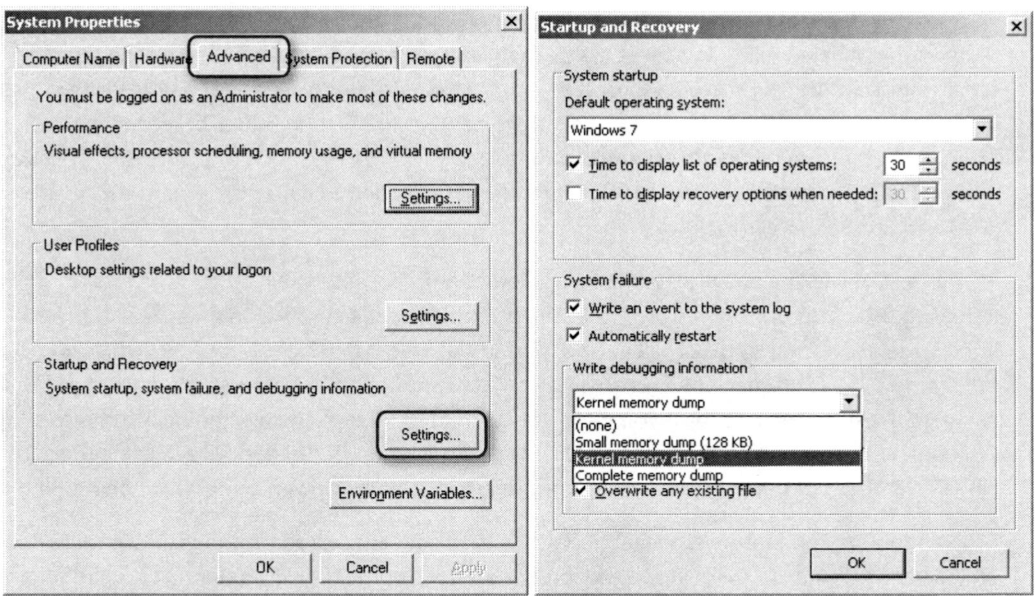

FIGURE 4-16 Automatic kernel-mode crash-dump generation settings (Windows 7).

As you see in the figure, the system is configured by default to automatically reboot when a kernel bug check occurs. In such occurrences, however, the system also generates a crash dump before rebooting and saves it under *%SystemRoot%\memory.dmp,* overwriting any existing dump that was previously saved there. This means that location will always have the last system crash dump.

The different types of kernel-mode crash dumps you can ask the system to generate deserve further explanation because they have different meanings from their user-mode counterparts:

- **Kernel memory dumps** This is the default type that's collected on kernel crashes in Windows 7. It contains the kernel-mode memory pages at the time of the crash, but not any user-mode pages. This means you won't be able to view the user-mode frames in thread call stacks when analyzing these dump files, though it's rare that you would need that information when investigating a kernel bug check.

- **Complete memory dumps** This is the most comprehensive memory dump type. It contains a dump of the entire physical memory (RAM), including resident user-mode pages at the time of the crash. The generated dump file can be quite large, though. For example, on a machine with 1 GB of RAM, the resulting dump will also roughly be about 1 GB large. Note also that this option is not always available (for instance, on computers with 2 GB or more of RAM) in the previous configuration UI.
- **Small memory dumps** This memory dump type is the smallest of the three types. It contains only information about the current process and thread context, the bug check stop code, and the kernel portion of the stack trace that caused the crash.

You can also force a kernel-mode crash-dump generation to occur in a number of ways. If you have a host kernel debugger attached to the target, the *.crash* command can be used to induce a bug check on the target. If you don't have a live kernel debugger, you can simply kill one of the critical system processes (*csrss.exe*, for example) or use a dedicated SysInternals tool (shown in Figure 4-17), which you can find at *http://download.sysinternals.com/files/notmyfault.zip*. This ZIP file also includes the tool's source code, which is actually straightforward because all it does is install a driver that enables it to indirectly induce bug checks from its main user-mode client executable process through this *myfault.sys* helper driver:

```
C:\notmyfault\exe\Release>NotMyfault.exe
```

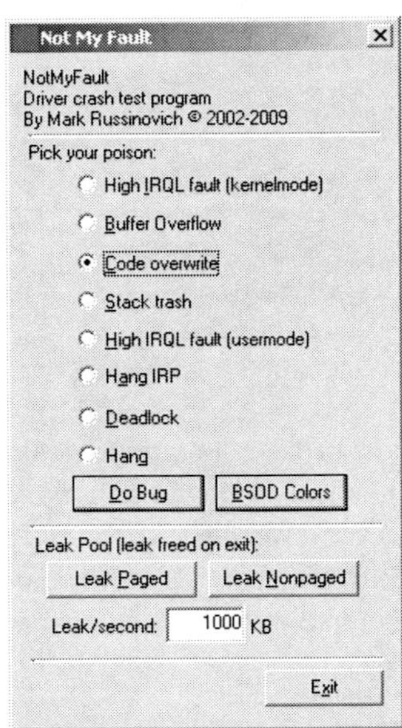

FIGURE 4-17 Inducing a kernel bug check.

As soon as you click Do Bug, the machine hits a bug check and reboots, generating a new crash dump in the process. After you reboot, you can open the saved crash dump by using the usual *–z* command-line option of WinDbg. The debugger will recognize that the dump is a kernel memory dump and, just like in the postmortem user-mode debugging case, the static kernel debugger commands and extensions will be available for you to use in your postmortem analysis, as shown in the following listing.

```
"C:\Program Files\Debugging Tools for Windows (x86)\windbg.exe" -z C:\Windows\MEMORY.DMP
...
Kernel Summary Dump File: Only kernel address space is available

0: kd> .symfix
0: kd> .reload
0: kd> !process -1 0
PROCESS 84d14468  SessionId: 1  Cid: 0e28    Peb: 7ffdf000  ParentCid: 1488
    Image: NotMyfault.exe
0: kd> !analyze -v
*************************************
*        Bugcheck Analysis          *
*************************************
ATTEMPTED_WRITE_TO_READONLY_MEMORY (be)
An attempt was made to write to readonly memory.
...
STACK_TEXT:
97d6db34 82a7d3e8 00000001 82ac6b20 00000000 nt!MmAccessFault+0x106
97d6db34 a3d567c0 00000001 82ac6b20 00000000 nt!KiTrap0E+0xdc
WARNING: Stack unwind information not available. Following frames may be wrong.
97d6dbc4 a3d568ac 851e1c98 00000001 00000000 myfault+0x7c0
97d6dbfc 82a7358e 84d5dc70 84d1d150 84d1d150 myfault+0x8ac
97d6dc14 82c66a31 851e1c98 84d1d150 84d1d1c0 nt!IofCallDriver+0x63
97d6dc34 82c69c03 84d5dc70 851e1c98 00000000 nt!IopSynchronousServiceTail+0x1f8
97d6dcd0 82cb049c 84d5dc70 84d1d150 00000000 nt!IopXxxControlFile+0x6aa
97d6dd04 82a7a1fa 000000a8 00000000 00000000 nt!NtDeviceIoControlFile+0x2a
97d6dd04 775c70b4 000000a8 00000000 00000000 nt!KiFastCallEntry+0x12a
0012f994 00000000 00000000 00000000 00000000 0x775c70b4

IMAGE_NAME:  myfault.sys
...
```

Notice that the stack trace of the thread that crashed shows only the kernel-mode frames, given this was a kernel memory dump (the default option). If this was a complete memory dump, you would also be able to see the user-mode portion of the stack.

Finally, note that you can also use the *.dump* command in the host kernel debugger to generate a *complete memory dump* of a target machine and save its current state without necessarily inducing a crash. You can't generate a *kernel memory dump* using this method, however, because the code that figures out the kernel memory pages to collect isn't available to the debuggers. The only two options from the kernel debugger are either to generate a small memory dump (the */m* option) or create a complete memory dump (the */f* option).

Complete memory dumps are required for any type of postmortem analysis of *soft* hangs, such as deadlocks in user-mode processes. However, they are best induced locally because they can take a very long time to create using the *.dump* command, depending on the type of cabling protocol that you're using to connect the host and target machines. In COM serial port communication (even when virtualized using named pipes), for instance, the slow speed of the protocol can become a major problem when trying to capture a complete memory dump over the debugger. Reading 2 GB of RAM at a maximum speed of 115,200 bits per second can take days to complete! This is an area where 1394 cabling excels. It remains the best protocol available when it comes to capturing complete memory dumps because FireWire supports Direct Memory Access (DMA) to the target machine's physical RAM.

Summary

This chapter offered a hands-on overview of postmortem debugging in Windows. It also covered the very useful JIT debugging mechanism for user-mode processes. After reading this chapter and studying its topics, there's no reason why those familiar, hard-to-reproduce crashes should escape your debugging reach anymore.

Through several experiments in this chapter, you learned a set of complementary techniques you can apply directly when you next encounter a crash in your code or other third-party software. As you wrap up this chapter, the following points are worth a recap:

- JIT debugging is useful when you want to stop a process just as it's about to crash and exit, giving you an opportunity to investigate the root cause of the unhandled exception. The system allows you to specify your native JIT debugger on the machine by using a registry key called *AeDebug*.
- You can set WinDbg as your default JIT debugger by simply running the *windbg.exe /I* command from an elevated administrative command prompt. This is preferred over manually editing the *AeDebug* key in the registry because it takes care of updating both the 32-bit and 64-bit views of the registry when you're running on 64-bit Windows.
- The Visual Studio debugger can also be used as your default native JIT debugger. It gives you the unique ability to perform both source-level .NET JIT debugging and script JIT debugging. Script JIT debugging, in particular, isn't based on SEH exceptions or the *AeDebug* registry key, so it requires intimate collaboration with the Process Debug Manager (PDM) component on the scripting host side, which WinDbg doesn't have.
- You can ask the Windows Error Reporting (WER) components in the system to generate memory dumps and save them to a location of your choice when user-mode processes crash. You can do that by using a registry key called *LocalDumps*. This is useful if you want to save the state of the crash and analyze it in postmortem fashion on a different machine.
- Different forms of user-mode and kernel-mode dumps exist with respective tradeoffs between the size that they occupy on disk and the amount of information that they capture. In user mode, minidumps with *all* flags are the most extensive form (*.dump /ma*), while in kernel mode, complete memory dumps are the largest form of kernel dumps and collect the entire

contents of physical RAM on the machine. In most cases, however, the kernel-only memory dumps that get captured by default on system bug checks are sufficient to investigate those kernel-side crashes.

- You can open dump files in WinDbg by using the *–z* command-line option. The *!analyze* debugger extension is usually your first step when analyzing a native crash dump file. This command works equally well in the kernel debugger. In fact, it also works in live debugging scenarios too!
- Another useful command when analyzing native user-mode crash dumps is the *.ecxr* command, which allows you to change the current thread context to that of the SEH exception and set the CPU registers (most notably, the current stack and instruction pointers) to their values at the time of the initial faulting instruction so that you can see the true call site that triggered the crash.
- Debugging crash dumps of .NET processes in WinDbg requires you to find the SOS extension that matches the CLR version and architecture used in the process that crashed. In addition, it's also best to use the debugger binaries from the same target architecture to analyze managed-code dump files. Once you get past this initial setup hurdle and can successfully execute SOS commands, the *!pe* command allows you to easily find the chain of exceptions that was responsible for the crash of the process.
- Starting with .NET 4.0 and Visual Studio 2010, you are also able to perform source-level postmortem debugging of .NET crash dumps using Visual Studio.
- In dump debugging investigations, remember to form a set of hypotheses about what might have led to the crash and validate their plausibility by looking at information from the memory dump, such as the values of global variables or the state of threads in the process relative to each other at the time of the crash. In the case of complete system memory dumps, you also have the ability to look at the state of other processes, which can be useful when interprocess communication such as COM or Remote Procedure Calls (RPCs) are at play. More important, understanding that dump debugging calls for a different mindset from what you're used to in regular live debugging is often the first step in successful crash-dump investigations.

CHAPTER 5

Beyond the Basics

In this chapter

Now that you're familiar with the Microsoft Windows debugger types and the system foundations that support their basic mechanisms, it's time to move beyond the basics and examine some additional features and strategies that are often needed for carrying out successful debugging investigations. After covering a few advanced debugger capabilities, this chapter introduces the important Global Flags editor tool (GFLAGS) and the debugging hooks in the Windows operating system that it allows you to control. As you'll see in practical case studies in the chapters that follow in this part of the book, these hooks can be particularly helpful to track down common code defects, including heap corruptions, memory leaks, and many more insidious bugs.

Noninvasive Debugging

You can use noninvasive debugging to inspect a memory snapshot of the target process without fully attaching to it as a user-mode debugger. WinDbg supports this convenient feature, which can be useful when a second debugger—such as the Microsoft Visual Studio debugger—is already used to actively debug the target. In that case, you can attach an instance of WinDbg in noninvasive mode and inspect a snapshot of the process virtual memory, with all the power of the WinDbg debugging environment. Once you are done observing the target, you can then detach WinDbg and go back to controlling it using the original debugger. This enables you to use WinDbg alongside the Visual Studio debugger and take advantage of their respective strengths at the same time.

In noninvasive debugging, the debugger doesn't receive any debug events from the target process, so it can't control it in this mode. Instead, the debugger simply suspends the threads in the target and executes the static debugger commands you enter, allowing you to inspect and modify the virtual address space of the target process. Commands used for tasks such as stack back-tracing (*k** commands), inspecting register and memory values (*dd*, *db*, and so on), or modifying process memory (*ed*, *eb*, and so on) are all supported. You can even generate memory dumps for later analysis by using the *.dump* command. What the debugger isn't able to do is actively control the target in this mode, so you won't be able to set breakpoints or let the target continue its execution. In this sense, the noninvasive form of user-mode debugging is similar to the live form of kernel-mode debugging introduced back in Chapter 2, "Getting Started," only the target machine isn't frozen in the case of live kernel debugging.

A noninvasive debugging session can be started by using the Attach To Process menu action in the *windbg.exe* user interface (UI) (the F6 shortcut) and selecting the Noninvasive option at the bottom of the Attach dialog box, as shown in Figure 5-1. Alternatively, you can use the *–pv* command-line option of WinDbg to achieve the same goal (as you'll shortly see in this section).

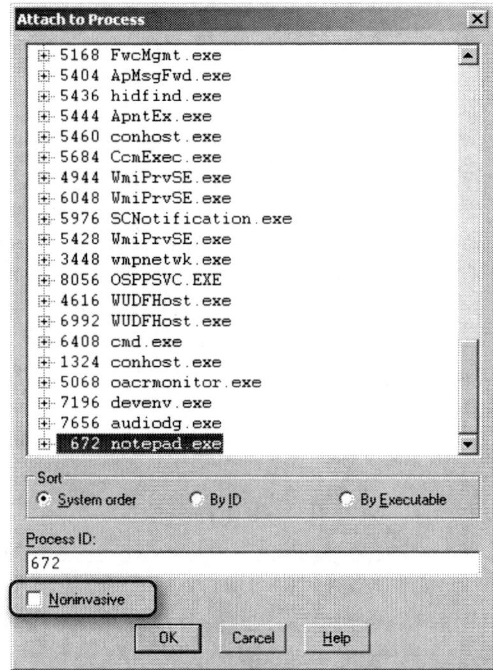

FIGURE 5-1 Using WinDbg for noninvasive user-mode debugging.

When a process is being debugged using a user-mode debugger, the system sets a field in the target process environment block (PEB) structure to reflect that fact. Using the *!peb* debugger command, which dumps the contents of the PEB structure of the target process, you can see this *BeingDebugged* field is *false* in noninvasive debugging sessions, meaning the target isn't really considered by the Windows operating system (OS) to be under the control of a debugger in that case.

This is demonstrated in the following listing, where *windbg.exe* is used as a noninvasive debugger for a running instance of *notepad.exe*.

```
C:\Program Files\Debugging Tools for Windows (x86)>start notepad
C:\Program Files\Debugging Tools for Windows (x86)>windbg.exe -pv -pn notepad.exe
0:000> .symfix
0:000> .reload
0:000> !peb
PEB at 7ffdb000
    BeingDebugged:            No
    CurrentDirectory:  'C:\Program Files\Debugging Tools for Windows (x86)\'
    ImageFile:    'C:\Windows\system32\notepad.exe'
...
0:000> g
     ^ No runnable debuggees error in 'g'
```

After you are done inspecting the target noninvasively, you can detach from it using the *qd* ("quit and detach") command, which lets the target out of the suspended state. Also, using the *q* command to exit a noninvasive debugging session doesn't terminate the target as it does in regular user-mode debugging, so it's equivalent to the *qd* command in this case.

```
0:000> qd
```

Note It is possible to fully attach *windbg.exe* to a user-mode process even when that process is already being debugged. This can be done by using the *–pe* command-line option when you attach the second WinDbg instance, as illustrated in the following sequence. Make sure you close all existing instances of *notepad.exe* before you execute these steps so that the *–pn* option used to attach to a process by name will not complain about the existence of more than one instance of that process.

```
---- run notepad.exe under the first debugger ----
windbg.exe notepad.exe

---- "Regular" attach attempt fails: notepad.exe is already being debugged ----
windbg.exe -pn notepad.exe
Cannot debug pid 1768, NTSTATUS 0xC0000048
    "An attempt to set a process's DebugPort or ExceptionPort was made, but a port already
exists in the process or an attempt to set an ALPC port's associated completion port was
made, but it is already set."

---- "/pe" attach succeeds despite the first debugger ----
windbg.exe -pe -pn notepad.exe
```

Unlike the *–pv* (noninvasive attach) option, though, the *–pe* (existing debug port attach) option is meant for scenarios where the first debugger instance freezes or stops working and isn't guaranteed to work reliably when the first debugger is still operational. This is because both debugger instances will then be competing for the debug events emitted by the target process. For example, a code breakpoint inserted using one debugger instance could end up being handled by the other one!

Data Breakpoints

Data breakpoints can be particularly useful when debugging conditions where it isn't *a priori* obvious how a given variable in the program is getting modified. This book contains several examples where this technique proves particularly effective in trying to answer questions such as who is responsible for changing the value of a variable or a field within a data structure. You've in fact already seen an application of this technique back in Chapter 2, where you used a data breakpoint to take full advantage of the global system scope provided by kernel-mode debugging and were able to find out that the *notepad.exe* main UI thread was being unblocked by new messages received from the kernel-mode portion of the Windows subsystem (*win32k.sys*).

In WinDbg, the *ba* ("break on access") debugger command is used to set data breakpoints that monitor when the specified memory location is either read from, written to, or executed by the processor. This last category of breakpoints (execution data breakpoints) is similar in effect to code breakpoints, even though they're implemented in a fundamentally different way by the operating system and CPU, as you'll shortly see.

As an illustration for how to use this command, the following debugger listing uses the *ba* command to set an execution (*e*) data breakpoint to be raised whenever the virtual address (*1*, which indicates a 1-byte range) referenced by the symbolic name *ntdll!NtCreateFile* is executed by the processor, which is essentially equivalent to a code breakpoint (*bp*) in this particular case.

```
0:000> vercommand
command line: '"c:\Program Files\Debugging Tools for Windows (x86)\windbg.exe"  c:\Windows\
system32\notepad.exe'
0:000> .symfix
0:000> .reload
0:000> bp notepad!WinMain
0:000> g
Breakpoint 0 hit
notepad!WinMain:
0:000> ba e1 ntdll!NtCreateFile
0:000> g
Breakpoint 1 hit
ntdll!NtCreateFile:
0:000> k
ChildEBP RetAddr
001bf028 751da939 ntdll!NtCreateFile
001bf0cc 769e03de KERNELBASE!CreateFileW+0x35e
...
0:000> $ Terminate this debugging session...
0:000> q
```

Similarly, the following listing shows a read (*r*) data breakpoint, which will be hit each time the processor executes a read instruction from the address (4 bytes in the case of a 32-bit processor) of a global variable in the *ntdll.dll* module.

```
0:000> vercommand
command line: '"c:\Program Files\Debugging Tools for Windows (x86)\windbg.exe"  c:\Windows\
system32\notepad.exe'
0:000> .symfix
```

```
0:000> .reload
0:000> bp notepad!WinMain
0:000> g
Breakpoint 0 hit
notepad!WinMain:
0:000> x ntdll!g_*
7763d968 ntdll!g_dwLastErrorToBreakOn = <no type information>
...
0:000> ba r4 7763d968
0:000> g
Breakpoint 1 hit
ntdll!RtlSetLastWin32Error+0x11:
0:000> k
ChildEBP RetAddr
0022f6f0 759b6b65 ntdll!RtlSetLastWin32Error+0x11
0022f700 759b91b5 KERNELBASE!BaseSetLastNTError+0x18
0022f748 759b88ca KERNELBASE!GetModuleHandleForUnicodeString+0xa1
0022fbc0 759bd15f KERNELBASE!BasepGetModuleHandleExW+0x181
0022fbdc 7690219d KERNELBASE!GetModuleHandleExW+0x2b
0022fc78 769009db ole32!IsRunningInRPCSS+0x75
0022fc90 002a143a ole32!CoInitializeEx+0x79
0022fcc4 002a16ec notepad!WinMain+0x35
...
0:000> $ Terminate this debugging session...
0:000> q
```

Deep Inside User-Mode and Kernel-Mode Data Breakpoints

In the previous examples, you might have noticed that you had to advance to the main entry point of the program first before you could add your data breakpoints. As it turns out, the debugger won't allow you to insert such breakpoints during the post-process initialization breakpoint that you see when you first execute a process under the WinDbg user-mode debugger, as demonstrated in the following listing.

```
0:000> vercommand
command line: '"c:\Program Files\Debugging Tools for Windows (x86)\windbg.exe"  notepad'
0:000> .symfix
0:000> .reload
0:000> x ntdll!*tobreak*
76fbd968 ntdll!g_dwLastErrorToBreakOn = <no type information>
0:000> ba r4 76fbd968
        ^ Unable to set breakpoint error
The system resets thread contexts after the process
breakpoint so hardware breakpoints cannot be set.
Go to the executable's entry point and set it then.
 'ba r4 76fbd968'
0:000> q
```

So, why is the debugger talking about thread contexts or *hardware* breakpoints here? To understand this, you need to go deeper and learn how data breakpoints are internally implemented by the system. Unlike code breakpoints, which are implemented in software by modifying the target memory in-place and inserting the *int 3* debug break instruction (as you saw in Chapter 3, "How Windows Debuggers Work"), data breakpoints do not change the code in memory and instead use dedicated CPU *debug registers* to implement their functionality. This is why data breakpoints are also called *hardware* breakpoints.

Both the *x86* and *x64* families of processors have eight debug registers, named DR0, DR1, and so on, through DR7. However, only the first four registers can be used for storing the memory location (virtual address) of a data breakpoint. DR4 and DR5 are reserved registers. The DR6 and DR7 registers deserve more explanation because, though they aren't used to directly hold data breakpoints, they're used to help track the breakpoints set using the first four debug registers. More specifically, DR6 is a status register whose bits are context-dependent and provide the debuggers with more information about certain exceptions. For example, the single-step bit mask (0x4000) is used to determine whether the received debug event is raised in response to a single-step exception or a data breakpoint because they are both raised with the STATUS_SINGLE_STEP Structured Exception Handling (SEH) exception code. DR6 also contains other bits to indicate which one of the four possible data breakpoints was hit, which is precisely why the DR6 register is called the *debug status register*. Finally, DR7 is called the *debug control register* and is used to track global information about the CPU data breakpoints, including whether the breakpoints stored in DR0, DR1, DR2, and DR3 are enabled or disabled and also the type (read/write or execute) of each of the four breakpoints. Figure 5-2 recaps the available debug registers and their respective roles.

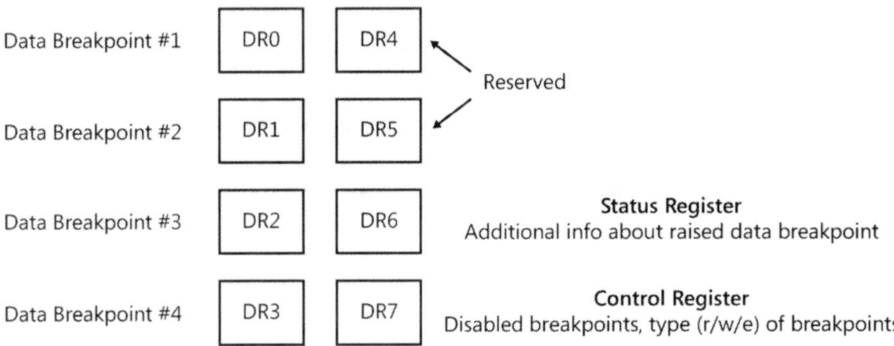

FIGURE 5-2 CPU debug registers and data breakpoints.

Be aware that the CPU debug registers (as well as other registers) are saved as part of the user-mode thread context so that when the thread is switched onto the CPU for execution, the values saved in its thread context are loaded into the physical CPU registers, providing the thread with the same context it had when its execution was preempted earlier by the operating system.

When a data breakpoint is set inside a user-mode debugger in particular, the debugger enumerates all the threads inside the target process and calls the *kernel32!SetThreadContext* Win32 function for each one of them to set the appropriate DR register values. Data breakpoints set inside a kernel-mode debugger are implemented similarly, except they get saved in a special field of the processor control block (PRCB)—a structure used by the operating system to store per-processor information—so that they also can get applied to new threads created on the target machine.

This explains why data breakpoints applied inside a user-mode debugger are visible only in that particular debugging session despite the fact that the debug registers are global (per CPU). Because the thread contexts in other user-mode processes won't be affected by the data breakpoints inserted in other user-mode debugging sessions, those breakpoints will be visible only when the CPU switches to the threads of the target process in those sessions. This results in exactly the behavior you would expect—namely, that data breakpoints from a user-mode debugger are visible only within the target process in that debugging session.

In addition, data breakpoints defined inside a user-mode debugger do not interfere with those defined in the kernel-mode debugger. The user-mode debugger always resets the contexts of the threads in its target process, so data breakpoints defined inside the kernel-mode debugger are never seen in any user-mode debugger instances on the target machine. This explains why the debugger didn't let you set data breakpoints during the early NTDLL post-process initialization breakpoint, because they would end up being cleared by the user-mode debugger.

Clearing Kernel-Mode Data Breakpoints

When hardware breakpoints are used in the kernel-mode debugger, they sometimes have a tendency to stick around even after they get cleared by the user using the *bc* debugger command. The reason for this is that although the *bc* command does indeed clear the breakpoints in the kernel-mode debugger itself, some threads on the target machine might have cached the data breakpoints in their contexts; when the target resumes, those threads appear to retain the breakpoint when they get to run on the CPU after the *g* command. For example, if you set a data breakpoint at a common function, such as the *user32!GetMessageW* API used in the message loop of every user-mode GUI application, you can see that it sometimes survives past the *bc* command, as illustrated in the following listing.

```
0: kd> $ Switch to a process context that has the DLL loaded (for example: explorer.exe)
0: kd> !process 0 0 explorer.exe
PROCESS 866188d8  SessionId: 1  Cid: 0608    Peb: 7ffdf000  ParentCid: 0ccc
    Image: explorer.exe
0: kd> .process /i 866188d8
0: kd> g
Break instruction exception - code 80000003 (first chance)
0: kd> .reload /user
kd> x user32!GetMessageW
76348f97 USER32!GetMessageW = <no type information>
0: kd> ba e1 USER32!GetMessageW
0: kd> $ Data breakpoints are raised as STATUS_SINGLE_STEP SEH exceptions
0: kd> g
Single step exception - code 80000004 (first chance)
USER32!GetMessageW:
0: kd> g
Single step exception - code 80000004 (first chance)
USER32!GetMessageW:
0: kd> bl
 0 e 76348f97 e 1 0001 (0001) USER32!GetMessageW
0: kd> $ Now clear the data breakpoint...
0: kd> bc 0
```

```
0: kd> g
Single step exception - code 80000004 (first chance)
USER32!GetMessageW:
0: kd> $ Notice you're still hitting the breakpoint even though bl shows an empty
0: kd> $  breakpoints list
0: kd> bl
```

Because you now know that data breakpoints are saved in the processor debug registers, however, you can quickly get yourself out of this predicament and forcibly clear the data breakpoint by manually resetting the debug register using the *r* debugger command directly, as shown in the following listing.

```
0: kd> $ Notice that the DR0 register is still set to the address of user32!GetMessageW
0: kd> r dr0
dr0=76348f97
0: kd> $ Reset the data breakpoint and disable breakpoints in the control register too
0: kd> r dr0=0
0: kd> r dr7=0
0: kd> g
```

Execution Data Breakpoints vs. Code Breakpoints

Execution data breakpoints can be used as an alternative to code (software) breakpoints. Despite data breakpoints (*ba*) being in limited supply (a maximum of four), they can prove a better choice than software breakpoints (*bp*, *bu*, or *bm*), specifically during kernel-mode debugging.

Code breakpoints are inserted as a debug break instruction into the target code page in memory by the user-mode or kernel-mode debuggers. A subtle problem with the way code breakpoints in the kernel-mode debugging case are implemented happens when a code page is made private to a process because of the *copy-on-write* OS mechanism. When a user-mode debugger is used to debug a process on the target machine of a kernel-mode debugging session, and both the user-mode and kernel-mode debuggers attempt to insert a code breakpoint into the same memory location relative to that process, the extra private code page created by the user-mode debugger's attempt to insert a code breakpoint might not be tracked correctly by the kernel-mode debugger when it inserts or removes its own copy of the code breakpoint. For this reason, data breakpoints are usually more reliable than code breakpoints in kernel debugging sessions.

Another issue is that code breakpoint addresses are interpreted relative to the current process context during a kernel debugging session, which is unlikely to be that of the process of interest after you break into the host kernel debugger. To illustrate this point, consider the following example that has an instance of the *notepad.exe* process already running on the target machine. After you break into the kernel-mode debugger, try to set a software breakpoint in code that is private to that *notepad.exe* process, as shown in the following listing.

```
kd> $ Notice that you are not in the NOTEPAD process here!
kd> !process -1 0
PROCESS 84a2dab0  SessionId: none  Cid: 0004    Peb: 00000000  ParentCid: 0000
    Image: System
```

```
kd> !process 0 0 notepad.exe
PROCESS 89a2b030  SessionId: 1  Cid: 02e0    Peb: 7ffdb000  ParentCid: 0d10
    Image: notepad.exe
kd> $ This only loads the user-mode symbols for notepad.exe. The target is still frozen
kd> .process /r /p 89a2b030
kd> !process 89a2b030 7
PROCESS 89a2b030  SessionId: 1  Cid: 02e0    Peb: 7ffdb000  ParentCid: 0d10
    Image: notepad.exe...
        0006f860 00e3148a USER32!GetMessageW+0x33
        0006f8a0 00e316ec notepad!WinMain+0xe6
        0006f930 76f21174 notepad!__mainCRTStartup+0x140
...
kd> u 00e3148a
notepad!WinMain+0xe6
00e3148a 85c0            test    eax,eax
00e3148c 0f8453050000    je      notepad!WinMain+0xea (00e319e5)
kd> bp 00e3148a
kd> g
```

Notice how you get no hits for the breakpoint even after moving the main *notepad.exe* window on the target machine, which should certainly have sent a message to the main UI thread's message loop and caused your breakpoint to be reached! Because *0x00e3148a* probably did not represent a valid virtual address (or, more likely, mapped to a random address) in the current process context, the breakpoint insertion actually failed. If you repeat the same experiment, but instead use a data breakpoint this time, you'll see that the breakpoint is successfully hit.

```
kd> ba e1 00e3148a
kd> g
Single step exception - code 80000004 (first chance)
notepad!WinMain+0xe6:
kd> !process -1 0
PROCESS 89a2b030  SessionId: 1  Cid: 02e0    Peb: 7ffdb000  ParentCid: 0d10
    Image: notepad.exe
```

If you really wanted a software breakpoint in this case, you could have used the *.process /i* command first, of course, as detailed back in Chapter 2 to let the target machine run and break right back inside the *notepad.exe* process context before inserting the code breakpoint.

The advantage to using an execution data breakpoint over a code breakpoint is that you don't have to let the target machine run (even for the very short time it takes to handle an invasive process context switch) before you are able to insert the breakpoint. For the sake of brevity, some kernel-mode debugging experiments in this book use execution data breakpoints (*ba e1*) in place of code breakpoints (*bp*, *bu*, or *bm*) to avoid the extra step. The drawback to data breakpoints is that the breakpoint might also get hit by unrelated code from other processes if it happens to get loaded by chance at the same virtual address, though you can use the */p* option of the *ba* command to further restrict the scope of the data breakpoint to a specific process, just as you are able to do with the *bp* command.

User-Mode Debugger Data Breakpoints in Action: C++ Global Objects and the C Runtime Library

To demonstrate the value of data breakpoints, consider what happens when the C runtime library (CRT) is used in a C++ program: the entry point of the executable module ends up being provided by the CRT during the compilation process. This generic entry point performs additional CRT initialization steps before actually invoking the user-provided main function of the program. To see this in action, you can use the following C++ sample program from the companion source code, which you can compile using the procedure described back in the Introduction of this book.

```
//
// C:\book\code\chapter_05\CrtCleanup>main.cpp
//
class CBuffer :
    CZeroInit<CBuffer>
{
public:
    HRESULT
    Init()
    {
        // ...
    }

private:
    CAutoPtr<BYTE> m_spFirstBuffer;
    CAutoPtr<BYTE> m_spSecondBuffer;
    static const BUFFER_SIZE = 1024;
};

class CMainApp
{
public:
    HRESULT
    MainHR(
        VOID
        )
    {
        ChkProlog();

        wprintf(L"Initializing Global C++ Object...\n");
        ChkHr(g_buffer.Init());

        ChkNoCleanup();
    }

private:
    static CBuffer g_buffer;
};
CBuffer CMainApp::g_buffer;
```

Under a user-mode debugger, you'll see that the true entry point to the program is a generic function called *__wmainCRTStartup*, which is supplied by the CRT and wraps the user-provided entry point function.

```
0:000> vercommand
command line: '"c:\Program Files\Debugging Tools for Windows (x86)\windbg.exe"
c:\book\code\chapter_05\CrtCleanup\objfre_win7_x86\i386\crtcleanup.exe'
0:000> .symfix
0:000> .reload
0:000> bp wmain
0:000> g
Breakpoint 0 hit
crtcleanup!wmain:
0:000> k
ChildEBP RetAddr
0019f9bc 00d017d8 crtcleanup!wmain
0019fa00 75883677 crtcleanup!__wmainCRTStartup+0x102
0019fa0c 77cd9f02 kernel32!BaseThreadInitThunk+0xe
0019fa4c 77cd9ed5 ntdll32!__RtlUserThreadStart+0x70
0019fa64 00000000 ntdll32!_RtlUserThreadStart+0x1b
0:000> q
```

One of the important jobs that the CRT main function takes care of is calling the constructors and destructors of all the C++ global and static objects in the executable module, which you can confirm by using a data breakpoint. In the previous example, a global C++ object called *g_buffer* is used by the program. That object doesn't have an explicit destructor, so you won't be able to use a source-level code breakpoint to see when it gets invoked (though you could still set a code breakpoint directly at *crtcleanup!CBuffer::~CBuffer* in the debugger's command window). That being said, you also know that the default destructor inserted by the compiler eventually needs to free the two smart-pointer member objects that the class has. This means that a data write access will be performed to those memory locations when the destructor for *g_buffer* is called, so a data breakpoint can be used to break into the debugger whenever the global object's destructor is called. This is illustrated in the following listing.

```
0:000> vercommand
command line: '"c:\Program Files\Debugging Tools for Windows (x86)\windbg.exe"
c:\book\code\chapter_05\CrtCleanup\objfre_win7_x86\i386\crtcleanup.exe'
0:000> .symfix
0:000> .reload
0:000> bp wmain
0:000> g
Breakpoint 0 hit
crtcleanup!wmain:
0:000> x crtcleanup!*g_buffer*
008c303c crtcleanup!CMainApp::g_buffer = class CBuffer
008c10ac crtcleanup!CMainApp::g_buffer$initializer$ = 0x008c1e1d
008c1e59 crtcleanup!'dynamic atexit destructor for 'CMainApp::g_buffer'' (void)
008c1e1d crtcleanup!'dynamic initializer for 'CMainApp::g_buffer'' (void)
0:000> dt crtcleanup!CMainApp::g_buffer
   +0x000 m_spFirstBuffer  : ATL::CAutoPtr<unsigned char>
   +0x004 m_spSecondBuffer : ATL::CAutoPtr<unsigned char>
   =008c0000 BUFFER_SIZE      : 0x905a4d
```

```
0:000> $ The default C++ destructor for g_buffer will also call the destructor of the
0:000> $ m_spSecondBuffer field member, for example, so set a "write" data breakpoint there
0:000> ba w4 0x008c303c+4
0:000> $ The first breakpoint hit is the Init call in MainHR, so skip it...
0:000> g
Breakpoint 1 hit
crtcleanup!CBuffer::Init+0x57:
0:000> $ The second breakpoint hit happens during process shutdown
0:000> g
Breakpoint 1 hit
crtcleanup!CBuffer::~CBuffer+0x11:
0:000> k
ChildEBP RetAddr
0017fabc 7603c3e9 crtcleanup!CBuffer::~CBuffer+0x11
0017faf0 760436bb msvcrt!_cinit+0xc1
0017fb04 008c1787 msvcrt!exit+0x11
0017fb40 75ea3677 crtcleanup!__wmainCRTStartup+0x118
0017fb4c 77069f02 kernel32!BaseThreadInitThunk+0xe
0017fb8c 77069ed5 ntdll!__RtlUserThreadStart+0x70
0017fba4 00000000 ntdll!_RtlUserThreadStart+0x1b
0:000> g
ntdll!NtTerminateProcess+0x12:
7704fc52 83c404          add     esp,4
0:000> q
```

You can see that the CRT main function calls *msvcrt!exit*, which destroys the C++ global objects prior to the process shutting down. Note, however, that the destructors for global C++ objects are called only when performing a regular process shutdown and this cleanup doesn't get a chance to run when the process is abruptly stopped using the *TerminateProcess* Win32 API, such as when the *kill.exe* utility is used to forcibly terminate a process instance. You can verify this because the data breakpoint used in the previous experiment isn't hit in that case. Though the memory won't be leaked as the process disappears along with all of its associated resources, invariants might get broken and your program needs to account for that when it starts up again (executing any necessary recovery steps), given that you can't depend on C++ destructors running all the time before your process exits.

Kernel-Mode Debugger Data Breakpoints in Action: Waiting for a Process to Exit

At the heart of the Windows concurrency model is the ability for threads to wait on a set of *dispatcher objects* to become signaled. Threads, processes, events, semaphores, and mutexes are all examples of kernel dispatcher objects in the Windows operating system. A user-mode application is able to wait on any of these objects to become *signaled* by using the generic *WaitForSingleObject(Ex)* Win32 API to wait for a single object, or the *WaitForMultipleObjects(Ex)* Win32 API when having to instead wait for a set of dispatcher objects to become signaled at the same time.

Note that even though the Win32 API offers this consistent scheme for true waiting in Windows, each kernel dispatcher object has its own semantics for when it gets signaled or reset. A semaphore, for instance, is automatically signaled by the kernel when its internal count drops to 0 while an event object becomes signaled only when explicitly set by a thread of execution. Similarly, a process object is also automatically signaled by the OS when its last thread of execution exits. This is why you're able to wait on a process termination event in Windows by directly using the user-mode handle to the process object. The following kernel debugger listing uses the *dt* ("dump type") command to show the header structure shared by all the dispatcher objects in the system and its internal *SignalState* field, which is used internally to keep track of the signal state of the object.

```
0: kd> .symfix
0: kd> .reload
0: kd> $ Event object
0: kd> dt nt!_KEVENT
   +0x000 Header           : _DISPATCHER_HEADER
0: kd> $ Mutex object
0: kd> dt nt!_KMUTANT
   +0x000 Header           : _DISPATCHER_HEADER
   +0x010 MutantListEntry  : _LIST_ENTRY
   +0x018 OwnerThread      : Ptr32 _KTHREAD
   +0x01c Abandoned        : UChar
   +0x01d ApcDisable       : UChar
0: kd> $ Semaphore object
0: kd> dt nt!_KSEMAPHORE
   +0x000 Header           : _DISPATCHER_HEADER
   +0x010 Limit            : Int4B
0: kd> $ Process object
0: kd> dt nt!_KPROCESS
   +0x000 Header           : _DISPATCHER_HEADER
...
0: kd> $ Common dispatcher header structure
0: kd> dt nt!_DISPATCHER_HEADER
   +0x000 Type             : UChar
   +0x004 SignalState      : Int4B
...
```

To watch how process objects get signaled in Windows, you can again use a data breakpoint. The key here is that all dispatcher objects track their signal state as part of their kernel object header structure, so you know the *SignalState* field has to be accessed (modified) by code in the operating system's kernel when the object gets signaled. Because the dispatcher objects are signaled in kernel mode, you need a kernel debugging session. Start a *notepad.exe* process instance on the target machine of this session, and then set a data breakpoint to track down when its corresponding process object gets signaled. Notice that, initially, the process object isn't signaled (the signal state is *0*) because it's still running on the target machine.

```
kd> !process 0 0 notepad.exe
PROCESS 892d7030  SessionId: 1  Cid: 0b2c    Peb: 7ffd4000  ParentCid: 0a30
    Image: notepad.exe
kd> $ the notepad.exe process object is not signaled
kd> dt nt!_KPROCESS 892d7030 Header.SignalState
   +0x000 Header            :
      +0x004 SignalState         : 0n0
kd> ba w4 892d7030+4
kd> g
```

If you now close the previous *notepad.exe* instance on the target machine, you immediately break into the host kernel debugger with the following stack trace, whether the termination was orderly (by using the Alt+F4 shortcut, for example) or abrupt through the use of the *TerminateProcess* Win32 API (by using the *kill.exe* utility, for example).

```
Breakpoint 0 hit
kd> k
ChildEBP RetAddr
97c81c88 82855d61 nt!KeSetProcess+0x59
97c81cfc 8286ed37 nt!PspExitThread+0x6c2
97c81d24 8265047a nt!NtTerminateProcess+0x1fa
97c81d24 776664f4 nt!KiFastCallEntry+0x12a
001bfdb0 00000000 ntdll!KiFastSystemCallRet
kd> dt nt!_KPROCESS 892d7030 Header.SignalState
   +0x000 Header              :
      +0x004 SignalState         : 0n1
kd> bc 0
kd> g
```

As you see in the preceding call stack, process objects are signaled by the kernel when their last thread exits as part of their run-down code path. Notice the call to *nt!PspExitThread* in the previous call stack, where the process object is signaled as its main, and last, thread exits.

Advanced Example: Who Is Changing a Registry Value?

Data breakpoints can be used whenever there is a need to break inside the debugger just as a memory location of interest is about to be manipulated (that is, executed, read, or written into). In the example described in this section, this strategy will be applied beyond its common usage pattern of monitoring when program variables are modified to answer the following question: why does a registry value change as a result of running a given test scenario?

Although this particular experiment is more of a pedantic exercise than a practical need, it has the side benefit of showcasing the use of the *!reg* debugger extension command, which is especially useful in postmortem debugging scenarios when trying to extract registry values from a kernel-mode memory dump. In practice, though, you usually will prefer to answer this question using a tracing tool, such as the Process Monitor tool from the SysInternals suite or the Windows Performance Toolkit (WPT) covered later in this book, which both allow you to monitor registry access events in the system. Having said that, you can also use a kernel debugger to solve this problem.

When using the kernel debugger, you can inspect kernel-mode memory, including the in-memory representation of the loaded registry hives and keys. The first task is to determine the location where the registry value you are interested in monitoring resides in memory. Once you know that, it's easy to set a write data breakpoint, run the scenario that modifies the value on the target machine, and watch with satisfaction as you break into the host kernel debugger just as the registry value is about to get modified.

The various options of the *!reg* debugger extension command refer to terms such as *hives*, *bins*, *cells*, and *key nodes*. These are all concepts that the kernel configuration manager (CM) uses to represent the registry contents on disk, as summarized in Table 5-1.

TABLE 5-1 Important Windows Registry Storage Concepts

Term	Description
Hive	A logical grouping of keys, subkeys, and registry values persisted to disk as a binary file. The OS registry is composed of a collection of hives.
Bin	Each hive is partitioned into fixed-sized (4-KB) blocks called bins.
Cell	Cells are variable-length containers that hold the data stored in the registry hives. There are different types of cells, each representing a possible container: a registry value, a registry key, a subkey or value list, or a key's security descriptor. Because cells have variable lengths, they're referenced using what is called a cell index.
Cell index	A cell index represents an offset to a cell element in a given registry hive. The configuration manager translates cell indices to the location of their cells using two levels of indirection, much in the same way that the memory manager maps virtual memory to physical memory addresses.

At the memory-representation level, open registry keys are maintained by the kernel's configuration manager in a global hash table so that it can quickly determine if a requested key needs to be loaded or if it has already been retrieved. In the latter case, it simply returns an additional reference to its object. Each open key in the table is represented in memory using a helper data structure called KCB, or *Key Control Block*. This structure contains a lot of useful information about the key, such as its reference count, name, cell index, containing hive, last write time, security descriptor, and much more. It is also typically where you start your scan of kernel memory to find the virtual memory addresses of registry values. The following live kernel debugger listing shows the fields of the KCB data structure in the OS.

```
lkd> dt nt!_CM_KEY_CONTROL_BLOCK
   +0x000 RefCount         : Uint4B ...
   +0x014 KeyHive          : Ptr32 _HHIVE
   +0x018 KeyCell          : Uint4B ...
   +0x02c NameBlock        : Ptr32 _CM_NAME_CONTROL_BLOCK
   +0x030 CachedSecurity   : Ptr32 _CM_KEY_SECURITY_CACHE ...
   +0x058 KcbLastWriteTime : _LARGE_INTEGER
...
```

In the following example, you'll see how you can monitor changes to the *Auto* registry value under the *AeDebug* native JIT debugger registry key by using a data breakpoint in the kernel debugger. For this experiment to work, this key should first be loaded into memory, so make sure you open it at least once on the target machine (for example, using the *regedit.exe* tool). You can now use the *openkeys* option of the *!reg* debugger command to list all the registry keys that have been loaded to memory on the target machine to this point (which is tracked as part of a global hash table in the kernel configuration manager). The output from this command is often relatively large (because it includes all open keys on the target!), so you can also use *.logopen* and *.logclose* around the command to save its output into a text file that you can then easily search using a text editor such as *notepad.exe*.

```
0: kd> .logopen c:\temp\log.txt
0: kd> !reg openkeys
0: kd> .logclose
```

By searching the output log.txt file from the previous listing for occurrences of *AeDebug*, you'll find an entry that describes that open key, along with its cell index and KCB.

```
Hive: \REGISTRY\MACHINE\SOFTWARE
...
   293ad50e kcb=a7075788 cell=00286ce0 f=00200000 \REGISTRY\MACHINE\SOFTWARE\MICROSOFT\WINDOWS
NT\CURRENTVERSION\AEDEBUG
```

The KCB memory address obtained from the preceding search, in particular, has all the information you need about the *AeDebug* key, which you can dump by using the *!reg* command again.

```
0: kd> !reg kcb a7075788
Key              : \REGISTRY\MACHINE\SOFTWARE\MICROSOFT\WINDOWS NT\CURRENTVERSION\AEDEBUG
RefCount         : 2
Flags            : CompressedName,
ExtFlags         :
Parent           : 0x93f35a08
KeyHive          : 0x8cfd8640
KeyCell          : 0x286ce0 [cell index]
...
```

Given a cell index and a hive, you can use the *!reg* command to get to the actual virtual address of the cell (called *pcell* by this debugger extension), as illustrated in the following debugger command.

```
0: kd> !reg cellindex 0x8cfd8640 0x286ce0
Map = 8f0fa000 Type = 0 Table = 1 Block = 86 Offset = ce0
MapTable     = 8f0fd000
BlockAddress = 8f806000
pcell:  8f806ce4
```

This is the address of the *AeDebug* key node in memory. (Notice it is a kernel-mode memory address.) From this address, you can list the values under the key by using the *valuelist* option of the *!reg* command, which takes the hive and key node addresses as parameters.

```
0: kd> !reg valuelist 0x8cfd8640 0x8f806ce4
Dumping ValueList of Key <AeDebug> :
[Idx]      [ValAddr]      [ValueName]
[    0]    8f9a6da4       Debugger
[    1]    8f9a6dec       Auto
 Use '!reg kvalue <ValAddr>' to dump the value
```

As expected, there are two values under the *AeDebug* key. The *Debugger* string (REG_SZ) value can be found by following the address of the key value provided by the previous command.

```
0: kd> !reg kvalue 8f9a6da4
Signature: CM_KEY_VALUE_SIGNATURE (kv)
Name      : Debugger {compressed}
DataLength: 6c
```

```
Data       : 1ce13f0  [cell index]
Type       : 1
0: kd> !reg cellindex 0x8cfd8640  1ce13f0
pcell:  916613f4
0: kd> du 916613f4
916613f4  ""c:\Windows\system32\vsjitdebugg"
91661434  "er.exe" -p %ld -e %ld"
```

Similarly, you can also find the address where the *Auto* value is located in memory. The only difference compared to the *Debugger* value is that the *Auto* value is stored directly in the *Data* field, given it's a small value that can fit inside that field. Notice, in particular, that the data length has the highest bit set, which indicates that the data is stored in-place rather than using a cell index (as was the case for the *Debugger* value).

```
0: kd> !reg kvalue 8f9a6dec
Signature: CM_KEY_VALUE_SIGNATURE (kv)
Name       : Auto {compressed}
DataLength: 80000004
Data       : 31  [cell index]
Type       : 1
0: kd> $ The '1' character maps to 0x31 in ASCII encoding
0: kd> ? '1'
Evaluate expression: 49 = 00000031
0: kd> db 8f9a6dec
8f9a6dec  76 6b 04 00 04 00 00 80-31 00 00 00 01 00 00 00  vk......1.......
```

Now that you know the memory location where the *Auto* registry value is stored, the rest of the experiment follows without any difficulties. First, set a write breakpoint at that memory location.

```
0: kd> ba w4 8f9a6dec+8
0: kd> g
```

You can then use *regedit.exe* on the target machine to change the key value. As soon as you do that, you break right back into the kernel debugger as the data breakpoint is hit. In this case, the process that was trying to modify the registry key was already known (*regedit.exe*), but this technique works equally well even if you don't know beforehand where the modification attempt is coming from.

```
Breakpoint 0 hit
nt!CmpSetValueKeyExisting+0xda:
0: kd> !process -1 0
PROCESS 8a10fd40  SessionId: 1  Cid: 09fc    Peb: 7ffd9000  ParentCid: 17d8
    Image: regedit.exe
0: kd> .reload /user
0: kd> k
ChildEBP RetAddr
a895fb94 82a1e14a nt!CmpSetValueKeyExisting+0xda
a895fc58 82a1e7cf nt!CmSetValueKey+0x7af
a895fd14 828511fa nt!NtSetValueKey+0x32b
a895fd14 76e370b4 nt!KiFastCallEntry+0x12a
0025eee0 76e36814 ntdll!KiFastSystemCallRet
```

```
0025eee4 752d97c4 ntdll!ZwSetValueKey+0xc
0025ef24 752d98fd kernel32!LocalBaseRegSetValue+0x158
0025ef88 00e00a05 kernel32!RegSetValueExW+0x159
0025f210 00df40f2 regedit!RegEdit_EditCurrentValueListItem+0x279
0025f220 00df2b59 regedit!RegEdit_OnNotify+0x3d
0025f238 76cdc4e7 regedit!RegEditWndProc+0x210
0025f264 76cdc5e7 USER32!InternalCallWinProc+0x23
0025f2dc 76cd5294 USER32!UserCallWinProcCheckWow+0x14b
0025f31c 76cd5582 USER32!SendMessageWorker+0x4d0
0025f33c 73ebc05c USER32!SendMessageW+0x7c
0025f3d8 73f61641 COMCTL32!CCSendNotify+0xc19
0025f488 73f330df COMCTL32!CLVMouseManager::HandleMouse+0x591
0025f4a4 73f32147 COMCTL32!CLVMouseManager::OnButtonDown+0x18
0025f624 73ebfe70 COMCTL32!CListView::WndProc+0x94a
0025f64c 76cdc4e7 COMCTL32!CListView::s_WndProc+0x4e8
0025f678 76cdc5e7 USER32!InternalCallWinProc+0x23
0025f6f0 76cdcc19 USER32!UserCallWinProcCheckWow+0x14b
0025f750 76cdcc70 USER32!DispatchMessageWorker+0x35e
0025f760 00df2ac6 USER32!DispatchMessageW+0xf
0025f79c 00df1b25 regedit!WinMain+0x152
...
```

Scripting the Debugger

The Windows debuggers offer several unique features that the Visual Studio 2010 debugger does not support: kernel-mode debugging, extensions, and cooperative remote debugging, to cite a few. The ability to script the debugger using text files is yet another one of those powerful debugging features.

Replaying Commands Using Debugger Scripts

When trying to narrow down where a certain failure is happening and debug the code that caused it, it is common to go past the point of the failure and have a need to restart the process again. Once you spot the location of the failing function, you typically want to rerun the scenario (with potentially different inputs) and get to the point of failure without having to retype the sequence of debugger commands. This is one situation where scripting the debugger comes in handy.

As an illustration of how this works, the following script records steps for fixing the debugger symbols search path so that it points to the Microsoft public symbols server, waiting for the CLR version 4 execution engine DLL to first get loaded and then loading the SOS extension from the same location. These steps are common when debugging managed programs using the SOS debugger extension because the version of the extension must always match that of the CLR of the target process. Automating this with a script is certainly more efficient than having to type the same commands every time you need to debug a managed process.

```
$$
$$ C:\book\code\chapter_05\Scripts\loadv4sos.txt
$$
.symfix
.reload
sxe ld clr.dll
g
.loadby sos clr
!eeversion
```

There are two ways you can invoke this script and execute its commands in WinDbg:

- The first approach is to run the target process under the debugger and then execute the script using the *$$><* debugger command (or *$$>a<* when the script requires additional arguments), as shown in the following listing.

```
0:000> vercommand
command line: '"c:\Program Files\Debugging Tools for Windows (x86)\windbg.exe"  C:\book\
code\chapter_05\HelloWorld\main.exe'
0:000> $$>< C:\book\code\chapter_05\Scripts\loadv4sos.txt
Reloading current modules.....
ModLoad: 5d560000 5dbce000   C:\Windows\Microsoft.NET\Framework\v4.0.30319\clr.dll
4.0.30319.239 retail
GC Heap not initialized, so GC mode is not determined yet.
In plan phase of garbage collection
SOS Version: 4.0.30319.239 retail build
```

- The other way is to run the script by using the *–c* WinDbg command-line option to specify an extra command to execute when the debugging session starts up. This runs the script as the very first command in the debugging session, as illustrated in the following listing.

```
C:\book\code\chapter_05>"C:\Program Files\Debugging Tools for Windows (x86)\windbg.exe"
-c "$$>< scripts\loadv4sos.txt" HelloWorld\main.exe
CommandLine: HelloWorld\main.exe
ntdll!LdrpDoDebuggerBreak+0x2c:
770104f6 cc              int     3
Processing initial command '$$>< scripts\loadv4sos.txt'
0:000> $$>< scripts\loadv4sos.txt
Reloading current modules.....
ModLoad: 5d560000 5dbce000   C:\Windows\Microsoft.NET\Framework\v4.0.30319\clr.dll
4.0.30319.239 retail
GC Heap not initialized, so GC mode is not determined yet.
In plan phase of garbage collection
SOS Version: 4.0.30319.239 retail build
```

There are a few ways the debugger can help you capture the history of commands you want to replay using a script. For example, you can dump the commands typed within a debugger session by using the *.write_cmd_hist* command. Unfortunately, this displays the history of the commands in reverse order, so you need to process the output file to get the commands in the right order. Nevertheless, this can still be a good starting point for saving a debugger script for your scenario.

Alternatively, the *.logopen* and *.logclose* commands can also be used to save the command history into a text file. Unlike using the *.write_cmd_hist* command, you need to remember to start the logging at the beginning of your experiment for this to work. In addition, this approach also saves the output of the commands, so you need to edit the log file and remove that output before the file can serve as a script that can be replayed in *windbg.exe*.

You can automate a plethora of debugging tasks using the scripting support in the Windows debuggers: you can define variables, access pseudo-register values, and even have loops or conditions in your scripts. You can find several helpful examples for writing your debugger scripts at *http://blogs.msdn.com/debuggingtoolbox*.

Debugger Pseudo-Registers

Pseudo-registers are variables maintained by the debugger engine. They can be either user-defined or hold predefined aliases to common debugging information within the debugging session. These variables are particularly useful for control flow statements in debugger scripts because you can use them to add loops and conditions to the scripts you write.

Pseudo-register names in the WinDbg debugger begin with the *$* sign, unlike real CPU register names, such as *ecx* or *eip*, which do not need to be preceded with the *$* sign. Some of the most useful predefined pseudo-registers are *$ra* (the current return address), *$teb* (the current thread environment block), and *$peb* (the current process environment block). To display the value of a pseudo-register in WinDbg (user-mode or kernel-mode debugging), it is typically a good idea to add the @ sign before the *$* sign to let the debugger know that the token that follows is a pseudo-register and not a symbol name (such as a function name, variable name, and so on) that the debugger needs to resolve. For example, notice how the value of the *@$ra* pseudo-register in the following listing matches the one you see in the *k* stack back-trace command.

```
0:004> k
ChildEBP RetAddr
0421fdd8 7700f161 ntdll!DbgBreakPoint
0421fe08 761fed6c ntdll!DbgUiRemoteBreakin+0x3c
0421fe14 76fd37f5 KERNEL32!BaseThreadInitThunk+0xe
0421fe54 76fd37c8 ntdll!__RtlUserThreadStart+0x70
0421fe6c 00000000 ntdll!_RtlUserThreadStart+0x1b
0:004> r @$ra
$ra=7700f161
```

There are also a few other pseudo-registers that are specific to kernel-mode debugging. For example, the following kernel-debugging session shows the address of the current thread object using the *@$thread* debugger pseudo-register. Notice that this value also matches the one displayed by the *!thread* command.

```
lkd> r @$thread
$thread=851c83f8
lkd> !thread -1 0
THREAD 851c83f8  Cid 1850.17fc  Teb: 7ffdf000 Win32Thread: 00000000 RUNNING on processor 0
```

Another useful kernel debugger pseudo-register is the *@$proc* variable, which is an alias to the current process context in the debugger. You can use this pseudo-register to avoid having to find and type that virtual address by hand (using the *!process* command with the *–1* special option). As an illustration, the following debugging listing shows how to set an execution data breakpoint and restrict its scope to the current process context (*explorer.exe* in this experiment) using the *@$proc* pseudo-register.

```
kd> !process 0 0 explorer.exe
PROCESS 8535d8a0  SessionId: 1  Cid: 0268    Peb: 7ffd9000  ParentCid: 01b0
    Image: explorer.exe
kd> .process /i 8535d8a0
kd> g
Break instruction exception - code 80000003 (first chance)
8267f110 cc              int     3
kd> ba e1 /p @$proc nt!NtCreateFile
kd> bl
 0 e 828551e4 e 1 0001 (0001) nt!NtCreateFile
     Match process data 8535d8a0
kd> g
Breakpoint 0 hit
nt!NtCreateFile:
kd> !process -1 0
PROCESS 8535d8a0  SessionId: 1  Cid: 0268    Peb: 7ffd9000  ParentCid: 01b0
    Image: explorer.exe
```

Table 5-2 lists the debugger pseudo-registers you'll find most useful when writing scripts, as well as during your regular live and postmortem debugging. A more exhaustive list can be found on the MSDN website at *http://msdn.microsoft.com/en-us/library/windows/hardware/ff553485(v=vs.85).aspx*.

TABLE 5-2 Common WinDbg Pseudo-Registers

Name	Description	Applicability
@$ra	Return address after the current function scope is done executing.	User-mode and kernel-mode debugging
@$peb	Process environment block structure of the current process context.	User-mode and kernel-mode debugging
@$teb	Thread environment block structure of the current thread context.	User-mode and kernel-mode debugging
@$thread	*nt!_ETHREAD* structure of the current thread context.	Kernel-mode debugging
@$proc	*nt!_EPROCESS* structure of the current process context.	Kernel-mode debugging

Name	Description	Applicability
@$ip	Value of the instruction pointer register (*eip* on *x86* and *rip* on *x64*).	User-mode and kernel-mode debugging
@$retreg	The main return value register (*eax* on *x86* and *rax* on *x64*).	User-mode and kernel-mode debugging
@$ptrsize	The size of a pointer.	User-mode and kernel-mode debugging
@$t0, @$t1, ..., @$t19	Twenty user-defined pseudo-registers that can hold any integer value. Particularly useful as loop variables.	User-mode and kernel-mode debugging

Resolving C++ Template Names in Debugger Scripts

If you try to set a breakpoint using the name of a C++ template function, you'll see that you are unable to do so, at least not in the most obvious way! The following listing provides an illustration of the behavior you'll observe if you try to set a breakpoint in a template function from the C++ Standard Template Library (STL) using the *bp* command, for example.

```
0:000> vercommand
command line: '"c:\Program Files\Debugging Tools for Windows (x86)\windbg.exe"
c:\book\code\chapter_05\StlSample\objfre_win7_x86\i386\stlsample.exe'
0:000> .symfix
0:000> .reload
0:000> x stlsample!*begin*
...
00bd14f4 stlsample!std::basic_string<char,std::char_traits<char>,std::allocator<char>,
_STL70>::begin
0:000> bp stlsample!std::basic_string<char,std::char_traits<char>,std::allocator<char>,
_STL70>::begin
Couldn't resolve error at 'stlsample!std::basic_string<char,std::char_traits<char>,
std::allocator<char>,_STL70>::begin'
```

The reason the breakpoint couldn't be resolved is that the debugger thinks the opening "<" sign before the *char* template type is a redirection character. To tell the debugger to treat the entire string as a symbol name, the "*@!*" character sequence can be prepended to the symbol name, as illustrated here:

```
0:000> bp @!"stlsample!std::basic_string<char,std::char_traits<char>,std::allocator<char>,
_STL70>::begin"
0:000> g
Breakpoint 0 hit
...
0:000> k
ChildEBP RetAddr
0025faf0 00bd193a stlsample!std::basic_string<char,std::char_traits<char>,std::allocator<char
>,_STL70>::begin [c:\ddk\7600.16385.1\inc\api\crt\stl70\xstring @ 1177]
0025fb28 00bd1982 stlsample!CMainApp::MainHR+0x3a
0025fb2c 00bd1de0 stlsample!wmain+0x5
...
```

All the other commands that also expect a symbol name, such as the *.open* and *lsa* debugger commands that can be used to display the source code corresponding to a code address, also work when the *@!* prefix is included before the template function name.

```
0:000> .open -a @!"stlsample!std::basic_string<char,std::char_traits<char>,
std::allocator<char>,_STL70>::begin"
0:000> lsa @!"stlsample!std::basic_string<char,std::char_traits<char>,
std::allocator<char>,_STL70>::begin"
  1173:         return (*this);
  1174:         }
  1175:
  1176:         iterator __CLR_OR_THIS_CALL begin()
> 1177:         {    // return iterator for beginning of mutable sequence
  1178:         return (_STRING_ITERATOR(_Myptr()));
  1179:         }
...
0:000> q
```

Although this is not essential to know in live debugging scenarios (the *x* command could be used first to get the hexadecimal address of the template function, and that address could then be used directly with the *bp* command), this trick proves particularly useful when scripting the debugger because the address of the C++ template function could change from one run to the next, making it necessary to be able to set the breakpoint using the function's symbolic name.

Scripts in Action: Listing Windows Service Processes in the Kernel Debugger

One of the common needs when conducting system debugging experiments using the kernel debugger is to figure out which of the running *svchost.exe* instances on the target machine corresponds to the service you're interested in debugging without having to let the target go. For example, you might want to view the state of the active threads in the *DComLaunch* service while investigating COM activation issues, but to do so, you need to be able to tell its host service from the other *svchost.exe* instances on the target machine.

```
0: kd> !process 0 0 svchost.exe
PROCESS 8a5fdd40  SessionId: 0  Cid: 02c8    Peb: 7ffde000  ParentCid: 0244
    Image: svchost.exe
PROCESS 8a5bbd40  SessionId: 0  Cid: 0314    Peb: 7ffdc000  ParentCid: 0244
    Image: svchost.exe
...
0: kd> ? 0x02c8
Evaluate expression: 712 = 000002c8
```

Of course, you could go to the target machine and type **tlist.exe /s** on a command prompt to list the services that are currently running on the target, allowing you to find the process ID (PID) of the *svchost.exe* instance corresponding to the *DComLaunch* service, as shown in the following command.

```
C:\Program Files\Debugging Tools for Windows (x86)>tlist.exe -s
   0 System Process
   4 System
...
   712 svchost.exe     Svcs:  DcomLaunch,PlugPlay,Power
```

You might not want to let the target go and lose the current break-in state, though. Unfortunately, this leaves you with relying on trial and error to figure out the correct *svchost.exe* process. In this case, applying the *!peb* command to the first *svchost.exe* instance on the target machine shows that *DComLaunch* is hosted by that process, but you wouldn't have been nearly as lucky had it been another *svchost.exe* instance.

```
0: kd> .process /r /p 8a5fdd40
0: kd> !peb
PEB at 7ffde000 ...
    CommandLine:  'C:\Windows\system32\svchost.exe -k DcomLaunch'
```

A possible solution that allows you to find the *svchost.exe* instance without this guesswork is to walk the list of service entries maintained by the service control manager (SCM) system process (*services.exe*). The head of that list is stored in the *services!ImageDatabase* global variable. Though visible in the Windows public symbols, this is an internal variable, of course, and it should be used solely for debugging purposes.

```
0: kd> vertarget
Windows 7 Kernel Version 7600 MP (2 procs) Free x86 compatible
Built by: 7600.16695.x86fre.win7_gdr.101026-1503
0: kd> .symfix
0: kd> .reload
0: kd> !process 0 0 services.exe
PROCESS 8a5dd478  SessionId: 0  Cid: 0244    Peb: 7ffd4000  ParentCid: 01d0
    Image: services.exe
0: kd> .process /r /p 8a5dd478
0: kd> $$>< C:\book\code\chapter_05\Scripts\win7services_x86.txt
Dumping running services list...
Service Image Name: C:\Windows\system32\svchost.exe -k DcomLaunch
Service Image PID: 0x000002c8
Service Image Name: C:\Windows\system32\svchost.exe -k RPCSS
Service Image PID: 0x00000314
...
```

The script used in the previous listing is quite simple. It starts at the head of the list and walks over each record in the list using a pseudo-register variable (*$t1*), each time displaying the command line and PID of the service process in question. Because it makes assumptions about field offsets inside the internal service image record structure, this script (listed next) is tested to work on Windows 7, but it might need to be adjusted slightly on other versions of Windows (and, potentially, even on future service packs of Windows 7). Another variant of this same script for 64-bit Windows 7, where the structure size and field offsets are also different, is included in the companion source code (named *win7services_x64.txt* under the same directory).

```
$$
$$ C:\book\code\chapter_05\Scripts\win7services_x86.txt
$$
.echo Dumping running services list...
r $t1=services!ImageDatabase;
r $t1 = poi(@$t1 + 0x04);

.for (; @$t1 != 0; r $t1 = poi(@$t1 + 0x04))
{
    .printf "Service Image Name: %mu\n", poi(@$t1+8);
    .printf "Service Image PID: 0x%p\n", poi(@$t1+c);
}
```

WOW64 Debugging

When 64-bit Windows was introduced about a decade ago, there was a need to be able to run existing *x86* applications on the new 64-bit versions of Windows. Even though the *x64* family of processors provides native support for running *x86* applications using the *x86* registers (*eax*, *ecx*, and so on), there is only one *x64* Windows kernel, and it runs in native 64-bit mode. This means a marshaling layer at the OS level is required for *x86* user-mode processes to be able to make successful system calls through the public Win32 API. This layer is known as *Windows 32-bit on Windows 64-bit*, or simply *WOW64*.

The WOW64 Environment

To understand WOW64 debugging, you'll find it useful to quickly revisit the architecture of the WOW64 environment and how *x64* Windows supports executing *x86* processes. The WOW64 layer runs completely in user mode. It intercepts system service calls from the 32-bit versions of *ntdll.dll* and *user32.dll* on behalf of 32-bit applications, and then translates them into 64-bit kernel calls, converting arguments so that pointer sizes and stack frames are set up correctly. Each thread in a WOW64 process, in fact, has two user-mode stacks (a 32-bit stack and a 64-bit stack), in addition to the usual kernel-mode stack used when the thread enters kernel mode via a system call. This conversion process is called *thunking* or *marshaling* the system call and is implemented by the *wow64.dll* DLL for the regular *ntdll* system calls and the *wow64win.dll* DLL for the GDI32/USER32 system calls into the kernel portion of the Windows GUI subsystem (*win32k.sys*). These layers, in turn, use the *wow64cpu.dll* DLL, which implements the 64-bit mode switch instructions in assembly language.

The three aforementioned native DLLs are special 64-bit DLLs allowed to run in WOW64 processes. In fact, the native *ntdll.dll* module is the only other 64-bit DLL that can be loaded into a WOW64 process. The loader code (implemented by this DLL) is responsible for detecting the *bitness* of the process right after it's created by the 64-bit kernel and handing control over to the WOW64 layer, which in turn loads the 32-bit *ntdll.dll* and executes the 32-bit loader code in that DLL. Conversely, a native (64-bit) process also is not allowed to load 32-bit DLLs, which explains why you can't use 32-bit debugger extensions in the 64-bit version of the Windows debuggers, for example.

Figure 5-3 illustrates the layers involved in the communication between WOW64 processes and the system services inside the 64-bit OS executive.

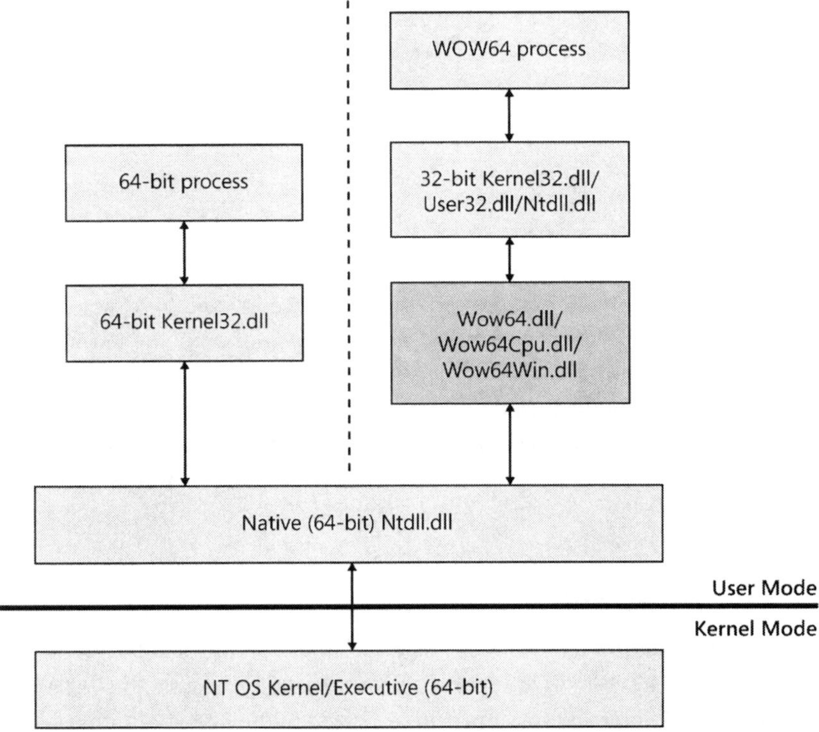

FIGURE 5-3 WOW64 architecture overview.

Debugging of WOW64 Processes

You can use either an *x86* or *x64* user-mode debugger to debug WOW64 processes. One problem, however, when using an *x64* debugger with a WOW64 target process is that, because the debugger extension DLLs are loaded into the debugger's address space, *x86* extensions cannot be loaded into the *x64* debugger. This is one of several reasons why it is usually best to use an *x86* user-mode debugger when debugging WOW64 processes and an *x64* user-mode debugger when debugging native 64-bit processes.

User-mode debugging generally does not allow you to see the interactions between your application and other user-mode processes, nor does it allow you to see the (64-bit) kernel side of your system calls. If you're interested in those interactions, you need to use a kernel-mode debugger.

Kernel-mode debugging of WOW64 programs is certainly possible, but with the power afforded by a kernel-mode debugger also comes a need to better understand the WOW64 architecture to be able to separate the application's 32-bit user-mode stack from the WOW64 layer and the 64-bit kernel-mode stack. If you start the WOW64 version of *notepad.exe* (from *%SystemRoot%\SysWow64\notepad.exe*) on a 64-bit target machine, and then break into the kernel debugger and dump the active call stacks in that *notepad.exe* process instance, you'll notice that the user-mode portion of the stack traces isn't readily visible, as shown in the following listing.

```
kd> vertarget
Windows 7 Kernel Version 7600 MP (1 procs) Free x64
Built by: 7600.16385.amd64fre.win7_rtm.090713-1255
kd> .symfix
kd> .reload
kd> !process 0 0 notepad.exe
PROCESS fffffa800a2fa060
    Image: notepad.exe
kd> .process /r /p fffffa800a2fa060
kd> !process fffffa800a2fa060 7
   THREAD fffffa800a69a910  Cid 035c.0f78  Teb: 000000007efdb000 ...
        Win32 Start Address notepad!WinMainCRTStartup (0x0000000000bb3689)
        Child-SP          RetAddr           : Call Site
        fffff880'048e3730 fffff800'014d7052 : nt!KiSwapContext+0x7a
        fffff880'048e3870 fffff800'014d91af : nt!KiCommitThreadWait+0x1d2
        fffff880'048e3900 fffff960'0015b447 : nt!KeWaitForSingleObject+0x19f
        fffff880'048e39a0 fffff960'0015b4e9 : win32k!xxxRealSleepThread+0x257
        fffff880'048e3a40 fffff960'00159b14 : win32k!xxxSleepThread+0x59
        fffff880'048e3a70 fffff960'00159c19 : win32k!xxxRealInternalGetMessage+0x7dc
        fffff880'048e3b50 fffff960'0015b615 : win32k!xxxInternalGetMessage+0x35
        fffff880'048e3b90 fffff800'014cf153 : win32k!NtUserGetMessage+0x75
        fffff880'048e3c20 00000000'7403fc2a : nt!KiSystemServiceCopyEnd+0x13
        00000000'0008df78 00000000'7401ac48 : wow64win!NtUserGetMessage+0xa
        00000000'0008df80 00000000'7406cf87 : wow64win!whNtUserGetMessage+0x30
        00000000'0008dfe0 00000000'73ff276d : wow64!Wow64SystemServiceEx+0xd7
<<<< 32-bit user-mode stack frames are missing! >>>>
        00000000'0008e8a0 00000000'7406d07e : wow64cpu!ServiceNoTurbo+0x24
        00000000'0008e960 00000000'7406c549 : wow64!RunCpuSimulation+0xa
        00000000'0008e9b0 00000000'775b84c8 : wow64!Wow64LdrpInitialize+0x429
        00000000'0008ef00 00000000'775b7623 : ntdll!LdrpInitializeProcess+0x17e2
```

Notice that you can see only the 64-bit stack of the thread, which only goes as deep as the *wow64.dll* thunking layer DLL, and the user-mode call stack (corresponding to the 32-bit, user-mode stack of the thread) is missing from this picture. To see that information, you can use the *.thread /w* command to set the current thread context and load the WOW64 symbols. This requires you to first load the *wow64exts.dll* debugger extension, as demonstrated in the following listing.

```
kd:x86> $ Loading WOW64 symbols warns you that you must first load the wow64exts extension
kd> .thread /r /p /w fffffa800a69a910
Loading User Symbols.....
Loading Wow64 Symbols.........................
```

```
The wow64exts extension must be loaded to access 32-bit state.
.load wow64exts will do this if you haven't loaded it already.
x86 context set
kd:x86> .load wow64exts
kd:x86> $ Reload the WOW64 symbols again now that the extension is loaded...
kd:x86> .thread /r /p /w fffffa800a69a910
The context is partially valid. Only x86 user-mode context is available
Loading User Symbols.....
Loading Wow64 Symbols........................
Current mode must be kd-native and must allow x86 to retrieve WOW context
kd:x86> k
  *** Stack trace for last set context - .thread/.cxr resets it
ChildEBP          RetAddr
WARNING: Frame IP not in any known module. Following frames may be wrong.
0a69a910 00000000 0x1479dda
```

The reason you were still unable to get the correct call stack is that the *.thread* command needs to be run from the 64-bit thread context in the debugger for it to successfully decode the WOW64 symbols (as indicated by the bold line preceding the *k* command in the previous listing). Because the first *.thread /w* command you issued in the previous listing transitioned you into the *x86* (*kd:x86*) thread context, however, you need to go back to the 64-bit thread context and reload the symbols using the *.thread /r* command. You can do that by using the *.effmach* debugger command, which is used to set the CPU context (32-bit or 64-bit) in the debugger explicitly. You're now finally able to see the 32-bit portion of the thread's stack trace!

```
kd:x86> .effmach amd64
Effective machine: x64 (AMD64)
kd> .thread /r /p /w fffffa800a69a910
Loading User Symbols.....
Loading Wow64 Symbols........................
x86 context set
kd:x86> k
ChildEBP          RetAddr
0022fd34 75f07ebd USER32!NtUserGetMessage+0x15
0022fd50 00b7148a USER32!GetMessageW+0x33
0022fd90 00b716ec notepad!WinMain+0xe6
0022fe20 74db3677 notepad!__mainCRTStartup+0x140
0022fe2c 77199d72 kernel32!BaseThreadInitThunk+0xe
0022fe6c 77199d45 ntdll_77160000!__RtlUserThreadStart+0x70
0022fe84 00000000 ntdll_77160000!_RtlUserThreadStart+0x1b
kd:x86> .effmach amd64
Effective machine: x64 (AMD64)
kd> $ Notice the 32-bit ntdll.dll is loaded into the WOW64 process address space
kd> lmv m ntdll_77160000
    Image path: C:\Windows\SysWOW64\ntdll.dll
```

Finally, note that the *.effmach* debugger command also works in the user-mode debugger. So, if you ever have to use a 64-bit user-mode debugger to debug a WOW64 process, you can use that command to switch the CPU context as needed so that you can view the 32-bit, user-mode stack, as illustrated in the following debugger listing.

```
C:\Program Files\Debugging Tools for Windows (x64)>start c:\Windows\SysWOW64\notepad.exe
C:\Program Files\Debugging Tools for Windows (x64)>windbg.exe -pn notepad.exe
```

```
0:001> .symfix
0:001> .reload
0:001> ~0s
0:000> k
Child-SP          RetAddr           Call Site
00000000'0012df78 00000000'7409aea8 wow64win!NtUserGetMessage+0xa
00000000'0012df80 00000000'740ecf87 wow64win!whNtUserGetMessage+0x30
00000000'0012dfe0 00000000'7407276d wow64!Wow64SystemServiceEx+0xd7
00000000'0012e8a0 00000000'740ed07e wow64cpu!ServiceNoTurbo+0x24
00000000'0012e960 00000000'740ec549 wow64!RunCpuSimulation+0xa
00000000'0012e9b0 00000000'77b0ae27 wow64!Wow64LdrpInitialize+0x429
00000000'0012ef00 00000000'77b072f8 ntdll!LdrpInitializeProcess+0x1780
00000000'0012f400 00000000'77af2ace ntdll!_LdrpInitialize+0x147c8
00000000'0012f470 00000000'00000000 ntdll!LdrInitializeThunk+0xe
<<<< 32-bit user-mode stack frames are missing!
0:000> .effmach x86
Effective machine: x86 compatible (x86)
0:000:x86> k
ChildEBP RetAddr
002bf76c 772f7ebd USER32!NtUserGetMessage+0x15
002bf788 008d148a USER32!GetMessageW+0x33
002bf7c8 008d16ec notepad!WinMain+0xe6
002bf858 75883677 notepad!_initterm_e+0x1a1
002bf864 77cd9f02 kernel32!BaseThreadInitThunk+0xe
002bf8a4 77cd9ed5 ntdll32!__RtlUserThreadStart+0x70
002bf8bc 00000000 ntdll32!_RtlUserThreadStart+0x1b
0:000:x86> $ Terminate this debugging session...
0:000:x86> q
```

Windows Debugging Hooks (GFLAGS)

To facilitate debugging of Windows applications as well as the system code itself, Windows supports several debugging hooks for developers to alter how applications interact with the core system components that support them, both in user mode (heap allocator, module loader, and so on) as well as in kernel mode. These hooks are enabled using a set of predefined bits in a DWORD registry value known as the *NT global flag*, and they can be used in a variety of debugging investigations, ranging from catching the source of heap corruptions to stress failures and memory-leak investigations.

Systemwide vs. Process-Specific NT Global Flags

The NT global flag is a 32-bit value that's composed of a set of bits, each representing a particular debugging hook. There are essentially two possible scopes for the bits in the NT global flag because they can be applied either systemwide or per-process. A kernel-mode global variable (*nt!NtGlobalFlag*) is used by the OS to track the value of the systemwide flag. This global variable is propagated to each user-mode process at process creation time. It's saved in its process environment block (in the *NtGlobalFlag* field of the *ntdll!_PEB* structure) unless the user-mode process was explicitly given an NT global flag of its own in the registry—in which case, the per-process value takes precedence over the systemwide value. Figure 5-4 illustrates this hierarchy.

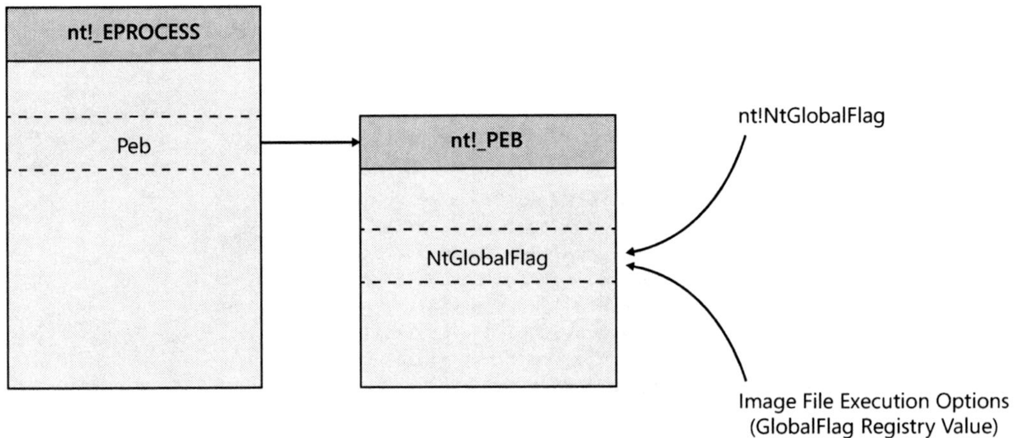

FIGURE 5-4 Process NT global flag hierarchy.

The bits encoded into the NT global flag DWORD value are described on the MSDN website at *http://msdn.microsoft.com/en-us/library/windows/hardware/ff549596(v=vs.85).aspx*. Naturally, a single bit isn't always sufficient to encode all the information related to a debugging hook, so some hooks use extended values once the OS determines that the primary control bit in the NT global flag is enabled. An important example of this is the Application Verifier tool (covered in more detail in Chapter 6, "Code Analysis Tools"), which gets enabled using a bit in the NT global flag, and then uses an additional registry value (*VerifierFlags*) to enable or disable Application Verifier hooks in a more granular way.

The GFLAGS Tool

Fortunately, there is a GUI tool for editing the systemwide and per-process NT global flag, so you don't have to remember the meaning of each bit. This important tool is *gflags.exe* and also comes as part of the Windows debuggers package. For the most part, this tool is a front-end UI for editing the values in the registry, though it's also able to edit the NT systemwide global flag in a volatile way that doesn't get persisted across OS reboots. Because both the systemwide and per-process NT global flag values are stored in admin-protected registry locations, you need to run this tool with administrative privileges, though the tool automatically asks for elevation when necessary. Figure 5-5 shows the main UI you see when starting this tool.

```
C:\Program Files\Debugging Tools for Windows (x86)>gflags.exe
```

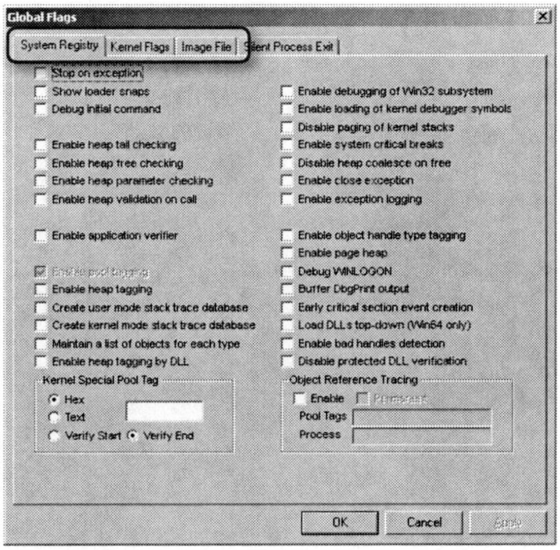

FIGURE 5-5 The GFLAGS graphical user-interface tool.

You'll notice three tabs that can be used to control the NT global flag and a few other hooks. The System Registry (leftmost) tab controls the value of the systemwide NT global flag DWORD in the registry. The changes performed using this tab are physically reflected under the session manager registry key, so they're persisted across reboots and are used again by the system to seed the value of *nt!NtGlobalFlag* during the next OS startup. Notice there is no "s" at the end of the *GlobalFlag* value name, unlike the name of the tool itself!

```
Windows Registry Editor Version 5.00

[HKEY_LOCAL_MACHINE\SYSTEM\CurrentControlSet\Control\Session Manager]
"GlobalFlag"=dword:00000400
```

The Kernel Flags tab can be used to directly set the value of *nt!NtGlobalFlag* for the current boot without a need for a reboot. Unlike the first tab, changes done using this second tab aren't persisted across reboots. Note that not all global flag bits can take effect in this manner because a few of them are read during OS boot and can't be changed while the machine is running. This is why you'll see a few options from the first tab missing from this second one. In particular, notice the absence of the Create Kernel Mode Stack Trace Database (kst) and Maintain A List Of Objects For Each Type (otl) options, for example. These bits need to be initialized during boot and can't be set on the fly while the machine is running.

Finally, the Image File tab, shown in Figure 5-6, is used to control the per-process *GlobalFlag* value, which gets stored under a registry key called *Image File Execution Options*.

```
Windows Registry Editor Version 5.00

[HKEY_LOCAL_MACHINE\SOFTWARE\Microsoft\Windows NT\CurrentVersion\Image File Execution Options\
notepad.exe]
"GlobalFlag"=dword:02000000
```

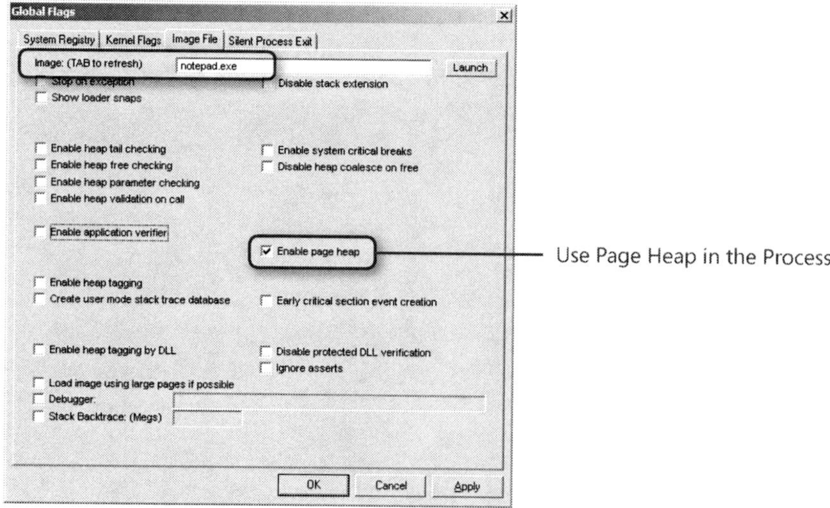

FIGURE 5-6 Configuring the per-process global flag in the GFLAGS tool.

Following is a list of a few details that many developers who are new to GFLAGS find confusing when dealing with this third tab:

- The text box expects a string representing an *image name* and not a *file name/path*. This means you should simply enter the name of the image in this text box and not the path to the executable. In the previous case, this means using *notepad.exe* and not *C:\Windows\System32\notepad.exe*!
- You need to include the extension as part of the image name. The registry key that the UI tool writes is directly derived from the string you enter in the text box, and it needs to contain the *.exe extension*. In the previous example, this means using *notepad.exe* and not just simply *notepad*!
- Any changes you make using the GFLAGS tool (or even changes you make directly in the registry) are reflected only in new instances of the process. This is because the NT global flag is read from the registry and propagated to the PEB structure during the process startup code path.

Once you've set the per-process NT global flag bits using the GFLAGS tool and clicked either Apply or OK, you can verify that the registry has a new value defined for the executable image you specified on the Image File tab of the UI (*notepad.exe*), as shown in Figure 5-7.

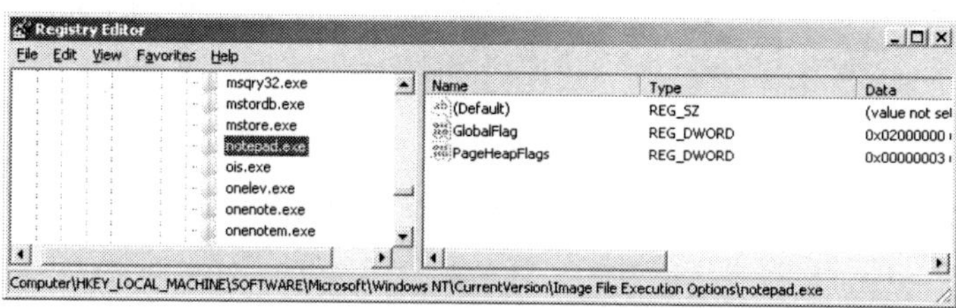

FIGURE 5-7 Per-process NT global flag value in the registry.

Notice that the page heap bit that was selected in the UI during this experiment also uses an extra registry value (*PageHeapFlags*) to control more granular flags for that debugging hook and that the GFLAGS tool automatically populated that registry value, too. The page-heap feature is useful when debugging heap corruptions and will be covered in more detail in Chapter 8, "Common Debugging Scenarios, Part 1."

Warning Ideally, you should always use the *gflags.exe* tool when setting the NT global flag for your images rather than edit the registry manually. If you want to change the registry directly, however, be aware that on 64-bit versions of Windows, you need to edit the registry view corresponding to the bitness of your target image. Remember that WOW64 programs have their own view of the software hive under the *Wow6432Node* registry key, which means you need to update the following registry key if *TestImage.exe* is an *x86* executable, for example:

```
Windows Registry Editor Version 5.00

[HKEY_LOCAL_MACHINE\SOFTWARE\Wow6432Node\Microsoft\Windows NT\CurrentVersion\Image File
Execution Options\TestImage.exe]
"GlobalFlag"=dword:00000100
...
```

The *gflags.exe* tool is kind enough to edit both the native and WOW64 registry views for you, so things will "just work" regardless of whether you specify the name of a native *x64* or *x86* image in the tool's UI.

The *!gflag* Debugger Extension Command

The *!gflag* (no "s" at the end!) extension command can be used from a user-mode debugger to read the value of the per-process NT global flag in the current process environment block. You can also use the *–?* option of this extension command to discover the meaning of each possible bit in the NT global flag, as shown in the following listing.

```
0:000> !gflag
Current NtGlobalFlag contents: 0x02000000
    hpa - Place heap allocations at ends of pages
0:000> !gflag -?
usage: !gflag [-? | flags]
Valid abbreviations are:
    soe - Stop On Exception
    sls - Show Loader Snaps
    htc - Enable heap tail checking
    hfc - Enable heap free checking
    hpc - Enable heap parameter checking
    hvc - Enable heap validation on call
    vrf - Enable application verifier
    htg - Enable heap tagging
    ust - Create user mode stack trace database
    htd - Enable heap tagging by DLL
```

```
    dse - Disable stack extensions
    scb - Enable system critical breaks
    dhc - Disable Heap Coalesce on Free
    hpa - Place heap allocations at ends of pages
...
```

Similarly, this same extension command can be used under a kernel-mode debugger, but in that case it displays the current value of the *nt!NtGlobalFlag* global kernel variable:

```
0: kd> dd nt!NtGlobalFlag
82ba8928  00040400 00000000 00000000 00000000
0: kd> !gflag
Current NtGlobalFlag contents: 0x00000400
    ptg - Enable pool tagging
0: kd> !gflag -?
Valid abbreviations are:
    soe - Stop On Exception
    sls - Show Loader Snaps
    dic - Debug Initial Command
    shg - Stop on Hung GUI
    htc - Enable heap tail checking
    hfc - Enable heap free checking
    hpc - Enable heap parameter checking
    hvc - Enable heap validation on call
    vrf - Enable application verifier
    ptg - Enable pool tagging
    htg - Enable heap tagging
    ust - Create user mode stack trace database
    kst - Create kernel mode stack trace database
    otl - Maintain a list of objects for each type
...
```

The *!gflag* command also can be used to dynamically enable or disable (using the + and – signs, respectively) global flag bits for the system so that they're inherited by new processes that get started on the target machine. For example, the following debugger listing shows how to enable the "stop on exception" bit, which causes the kernel debugger to start catching unhandled exceptions thrown by user-mode processes on the target machine.

```
0: kd> $ Use the "!gflag" command to (indirectly) edit the value of the NtGlobalFlag variable
0: kd> !gflag +soe
Current NtGlobalFlag contents: 0x00000401
    soe - Stop On Exception
    ptg - Enable pool tagging
0: kd> $ You could also use the "ed" command to directly edit the value of NtGlobalFlag
0: kd> ed nt!NtGlobalFlag 0
```

Practical uses of various bits in the NT global flag, including the "stop on exception" bit, will be covered in more detail in future chapters.

Impact of User-Mode Debuggers on the Value of the NT Global Flag

If you're using the *!gflag* extension in a user-mode debugging session, be aware that the process-initialization code in the *ntdll.dll* system module automatically enables a few default bits in the process global flag when the process is started under a user-mode debugger. This is done only when no value is explicitly set for the global flag of the image in the registry. As an illustration, the following listing shows the value of the NT global flag in the PEB of a *notepad.exe* process instance when the *notepad.exe* image has no explicit global flag specified in the registry.

```
0:000> vercommand
command line: '"c:\Program Files\Debugging Tools for Windows (x86)\windbg.exe"
c:\Windows\system32\notepad.exe'
0:000> !gflag
Current NtGlobalFlag contents: 0x00000070
    htc - Enable heap tail checking
    hfc - Enable heap free checking
    hpc - Enable heap parameter checking
0:000> $ use the @$peb pseudo-register as an alias to the address of the PEB structure
0:000> dt ntdll!_PEB @$peb NtGlobalFlag
   +0x068 NtGlobalFlag : 0x70
```

As you can see, a few heap-debugging features are enabled by default to make it easier to investigate heap-corruption bugs in the user-mode debugger. This is why you will sometimes catch heap corruptions (such as writing past the end of a buffer) and immediately hit an access violation under a user-mode debugger when the application might otherwise not consistently hit the crash outside of the debugger. This being said, the NT debug-heap settings enabled by the presence of a user-mode debugger are relatively unsophisticated, and a better way to catch heap corruptions is to enable the page-heap global flag bit for the target executable image—a technique detailed in Chapter 8.

If you really want to, you also can disable this debugger side effect by setting the _NO_DEBUG_HEAP environment variable before starting the process, or by passing the *–dh* command-line option when starting WinDbg. This asks the heap-manager code in the OS to always use the regular (nondebug) heap. Alternatively, you can just start the process and later attach the debugger to it—in which case, the NT debug heap won't be automatically enabled for the process, either.

The Image File Execution Options Hooks

The NT global flag described in this chapter is just one of many per-image debugger hooks the OS exposes under the Image File Execution Options (IFEO) registry key. Although the NT global flag itself is applicable only to executable images, there are other debugging hooks that also apply to DLL images, which is why the names of the images you enter in the GFLAGS UI need to include the module extension too (*.exe*, in the case of the NT global flag).

An example of a DLL-specific IFEO hook is the *BreakOnDllLoad* value used to break into the debugger when the target DLL image is loaded—a technique that will be covered in more detail in Chapter 7, "Expert Debugging Tricks." In addition, EXE-specific debugging hooks other than the NT global flag also exist. An important example is the "startup debugger" registry value, which is also covered in Chapter 7. Knowing when to apply these hooks and how to use them in practice can sometimes make the difference between a long, futile debugging investigation and an efficient one that takes only a few minutes to wrap up.

Summary

This chapter introduced you to several important debugging features in Windows. As you move to the following chapters, here is a quick recap of a few key things you learned:

- Noninvasive debugging can be used to combine a WinDbg inspection with other debuggers, such as the Visual Studio debugger. This can sometimes allow you to get the best of both debuggers for your test scenario.
- Data (also known as *hardware*) breakpoints are a powerful debugging technique you can use to detect attempts to access (write, read, and execute) global variables or code locations. They come in a limited supply, however, because the number available is capped by the number of dedicated debug registers in the processor. So, you should consider the alternative of using code (also known as *software*) breakpoints, at least for the "execution" type of data breakpoints.
- If you find yourself repeating the same commands in your WinDbg debugging experiments, consider automating those steps by using a script. Scripts are also useful when you need to automate routines such as walking over a linked list and displaying its elements in the debugger.
- If you're debugging a 32-bit image on 64-bit Windows, you should prefer using a 32-bit, user-mode debugger. If you must use a 64-bit user-mode debugger, you should know about the *.effmach* command, which allows you to easily switch the processor context and view the 32-bit, user-mode stack frames of the WOW64 process.
- Debugging a WOW64 process using a host kernel debugger requires a basic understanding of the internals of the WOW64 environment. The */w* option of the *.thread* command is used to reload the WOW64 symbols, and the *.effmach* command can again be used to switch the processor context so that you can see the 32-bit, user-mode stack frames in the WOW64 process.
- This chapter concluded by introducing the Image File Execution Options concept—more specifically, the NT global flag and the *gflags.exe* UI tool used to edit its value in the registry. The IFEO hooks can be useful in debugging investigations on Windows, and future chapters will demonstrate that with several practical examples. In fact, the next chapter, which introduces tools for static and run-time code analysis in Windows, covers an important bit in the NT global flag, which is used to enable the run-time code-analysis capabilities of the indispensable Application Verifier tool.

CHAPTER 6

Code Analysis Tools

In this chapter

Preventative strategies to discover bugs early during the software development cycle are very important because using the debuggers to investigate bugs in a reactive manner after they're found in shipped software is an expensive and woefully inefficient approach. It's generally accepted that the longer it takes to find a bug, the more costly it becomes to fix it and update the code. In addition to the obvious business disruptions that these latent bugs often cause, they also have tremendous negative effects on the perception the customer base has of the software.

This chapter covers two approaches that are often used in Microsoft Windows to automate the process of discovering defects that otherwise can go unnoticed until they result in random crashes and other insidious bugs. The chapter starts by covering static code analysis and the Visual C++ (VC++) Standard Annotation Language (SAL). It then follows with detailed coverage of the Application Verifier tool, which extends the NT global flag debugging hook covered in the "Windows Debugging Hooks (GFLAGS)" section of Chapter 5, "Beyond the Basics," and provides additional run-time verification capabilities for native code in Windows.

Static Code Analysis

Microsoft Visual Studio 2010 supports static code analysis for both native and .NET code, though this feature is available only in the Premium and Ultimate editions, including the free, time-limited trial versions of those editions. You can also take advantage of static code analysis techniques even if you can't or simply don't want to build your code using the Visual Studio environment, as will be demonstrated later in this section.

Catching Your First Crashing Bug Using VC++ Static Code Analysis

The best way to understand the value of static code analysis is to see it in action catching a serious bug in your code. Consider the following C++ code sample from the companion source code.

```
//
// C:\book\code\chapter_06\FormatString>main.cpp
//
static
HRESULT
MainHR(
    VOID
    )
{
    ChkProlog();

    // BUG! Use of %s with an integer argument type
    wprintf(L"Error code value is: %s\n", E_ACCESSDENIED);

    ChkNoCleanup();
}
```

The bug, in this case, is that the code uses an incorrect format string in the *wprintf* call, trying to format an integer HRESULT value as a string (*%s*). The companion source code contains a Visual Studio 2010 project for the previous code sample. You'll see a menu item called Analyze and an option under it to start a static code analysis run for the project, as shown in Figure 6-1.

```
C:\book\code\chapter_06\FormatString>FormatString.sln
```

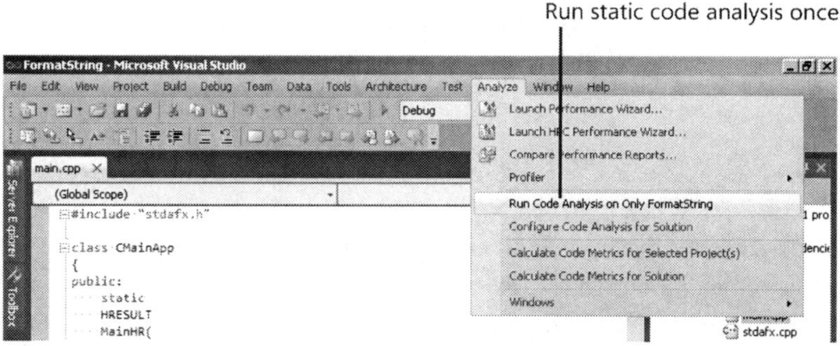

FIGURE 6-1 Running static code analysis for a Visual Studio 2010 project.

You could also configure the project so that C/C++ static code analysis is run automatically every time you rebuild. To do so, you can use the Ctrl+Enter shortcut to invoke the project properties dialog box, and then select the corresponding check box in the Code Analysis node under the Configuration Properties tree, as illustrated in Figure 6-2.

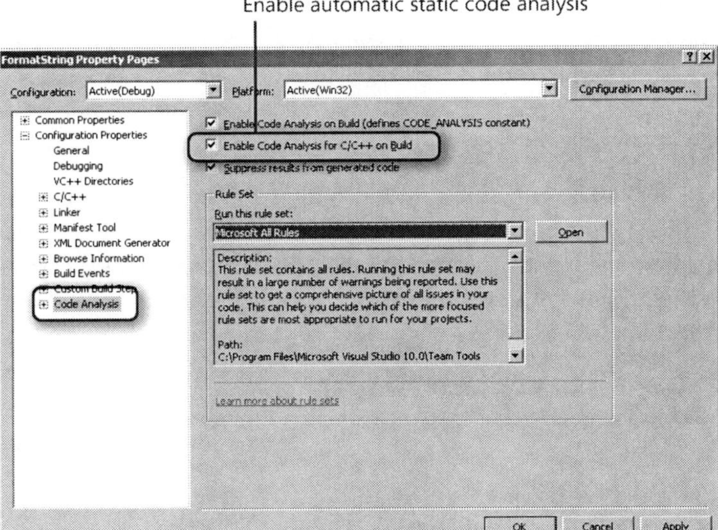

FIGURE 6-2 Enabling automatic code analysis for Visual Studio 2010 projects.

By using either one of the aforementioned two approaches to run static code analysis, you'll see a warning printed as part of building the Visual C++ project, pointing out the exact location of the bug in the initial code. Visual Studio also allows you to conveniently double-click the line of the warning in the build's output window and quickly navigate to the call site of the warning in the source code, as demonstrated in Figure 6-3. The text of the warning (shown next) in this example indicates a bad format string bug.

```
1>   Running Code Analysis for C/C++...
1>c:\book\code\chapter_06\formatstring\main.cpp(14): warning C6067: Parameter '2' in call to
'wprintf' must be the address of the string
```

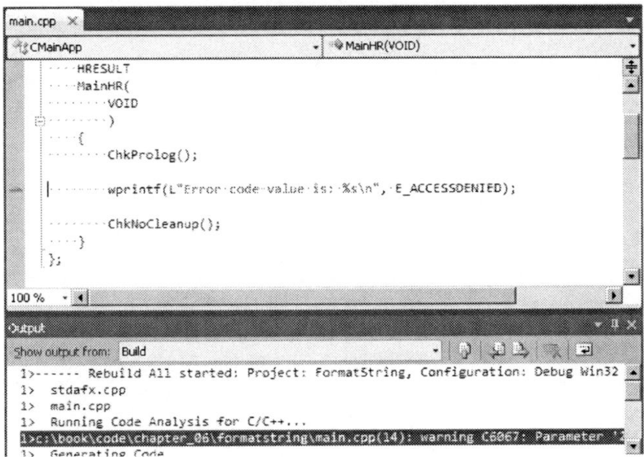

FIGURE 6-3 C/C++ code analysis warnings in the build output window.

Not all warnings are indicative of a serious bug. Some warnings, such as declaring unused variables, are benign. Other warnings, such as the one at play in this example, might point to serious code defects. As a general rule, you need to carefully review all the static-analysis warnings displayed during the build process.

In the previous example, the VC++ static-analysis feature was able to spot the defect before you even had to run the program and hit the crash. As it turns out in this particular case, the crash is also easily reproducible inside of a user-mode debugger, as demonstrated in the following debugging session, which starts the same program under WinDbg and simply lets it run using the *g* command. Notice that the program consistently hits a Structured Exception Handling (SEH) access violation exception inside the *wprintf* function call.

```
"C:\Program Files\Debugging Tools for Windows (x86)\windbg.exe"
C:\book\code\chapter_06\formatstring\objfre_win7_x86\i386\FormatStringBug.exe
0:000> g
...
(1e9c.16f0): Access violation - code c0000005 (first chance)
75a0ba16 66833800        cmp     word ptr [eax],0        ds:002b:80070005=????
0:000> .symfix
0:000> .reload
0:000> .lastevent
Last event: 1e9c.16f0: Access violation - code c0000005 (first chance)
0:000> k
ChildEBP RetAddr
0020faa8 75a25e29 msvcrt!_woutput_l+0x98b
0020faf0 0048147e msvcrt!wprintf+0x5f
0020fafc 00481497 FormatStringBug!CMainApp::MainHR+0x10
0020fb04 00481624 FormatStringBug!wmain+0x8
...
```

In the instruction that the program was executing when it crashed you can clearly see that there was an attempt to dereference the address pointed to by the *eax* register (because the *wprintf* function call assumes it's a string pointer, per the format string you provided!). However, *eax* holds the E_ACCESSDENIED value (*0x8007005*), which results in access to invalid memory, as confirmed by the *db* ("dump bytes") command in the following listing.

```
0:000> u
msvcrt!_woutput_l+0x98b:
75a0ba16 66833800        cmp     word ptr [eax],0
0:000> r
eax=80070005 ebx=80070005 ecx=00000007 edx=00000073 esi=7ffffffe edi=00481172
...
0:000> db 80070005
80070005  ?? ?? ?? ?? ?? ?? ?? ??-?? ?? ?? ?? ?? ?? ?? ??  ????????????????
...
0:000> $ Terminate this debugging session now...
0:000> q
```

Although this case could be easily caught, given that it would result in a crash every time the program is run (assuming, of course, that the code path is hit at run time), there are many other cases where you might not be as lucky. Rare code paths are not always hit during your test runs, and memory corruption bugs are not always easily reproducible. So, even if static analysis helps catch just one serious bug you otherwise would have missed in your regular testing, it is well worth the effort to set it up for your projects.

SAL Annotations

One key limitation in the engine that Visual C++ uses for static analysis is that it doesn't know the shape of the data coming in and out of function calls. For this reason, VC++ static analysis needs help to learn the contracts between functions and their callers. This is exactly the purpose of SAL annotations, which enable developers to describe their expectations of the arguments passed to the functions or APIs they write. The syntax for SAL annotations is described at a high level in the MSDN website—for example, at *http://msdn.microsoft.com/en-us/library/ms235402(v=VS.80).aspx.*

Catching a Buffer Overrun Bug Using SAL Annotations

To illustrate the value of SAL annotations in static code analysis, this section uses the following C++ program from the companion source code.

```
//
// C:\book\code\chapter_06\BufferOverrun>main.cpp
//
class CMainApp
{
private:
    static
    HRESULT
    FillString(
        __in WCHAR ch,
        __in DWORD cchBuffer,
        __out_ecount(cchBuffer) WCHAR* pwszBuffer
        )
    {
        ChkProlog();

        for (DWORD i=0; i < cchBuffer; i++)
        {
            pwszBuffer[i] = ch;
        }

        ChkNoCleanup();
    }
```

```
public:
    static
    HRESULT
    MainHR()
    {
        WCHAR wszBuffer[MAX_PATH];

        ChkProlog();

        // BUG! Use of incorrect size in the function call
        ChkHr(FillString(L'\0', sizeof(wszBuffer), wszBuffer));

        ChkNoCleanup();
    }
};
```

This program has a very serious bug: the *FillString* function expects the *cchBuffer* argument to represent the length of *pwszBuffer* in number of characters ("elements count," or *ecount*), which is expressed with the *__out_ecount* SAL annotation in the previous example. The caller, however, makes the mistake of passing in the size of the input buffer as a number of bytes (*sizeof(wszBuffer)*). This causes the *FillString* function to write past the end of the buffer, resulting in what is known as a *buffer overrun* (or *overflow*).

Fortunately, because this C++ program used SAL to annotate the arguments to the *FillString* function and describe the assumptions made by that function about the arguments it receives, the VC++ static-analysis engine is able to consume those SAL annotations and check for the possibility of broken invariants. Visual Studio 2010 is again able to pinpoint the nature of the problem and the exact line of source code that was responsible for the issue, as shown in Figure 6-4. Unlike the first example in this section, however, this bug would cause random crashes, depending on the memory being overwritten by the buffer overrun, so catching it with static code analysis is all the more welcome. Notice that the static code analysis warning (shown next) also provides you with the likely cause of the buffer overrun in this case.

```
C:\book\code\chapter_06\BufferOverrun>BufferOverrun.sln
1>   Running Code Analysis for C/C++...
1>c:\book\code\chapter_06\bufferoverrun\main.cpp(33): warning C6057: Buffer overrun due to
number of characters/number of bytes mismatch in call to 'CMainApp::FillString'
```

Note that without the SAL annotations in the *FillString* function, Visual Studio flags the buffer overrun bug only as a "possible warning" because it's not able to ascertain whether the argument to the *FillString* function is supposed to be a number of character elements or a number of bytes. By adding SAL annotations, you eliminate any doubt on the part of the static code analysis engine, which is then able to report that a buffer overrun bug is at play.

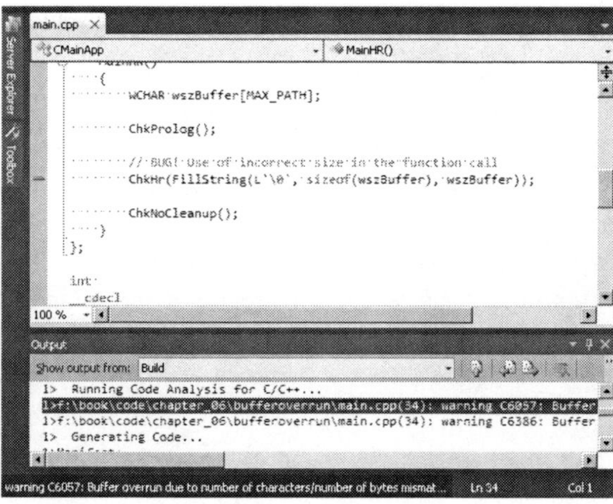

FIGURE 6-4 Catching a buffer overrun bug using SAL annotations.

The Evils of Buffer Overruns

Even if static analysis catches only a single buffer overrun bug in your code, it is probably still well worth the time investment you made to use it. When a function copies user-supplied input data into a local array without proper bounds checking, for example, it might end up copying data from the potentially malicious user input and overwriting addresses higher up on the call stack, including the return address of the function. This can allow an attacker to run her malicious code with the privileges of the vulnerable process! The notorious Blaster virus (MS03-26 security bulletin) was an exploit of a buffer overrun in the *RpcSs* service, which ran with *LocalSystem* privileges prior to Windows XP Service Pack 2. Similarly, the JPEG GDI+ buffer overrun (MS04-28 security bulletin) affected Internet Explorer, and machines with non-updated browser versions ran the risk of getting infected when visiting a compromised website through a maliciously crafted JPEG image file.

Buffer overruns are equally exploitable, even if the memory is allocated on the heap. In that case, the buffer overflow can be exploited by overwriting C++ virtual function pointers or other function pointers on the heap to make them point to the malicious code, which is typically also bundled into the properly crafted malicious input buffer, usually called the *shellcode*. There is plenty of fascinating literature on the Web detailing how to exploit buffer overruns. In particular, the free articles published in the issues of PHRACK magazine (*http://www.phrack.org*) in the late 1990s are certainly worth a read. In particular, the articles at *http://www.phrack.org/issues.html?issue=49&id=14#article* and *http://www.phrack.org/issues.html?issue=56&id=8#article* are great introductions to stack-based and heap-based buffer overrun exploitation. Although those articles address primarily the art of exploiting buffer overruns, they also provide an introduction to the enemy's tools as well as a historical chronology of large-scale exploits, especially as new mitigations made their way into the operating system. Ironically, the goal of those mitigations is to make the process crash in the presence of an exploit rather than allow an elevation of privilege. This is one case where an immediate crash is certainly better than the alternative!

SAL in the Win32 API Headers

In the buffer overrun example presented earlier, you were responsible for writing both ends of the function call, but you can easily see why SAL annotations are even more useful when the consumers and providers of an API aren't the same individuals. This is the case for the entire Win32 API layer provided by Microsoft and that gets consumed by the rest of the Windows developers at large. Fortunately, the Win32 API layer is now almost entirely annotated with SAL, as you can see in the function declarations inside the public Win32 Software Development Kit (SDK) header files. For example, here is how the arguments for the common *WriteFile* Win32 API are annotated using SAL.

```
//
// C:\ddk\7600.16385.1\inc\api>WINBASE.H
//
WINBASEAPI
BOOL
WINAPI
WriteFile(
    __in        HANDLE hFile,
    __in_bcount_opt(nNumberOfBytesToWrite) LPCVOID lpBuffer,
    __in        DWORD nNumberOfBytesToWrite,
    __out_opt   LPDWORD lpNumberOfBytesWritten,
    __inout_opt LPOVERLAPPED lpOverlapped
    );
```

Even if you don't explicitly annotate your code to use SAL, you can still benefit from the annotations provided by Microsoft for the Win32 API calls your programs make. That being said, using SAL in your code is highly beneficial, as demonstrated by the buffer overrun example from this section. All the C++ samples from this book's companion source code are also annotated so that you can get used to the syntax and start taking advantage of SAL annotations in your own projects.

Other Static Analysis Tools

There are also standalone tools that can be used for static code analysis if your code is compiled outside the Visual Studio environment. This section will cover two such options: OACR, which can be used for C/C++ static analysis in the Driver Development Kit (DDK) build environment, and the FxCop tool, which can be used for analyzing .NET code.

OACR in the DDK Build Environment

OACR stands for *Office Auto Code Review* and is a static-analysis system that was developed about a decade ago, originally for Microsoft's own use when compiling its products. It was then also integrated into the build environment included with the DDK, which is used by the C++ samples in the companion source code. Its main idea was to extend and automate the very good practice of peer code reviews, where changes are reviewed by at least one other developer before being allowed to be committed to the source code depot that's visible to the rest of the team.

OACR uses a similar C++ code analysis engine to the one used by the Visual C++ compiler (*/analyze* switch of the *cl.exe* C++ compiler) and Visual Studio 2010 environment. When using the DDK build environment, an OACR monitor runs in the background watching for when a C or C++ project gets compiled. After the build is done, it will typically take a little while—depending on the size of the project—for OACR to process all of the files in the project.

A notification area status icon shows when the static analysis is in progress or complete. A green icon indicates that the project is clean from both OACR warnings and errors, a yellow icon indicates the project contains at least one OACR warning, and a red icon indicates at least one OACR error (the most severe type of violation). For example, the icon shown in Figure 6-5 indicates that OACR is still processing the source files from the last build operation, which is indicated using the progress sign at the bottom-right corner of the icon.

```
C:\book\code\chapter_06\FormatString>build -cCZ
```

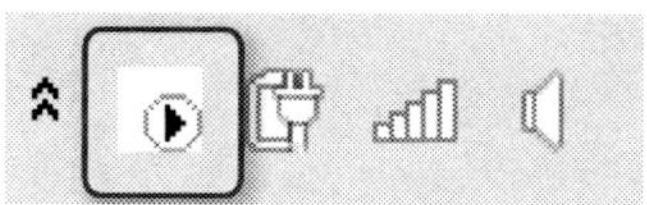

FIGURE 6-5 OACR status icon in the notification area.

After the static-analysis run is complete, you can view any reported OACR warnings or errors by right-clicking the OACR status icon, as illustrated in Figure 6-6.

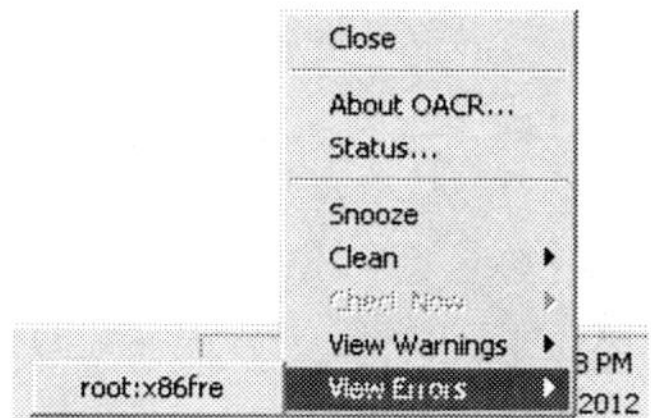

FIGURE 6-6 Starting the OACR warnings and errors viewer UI.

After selecting the target build platform (*x86* or *x64*), you'll see a list of the violations in the project. You can then click the line representing each violation in the list and view more details about it, as shown in Figure 6-7.

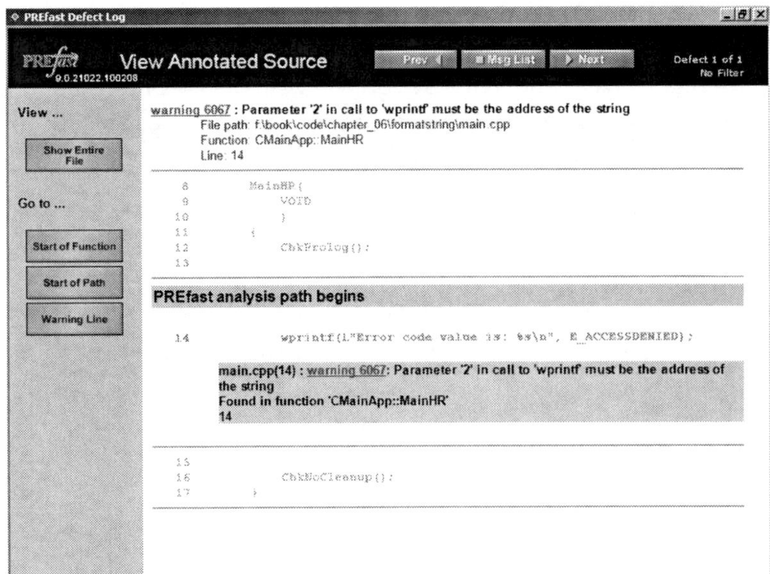

FIGURE 6-7 Viewing violation details in the OACR viewer UI.

You can also reset all previous OACR warnings from the DDK build environment window by using the *clean* option of the *oacr.bat* batch file. Notice how the notification area icon switches to a green color after you execute this command:

```
C:\book\code\chapter_06\FormatString>oacr clean all
```

To go back to the default behavior and enable OACR processing again, you can explicitly use the *set* option of the *oacr.bat* batch file. OACR processing will then be resumed the next time a build is attempted inside the DDK build window.

```
C:\book\code\chapter_06\FormatString>oacr set all
C:\book\code\chapter_06\FormatString>build -cCZ
```

Standalone FxCop Tool

There is also a static-analysis engine for .NET projects in Visual Studio 2010, which can similarly be enabled using the Code Analysis menu. This same engine is also shipped as a standalone tool with the Windows 7 SDK. This tool is called FxCop, highlighting the fact that it can be used to enforce rules and best practices for code built using the .NET Framework.

After completing a full install of the Windows 7 SDK, you'll find the setup program for installing this standalone FxCop version under the directory location where you chose to install the SDK. With the default installation path, you can use the following command to start the FxCop installation process, which brings up the setup user interface depicted in Figure 6-8.

```
C:\Program Files\Microsoft SDKs\Windows\v7.1\Bin\FXCop>FxCopSetup.exe
```

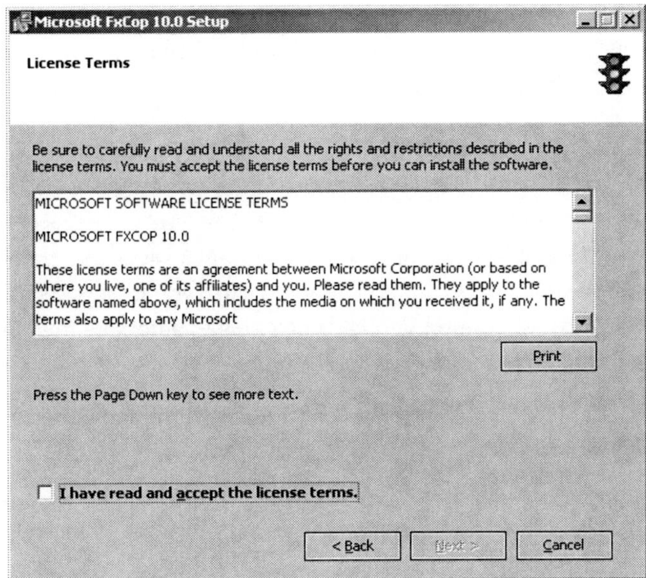

FIGURE 6-8 FxCop installation setup program.

Unlike VC++ static code analysis, .NET code analysis using FxCop is executed over the target assembly image and not its corresponding source code. You can add target assemblies in the FxCop tool UI and run its static-analysis engine to find violations for a set of predefined rules, as demonstrated in Figure 6-9.

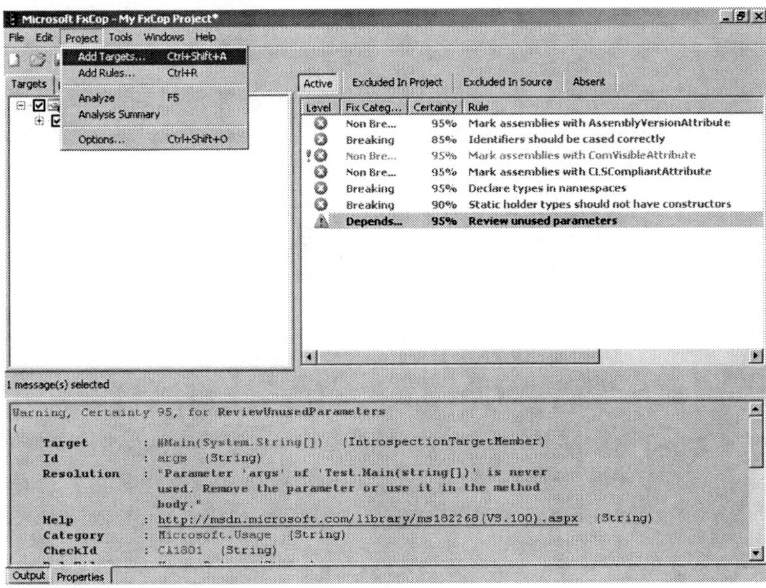

FIGURE 6-9 Static code analysis in the FxCop user interface.

The MSDN website has more detailed coverage of how to use FxCop and the various static-analysis rules it supports. If you're interested in learning more about the capabilities of that tool, you can start at *http://msdn.microsoft.com/en-us/library/bb429476(v=vs.80).aspx*.

Runtime Code Analysis

This section covers the Application Verifier tool, which is the de facto runtime analysis tool for native code in Windows. This tool relies on support in the operating system to catch common misuses of system APIs. With that intimate support, the Application Verifier tool is able to automate the hunt for many hard-to-reproduce code bugs, including the following ones:

- A variety of heap corruption bugs, including many cases of buffer overruns and underruns, double-frees, and invalid memory addresses
- Use of bad resource handles, such as handles that have already been closed or the use of NULL or default handles (such as the handle returned by the *GetCurrentProcess* Win32 API) when not allowed
- Critical section leaks in dynamic-link library (DLL) modules, as well as a host of other critical section usage bugs (double release, use before initialization, and so on)
- Orphaned locks, such as when you call *ExitThread* or *TerminateThread* without releasing a lock that was acquired in the thread callback routine
- Many more bugs with each new release of the tool—because the Windows team at Microsoft extends the tool to cover more common bugs and code defects with every new release of Windows

Because API misuses are raised as runtime assertions that would otherwise go unhandled and lead to the process crashing, the Application Verifier tool is usually best used when the target application is also executed under the control of a debugger so that any potential verifier assertions/breaks can be caught and analyzed inside the debugger. Although verifier assertions can also be caught using the Visual Studio debugger, the tight integration between the verifier debug output and the Windows debuggers extension commands makes WinDbg the companion debugger of choice for Application Verifier experiments.

Catching Your First Bug Using the Application Verifier Tool

The Application Verifier tool is free and can be obtained from the Microsoft Download Center at *http://www.microsoft.com/download/en/details.aspx?id=20028*. By default, the installation setup program places the tool under the *system32* directory. You can then start it either directly by running the *AppVerif.exe* executable or by using its shortcut from the Start menu, as shown in Figure 6-10. The tool also has a nice integrated Help file you can invoke by using the F1 shortcut.

```
C:\Windows\System32>AppVerif.exe
```

FIGURE 6-10 Starting Application Verifier from the Windows Start menu.

When you start the Application Verifier tool, by using the Ctrl+A shortcut you can enable verifier checks for any application on the machine by adding its main executable to the list of applications. As an example, start the Application Verifier and use the Ctrl+A shortcut to enable it for the *DoubleFreeBug.exe* executable image, as shown in Figure 6-11. For this first experiment, you can leave the selected Tests on the right half of the main window to their defaults and simply click Save to commit the changes before exiting the tool.

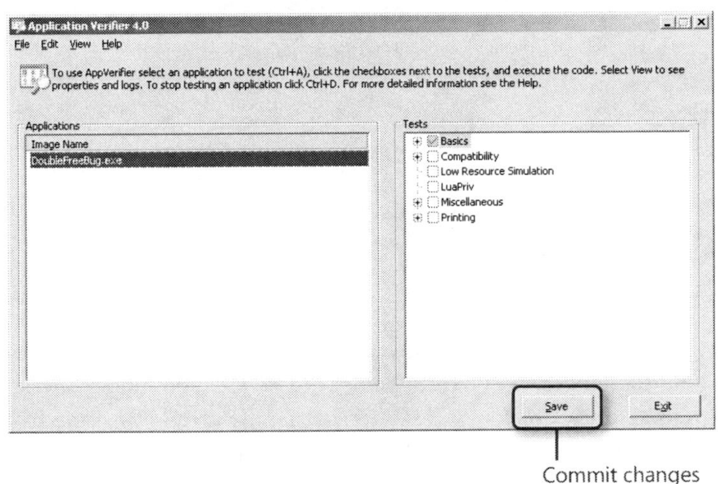

FIGURE 6-11 Enabling basic Application Verifier settings for a C/C++ application.

The C++ program referenced in the previous step is a sample from the companion source code, which has a serious (and relatively common) bug where the cleanup code results in a double-free bug, as you can see in the following listing.

```
//
// C:\book\code\chapter_06\DoubleFree>main.cpp
//
static
HRESULT
MainHR()
{
    CHAR* psz = NULL;

    ChkProlog();

    psz = new CHAR[10];
    ChkAlloc(psz);

    delete[] psz;
    //psz = NULL;

    ChkCleanup();

    // BUG! Double-free of the psz buffer
    //if (psz)
    {
        delete[] psz;
    }

    ChkEpilog();
}
```

If you run this program in standalone mode, it either crashes (unhandled verifier break assertion) or brings up the Just-in-Time (JIT) debugger attach dialog box if a native debugger was previously registered on the machine. If you run the program directly under the WinDbg debugger, though, you'll immediately hit the following verifier break message. Notice that the verifier was able to spot the exact nature of the bug in this case (a "double-free" of a heap block) and triggered the verifier debug break to alert you to the problem.

```
0:000> vercommand
command line: '"c:\Program Files\Debugging Tools for Windows (x86)\windbg.exe"
c:\book\code\chapter_06\DoubleFree\objfre_win7_x86\i386\DoubleFreeBug.exe'
0:000> g
=======================================
VERIFIER STOP 00000007: pid 0x854: Heap block already freed.
    00091000 : Heap handle for the heap owning the block.
    02E30034 : Heap block being freed again.
    0000000A : Size of the heap block.
    00000000 : Not used
```

```
=======================================
(854.1520): Break instruction exception - code 80000003 (first chance)
ntdll!DbgBreakPoint:
774f40f0 cc              int     3
```

You can also see that this runtime assertion was raised by code in the system on behalf of the user-mode program when the attempt to free the same memory buffer was made the second time.

```
0:000> .symfix
0:000> .reload
0:000> k
ChildEBP RetAddr
0006f5d0 59483b68 ntdll!DbgBreakPoint
0006f7d8 594878c9 vrfcore!VerifierStopMessageEx+0x4d1
0006f7fc 10589d3c vrfcore!VfCoreRedirectedStopMessage+0x81
0006f860 10586e4d verifier!AVrfpDphReportCorruptedBlock+0x10c
0006f8c4 105895cc verifier!AVrfpDphFindBusyMemoryNoCheck+0x7d
0006f8e0 77586c1d verifier!AVrfDebugPageHeapSize+0x5c
0006f928 77549359 ntdll!RtlDebugSizeHeap+0x2b
0006f940 58081009 ntdll!RtlSizeHeap+0x27
0006f95c 0069130c vfbasics!AVrfpHeapFree+0x2a
0006f970 00691568 DoubleFreeBug!MemoryFree+0x17
0006f980 00691580 DoubleFreeBug!CMainApp::MainHR+0x2e
[c:\book\code\chapter_06\doublefree\main.cpp @ 28]
0006f988 0069170d DoubleFreeBug!wmain+0x8
0006f9cc 76e4ed6c DoubleFreeBug!__wmainCRTStartup+0x102
...
0:000> q
```

A Behind-the-Scenes Look: Verifier Support in the Operating System

Often, when learning about a new technology, it can be enlightening to get a feel for the core of the area by trying to build something from the ground up. Think back to your first "Hello World!" C++ program or your first C# web service developed using a rudimentary text editor and command-line build tools, and remember how it helped you see through the clutter and gain a better knowledge of the technologies involved. This is certainly not to advocate the blind and obstinate use of command-line tools over the more efficient visual tools; I say it more to stress once again that understanding how tools and programming languages work internally leads to increased proficiency when using higher-level abstractions or development environments. Following this model, this section will demonstrate the operating system's (OS) verifier features without using the Application Verifier tool.

To get this experiment started, you'll need to enable the Application Verifier hooks for your target executable image. You can, for instance, use the following C++ program from the companion source code, which incorrectly passes a thread handle instead of a process handle when calling the *TerminateProcess* Win32 API to request a forced process termination.

```
//
// C:\book\code\chapter_06\BadHandle>main.cpp
//
static
HRESULT
MainHR()
{
    CHandle shThread;

    ChkProlog();

    shThread.Attach(OpenThread(
        THREAD_ALL_ACCESS, FALSE, GetCurrentThreadId()));
    ChkWin32(shThread);

    // BUG! Use of a thread instead of a process handle
    ChkWin32(TerminateProcess(shThread, EXIT_SUCCESS));

    ChkNoCleanup();
}
```

When you run this program without any verifier settings turned on, you'll see that it fails and reports an error HRESULT (*0x80070006*).

```
C:\book\code\chapter_06\BadHandle>objfre_win7_x86\i386\BadHandleBug.exe
HRESULT: 0x80070006
```

This is an invalid handle error, which you can confirm by using the *!error* debugger extension command, as shown in the following listing.

```
0:000> vercommand
command line: '"c:\Program Files\Debugging Tools for Windows (x86)\windbg.exe"  notepad.exe'
0:000> !error 0x80070006
Error code: (HRESULT) 0x80070006 (2147942406) - The handle is invalid.
0:000> q
```

The problem now is to determine where exactly this error came from, which is not always a straightforward exercise, especially if you have a large application with many Win32 API calls that take handle parameters. This is where the Application Verifier hooks can be very helpful. You can use the GFLAGS tool to enable default OS-supplied verifier hooks for this sample program by simply selecting the corresponding option in the UI, as illustrated in Figure 6-12. This is, in fact, one of the things that the Application Verifier tool configures when you use its user interface to enable the verifier hooks for an executable image.

```
"C:\Program Files\Debugging Tools for Windows (x86)\gflags.exe"
```

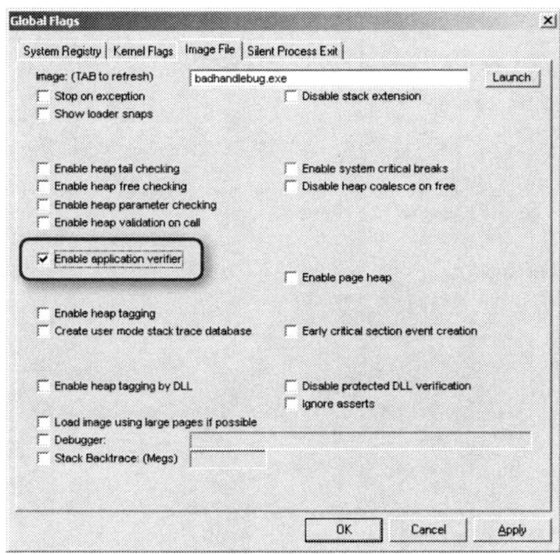

FIGURE 6-12 Enabling the default Application Verifier hooks in the OS using the *gflags.exe* tool.

The previous step simply turns on bit 0x100 in the NT global flag for the process image. By doing so, you are essentially letting the OS know you want common Application Verifier hooks enabled for future instances of the process. The first thing you will notice is that a new DLL called *verifier.dll* is now loaded right after *ntdll.dll* is mapped into the process address space when you run the process under the user-mode debugger, as shown in the following listing. The *verifier.dll* module hosts the core verifier engine in the OS.

```
0:000> vercommand
command line: '"c:\Program Files\Debugging Tools for Windows (x86)\windbg.exe"
c:\book\code\chapter_06\BadHandle\objfre_win7_x86\i386\BadHandleBug.exe'
0:000> lm
start    end        module name
00980000 00985000   BadHandleBug   (deferred)
65e80000 65ee0000   verifier   (deferred)
75870000 75970000   kernel32   (deferred)
75980000 759c6000   KERNELBASE   (deferred)
75a00000 75aac000   msvcrt     (deferred)
77ca0000 77e20000   ntdll      (pdb symbols)
0:000> lmv m verifier
start    end        module name
65e80000 65ee0000   verifier   (deferred)
    Image path: C:\Windows\system32\verifier.dll
    FileDescription:  Standard application verifier provider dll
...
0:000> .symfix
0:000> .reload
0:000> !gflag
Current NtGlobalFlag contents: 0x00000100
    vrf - Enable application verifier
```

If you let the program "go" under the debugger now, you'll immediately hit a verifier break indicating the use of an invalid handle type, as well as the stack trace that raised that verifier stop message.

```
0:000> g
=======================================
VERIFIER STOP 00000305: pid 0x1B88: Incorrect object type for handle.
    000000D4 : Handle value.
    0008FAB8 : Object type name. Use du to display it
    5F945100 : Expected object type name. Use du to display it
    00000000 : Not used.
=======================================
This verifier stop is continuable.
After debugging it use 'go' to continue.
=======================================
(1b88.e44): Break instruction exception - code 80000003 (first chance)
verifier!VerifierStopMessageEx+0x5ce:
5f94c0de cc              int     3
0:000> k
ChildEBP RetAddr
0008fa24 5f95fb7f verifier!VerifierStopMessageEx+0x5ce
0008fadc 5f960324 verifier!AVrfpCheckObjectType+0xb2
0008faf0 75803c22 verifier!AVrfpNtTerminateProcess+0x25
0008fb00 00261554 KERNELBASE!TerminateProcess+0x2c
0008fb1c 00261599 BadHandleBug!CMainApp::MainHR+0x2e
0008fb24 00261726 BadHandleBug!wmain+0x8
...
```

As you can see, the verifier break assertion is raised in the *verifier.dll* layer. The idea behind verifier checks is to update the import table entries corresponding to a few common Win32 API calls. You'll notice, in particular, that the import entry of the *ntdll!NtTerminateProcess* function call, which is invoked by the *TerminateProcess* Win32 API, is altered to point to the *verifier.dll* version of the same function, as demonstrated in the following listing. By using the *uf* ("unassemble function") debugger command, which can help you display the full disassembly of a function routine inside the debugger, you can see that the function performs the verifier checks before calling back into the real *NtTerminateProcess* Win32 API.

```
0:000> x kernelbase!*terminateprocess*
75830ae4 KERNELBASE!NtTerminateProcess = <no type information>
75803bfc KERNELBASE!TerminateProcess = <no type information>
757f11dc KERNELBASE!_imp__NtTerminateProcess = <no type information>
0:000> dd 757f11dc
757f11dc  5f9602ff 7751dfdc 775062a8 77507105
0:000> uf 5f9602ff
verifier!AVrfpNtTerminateProcess:
5f9602ff 8bff            mov     edi,edi
5f960301 55              push    ebp
```

```
5f960302 8bec            mov     ebp,esp
5f960304 56              push    esi
5f960305 6a3a            push    3Ah
5f960307 68402e975f      push    offset verifier!AVrfpNtdllThunks (5f972e40)
5f96030c e80043ffff      call    verifier!AVrfpGetThunkDescriptor (5f954611)
5f960311 837d0800        cmp     dword ptr [ebp+8],0
5f960315 8b7004          mov     esi,dword ptr [eax+4]
5f960318 740a            je      verifier!AVrfpNtTerminateProcess+0x25 (5f960324)
verifier!AVrfpNtTerminateProcess+0x1b:
5f96031a 6a02            push    2
5f96031c ff7508          push    dword ptr [ebp+8]
5f96031f e88ef8ffff      call    verifier!AVrfpHandleSanityChecks (5f95fbb2)
verifier!AVrfpNtTerminateProcess+0x25:
5f960324 ff750c          push    dword ptr [ebp+0Ch]
5f960327 ff7508          push    dword ptr [ebp+8]
5f96032a ffd6            call    esi
5f96032c 5e              pop     esi
5f96032d 5d              pop     ebp
5f96032e c20800          ret     8
0:000> q
```

One immediate corollary of the fact that Application Verifier checks are inserted at run time by updating the import table of the modules consuming the hooked APIs is that those hooks are relevant only in the context of user-mode code. For kernel-mode drivers, Microsoft ships another tool with the operating system, called the *driver verifier tool* (*verifier.exe*).

Also, if you've noticed, all you really did so far in this particular experiment was set a bit in the *GlobalFlag* Image File Execution Options (IFEO) registry value for the target executable image. That was, by itself, enough to enable a default set of verifier checks. As it turns out, you can also control which checks to enable by using a second DWORD registry value named *VerifierFlags*, which also lives under the IFEO registry key for the target executable image. Notice the "s" at the end of the value name of this second flag, unlike the NT global flag value, which does not have an "s" at the end!

Being able to control this second registry value is one key advantage to using the Application Verifier tool UI over enabling the verifier checks using GFLAGS. If you go back and edit the verifier settings for the program used in this experiment by using the Application Verifier UI, you'll observe after you click the Save button that both the *GlobalFlag* and *VerifierFlags* registry values are automatically populated by the tool, as demonstrated in Figure 6-13, which depicts the IFEO key for the target process image (*BadHandleBug.exe* in this case).

```
[HKEY_LOCAL_MACHINE\SOFTWARE\Microsoft\Windows NT\CurrentVersion\Image File Execution Options\
BadHandleBug.exe]
```

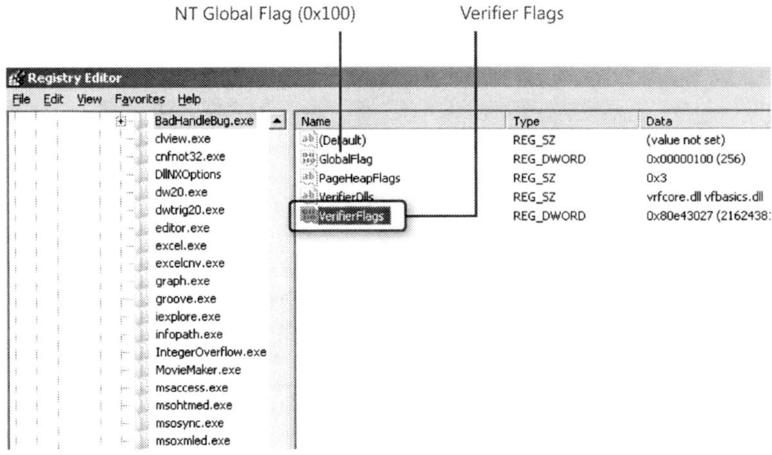

FIGURE 6-13 Application Verifier settings in the system registry when using the UI tool.

The *!avrf* Debugger Extension Command

The *!avrf* extension command is a useful debugger command that can be used to view the verifier flags in effect for the process you're debugging, akin to how the *!gflag* command is used to view the NT global flag. However, there is an unfortunate catch you need to be aware of, and the *!avrf* command will give you the following error if you simply set your debugger symbols search path to the Microsoft public symbols server.

```
0:000> .symfix
0:000> .reload
0:000> !avrf
Verifier package version >= 3.00
No type information found for '_AVRF_EXCEPTION_LOG_ENTRY'.
Please fix the symbols for 'vfbasics.dll'.
0:000> q
```

This is because *vfbasics.dll* is installed as part of the application verifier tool along with its private symbols under the *system32* directory. However, this DLL (along with a few others that also come with the Application Verifier tool's MSI setup) also has public symbols on the Microsoft symbols server, which don't have the type definitions needed by the extension to function properly! To work around this problem, you should set your symbols path so that the local *system32* path comes *before* the Microsoft symbols server so that *vfbasics.pdb* is found first under the *system32* directory.

If you restart your debugging session and set the symbols path this way, you'll see the correct output from the *!avrf* extension command.

```
0:000> vercommand
command line: '"c:\Program Files\Debugging Tools for Windows (x86)\windbg.exe"
objfre_win7_x86\i386\BadHandleBug.exe'
0:000> .sympath c:\windows\system32;srv*c:\localsymbolcache*http://msdl.microsoft.com/download/
symbols
```

```
0:000> .reload
0:000> !avrf
Verifier package version >= 3.00
Application verifier settings (80643027):
   - full page heap
   - Handles
   - Locks
   - Memory
   - TLS
   - Exceptions
   - Threadpool
   - Leak
No verifier stop active.
0:000> q
```

Note You can also solve the previous problem and not have to explicitly prefix the *system32* path to your debugger symbols search path if you manually copy the private PDB symbol files for all the verifier DLLs from the *system32* directory, where they get installed by default to your local debugger symbols cache path.

In the previous case, there was no active verifier stop, so the *!avrf* command simply displayed the active configuration in effect for the process (similar to what the *!gflag* command does for the NT global flag). A more useful application of the *!avrf* command is after a verifier stop is hit inside the debugger, in which case the command provides more information on the nature of the verifier break and a few hints on how to investigate it, as illustrated in the following continuation of the previous debugging session.

```
0:000> g
VERIFIER STOP 00000305: pid 0x720: Incorrect object type for handle.
...
0:000> !avrf
...
*******************************************************
*           Exception Analysis                        *
*******************************************************
APPLICATION_VERIFIER_HANDLES_INCORRECT_OBJECT_TYPE (305)
Incorrect object type for handle.
This stop is generated if the current thread is calling an API with a handle to
an object with an incorrect object type. E.g. calling SetEvent with a semaphore
handle as parameter will generate this stop. To debug this stop:
$ kb - to display the current stack trace. The culprit is probably the DLL
that is calling into verifier.dll;
$ du parameter2 - to display the actual type of the handle. The handle value
is parameter1. In the example above, this will display: Semaphore.
$ du parameter3 - to display the object type expected by the API. In the example above,
this name will be: Event.
$ !htrace parameter1 might be helpful because it will display the stack
trace for the recent open/close operations on this handle.
```

```
Arguments:
Arg1: 0000047c, Handle value.
Arg2: 0014f830, Object type name. Use du to display it
Arg3: 70be46f8, Expected object type name. Use du to display it
Arg4: 00000000, Not used.
...
FOLLOWUP_IP:
BadHandleBug!CMainApp::MainHR+49 [c:\book\code\chapter_06\badhandle\main.cpp @ 19]
...
0:000> q
```

Finally, note that not unlike how the OS enables a few debug heap options by default when running under a user-mode debugger and no explicit *GlobalFlag* value is specified, a similar dynamic occurs for the *VerifierFlags* registry value as the OS enables a few verifier bits by default when the primary application verifier bit in the NT global flag is set. (Although in this case, this happens whether the program is run under a user-mode debugger or not.) This explains why you were able to catch the handle-type mismatch issue in the experiment you conducted earlier, where all you did was simply set the verifier bit using the GFLAGS tool.

To confirm the previous point, delete the *BadHandleBug.exe* application from the Application Verifier UI using the Ctrl+D shortcut, and then use the GFLAGS tool again to enable the verifier bit in the NT global flag for the target image, as was demonstrated in Figure 6-12. After these changes are made, the IFEO registry key for the *BadHandleBug.exe* image should have only one DWORD value (*GlobalFlag*) that's set to 0x100, as shown in Figure 6-14.

```
[HKEY_LOCAL_MACHINE\SOFTWARE\Microsoft\Windows NT\CurrentVersion\Image File Execution Options\
BadHandleBug.exe]
```

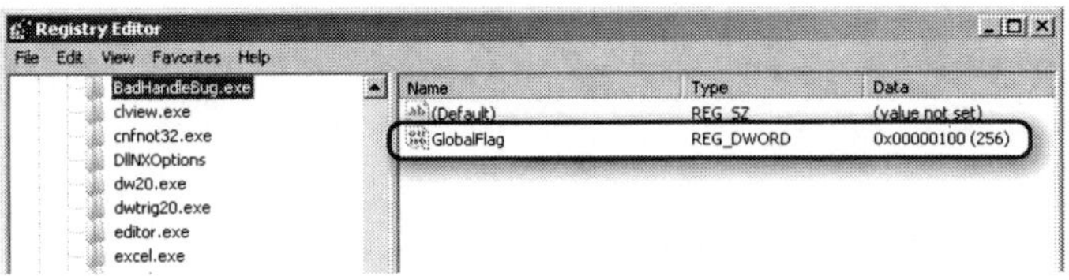

FIGURE 6-14 Enabling the Application Verifier with the default system checks.

You'll notice that handle checks are one of the default categories enabled by the system when no *VerifierFlags* value is provided for the target image but the main 0x100 verifier bit in the NT global flag is set, as confirmed by the output of the *!avrf* extension command in the following listing.

```
0:000> vercommand
command line: '"c:\Program Files\Debugging Tools for Windows (x86)\windbg.exe"
c:\book\code\chapter_06\BadHandle\objfre_win7_x86\i386\BadHandleBug.exe'
0:000> .sympath c:\windows\system32;srv*c:\localsymbolcache*http://msdl.microsoft.com/download/
symbols
0:000> .reload
```

```
0:000> !avrf
Application verifier settings (00048004):
   - fast fill heap (a.k.a light page heap)
   - lock checks (critical section verifier)
   - handle checks
No verifier stop active.
0:000> q
```

The Application Verifier as a Quality Assurance Tool

The Application Verifier is a great addition to your arsenal of quality assurance tools. Like the NT global flag, the Application Verifier settings can also be applied either to a single process (the default operating mode exposed in the UI of the tool) or systemwide. Enabling the Application Verifier settings systemwide can also be done by using the System Registry tab in the GFLAGS tool to edit the NT global flag value under the session manager registry key. This testing environment is used, for example, by the Windows product group at Microsoft when executing the daily automated test passes used to catch regression bugs.

```
Windows Registry Editor Version 5.00

[HKEY_LOCAL_MACHINE\SYSTEM\CurrentControlSet\Control\Session Manager]
"GlobalFlag"=dword:00000100
```

When enabling Application Verifier settings systemwide, the *verifier.dll* module gets loaded into every user-mode process on the system. Note, however, that one key difference from the per-process Application Verifier behavior is that there is no way to enable additional verifier checks (providers) systemwide. If you really need to do that, you can use the Application Verifier tool UI and manually enable the providers for each process you're interested in.

At Microsoft, running the Application Verifier tool is a mandatory step before signing off any public product release. This is a good practice that you might also want to follow with your own products. There is simply no excuse for missing bugs that can easily be detected in a matter of minutes by this excellent tool.

Summary

This chapter covered a few code analysis tools you can use in Windows to automate the process of finding code defects early, before you need to call on the debuggers to investigate bugs that eventually get uncovered either by ad-hoc testing or, worse, as they surface in customer or production environments.

The following points summarize some of the static and runtime code analysis strategies discussed in this chapter and their key characteristics:

- Static code analysis tries to automate the best practice of using peer code reviews by statically scanning the source code or program binaries for common code defects.

- Visual Studio 2010 supports static code analysis of both C/C++ and .NET code. The underlying engines are different, though. In the case of C/C++, Visual Studio uses the engine behind the VC++ */analyze* compiler option, also used in the DDK build environment and its OACR static-analysis system. In the case of .NET, Visual Studio uses the FxCop engine, which is also available as a standalone tool that comes with the Windows 7 and .NET Framework 4.0 SDK.
- SAL annotations are needed by the VC++ static-analysis engine so that it will know the shape of the parameters passed in and out of function calls. Most of the Win32 API is currently annotated, which means you can take advantage of SAL in your static analysis even if your code doesn't directly use it.
- Using SAL in your native code can help the VC++ static-analysis engine catch more issues in your code. So, learning how to use SAL can help you take full advantage of the Visual C/C++ static-analysis engine. Most of the internal Windows source code also uses SAL specifically for this reason.
- The Application Verifier tool is the de facto runtime code analysis tool for native code in Windows. It works by replacing the import table entries for common system APIs with calls that first perform additional verifier checks before eventually making the requested call. Many API misuse bugs can be automatically detected by simply enabling this tool and running the application.
- The Application Verifier tool is focused only on native, user-mode code runtime analysis and doesn't target kernel code. Drivers also have an inbox runtime tool, called the driver verifier tool, which can be used to enable several checks in the OS code that detect common bugs and raise them as kernel bug checks that can be analyzed by using a kernel-mode debugger.
- Application Verifier breaks are raised as runtime assertions (SEH exceptions) that would go unhandled if the process was not run under a debugger, causing it to simply die unless a native JIT debugger was configured on the machine under the *AeDebug* registry key. This is why it's usually best to run the target application under a debugger during Application Verifier testing so that you automatically catch any verifier stops that might get reported using the attached debugger.

CHAPTER 7

Expert Debugging Tricks

In this chapter

After you begin using the debuggers in even moderately complex scenarios, you'll quickly realize that you often need to accomplish a small set of fairly common tasks. You might want, for example, to know if there are additional processes that get created when executing your test scenario. You might also need to start them directly under the control of a debugger so that you can debug their startup code path. In other cases, you might have to wait for a specific dynamic-link library (DLL) module to get loaded before setting code breakpoints at a function that it hosts.

When I was learning user-mode debugging, I often found myself frustrated by the fact that the documentation of the debuggers didn't directly help me with the aforementioned needs. I could find information on how to use a number of commands, but putting them together to accomplish useful tasks was often an arduous trial-and-error exercise. When I later started using kernel-mode debugging more systematically as a useful complement to user-mode debugging, I had to go through the same learning process. To my surprise, I found that some tasks that were natively supported by user-mode debugger commands, such as freezing threads or waiting for a DLL to get loaded, did not have any direct equivalents in the kernel-mode debugger. Not even reading the entire commands-centric documentation could help me in that case!

The goal of this chapter is to take a scenario-centric approach and distill some of the most efficient ways to achieve those common tasks inside the user-mode and kernel-mode debuggers. The chapter starts with user-mode debugging tricks before closing with a few generic techniques that will help you make the most out of your use of kernel-mode debugging.

Essential Tricks

In this first section, you'll learn how to get the programs you're debugging under the control of a user-mode debugger when a new process starts up or when a DLL is mapped into the address space of a user-mode process. These two categories of events often represent critical junctures in the lifetime of the scenarios you debug because they allow you to break into the debugger early enough, which then puts you in position to issue the commands you need to debug their behaviors.

Waiting for a Debugger to Attach to the Target

If you can change the source code of your application, one easy way to block at key junctures during your program's execution and give yourself a chance to attach a user-mode debugger is to simply insert an infinite loop based on the value of a global Boolean flag. After you attach the debugger, you can then change the value of the conditional flag in memory directly from the debugger and force the loop to exit so that the program continues its normal execution. You should remove this infinite loop, of course, as soon as you're done with your debugging experiment.

Despite its surprising simplicity, this approach derives several advantages from the powerful debugger "attach" mechanism. In particular, the user-mode debugger can be started within the security context of your choice. If you simply inserted a debug break instead of using the debugger wait loop idea suggested here, the Just-in-Time (JIT) debugging sequence (which was explained in Chapter 4, "Postmortem Debugging") would start the debugger within the same security context as the target process, which can sometimes be insufficient when the target process happens to be running with low privileges.

The previous trick can also be applied in .NET code or even scripts. To provide a practical illustration, you'll now apply this technique to debug the "startup" code path of the following JScript example from the companion source code.

```
//
// C:\book\code\chapter_07\WaitForDebugger>test.js
//
var g_bAttached;
function WaitForDebugger()
{
    g_fAttached = false;
    while (!g_bAttached);
}

function main()
{
    WaitForDebugger();
    RunScript();
}
```

You'll need to run the previous script with the *//D* (double-slash) command-line option so that the script-debugging support in the host process gets enabled. As discussed back in the "Script Debugging" section of Chapter 3, "How Windows Debuggers Work," the Process Debug Manager (PDM) needs to be explicitly enabled for script debugging to work. In the case of the *cscript.exe* host, this is done by using the *//D* option.

```
C:\book\code\chapter_07\WaitForDebugger>cscript test.js //D
```

The script then blocks when it hits the *WaitForDebugger* function, and you can then attach the Microsoft Visual Studio debugger to it by using the Debug\Attach To Process menu action, as usual. Remember to run Visual Studio with the same privileges as the target-script host process. So, if you ran the script from an elevated administrative command prompt, you also need to start the Visual Studio process with the same elevated privileges. You should then select the target *cscript.exe* host process from the list of active processes, as illustrated in Figure 7-1.

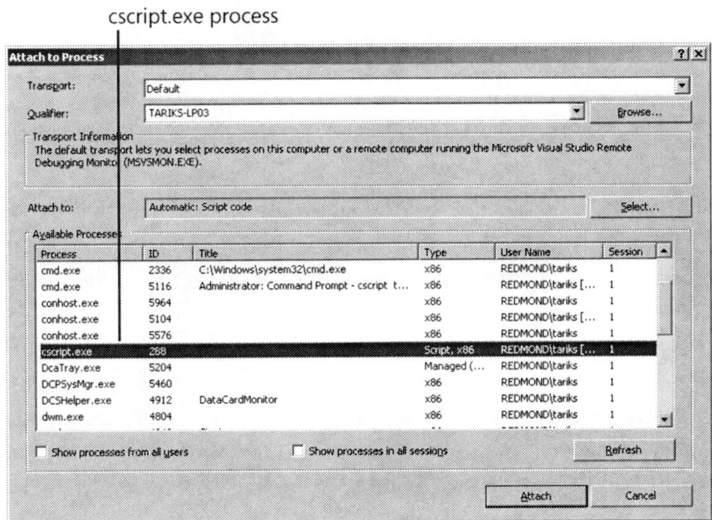

FIGURE 7-1 Attaching the Visual Studio 2010 debugger to the blocked script.

Once the "attach" operation is completed, you can use the Debug\Break All menu action (or the Ctrl+Alt+Break shortcut) to issue a break-in request. Using the locals window, which you can invoke using the Debug\Windows\Locals menu action, you can then forcibly change the value of the flag to *true*, as illustrated in Figure 7-2. This unblocks the infinite wait loop and allows you to continue debugging the script and step through its source code using the usual F10 (step-over) and F11 (step-into) shortcuts.

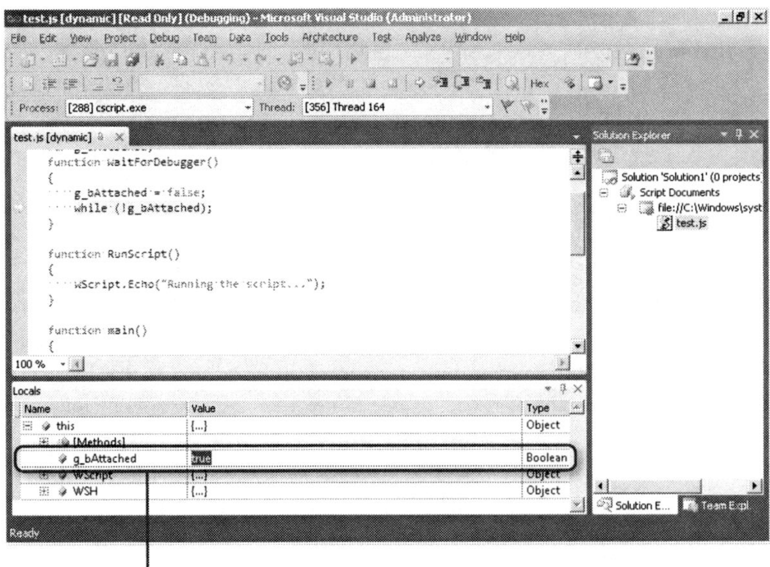

Set conditional flag to true after breaking in.

FIGURE 7-2 Unblocking the infinite wait loop by manually editing the value of the conditional flag.

The technique described in this section allows you to stop anywhere within your source code (akin to an artificial breakpoint). The key drawback to it, however, is that it requires you to change the source code and rebuild the target binary (for native and .NET code, at least) in order for it to work. This is not always possible—in particular, when you're debugging system code or third-party software for which you don't have the source code. So, the rest of this section will focus on alternative techniques that, although not as generic as the previous trick, will at least help you stop under the debugger when DLL module load events occur or new processes are created. Once you're able to intercept these two important events, you will be able to also set additional breakpoints and stop at other junctures over the course of the scenario you're debugging—just as you can do when using the "attach" wait loop trick.

Breaking on DLL Load Events

Breaking on DLL load events can be useful in many situations. In particular, breaking into the debugger just as a DLL is mapped into the target process gives you the opportunity to look up its symbols (using the *x* command) and then set breakpoints at functions from that DLL before the code it hosts gets to run. In several scenarios, the DLLs you write get loaded into system-provided host processes, such as the *dllhost.exe* surrogate process for DLL COM servers and the *svchost.exe* process for DLL Windows services. In such cases, you are not in control of precisely when and where your DLL module gets loaded, so you need to wait until the DLL is mapped before you can set other breakpoints in your code. Without this capability, it might be too late to step into the code you're interested in by the time the host process starts up and you then try to attach to it using a user-mode debugger.

Breaking on DLL Load Events in the WinDbg Debugger

The WinDbg user-mode debugger supports breaking on DLL load events natively, which you can do by using the *sxe ld [module_name]* (stop on module load "exception") command. You probably remember the *sxe ld* command from the examples used to introduce the SOS debugger extension in the "Managed-Code Debugging" section in Chapter 3. In that case, the command was used to wait for the Common Language Runtime (CLR) execution engine DLL to get mapped into the target address space before then loading the matching *sos.dll* extension from the same directory by using the *.loadby* command.

The *sxe ld* command also supports wildcard characters in the module name argument it takes. As an illustration, the following listing starts a user-mode debugging session with *notepad.exe* as the target process, and then instructs the debugger to break in whenever a new DLL is loaded into the *notepad.exe* target process. Notice that you're able to list the module name of each new DLL as it gets loaded. You can also compare the *ModLoad* message logged by the debugger with the output from the *.lastevent* command, which shows the last event that caused the debugger break-in (a DLL module load in the case of this listing). Note, finally, that when you use the *sxe ld* command twice during the same debugging session, the last one wins and replaces the match pattern specified in the first command.

```
0:000> vercommand
command line: '"c:\Program Files\Debugging Tools for Windows (x86)\windbg.exe"  notepad.exe'
0:000> .symfix
0:000> .reload
0:000> sxe ld *.dll
0:000> g
ModLoad: 76da0000 76dbf000   C:\Windows\system32\IMM32.DLL
ntdll!KiFastSystemCallRet:
777370b4 c3              ret
0:000> .lastevent
Last event: 1490.1dc8: Load module C:\Windows\system32\IMM32.DLL at 76da0000
0:000> g
ModLoad: 77260000 7732c000   C:\Windows\system32\MSCTF.dll
ntdll!KiFastSystemCallRet:
777370b4 c3              ret
0:000> .lastevent
Last event: 1490.1dc8: Load module C:\Windows\system32\MSCTF.dll at 77260000
```

When you no longer want to break into the debugger in response to these module load events, you can simply use the *sxd ld* (disable load "exception" handling) command, as shown in the following listing.

```
0:000> sxd ld
0:000> $ Notice the debugger no longer stops on new module load events now...
0:000> g
0:000> $ Terminate this debugging session
0:000> q
```

As mentioned at the top of this section, a common use case of the *sxe ld* command is when you need to set code breakpoints in DLL modules but can't simply let the DLL load first because the code might get executed before you can complete a regular debugger attach. To illustrate this case, the companion source code contains a simple C++ tool that can be used to load DLL modules dynamically.

```
//
// C:\book\code\tools\dllhost>main.cpp
//
static
HRESULT
MainHR(
    __in int argc,
    __in_ecount(argc) WCHAR* argv[]
    )
{
...
    hModule = ::LoadLibraryW(argv[1]);
    ChkWin32(hModule);
    FreeLibrary(hModule);
...
}
```

After you compile the previous sample (using the procedure described in the Introduction), you can use the following listing to break into the debugger when the target module is loaded, and insert a breakpoint at the *DllMain* entry point code of that DLL using the *bp* command so that you can then debug the startup code path of the target DLL.

```
0:000> vercommand
command line: '"c:\Program Files\Debugging Tools for Windows (x86)\windbg.exe"
c:\book\code\tools\DllHost\objfre_win7_x86\i386\host.exe
c:\book\code\chapter_07\BreakOnDllLoad\objfre_win7_x86\i386\DllModule.dll'
0:000> .symfix
0:000> .reload
0:000> sxe ld DllModule.dll
0:000> g
...
777370b4 c3              ret
0:000> .lastevent
Last event: 1eb4.16a0: Load module
c:\book\code\chapter_07\BreakOnDllLoad\objfre_win7_x86\i386\DllModule.dll at 73ec0000
...
0:000> $ set a breakpoint at the DLL entry point function
0:000> bp dllmodule!DllMain
0:000> g
Breakpoint 0 hit
DllModule!DllMain:
```

Figure 7-3 depicts the state of the debugging session at the end of the previous listing. You can now step through the startup code of the DLL (*DllMain* routine) and set any additional breakpoints you need to debug the code in the DLL module.

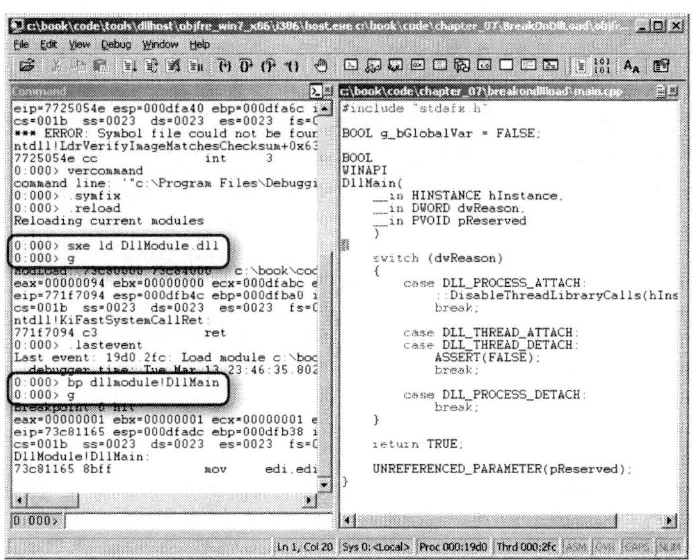

FIGURE 7-3 Debugging the startup code path of DLL modules.

When you're done debugging the DLL, you can exit the user-mode debugging session using either the *q* (quit and terminate the target) or *qd* (quit and detach without terminating the target) command, as usual.

```
0:000> $ Terminate this debugging session now...
0:000> q
```

Breaking on DLL Load Events in the Visual Studio Debugger

Visual Studio has no direct equivalent to the *sxe ld* command because this isn't often needed in that case, where you're usually debugging your own code. The Visual Studio debugger is also kind enough to let you set source-level breakpoints (using the F9 shortcut) in the DLL modules you compile without having to worry about when they get loaded, as long as you have the source code (and private symbols) for them.

That being said, however, you might still want to break into the Visual Studio debugger when a system DLL (such as the CLR execution engine DLL) gets loaded. Fortunately, an alternative solution exists, though the way it works internally is fundamentally different from how the *sxe ld* command is implemented in WinDbg. The idea behind this trick is to take advantage of an existing debugging hook in the system that you can enable using the *BreakOnDllLoad* Image File Execution Option (IFEO). The effect of this hook is to instruct the module loader of the operating system (OS) to raise a debug break instruction whenever the specified image name is about to get loaded into a user-mode process. Note that the system does so only when the target process happens to be under the control of a user-mode debugger, so the hook has no effect when you run the scenario in standalone mode.

The Global Flags editor (GFLAGS) tool covered in Chapter 5, "Beyond the Basics," doesn't support this particular IFEO value, so you'll need to edit the registry manually. If you're running your experiment on 64-bit Windows, in particular, you need to modify the 32-bit view of the registry if your target is a WOW64 process. The companion source code has a wrapper script to help you make these registry modifications without having to worry about these details. The following command, for example, enables this hook for the *advapi32.dll* Win32 DLL. Remember to run the command from an elevated administrative command prompt so that you can modify the target IFEO registry key successfully.

```
C:\book\code\chapter_07\scripts>configure_breakondllload.cmd -enable advapi32.dll
```

You can verify whether the previous command was successful by inspecting the IFEO key for the *advapi32.dll* image in the registry. If everything worked correctly, there should be a new REG_DWORD value, named *BreakOnDllLoad*, under the IFEO key, and its value should be set to *1*, as shown in Figure 7-4.

```
[HKEY_LOCAL_MACHINE\SOFTWARE\Microsoft\Windows NT\CurrentVersion\Image File Execution Options
\advapi32.dll]
```

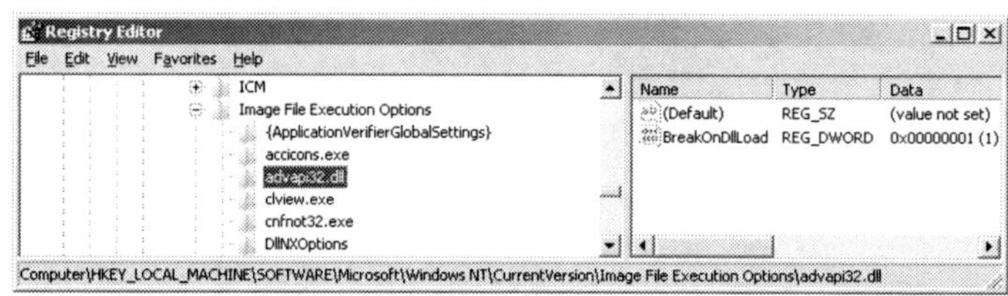

FIGURE 7-4 The *BreakOnDllLoad* value under the IFEO registry key.

To see how this works in practice, the companion source code has a Visual Studio 2010 C++ project where the main function simply loads the *advapi32.dll* module. If you open that project and execute it using the F5 shortcut, a debug break instruction will be issued by the system when the module is loaded. The Visual Studio debugger, acting as a native user-mode debugger, will then catch it and display the dialog box shown in Figure 7-5.

```
C:\book\code\chapter_07\BreakOnDllLoadVs>BreakOnDllLoad.sln
```

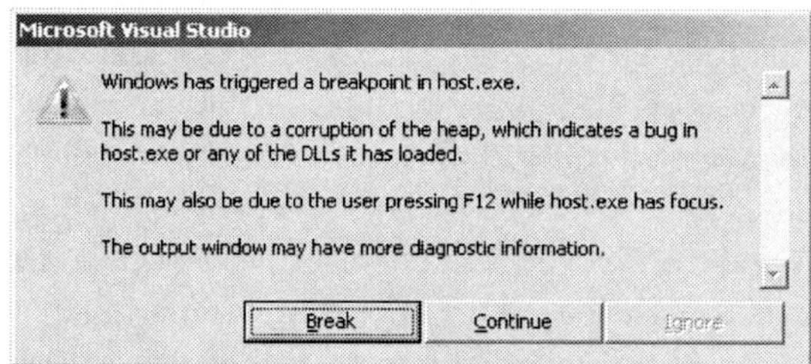

FIGURE 7-5 Module load event triggering a debug break dialog box in Visual Studio 2010.

The message in that dialog box is a bit misleading and incorrectly indicates that there is a bug in the target process, though this Structured Exception Handling (SEH) exception was an intentional debug break inserted by the system on your behalf and so isn't really a code bug. When you see the dialog box, you can click the Break button shown in Figure 7-5, which will break in to the debugger at the source line that tried to load *advapi32.dll*, as shown in Figure 7-6.

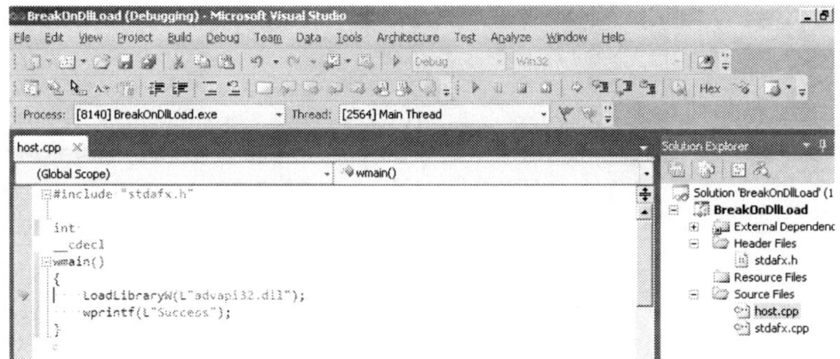

FIGURE 7-6 Breaking on a DLL load event in the Visual Studio debugger.

Don't forget to delete the *BreakOnDllLoad* registry key after you're done with this debugging experiment; otherwise, it will cause all user-mode debuggers (including WinDbg!) to break in while debugging any process that tries to load *advapi32.dll* on the system. You can use the same script you used earlier to delete the *BreakOnDllLoad* value under the IFEO key for the *advapi32.dll* image, as demonstrated in the following command.

```
C:\book\code\chapter_07\scripts>configure_breakondllload.cmd -disable advapi32.dll
```

Debugging Process Startup

One of the most common debugging needs is the ability to get a new process to stop inside a user-mode debugger at startup time. Not only is that behavior required to debug code that runs early as part of the startup code path, but this can also prove particularly useful when debugging large scenarios that involve the creation of multiple processes as part of a long sequence of events. In this fairly common case, it can be difficult to know when the process you're trying to debug will be started, let alone be able to issue the regular debugger attach request (using the F6 shortcut, for example, in the case of WinDbg) so that it coincides exactly with the start of the new process. Fortunately, there is an OS debugging hook that allows you to specify a *startup debugger* whenever an executable image is started.

Startup Debugging in Action

The startup debugger is another IFEO debugging hook you can configure using the GFLAGS tool. For example, Figure 7-7 illustrates how you can enable this hook for *notepad.exe*: enter the image name (with the extension!) in the Image text box and press Tab. Then, select the Debugger option and enter the full path to the debugger program in the corresponding text box.

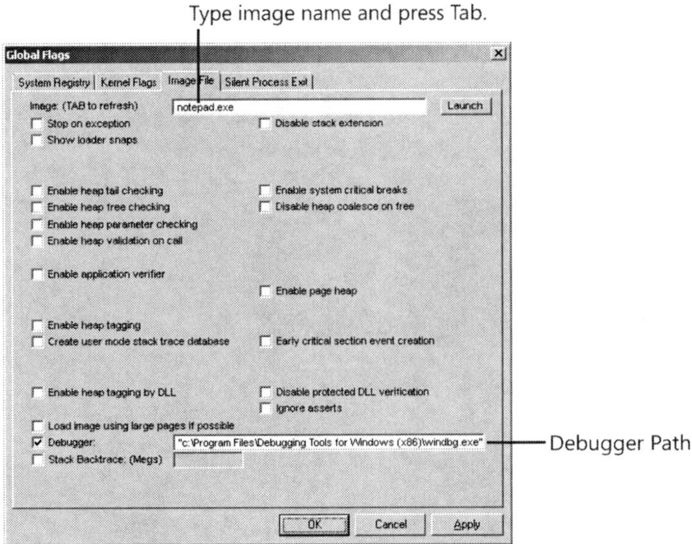

FIGURE 7-7 Configuring the startup debugger for an executable image name using GFLAGS.

Once you click OK to commit the configuration, the GFLAGS tool inserts the following *Debugger* registry value under the IFEO key for the target image name, with the full debugger's path you provided in the UI as its string value:

```
Windows Registry Editor Version 5.00

[HKEY_LOCAL_MACHINE\SOFTWARE\Microsoft\Windows NT\CurrentVersion\Image File Execution Options
\notepad.exe]
"Debugger"="c:\\Program Files\\Debugging Tools for Windows (x86)\\windbg.exe"
```

Notice now that whenever you start a new instance of *notepad.exe*, the new process starts directly under the *windbg.exe* debugger. You can then, in particular, set a breakpoint at the main entry point of the process and debug the early stages of its execution, as illustrated in Figure 7-8, which depicts the debugging session corresponding to the following listing.

```
C:\Windows\system32>notepad
...
0:000> vercommand
command line: '"c:\Program Files\Debugging Tools for Windows (x86)\windbg.exe" notepad'
0:000> .symfix
0:000> .reload
0:000> x notepad!*main*
006c1320 notepad!_imp____getmainargs = <no type information>
006c1405 notepad!WinMain = <no type information>
006c3689 notepad!WinMainCRTStartup = <no type information>
0:000> bp notepad!WinMain
0:000> g
(1fec.11cc): Break instruction exception - code 80000003 (first chance)
ntdll!LdrpRunInitializeRoutines+0x211:
7741d75a cc              int     3
```

```
0:000> g
Breakpoint 0 hit
notepad!WinMain:
...
0:000> q
```

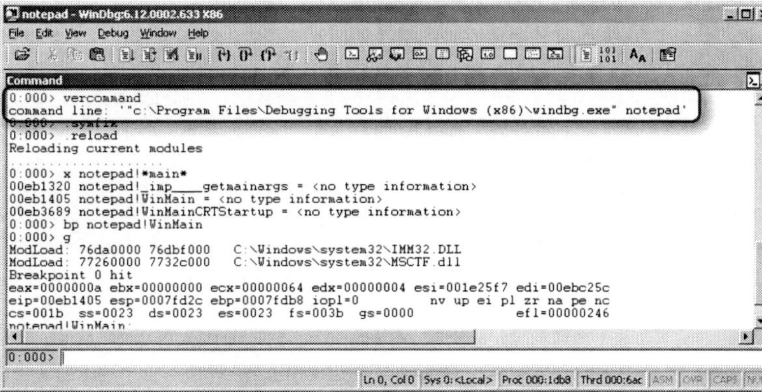

FIGURE 7-8 Debugging the startup code path using the startup debugger IFEO.

Because the startup debugger configuration affects every new instance of the executable program, don't forget to reset it as soon as you're finished with your debugging investigation. You can do so, for example, by clearing the Debugger option for the target image using the GFLAGS tool, as shown in Figure 7-9.

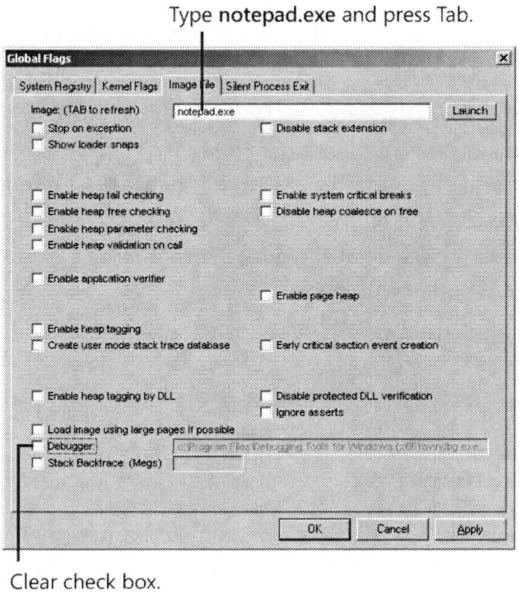

Type **notepad.exe** and press Tab.

Clear check box.

FIGURE 7-9 Clearing the startup debugger for a process image in GFLAGS.

How the Startup Debugger Hook Works

When a startup debugger is configured for a user-mode executable image, the loader code in *ntdll.dll* concatenates the IFEO startup debugger string value read from the registry with the initial command line before proceeding to start new instances of the target process. It then uses this newly constructed command line (*"c:\Program Files\Debugging Tools for Windows (x86)\windbg.exe" notepad.exe* in the previous case) in place of the original one (*notepad.exe*) to start the new process. There are two important observations that follow from the way this scheme works:

- New instances of the target process will be started directly under the user-mode startup debugger when using this method.
- The debugger process will be running with the same user context as the original process. So, when the target instance is started with restricted privileges, that might also affect your ability to perform privileged operations in the debugger, such as accessing symbol files on remote network shares.

The generic way in which this feature is implemented in the operating system allows it to support any user-mode debugger. In particular, because all the loader does is concatenate the *Debugger* string value from the registry with the original command line, it's also possible to employ Visual Studio as your startup debugger by using the */debugExe* option of the *devenv.exe* Visual Studio debugger process, as shown in the following registry configuration.

```
Windows Registry Editor Version 5.00

[HKEY_LOCAL_MACHINE\SOFTWARE\Microsoft\Windows NT\CurrentVersion\Image File Execution Options
\notepad.exe]
"Debugger"="\"c:\\Program Files\\Microsoft Visual Studio 10.0\\Common7\\IDE\\devenv.exe\"
 -debugexe"
```

Another useful extension of the startup debugging idea is to combine it with the ability to script the Windows debuggers. For example, the following startup debugger configuration allows you not only to get new instances of the *notepad.exe* process to automatically start under the debugger, but it also executes the *StopAtMain.txt* script when the debugger instance starts up. This can make your debugging iterations more efficient by saving you the hassle of retyping the common commands you know you'll always need to run to start your debugging investigation.

```
Windows Registry Editor Version 5.00

[HKEY_LOCAL_MACHINE\SOFTWARE\Microsoft\Windows NT\CurrentVersion\Image File Execution Options
\notepad.exe]
"Debugger"="\"c:\\Program Files\\Debugging Tools for Windows (x86)\\windbg.exe\" -c
\"$$><C:\\book\\code\\chapter_07\\Scripts\\StopAtMain.txt\""
```

In the previous configuration, notice the use of the *–c* command-line option of *windbg.exe*, which was covered back in the "Scripting the Debugger" section of Chapter 5, to execute a script as the first command after the startup debugger is started. The script, in this case, simply fixes up the symbols search path to include the Microsoft public symbols server, reloads the symbols, and then sets a breakpoint at the entry point of *notepad.exe*.

```
$$
$$ C:\book\code\chapter_07\Scripts>StopAtMain.txt
$$
.symfix
.reload
bp notepad!WinMain
g
k
```

With the previous setup, you'll stop under the startup debugger right at the main entry point of *notepad.exe* whenever a new instance of that process is started on the machine, as shown in Figure 7-10.

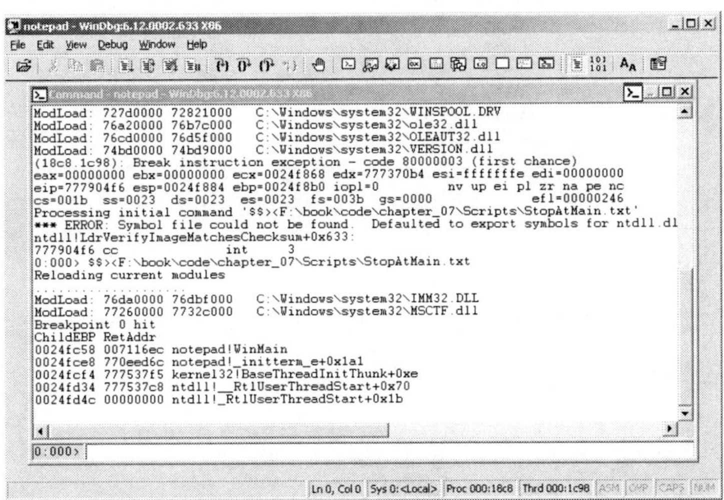

FIGURE 7-10 Performing efficient debugging iterations by combining debugger scripts with the startup debugger IFEO.

Startup Debugging of Service Processes in Session 0

In some cases, the process you're interested in debugging is started in the noninteractive system session (session 0). For example, this is the case for Windows services, which get started by the NT Service Control Manager (*services.exe*) in session 0. The OS loader code that implements the startup debugging scheme starts the startup debugger in the same session as the target process, so you will never be able to see its new instance or interact with it. Fortunately, however, the same technique can be adjusted to cover this scenario as well and allow you to debug the startup code path of processes that run in session 0.

Just as you were able to carefully craft a startup debugger string that allowed you to execute WinDbg debugger scripts, you can also use the *–server* debugger command-line option to have the WinDbg startup debugger instance in session 0 open a remote server and wait for a client to connect to it. You could then use the *–remote* debugger command-line option to start issuing commands to the remote ("invisible") WinDbg instance right from your current user session.

To see how this works in practice, you'll now apply this idea to debug the startup code path of the crashing Windows service example that was used in Chapter 4. Back then, you were able to debug the access violation in that service by using the *LocalDumps* registry key and postmortem (crash dump) debugging. However, what if you instead wanted to use live debugging to step through the startup code path until you hit the crash call site? As it turns out, the startup debugging trick described in this section will allow you to do just that.

As covered in Chapter 4, the first step in that experiment was to register the test service on the machine, which you can do from your Driver Development Kit (DDK) build window by using the *setup.bat* helper script, as shown in the following commands. Note that you'll need to run your DDK build window in an elevated administrative command prompt, just as you did when you executed this experiment back in Chapter 4.

```
C:\book\code\chapter_04\ServiceCrash>build -cCZ
C:\book\code\chapter_04\ServiceCrash>setup.bat
```

You can now configure the startup debugger for the service image name using the GFLAGS tool and the following string value:

```
Windows Registry Editor Version 5.00

[HKEY_LOCAL_MACHINE\SOFTWARE\Microsoft\Windows NT\CurrentVersion\Image File Execution Options
\ServiceWithCrash.exe]
"Debugger"="\"c:\\Program Files\\Debugging Tools for Windows (x86)\\windbg.exe\" -server
 tcp:port=4445 -Q"
```

Notice that starting the service now seems to block as the target service process is started under WinDbg in session 0.

```
net start ServiceWithCrash
```

You can then connect from your user session to the invisible remote instance of *windbg.exe* that's running in session 0, set a breakpoint at the main entry point of the Windows service, and start debugging the service process, as usual. However, there is another catch! After a short period of time, your session will time out and you'll see the error message shown in Figure 7-11.

```
"C:\Program Files\Debugging Tools for Windows (x86)\windbg.exe" -remote tcp:port=4445
...
0:000> .symfix
0:000> .reload
0:000> x servicewithcrash!*main*
00fb2000 ServiceWithCrash!__native_dllmain_reason = 0xffffffff
00fb2058 ServiceWithCrash!mainret = 0n0
```

```
00fb1399 ServiceWithCrash!CMainApp::MainHR (void)
00fb13ec ServiceWithCrash!wmain (void)
...
0:000> bp ServiceWithCrash!wmain
0:000> g
(1dfc.1ef8): Break instruction exception - code 80000003 (first chance)
ntdll!LdrpRunInitializeRoutines+0x211:
7741d75a cc              int     3
0:000> g
Breakpoint 0 hit
ServiceWithCrash!wmain:
```

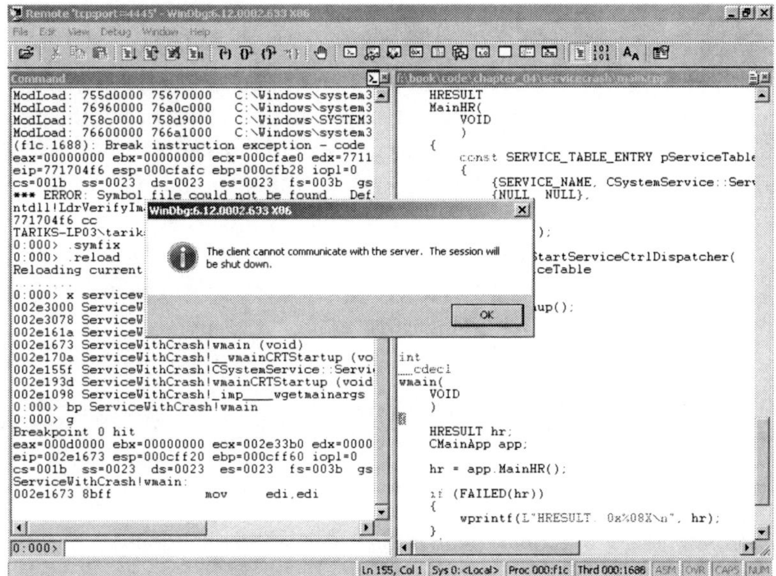

FIGURE 7-11 Service control manager handshake timeout.

This timeout happens because the NT service control manager (SCM) process expects any new services that it starts to report the "running" status within a reasonable time, set by default to 30 seconds. (Otherwise, the SCM assumes they might have crashed or simply had a code bug and forgot to report their status.) In this case, the program had not progressed to that point yet, given that you were still stopped at its main entry point inside the debugger, so the SCM decided to terminate the target while you were still debugging it. To prevent this from happening, you can override this default timeout in the registry by setting the *ServicesPipeTimeout* registry value to a large timeout value so that this artifact doesn't interfere with your debugging of the startup code path anymore. In Figure 7-12, the timeout value is set to 24 hours (86,400,000 milliseconds), for example. Note that an extra reboot is required for the SCM process (*services.exe*) to reflect this new configuration value.

```
[HKEY_LOCAL_MACHINE\SYSTEM\CurrentControlSet\Control]
```

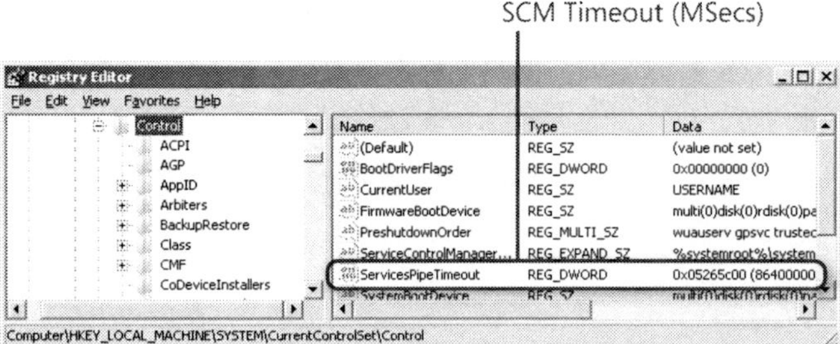

FIGURE 7-12 Changing the SCM timeout in the registry.

After you reboot and this new timeout value takes effect, you'll be able to debug the startup code path of the service using live debugging, set breakpoints, and step through the process execution all the way to the point of the crash call site. Note also that when you close the instance of the debugger that's local to your session, the service process (and its startup debugger instance in session 0) will still be active (unless you use the *qq* command to close both the local and remote debugger instances simultaneously). So, if you want to be able to restart the service and try the experiment again, you need to forcibly kill any orphaned service process instance (or the associated *windbg.exe* startup debugger instance). The SCM will refuse to start a new instance of the service until you terminate the orphaned service process, as illustrated in the following listing.

```
net start ServiceWithCrash
The service is starting or stopping.  Please try again later.
"C:\Program Files\Debugging Tools for Windows (x86)\kill.exe" -f windbg*
process windbg.exe (5892) - '' killed
net start ServiceWithCrash
```

Timeout issues are a problem you'll sometimes need to deal with when debugging the startup code path, especially in situations involving interprocess handshakes between the activator process and the new child process you're trying to debug. Fortunately, however, these timeouts are usually configurable, just like in the NT SCM case that you saw here.

Debugging Child Processes

Another way to debug the startup code path of new processes is to use the native child-debugging support in WinDbg. This is akin to how you can break in to WinDbg as new DLL modules get loaded into your target process address space, except here you are breaking in whenever a new child process is created by the target process (or by one of its children).

If you can use the startup-debugger IFEO hook to debug the startup code path of any user-mode process (not just direct child processes), why would you ever need to use child debugging, you might ask? The answer is that the startup-debugger technique doesn't work all the time because it breaks the regular parent/child relationship between the creator process and the target you're debugging, as you'll shortly see in this section. Child debugging is also easy to enable without having global impact and without the need to change an admin-protected location in the system registry.

Finally, child debugging can be used beyond just startup debugging—in particular, to discover any new child processes that get created as part of running your test scenario. This isn't something you are able to do using the startup-debugger hook, which requires you to already know the name of the process image when you add the IFEO hook to the registry. The next example that you'll see in this section will demonstrate this unique feature of child debugging.

Child Debugging in Action

You can enable child debugging for the target process in a user-mode WinDbg debugging session in one of two ways:

- Using the *–o* command-line option, which starts the target process with child debugging enabled
- Using the *.childdbg 1* command after you attach to an existing process

To see how this works in practice, you'll now try a fun experiment where you'll be able to witness all the processes that get started by Visual Studio as part of compiling a C++ project inside the Integrated Development Environment (IDE). To do so, you can open an existing Visual Studio 2010 project, such as the one used earlier in this chapter to illustrate breaking on DLL load events in Visual Studio. After the Visual Studio IDE is started, attach WinDbg to the new Visual Studio process instance (*devenv.exe*), as demonstrated in Figure 7-13.

```
C:\book\code\chapter_07\BreakOnDllLoadVs>BreakOnDllLoad.sln
```

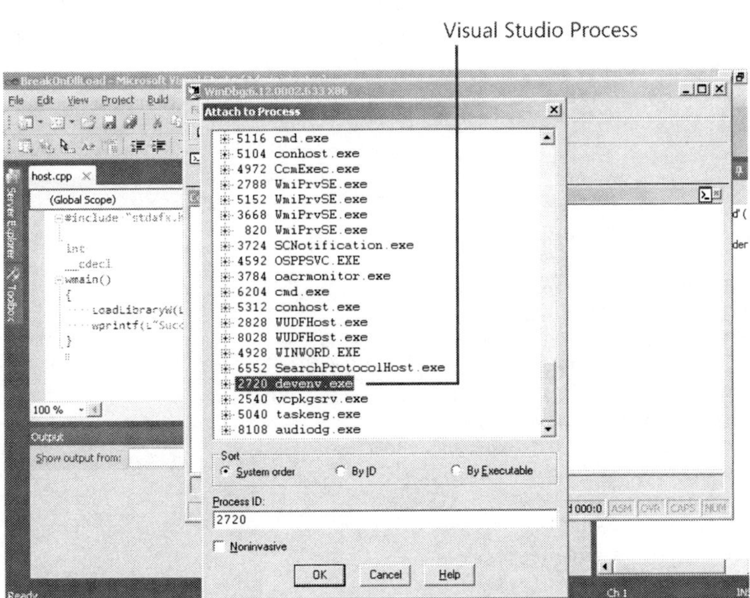

FIGURE 7-13 Attaching WinDbg as a debugger to the Visual Studio 2010 process (*devenv.exe*).

In the new *windbg.exe* user-mode debugging session (with Visual Studio as the target), turn on child debugging as follows:

```
0:031> .childdbg 1
Processes created by the current process will be debugged
0:031> g
```

You'll now break back into the debugger whenever the target (*devenv.exe*) creates any child process. Because the child-debugging property is also inherited by all the new child processes, you'll also break into the debugger when the first-level child processes create new child processes of their own too. To see this in action, rebuild the Visual Studio project and watch as you break back into WinDbg when Visual Studio creates the *MSBuild.exe* process to carry out the build task.

```
1:034> $ Display all process contexts in the current debugging session
1:034> |
   0    id: 154c    attach    name: C:\Program Files\Microsoft Visual Studio 10.0\Common7\IDE\
devenv.exe
.  1    id: 177c    child    name: MSBuild.exe
```

Notice the debugger command prompt now starts with *1*, indicating the current process context in the debugger is process #1 (*MSBuild.exe*), with the main *devenv.exe* process being the other process (process #0) in the debugging session. The three digits following the colon indicate, as usual, the thread number. In the case of child-process debugging, the | command is used to view the available process contexts within the user-mode debugging session. This command is similar to the ~ debugger command, except ~ applies to thread contexts instead. As with the ~ command, you can also use | with the *s* suffix to change the process context in the debugger. For example, *|0s* switches the process context back to *devenv.exe*, where commands you issue in the debugger start applying to that process. For example, the following listing displays the call stacks for threads in *devenv.exe*.

```
1:034> |0s
1:034> .symfix
1:034> .reload
0:001> ~*k
   0  Id: 154c.1264 Suspend: 1 Teb: 7ffde000 Unfrozen
ChildEBP RetAddr
002ff8cc 76eabd1e ntdll!KiFastSystemCallRet
002ff914 772062f9 kernel32!WaitForMultipleObjectsEx+0x8e
002ff968 5caddc17 USER32!RealMsgWaitForMultipleObjectsEx+0x13c
002ff9b8 5cae30cb msenv!CMsoCMHandler::EnvironmentMsgLoop+0x139
002ff9f8 5cae2ffc msenv!CMsoCMHandler::FPushMessageLoop+0x156
002ffa1c 5cae2f5d msenv!SCM::FPushMessageLoop+0xab
002ffa38 5cae2f2a msenv!SCM_MsoCompMgr::FPushMessageLoop+0x2a
002ffa58 5cae2e6c msenv!CMsoComponent::PushMsgLoop+0x28
002ffaf0 5c9fdb92 msenv!VStudioMainLogged+0x553
002ffb1c 2fc67435 msenv!VStudioMain+0xbc
002ffb54 2fc70445 devenv!util_CallVsMain+0xfd
002ffe40 2fc7167c devenv!CDevEnvAppId::Run+0x938
002ffe74 2fc716ec devenv!WinMain+0x9c
...
```

Continuing your experiment, you can now watch every new child that gets created as part of the compilation sequence. You can also issue the *!peb* extension command in the right process context to figure out the command line for a process in your child-debugging session, as demonstrated in the following listing.

```
0:001> $ Switch back to process #1 (MSBuild.exe)...
0:001> |1s
1:034> .symfix
1:034> .reload
1:034> !peb
PEB at 7ffdf000
    InheritedAddressSpace:    No
    ReadImageFileExecOptions: No
    BeingDebugged:            Yes
...
    CommandLine:  'C:\Windows\Microsoft.NET\Framework\v4.0.30319\MSBuild.exe /nologo /nodemode:1
/nr'
1:034> $ More child processes...
1:034> g
(15ec.1540): Break instruction exception - code 80000003 (first chance)
...
2:003> g
3:045> g
4:062> g
5:065> |
   0    id: 154c    attach    name: C:\Program Files\Microsoft Visual Studio 10.0\Common7\IDE\
devenv.exe
   1    id: 177c    child     name: MSBuild.exe
   2    id: 15ec    child     name: MSBuild.exe
   3    id: 12c0    child     name: MSBuild.exe
   4    id: 950     child     name: Tracker.exe
.  5    id: 6fc     child     name: cl.exe
...
5:065> $ Terminate the debugging session without terminating the target...
5:065> qd
```

How Child Debugging Works

Child debugging uses support in the OS that allows a debug port object to be shared by more than one process. A user-mode debugger can then attach to that debug port object and start receiving events from all the processes that share the port. Every debug event that the system generates on behalf of those processes also contains the identity of the originating process, allowing a debugger that's capable of child debugging to handle the entirety of those events in the same debugging session, as you can confirm by looking at the definition of the _DEBUG_EVENT data structure.

```
//
// C:\DDK\7600.16385.1\inc\api>winbase.h
//
typedef struct _DEBUG_EVENT {
    DWORD dwDebugEventCode;
    DWORD dwProcessId;
    DWORD dwThreadId;
    union {
        EXCEPTION_DEBUG_INFO Exception;
        CREATE_THREAD_DEBUG_INFO CreateThread;
        CREATE_PROCESS_DEBUG_INFO CreateProcessInfo;
```

```
        EXIT_THREAD_DEBUG_INFO ExitThread;
        EXIT_PROCESS_DEBUG_INFO ExitProcess;
        LOAD_DLL_DEBUG_INFO LoadDll;
        UNLOAD_DLL_DEBUG_INFO UnloadDll;
        OUTPUT_DEBUG_STRING_INFO DebugString;
        RIP_INFO RipInfo;
    } u;
} DEBUG_EVENT, *LPDEBUG_EVENT;
```

The operating system allows a parent process to share its debug port with its children by setting a bit (*NoDebugInherit*) in its *nt!_EPROCESS* executive object structure, as you can see when dumping that structure using the *dt* ("dump type") command.

```
lkd> dt nt!_EPROCESS
...
   +0x270 Flags              : Uint4B
   +0x270 CreateReported     : Pos 0, 1 Bit
   +0x270 NoDebugInherit     : Pos 1, 1 Bit
   +0x270 ProcessExiting     : Pos 2, 1 Bit
   +0x270 ProcessDelete      : Pos 3, 1 Bit
...
```

This bit can be set at the Win32 API layer at process creation time using the DEBUG_PROCESS flag of the *kernel32!CreateProcessW* Win32 API call. This is how the *–o* command-line option of *windbg.exe* works, altering the debugger's default behavior when it creates the target command line to use DEBUG_PROCESS instead of DEBUG_ONLY_THIS_PROCESS. It's also possible to enable debug port inheritance at run time after the target has started by clearing the *NoDebugInherit* bit, which is how the *.childdbg* debugger command is internally implemented.

Child debugging also requires work on the part of the debugger. Visual Studio (at least up to its 2010 version), for instance, supports handling debug events only from a single process and, as a result, doesn't support child debugging. In part, this can be attributed to the fact that Visual Studio is optimized for debugging "just your code," which allows its debugging user interface to remain simple for its core scenarios. By contrast, WinDbg is able to support child debugging as a native concept and implements its main debugger loop and user interface so that they're both capable of handling events from more than one process.

Child Debugging as a "Startup Debugger" Alternative

Child debugging can also be used as a way to debug the startup code path of a process, provided that you also know what the parent of that process is going to be. Child debugging works only for *true* child processes of the target process, though. For example, if your program calls a COM object implemented in an out-of-process server executable, you won't be able to trap the creation event of the new server process using child debugging in your own client process because the COM server executable is ultimately created by the COM service control manager (*RpcSs/DComLaunch* services), and not by your client process.

In the COM out-of-process activation case, you could certainly attach a user-mode debugger to the *DComLaunch* service host process instance and enable child debugging for that process so that you get notified whenever a new COM server executable is created by the COM SCM. One problem you must deal with, however, when applying this method and attaching a user-mode debugger to system processes is that you might end up introducing artificial deadlocks. In the case of Windows services, for example, you might be tempted to attach WinDbg to the NT SCM process (*services.exe*) and use child debugging instead of the startup-debugger IFEO hook used earlier to step through the startup code path of a test service. By inadvertently suspending the NT SCM while debugging its child service process using the same debug port, however, a debugger command (such as one downloading symbols off the network) could call back to the NT SCM process and hang the debugger due to *services.exe* being already frozen under the user-mode debugger!

Although the startup-debugger approach avoids the previous problem when dealing with child processes of system processes, it unfortunately also has one serious drawback, which stems from the way the OS loader replaces the initial target command line by starting the debugger process instead. This scheme has the side effect of breaking the parent/child link as the startup debugger becomes the parent of the child process, which alters the process hierarchy compared to when the scenario is not being debugged. This can sometimes break the normal operations of the application. Although these scenarios are fortunately rare, they do exist in practice and the next section will detail one such example that involves MSI (Microsoft Windows Installer) setup custom actions.

Table 7-1 recaps the relative advantages of child debugging and the startup-debugger IFEO configuration when it comes to stepping through the startup code path of new processes.

TABLE 7-1 Startup Debugging Techniques

Technique	Advantages	Drawbacks
Startup-Debugger IFEO Hook	■ Extensible scheme that works well with both WinDbg and the Visual Studio debugger ■ Can be combined with WinDbg scripts for efficient debugging iterations	■ Requires global registry changes that affect all new instances of the target image name ■ Requires administrative privileges to change the IFEO registry location ■ The security context of the debugger is determined by that of the target ■ Breaks the parent/child hierarchy because it inserts the debugger process in between the creator and child (target) processes
Child Debugging	■ Easy to enable in WinDbg ■ Works without any global system changes, and its effect is limited to the current debugging session ■ Can be used by regular users on the machine ■ You can also control the security context of the debugger before attaching to the parent process	■ Works only for true child processes ■ Can cause hangs when used with critical system processes ■ Not supported when you want to debug the startup code path using the Visual Studio debugger

Example: The Case of MSI Custom Actions

To illustrate the fact that preserving the parent/child relationship between processes can sometimes be important, I'll now show you a real-life case involving MSI custom actions. Even if you never intend to write MSI setups, you'll find this section useful as a practical illustration for several of the topics covered so far in this chapter.

The MSI setup technology supports a plug-in model that allows you to write *custom action* DLLs for operations that aren't natively covered by existing MSI tasks. These custom actions get loaded into the system-provided *msiexec.exe* host process, so being able to perform process startup debugging in this case also enables you to debug the custom action code. This worker process instance of *msiexec.exe* gets started by a Windows service named *MsiServer* (also hosted in the same *msiexec.exe* binary), which runs in the *LocalSystem* security context.

The sequence of events from when you double-click the MSI setup in the Windows explorer UI (step #1) to when the custom action code executes is summarized in Figure 7-14. To debug the custom action, you need to be able to step through the new worker *msiexec.exe* process instance as soon as it's created by the *MsiServer* service (step #2).

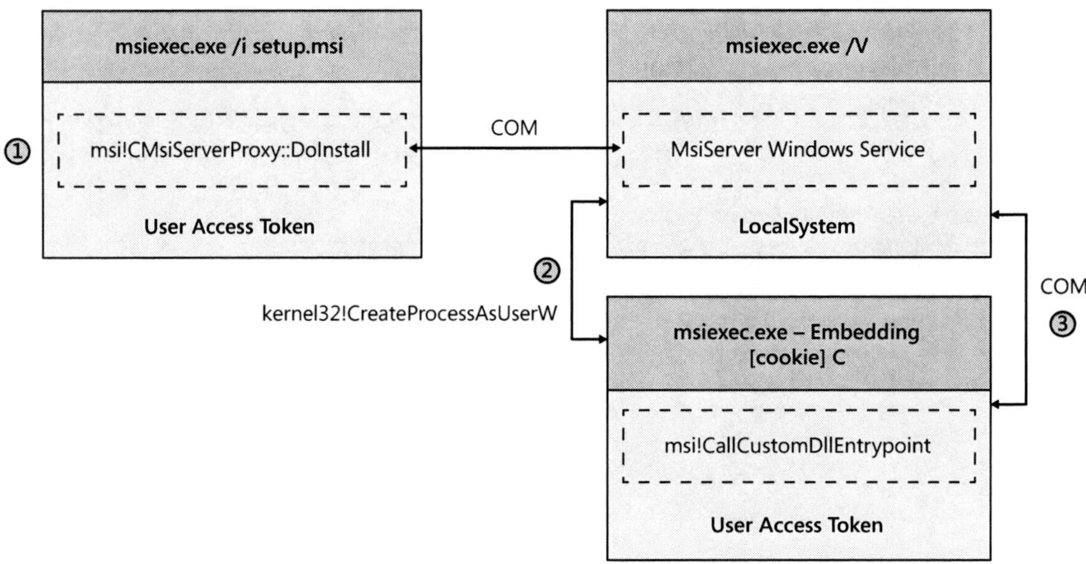

FIGURE 7-14 Execution of MSI custom actions.

For this experiment, you'll use a sample MSI included with the companion source code that has a fairly straightforward custom action and is authored using the Windows Installer XML (WIX) declarative language. Though it's not required to follow this experiment, you might want to rebuild the MSI rather than reuse the one that already comes with the companion source code. If you want to do that, you need to download the WIX toolset, which is available as an open-source project download at *http://wix.sourceforge.net/* and use the *compile.bat* batch file provided in the companion source code to regenerate the MSI.

```
C:\book\code\chapter_07\MsiCustomAction\Setup>compile.bat
```

When you execute the MSI setup and accept the end-user license agreement (EULA), the setup program proceeds forward and stops (for convenience) at the confirmation dialog box shown in Figure 7-15 before executing the custom action. Before you click Finish to complete the setup, make sure you select the Launch Custom Action option at the bottom of the dialog box.

```
C:\book\code\chapter_07\MsiCustomAction\Setup>setup.msi
```

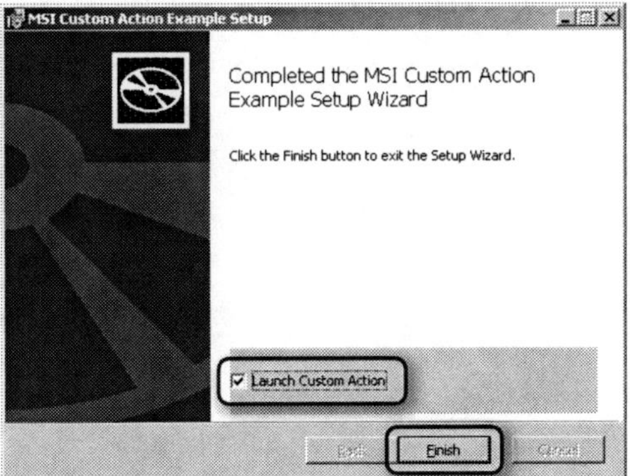

FIGURE 7-15 MSI custom action sample.

Notice that after you click Finish, an empty file is created as a result of running the MSI custom action, indicating that it completed successfully. The code of the custom action is shown here.

```
//
// C:\book\code\chapter_07\MsiCustomAction\CustomActionDll>main.cpp
//
extern "C"
UINT
WINAPI
TestCustomAction(
    __in MSIHANDLE hInstall
    )
{
    ...
    shFile.Attach(CreateFile(
        L"c:\\temp\\abc.txt",
        GENERIC_WRITE,
        FILE_SHARE_READ,
        NULL,
        CREATE_ALWAYS,
        0,
        NULL
        ));
    ...
}
```

To repeat the previous MSI setup sequence as if it was a first-time installation, run *setup.msi* again and choose the option to remove the application. The next time you execute *setup.msi*, you'll go through the same flow as when you first ran the experiment.

As mentioned earlier, the startup-debugger IFEO hook breaks this scenario. To see this in action, follow these steps:

1. Run *setup.msi* until you get to the dialog box shown in Figure 7-15.
2. Add *windbg.exe* as the startup debugger for *msiexec.exe* by using the GFLAGS tool to edit the IFEO *Debugger* registry value.

```
Windows Registry Editor Version 5.00

[HKEY_LOCAL_MACHINE\SOFTWARE\Microsoft\Windows NT\CurrentVersion\Image File Execution Options\msiexec.exe]
"Debugger"="C:\\Program Files\\Debugging Tools for Windows (x86)\\windbg.exe"
```

3. Click Finish to complete the MSI setup and execute the custom action.

Unfortunately, the scenario no longer works, and you now get the cryptic error message shown in Figure 7-16.

FIGURE 7-16 MSI custom action error in the presence of a startup debugger for *msiexec.exe*.

This failure occurs because *MsiServer* stores the process ID (PID) of the worker process it creates and allows the new *msiexec.exe* process instance to register back with it only if its PID matches the one it knows about. When a startup debugger is inserted into the picture, however, the PID saved by *MsiServer* when creating the new process is that of the debugger and not of the child worker process! This private interprocess-communication handshake protocol ideally should have been implemented in a way that still allowed the startup debugger technique to work. A common design pattern to address similar situations is to pass *connection data* as part of the command line used to create the child process, which is precisely how the Windows Error Reporting (WER) code, for instance, allows the JIT debugger to communicate with the initial faulting process that threw the unhandled exception.

Fortunately, child debugging works well as an alternative to the startup-debugger IFEO in this case. By attaching a user-mode debugger to the *MsiServer* service process, you can enable child debugging so that you break in to the debugger when the new *msiexec.exe* process gets started, and before the custom action is executed. You can use the *–s* option of the *tlist.exe* tool to find the process ID of the *MsiServer* service, as shown in the following command.

```
"C:\Program Files\Debugging Tools for Windows (x86)\tlist.exe" -s
6468 msiexec.exe      Svcs:  msiserver
...
```

Using the PID obtained in the previous step, attach *windbg.exe* to the service process and enable child debugging using the *.childdbg* command, as demonstrated in the following listing. Make sure you execute the WinDbg debugger from an elevated administrative command prompt so that it is allowed to attach to this *LocalSystem* service.

```
"C:\Program Files\Debugging Tools for Windows (x86)\windbg.exe" -p 6468
0:006> .symfix
0:006> .reload
0:006> !peb
...
    CommandLine:  'C:\Windows\system32\msiexec.exe /V'
0:006> .childdbg 1
Processes created by the current process will be debugged
0:006> g
```

After you click Finish in the dialog box shown in Figure 7-15, you'll immediately break in to the debugger as the new instance of *msiexec.exe* gets created by the service to host the custom action DLL, as shown in the following listing.

```
(1bf8.1410): Break instruction exception - code 80000003 (first chance)
1:008> |
   0    id: 1944    attach  name: C:\Windows\system32\msiexec.exe
.  1    id: 1bf8    child   name: msiexec.exe
1:008> !peb
...
    CommandLine:  'C:\Windows\system32\MsiExec.exe -Embedding 5EA589DCD1565F851BE1C0312959399F
C'
```

You can now use the *sxe ld* command to break inside the debugger when the custom action DLL gets loaded into the process. Note that the MSI custom action DLL isn't installed with the rest of the application files on the deployment machine. Instead, the MSI setup extracts it to a temporary location and gives it a different name. However, the MSI framework always gives this file a **.tmp* extension, so you don't need to know its exact name when using the *sxe ld* command, given you can use the **.tmp* match pattern with the *sxe ld* command. Once the symbols for the custom action DLL are loaded, you can finally set a breakpoint directly at its entry point, as illustrated in the following listing.

```
1:008> sxe ld *.tmp
1:008> g
ModLoad: 74b20000 74b25000   C:\Users\tariks\AppData\Local\Temp\MSI9953.tmp
1:014> .sympath+ C:\book\code\chapter_07\MsiCustomAction\CustomActionDll\objfre_win7_x86\i386
1:014> .srcpath+ C:\book\code
1:014> .reload
1:014> k
```

```
ChildEBP RetAddr
...
0268f4cc 752e1e23 KERNELBASE!LoadLibraryExW+0x178
0268f4e0 73da9c85 kernel32!LoadLibraryW+0x11
0268f818 752e3677 msi!CMsiCustomAction::CustomActionThread+0x84
...
1:014> $ Go to the return address from LoadLibrary so the DLL is fully loaded
1:014> g 73da9c85
msi!CMsiCustomAction::CustomActionThread+0x84:
1:014> x MSI9953!*customaction*
74b21503          MSI9953!TestCustomAction (unsigned long)
1:014> bp MSI9953!TestCustomAction
1:014> g
Breakpoint 0 hit
1:014> k
ChildEBP RetAddr
0268f4b8 73deb67c MSI9953!TestCustomAction [c:\book\code\chapter_07\msicustomaction\
customactiondll\main.cpp @ 15]
0268f4d4 73da9e31 msi!CallCustomDllEntrypoint+0x25
0268f818 752e3677 msi!CMsiCustomAction::CustomActionThread+0x230
...
```

Now that you're stopped in the debugger right at the beginning of the custom action function, you can finally step through it and debug it line by line.

Debugging MSI Custom Actions Using the *MsiBreak* Environment Variable

The MSI code in Windows also provides another custom hook that makes it easier for developers to debug their custom actions. However, this hook is entirely specific to MSI and does not represent an extensible strategy. You'll find it very convenient if you already know the name of the MSI custom action.

```
C:\book\code\chapter_07\MsiCustomAction\Setup>set MsiBreak=WriteTmpFile
C:\book\code\chapter_07\MsiCustomAction\Setup>setup.msi
```

You will now see a command prompt giving you the PID of the MSI host process for the custom action and allowing you to attach to it (after the custom-action DLL has already been loaded!) and step through your custom-action DLL code in the same way you just did, except without having to enable child debugging.

Another method many setup developers use is to simply instrument the entry point of their custom action with a debug break that they're then able to catch using a JIT debugger. You can also add an infinite "attach" wait loop at the start of the custom action, as described in the beginning of this chapter. Both of these methods require regenerating the MSI binary, however. Also, unlike the child debugging method shown in this section, which requires virtually no prior knowledge of the custom action, the alternative approaches presented here work only if you own the custom action and have access to its source code.

More Useful Tricks

This section contains a few more important user-mode debugging tricks you'll also find useful during your user-mode debugging investigations.

Debugging Error-Code Failures

You probably have encountered situations where a large application starts failing after a new configuration or environment change (such as when rolling out a new update), often with low-level, uninformative error codes such as ERROR_ACCESS_DENIED or ERROR_FILE_NOT_FOUND. This section will arm you with a few investigative techniques that can help you debug those situations more efficiently, especially when the task of reviewing the application's source code or stepping through its code in the debugger one instruction at a time happens to be a tedious and unappealing approach.

Debugging Win32 API Failures

Low-level error codes are often returned from system calls made through the Win32 API layer. An efficient way to start figuring out which internal Win32 function raised a given error code is to use a little-known debugging hook inside the *ntdll.dll* system module. This trick relies on the internal *ntdll!g_dwLastErrorToBreakOn* global variable and causes the process to break immediately inside the debugger as soon as an *ntdll.dll* function fails with the error code that you set this variable value to be.

Warning The *ntdll!g_dwLastErrorToBreakOn* hook is undocumented and could very well be removed by Microsoft in future versions of Windows. However, there is no reason why you can't take advantage of it for debugging purposes only.

To illustrate how to apply this useful technique, I'll show you how to use it to discover the call site at the origin of the failure to delete system files, even from within an elevated administrative command-prompt window.

```
C:\Windows\system32>del kernel32.dll
Access is denied.
```

All you have to do to find the call site of the "access denied" failure is attach a debugger to the *cmd.exe* process, set the value of the global variable in memory (by using the *ed* debugger command to edit the DWORD value in memory), and then simply watch as you stop exactly at the point of failure. This saves you the hassle of having to step through the code, and it lets the debugger do the work on your behalf.

```
0:003> .symfix
0:003> .reload
0:003> x ntdll!g_dwLastErrorToBreakOn
7793d748 ntdll!g_dwLastErrorToBreakOn = <no type information>
0:003> !error 5
Error code: (Win32) 0x5 (5) - Access is denied.
0:003> ed ntdll!g_dwLastErrorToBreakOn 5
0:003> g
```

As soon as you run the command to delete the system file in the target command-prompt window after the previous listing, you'll see that the debugger breaks in with the following call stack, which shows that the error was returned from a call to the *DeleteFile* Win32 API.

```
(13b0.c94): Break instruction exception - code 80000003 (first chance)
0:000> k
ChildEBP RetAddr
0013e858 75c46b65 ntdll!RtlSetLastWin32Error+0x1c
0013e868 75c4dc0d KERNELBASE!BaseSetLastNTError+0x18
0013e8d0 4abba7bd KERNELBASE!DeleteFileW+0x106
...
0013f9d0 4abc76f0 cmd!Dispatch+0x14b
0013fa14 4abb835e cmd!main+0x21a
...
```

By following the saved frame pointer for the *KernelBase!DeleteFileW* call frame as explained in the "Listing Parameters and Locals for System Code" section of Chapter 2, "Getting Started," you can also find the first argument to this Win32 API call, which turns out to be precisely the file path you used in your *del* command, as shown by the *du* ("dump unicode string") command in the following listing.

```
0:000> dd 0013e8d0
0013e8d0  0013ed14 4abba7bd 0013e8f8 002ba698
0:000> du 0013e8f8
0013e8f8  "c:\Windows\system32\kernel32.dll"
0:000> qd
```

You now see that the error code is coming from the *DeleteFile* Win32 API call, but that still doesn't tell you why the "access denied" failure happened. However, now that you know for sure the exact operation that returned the error code, you can fairly assume that the access-control rules applied to system files don't allow administrators to delete them, which is done to prevent accidental deletions of critical system files.

Note that the first break into the debugger when using this technique might not be the one you're looking for, especially for common error codes that might be expected and handled by other parts of the system (such as the ERROR_INSUFFICIENT_BUFFER error code). Also, this trick works only when the Win32 API responsible for the error code happens to set the last error before returning. This is because the return-code comparison used to see whether a debug break should be raised is done by the system in *ntdll!RtlSetLastWin32Error*, as you're able to observe in the previous call stack.

Fortunately, the majority of Win32 API calls are in this category and will save their return error codes in the thread environment block (TEB) using the *kernel32!SetLastError* Win32 API—in turn, calling the previous *ntdll.dll* function—before exiting.

Observing Low-Level Resource Access Failures with the Process Monitor Tool

Another approach for debugging issues suspected to be due to a security access check or other low-level errors while accessing system resources (such as files and registry keys) is to use the Process Monitor tool from the SysInternals suite, which you can download for free from *http://technet.microsoft.com/en-us/sysinternals/bb842062*, as described back in the Introduction of this book.

Process Monitor records every resource (I/O) access on the system and displays it in a nice end-user interface, along with the success or failure error codes returned from each operation. By running this tool and starting the failing scenario in parallel, you can search the tool's UI output using the Ctrl+F shortcut and find the resource that the target process failed to access.

For example, Figure 7-17 shows the result of running the same experiment of attempting to delete a system file from an elevated administrative command prompt, only this time you also have Process Monitor record the I/O operations on the machine while issuing the command. Notice that searching for the string "denied" in the output from the tool yields all the APIs that returned "access denied" failures, including the *DeleteFile* API.

```
C:\pstools>ProcMon.exe
C:\pstools>del c:\Windows\system32\kernel32.dll
Access is denied.
```

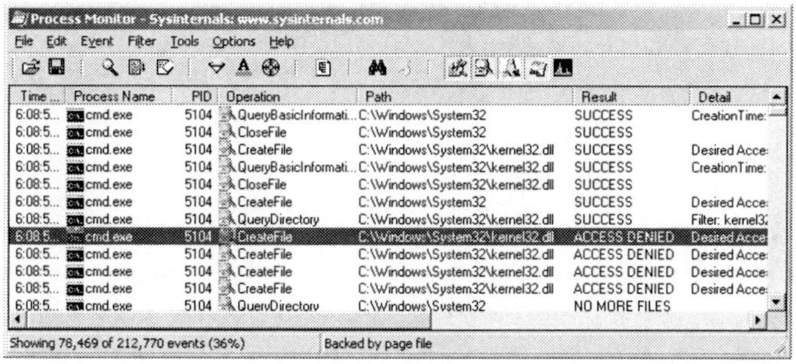

FIGURE 7-17 Using Process Monitor to trace an "access denied" failure.

By double-clicking the line you are interested in, you can also obtain the stack trace for the failing call, assuming you have Internet access to the Microsoft public symbols server, which Process Monitor looks up automatically when resolving symbols in system binaries. Figure 7-18 shows the stack trace of the failed attempt to delete the system file in the *cmd.exe* process context.

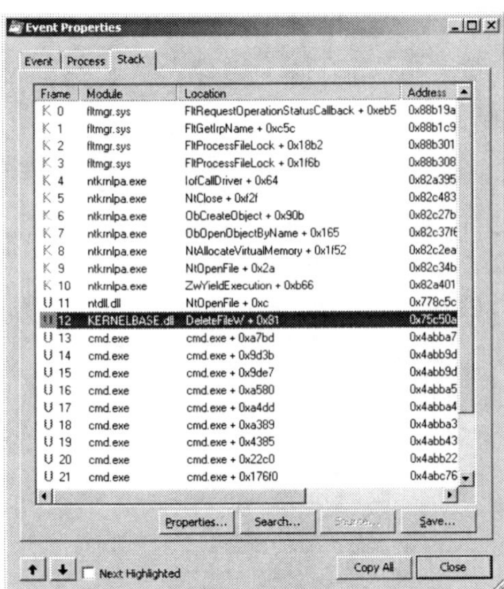

FIGURE 7-18 Call stacks of resource access attempts in the Process Monitor tool.

Unlike the *ntdll.dll* hook, the Process Monitor method does not work for all Win32 functions. More specifically, any Win32 API that does not result in a transition to kernel mode for a resource-access attempt will escape the reach of Process Monitor. An example is any failure raised in a Win32 API that's implemented entirely in user mode, such as the *advapi32!CryptEncrypt* API. This is because Process Monitor works by unpacking and installing a temporary filter device driver to record the I/O accesses, so it observes only those types of failures. Also, neither the *ntdll!g_dwLastErrorToBreakOn* debugging hook nor Process Monitor work for higher-level, non-Win32 error codes because tracking such failures requires additional instrumentation. The next section will present a trick that allows you to do just that.

Debugging High-Level, Error-Code Failures

You can extend the idea of the *ntdll.dll* hook covered earlier to your own code as long as you have instrumented all of your functions to use common error-handling macros, such as the ones used in the C++ companion source code of this book. Although the *ntdll.dll* hook allows you to track failures at the Win32 API level, it doesn't help you debug error codes raised at higher layers in your application.

Because all the C++ code samples in the companion source code use the same error-handling macros, it is easy to modify the definition of those macros and insert a debugging hook to report HRESULT failures by raising a debug break instruction. In fact, this lightweight instrumentation is already enabled by default in the companion source code. If you choose to use that same error-handling scheme in your code, you'll find this hook particularly helpful in debugging your code in production environments, just as the *ntdll.dll* hook allows you to debug Win32 API failures.

The following listing shows the one-line macro that's appended to the error-handling macros (*ChkHr*, *ChkWin32*, and so on) from the C++ companion source code.

```
//
// C:\book\code\common\corelib>chkmacros.h
//
#define ___ChkMacroEndDefault___() \
    ; \
            CBreakOnFailure::CheckToBreakOnFailure(__hr); goto Exit; \
```

The *CheckToBreakOnFailure* function (shown next) looks at the value of a predefined global variable and issues a debug break if needed. Notice how the function is declared *no-inline*, so its impact on the size of the resulting binaries is kept to a minimum.

```
//
// C:\book\code\common\corelib>coredefs.h
//
class CBreakOnFailure
{
public:
    DECLSPEC_NOINLINE
    static
    VOID
    CheckToBreakOnFailure(
        __in_opt HRESULT hResult
        )
    {
        if (g_hResultToBreakOn != S_OK && FAILED(hResult))
        {
            //
            // -1 (0xFFFFFFFF) is a special code to cause a debugger
            // break-in for any error failure
            //
            if (g_hResultToBreakOn == hResult ||
                g_hResultToBreakOn == static_cast<HRESULT>(-1))
            {
                __debugbreak();
            }
        }
    }

private:
    static HRESULT g_hResultToBreakOn;
};
```

With this custom hook in place, you can break on failures by simply setting the global *g_hResultToBreakOn* variable to *0xFFFFFFFF (-1)* in the debugger. This can be very convenient because it allows you to quickly determine the code paths that result in failures inside your code, though you should also remember that errors are sometimes caught and can be expected and handled.

Just as in the case of the *ntdll.dll* hook, you can narrow the search and break only when a specific error code occurs, such as when an "access denied" error is raised in your code. For example, you'll now apply this hook to determine why the following C++ program from the companion source code returns E_ACCESSDENIED.

```
C:\book\code\chapter_07\BreakOnFailure>objfre_win7_x86\i386\breakonfailure.exe
HRESULT: 0x80070005
```

By simply setting the value of the global variable to E_ACCESSDENIED (*0x80070005*), you'll be able to let the target run (using the *g* command) and break in as soon as the "access denied" error is raised without having to manually step through the code!

```
0:000> vercommand
command line: '"c:\Program Files\Debugging Tools for Windows (x86)\windbg.exe"
c:\book\code\chapter_07\BreakOnFailure\objfre_win7_x86\i386\breakonfailure.exe'
0:000> .symfix
0:000> .reload
0:000> bp breakonfailure!wmain
0:000> g
Breakpoint 0 hit
breakonfailure!wmain:
0:000> x breakonfailure!*tobreak*
0043201c breakonfailure!CBreakOnFailure::g_hResultToBreakOn = 0x00000000
004311c5 breakonfailure!CBreakOnFailure::CheckToBreakOnFailure (HRESULT)
0:000> ed 0043201c 0x80070005
0:000> g
(51c.124c): Break instruction exception - code 80000003 (first chance)
...
0:000> $ The frame in bold below is where E_ACCESSDENIED was raised
0:000> k
ChildEBP RetAddr
000af7c0 004311fb breakonfailure!CBreakOnFailure::CheckToBreakOnFailure+0x1e
[c:\book\code\common\corelib\coredefs.h @ 103]
000af7cc 00431218 breakonfailure!CBreakOnFailureApp::MainHR+0xe
[c:\book\code\chapter_07\breakonfailure\main.cpp @ 11]
000af7d8 004313a3 breakonfailure!wmain+0xe
[c:\book\code\chapter_07\breakonfailure\main.cpp @ 36]
...
0:000> q
```

Note that if a failure is raised by a DLL module that uses the *Chk** macros instead of the main executable module, you need to edit the *g_hResultToBreakOn* global variable corresponding to that DLL module instead. This is because each module has its own separate *g_hResultToBreakOn* global variable.

Tracking Down Error Codes the Brute-Force Way

As is often the case in software engineering, simple ideas sometimes yield surprisingly good and satisfactory results. If you consider the problem of trying to find where a given error code is raised in a program, the most naïve idea that comes to mind is to keep stepping into function calls until one of them returns the error code in question. This approach doesn't require any tracing support, whether it's explicit or done on your behalf by the code in the operating system.

Fortunately, the debugger can be used to automate the process of stepping into function calls (using the *t* debugger command) repeatedly by using the *.for* command. Given that the return code of function calls is usually stored in a known register (the *eax* register on *x86*, for example), you can use a loop such as the one shown in the following script to accomplish the task at hand. Notice how *r?* is used in this script to define pseudo-registers of the same type and size so that they can be compared within the *.for* loop. You can also adapt this script easily to the *x64* platform, where the *rax* register is often used to hold the return value of function calls.

```
$$
$$ C:\book\code\chapter_07\Scripts\FindError_x86.txt
$$
.if (${/d:$arg1})
{
    r? $t1 = ((DWORD*) @eax);
    r $t2 = $arg1;
    r? $t2 = ((DWORD*) @$t2);
    .for (; @$t1 != @$t2; r $t1=@eax)
    {
        t; r @eax;
    }
}
.else
{
    .echo An error value is required with this script
    .echo For example: $$>a< FindError_x86.txt 0x80070005
}
```

You can now apply this script to again find the call site where E_ACCESSDENIED is raised inside the C++ sample, which was used previously in this section to illustrate the custom debugging hook in the *Chk** macros from the companion source code.

```
0:000> vercommand
command line: '"c:\Program Files\Debugging Tools for Windows (x86)\windbg.exe"  C:\book\code\
chapter_07\BreakOnFailure\objfre_win7_x86\i386\breakonfailure.exe'
0:000> bp breakonfailure!wmain
0:000> g
Breakpoint 0 hit
breakonfailure!wmain:
0:000> $ Keep stepping into (t) code till E_ACCESSDENIED is returned
0:000> $$>a< C:\book\code\chapter_07\scripts\FindError_x86.txt 0x80070005
```

```
eax=000b0000
eax=000b0000
...
eax=00000000
eax=80070005
0:000> k
ChildEBP RetAddr
0018fe3c 002e1218 breakonfailure!CBreakOnFailureApp::MainHR+0x17
0018fe48 002e13a3 breakonfailure!wmain+0xe
...
0:000> q
```

In this particular case, the trick worked well. However, running a process one instruction at a time slows down execution, especially if the target process is large and the error code of interest is raised too deep during its execution. However, you can work around this issue by progressing as far ahead as you can in the execution of the process before starting the loop. This was also the case in the previous example because it was known that the error had to be raised after the main entry point. So, a breakpoint was set there first, and only after it was hit did it become necessary to trace execution one instruction at a time.

Also, this primitive method will work well only if the error you're trying to track down doesn't look like a regular number, given that the *eax* register can also be used for purposes other than receiving the return code from function calls. This means that it's more likely to work well with HRESULT values than with Win32 error values, where you might get many more false hits.

Breaking on First-Chance Exception Notifications

By default, the WinDbg user-mode debugger simply logs first-chance exception notifications when given a chance to respond to them and breaks only on second-chance (unhandled SEH exception) notifications. This is because first-chance notifications are often benign and can be ignored. It is possible, however, to change this default behavior and break on first-chance notifications by using the *sxe* ("enable exception stops") debugger command. This is especially useful in .NET programs, where exceptions are often caught by applications before more generic ones are thrown. To stop at these first-chance CLR exception notifications, for example, you can use the following command:

```
0:000> sxe clr
```

You can also use the *sxe* * command to break on all first-chance notifications. In fact, the *sxe* command allows you to also control the behavior of the debugger in the face of other debug events. Using the *sx* debugger command, you can see the default behavior in place for the various events that can be controlled by *sxe*. Notice, in particular, that the handling in effect for the module load (*ld*) events covered earlier in this chapter is also displayed by this command (in this particular case, the last *sxe ld* command was for **.tmp*).

```
0:000> sx
  ct - Create thread - ignore
  et - Exit thread - ignore
```

```
 cpr - Create process - ignore
 epr - Exit process - break
  ld - Load module - output
       (only break for *.tmp)
...
  av - Access violation - break - not handled
asrt - Assertion failure - break - not handled
 aph - Application hang - break - not handled
 bpe - Break instruction exception - break
bpec - Break instruction exception continue - handled
  eh - C++ EH exception - second-chance break - not handled
 clr - CLR exception - break - not handled
clrn - CLR notification exception - second-chance break - handled
...
```

The debugger will now "break" on first-chance CLR exception notifications. If you no longer want the debugger to do so and want to revert to the default behavior of breaking only on unhandled .NET exceptions, you can use the *sxd* command to clear the configuration, as demonstrated in the following listing.

```
0:000> sxd clr
0:000> sx
...
 clr - CLR exception - second-chance break - not handled
```

You can also reset all the exception and debug event filter states to their default settings by using the *sxr* ("reset exception stops") command.

```
0:000> sxr
sx state reset to defaults
```

Similarly, you can also break on first-chance exception notifications in Visual Studio by using the Debug\Exceptions menu selection to choose the exception categories you want to observe.

Freezing Threads

Freezing and unfreezing threads can be useful when debugging code bugs in multithreaded programs that reproduce only under a set of timing conditions between the threads in the process (also known as *race conditions*). By using this trick, you can control when threads get to run relative to each other and reproduce bugs that are otherwise hard to hit outside of the debugger.

You must be vigilant, however, when using this technique and pick safe points during the execution of the threads you're targeting before you freeze them. If you freeze the threads while critical exclusive locks are still being held, for example, you might end up introducing artificial deadlocks in the target program you're debugging. On the bright side, though, if you are able to simulate a broken code invariant through a combination of freeze and unfreeze commands in the debugger, it's likely you've uncovered a valid race condition bug in your code!

Freezing and Unfreezing Threads

Freezing a thread in the *windbg.exe* user-mode debugger is relatively easy. For example, the following listing shows how to freeze thread 9 in the target process.

```
0:013> ~
...
   9  Id: 1a08.ca8 Suspend: 1 Teb: 7ef9d000 Unfrozen
. 13  Id: 1a08.2d8 Suspend: 1 Teb: 7ef91000 Unfrozen
0:013> ~9f
0:013> ~
...
   9  Id: 1a08.ca8 Suspend: 1 Teb: 7ef9d000 Frozen
. 13  Id: 1a08.2d8 Suspend: 1 Teb: 7ef91000 Unfrozen
0:013> g
System 0: 1 of 14 threads are frozen
System 0: 1 of 13 threads were frozen
System 0: 1 of 13 threads are frozen
```

You can choose to unfreeze this thread again at any time by breaking back into the debugger and using the *~9u* command, as shown in the following listing.

```
ntdll!DbgBreakPoint:
776f000c cc              int     3
0:010> ~9u
0:010> g
```

Similarly, you can easily freeze and unfreeze threads in the Threads debug window of the Visual Studio debugger, which you can access from the Debug\Windows menu selection.

The Difference Between Freezing and Suspending Threads

User-mode programs are able to suspend threads by calling the *SuspendThread* Win32 API. The kernel keeps track of how many times a thread has been suspended in the associated kernel thread object. When the thread is resumed using the *ResumeThread* Win32 API, the suspend count is decremented by one.

Internally, the kernel sends a signal (an asynchronous procedure call) to the target thread when it's first suspended, which causes it to enter a wait state on an internal semaphore object. The thread is then unblocked when that helper semaphore object is signaled by the OS as the thread's *suspend count* drops back down to 0.

```
lkd> dt nt!_KTHREAD
...
   +0x188 SuspendCount      : Char
   +0x1c8 SuspendSemaphore : _KSEMAPHORE
...
```

When a process is broken into in the debugger, you can see (using the ~ command) that all of its threads have been suspended by the debugger process, so the target remains in a stable state while you're looking at a snapshot during its execution.

```
0:000> vercommand
command line: '"c:\Program Files\Debugging Tools for Windows (x86)\windbg.exe"  c:\Windows\
System32\notepad.exe'
0:000> $ List all the threads in the target
0:000> ~
.  0  Id: 1a24.19f4 Suspend: 1 Teb: 7efdd000 Unfrozen
0:000> $ Terminate the debugging session
0:000> q
```

You can suspend and resume threads in the debugger by using the *~n* and *~m* commands, respectively. This can sometimes be useful when dealing with bugs related to unbalanced calls (usually resulting in deadlock conditions) for suspending and resuming threads by the target program. The difference between these commands and the *~f* and *~u* commands (used to freeze and unfreeze threads, respectively) is that every *~n* increments the thread's suspend count by one, whereas the *~f* command simply instructs the debugger not to resume the thread that it had previously suspended at the break-in time. In that sense, *~f* and *~u* are really debugger concepts, whereas *~n* and *~m* mimic the suspend/resume semantics in the operating system.

Kernel-Mode Debugging Tricks

To close this chapter, the following section will walk you through several kernel-mode debugging techniques for accomplishing many of the tasks shown earlier in this chapter in the sections covering user-mode debugging tricks. The way you go about achieving some debugging tasks can sometimes differ greatly between user-mode and kernel-mode debugging. You'll see, in particular, that freezing threads, breaking on DLL load events within a user-mode process, and trapping process creation events require a different set of tricks when using the kernel-mode debugger.

Breaking on User-Mode Process Creation

When studying system components and their interactions, it can be useful to break into the debugger every time a new user-mode process is started on the target machine. This is arguably one of the most useful kernel-mode debugging tricks because it allows you to take full advantage of the global system scope that this type of debugging provides. It also opens the door for different and sometimes easier ways to debug the startup code path of new processes and the DLLs that they load by using kernel debugging as a complement to user-mode debugging.

The *nt!PspInsertProcess* Kernel-Mode Breakpoint

The idea behind this trick is simple: every new user-mode process creation attempt first goes to the kernel and calls *n!PspAllocateProcess* to create an executive object (*nt!_EPROCESS*) for the new process. It then calls *nt!PspInsertProcess* to insert it into a linked list of active process structures that the executive maintains. This means, in particular, that setting a breakpoint at one of these internal function calls using a kernel debugger allows you to *trap* every process-creation attempt on the target. You stop inside the debugger as a new process gets created, but before any code from it gets to run, because that happens only when the process creation system call returns to user mode and completes the process initialization in the NTDLL system module.

The *nt!PspInsertProcess* breakpoint is usually a better point to break than *nt!PspAllocateProcess* because the new process structure has been populated by that time, allowing you to easily find the identity of the new process from its associated executive structure, which is passed as the first argument to the *nt!PspInsertProcess* call. If you look closer at the disassembly of this function, you'll see that a register is used to hold the value of this parameter during the function call. In the *x86* version of the Windows 7 operating system, that register happens to be *eax*. Different registers will be used on each CPU architecture, but the following listing provides an illustration of how you can infer that information from the first few disassembly instructions in this call.

```
0: kd> vertarget
Windows 7 Kernel Version 7601 (Service Pack 1) MP (2 procs) Free x86 compatible
Built by: 7601.17640.x86fre.win7sp1_gdr.110622-1506
0: kd> .symfix
0: kd> .reload
0: kd> u nt!PspInsertProcess L20
82a7b003 8bff             mov     edi,edi
82a7b005 55               push    ebp
82a7b006 8bec             mov     ebp,esp
82a7b008 83e4f8           and     esp,0FFFFFFF8h
82a7b00b 83ec1c           sub     esp,1Ch
82a7b00e 53               push    ebx
82a7b00f 648b1d24010000   mov     ebx,dword ptr fs:[124h]
82a7b016 56               push    esi
82a7b017 57               push    edi
82a7b018 8bf8             mov     edi,eax
82a7b01a 8b4350           mov     eax,dword ptr [ebx+50h]
82a7b01d 8b8fb4000000     mov     ecx,dword ptr [edi+0B4h]
82a7b023 8944241c         mov     dword ptr [esp+1Ch],eax
82a7b027 8b87f4000000     mov     eax,dword ptr [edi+0F4h]
82a7b02d 894808           mov     dword ptr [eax+8],ecx
82a7b030 33d2             xor     edx,edx
82a7b032 b981000000       mov     ecx,81h
82a7b037 895c2418         mov     dword ptr [esp+18h],ebx
82a7b03b e8f4faffff       call    nt!SeAuditingWithTokenForSubcategory (82a7ab34)
82a7b040 84c0             test    al,al
82a7b042 7407             je      nt!PspInsertProcess+0x48 (82a7b04b)
82a7b044 8bc7             mov     eax,edi
82a7b046 e8cdfa0000       call    nt!SeAuditProcessCreation (82a8ab18)
...
```

The *nt!SeAuditProcessCreation* function call that happens a few assembly instructions into the *nt!PspInsertProcess* call is also passed the same process executive structure. The instructions that appear in bold text in the previous listing show that this argument ultimately can be traced back to the *eax* register.

This means that once you reach the *nt!PspInsertProcess* breakpoint in the kernel debugger, you can quickly examine the *ImageFileName* field in the new *_EPROCESS* structure saved in the *eax* register to determine the name of the process that's about to get created. In the following debugger listing, the breakpoint is hit after an attempt to start a new *notepad.exe* process instance on the target machine, which you're able to quickly confirm using the *dt* command. You can also append the field name to the command, which allows you to restrict the output to only dump the value of that particular field instead of the entire process executive structure, as shown in the following listing.

```
0: kd> bp nt!PspInsertProcess
0: kd> g
0: kd> dt nt!_EPROCESS @eax ImageFileName
   +0x16c ImageFileName : [15]  "notepad.exe"
```

Finally, note that this breakpoint will be hit quite often—in fact, every time a new process is created—so make sure you disable or clear it at the end of your experimentation.

```
1: kd> bl
 0 e 82a7b003     0001 (0001) nt!PspInsertProcess
1: kd> bd 0
1: kd> g
```

Breaking on Instances of a Particular Process Only

Although the global scope of the previous breakpoint can be useful when you are discovering the processes that get created as part of running your test scenario, you might also find that you're breaking into the kernel debugger more often than you would like to because of interference from other tasks that happen to be running on the target machine at the same time.

You can extend the idea of the previous breakpoint and restrict its scope to only instances of the process that you're interested in observing, though. The key behind the trick presented in this section is the powerful concept of *conditional breakpoints*. A conditional breakpoint is just like any other regular breakpoint, except it allows you to run a command of your choice when a breakpoint hit occurs, giving you an opportunity to examine the state of the memory and registers and automatically skip the breakpoint if you want to. You can also run a set of commands (grouped in a script, for instance) when handling a conditional breakpoint. To provide a practical illustration, you can use the following breakpoint so that you break into the kernel debugger only when instances of *notepad.exe* are created and ignore all the other processes on the system.

```
0: kd> bp nt!PspInsertProcess
"$$<C:\\book\\code\\chapter_07\\Scripts\\BreakOnProcessInKD_x86.txt"
breakpoint 0 redefined
0: kd> g
```

The script used in the previous listing targets the *x86* version of the Windows 7 OS, but you can easily adjust it to cover other versions or CPU platforms by changing the first line in the script.

```
$$
$$ C:\book\code\chapter_07\Scripts>BreakOnProcessInKD_x86.txt
$$ This script assumes the Windows 7 OS.
$$
r? $t1 = ((nt!_EPROCESS*) @eax);
as /ma ${/v:NewImageName} @@c++(@$t1->ImageFileName);
.echo ${NewImageName}
j ($spat("${NewImageName}", "notepad*") == 0) gc;
```

Several commands in the previous script need further explanation. First, the *r?* command is used to define a strongly typed pseudo-register. The second line then defines an ASCII (*/ma*) string variable ("alias") and assigns to it the value of the *ImageFileName* field in the executive process structure. Notice the use of the *@@C++* prefix to indicate that the pointer dereference in the parentheses is to be interpreted as a C++ expression. The last line in the script then uses the *$spat* operator and performs a regular expression evaluation of the new image name against the *notepad** pattern. (You can apply the same idea to other processes by simply modifying this last line.) The *gc* command is finally used when you decide to ignore the conditional breakpoint and continue.

You can learn more about conditional breakpoints in the MASM (Macro Assembler) sections of the WinDbg documentation Help index. As a fun challenge to test your understanding of the material described there, try to apply the idea demonstrated in the previous script to establish a conditional breakpoint (either using a user-mode or kernel-mode debugger) that allows you to break when a file with a particular name (or one that matches a given pattern) is created during your test scenario.

Tracing Processes Started During the Windows Boot Sequence

You can apply the technique described in this section to list the new processes started as part of the boot sequence in Windows 7, for example. The first thing you'll need to do, though, is make sure to break into the kernel debugger at the start of the boot sequence after the target is rebooted because the kernel debugger will not break on boot by default.

One easy way to do this is to use the *sxe ld* command to break when the *nt* kernel module is loaded at the beginning of the boot sequence. Remember that this command controls how module load events are handled on the debugger side, so unlike a breakpoint, it will survive a reboot. In the following listing, the *.reboot* command is used to initiate a reboot of the target machine from the host kernel debugger. Thanks to the *sxe ld* command you issued prior to the reboot, the kernel debugger stops at the beginning of the boot sequence.

```
0: kd> sxe ld:nt
0: kd> .reboot
Waiting to reconnect...
Windows 7 Kernel Version 7601 MP (1 procs) Free x86 compatible
nt!DbgLoadImageSymbols+0x47:
8281b578 cc              int     3
kd> .lastevent
Last event: Load module ntkrnlpa.exe at 8283b000
```

You can now insert the *nt!PspInsertProcess* breakpoint and list the processes that get created on the target machine without stopping inside the host debugger by using the conditional breakpoint shown in the following listing, which simply logs the name of each new process it encounters and continues. Remember also to disable the module load handling (*sxd ld*) now that you don't need it anymore.

```
kd> sxd ld
kd> bp nt!PspInsertProcess "dt nt!_EPROCESS @eax ImageFileName; gc"
kd> g
   +0x16c ImageFileName : [15]  "smss.exe"
   +0x16c ImageFileName : [15]  "csrss.exe"
...
```

Debugging the Startup of User-Mode Processes

As you just saw in the previous section, it is possible to trap user-mode process creation events in the kernel-mode debugger. The only problem when applying that idea to debug the startup code path of a user-mode process is that the *nt!PspInsertProcess* breakpoint is hit in the context of the parent process and the symbols for the new child process have not yet been loaded at the time.

One technique you can use to work around this problem is to simulate being under the control of a user-mode debugger even though you're only using a host kernel debugger. The key idea behind this useful trick is that the system determines that a process is under the control of a user-mode debugger by looking at a byte (*BeingDebugged*) in its process environment block (PEB) structure. So, if you forcibly set that field from within the kernel debugger, debug breaks generated by the system and destined for user-mode debuggers can be caught inside the kernel-mode debugger.

```
1: kd> dt ntdll!_PEB
   +0x000 InheritedAddressSpace : UChar
   +0x001 ReadImageFileExecOptions : UChar
   +0x002 BeingDebugged    : UChar
...
```

To see how this works in practice, you'll use this idea to set a breakpoint at the main function of a new *notepad.exe* process using a kernel-mode debugging session. When you hit the *nt!PspInsertProcess* breakpoint, you can switch the process context to that of the new process so that the *$peb* pseudo-register in the debugger is pointing to the process environment block of the new child process rather than that of its parent. You can then simply edit the *BeingDebugged* field in memory by using the *eb* ("edit byte") command (which is the byte at offset "+2" after the start of the PEB structure), as demonstrated in the following listing.

```
0: kd> vertarget
Windows 7 Kernel Version 7600 MP (2 procs) Free x86 compatible
...
0: kd> bp nt!PspInsertProcess
0: kd> g
Breakpoint 0 hit
nt!PspInsertProcess:
0: kd> dt @eax nt!_EPROCESS ImageFileName
   +0x16c ImageFileName : [15]  "notepad.exe"
0: kd> $ notice that you can't resolve notepad.exe symbols at this point yet!
0: kd> x notepad!*main*
              ^ Couldn't resolve 'x notepad'
0: kd> .process /r /p @eax
0: kd> eb @$peb+2 1
0: kd> g
Break instruction exception - code 80000003 (first chance)
001b:76e2ebbe cc              int     3
0: kd> k
ChildEBP RetAddr
000af7a4 77280dc0 ntdll!LdrpDoDebuggerBreak+0x2c
000af904 77266077 ntdll!LdrpInitializeProcess+0x11a9
000af954 77263663 ntdll!_LdrpInitialize+0x78
000af964 00000000 ntdll!LdrInitializeThunk+0x10
```

Notice how you were able to simulate the *ntdll.dll* process initialization breakpoint usually hit during user-mode debugging even though you were using only a kernel-mode debugger! By doing so, you managed to move just far enough in the child process execution that its symbols are available, but not so far that you entirely miss the startup code you're interested in being able to debug. The following listing uses the *x* command first to list the symbols of the *notepad.exe* process and then sets a breakpoint at the main entry point of that process, allowing you to then debug the startup code path of the user-mode process using the kernel debugger.

```
1: kd> !process -1 0
PROCESS 8585b030  SessionId: 1  Cid: 15a4    Peb: 7ffd8000  ParentCid: 0374
    Image: notepad.exe
0: kd> .reload /user
0: kd> x notepad!*main*
00c51405          notepad!WinMain = <no type information>
...
0: kd> bp notepad!WinMain
0: kd> g
Breakpoint 1 hit
notepad!WinMain:
```

Breaking on DLL Load Events

Breaking when a DLL is loaded into the address space of a specific user-mode process when using the kernel-mode debugger is trickier than when using a user-mode debugger because the *sxe ld* command works differently for user-mode modules in the two cases. If you try to use it with a user-mode module in the kernel debugger, you'll be disappointed to see that it has no effect.

However, you can again simulate being under the user-mode debugger (just as you did in the previous section) and use the *BreakOnDllLoad* IFEO hook to catch DLL module load events as debug breaks in the kernel-mode debugger. Because the OS module loader honors the *BreakOnDllLoad* hook only when the target process is running (or appears to be running) under the control of a user-mode debugger, you'll again need to forcibly overwrite the *BeingDebugged* field in the process PEB for this trick to work under the kernel-mode debugger.

To see this in action, you'll now use this technique to break into the debugger when the *secur32.dll* system DLL gets loaded by *notepad.exe*. The first step is to add the *BreakOnDllLoad* hook for the *secur32.dll* image on the target machine, just as you saw back in the "Breaking on DLL Load Events in the Visual Studio Debugger" section earlier in this chapter.

```
C:\book\code\chapter_07\scripts>configure_breakondllload.cmd -enable secur32.dll
```

You can then add the familiar *nt!PspInsertProcess* breakpoint using the host kernel debugger so that you get notified when new processes are created on the target machine.

```
0: kd> bp nt!PspInsertProcess
0: kd> g
```

Back on the target machine, start a new instance of *notepad.exe*. When the previous breakpoint is reached in the host kernel debugger, you can then apply the trick shown earlier to simulate being under the user-mode debugger, as shown in the following listing.

```
Breakpoint 0 hit
1: kd> dt nt!_EPROCESS @eax ImageFileName
   +0x16c ImageFileName : [15]  "notepad.exe"
1: kd> .process /r /p @eax
1: kd> eb @$peb+2 1
1: kd> g
Break instruction exception - code 80000003 (first chance)
001b:772a04f6 cc              int     3
1: kd> !process -1 0
PROCESS 8642f428  SessionId: 1  Cid: 1170    Peb: 7ffdf000  ParentCid: 17cc
    Image: notepad.exe
1: kd> g
```

As you can see, the *secur32.dll* isn't loaded as a static dependency in *notepad.exe*. However, if you now invoke the File\Open dialog box using the Ctrl+O shortcut in *notepad.exe*, you'll see that *secur32.dll* gets loaded as part of that sequence, with the following stack trace.

```
Break instruction exception - code 80000003 (first chance)
1: kd> .reload /user
1: kd> k
ChildEBP RetAddr
0022dc34 774801db ntdll!LdrpRunInitializeRoutines+0x211
0022dda0 7747f5f9 ntdll!LdrpLoadDll+0x4d1
0022ddd4 7582b8a4 ntdll!LdrLoadDll+0x92
0022de0c 75b6a293 KERNELBASE!LoadLibraryExW+0x15a
0022de28 75b6a218 ole32!LoadLibraryWithLogging+0x16
0022de4c 75b6a107 ole32!CClassCache::CDllPathEntry::LoadDll+0xa9
...
```

Notice that you can now list the symbols of the *secur32.dll* module using the *x* command, meaning that you can also set breakpoints in functions from this module in the context of the new user-mode process, as you set out to accomplish.

```
1: kd> .reload /user
1: kd> x secur32!g_*
75175688          Secur32!g_bInitOK = <no type information>
7517568c          Secur32!g_dwOpenCount = <no type information>
75175680          Secur32!g_pCounterBlock = <no type information>
75175684          Secur32!g_hLsaSharedMemory = <no type information>
```

When you're done with this experiment, don't forget to delete the *BreakOnDllLoad* hook you added on the target machine, which you can do using the following command.

```
C:\book\code\chapter_07\scripts>configure_breakondllload.cmd -disable secur32.dll
```

Breaking on Unhandled SEH Exceptions

By default, the kernel debugger doesn't catch unhandled exceptions in user-mode processes, even when no user-mode debugger is attached to the process on the target machine. You can change this default behavior, though. This is configurable via one of the bits in the NT global flag called "stop on exception" (*soe*). So, you can use the *!gflag* extension command to enable that bit, allowing you to debug user-mode crashes in the kernel-mode debugger.

```
0: kd> !gflag +soe
Current NtGlobalFlag contents: 0x00040401
    soe - Stop On Exception
    ptg - Enable pool tagging
    ksl - Enable loading of kernel debugger symbols
0: kd> g
```

To see this in action, you can execute a user-mode process that crashes on the target machine. For example, you can use the *NullDereference.exe* example from Chapter 4. As soon as you execute that process on the target machine, you'll see the following access-violation event in the host kernel debugger.

```
Access violation - code c0000005 (first chance)...
0: kd> .sympath+ C:\book\code\chapter_04\NullDereference\objfre_win7_x86\i386
0: kd> .srcpath+ C:\book\code
0: kd> .reload /user
0: kd> k
ChildEBP RetAddr
0014fc70 00671364 NullDereference!wmain+0x9
0014fcb4 756eed6c NullDereference!__wmainCRTStartup+0x102
0014fcc0 772637f5 kernel32!BaseThreadInitThunk+0xe
0014fd00 772637c8 ntdll!__RtlUserThreadStart+0x70
0014fd18 00000000 ntdll!_RtlUserThreadStart+0x1b
```

When you no longer want this behavior and prefer to let user-mode debuggers on the target machine crash without further debugging, you can disable the *soe* bit using the *!gflag* extension command again, as demonstrated in the following listing.

```
0: kd> !gflag -soe
```

Freezing Threads

The *~f* and *~u* user-mode debugger commands that are used to freeze and unfreeze threads, respectively, rely on the *SuspendThread* and *ResumeThread* functions at the Win32 API layer, so they're not available during kernel-mode debugging. Fortunately, there is another way to simulate the same behavior under the kernel-mode debugger.

This technique is another case illustrating why simple engineering is also good engineering: the most obvious way of suspending a thread is to simply make it spin in an infinite loop. As it turns out, you can do that relatively easily by inserting a "jump to self" instruction at the current address executed by the thread you want to freeze.

To illustrate this technique, you'll now apply it to freeze the main UI thread of a running *notepad .exe* instance on the target machine of a kernel debugging session. When freezing threads, it's important to pick safe points during the execution of the program. A good choice in this case is somewhere in the private *notepad.exe* code implementing the UI message loop rather than in the kernel code that's at the top of the stack of the main thread. Freezing it in the kernel code would freeze the entire target machine and not just the UI code in *notepad.exe*, given that same kernel code is also used by the other threads on the target that are waiting to get unblocked. The following listing switches over to the context of the target *notepad.exe* instance, and then breaks into the debugger when the *GetMessage* API returns to its calling message loop in the *WinMain* function.

```
0: kd> !process 0 0 notepad.exe
PROCESS 85d43c88  SessionId: 1  Cid: 1350    Peb: 7ffdd000  ParentCid: 17cc
    Image: notepad.exe
0: kd> .process /i 85d43c88
0: kd> g
Break instruction exception - code 80000003 (first chance)
0: kd> .reload /user
0: kd> !process -1 2
PROCESS 85d43c88  SessionId: 1  Cid: 1350    Peb: 7ffdd000  ParentCid: 17cc
    Image: notepad.exe
        THREAD 86fe8030  Cid 1350.08a8  Teb: 7ffdf000 Win32Thread: ffae0318 WAIT:
            858c8780  SynchronizationEvent
0: kd> .thread 86fe8030
Implicit thread is now 86fe8030
0: kd> k
ChildEBP RetAddr
9635db10 828b965d nt!KiSwapContext+0x26
9635db48 828b84b7 nt!KiSwapThread+0x266
9635db70 828b20cf nt!KiCommitThreadWait+0x1df
9635dbe8 9655a736 nt!KeWaitForSingleObject+0x393
9635dc44 9655a543 win32k!xxxRealSleepThread+0x1d7
9635dc60 965575b0 win32k!xxxSleepThread+0x2d
9635dcb8 9655ab02 win32k!xxxRealInternalGetMessage+0x4b2
9635dd1c 828791fa win32k!NtUserGetMessage+0x3f
9635dd1c 772470b4 nt!KiFastCallEntry+0x12a
001af6b4 7602cde0 ntdll!KiFastSystemCallRet
001af6b8 7602ce13 USER32!NtUserGetMessage+0xc
001af6d4 0069148a USER32!GetMessageW+0x33
001af714 006916ec notepad!WinMain+0xe6
...
0: kd> g 0069148a
notepad!WinMain+0xe6:
001b:0069148a 85c0            test    eax,eax
```

Now that you picked a good safe point to freeze the thread at, you can insert an instruction to "jump" back to the same location by using the *a* ("assemble") debugger command. This command allows you to type the instructions to write at the target memory location. Like with other debugger commands involving editing or reading memory, the "." alias can also be used as a shortcut for the current instruction pointer register. Once you're done entering the "jump to self" instruction (represented by the *jmp 0x0069148a* instruction in this listing), type one final **ENTER** to exit the "edit" mode that the *a* command places the debugger in, as illustrated in the following listing.

```
1: kd> u .
notepad!WinMain+0xe6:
001b:0069148a 85c0            test    eax,eax
001b:0069148c 0f8453050000    je      notepad!WinMain+0xea (006919e5)
...
1: kd> $ Make sure you prefix the address with 0x when using the a command
1: kd> a .
001b:0069148a jmp 0x0069148a
jmp 0x0069148a
001b:0069148c
1: kd> u .
notepad!WinMain+0xe6:
001b:0069148a ebfe            jmp     notepad!WinMain+0xe6 (0069148a)
001b:0069148c 0f8453050000    je      notepad!WinMain+0xea (006919e5)
1: kd> g
```

Notice, as shown in Figure 7-19, that the *notepad.exe* process now becomes unresponsive when you interact with its main window on the target machine.

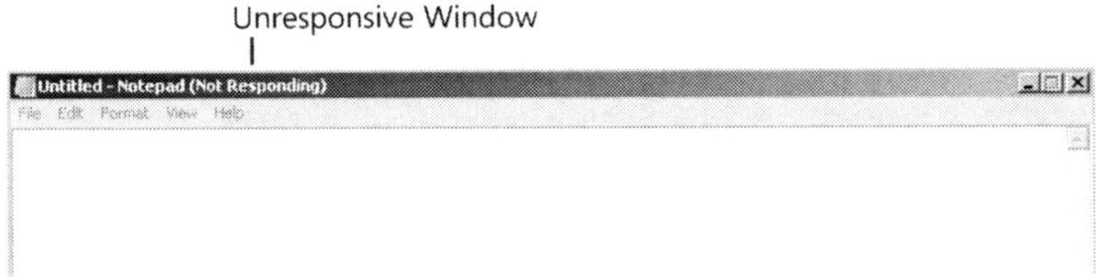

FIGURE 7-19 Freezing the main UI thread of *notepad.exe*.

You can unfreeze the main UI thread (in turn, making the target *notepad.exe* instance responsive again) by restoring the original instruction you previously overwrote with the "jump to self" infinite loop. When freezing threads using this trick, you should always write down the initial instructions before you overwrite them so that you're able to restore them later when you need to unfreeze the thread. Note that because the memory address you need to overwrite is in user mode, you must first switch back to the context of the target user-mode process so that the address is interpreted relative to that process context, as demonstrated in the following listing.

```
0: kd> !process 0 0 notepad.exe
PROCESS 85d43c88  SessionId: 1  Cid: 1350    Peb: 7ffdd000  ParentCid: 17cc
    Image: notepad.exe
0: kd> .process /i 85d43c88
0: kd> g
Break instruction exception - code 80000003 (first chance)
0: kd> eb 0x0069148a 85 c0
0: kd> g
```

Note that the technique described in this section also works for threads executing inside the kernel (assuming again that you pick safe points). In fact, it can also be used in user-mode debuggers too!

Finally, if you look closely at the disassembly resulting from the jump to the current address, you can see that the debugger ended up translating the "jump to self" instruction you provided into the more efficient *"0xeb 0xfe"* 2-bytes equivalent. In *x86/x64*, the *0xeb* byte is the hexadecimal operation code (opcode) for a short jump, meaning a jump using a relative offset instead of an absolute target address. The debugger was smart enough in this case to recognize that the jump instruction could be encoded more efficiently as a short jump using –2 (*0xfe* two's complement) as a relative offset. The main takeaway from this observation is that the "jump to self" trick will end up overwriting 2 bytes on *x86* and *x64*, so you'll need to write aside the two original bytes so that you can restore them later when you need to unfreeze the thread. In addition, this observation means you can also insert the "jump to self" instruction by using the *eb* command to modify the memory directly instead of the *a* command, without having to explicitly provide the address of the "jump to self" instruction you want to insert.

Summary

This chapter contained a compilation of several generic techniques that put you in position to start examining the state of a process or the entire system using user-mode or kernel-mode debuggers. Being able to respond to some of the important events described in this chapter is often a key ingredient to efficient debugging investigations. In particular, you now know how to use the following tricks after reading this chapter:

- Insert an infinite debugger wait loop to wait anywhere in your source code until a debugger of your choice is attached. This method is very powerful because it can be used in scripts, managed code, or native code, though it also requires you to change the source code of the application, which is not always possible.
- Debug the startup path of a process in both user-mode and kernel-mode debugging sessions. The strategies for doing so are quite different, though: using child debugging and using the "startup-debugger" IFEO hook are common approaches when using a user-mode debugger, and the useful kernel-mode *nt!PspInsertProcess* breakpoint can be used for this purpose in the case of kernel-mode debugging.
- Set breakpoints at DLL modules that get dynamically loaded into host processes by first responding to their DLL load events and resolving their symbols at that point.
- Freeze and unfreeze threads so that you can simulate race condition bugs inside the debugger or simply focus on stepping through the code of a single thread in a multithreaded application.
- Investigate error-code failures, and efficiently track down the call sites that trigger them. This topic will be revisited when tracing is covered later in this book because tracing strategies also can be useful for this type of investigation, just like you saw earlier in this chapter when you used the Process Monitor tool to track down resource-access failures.

While this chapter focused on learning how to maneuver the debugger so that you're able to stop at key junctures during the execution of an application, the next two chapters will cover strategies for tackling investigations of common code defects. They will discuss how to complete the usual debugging iterations where you first control the target's execution and break into the debugger as needed, and then deftly analyze the state at each juncture so that you can form a full picture of the behavior of the code you're debugging.

CHAPTER 8

Common Debugging Scenarios, Part 1

In this chapter

This chapter presents various examples of crashes and resource leaks, and it shows the most efficient strategies to debug them. Because these reliability bugs are sometimes hard to reproduce, this chapter also covers the techniques required to get more consistent reproducible cases for each bug category, which enables you to then inspect the failures using the debugger.

The examples presented in this chapter demonstrate how to apply many of the concepts and tools introduced in the previous chapters, including the Application Verifier tool covered in Chapter 6, "Code Analysis Tools," and the GFLAGS tool introduced back in Chapter 5, "Beyond the Basics." Your goal, by the end of this chapter, should be to form a set of basic first steps you can use to start your debugging investigations when faced with the common code-defect categories covered in this chapter.

Debugging Access Violations

One of the most common causes of program crashes is attempting to access invalid memory, also known as memory *access violations*. This section starts by defining this category of crashes more formally and then shows how you can investigate their immediate cause by using the *!analyze* extension command of the WinDbg debugger.

Understanding Memory Access Violations

Memory in user-mode programs comes, either directly or indirectly, from virtual allocations in the operating system using the *VirtualAlloc* Win32 API. The virtual memory is first *reserved* by the application in units of fixed size called *pages* and then must be *committed* before the program proceeds to access it. When you use the NT heap manager, in particular, this is done automatically for you when you use that user-mode virtual memory management layer. The "commit" step ensures that the memory manager in the operating system's (OS) kernel has reserved storage for the page in the page file and might fail—for example, if the maximum size limit set for the page file on disk is reached under high-memory usage. Note that a successful "commit" is simply a promise by the OS to make the memory available when it's later used by the program (which is why the OS needs to verify in this step that it will be able to insert the page into the page file, if needed, without going over the user-defined page file size limit), but this step doesn't eagerly consume any physical resources—neither physical RAM nor page-file disk space. Only after the page is touched does the OS use the appropriate resource to back it.

Any attempt to reference a virtual address without its memory page having been previously committed will result in a special Structured Exception Handling (SEH) exception known as a memory access violation. The telltale sign that you're looking at memory that's not properly committed is that you'll see the *??* pattern when using the debugger to dump the values stored in the addresses around that memory location. There are many ways that programs can encounter this condition, such as the following:

- Trying to access deleted memory
- Attempting to execute code in an unloaded DLL module
- Dereferencing the system-reserved NULL pointer address (which is probably the most frequent case of all access-violation types)

All these actions are illegal memory accesses that can trigger an access violation. The following debugger listing illustrates the last case, where the *db* ("dump memory as a sequence of bytes") command is used to view the values located at virtual address 0 (NULL address).

```
0:000> db 0
00000000  ?? ?? ?? ?? ?? ?? ?? ??-?? ?? ?? ?? ?? ?? ?? ??  ????????????????
```

The second case that can result in an access-violation exception is when a program tries to access a page in violation of the CPU protections that were assigned to it. Memory pages can be marked as read-only, write-only, execute-only, or any combination of the previous flags. Trying to write to read-only memory, for example, will also lead to an access violation even if the page is committed and contains valid data.

To recap, access violations occur in one of the following scenarios:

- An attempt to access noncommitted memory
- An attempt to use memory in a way that's not allowed by the CPU protections applied to the page that contains it

The *!analyze* Debugger Extension Command

The *!analyze* debugger extension command is usually your first step in trying to determine the cause of an access violation; it typically does a good job of providing you with the immediate reason for the exception. You've already seen this command in action back in Chapter 4, "Postmortem Debugging," but the same command works in live debugging too. Sometimes this extension command is sufficient to directly pinpoint the nature of the bug that led to the access violation. In other cases, the code that results in the access violation isn't the true culprit, and another code path—or even a different thread—could have been responsible for the memory corruption. Tracking down the root cause of these memory corruptions often calls for more careful analysis, and it might require you to enable *debug* hooks in the OS, as you'll see in the following sections describing heap and stack memory corruptions.

If you compile the following C++ code sample from the companion source code (using the instructions described back in the Introduction of this book), you'll see that it immediately hits an access violation when you execute it.

```
//
// C:\book\code\chapter_08\IllegalWriteAV>main.cpp
//
WCHAR* g_pwszMessage = L"Hello World";

int
__cdecl
wmain()
{
    g_pwszMessage[0] = L'a';
    return 0;
}
```

This program causes an access violation because the Microsoft Visual C++ (VC++) compiler used in the Driver Development Kit (DDK) build environment recognized the string literal and placed it in a read-only section of the executable image. Even though the data referenced by the pointer variable wasn't explicitly declared constant, it's still legal for the compiler to store string literals in read-only memory. When the program then tries to overwrite the first character in the string, an access violation fault ensues, as reported by the *!analyze* extension command in the following listing, where the *–v* option is used to request additional verbose output from the command.

```
0:000> vercommand
command line: '"c:\Program Files\Debugging Tools for Windows (x86)\windbg.exe"
c:\book\code\chapter_08\IllegalWriteAV\objfre_win7_x86\i386\IllegalWriteAv.exe'
0:000> g
(1be8.1bd8): Access violation - code c0000005 (first chance)
0:000> g
(1be8.1bd8): Access violation - code c0000005 (!!! second chance !!!)
0:000> .lastevent
Last event: 1be8.1bd8: Access violation - code c0000005 (!!! second chance !!!)
0:000> .symfix
```

```
0:000> .reload
0:000> !analyze -v
...
ExceptionAddress: 00b5199c (IllegalWriteAv!wmain+0x00000009)
   ExceptionCode: c0000005 (Access violation)
  ExceptionFlags: 00000000
NumberParameters: 2
   Parameter[0]: 00000001
   Parameter[1]: 00b511b0
Attempt to write to address 00b511b0

FAULTING_SOURCE_CODE:
     5: int
     6: __cdecl
     7: wmain()
     8: {
>    9:     g_pwszMessage[0] = L'a';
    10:     return 0;
    11: }
    12:
```

In this particular case, the bug was straightforward and the *!analyze* command was able to accurately pinpoint the root cause of the access violation (which was an attempt to write to read-only memory), as well as the exact source line that triggered the violation.

Note that had you declared the global variable in the previous example with the *const* modifier to indicate that it was pointing to constant data, the compiler would've caught this error for you at compile time. This is why it's important to use the correct modifiers when declaring variables, especially those with global scope.

```
//
// The Correct variable declaration in this case...
//
const WCHAR* g_pwszMessage = L"Hello World";
```

Finally, even though the example provided in this section might sound contrived, the bug it describes isn't uncommon at all. For example, this same bug happens when you use a string literal as the command line in the *CreateProcess* Win32 API call. The *lpCommandLine* argument to that API is declared as LPWSTR, not LPCWSTR (a constant pointer to a unicode string of wide characters), reflecting the API's intention that it might modify (write to) the string argument you provide to it. This is why the *WorkerProcess* sample from this book's companion source code uses a C++ helper function (*LaunchProcess*) that wraps the *CreateProcess* Win32 API and accepts a constant command-line string when starting a new process. You can use this helper function so that you can write your code in a more natural way without having to worry about this pitfall.

Debugging Heap Corruptions

Heap corruptions are one of the most common causes of access violations. Unfortunately, they're also often hard to diagnose because the instruction that ultimately triggers the access violation is usually not at fault and might simply have fallen victim to other code in the user-mode process that corrupted the shared memory well before that point in the program's execution. Remember that access violations are raised by the operating system only on access to uncommitted or protected pages. For example, you would be successful in writing past the end of an allocated buffer and go undetected as long as you didn't write data to any other uncommitted pages. If that buffer overrun corrupts other data that gets dereferenced later in the program, the access violation might not happen until that point during the process lifetime.

If you're writing native C/C++ code, this section will show you a few techniques to help you track down heap corruptions in allocators that are based on the NT heap manager. If, instead, you're writing your code using the Microsoft .NET Framework, there is good news: one of the main value propositions of the safe managed environment provided by the .NET Common Language Runtime (CLR) is that it insulates you from these types of bugs (barring bugs in the CLR native code itself, of course). That is, it protects you until you need to interoperate with native code (using the P/Invoke or COM Interop features, for example), at which point you could still write code that causes memory corruptions, just as you have the potential to do in pure native scenarios. The latter part of this section will cover this case.

Debugging Native Heap Corruptions

The majority of well-known custom allocators in Microsoft Windows are built on top of the NT heap manager APIs in *ntdll.dll* (*RtlAllocateHeap/RtlFreeHeap*). This includes the C runtime library's *malloc/free* and *new/delete*, the COM framework's *SysAllocString*, as well as Win32's *LocalAlloc*, *GlobalAlloc*, and *HeapAlloc*. Though these allocators create different heaps to store the memory they allocate, they all end up calling the NT heap implementation in *ntdll.dll*.

As stated earlier, one complicating factor when debugging heap corruptions is that the program might crash well after the memory corruption had taken place. It might also go completely undetected in some runs of the program only to surface unexpectedly in others. Fortunately, you can use several debugging features in the NT heap manager to help catch heap corruptions closer to where they happen, with the ideal case being an immediate crash at the point of the transgression. Although these debugging aids require you to run the scenario again and hope for a repro after the debugging features are enabled, they're still the best way to track down heap memory corruptions. They're also particularly useful during automated testing because they make it much more possible to catch all heap corruption bugs in your code base before they cause mayhem in the wild.

The most important of these heap-corruption debugging aids is a set of options commonly known as the *page heap*, which will be the main focus of this section.

Introducing the Page Heap

Page heap is a complete (parallel) NT heap implementation with a number of debug checks to help catch corruptions as soon as they occur, as opposed to relying on the OS to eventually raise an access violation when an illegal memory page access later takes place.

Because the page heap affects the behavior of the NT heap manager, it also helps you debug heap corruptions even when your programs use higher-level, memory-management primitives such as the C runtime library allocators, given that those allocators are also built on top of the NT heap allocators. If, for any reason, you write an allocator that's not based on the NT heap layer, it is certainly a good idea to at least have a special mode in which all you do is redirect your allocator to invoke the NT heap functions so that you can take advantage of the page-heap feature for debugging corruptions in the programs that use your custom allocator. Figure 8-1 illustrates the position of the page-heap implementation at the NT heap layer relative to other well-known, user-mode allocators in Windows.

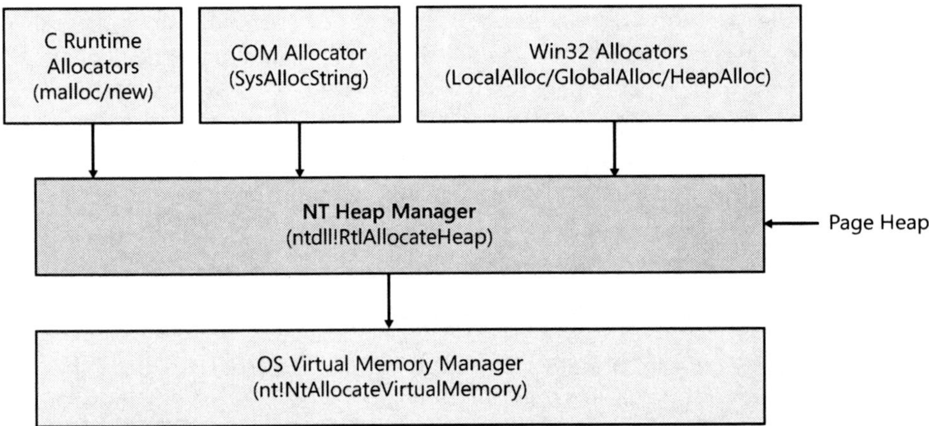

FIGURE 8-1 Page heap position in the hierarchy of common allocators in Windows.

Page heap can be easily enabled using the Application Verifier tool, as you'll see later in this section. In fact, it's enabled by default with the basic settings in the Application Verifier UI. In its full form, page heap allows you to catch most heap-corruption bugs, and your reach is limited only by how comprehensive your test coverage is. Most notably, you can automate the catching of the following categories of bugs:

- Use of invalid heap pointers
- Use of the wrong heaps—for example, allocating memory using *SysAllocString* and freeing it using *free*
- Double-free bugs
- Use of memory after it has been freed
- Access to memory before or after the end of an allocated buffer (heap-based underruns and overruns)

How Page Heap Works

The idea behind page heap is simple: if the heap implementation places each allocation at the end of its own dedicated memory page or pages and reserves the adjacent page right after it without committing it, an access to write past the end of the buffer—even an off-by-one bug—will be caught immediately, making it much easier to diagnose the root cause of the corruption. By giving each allocation its own page (or pages, depending on its size), the page heap implementation also can insert a block header before the actual application buffer and use this header to describe the state of the allocated buffer, such as whether it has been freed and where it was last allocated or deleted. This opens the door to a number of useful debugging features, such as being able to find precisely how each buffer on the heap was allocated and freed and detect when the buffer gets used while in an invalid state.

There is a small catch, though. The NT heap manager has always guaranteed that the buffers it returns to the application are 8-bytes-aligned on 32-bit Windows, and 16-bytes-aligned on 64-bit Windows. However, it isn't possible for the page heap to both place the allocations at the end of a page and satisfy the alignment requirement. The page-heap implementation handles this dilemma by giving priority to the alignment requirement (so that replacing the regular NT heap with the page heap won't introduce artificial bugs in the target program) and uses a known fill pattern to pad the allocation so that it ends on a page boundary. When the memory is freed, the page heap checks this fill pattern and, if it's corrupted, raises an error. This ensures that the corruption is detected at *free* time, so you still need to track down when the buffer got corrupted. It's certainly better than the alternative of having to investigate random crashes without page heap, though. That being said, if you know that your application doesn't rely on the alignment guarantee from the NT heap manager, you can use a page-heap option to enable unaligned allocations so that you immediately catch the memory corruption as it happens rather than waiting till free time.

The form of page heap described so far is called *full page heap* because it uses guard pages for every allocation. This means two memory pages for even small allocations. For programs with heavy memory usage, you could possibly run out of virtual memory space when using full page heap, particularly on 32-bit Windows. Even when you're running your test on 64-bit Windows and you define a large-enough size for the page file on disk to avoid failing memory allocations, your program might start experiencing a lot of thrashing and the timing of your test case might end up fundamentally changed, possibly causing the bug to no longer reproduce when using the full page heap in place of the regular NT heap.

There are two good ways to soften the memory impact of the full page heap:

- The first is to use a variant called *light page heap*, where no guard pages are used for allocations. Instead, the idea of using a fill pattern is extended to "guard" the boundaries of the block descriptor header and application buffer. The drawback to light page heap is that you catch corruptions only at free time, when it might not be obvious who was previously responsible for the corruption during the lifetime of the buffer.
- The other approach to deal with the memory impact of the full page heap is to use it in a more surgical manner instead of throughout the target process. For example, if you know the heap corruption occurs due to a specific dynamic-link library (DLL) module, you can restrict

the scope of full page heap in the process to only that single DLL. As you'll shortly see, you can choose from several other options to control the granularity of full-page-heap applicability so that you can take advantage of its benefits even in situations where its impact on memory usage (when used indiscriminately) might not be acceptable.

Figure 8-2 offers a comparative view of each block allocation in the light-page-heap and full-page-heap schemes. Notice that allocations are placed at the end of pages and that an additional guard page is inserted right after the allocation in the case of full page heap. Light page heap, on the other hand, uses only fill patterns to detect corruptions in the allocated buffer.

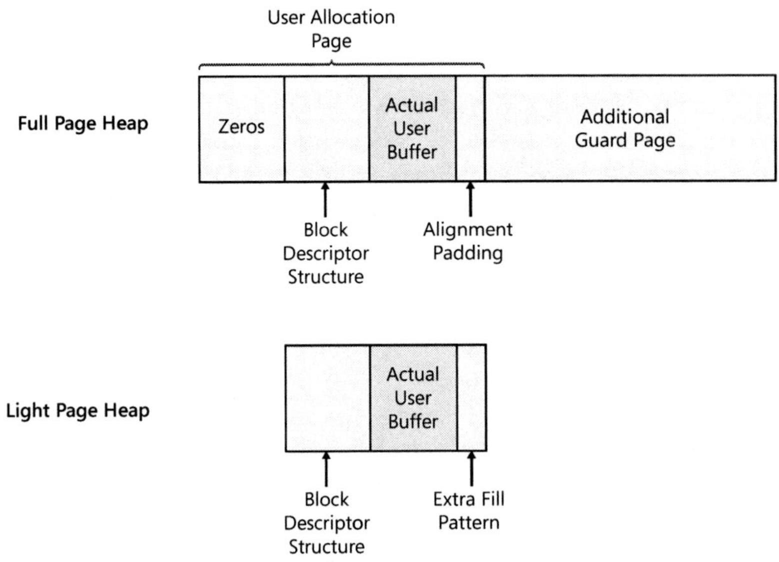

FIGURE 8-2 Memory allocations in the light-page-heap and full-page-heap schemes.

You can also dump the block structure used to describe each allocation in the page heap using the *dt* ("dump type") command in WinDbg, as shown in the following listing. You'll notice the *StartStamp* and *StopStamp* fill pattern fields bordering both ends of the block descriptor structure. This important data structure is also documented on the MSDN website at *http://msdn.microsoft.com/en-us/library/ms220938.aspx*.

```
0:000> dt _DPH_BLOCK_INFORMATION
ntdll!_DPH_BLOCK_INFORMATION
   +0x000 StartStamp       : Uint4B
   +0x004 Heap             : Ptr32 Void
   +0x008 RequestedSize    : Uint4B
   +0x00c ActualSize       : Uint4B
   +0x010 FreeQueue        : _LIST_ENTRY
   +0x010 FreePushList     : _SINGLE_LIST_ENTRY
   +0x010 TraceIndex       : Uint2B
   +0x018 StackTrace       : Ptr32 Void
   +0x01c EndStamp         : Uint4B
```

Enabling Page Heap for a Target Process

You can enable page-heap settings using either the GFLAGS tool or the Application Verifier tool. Though both tools allow you to configure the various settings of page heap from the command line, the Application Verifier tool has a convenient user interface to do so, while the *gflags.exe* user interface allows you only to set full page heap, without extra customizations. For this reason, you'll be using the Application Verifier tool in the experiment shown as part of this section, which consists of debugging the heap-memory corruption exhibited by the following C++ program from the companion source code.

```
//
// C:\book\code\chapter_08\HeapCorruption>main.cpp
//
static
HRESULT
MainHR()
{
    CAutoPtr<WCHAR> pwszBuffer;
    const WCHAR* pwszStringToCopy = L"abc.txt";

    ChkProlog();

    pwszBuffer.Attach(new WCHAR[wcslen(pwszStringToCopy)]);
    ChkAlloc(pwszBuffer);

    // BUG! destination buffer is smaller than the number of bytes copied
    wcscpy(pwszBuffer, pwszStringToCopy);
    wprintf(L"Copied string is %s\n", pwszBuffer);

    ChkNoCleanup();
}
```

When you run this program in standalone mode without any global flags, you'll see that it seems to work and complete successfully.

```
C:\book\code\chapter_08\HeapCorruption>objfre_win7_x86\i386\OffByOne.exe
Copied string is abc.txt
Success.
```

However, there is a very serious bug in this code because it writes two bytes (L'*\0*' null terminator unicode character) past the end of the allocated area, which didn't account for that character, resulting in a heap-based buffer overrun. This is why *wcscpy* is a dangerous function that you should avoid in your code in the first place and replace with safer alternatives, such as *wcscpy_s*. In fact, C/C++ static code analysis (either inside the DDK build environment or Visual Studio) will flag the usage as an error and give the following message when you compile the previous program.

```
main.cpp(18) : warning 28719: Banned API Usage: wcscpy is a Banned API as listed in dontuse.h
for security purposes.
Found in function 'CMainApp::MainHR'
```

Fortunately, even if you didn't configure static analysis for your project or if you foolishly decided to ignore the static-analysis error message, you can still catch this serious bug at run time using the Application Verifier tool. The default Application Verifier settings already include a Heaps category, which enables the full flavor of page heap on your behalf, as illustrated in Figure 8-3.

```
C:\Windows\System32>appverif.exe
```

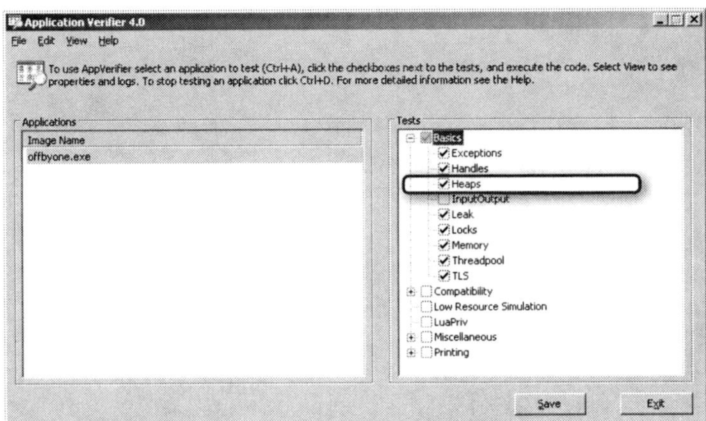

FIGURE 8-3 Enabling page heap in the Application Verifier user interface.

As soon as you run the program now under a user-mode debugger, you'll hit the following verifier stop. You can then use the *!avrf* extension command that was introduced in Chapter 6 to display additional details about the reason for the verifier stop, as shown in the following listing.

```
0:000> vercommand
command line: '"c:\Program Files\Debugging Tools for Windows (x86)\windbg.exe"
c:\book\code\chapter_08\HeapCorruption\objfre_win7_x86\i386\OffByOne.exe'
0:000> .sympath
c:\windows\system32;srv*c:\localsymbolcache*http://msdl.microsoft.com/download/symbols
0:000> .reload
0:000> !gflag
Current NtGlobalFlag contents: 0x02000100
    vrf - Enable application verifier
    hpa - Place heap allocations at ends of pages
0:000> g
VERIFIER STOP 0000000F: pid 0xCD4: Corrupted suffix pattern for heap block.
...
0:000> !avrf
Verifier package version >= 3.00
Application verifier settings (80643027):
   - full page heap
   - Handles
...
APPLICATION_VERIFIER_HEAPS_CORRUPTED_HEAP_BLOCK_SUFFIX (f)
Corrupted suffix pattern for heap block.
...
```

```
You just have access to the free moment (stop happened here) and the
allocation stack trace (!heap -p -a HEAP_BLOCK_ADDRESS)
Arguments:
Arg1: 000a1000, Heap handle used in the call.
Arg2: 02e28ff0, Heap block involved in the operation.
Arg3: 0000000e, Size of the heap block.
Arg4: 02e28ffe, Corruption address.
```

The *!heap* Debugger Extension Command

The previous verifier message provides a detailed explanation of the issue that caused the verifier stop. As you can see in the lines marked in bold type in the previous debugger listing, the suffix inserted to pad the allocation to a page boundary was corrupted with the extra null terminator character, but the corruption fell short of touching the next guard page. In this case, both the light and full page heaps would yield the same result and catch the bug only when the corrupted buffer is freed.

The output from the *!avrf* command also suggests that you use the *!heap* command to find the call stack of the allocation site (*!heap -p -a <address_of_corruption>*), where the *–p* option is used to tell the *!heap* extension command that page heap information is being requested. Sure enough, that command gives you the precise call stack of the allocation, which matches the explicit *new* operator overload used in the book's C++ companion source code.

```
0:000> !heap -p -a 02e28ffe
    address 02e28ffe found in
    _DPH_HEAP_ROOT @ a1000
    in busy allocation (  DPH_HEAP_BLOCK:  UserAddr  UserSize - VirtAddr VirtSize)
                             2e10034:         2e28ff0   e        - 2e28000  2000
    6e4f8e89 verifier!AVrfDebugPageHeapAllocate+0x00000229
    77565e26 ntdll!RtlDebugAllocateHeap+0x00000030
    7752a376 ntdll!RtlpAllocateHeap+0x000000c4
    774f5ae0 ntdll!RtlAllocateHeap+0x0000023a
    6a2bfd2c vfbasics!AVrfpRtlAllocateHeap+0x000000b1
    004f132c OffByOne!MemoryAlloc+0x00000017
    004f15c4 OffByOne!CMainApp::MainHR+0x00000033
    76ffed6c kernel32!BaseThreadInitThunk+0x0000000e
    775037f5 ntdll!__RtlUserThreadStart+0x00000070
    775037c8 ntdll!_RtlUserThreadStart+0x0000001b
```

The previous listing also provides the address of the buffer returned to the application (the *UserAddr* value). You can use the *db* command to verify that this user allocation is indeed put on a page boundary, and that the only bytes that were overwritten were the padding bytes. The guard page that followed (marked with the *??* signs in the following listing) stayed completely intact, so no access violation was generated at the time of the buffer overrun.

```
0:000> db 2e28ff0
02e28ff0  61 00 62 00 63 00 2e 00-74 00 78 00 74 00 00 00  a.b.c...t.x.t...
02e29000  ?? ?? ?? ?? ?? ?? ?? ??-?? ?? ?? ?? ?? ?? ?? ??  ????????????????
...
```

You can also manually examine the page-heap block header structure located just before the user allocation address. The size of that structure is 0x20 on 32-bit Windows and 0x40 on 64-bit Windows, which you can have the debugger compute for you as well by using the *??* command, which can be used to evaluate C++ expressions, as demonstrated in the following listing.

```
0:000> ?? sizeof(ntdll!_DPH_BLOCK_INFORMATION)
unsigned int 0x20
0:000> db 02e28ff0-20
02e28fd0  bb bb cd ab 00 10 0a 00-0e 00 00 00 00 10 00 00  ................
02e28fe0  00 00 00 00 00 00 00 00-f4 d7 51 00 bb bb ba dc  ..........Q.....
02e28ff0  61 00 62 00 63 00 2e 00-74 00 78 00 74 00 00 00  a.b.c...t.x.t...
0:000> dt ntdll!_DPH_BLOCK_INFORMATION 02e28ff0-20
   +0x000 StartStamp       : 0xabcdbbbb
   +0x004 Heap             : 0x000a1000 Void
   +0x008 RequestedSize    : 0xe
   +0x00c ActualSize       : 0x1000
   +0x010 FreeQueue        : _LIST_ENTRY [ 0x0 - 0x0 ]
   +0x010 FreePushList     : _SINGLE_LIST_ENTRY
   +0x010 TraceIndex       : 0
   +0x018 StackTrace       : 0x0051d7f4 Void
   +0x01c EndStamp         : 0xdcbabbbb
```

Notice the distinct fill patterns at the start and end of the block descriptor structure. The various page-heap fill patterns use values that look like kernel-mode addresses so that any attempts to use them as pointers generate an immediate access violation.

The *StackTrace* field in the page-heap block descriptor structure is important and deserves further explanation. It represents a pointer to the start of an array holding the hexadecimal addresses of the call frames from the time of the allocation, so the *dps* ("dump memory as a sequence of function pointer values") command can be used to walk the values in this array, printing the symbolic name (when available) corresponding to every call frame. This is another way to find the call stack of the allocation site without using the *!heap* command. In the following listing, the *dps* command is used with the *StackTrace* address value obtained in the previous listing to once again display the allocation call stack of the corrupted buffer.

```
0:000> dps 0x0051d7f4
0051d7f4  0051c66c
0051d7f8  00005001
0051d7fc  000b0000
0051d800  6e4f8e89 verifier!AVrfDebugPageHeapAllocate+0x229
0051d804  77565e26 ntdll!RtlDebugAllocateHeap+0x30
0051d808  7752a376 ntdll!RtlpAllocateHeap+0xc4
0051d80c  774f5ae0 ntdll!RtlAllocateHeap+0x23a
0051d810  6a2bfd2c vfbasics!AVrfpRtlAllocateHeap+0xb1
0051d814  004f132c OffByOne!MemoryAlloc+0x17
0051d818  004f15c4 OffByOne!CMainApp::MainHR+0x33
...
0:000> $ Terminate this debugging session...
0:000> q
```

The *dps* command is useful in its own right because of its basic, yet very powerful nature. You'll see in the following section that this command can also be helpful when debugging stack memory corruptions, for example.

Customizing Page Heap for Your Situation

You need to worry about customizing the scope of page heap only if you find that the extra memory consumption resulting from enabling full page heap affects the functionality of your application. If you find yourself in this situation, you can alter the page-heap options by right-clicking on the Heaps option in the Application Verifier UI, which gives you the ability to configure additional properties, as shown in Figure 8-4.

```
C:\Windows\System32>appverif.exe
```

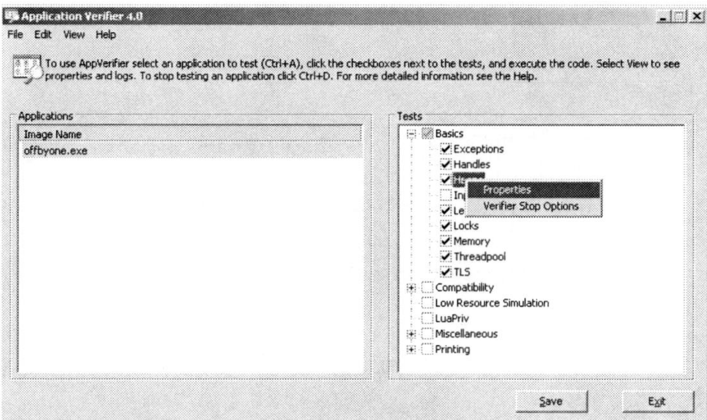

FIGURE 8-4 Customizing the page-heap settings using the Application Verifier user interface.

A new dialog box with several configuration options, shown in Figure 8-5, is then displayed. You can see how these options get reflected in the registry by looking at the Image File Execution Options (IFEO) registry key for the target image after you change the setting in this UI dialog box.

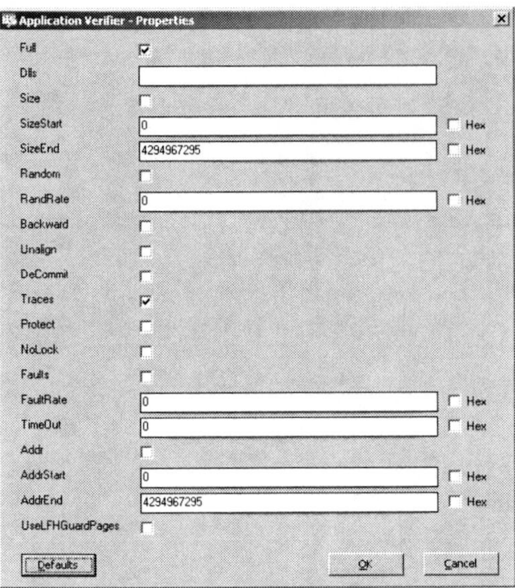

FIGURE 8-5 Page-heap configuration options in the Application Verifier user interface.

Looking at the available configuration options, you'll recognize many internal page-heap concepts discussed earlier in this section. Table 8-1 describes a few useful choices you have when configuring page heap and the scenarios in which you might want to use them.

TABLE 8-1 Page-Heap Settings and Their Applications

Application Verifier UI Option	Scenario Applicability
Dlls	Reduces the amount of memory consumed by the full page heap by restricting its scope to only a subset of DLLs in the target process. Light page heap is still used for the rest of the process when this option is specified.
Size, SizeStart, and SizeEnd	Reduces the amount of memory consumed by the full page heap by restricting its scope to only allocations whose size falls within the interval defined by the start and end values (in bytes). Allocations outside of this range will use light page heap.
Random and RandRate	Can also be used to reduce the amount of memory consumed by full page heap. It does so by randomly alternating between full-page-heap and light-page-heap allocations in the target program. The RandRate integer value is a probability between 0 and 100 percent for how often full page heap should be used vs. light page heap.
Backward	Causes the full page heap to place allocations at the start instead of at the end of memory pages. The guard page is inserted before the allocation in this case, which allows you to catch buffer underrun bugs, when the normal mode allows you to catch buffer overruns.
Unalign	Instructs the full page heap to place allocations at the end of their memory page without any suffix fill pattern, even if it means an unaligned buffer is returned to the application. This is useful when you need to catch a memory corruption immediately (access violation) and you know that your program doesn't make assumptions about allocations being aligned on 8-byte or 16-byte boundaries.

As an illustration, choose the Unalign option n the UI shown in Figure 8-5 for the *offbyone.exe* example used in this section, and then commit the configuration change by clicking OK. When you run the *offbyone.exe* C++ program again and simply let it "go" in the debugger, you'll immediately hit an access violation precisely at the line that was responsible for the buffer overrun without having to wait for the detection to occur at free time, as was previously the case when full page heap with aligned allocations was applied to the same program. Figure 8-6 illustrates this experiment.

```
C:\book\code\chapter_08\HeapCorruption>windbg.exe objfre_win7_x86\i386\OffByOne.exe
```

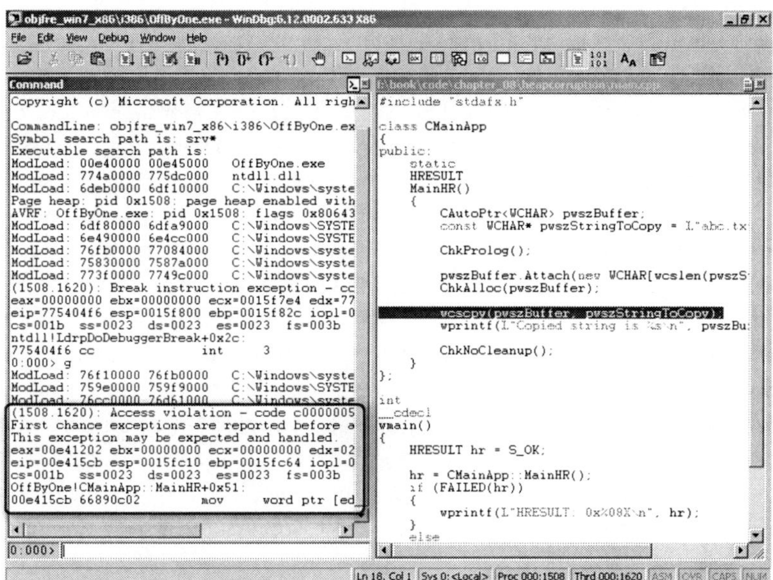

FIGURE 8-6 Catching the buffer overrun bug with an immediate access violation using the full page heap with unaligned allocations.

Debugging Managed (GC) Heap Corruptions

Despite the safety guarantees of the managed execution environment offered by the CLR, .NET applications aren't completely immune to heap corruptions. Even ignoring any rare bugs that might slip into the CLR itself, .NET programs often end up needing to interoperate with existing Win32 DLLs or consuming COM objects written in native C/C++ code. Corruptions can happen as a result of coding mistakes, such as the ones listed here:

- Executing *unsafe* C# code that manipulates C-style pointers to managed memory in incorrect ways
- Incorrect *P/Invoke* method declarations (such as wrong argument types) resulting in the managed object parameters getting potentially overrun or corrupted by the native side of the function call

- Attempts to use managed objects (such as callback delegates) by native code after they've been collected or relocated (if the objects are still *rooted* but were not correctly pinned on the managed heap) by the periodic garbage collections performed by the CLR execution engine, resulting in random access violations

The CLR uses its own heap because it uses garbage collection (GC) as a policy to free the memory it allocates, unlike the NT heap, which returns the freed memory immediately to the pool available to future allocations. In the GC heap, objects are allocated sequentially by simply sliding an index pointer when new objects are created.

When the CLR execution engine environment decides that memory should be reclaimed, it does so in bulk and walks the objects graph, marks objects that are referenced by other *root* objects (static variables, local parameters, arguments on the stack, and so on), and then sweeps any unmarked objects in its second pass. In this *mark-and-sweep* scheme, the garbage collector can also decide to reduce fragmentation and compact the heap, moving where the objects are physically stored and updating all object references accordingly. All the managed threads are suspended while garbage collections are in progress, so this compaction step is safe because the target code being managed by the CLR execution engine gets to run again only after all the object references are updated to point to the new, correct locations on the GC heap. Note that the CLR garbage collector performs this compaction step only when it deems it necessary to do so. Note also that it uses the concept of generations to partition the GC-heap space based on the *age* of the objects so that only the young objects generation (*gen0*) has to be traversed frequently, thereby reducing the amount of heap memory that has to be scanned during the mark-and-sweep phase. This, in turn, reduces the time it takes to perform garbage collections, which is very important for applications that consume a lot of memory, given that the entire managed-code execution in the process gets stalled during these periodic collections.

The *!VerifyHeap* SOS Command

When memory in the managed heap that's maintained by the CLR garbage collector gets corrupted, an access violation might eventually take place. These corruptions might also go completely undetected for several runs of the application, just as in the case of NT-heap corruptions. In fact, managed-heap corruptions can be even harder to track down than are NT-heap corruptions because of the added unpredictability introduced by the fact that the CLR garbage collector runs periodically in a background thread and can potentially move objects on the GC heap to different memory locations to more efficiently use the space available on the managed heap. Just like in the case of the page heap, the main idea behind debugging aids in managed-heap corruptions is to make the program crash closer to the point of corruption. In the managed-heap case, this is done by forcing garbage collections more often than usual in the hope of hitting an access violation before objects are potentially displaced by additional collections.

To illustrate this idea and a few CLR hooks that implement it, consider the following sample C# program from the companion source code, which is compiled using the */unsafe* C# compiler option and uses *unsafe* code to manipulate raw pointers directly in the managed *memcpy* helper function shown here.

```
//
// C:\book\code\chapter_08\GcHeapCorruption>test.cs
//
public static void Main()
{
    byte[] dstArray = new byte[3];
    byte[] srcArray = new byte[] { 1, 2, 3, 4, 5, 6, 7, 8, 9, 10 };
    Console.WriteLine("Starting...");
    for ( ; ; )
    {
        // BUG! destination array is smaller than the number of bytes
        // copied in the "unsafe" memcpy routine.
        memcpy(dstArray, srcArray, srcArray.Length);
        PrintByteArray(dstArray);
    }
}

private unsafe static void memcpy(
    byte[] dst,
    byte[] src,
    int size
    )
{
    int n;
    fixed (byte* m1 = src, m2 = dst)
    {
        byte* pSrc = m1;
        byte* pDst = m2;
        for (n = 0; n < size; n++)
        {
            *pDst++ = *pSrc++;
        }
    }
}
```

The goal now is to see if you can debug the root cause of this bug back to its call site in the source code. As you'll see, this is one of the more complicated bugs to investigate because of the apparent randomness of where the corruption is eventually caught. If you run this program under the debugger, you'll see that after a few iterations, the following access violation is raised in the process.

```
0:000> vercommand
command line: '"c:\Program Files\Debugging Tools for Windows (x86)\windbg.exe"
c:\book\code\chapter_08\GcHeapCorruption\test.exe'
0:000> .symfix
0:000> .reload
0:000> g
(13b4.11a4): Access violation - code c0000005 (first chance)
clr!WKS::gc_heap::update_brick_table+0x8d:
5bca8271 66893453        mov     word ptr [ebx+edx*2],si  ds:0023:006e0000=????
```

```
0:000> k
ChildEBP RetAddr
0013ea9c 5bca840b clr!WKS::gc_heap::update_brick_table+0x8d
0013eb80 5bca59b4 clr!WKS::gc_heap::plan_phase+0x401
0013eba4 5bca5f55 clr!WKS::gc_heap::gc1+0x140
0013ec28 5bca5d02 clr!WKS::gc_heap::garbage_collect+0x3ae
0013ec54 5bca6d72 clr!WKS::GCHeap::GarbageCollectGeneration+0x17b
0013ec78 5bca5165 clr!WKS::gc_heap::try_allocate_more_space+0x162
0013ec8c 5bca5448 clr!WKS::gc_heap::allocate_more_space+0x13
0013ecac 5bb37333 clr!WKS::GCHeap::Alloc+0x3d
...
0013ecc8 5bb2091a clr!Alloc+0x8d
0013ed64 5bb209a6 clr!AllocateArrayEx+0x1f5
0013ee28 5af55336 clr!JIT_NewArr1+0x1b4
0013ee40 5af42c58 mscorlib_ni+0x225336
...
```

The access violation appears to be occurring inside the CLR execution engine DLL (*clr.dll*) and, more specifically, during a garbage collection after a request was made to allocate a new array. The bug here isn't in the CLR, of course—it's in the managed application itself. The CLR has simply fallen victim to executing in the same user-mode process address space as the offending code. The challenge is to find out why (and where) the corruption initially occurred. Using the SOS extension, which was introduced back in Chapter 3, "How Windows Debuggers Work," you can see the managed call stack that triggered the garbage collection, which you can dump using the *!clrstack* command. Notice that the new allocation request wasn't directly made by your code, but rather in a function you called inside the *mscorlib.dll* managed assembly from the .NET Framework.

```
0:000> .loadby sos clr
0:000> !clrstack
Child SP IP       Call Site
0013ee30 5af55336 System.IO.TextWriter.Write(System.String, System.Object)
0013ee4c 5af42c58 System.IO.TextWriter+SyncTextWriter.Write(System.String, System.Object)
0013ee60 5af5671f System.Console.Write(System.String, System.Object)
0013ee70 003a0311 Test.PrintByteArray(Byte[])
 [c:\book\code\chapter_08\GcHeapCorruption\test.cs @ 45]
0013ee9c 003a0111 Test.Main() [c:\book\code\chapter_08\GcHeapCorruption\test.cs @ 15]
```

The best tool available to start investigating GC-heap corruptions is the *!VerifyHeap* command from the SOS debugger extension. This command traverses the objects on the managed heap sequentially, trying to determine if their fields look valid. The following pseudo-code snippet is a close approximation of how this command is implemented.

```
//
// Pseudo-code of !VerifyHeap SOS command
//
o = GetFirstObject();
while (o != GetLastObject())
{
    ValidateObject(o);
    o = Align((Object*) o + o.GetSize());
}
```

Unfortunately, this useful command doesn't work in this case because the CLR was in the middle of a garbage collection and the objects on the managed heap couldn't be traversed in this state, as shown in the following listing.

```
0:000> !verifyheap
-verify will only produce output if there are errors in the heap
The garbage collector data structures are not in a valid state for traversal.
It is either in the "plan phase," where objects are being moved around, or
we are at the initialization or shutdown of the gc heap. Commands related to
displaying, finding or traversing objects as well as gc heap segments may not
work properly. !dumpheap and !verifyheap may incorrectly complain of heap
consistency errors.
```

The solution to this problem is a useful CLR configuration that performs a GC-heap validation every time a garbage collection occurs. This also increases the probability of catching the corruption closer to its source. Unfortunately, you also need to restart the experiment and run the program again after this setting is enabled. You can do that either as a global setting in the registry or through a case-insensitive environment variable (*COMPLUS_HeapVerify*) so that you can keep the locality of the configuration to the command window you're running your program from.

Warning The *HeapVerify* CLR hook isn't explicitly documented on MSDN. So, you can use it for debugging purposes in the versions of the .NET Framework that support it (including version 4.0), but it might get removed without notice in future releases.

```
C:\book\code\chapter_08\GcHeapCorruption>set COMPLUS_HeapVerify=1
C:\book\code\chapter_08\GcHeapCorruption>"C:\Program Files\Debugging Tools for Windows (x86)\
windbg.exe" test.exe
...
0:000> .symfix
0:000> .reload
0:000> g
KERNELBASE!DebugBreak+0x2:
758e3e2e cc              int     3
0:000> k
ChildEBP RetAddr
002feda0 5bdae0aa KERNELBASE!DebugBreak+0x2
002fedf0 5bdae6d2 clr!Object::ValidateInner+0xdb
002fee00 5bde32df clr!Object::ValidateHeap+0xf
002fee50 5bde5f86 clr!WKS::gc_heap::verify_heap+0x3be
002feed8 5bca5d02 clr!WKS::gc_heap::garbage_collect+0x2ca
002fef04 5bca6d72 clr!WKS::GCHeap::GarbageCollectGeneration+0x17b
002fef28 5bca5165 clr!WKS::gc_heap::try_allocate_more_space+0x162
...
0:000> .lastevent
Last event: 1d70.15ec: Break instruction exception - code 80000003 (first chance)
```

Notice that you're now getting a debug break SEH exception. This debug break is raised by the *verify_heap* method in the CLR garbage collector code. This is the telltale sign that you're dealing with a managed-heap-corruption case.

When you run the *!verifyheap* command again, you can see that it reports that the GC heap has a corruption and gives you the last object that it thinks is still valid.

```
0:000> .loadby sos clr
0:000> !verifyheap
-verify will only produce output if there are errors in the heap
object 01edb318: does not have valid MT
curr_object:      01edb318
Last good object: 01edb308
```

By inspecting the last "good" object using the *!do* ("dump object") SOS command, you can see that it's a byte array with three elements.

```
0:000> !do 01edb308
Name:        System.Byte[]
MethodTable: 5b0548c4
EEClass:     5ad8af0c
Size:        15(0xf) bytes
Array:       Rank 1, Number of elements 3, Type Byte
```

The next (bad) object detected by the *!verifyheap* command is located 16 bytes after this seemingly good object, at address *0x01edb318* in the case of this experiment. The *!do* command won't be able to display it given that it's corrupted, but you can still look at the memory contents at that location using the regular *db* ("dump bytes") command.

```
0:000> !do 01edb318
<Note: this object has an invalid CLASS field>
0:000> $ dump memory starting at the header of the last good (previous) object
0:000> db 01edb308-4
[PREVIOUS OBJECT - "GOOD"]
[HEADER] 00 00 00 00 [OBJECT POINTER] [Method Table] c4 48 05 5b
[SIZE] 03 00 00 00 [ELEMENTS] 01 02 03 [END OF OBJECT]
[UNUSED] 04
[NEW OBJECT - "BAD"]
[HEADER] 05 06 07 08 [OBJECT POINTER] [Method Table] 09 0a 05 5b
[SIZE] 0a 00 00 00 [ELEMENTS] 01 02 03 04 05 06 07 08 09 0a...
```

In the previous listing, I took the liberty of formatting the output of the *db* command so that it's easier to parse. As shown in Figure 8-7, every one-dimensional, primitive-type array has an integer length, followed by the element values. As with any other .NET object, the total size of the object includes an additional header field (also called a *sync block*) that precedes the actual object pointer. The object then starts with a pointer to a method table structure (akin to a virtual table in C++) that describes the type of the managed object. In the previous case, the good object had a total size of 15 bytes, which is consistent with what was previously reported by the *!do* command.

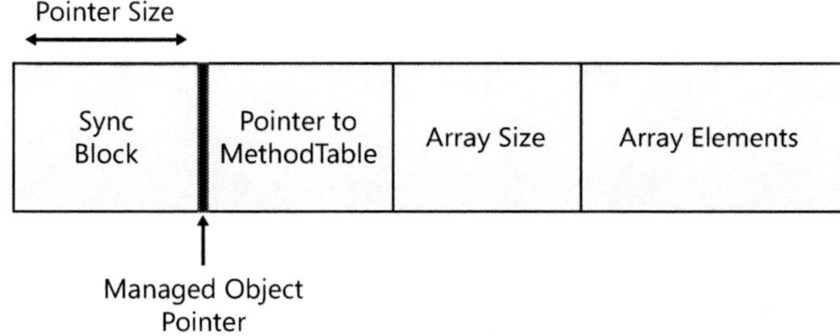

FIGURE 8-7 Layout of one-dimensional arrays of nonpointer elements in .NET.

With this knowledge, you can now form a theory as to what might have led to the corruption. In the previous debugger listing, it looks like the second (bad) object is a 10-element array that has an invalid method table pointer (and sync block header too), because the leading two bytes in that first field were presumably overwritten by a copy to the previous ("good") three-element array that overstepped its bounds (resulting in a buffer overrun!). By looking at the managed call stack at the point of the debug break, you know that it's now time to close the debugging session and go look at the frames from your program that appear on that call stack. In this case, it's easy to review the source code and find the bug during the unsafe *memcpy* call in the *Test.Main* method frame.

```
0:000> $ Terminate the debugging session now that you found the call site of the bug...
0:000> q
```

There are cases where it might be difficult to find the site of the corruption from the state of the heap if the garbage collection occurs much later than the corruption. So, you might also want to increase the number of GC occurrences so that the *COMPLUS_HeapVerify* setting results in even more frequent heap validations. This can be done using another internal CLR configuration called *GCStress*.

Warning Like the *HeapVerify* setting, the *GCStress* CLR configuration isn't officially documented, either. The *GCStress* setting can also cause the target process to run very slowly (especially if the application is a large one). So, you should use it only if you feel desperate and have already exhausted all the other options (such as the one you're about to learn in the next section, which deals with the common case of heap corruptions during managed/native transitions).

In the case of the previous managed-heap corruption, using the *COMPLUS_GCStress* setting causes a much quicker demise of the target process, showing that the very first *memcpy* corrupted the heap. This is illustrated in Figure 8-8. With this additional setting, in fact, you hit the debug break even without the artificial loop that was used in this example to increase the likelihood of hitting an access violation during the lifetime of the process.

```
C:\book\code\chapter_08\GcHeapCorruption>set COMPLUS_HeapVerify=1
C:\book\code\chapter_08\GcHeapCorruption>set COMPLUS_GCStress=3
C:\book\code\chapter_08\GcHeapCorruption>"C:\Program Files\Debugging Tools for Windows (x86)\
windbg.exe" test.exe
```

```
...
0:000> g
(1a2c.1fac): Access violation - code c0000005 (first chance)
...
0:000> .symfix
0:000> .reload
0:000> .loadby sos çlr
0:000> !clrstack
Child SP IP       Call Site
003bf3bc 65ed1d3e [PrestubMethodFrame: 003bf3bc] Test.PrintByteArray(Byte[])
003bf3cc 00270111 Test.Main()
0:000> q
```

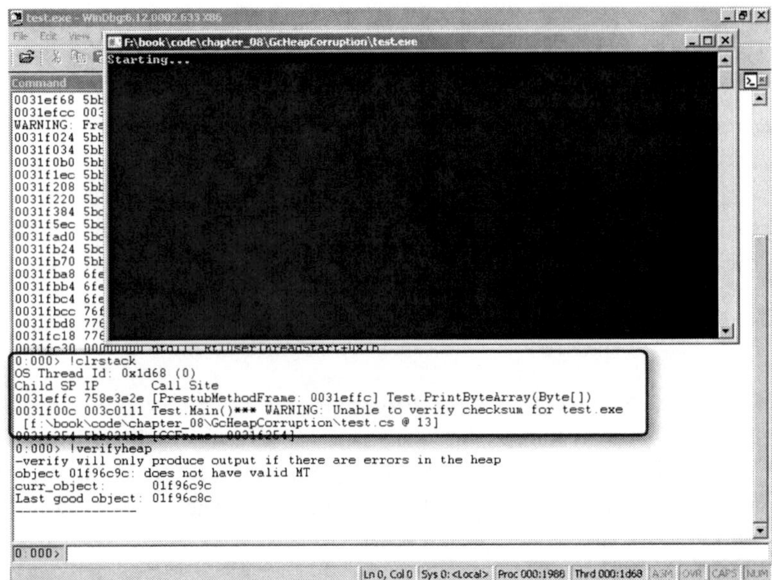

FIGURE 8-8 Catching the managed-heap corruption using the *HeapVerify* and *GCStress* settings.

You're now able to hit the debug break with your code at the top of the managed call stack. All you need to do is look at the source code of the *Main* method in your program and review the function call preceding the *PrintByteArray* function. In this case, this immediately points to the *memcpy* method as the initial source of the GC-heap corruption.

Managed Debugging Assistants

Although the previous case was a heap corruption due to a bug in a C# program using unsafe code (raw memory pointers), the bulk of GC-heap corruptions in .NET programs take place when managed-code developers try to interoperate with native code. Luckily, this type of GC corruption is also easier to debug, though the same idea of increasing the frequency of garbage collections and verifying the heap on each GC occurrence is still at the center of these investigations.

The CLR supports two dedicated settings to trigger a garbage collection during managed-to-unmanaged and unmanaged-to-managed transitions, which can be used to reduce the unpredictability associated with GC occurrences moving managed objects around or collecting them when they're determined to no longer be rooted. Remember that the native code you invoke in your .NET programs is completely unaware of garbage collections, so the addresses of the objects passed during calls to native code must stay fixed during the transition, and the occurrence of a garbage collection right before each transition will expose any bugs where the objects aren't properly *pinned*.

These settings are controlled using two special CLR *managed debugging assistants* (MDAs). In many ways, managed debugging assistants serve a purpose similar to that of Image File Execution Options (IFEO). The difference is that they let you configure the execution engine's behavior in your .NET programs, while the IFEO settings allow you to configure how the system executes your user-mode (both managed and native) programs. If you're writing a .NET application that calls native code directly, you should definitely consider running your testing with these MDAs enabled to proactively catch any latent bugs your interoperability layer might have. The complete list of supported MDAs can be found on MSDN at *http://msdn.microsoft.com/en-us/library/d21c150d.aspx*, which also includes the two MDAs you're about to use in this section.

To see how this works in practice, consider the following C# sample from the companion source code.

```
//
// C:\book\code\chapter_08\PInvokeCorruption>test.cs
//
public static void Main()
{
    byte[] buffer = new byte[8]; // <<< window title text will be truncated
    IntPtr hwnd = FindWindow("notepad", null);
    if (hwnd != IntPtr.Zero)
    {
        // BUG! the nMaxCount parameter passed in exceeds the destination
        // buffer's size
        GetWindowText(hwnd, buffer, 256);
        Console.WriteLine(System.Text.UnicodeEncoding.Unicode.GetString(buffer));
        Console.WriteLine("Success");
    }
}

[DllImport("user32.dll", CharSet = CharSet.Auto)]
internal static extern int GetWindowText(
    IntPtr hWnd,
    [Out] byte[] lpString,
    int nMaxCount
    );

[DllImport("user32.dll", CharSet = CharSet.Auto)]
internal static extern IntPtr FindWindow(
    string lpClassName,
    string lpWindowName
    );
```

This program tries to obtain the window title of a running *notepad.exe* instance. It also seems to run without encountering any problems, despite having a serious heap-corruption bug. Remember that memory corruptions do not consistently result in immediate crashes and might start happening as you add unrelated code to your program, making them that much harder to reproduce and investigate.

```
C:\book\code\chapter_08\PInvokeCorruption>notepad.exe
C:\book\code\chapter_08\PInvokeCorruption>test.exe
Starting...
Unti
Success
```

The same directory in the companion source code contains a configuration file that enables garbage collections both during managed-to-unmanaged and unmanaged-to-managed code transitions.

```
<!-- test.exe.mda.config -->
<mdaConfig>
  <assistants>
    <gcManagedToUnmanaged/>
    <gcUnmanagedToManaged/>
  </assistants>
</mdaConfig>
```

However, for these settings to take effect, you also need to set another environment variable (*COMPLUS_Mda*), which instructs the CLR to read the MDAs from this configuration file when the application starts up.

```
C:\book\code\chapter_08\PInvokeCorruption>set COMPLUS_MDA=1
C:\book\code\chapter_08\PInvokeCorruption>"C:\Program Files\Debugging Tools for Windows (x86)\
windbg.exe" test.exe
...
0:000> .symfix
0:000> .reload
0:000> g
(b38.1170): Access violation - code c0000005 (first chance)
clr!WKS::gc_heap::relocate_address+0xb:
5b738f7f 8b38            mov     edi,dword ptr [eax]  ds:0023:01fb2000=????????
0:000> k
ChildEBP RetAddr
002eea70 5b739d81 clr!WKS::gc_heap::relocate_address+0xb
002eea98 5b7392eb clr!WKS::gc_heap::relocate_survivors_in_plug+0x78
002eeacc 5b73909b clr!WKS::gc_heap::relocate_survivors+0x72
002eeb08 5b736035 clr!WKS::gc_heap::relocate_phase+0x76
002eebe4 5b7359b4 clr!WKS::gc_heap::plan_phase+0x851
002eec08 5b735f55 clr!WKS::gc_heap::gc1+0x140
002eec8c 5b735d02 clr!WKS::gc_heap::garbage_collect+0x3ae
002eecb8 5b6b5d0d clr!WKS::GCHeap::GarbageCollectGeneration+0x17b
002eecc8 5b6b5d4d clr!WKS::GCHeap::GarbageCollectTry+0x24
002eece8 5b79f45d clr!WKS::GCHeap::GarbageCollect+0x69
```

```
002eed60 5b8b6441 clr!TriggerGCForMDAInternal+0xb9
...
0:000> .loadby sos clr
0:000> !clrstack
System.StubHelpers.StubHelpers.TriggerGCForMDA()
0020edcc 003b09a2 DomainBoundILStubClass.IL_STUB_PInvoke(IntPtr, Byte[], Int32)
0020edd0 003b0201 [InlinedCallFrame: 0020edd0] Test.GetWindowText(IntPtr, Byte[], Int32)
0020ee74 003b0201 Test.Main()
```

At this point, you're able to consistently reproduce the corruption thanks to the MDA, which is often half the battle in memory-corruption investigations. You can apply the same techniques demonstrated earlier in this section to debug this heap corruption—including the *!verifyheap* command from the SOS extension and the *COMPLUS_HeapVerify* hook—except it's easier to track down the corrupted objects in this case because they're likely to come directly from the P/Invoke that's in progress and that happened to trigger the MDA (the *Test.GetWindowText* call in this case).

Debugging Stack Corruptions

Unlike heap corruptions, which benefit from a comprehensive set of debugging hooks, stack corruptions can sometimes be harder to diagnose because there are many more ways for a program to consume the values saved on the stack. So, latent stack-memory corruptions sometimes can go undetected for a long time before they cause the program to fail.

This section presents a few high-level strategies that will get you started when you're faced with stack corruptions. There will also be scenarios that require more in-depth analysis of the code paths that could have led to the corruption. Generally speaking, though, even those situations use the same debugging techniques, with the difference being persistence and a healthy dose of analytical problem solving to methodically form hypotheses and then progressively eliminate those that don't hold true, until you're able to unveil the mystery and find the correct solution.

Stack-Based Buffer Overruns

A common case that leads to stack-memory corruptions is when local array variables are overrun due to coding mistakes, causing data to be written past the end of the buffer and potentially overwriting values higher up on the stack, such as the return address of the function. In Chapter 2, you saw how the stack in the standard calling convention held function parameters as well as local variables, and you used that knowledge to derive those values even if you were debugging system code with only the public symbols from Microsoft. One detail that was left out back then was that the compiler typically also inserts an additional value right after the current frame pointer and before the local variables. The compiler does this based on heuristics such as the type of local variables in the function being invoked and whether it has array types, for example. This value is a *guard* against buffer overruns and is added when the */GS* VC++ compiler flag is used, as illustrated in Figure 8-9.

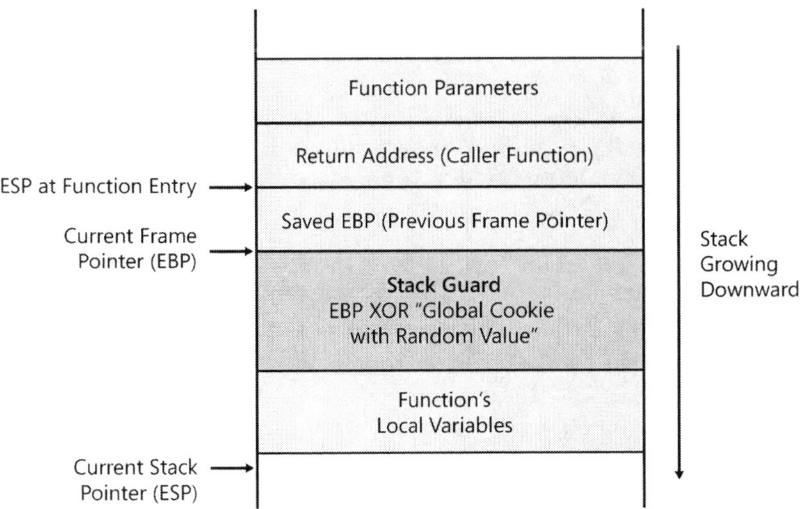

FIGURE 8-9 Stack guard location with the */GS* Visual C++ compiler feature (*x86* platform).

By including this stack-guard value, the compiler is able to insert code to check its consistency before the function returns by comparing it to the global *cookie* value from the module, which is more immune to overruns of local variables on the stack. If a local variable array of elements is overrun, for example, chances are the stack-guard value will be modified but not the global per-module cookie variable, which resides in one of the program sections, usually far away from the stack space. When that situation is detected, the code inserted by the VC++ compiler for you to check the stack-guard consistency terminates the process immediately rather than allowing the return address on the stack to get overwritten by the malicious buffer, thus preventing this class of exploitable buffer overruns from taking place. Incidentally, this also means that the stack-memory corruption is detected quickly before the offending function returns control to the caller.

Warning Fortunately, the */GS* switch is turned on by default in both the DDK and Visual Studio 2010 build environments. Obviously, you should never disable this option when compiling your C/C++ code because its security benefits far outweigh the very small performance penalty it adds to the generated code.

To see the stack-guard consistency check in action, compile and run the following C++ program from the companion source code, which is similar to the heap-corruption example shown earlier in this chapter, except the destination buffer is now declared as a local variable on the stack.

```
//
// C:\book\code\chapter_08\StackCorruption\BufferOverflow>main.cpp
//
static
HRESULT
MainHR()
{
    WCHAR pwszBuffer[] = L"12";
    const WCHAR* pwszStringToCopy = L"abcdefghijklmnopqrstuvwxyz";

    ChkProlog();

    // BUG! destination buffer is smaller than the number of bytes copied
    wcscpy(pwszBuffer, pwszStringToCopy);
    wprintf(L"Copied string is %s\n", pwszBuffer);

    ChkNoCleanup();
}
```

As soon as you run this code, you'll see that it exits early with the following stack trace, showing that the compiler-generated code (*__report_gsfailure*) did immediately catch the stack-based buffer overrun in this case.

```
C:\book\code\chapter_08\StackCorruption\BufferOverflow>"C:\Program Files\Debugging Tools for
Windows (x86)\windbg.exe" objfre_win7_x86\i386\StackCorruption.exe
...
0:000> g
STATUS_STACK_BUFFER_OVERRUN encountered
(ea0.484): Break instruction exception - code 80000003 (first chance)
...
0:000> .symfix
0:000> .reload
0:000> k
ChildEBP RetAddr
000df658 001419f5 kernel32!UnhandledExceptionFilter+0x5f
000df98c 001412cc StackCorruption!__report_gsfailure+0xce
000df9a0 006a0069 StackCorruption!CMainApp::MainHR+0x53 [c:\book\code\chapter_08\
stackcorruption\bufferoverflow\main.cpp @ 20]
...
0:000> q
```

Using Data Breakpoints in Stack Corruption Investigations

Data breakpoints can be especially useful in tracking down the call sites of stack corruptions because they can let you break into the debugger just as memory is about to get corrupted, assuming you know the address that gets corrupted during the program's execution. In the previous example of a stack-based buffer overrun, you were able to determine that the code in *MainHR* function had a stack-memory corruption, but the exact call site where that corruption occurred is still unclear. In this particular case, a quick code review is sufficient to make that determination, but that might not be nearly as easy in other scenarios.

You can use a write-data breakpoint to let the debugger help you find why the stack-guard value is being corrupted. For example, you can set a breakpoint in *MainHR*, let the target execute to the point where the stack-guard value is populated during the function's assembly prolog, and then set the data breakpoint to "watch" write modifications of the stack-guard memory location, as illustrated in the following listing.

```
0:000> vercommand
command line: '"c:\Program Files\Debugging Tools for Windows (x86)\windbg.exe"
c:\book\code\chapter_08\StackCorruption\BufferOverflow\objfre_win7_x86\i386\StackCorruption.exe'
0:000> bp StackCorruption!CMainApp::MainHR
0:000> g
Breakpoint 0 hit
StackCorruption!CMainApp::MainHR:
0:000> u
StackCorruption!CMainApp::MainHR
[c:\book\code\chapter_08\stackcorruption\bufferoverflow\main.cpp @ 9]:
00bd14c2 8bff            mov     edi,edi
00bd14c4 55              push    ebp
00bd14c5 8bec            mov     ebp,esp
00bd14c7 83ec0c          sub     esp,0Ch
00bd14ca a10030bd00      mov     eax,dword ptr [StackCorruption!__security_cookie (00bd3000)]
00bd14cf 33c5            xor     eax,ebp
00bd14d1 8945fc          mov     dword ptr [ebp-4],eax
00bd14d4 56              push    esi
0:000> g 00bd14d4
StackCorruption!CMainApp::MainHR+0x12:
00bd14d4 56              push    esi
0:000> ba w4 (ebp-4)
```

Now that you've activated this breakpoint, you can let the target continue its execution and watch with satisfaction as you break exactly at the call site of the buffer overrun—namely, at the ill-advised *wcscpy* function call, as shown in Figure 8-10.

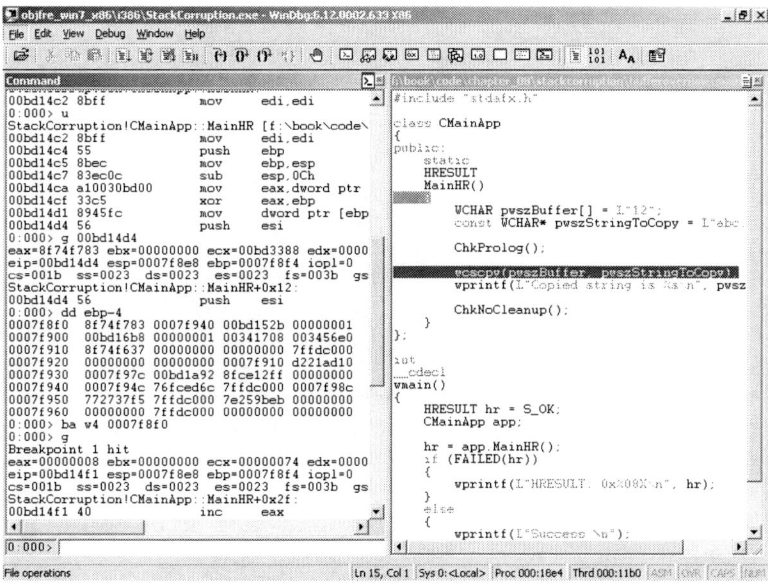

FIGURE 8-10 Catching the stack corruption call site using a data breakpoint.

Reconstructing Call Frames from Corrupted Stacks

In some stack-memory corruptions, the condition of the stack might be such that the regular *k* debugger command isn't able to reconstruct the thread's call stack properly. This is because the *k* command relies on the chain of frame pointers and return addresses saved on the stack, so it might not work if that chain itself is corrupted. All hope isn't lost, though. The useful *dps* command mentioned earlier in "The *!heap* Debugger Extension Command" section of this chapter can still be used to traverse the stack manually and decode raw addresses (including valid return addresses saved on the stack memory) to their corresponding symbols, even if some return addresses in the chain are corrupted.

To see this in action, consider the following program from the companion source code, where the previous frame pointer and return address values from *FunctionCall4* are overwritten on purpose so that the regular *k* command wouldn't work.

```
//
// C:\book\code\chapter_08\StackCorruption\BadCallStack>main.cpp
//
DECLSPEC_NOINLINE
static
VOID
FunctionCall4()
{
    volatile PVOID p;
    wprintf(L"Local variable address is %x\n", &p);
```

```
    //
    // Overwrite the saved frame pointer and return address using offsets
    // from the address on the stack of the local variable
    //
    *(&p + 1) = 0;
    *(&p + 2) = 0;
    *(&p + 3) = 0;
    *(&p + 4) = 0;
    DebugBreak();
}
```

When you run this program, you'll see that the *k* command fails to reconstruct the call stack at the time of the debug break. Notice that the output from the command stops right after the *FunctionCall4* function and isn't able to walk the stack up any further, as illustrated in the following listing.

```
0:000> vercommand
command line: '"c:\Program Files\Debugging Tools for Windows (x86)\windbg.exe"
c:\book\code\chapter_08\StackCorruption\BadCallStack\objfre_win7_x86\i386\BadCallStack.exe'
0:000> g
(11b8.b84): Break instruction exception - code 80000003 (first chance)
KERNELBASE!DebugBreak+0x2:
0:000> k
ChildEBP RetAddr
000af9ec 000314a5 KERNELBASE!DebugBreak+0x2
000af9fc 00000000 BadCallStack!CMainApp::FunctionCall4+0x2c [c:\book\code\chapter_08\
stackcorruption\badcallstack\main.cpp @ 66]
```

Fortunately, the *dps* command can give you an idea of what return addresses happen to reside on the stack, which can be very helpful in stack-memory corruptions that render the *k* command unusable, such as the one shown in this example. The *dps* command accepts a memory address as a parameter and starts walking the memory from that address one pointer at a time, trying to interpret each value as a symbol name. It also accepts another (optional) parameter to specify how many bytes should be read following the start address. If you start from the current memory address held by the stack pointer register, you can see the rest of the thread's call stack, as shown in the following listing.

```
0:000> dps esp L40
000af9f0  000314a5 BadCallStack!CMainApp::FunctionCall4+0x2c
[c:\book\code\chapter_08\stackcorruption\badcallstack\main.cpp @ 66]
000af9f4  00031178 BadCallStack!'string'
000af9f8  00000000
000af9fc  00000000
000afa00  00000000
000afa04  00000000
000afa08  00031649 BadCallStack!CMainApp::FunctionCall2+0x16
[c:\book\code\chapter_08\stackcorruption\badcallstack\main.cpp @ 37]
000afa0c  76aa5de3 msvcrt!wprintf
000afa10  0003169e BadCallStack!CMainApp::FunctionCall1+0x16
[c:\book\code\chapter_08\stackcorruption\badcallstack\main.cpp @ 27]
000afa14  76aa5de3 msvcrt!wprintf
```

```
000afa18  0003171a BadCallStack!CMainApp::MainHR+0x16
[c:\book\code\chapter_08\stackcorruption\badcallstack\main.cpp @ 15]
000afa1c  00000001
000afa20  0003173a BadCallStack!wmain+0x8
[c:\book\code\chapter_08\stackcorruption\badcallstack\main.cpp @ 75]
000afa24  00000001
000afa28  000318c7 BadCallStack!__wmainCRTStartup+0x102
...
0:000> $ Terminate this debugging session now...
0:000> q
```

Naturally, some values on the stack do not represent code locations, so they won't have corresponding symbols. This is why you see a noncontinuous stack when you use the *dps* command, unlike the more polished output you get when using the *k* command. Conversely, the *dps* command might also dump misleading frames from function pointers that are stored on the stack, either as local variables or function parameters, so you should also filter those out when you look at the output from this command.

Debugging Stack Overflows

Each thread has a user-mode and kernel-mode stack, both with a maximum memory space they can't exceed. The kernel-mode stack is used when the thread transitions over to kernel mode during a system call. This stack is separate from the user-mode stack of the thread to ensure that the code in user mode can't compromise the security of the kernel.

Both the user-mode and kernel-mode stacks are used to hold local variables and keep track of function arguments and their return addresses. The kernel-mode stack is relatively small (16 KB) compared to the user-mode stack size, which in the case of C++ programs is set to a default value (1 MB) by the linker, although you can also override this default value at run time by using a non-zero *dwStackSize* parameter when creating threads using the *CreateThread* Win32 API. The 1 MB of pages on the stack are initially simply reserved, and they get committed one by one by the memory manager as the stack grows.

Understanding Stack Overflows

A stack overflow could happen if the OS memory manager fails to extend the stack due to a transient out-of-memory condition in the system. The more common case of stack overflows, though, happens when you exhaust all the available space on the stack (1 MB) and can no longer push any more items onto it. This usually happens as a result of excessive stack space utilization. For example, the following scenarios could lead to this condition:

- An infinite recursive loop bug.
- Excessive use of large stack-allocated, local variable arrays by functions on the call stack.

- Excessive use of dynamically allocated stack memory, either via a direct call to the *_alloca* C runtime (CRT) function or indirectly by calling a function that does so. An example is the *A2W* ASCII-to-Unicode ATL conversion macro, which ends up invoking that CRT function.

The following C++ example from the companion source code illustrates this last case.

```
//
// C:\book\code\chapter_08\StackOverflow>main.cpp
//
class CMainApp
{
public:
    static
    HRESULT
    MainHR()
    {
        const char* pszTest = "Test";
        int n;

        ChkProlog();

        USES_CONVERSION;
        for (n = 0; n < 1000000; n++)
        {
            wprintf(L"%s: %d.\n", A2W(pszTest), n);
        }

        ChkNoCleanup();
    }
};
```

When you compile and run this program, you'll see it vanish and exit early—in the absence of a native Just-In-Time (JIT) debugger—after only a few iterations, way short of the one million lines it set out to print.

```
C:\book\code\chapter_08\StackOverflow\objfre_win7_x86\i386>StackOverflow.exe
Test: 0.
Test: 1.
...
Test: 15454.
Test: 15455.
```

The *kf* Debugger Command

When you run the previous program under WinDbg, you can readily see that an unhandled stack overflow SEH exception was responsible for the early process demise, as shown in the following listing.

```
0:000> vercommand
command line: '"c:\Program Files\Debugging Tools for Windows (x86)\windbg.exe"
c:\book\code\chapter_08\StackOverflow\objfre_win7_x86\i386\StackOverflow.exe'
0:000> g
(18b4.1db4): Stack overflow - code c00000fd (first chance)
0:000> g
(18b4.1db4): Stack overflow - code c00000fd (!!! second chance !!!)
0:000> .symfix
0:000> .reload
0:000> k
ChildEBP RetAddr
00163010 75483b6b kernel32!WriteConsoleA+0x10
0016306c 76b44fc6 kernel32!WriteFile+0x7f
00163628 76b44da3 msvcrt!_write_nolock+0x3fb
0016366c 76b3f57e msvcrt!_write+0x9f
0016368c 76b5ccb5 msvcrt!_flush+0x3a
0016369c 76b56531 msvcrt!_ftbuf+0x1d
001636ec 00941a93 msvcrt!wprintf+0x69
0006faa8 00241556 StackOverflow!CMainApp::MainHR+0x51
[c:\book\code\chapter_08\stackoverflow\main.cpp @ 19]
0006fab0 002416e3 StackOverflow!wmain+0x8
[c:\book\code\chapter_08\stackoverflow\main.cpp @ 32]
...
```

The function call (*kernel32!WriteConsoleA*) that was being executed by the thread at the time of the stack overflow clearly is not the function responsible for causing it. To determine the culprit, you can use the *kf* debugger command, which displays the size of the memory consumed by each frame on the call stack, allowing you to quickly determine the function that was responsible for the thread's stack space running out. In the following listing, you can see that your *MainHR* function is consuming most of the stack space and therefore is likely the cause of the stack overflow exception.

```
0:000> kf
  Memory  ChildEBP RetAddr
          00163010 75483b6b kernel32!WriteConsoleA+0x10
       5c 0016306c 76b44fc6 kernel32!WriteFile+0x7f
      5bc 00163628 76b44da3 msvcrt!_write_nolock+0x3fb
       44 0016366c 76b3f57e msvcrt!_write+0x9f
       20 0016368c 76b5ccb5 msvcrt!_flush+0x3a
       10 0016369c 76b56531 msvcrt!_ftbuf+0x1d
       50 001636ec 00941a93 msvcrt!wprintf+0x69
    3c214 0019f900 00941acd StackOverflow!CMainApp::MainHR+0x51
       1c 0019f91c 0094299d StackOverflow!wmain+0x13
0:000> $ Terminate this debugging session now that you uncovered the culprit function...
0:000> q
```

It's true that you still don't know at this point why so much space on the stack was allocated by this function because you didn't directly allocate any memory on the stack. However, a quick look at *atlconv.h* from the ATL source code reveals that the *A2W* macro uses *_alloca* to allocate space on the stack and then fills that space with the unicode conversion of the string (using *AtlA2WHelper*, which is defined as an inlined function in the same header file). In general, you should avoid using the *A2W* ATL macro in your programs and use the *MultiByteToWideChar* Win32 API directly or alternatively wrap the macro within a helper function so that the *_alloca* stack allocation becomes transient on the stack.

It's never a good idea to allocate space on the stack inside of a large loop or a recursive call, and this example is a perfect illustration of the hazards involved in doing so. As tempting as it might sometimes be to try to reduce the number of heap allocations and replace them with buffers on the stack, this approach can do more harm than good when overused. In fact, it's very likely your performance problems aren't at all related to heap allocations in the first place, so you should always trace your bottlenecks with profiling tools before engaging in optimizations.

Debugging Handle Leaks

Handles in Windows are user-mode references to executive objects. Failure to properly close these object handles can result in the corresponding executive objects staying alive until the process eventually terminates its execution and its handle table is finally run down by the OS. Many developers fail to realize the severity of such bugs simply because a handle leak isn't visibly charged to the application's user-mode memory consumption in the task manager. However, handle leaks can sometimes be worse than user-mode memory leaks because the memory being leaked is from the kernel-mode memory pool shared by all the programs on the system.

A Handle Leak Example

For short-lived processes, the effect of a handle-leak bug is somewhat mitigated by the fact that it goes away when the process exits. With long-lived processes such as Windows services, however, handle leaks can become a serious problem. In the case of the IIS (Internet Information Server) web server, for example, a badly written ASP.NET application that uses the *advapi32!LogonUserW* Win32 API but doesn't diligently close the obtained access token handle after it's done using it would cause the token objects to stay alive and progressively leak kernel-mode memory space until the server runs out of memory.

The choice of this example is not entirely coincidental because this particular function isn't natively exposed in the .NET Framework (at least not in its early releases) and an ASP.NET application could need to invoke it directly through P/Invoke, exposing it to the potential of forgetting to close the access token handle. The following C# program suffers from this exact problem.

```
//
// C:\book\code\chapter_08\HandleLeak>HandleLeak.cs
//
public class Leak
{
    public static void Main()
    {
        //
        // Loop indefinitely to simulate a progressive handle leak
        //
        IntPtr userToken = IntPtr.Zero;
        for ( ; ; )
        {
            if (!LogonUserW(
                @"test_user_hl", @"localhost", @"$a1234%BC",
                LOGON32_LOGON_NETWORK_CLEARTEXT, LOGON32_PROVIDER_DEFAULT,
                out userToken))
            {
                throw new Win32Exception(Marshal.GetLastWin32Error());
            }
            // BUG! missing call to CloseHandle(userToken)
        }
    }
}
```

When you run this program (as shown next), you'll see that its handle count as reported by the task manager seems to grow unboundedly. In addition, you'll see that the kernel memory (represented by the Paged Pool and NP Pool columns in Figure 8-11) attributed to this C# program seems to also be growing indefinitely. Note that you need to run this experiment (at least the helper *adduser.bat* batch script) from an elevated command window because adding or deleting local user accounts requires full administrative privileges.

```
C:\book\code\chapter_08\HandleLeak>taskmgr.exe
C:\book\code\chapter_08\HandleLeak>adduser.bat
C:\book\code\chapter_08\HandleLeak>HandleLeak.exe
```

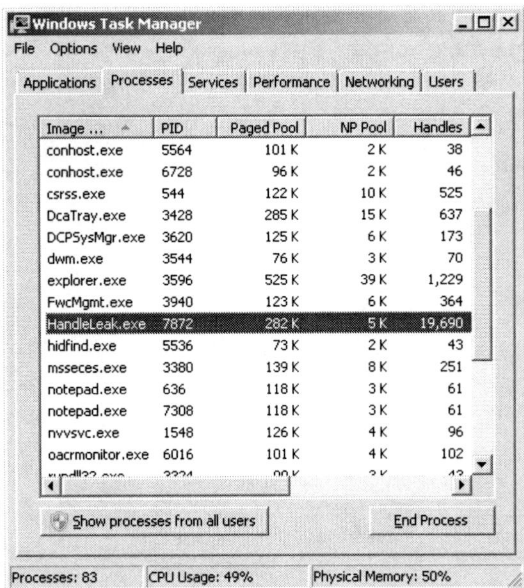

FIGURE 8-11 Handle-count and kernel-memory-usage columns in the task manager UI.

The *!htrace* Debugger Extension Command

Observing the steadily increasing trend exhibited by the number of handles in the previous program suggests that a progressive handle leak might be in play. The next steps involved in tracking down the root cause of a potential handle leak are usually to first figure out the handle type being leaked, and then the call site that's responsible for the open handle allocations. Fortunately, the *!htrace* Windows debugger extension command can be used to automate this process.

How *!htrace* Works

The *!htrace* extension command takes advantage of handle-tracing support in the Windows kernel. When this tracing mode is enabled for a user-mode process, the kernel starts keeping track of additional information about new handles inside that process as they get opened and closed. With this logging support, it becomes easier to track down the state of each handle, including its creation call stack. A private API is exposed at the NTDLL layer for user-mode debuggers to query this information and obtain a snapshot of all the active handles in the target process. This is precisely how the *!htrace* extension command works. In particular, the following options are supported when the command is used in a user-mode debugging session:

- ***!htrace –enable*** This command enables handle tracing for the target user-mode process. This is not required if you've already enabled the Application Verifier tool for the process, but it is needed if you want to dynamically enable tracing at run time without restarting the target. This option also captures a snapshot of the handles in the process handle table.

- ***!htrace –disable*** This command disables handle tracing for the target user-mode process. Do not forget to do this at the end of your debugging if you're operating over a server process that needs to remain running because handle tracing consumes precious kernel memory and shouldn't be left enabled on live production servers.
- ***!htrace –snapshot*** This command queries the kernel for a list of the handles that have been logged in the handle table of the target process.
- ***!htrace –diff*** This command is a convenient option that captures a new snapshot and automatically compares it to a snapshot that was established using the *–snapshot* or *–enable* options.

The previous options are implemented only in the user-mode debugger and aren't available when the *!htrace* command is used during kernel-mode debugging. There is no compelling reason why this is so; it was just never deemed necessary to implement these features in the kernel debugger version of the extension command. There is one additional usage scenario that's available both in user-mode and kernel-mode debugging sessions, though, because *!htrace* can also be used to dump the tracing information associated with a specific handle (or all the handles) from a user-mode process in both cases.

!htrace in Action

As a practical illustration for how to use the *!htrace* command, you'll now apply it to track down the root cause of the apparent token-handle leak exhibited by the .NET program shown earlier in this section, assuming all you knew was your observation in the task manager that the number of handles in the process seemed to be growing indefinitely. You'll also be performing this investigation without restarting the process, just as you would if this were a live production-server process.

While the target process is running, you can attach the *windbg.exe* user-mode debugger to it (using either the F6 shortcut or the *–pn* command-line option) and use the *!htrace* command with the *–enable* option to turn on handle tracing for the target process, as shown in the following listing.

```
"C:\Program Files\Debugging Tools for Windows (x86)\windbg.exe" -pn HandleLeak.exe
0:004> .symfix
0:004> .reload
0:004> !htrace -enable
Handle tracing enabled.
Handle tracing information snapshot successfully taken.
0:004> g
```

After letting the target run for a few seconds, you can break back into the debugger again (using the Debug\Break menu action) and use the *–diff* option of the *!htrace* command to capture a second snapshot. The *–diff* option also compares the current snapshot (the one it takes) to the snapshot that was taken earlier when the *–enable* option was issued. This is illustrated in the following listing.

```
(14c4.182c): Break instruction exception - code 80000003 (first chance)
ntdll!DbgBreakPoint:
772440f0 cc              int     3
0:007> !htrace -diff
Handle tracing information snapshot successfully taken.
```

```
0x5b3 new stack traces since the previous snapshot.
Ignoring handles that were already closed...
Outstanding handles opened since the previous snapshot:
--------------------------------------
Handle = 0x0000739c - OPEN
Thread ID = 0x00000c80, Process ID = 0x00000260

0x772558a4: ntdll!NtDuplicateObject+0x0000000c
0x75147b65: +0x75147b65
0x751177ab: +0x751177ab
0x75117c08: +0x75117c08
0x7520188b: +0x7520188b
0x76b904e8: RPCRT4!Invoke+0x0000002a
0x76bf5311: RPCRT4!NdrStubCall2+0x000002d6
0x76bf431d: RPCRT4!NdrServerCall2+0x00000019
0x76b9063c: RPCRT4!DispatchToStubInCNoAvrf+0x0000004a
0x76b907ca: RPCRT4!RPC_INTERFACE::DispatchToStubWorker+0x0000016c
0x76b906b6: RPCRT4!RPC_INTERFACE::DispatchToStub+0x0000008b
0x76b876db: RPCRT4!LRPC_SCALL::DispatchRequest+0x00000257
0x76b90ac6: RPCRT4!LRPC_SCALL::QueueOrDispatchCall+0x000000bd
0x76b90a85: RPCRT4!LRPC_SCALL::HandleRequest+0x0000034f
--------------------------------------
Handle = 0x00007398 - OPEN
Thread ID = 0x00000c80, Process ID = 0x00000260

0x772558a4: ntdll!NtDuplicateObject+0x0000000c
0x75147b65: +0x75147b65
0x751177ab: +0x751177ab
0x75117c08: +0x75117c08
0x7520188b: +0x7520188b
0x76b904e8: RPCRT4!Invoke+0x0000002a
0x76bf5311: RPCRT4!NdrStubCall2+0x000002d6
...
```

The previous listing provides you with a list of handles that were opened by the process without getting closed in the timeframe between the two snapshots. Notice several creation call stacks that look eerily similar, pointing to the possibility of the same call site being at the root of the leak. You can use the *!handle* extension command to confirm that all these handles are access token handles. For example, the following command takes one of the open handles obtained in the previous listing and dumps its properties.

```
0:007> !handle 0x0000739c f
Handle 739c
  Type             Token
...
```

Now that you know this is a token handle, you can use the *!token* command to see that it corresponds to the test account you created prior to running this experiment, as shown in the following listing.

```
0:007> !token -n 0x0000739c
TS Session ID: 0x1
User: S-1-5-21-3268063145-3624069009-1332808237-1016 (User: tariks-lp03\test_user_hl)
Groups:
...
```

To make further progress and find where these token handles are created in the target application, it's important to understand two subtle aspects:

- Handles in this list aren't necessarily true leaks because the handles might still get closed by the program at a later time. However, this provides you with a reduced subset of *potential handle leaks* you can start your investigation with.
- The handles displayed by the command are all relative to the target process. However, they might have been created in different process contexts! This can happen when another process prepares the handle by duplicating one of its handles using the *DuplicateHandle* Win32 API, with the target process (*hTargetProcessHandle*) as the third argument to the API call. Though this is typically an edge case, the current leak example falls precisely in this rare category.

The last observation is key to understanding why you weren't able to get proper call stacks for the handles displayed by the *!htrace –diff* command in the previous experiment. If you look closely at the first handle flagged by the *–diff* option as a potential handle leak, for instance, you'll see that it came from a different process, which also means that the saved address values for the functions on its creation call stack are meaningless in the context of the current target process. To see the proper call stack, you need to interpret those addresses relative to the creator process, which happens to be the *lsass.exe* local security authority subsystem process, which you're able to confirm by matching the creator process ID listed by the *!htrace* command with the *lsass.exe* process ID (PID) displayed by the *.tlist* command, as shown in the following listing. Note that the *.tlist* command shows the process ID values in decimal (*0n* prefix) while the *!htrace* extension displays them in hexadecimal (*0x* prefix). So, the *?* command is used to do the conversion in this listing.

```
0:007> !htrace 0x0000739c
Handle = 0x0000739c - OPEN
Thread ID = 0x00000c80, Process ID = 0x00000260

0x772558a4: ntdll!NtDuplicateObject+0x0000000c
0x75147b65: +0x75147b65
0x751177ab: +0x751177ab
0x75117c08: +0x75117c08
0x7520188b: +0x7520188b
...
0:007> ? 0x00000260
Evaluate expression: 608 = 00000260
0:007> $ .tlist displays the process IDs in decimal format
0:007> .tlist
  0n608 lsass.exe
 0n5316 HandleLeak.exe
...
```

The trick now is to interpret the addresses in the previous call stack relative to the address space of the *lsass.exe* process. Attaching a user-mode debugger to *lsass.exe* to see the code that the addresses on the call stack resolve to within that context might cause the system to deadlock if the user-mode debugger performs any actions that require an immediate response from the frozen *lsass.exe*. So, this is a good case for using a live kernel-mode debugging session, given that only static memory inspection is required. By setting the current process context in the live kernel debugger to that of *lsass.exe*, you can use the *!htrace* command to once again dump the trace information for the previous handle (with value *0x739c* in this experiment), except this time you're able to resolve the stack trace successfully.

```
lkd> .symfix
lkd> .reload
lkd> !process 0 0 lsass.exe
PROCESS 934d7ad8  SessionId: 0  Cid: 0260    Peb: 7ffde000  ParentCid: 0214
    Image: lsass.exe
lkd> !process 0 0 handleleak.exe
PROCESS 84c8fbb0  SessionId: 1  Cid: 14c4    Peb: 7ffdf000  ParentCid: 1150
    Image: HandleLeak.exe
lkd> .process /r /p 934d7ad8
lkd> !htrace 0x0000739c 84c8fbb0
Process 0x84c8fbb0
ObjectTable 0xb921ad38

Handle 0x739C - OPEN
Thread ID = 0x00000c80, Process ID = 0x00000260

0x82c8665b: nt!NtDuplicateObject+0xD9
0x82a921fa: nt!KiFastCallEntry+0x12A
0x772558a4: ntdll!NtDuplicateObject+0xC
0x75147b65: lsasrv!LsapDuplicateHandle+0x86
0x751177ab: lsasrv!LsapAuApiDispatchLogonUser+0x6CB
0x75117c08: lsasrv!SspiExLogonUser+0x29C
0x7520188b: SspiSrv!SspirLogonUser+0x175
0x76b904e8: RPCRT4!Invoke+0x2A
0x76bf5311: RPCRT4!NdrStubCall2+0x2D6
0x76bf431d: RPCRT4!NdrServerCall2+0x19
0x76b9063c: RPCRT4!DispatchToStubInCNoAvrf+0x4A
0x76b907ca: RPCRT4!RPC_INTERFACE::DispatchToStubWorker+0x16C
0x76b906b6: RPCRT4!RPC_INTERFACE::DispatchToStub+0x8B
0x76b876db: RPCRT4!LRPC_SCALL::DispatchRequest+0x257
0x76b90ac6: RPCRT4!LRPC_SCALL::QueueOrDispatchCall+0xBD
0x76b90a85: RPCRT4!LRPC_SCALL::HandleRequest+0x34F
```

This last call stack represents the server side of a local Remote Procedure Call (RPC) initiated by the *LogonUser* Win32 API. The new user is authenticated, and the corresponding token object is constructed inside the *lsass.exe* process. The handle value returned by the API to the client process is then created by the previous call stack, where *lsass.exe* duplicates its own user-mode handle to the new executive token object into the address space of the client. All that's left for you to do is review the source code of the target application and look for calls to *LogonUser* to check whether there are any instances where the code fails to close the token handle obtained from that API call.

Now that you've concluded your investigation, you can stop debugging the target process without terminating it by detaching the user-mode debugger you previously attached to it using the *qd* ("quit and detach") command. However, you should also remember to disable handle tracing before you detach from the target so that it's no longer consuming precious kernel-mode memory space, as shown in the following listing.

```
0:007> !htrace -disable
Handle tracing disabled.
0:007> qd
```

Limitations of Handle-Leak Detection Using *!htrace*

Note the following two limitations when using the *!htrace* technique:

- This method works only with true kernel handles. You cannot use the *!htrace* extension command to track down the source of graphics device interface (GDI) handle leaks or leaks of opaque handles to user-mode structures, such as those returned by the Win32 Crypto API (HCRYPTPROV, HCRYPTKEY, and so on).
- The call stacks captured in the handle-tracing code inside the kernel have a maximum depth that's not configurable. This means user-mode stacks that are too deep might end up getting truncated.

Nevertheless, *!htrace* remains the current tool of choice for debugging handle leaks on Windows, especially in live production environments where the ability to turn it on dynamically without having to restart the system or the target process is especially useful.

Debugging User-Mode Memory Leaks

Just like handle leaks, memory-leak bugs can have severe consequences on the reliability of your software and cause unpredictable failures. User-mode memory-leak bugs can happen at every layer of memory management in your program. For example, virtual memory can be leaked directly if calls to the *VirtualAlloc* API aren't properly paired up with matching calls to *VirtualFree*. Similarly, virtual memory can be leaked indirectly through heap allocations, like those coming from the NT heap or any of the allocators built on top of it (such as the C runtime allocators). This is usually the more common case in user-mode programs.

The underlying idea used in the *!htrace* command to detect handle leaks also plays a central role in memory-leak detection. If all allocations are recorded in a global data structure along with their respective call stacks and removed when they're freed, you could query this global table for the current active allocations in the module at any point in time and examine potential memory leaks this way. You'll recognize this basic idea throughout this section as several memory-leak debugging hooks and tools are introduced.

Detecting Resource Leaks Using the Application Verifier Tool

The Application Verifier tool can be used to detect resource leaks, including both memory and handle leaks. The clear advantages to this technique are its simplicity and that it allows you to automate the detection process and find memory-leak bugs proactively as part of your regular testing, before they ever get a chance to turn into out-of-memory failures under heavy load.

There are two important limitations you need to be aware of, though:

- Only leaks in DLL modules are caught using this method. Leaks in the main executable module aren't flagged with verifier stops in the debugger. This comes as a surprise to most people who are new to how the Application Verifier detects resource leaks. In the case of a

DLL module, leak checks are inserted as the DLL module is getting unloaded and the call to *kernel32!FreeLibrary* is detoured toward *verifier!AvrfpLdrUnloadDll*. There is no such verifier hook point when the main process exits, though.

- For handle leaks, the verification code relies on the handle allocation APIs getting re-routed to the verifier code, so not all handle types will be tracked—only those whose allocation API is patched by the Application Verifier hooks. In particular, the token handle-leak example shown in the previous section wouldn't be caught by enabling the verifier hooks for the target process, given that it occurs in a different process context (*lsass.exe*).

Despite these limitations, this technique is certainly a great place to start when trying to rid your code from resource leaks during the development or testing phase of your software, and you get it for free if you simply enable the basic Application Verifier hooks when running your existing tests.

To see resource-leak verifier stops in action, consider the following C++ sample from the companion source code, which intentionally leaks a heap allocation in a DLL module (as well as an event handle, for good measure!).

```
//
// C:\book\code\chapter_08\HeapLeak\DllHeapLeak>HeapLeak.cpp
//
BOOL
WINAPI
DllMain(
    __in HINSTANCE hInstance,
    __in DWORD dwReason,
    __in PVOID pReserved
    )
{
    switch (dwReason)
    {
        case DLL_PROCESS_ATTACH:
            ::DisableThreadLibraryCalls(hInstance);

            // BUG! Leaked NT heap memory allocation
            ::HeapAlloc(::GetProcessHeap(), 0, 50000);
            // BUG! Leaked event handle
            ::CreateEvent(NULL, FALSE, FALSE, NULL);
            break;
...
}
```

In this experiment, the previous DLL is dynamically loaded using the *host.exe* tool from the companion source code, which simply calls the *LoadLibrary* Win32 API to load the DLL in question. The first step is to enable the basic Application Verifier hooks (and the Leak category, in particular) for that target process image name (*host.exe*) using the Application Verifier tool, as shown in Figure 8-12.

```
C:\Windows\system32\appverif.exe
```

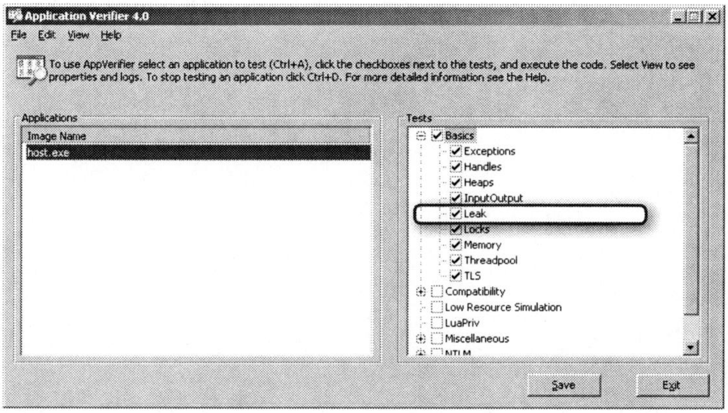

FIGURE 8-12 Enabling the basic Application Verifier hooks for *host.exe*.

When you now run the target *host.exe* program using the command line shown by the *vercommand* debugger command in the following listing, you immediately hit two verifier stops when the *HeapLeak.dll* module gets unloaded. The first verifier stop corresponds to the NT-heap memory leak, and the second one corresponds to the leaked event handle, as shown in the following listing.

```
0:000> vercommand
command line: '"c:\Program Files\Debugging Tools for Windows (x86)\windbg.exe"
c:\book\code\tools\dllhost\objfre_win7_x86\i386\host.exe
c:\book\code\chapter_08\HeapLeak\DllHeapLeak\objfre_win7_x86\i386\HeapLeak.dll'
0:000> .symfix
0:000> .reload
0:000> g
=======================================
VERIFIER STOP 00000900: pid 0x934: A heap allocation was leaked.
    0696ACB0 : Address of the leaked allocation. Run !heap -p -a <address> to get additional
information about the allocation.
    03E70E34 : Address to the allocation stack trace. Run dps <address> to view the allocation
stack.
...
0:000> g
=======================================
VERIFIER STOP 00000901: pid 0x934: A HANDLE was leaked.
    000001DC : Value of the leaked handle. Run !htrace <handle> to get additional information
about the handle if handle tracing is enabled.
    03E70E8C : Address to the allocation stack trace. Run dps <address> to view the allocation
stack.
...
```

When you enable the Leak category in the basic Application Verifier hooks, the verifier code in the target process starts saving the stack trace of every allocation in a global (per-module) data structure. So, when a leak is detected, you're able to use the *dps* command to dump the creation call stack array that was previously saved for the leaked resource. As you see in the previous listing, the verifier stop message gives you the address to use with this command, which represents a pointer to the base of the saved call-stack array.

```
0:000> dps 03E70E34
...
03e70e40  00000000
03e70e44  6d361349 HeapLeak!DllMain+0x2a
03e70e48  6d361642 HeapLeak!__DllMainCRTStartup+0xe1
...
03e70e70  753a1e23 kernel32!LoadLibraryW+0x11
03e70e74  00641543 host!CMainApp::MainHR+0x14
...
0:000> dps 03E70E8C
...
03e70e94  00130000
03e70e98  69ac2e58 vfbasics!AVrfpCreateEventA+0xb0
03e70e9c  6d361353 HeapLeak!DllMain+0x34
03e70ea0  6d361642 HeapLeak!__DllMainCRTStartup+0xe1
...
03e70ec8  753a1e23 kernel32!LoadLibraryW+0x11
03e70ecc  00641543 host!CMainApp::MainHR+0x14
...
0:000> q
```

Because both the full page heap and handle tracing were also enabled by the Application Verifier during this experiment, the *!heap* and *!htrace* commands covered earlier in this chapter can be used as alternative ways to obtain the allocation call stacks for the leaked NT-heap memory block and event handle, respectively. The verifier stop message from the previous experiment, in fact, also suggested those alternative approaches for obtaining the allocation sites, though the call stacks shown by those commands come from totally different tracking mechanisms than the one used by the verifier leak-detection code and displayed by the *dps* command.

Investigating Memory Leaks Using the UMDH Tool

The Application Verifier tool offers a good way to automate the task of finding resource leaks in DLL modules, but what about long-running processes such as standalone executable Windows services or long-lived worker processes? In those cases, you need a different method to track down any suspected memory leaks.

One approach is to use the built-in Event Tracing for Windows (ETW) instrumentation in the OS and the Windows Performance Toolkit to visualize memory-allocation trends in the target process and map suspected leaks to their originating call sites. This powerful method can be used to observe virtual allocations, heap allocations, and even kernel-mode pool allocations, but its coverage is deferred until the next part of this book when tracing methodologies are covered in more detail. Another available technique for memory leaks when using the NT heap manager is to use the special-purpose UMDH ("user-mode dump heap") tool. This section will demonstrate how you can use this tool to investigate NT-heap memory leaks.

How UMDH Works

The idea underlying the UMDH technique is similar to that of the *!htrace* command and also the DLL leak-detection scheme used by the Application Verifier tool. A global stack-trace database is again kept by the NT-heap code for all the active allocations in the process after a special bit in the NT global flag is set for the target executable image. The UMDH tool is then able to ask (via a private NTDLL API) for a snapshot of the database at any point in time. Just like *!htrace*, the UMDH tool also supports a *diff* option to compare two snapshots and provide you with a list of *potential memory leak* call stacks.

Keep in mind that just because a heap-allocation stack trace appears in a list obtained by comparing two snapshots, this doesn't mean that it's a true memory leak because the target process could free the memory later during its execution. However, having a list of potential suspects (with their call stacks!) is very helpful in memory-leak investigations, just as it is in handle-leak investigations. A good way to reduce the number of false positives is to take multiple snapshot comparisons and start your investigation with allocations that continue to grow larger as time goes on.

The UMDH tool relies on the NT-heap code in the target process maintaining an allocation stack-trace database. This behavior is primarily controlled by one of the bits in the NT global flag, which you can set by selecting the Create User Mode Stack Trace Database check box in the GFLAGS tool, as shown in Figure 8-13.

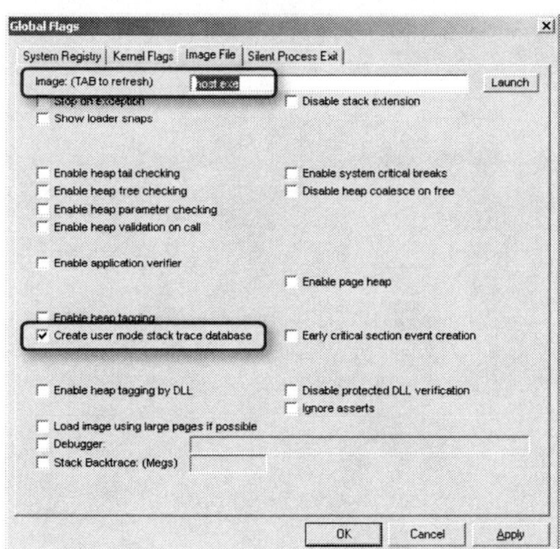

FIGURE 8-13 Setting the user-mode stack-trace database bit in the NT global flag using GFLAGS.

There are also two other ways to enable NT-heap allocation tracing in the target process:

- Enabling the Application Verifier hooks also automatically turns this tracing mode on for all future instances of the target process. This is convenient if you're already enabling the Application Verifier tool during your testing of the target application, saving you the inconvenience of having to use another tool (GFLAGS).

- Another way to get this tracing mode enabled is to simply run the *umdh.exe* tool against a running instance of the target process, as you will shortly see in the next section. This dynamically enables the tracing in the NT-heap-manager code that's running within the target process and starts capturing stack traces for all future NT-heap allocations. This is especially useful in live production environment investigations, where you might not want to restart the target process and lose the leak situation you might already have in place.

Note When *umdh.exe* is used to dynamically enable the user-mode, stack trace database for a running process, this setting doesn't get persisted to the IFEO registry key for the target image, so other instances of the target process remain unaffected. This is yet another advantage of this approach over using GFLAGS or the Application Verifier tool for NT-heap, memory-leak investigations in production environments because UMDH keeps the locality of the setting to the single process instance it's targeting.

UMDH in Action

You can find the *umdh.exe* tool in the same directory as the Windows debuggers. It's a command-line tool and isn't the friendliest of tools to use, though it gets the job done when it comes to NT-heap memory leaks. To see how this works in practice, consider the following C++ sample from the companion source code, which simply leaks heap-allocated memory in an infinite loop.

```
//
// C:\book\code\chapter_08\HeapLeak\ExeHeapLeak>main.cpp
//
BYTE* pMem;
for ( ; ; )
{
    // BUG! Leaked NT heap memory allocation
    pMem = new BYTE[1024];
    ChkAlloc(pMem);
}
```

To start this experiment, compile and run this program from a command prompt window.

```
C:\book\code\chapter_08\HeapLeak\ExeHeapLeak\objfre_win7_x86\i386>host.exe
```

While the process continues to run (and leak memory!), go to another command prompt and run the following two commands, which capture two snapshots of the heap allocation stack-trace database from the target process and save them into two files on disk (named *log1.txt* and *log2.txt* in this example).

```
C:\Program Files\Debugging Tools for Windows (x86)>umdh.exe -pn:host.exe -f:log1.txt
Warning: UMDH didn't find any allocations that have stacks collected.
Warning: UMDH has enabled allocation stack collection for the current running process.
```

```
Warning: To persist the setting for the application run GFLAGS.
Warning: A 32bit GFLAGS must be used. The command is:
Warning: gflags -i host.exe +ust

C:\Program Files\Debugging Tools for Windows (x86)>umdh.exe -pn:host.exe -f:log2.txt
```

Notice the bold line in the output from the first command, which automatically enabled allocation stack-trace collection for the target process. Now that you have these two snapshots, you can use the *umdh.exe* tool again to compare them (even on a different machine!) and examine the outstanding allocations that happened in the time interval between them.

```
C:\Program Files\Debugging Tools for Windows (x86)>umdh.exe log1.txt log2.txt
Warning: _NT_SYMBOL_PATH variable is not defined. Will be set to %windir%\symbols.
DBGHELP: host - private symbols & lines
        c:\book\code\chapter_08\HeapLeak\ExeHeapLeak\objfre_win7_x86\i386\host.pdb
DBGHELP: ntdll - export symbols
...
+   27000 ( 27000 -      0)      9c allocs        BackTrace1
+      9c (    9c -      0)       BackTrace1      allocations
        ntdll!RtlLogStackBackTrace+00000007
        ntdll!wcsnicmp+000001E4
        host!MemoryAlloc+00000017
        host!CMainApp::MainHR+00000018
        kernel32!BaseThreadInitThunk+00000012
        ntdll!RtlInitializeExceptionChain+000000EF
        ntdll!RtlInitializeExceptionChain+000000C2
Total increase ==  27000 requested +    9c0 overhead =  279c0
```

Notice that there are several allocations with the same call stack, strongly indicating that a heap memory leak might be at play. Notice also that the last *umdh.exe* command was able to automatically resolve the functions from the target process in the stack trace, given that it found the private symbol file in the same directory as the target executable in this case. Symbol resolution doesn't always work seamlessly, though, and UMDH often needs your help to locate the correct symbol files, as explained in the next section.

Resolving Symbols in UMDH

If you look closer at the call stack displayed earlier by the UMDH tool, you'll quickly realize that the first two frames at the top of the call stack, which correspond to functions from the *ntdll.dll* system module, look incorrect. The overloaded C++ *new* operator in the companion source code (*MemoryAlloc*) calls *HeapAlloc/RtlAllocateHeap* to allocate memory from the NT heap, but that call is nowhere to be found in the previous call stack!

To be able to resolve the symbols for system binaries in the stack traces displayed by the *umdh.exe* tool, you must first let the tool know where to locate those symbol files. UMDH, like many other command-line NT tools with no user interface to configure the symbols path, relies on the _NT_SYMBOL_PATH environment variable to find symbols.

Up until this point, the useful *.symfix* debugger command has been used to save you the hassle of having to manually set the Microsoft public symbols path, but you'll now need to get your hands dirty and set this variable by hand. Even so, you can still use the *.symfix* command in the WinDbg debugger, and then use the *.sympath* command to remind you of the symbols search path syntax expected in the _NT_SYMBOL_PATH variable. Note that you might also need to append the directory path for your own symbols to this variable if you are trying to resolve the symbols on a machine that's different from the one on which you built your code.

The syntax for this variable can be summarized as shown next, where you're also able to specify an optional local symbols cache directory for the symbols downloaded from a remote server by adding a path enclosed between * characters right before the server URL.

```
set _NT_SYMBOL_PATH=srv*<Local Cache Path Directory>*<Symbols Server Location URL>;<Local
Path1>;<Local Path2>;...
```

Notice that you're now able to obtain the correct call stack when using the *umdh.exe* tool's *diff* feature.

```
set _NT_SYMBOL_PATH=SRV*c:\LocalSymbolCache*http://msdl.microsoft.com/download/symbols
C:\Program Files\Debugging Tools for Windows (x86)>umdh.exe log1.txt log2.txt
+   27000 ( 27000 -      0)      9c allocs        BackTrace1
+      9c (    9c -      0)      BackTrace1       allocations
        ntdll!RtlLogStackBackTrace+00000007
        ntdll!RtlAllocateHeap+0000023A
        host!MemoryAlloc+00000017
        host!CMainApp::MainHR+00000018
        kernel32!BaseThreadInitThunk+0000000E
        ntdll!__RtlUserThreadStart+00000070
        ntdll!_RtlUserThreadStart+0000001B
Total increase ==  27000 requested +    9c0 overhead =  279c0
```

Extending the Strategy: A Custom Reference Stack-Trace Database

In both leak-detection techniques described so far in this section, the key feature that enabled you to find the site of the memory leak was a global database keeping track of the stack traces of outstanding allocations. As it turns out, implementing this functionality is relatively easy, and you can extend the strategy to other types of leaks. For example, the companion source code has a sample C++ class that can be used to track the call sites of leaked object references. This can be used, for instance, to instrument and find unbalanced object-reference counting or module-lock counting in a COM helper library (such as the Microsoft ATL library).

You can keep track of each added reference to an object in a global array (database), and if the client fails to release it, you can generate a debugger break before the program exits and output the stack trace that created the leaked object. Once you know a reference-counted object has been leaked, you can review the places in the source code that took references to the object to see whether any of them failed to release it. To keep the size of the database from becoming too large, the global database in this example keeps track of only the allocation stack traces, not the stack traces of every *AddRef* call site.

The most interesting part of this sample is the function that saves the stack trace at the time of the allocation, which uses the public *kernel32!CaptureStackBackTrace* Win32 API call.

```
//
// C:\book\code\chapter_08\RefCountDB>RefTracker.h
//
struct CObjRef :
    CZeroInit<CObjRef>,
    public CIUnknownImplT<false>
{
    VOID
    Init(
        __in const VOID* pObj
        )
    {
        USHORT nCount, n;
        PVOID pStackFrames[MAX_CAPTURED_STACK_DEPTH];

        m_pObj = pObj;
        m_nStackFrames = 0;
        nCount = CaptureStackBackTrace(
            1,
            ARRAYSIZE(pStackFrames),
            pStackFrames,
            NULL);
        ASSERT(nCount <= ARRAYSIZE(pStackFrames));

        m_spStackFrames.Attach((PVOID*)new BYTE[nCount * sizeof(PVOID)]);
        if (m_spStackFrames)
        {
            for (n = 0; n < nCount; n++)
            {
                m_spStackFrames[n] = pStackFrames[n];
            }
            m_nStackFrames = nCount;
        }
    }
...
    const VOID* m_pObj;
    CAutoPtr<PVOID> m_spStackFrames;
    int m_nStackFrames;
};
```

You can now associate an instance of this structure with every new reference-counted object and store those structures in a global array. Every subsequent *AddRef* and *Release* for the object will then increment and decrement the reference count of this structure. When the object finally gets deleted (that is, the reference count reaches zero), the corresponding structure can also be deleted from the global database array. The global array then constantly reflects all the current active (referenced) objects within the target module. This behavior allows you to obtain the allocation call stack of any leaked objects, which is usually only one step away from figuring out the site of the leaked *AddRef* call.

To see how this can be used in practice, you can run a test where you intentionally leak a reference to a memory address. If you also insert a call to detect leaks at process exit, your program would then hit a debugger break because the reference tracking code will find that the global stack-trace database (array) is not empty due to unbalanced reference counting. As the displayed message suggests, you can again use the *dps* command to dump the stack trace of the offending object instantiation site, which you're able to do with complete accuracy, as shown in the following debugger listing.

```
0:000> vercommand
command line: '"c:\Program Files\Debugging Tools for Windows (x86)\windbg.exe"
c:\book\code\chapter_08\RefCountDB\objfre_win7_x86\i386\RefCountDB.exe'
0:000> .symfix
0:000> .reload
0:000> g
  OBJECT LEAK:
   Address: 0x000E5388
   StackTrace: dps 0x000E53D8 L0x7
    0: 0x006020A4
    1: 0x0060211A
    2: 0x006021A0
    3: 0x006022DE
    4: 0x7623ED6C
    5: 0x7798377B
    6: 0x7798374E
0:000> dps 0x000E53D8 L0x7
000e53d8  006020a4 RefCountDB!CRefCountDatabase::AddRef+0x68
000e53dc  0060211a RefCountDB!CRefCountDatabase_AddRef+0x14
000e53e0  006021a0 RefCountDB!CIUnknownImplT<1>::CIUnknownImplT<1>+0x11
000e53e4  006022de RefCountDB!wmain+0x14 [c:\book\code\chapter_08\refcountdb\main.cpp @ 70]
000e53e8  7623ed6c kernel32!BaseThreadInitThunk+0xe
000e53ec  7798377b ntdll!__RtlUserThreadStart+0x70
000e53f0  7798374e ntdll!_RtlUserThreadStart+0x1b
0:000> q
```

Debugging Kernel-Mode Memory Leaks

The techniques described earlier for detecting user-mode, heap-memory leaks were all, in one way or another, based on instrumentation hooks implemented by Microsoft at the user-mode heap manager and verifier layers. Those approaches won't help much when the memory happens to be leaked on the kernel side of the fence. Fortunately, kernel-mode memory leaks are often easier to track down because allocations in kernel-mode code are relatively infrequent and more explicit than user-mode allocations, which often occur indirectly when using user-mode components and layers written by third-party vendors. Kernel-mode memory leaks are also easier to debug thanks to a great feature in the Windows memory manager called *pool tagging*, as you'll see later in this section.

Kernel Memory Basics

When Windows starts, the memory manager creates two dynamically sized memory pools for use by kernel-mode components: the *paged* and *nonpaged* pools. The nonpaged pool, as its name indicates, is a particularly scarce resource because its memory can't be paged out to disk and must remain resident in main memory at all times.

Both the paged and nonpaged pools can be viewed in the Performance tab of the Windows task manager or using the *!vm* kernel-debugger extension command. As you can see when using the *!vm* command, the Windows kernel creates multiple paged pools (not a single one) to relieve lock contention on multicore machines.

```
lkd> $ Nonpaged pool=32MB, paged pool=203MB in this example
lkd> !vm
*** Virtual Memory Usage ***
    Physical Memory:       262030 (   1048120 Kb)
    Page File: \??\C:\pagefile.sys
      Current:   1048576 Kb  Free Space:    510964 Kb
      Minimum:   1048576 Kb  Maximum:      4194304 Kb
    Available Pages:       149601 (    598404 Kb)
    NonPagedPool Usage:      8059 (     32236 Kb)
    NonPagedPool Max:      189951 (    759804 Kb)
    PagedPool 0 Usage:      40130 (    160520 Kb)
    PagedPool 1 Usage:       4084 (     16336 Kb)
    PagedPool 2 Usage:       2159 (      8636 Kb)
...
    PagedPool Usage:        50828 (    203312 Kb)
    PagedPool Maximum:     523264 (   2093056 Kb)
...
```

Figure 8-14 depicts the high-level breakdown of the 4-GB virtual memory address space in *x86* processes, including the position of the paged and nonpaged pools in kernel memory. The virtual address space of *x64* processes is much larger, but the core concepts remain the same.

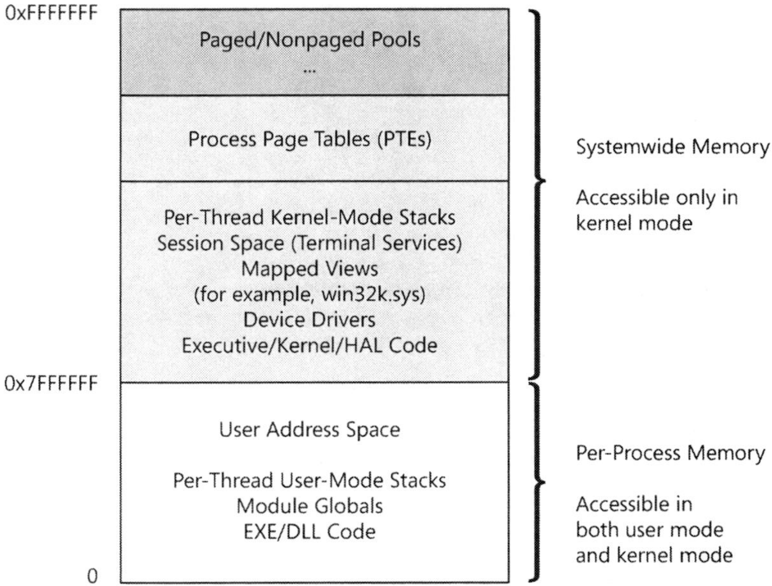

FIGURE 8-14 Paged and nonpaged pools in the virtual memory address space on *x86* Windows.

An unbounded, kernel-mode memory leak eventually leads to out-of-memory failures in the system as the pool resources dry up, so finding and fixing those bugs is of utmost importance.

Investigating Kernel-Mode Leaks Using Pool Tagging

To see how pool tagging can be used in kernel-mode, memory-leak investigations, consider the following C driver from the companion source code, which exposes a single I/O control code (user-mode API, if you will) that leaks 1 KB of memory each time it gets invoked by a user-mode client process. Notice how the leaked allocation is tagged with a special tag ('Dlek' in this example) identifying the owning component, which sets it apart from other kernel-mode allocations. It's typical for kernel-mode code to use the same tag for all the allocations that come from the same component, so it becomes easier to attribute memory consumption to the different kernel components present on the system.

```
//
// C:\book\code\chapter_08\DriverLeak\sys>main.h
//
#define DRV_CONTROL_DEVICE_NAME L"DrvCtrl"
#define DRV_POOL_TAG 'Dlek'
#define DRV_LEAK_ALLOCATION_SIZE 1024

#define IOCTL_DRV_TEST_API \
    CTL_CODE(FILE_DEVICE_UNKNOWN, 0xa01, METHOD_BUFFERED, FILE_READ_ACCESS)

//
// C:\book\code\chapter_08\DriverLeak\sys>main.c
//
NTSTATUS
DrvIoDispatch(
    __in PDEVICE_OBJECT DeviceObject,
    __inout PIRP Irp
    )
{
...
    switch (IrpSp->MajorFunction) {
...
        case IRP_MJ_DEVICE_CONTROL:
            switch (ControlCode) {
                case IOCTL_DRV_TEST_API:
                    Status = LeakRoutine(DRV_LEAK_ALLOCATION_SIZE);
                    Irp->IoStatus.Information = 0;
                    break;
            }
            break;
    }
...
}

NTSTATUS
LeakRoutine(
    __in ULONG Length
    )
{
    PVOID Buffer;
```

```
    PAGED_CODE();

    Buffer = ExAllocatePoolWithTag(PagedPool, Length, DRV_POOL_TAG);
    if (Buffer == NULL) {
        return STATUS_INSUFFICIENT_RESOURCES;
    }
    DRVPRINT("Allocated %d bytes at 0x%x.\n", Length, Buffer);
    //
    // BUG! Memory is Leaked here
    // ExFreePoolWithTag(Buffer, DRV_POOL_TAG);
    //
    return STATUS_SUCCESS;
}
```

The I/O manager code in the Windows kernel invokes the *LeakRoutine* dispatch routine for you when the test user-mode client application issues a *DeviceIOControl* Win32 API call to the device created by your test driver.

```
//
// C:\book\code\chapter_08\DriverLeak\test>main.cpp
//
static
HRESULT
MainHR(
    VOID
    )
{
    CHandle shLeakDrv;
    DWORD dwReturned, n;

    ChkProlog();

    shLeakDrv.Attach(CreateFile(
        L"\\\\.\\" DRV_CONTROL_DEVICE_NAME,
        GENERIC_READ,
        0, NULL, OPEN_EXISTING, FILE_ATTRIBUTE_NORMAL, NULL));
...
    for (n = 0; n < NUM_CALLS; n++)
    {
        ChkWin32(DeviceIoControl(
            shLeakDrv,
            IOCTL_DRV_TEST_API,
            NULL, 0, NULL, 0, &dwReturned, NULL));
    }

    ChkNoCleanup();
}
```

To follow this experiment, you need to set up a kernel-mode debugging session. First, you need to register the driver with the service control manager (SCM) on the target machine in this debugging session. The helper *CreateService.cmd* script in the *scm* folder helps you perform this driver registration step—a one-time requirement.

```
C:\book\code\chapter_08\DriverLeak\scm\createservice.cmd
sc.exe create drvleak type= kernel start= demand error= normal
binPath=\Systemroot\system32\drivers\drvleak.sys DisplayName= "drvleak kernel driver"
[SC] CreateService SUCCESS
```

All you have left to do is copy your test driver to the target location you used during the previous step. You then can start and stop the driver like any other user-mode Windows service. The presence of a kernel-mode debugger also has the convenient side effect of disabling driver-signing verification in the OS kernel, so you don't need to explicitly sign the *drvleak.sys* driver prior to conducting this debugging experiment.

```
copy C:\book\code\chapter_08\DriverLeak\sys\objfre_win7_x86\i386\drvleak.sys C:\Windows\
system32\drivers\.

net start drvleak
```

Now that the driver is started and loaded into kernel memory, you can start issuing I/O device control calls to the driver from the user-mode test application, which allows you to reproduce the pool memory leak.

```
C:\book\code\chapter_08\DriverLeak\test\objfre_win7_x86\i386\drvclient.exe
Success.
```

Several memory blocks are leaked after each run of this user-mode client application on the target machine. In fact, this memory is leaked even after you stop the driver!

```
net stop drvleak
```

To confirm this, you can use the *!poolused* kernel-debugger extension command, either in the host kernel debugger or from a live kernel-debugging session on the target machine, which will show several outstanding blocks with the 'Dlek' tag from your driver even after the driver is stopped and unloaded—a clear indication of a kernel-mode memory leak.

```
kd> .symfix
kd> .reload
kd> !poolused 4
 Sorting by Paged Pool Consumed
                  NonPaged                       Paged
 Tag      Allocs            Used      Allocs            Used
...
 kelD          0               0        1107         1142424   UNKNOWN pooltag 'kelD'
```

The tag (interpreted as a 4-byte integer value) is listed in little-endian order by the *!poolused* command. This is why it's displayed as 'kelD' and not the 'Dlek' value you used when allocating the pool memory in your driver. In this case, you own the code in question and can easily go back and review it for memory leaks with this pool tag. In other cases, you might be debugging a leak caused by a third-party driver. In those situations, you can force the kernel debugger to break on each allocation from the suspicious pool tag by editing the internal *nt!poolhittag* global variable using the kernel-mode debugger, which can help you figure out the call stack of the memory leak, as demonstrated in the following command.

```
kd> ed nt!poolhittag 'Dlek'
```

Starting the driver again on the target machine and running the user-mode *drvclient.exe* test application then causes the following debug break, which reveals the exact call site of the pool leak from the example used in this section.

```
kd> g
Break instruction exception - code 80000003 (first chance)
nt!ExAllocatePoolWithTag+0x881:
82924432 cc              int     3
kd> .reload /user
kd> k
ChildEBP RetAddr
a68e3bd4 89812067 nt!ExAllocatePoolWithTag+0x881
a68e3be8 8980f064 drvleak!LeakRoutine+0x15
a68e3bfc 828404ac drvleak!DrvIoDispatch+0x3c
a68e3c14 82a423be nt!IofCallDriver+0x63
a68e3c34 82a5f1af nt!IopSynchronousServiceTail+0x1f8
a68e3cd0 82a6198a nt!IopXxxControlFile+0x6aa
a68e3d04 8284743a nt!NtDeviceIoControlFile+0x2a
a68e3d04 77b76344 nt!KiFastCallEntry+0x12a
001df6d4 77b74b0c ntdll!KiFastSystemCallRet
001df6d8 75f0a08f ntdll!NtDeviceIoControlFile+0xc
001df738 775aec25 KERNELBASE!DeviceIoControl+0xf6
001df764 00781574 kernel32!DeviceIoControlImplementation+0x80
001df79c 007815bb drvclient!CMainApp::MainHR+0x72
[c:\book\code\chapter_08\driverleak\test\main.cpp @ 35]
kd> $ Disable the breakpoint now...
kd> ed nt!poolhittag 0
kd> g
```

Summary

This chapter covered debugging scenarios related to the reliability aspects of the code that you write. As you move to the next chapter and the second part in this selection of common debugging scenarios, the following points are worth emphasizing again:

- Crashes, corruptions, and memory leaks can all rear their heads in unpredictable ways. Often they do so at the most inopportune times, when the bottom line of your business might depend directly on the stability of your software and its uninterrupted operations.

- Getting a consistent repro for memory corruptions is a luxury you won't always have, so never ignore a crash just because you can't reproduce it consistently. If you get a crash dump or a live JIT debugging session for an unhandled exception, look carefully at the state of the program and try to form hypotheses as to why it might have gotten into that state. You might never get to see the crash again—until your end users hit it and you have to debug it under far less favorable conditions.

- Debugging tools and hooks that allow you to force your program to crash closer to the site of memory corruptions are invaluable. The NT page-heap feature uses this goal as the basis for its design, and you'll find many debugging hooks that use the same underlying idea. For native code, in particular, make sure you schedule regular runs of your tests after enabling the hooks provided by the Application Verifier tool.

- Tracking down leaks requires hooks to enable tracing the active allocations so that any leaked memory can be attributed to its origin in the source code through an allocation call stack. I'll expand on this idea later in this book and show how you can also use the built-in event-tracing instrumentation in the OS for analyzing memory usage in Part 3, "Observing and Analyzing Software Behavior."

- Helping developers be more productive while also writing more reliable software is one of the main value propositions of the .NET Framework. Even so, the safeguards of the managed environment provided by the CLR execution engine can be breached when you call native code and corrupt memory in the same process. So, having strategies for how to deal with corruption scenarios is important even when you write your code in .NET (and trust that the native code that forms the CLR itself, as well as the other managed .NET assemblies you call, will be free of such bugs).

In the next chapter, you'll continue complementing your arsenal with strategies to investigate common debugging scenarios in two fundamental areas of the Windows operating system: concurrency and security. These two topics permeate various areas of software development in Windows, which is why mastering them is important in a large number of debugging investigations.

CHAPTER 9

Common Debugging Scenarios, Part 2

In this chapter

Continuing with the theme of the previous chapter, you'll now study a few common debugging scenarios from two important areas of the operating system: concurrency and security. This chapter serves a dual purpose. First, it will arm you with a few techniques for debugging the concurrency and security aspects of the software you ship, which is particularly important given the ubiquity of these topics. Second, this chapter will also improve your familiarity with those fundamental areas, which can be useful when trying to understand some of the output and behaviors described by the debugging and tracing tools in Microsoft Windows.

Debugging Race Conditions

Multithreading is the source of a number of challenges that come with writing, maintaining, and debugging code with units of execution that can run in parallel. One basic challenge is the ability to use shared memory, such as global variables or the state provided as part of the thread context, from multiple threads. Broken invariants introduced by the parallel nature of a program and the relative order in which its threads get scheduled by the operating system are called *race conditions*.

Race condition bugs are often hard to reproduce because the sequence of events leading up to the failure path might depend on the order in which the threads were scheduled relative to each other. The best way to prevent these bugs is through careful reviews during the design and coding phases. Multithreaded programming is hard for mere mortals, unfortunately, so mistakes will be made even by the best engineers. That being said, the first step to avoiding these bugs is to learn how to recognize them. This section covers three common categories of race conditions that result from breaking any of the following basic rules:

- Modifying shared memory from multiple threads requires proper synchronization. This is the most common form of race conditions, which often leads to *logical* bugs where internal code invariants that would've held true in sequential execution get broken by nonsynchronized access to shared state from multiple threads. This category of race conditions is often more sinister than the next two because the program can simply yield incorrect results as opposed to something more visible like a process crash.
- The lifetime of any shared variables must be prolonged beyond that of the worker thread using them. Failure to do so will result in the thread accessing invalid memory after it has been freed, potentially causing an access violation.
- Code executed in worker threads must not be unloaded as long as there is a chance it might get invoked by the program. This is something you must take into consideration whenever you plan to execute code hosted in dynamic-link library (DLL) modules from worker threads. Any attempt to execute instructions or access global variables from unloaded DLL modules will result in an immediate access violation.

Shared-State Consistency Bugs

To get a better understanding of the potential ways in which race conditions are manifested when access to shared state isn't properly synchronized, consider the following C# program from the companion source code, where a global .NET object is used from multiple threads to hash the same input string.

```
//
// C:\book\code\chapter_09\HashRaceCondition\Bug>test.cs
//
class Program
{
    private static void ThreadProc(
        object data
        )
    {
        string hashValue = Convert.ToBase64String(
            g_hashFunc.ComputeHash(data as byte[]));
        Console.WriteLine("Thread #{0} done processing. Hash value was {1}",
            Thread.CurrentThread.ManagedThreadId, hashValue);
    }

    private static void Main(
        string[] args
        )
    {
```

```
        int n, numThreads;
        Thread[] threads;

        numThreads = (args.Length == 0) ? 1 : Convert.ToInt32(args[0]);
        threads = new Thread[numThreads];
        g_hashFunc = new SHA1CryptoServiceProvider();

        //
        // Start multiple threads to use the shared hash object
        //
        for (n = 0; n < threads.Length; n++)
        {
            threads[n] = new Thread(ThreadProc);
            threads[n].Start(Encoding.UTF8.GetBytes("abc"));
        }

        //
        // Wait for all the threads to finish
        //
        for (n = 0; n < threads.Length; n++)
        {
            threads[n].Join();
        }
    }
    private static HashAlgorithm g_hashFunc;
}
```

You would expect all the threads in this program to yield the same hash value, given that they're all hashing the same input string (*"abc"*). When you run the program with only one thread, notice that the hash value is consistent from one run to the next.

```
C:\book\code\chapter_09\HashRaceCondition\Bug>test.exe 1
Thread #3 done processing. Hash value was qZk+NkcGgWq6PiVxeFDCbJzQ2J0=

C:\book\code\chapter_09\HashRaceCondition\Bug>test.exe 1
Thread #3 done processing. Hash value was qZk+NkcGgWq6PiVxeFDCbJzQ2J0=
```

However, when you run the program with two threads, you start seeing different hash values sporadically. This is the telltale sign of a race condition, where the behavior of the program starts depending on the order in which the threads get to run on the CPU.

```
C:\book\code\chapter_09\HashRaceCondition\Bug>test.exe 2
Thread #3 done processing. Hash value was qZk+NkcGgWq6PiVxeFDCbJzQ2J0=
Thread #4 done processing. Hash value was qZk+NkcGgWq6PiVxeFDCbJzQ2J0=

C:\book\code\chapter_09\HashRaceCondition\Bug>test.exe 2
Thread #3 done processing. Hash value was +MHYcAb79+XMSwJsMTi8BGiD3HE=
Thread #4 done processing. Hash value was AAAAAAAAAAAAAAAAAAAAAAAAAAA=
```

In this case, some runs eventually end up with the program crashing with an unhandled .NET exception. This result is actually fortunate because it alerts you to the potential race condition even if you didn't realize the program had started behaving erratically and computing incorrect results.

```
C:\book\code\chapter_09\HashRaceCondition\Bug>test.exe 2
Thread #3 done processing. Hash value was qZk+NkcGgWq6PiVxeFDCbJzQ2J0=
Unhandled Exception: System.Security.Cryptography.CryptographicException: Hash not valid for use
in specified state.
```

There are several reasons why multiple threads cannot safely share the same hash object in .NET without additional synchronization. First, most .NET classes maintain internal state, so they aren't thread-safe unless it is explicitly stated otherwise in their documentation. Typically, this arrangement leaves the synchronization responsibilities up to the consumer of the class. Second, most popular hash functions, including the SHA-1 (pronounced "shaw one") hash function from the previous example, use a *chaining* mechanism to extend a basic compression function of a single block (64 bytes in the case of SHA-1) and turn it into a more general hashing scheme that can handle data of any size. In that sense, every hash operation is an iterative process in which the hash value is continuously updated (the *HashAlgorithm.HashUpdate* .NET method) as more blocks of data are hashed, and then eventually finalized with the last block of data (the *HashAlgorithm.HashFinal* .NET method). This means in particular that the hash algorithm implementation also keeps an internal state (the hash of the input bytes processed so far), which prevents hash objects from being shared between parallel threads of execution without applying a high-level lock over the entire hash computation operation.

Stress Testing and Reproducing Race Conditions

Just like in dealing with memory-corruption bugs, reproducing race conditions is often half the battle. Race conditions are usually hard to reproduce because the order of thread scheduling that causes the race condition to occur might be difficult to simulate in real-time execution. The smaller the time window of the race condition, the harder it becomes to hit it in a test environment. This is why increasing the number of times you execute the previous program also makes the crash more likely to occur. With a loop calling the program 10 times with 2 threads of execution in every run, for example, the hit rate is almost 100 percent.

```
C:\book\code\chapter_09\HashRaceCondition\Bug>runloop.bat test.exe 2
```

This important testing strategy is commonly known as *stress testing*. This type of testing tries to push the resource (memory, disk, CPU, and so on) consumption on a machine to the limit to simulate hard-to-reproduce conditions. It's also usually the best automated way to discover race conditions without source-code analysis, and it's one of the central strategies in ridding your code of these bugs. The Application Verifier tool can also be combined with stress runs to increase the likelihood of hitting debugger breaks during stress testing. Microsoft products, including Windows itself, are put under rigorous stress testing and usually have to pass strict quality metrics—surviving several consecutive days of stress testing being one of them—before they're finally declared ready to ship.

Simulating Race Conditions Under the Debugger

Once you suspect the presence of a race condition bug, you can use the Windows debuggers to simulate the conditions leading up to the failure. For example, by using the *~f* and *~u* (freeze and unfreeze threads) debugger commands covered in Chapter 7, "Expert Debugging Tricks," you can control the order in which threads are scheduled on the processor relative to each other. Once you identify a sequence that consistently leads to the race condition, you can prepare a debugger script and have a consistent way of reproducing the bug by replaying the script back inside the debugger. This allows you to quickly test your attempts at fixing the code bug and verify whether the program runs successfully after applying your fix.

You can apply this technique with the hash function example used at the start of this section. One way to force the race condition to happen consistently in the case of two worker threads is to stop one of them while it's in the middle of its hash operation, have the other thread run until it finalizes the hash value, and then resume the first thread before the second one has a chance to reset the Crypto API hash handle. The following script captures this sequence and will cause the program to fail every time.

```
$$
$$ C:\book\code\chapter_09\HashRaceCondition\Bug>RaceRepro.txt
$$
.symfix
.reload
bp advapi32!CryptHashData
bp advapi32!CryptCreateHash
$$ The first breakpoint is CryptCreateHash (constructor)
g
$$ The first thread hits CryptHashData (ComputeHash)
g
$$ Now freeze the first thread before continuing the hash operation
~f
$$ The next breakpoint is CryptHashData in the second thread
g
$$ Let the second thread complete the hash operation
g
$$ You've now hit CryptCreateHash: The second thread is re-initializing the
$$ hash object after the hash operation is over. Freeze the second thread now
$$ and unfreeze the first thread so it sees the hash in this finalized state.
~*u
~f
g
g
$$ You will always hit a managed code exception here
.loadby sos clr
!pe
```

This causes the first thread to try to use a Crypto API hash handle in the *finalized* state, which causes the Win32 function call to fail. This failure then gets remapped in the Microsoft .NET Framework to a managed-code exception, which is precisely the exception displayed by the *!pe* (print managed exception) SOS debugger extension command at the end of the previous debugger script. You now have a 100 percent reproduction of the failure.

```
C:\book\code\chapter_09\HashRaceCondition\Bug>"c:\Program Files\Debugging Tools for Windows
(x86)\windbg.exe" -c "$$>< racerepro.txt" test.exe 2
Processing initial command '$$>< racerepro.txt'
0:000> $$>< racerepro.txt
Reloading current modules
.....
Exception object: 028ba09c
Exception type: System.Security.Cryptography.CryptographicException
Message: Hash not valid for use in specified state.
...
```

Shared-State Consistency Bugs: A Few Suggested Fixes

The race condition example shown in this section can be avoided by assigning a dedicated hash object to each worker thread, or alternatively by using a lock to ensure no two threads are ever using the global singleton hash instance simultaneously while it's in the middle of a hash operation. These are essentially two extremes, though: the former requires the creation and destruction of an object for every thread. The latter forfeits any benefits you could get on a multicore machine. A better, more scalable, solution is to use the *object pooling* design pattern.

An object pool is a collection of objects that can be checked out from the pool and assigned to a thread to complete a certain operation and later returned to the pool in a reusable state once the worker thread is done using it. This design pattern can lead to better scalability when the act of resetting an object to a reusable state is cheaper than creating a brand new instance, and when the problem can benefit from parallelism at the same time. When using an object pool, it's typical to cap the number of objects in the pool to a predefined maximum limit. An implementation of this idea can be found in this book's companion source code, where the following generic C# object pool class is used to safely share a collection of .NET hash objects among multiple threads in the program.

```
//
// C:\book\code\chapter_09\HashRaceCondition\Fix>objectpool.cs
//
class ObjectPool<T>
    where T : class, new()
{
    public ObjectPool(
        int capacity
        )
    {
...
        m_objects = new Stack<T>(capacity);
```

```
        //
        // objects will be lazily created only as needed
        //
        for (n = 0; n < capacity; n++)
        {
            m_objects.Push(null);
        }
        m_objectsLock = new object();
        m_semaphore = new Semaphore(capacity, capacity);
    }

    public T GetObject()
    {
        T obj;

        m_semaphore.WaitOne();

        lock (m_objectsLock)
        {
            obj = m_objects.Pop();
        }

        if (obj == null)
        {
            obj = new T(); // delay-create the object
        }
        return obj;
    }

    public void ReleaseObject(
        T obj
        )
    {
...
        lock (m_objectsLock)
        {
            m_objects.Push(obj);
        }
        //
        // Signal that one more object is available in the pool
        //
        m_semaphore.Release();
    }

    private Stack<T> m_objects;
    private object m_objectsLock;
    private Semaphore m_semaphore;
}
```

Notice that the same stress test used earlier to show the race condition is now successful when using this generic class to implement concurrent, but synchronized use of the hash objects in the pool.

```
C:\book\code\chapter_09\HashRaceCondition\Fix>runloop.bat test.exe 2
...
Thread #3 done processing. Hash value was qZk+NkcGgWq6PiVxeFDCbJzQ2J0=
Thread #4 done processing. Hash value was qZk+NkcGgWq6PiVxeFDCbJzQ2J0=
Test completed in 16 ms
```

Shared-State Lifetime Management Bugs

Accessing shared state from worker threads requires careful management of the lifetime of that state relative to that of the threads consuming it, whether the state is an explicit thread context or global variables.

This category of race conditions is specific to native code. Worker threads in .NET can also be provided with an explicit shared state (opaque object) when they're created or use static (global) variables, but because the Common Language Runtime's (CLR) garbage collector automatically manages the lifetime of those objects and ensures they're not collected as long as they remain "rooted" by one of the threads in the managed process, the issues discussed in this section aren't a concern that .NET programmers need to worry about.

Thread Context Lifetime and Reference Counting

When you manually create a new thread in C/C++, you can use an opaque pointer variable (*lpParameter*) to share a context state with the new thread. When doing so, however, you should always remember that if this state is destroyed before the new thread callback routine is done using it; you end up with unpredictable crashes in your program, depending on the exact timing of when the state is destroyed. Consider the following C++ sample from this book's companion source code.

```
//
// C:\book\code\chapter_09\ThreadCtxLifetime\Bug>main.cpp
//
static
HRESULT
MainHR(
    VOID
    )
{
    CAutoPtr<CThreadParams> spParameter;
    CHandle shThreads[NUM_THREADS];
    int n;

    ChkProlog();
```

```
    spParameter.Attach(new CThreadParams());
    ChkAlloc(spParameter);
    ChkHr(spParameter->Init(L"Hello World!"));

    //
    // Create new worker threads with non-ref counted shared state
    //
    for (n = 0; n < ARRAYSIZE(shThreads); n++)
    {
        shThreads[n].Attach(::CreateThread(
            NULL, 0, WorkerThread, spParameter, 0, NULL));
        ChkWin32(shThreads[n]);
    }

    //
    // Do not Wait for the worker threads to exit
    //    DWORD nWait = WaitForMultipleObjects(ARRAYSIZE(shThreads),
    //        (HANDLE*)shThreads, TRUE, INFINITE);
    //    ChkWin32(nWait != WAIT_FAILED);
    //
    Sleep(10);

    ChkNoCleanup();
}
```

This code will probably appear to work as expected on a few runs of the program, but it has a serious race condition bug. Because the smart pointer holding the *spParameter* memory address will be destroyed when the *MainHR* function exits, its usage inside the worker-thread callback routines is unsafe. If you run the program enough times, you'll notice a few runs where the printed messages appear to be composed of garbage characters—the telltale sign of a memory corruption.

```
C:\book\code\chapter_09\ThreadCtxLifetime\Bug>objfre_win7_x86\i386\NoRefCountingBug.exe
Test message... Hello World!
Test message... Hello World!
Test message... Hello World!
Test message... Hello World!
Test message... Äello World!
Test message... Äello World!
Success.
Test message... okkkk
```

Now that you suspect a memory corruption is in play, you should enable the Application Verifier's basic hooks for this process image (*NoRefCountingBug.exe*), as demonstrated in Figure 9-1, so that you increase the likelihood of catching the memory corruption as an access violation, as you learned in the previous chapter.

```
C:\Windows\System32>appverif.exe
```

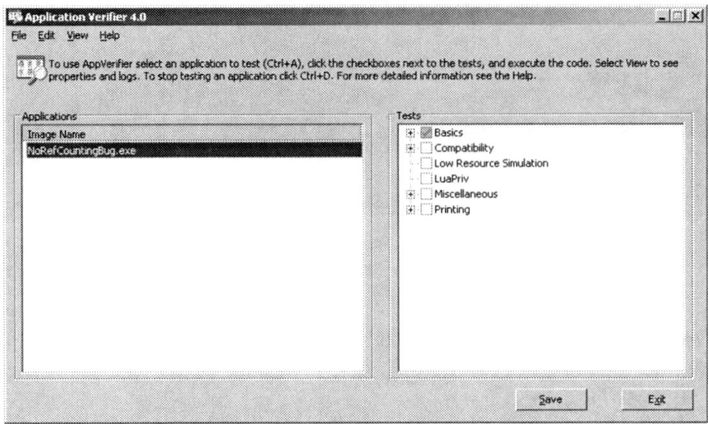

FIGURE 9-1 Catching the memory corruption as an access violation using the Application Verifier tool.

You'll now see the following access violation call stack when you run the program using the WinDbg debugger.

```
C:\book\code\chapter_09\ThreadCtxLifetime\Bug>"C:\Program Files\Debugging Tools for Windows
(x86)\windbg.exe" objfre_win7_x86\i386\NoRefCountingBug.exe
...
0:000> g
(cc0.1f80): Access violation - code c0000005 (first chance)
0:011> .symfix
0:011> .reload
0:011> k
ChildEBP RetAddr
033bfcfc 75e35e29 msvcrt!_woutput_l+0x98b
033bfd44 00031329 msvcrt!wprintf+0x5f
033bfd54 73f942f7 NoRefCountingBug!CMainApp::WorkerThread+0x15 [c:\book\code\chapter_09\
threadctxlifetime\bug\main.cpp @ 48]
0307fefc 7710ed6c vfbasics!AVrfpStandardThreadFunction+0x2f
0307ff08 7766377b kernel32!BaseThreadInitThunk+0xe
0307ff48 7766374e ntdll!__RtlUserThreadStart+0x70
0307ff60 00000000 ntdll!_RtlUserThreadStart+0x1b
```

By using the *!analyze* extension command, you'll see that the memory access violation was due to an attempt to read from noncommitted memory while trying to print the freed string buffer field from the shared *CThreadParams* structure—a structure that was destroyed earlier when it went out of scope at the exit of the *MainHR* function.

```
0:001> !analyze -v
...
ExceptionAddress: 7502ba16 (msvcrt!_woutput_l+0x0000098b)
   ExceptionCode: c0000005 (Access violation)
  ExceptionFlags: 00000000
NumberParameters: 2
   Parameter[0]: 00000000
   Parameter[1]: 06988fe0
Attempt to read from address 06988fe0
...
```

```
0:001> db 06988fe0
06988fe0  ?? ?? ?? ?? ?? ?? ?? ??-?? ?? ?? ?? ?? ?? ?? ??  ????????????????
...
0:001> $ Terminate this debugging session now...
0:001> q
```

There are a couple of ways to fix the race condition from the previous example:

- The first solution is to uncomment the two lines at the end of the *MainHR* code listing and use the *WaitForMultipleObjects* API to wait for the worker threads to complete before allowing the *MainHR* function to exit and the shared state to be destroyed.

- If waiting for the worker threads at the end of *MainHR* isn't the behavior you want, an alternative solution is to use reference counting. This generic technique is typically used to manage lifetime when a shared resource has multiple logical owners. It's applied, for instance, in COM to manage the lifetime of COM objects and server modules and lends itself well to state lifetime management in multithreaded applications too.

In this case, the worker threads need to keep the shared state alive until they're done using it. So, you can increment a reference count before the shared state is handed over to a new thread and decrement it at the time the respective thread callback exits, ensuring the state is deleted from memory only after the last thread releases its reference to it while exiting. The changes to fix the code shown earlier in this section are minimal.

```
//
// C:\book\code\chapter_09\ThreadCtxLifetime\Fix>main.cpp
//
static
DWORD
WINAPI
WorkerThread(
    __in LPVOID lpParameter
    )
{
    //
    // The reference count is automatically decremented when the callback exits
    // thanks to the CComPtr ATL smart pointer calling Release in its destructor
    //
    CComPtr<CThreadParams> spRefCountedParameter;
    spRefCountedParameter.Attach(reinterpret_cast<CThreadParams*>(lpParameter));

    wprintf(L"Test message... %s\n", spRefCountedParameter->m_spMessage);
    return EXIT_SUCCESS;
}
```

```
static
HRESULT
MainHR(
    VOID
    )

{
    CThreadParams* pRefCountedParameter;
    CComPtr<CThreadParams> spRefCountedParameter;
    CHandle shThreads[NUM_THREADS];
    DWORD dwLastError;
    int n;

    ChkProlog();

    spRefCountedParameter.Attach(new CThreadParams());
    ChkAlloc(spRefCountedParameter);
    pRefCountedParameter = static_cast<CThreadParams*>(spRefCountedParameter);
    ChkHr(spRefCountedParameter->Init(L"Hello World!"));

    //
    // Create new worker threads with reference-counted shared state
    //
    for (n = 0; n < ARRAYSIZE(shThreads); n++)
    {
        pRefCountedParameter->AddRef();
        shThreads[n].Attach(::CreateThread(
            NULL, 0, WorkerThread, pRefCountedParameter, 0, NULL));
        dwLastError = ::GetLastError();
        if (shThreads[n] == NULL)
        {
            pRefCountedParameter->Release();
        }
        ChkBool(shThreads[n], HRESULT_FROM_WIN32(dwLastError));
    }

    ChkNoCleanup();
}
```

The key to this implementation was the following reference-counting C++ class, from which the *CThreadParams* shared context was made to derive so that it could support the *AddRef* and *Release* operations needed for reference counting.

```
//
// C:\book\code\chapter_09\ThreadCtxLifetime\Fix>refcountimpl.h
//
class CRefCountImpl
{
public:
    //
    // Declare a virtual destructor to ensure that derived classes
    // will be destroyed properly
    //
    virtual
    ~CRefCountImpl() {}

    CRefCountImpl() : m_nRefs(1) {}

    VOID
    AddRef()
    {
        InterlockedIncrement(&m_nRefs);
    }

    VOID
    Release()
    {
        if (0 == InterlockedDecrement(&m_nRefs))
        {
            delete this;
        }
    }

private:
    LONG m_nRefs;
};

//
// C:\book\code\chapter_09\ThreadCtxLifetime\Fix>main.cpp
//
class CThreadParams :
    CZeroInit<CThreadParams>,
    public CRefCountImpl
{
...
```

To close this experiment, you can now run this version of the program and observe that it no longer hits the race condition or access violation. The number of messages displayed by the program still varies from one run to the next, depending on how many callbacks got to run before the main thread in the program exited and the process terminated, but the memory backing the shared state referenced in those callbacks is never deleted while they're still in progress.

```
C:\book\code\chapter_09\ThreadCtxLifetime\Fix>objfre_win7_x86\i386\CorrectRefCounting.exe
Test message... Hello World!
Test message... Hello World!
Test message... Hello World!
Success.
Test message... Hello World!
Test message... Hello World!
```

Global Variables in Worker Threads and the Process Rundown Sequence

Worker threads that are created for you by system components, such as the NT thread pool and the Remote Procedure Call (RPC) or COM runtime code, often need to use global (or static) variables because you don't create those threads or post their callbacks explicitly, which also means that you can't provide them with a state object. This section details why synchronization of the process rundown and thread-termination events is important to understand whenever global variables are used to hold state for worker threads. Just like the previous section, this issue applies only to native code, where global memory is freed by the C runtime library during the process rundown sequence.

All the (DLL and EXE) global and static C++ objects get destroyed automatically by the C runtime library before the process exits. If the process has worker threads still attempting to access that shared state after that point, access violations can occur as a result of the invalid memory access. The simplest way to avoid this problem is to wait for all the worker threads to finish their callbacks before letting the process exit. However, this is not always desirable, especially with worker threads whose callbacks aren't immediately cancelable. In some cases, a worker thread might be in the middle of an expensive, synchronous, third-party network API call that doesn't support cancellation, and you might not want to block the process exit waiting for it to complete. If you decide to solve this problem by simply abandoning the ongoing work in the worker thread and proceeding to exit the process anyway, you must understand how the rundown performed by the C runtime library fits in the DLL and process rundown sequence, and you need to take precautions so that your worker threads never try to access freed global or static objects.

When you use the C runtime library, the Microsoft Visual C++ compiler wraps your entry point function (*wmain*) in a C runtime-provided entry point (*__wmainCRTStartup*). The same is also true for DLL modules, where your *DllMain* entry point is also wrapped by a C runtime entry point for DLL modules. These C runtime entry points are responsible for initializing the C++ global and static objects in the module before calling your entry points. The main executable's C runtime entry point is also responsible for initiating the process rundown sequence right after your main function exits. This is done by calling *msvcrt!exit*, which performs the necessary shutdown tasks for the process, as illustrated in Figure 9-2.

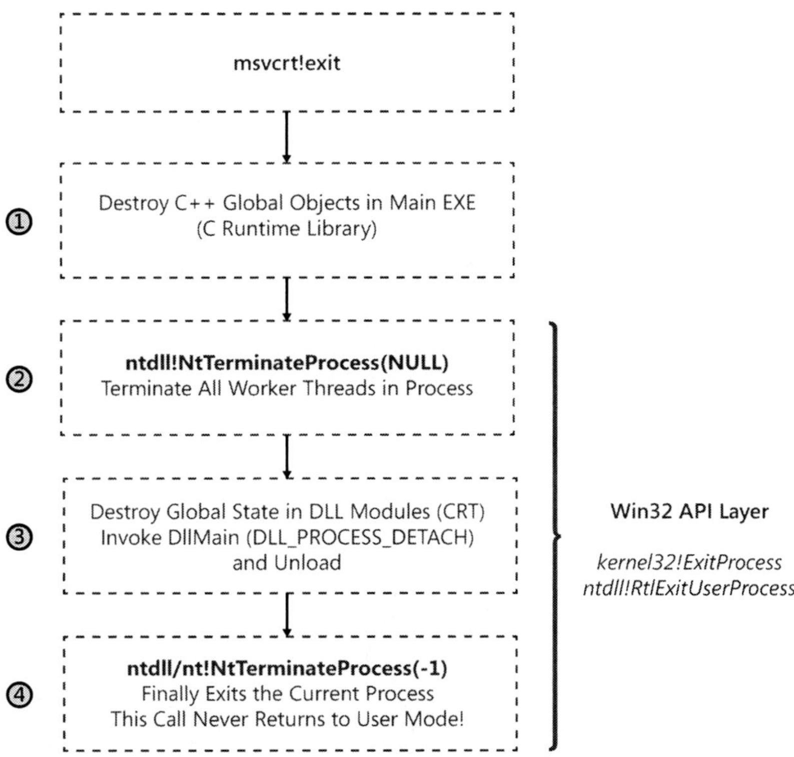

FIGURE 9-2 C++ global state destruction during the process rundown sequence.

As you can see in the previous diagram, the DLL and main EXE's global C++ objects are destroyed at different points during the process rundown sequence. The following two observations are worth noting:

- Global and static C++ objects in the main executable are destroyed *before* the worker threads in the process are terminated (steps 1 and 2 in the previous diagram). This means that you can't have dangling threads trying to access these global variables from the main executable. You need to write code in your worker threads to refrain from touching the main EXE's global state once the process shutdown is initiated. In addition, you need to add code in your main executable to inform the worker threads (via a global Boolean variable and an *InterlockedExchange* assignment, for instance) when the process is about to exit.
- The situation is less hazardous with global and static C++ objects from DLL modules. This is because the global state in DLL modules loaded into the process is destroyed only after the worker threads have been terminated (step 3 in the previous diagram). At that time, only the main thread in the process will be running, and it won't try to use any state from the DLL modules, given that it's right in the middle of finishing the rundown sequence and finally exiting the process. Note, however, that because all the worker threads got abruptly terminated during step 2, the C++ destructors from DLL modules that run later in step 3 should not make any assumptions about the state in which the objects happen to be when they're invoked. Fortunately, this *reverse hazard* isn't a common bug in practice because well-written C++ destructors don't make assumptions about invariants in the objects they free.

The companion source code contains an example of a race condition bug illustrating the first point I just listed, where dangling threads are left running during the process rundown and cause an access violation by using a global C++ object from the main executable after it has been destroyed by the C runtime library.

```
//
// C:\book\code\chapter_09\ExeGlobalsLifetime>bug.cpp
//
class CMainApp
{
private:
    static
    DWORD
    WINAPI
    WorkerThread(
        __in LPVOID lpParameter
        )
    {
        CThreadParams* pParameter =
            reinterpret_cast<CThreadParams*>(lpParameter);
        wprintf(L"Test message... %s\n", pParameter->m_spMessage);
        return EXIT_SUCCESS;
    }

public:
    static
    HRESULT
    MainHR()
    {
        CHandle shThreads[NUM_THREADS];
        int n;

        ChkProlog();

        ChkHr(g_params.Init(L"Hello World!"));
        for (n = 0; n < ARRAYSIZE(shThreads); n++)
        {
            shThreads[n].Attach(::CreateThread(
                NULL, 0, WorkerThread, &g_params, 0, NULL));
            ChkWin32(shThreads[n]);
        }
        //
        // Do not Wait for the worker threads to exit...
        //
        ChkNoCleanup();
    }

private:
    static const NUM_THREADS = 64;
    static CThreadParams g_params;
};
```

After enabling the Application Verifier tool for this test application (*bug.exe*), you'll get an access-violation exception in the same call stack you saw earlier when a thread context that wasn't properly reference-counted was used, except in this case the worker thread faults while trying to access the freed global C++ object holding the shared state.

```
C:\book\code\chapter_09\ExeGlobalsLifetime>"c:\Program Files\Debugging Tools for Windows
(x86)\windbg.exe" objfre_win7_x86\i386\bug.exe
...
0:000> g
(e90.1404): Access violation - code c0000005 (first chance)
...
0:030> .symfix
0:030> .reload
0:030> k
ChildEBP RetAddr
0336f718 75f95e29 msvcrt!_woutput_l+0x98b
0336f760 00e913b9 msvcrt!wprintf+0x5f
0336f770 71fb42f7 bug!CMainApp::WorkerThread+0x15
[c:\book\code\chapter_09\exeglobalslifetime\bug.cpp @ 48]
0336f7a8 7590ed6c vfbasics!AVrfpStandardThreadFunction+0x2f
...
```

Notice that the main thread (thread #0) in the process is deep in the middle of the rundown sequence—right in between steps 1 and 2 from the previous diagram—which explains the access violation, given that the global C++ object from the main executable had already been destroyed earlier in the *msvcrt!exit* function.

```
0:030> ~0s
0:000> $ Thread #0 is inside msvcrt!exit
0:000> k
ChildEBP RetAddr
0019f608 77456a24 ntdll!KiFastSystemCallRet
0019f60c 77442264 ntdll!NtWaitForSingleObject+0xc
0019f670 77442148 ntdll!RtlpWaitOnCriticalSection+0x13e
0019f698 77468ce6 ntdll!RtlEnterCriticalSection+0x150
0019f808 77468b10 ntdll!LdrGetDllHandleEx+0x2f7
0019f824 756689cc ntdll!LdrGetDllHandle+0x18
0019f878 756688ca KERNELBASE!GetModuleHandleForUnicodeString+0x22
0019fcf0 7566899a KERNELBASE!BasepGetModuleHandleExW+0x181
0019fd08 75f836f2 KERNELBASE!GetModuleHandleW+0x29
0019fd14 75f836d2 msvcrt!__crtCorExitProcess+0x10
0019fd20 75f83371 msvcrt!__crtExitProcess+0xd
0019fd58 75f836bb msvcrt!_cinit+0xea
0019fd6c 00e918da msvcrt!exit+0x11
0019fda8 7590ed6c bug!__wmainCRTStartup+0x118
0019fdb4 774737f5 kernel32!BaseThreadInitThunk+0xe
0019fdf4 774737c8 ntdll!__RtlUserThreadStart+0x70
0019fe0c 00000000 ntdll!_RtlUserThreadStart+0x1b
0:000> $ Terminate this debugging session now...
0:000> q
```

DLL Module Lifetime-Management Bugs

If your worker threads execute code that's hosted in a DLL, you must ensure that the DLL module is never unloaded while the thread callbacks are still in progress. This sounds obvious, but remember that you're not always in control of the environment (hosting process) into which the DLL modules you write get loaded. For example, you might be writing an API for use by other developers. The danger lies in the fact that your callers can invoke your API by dynamically loading the DLL hosting it. If that API internally starts new worker threads to complete its work asynchronously, and the code consuming it then unknowingly proceeds to unload the hosting DLL—something it's perfectly entitled to do because the fact that your API uses new threads is really an internal implementation detail—the worker threads are left executing unloaded memory, resulting in an immediate access violation.

To see this race condition bug in action, consider the following C++ host program from the companion source code, which loads a DLL and calls an exported API that spawns multiple threads to print "Hello World!" messages.

```
//
// C:\book\code\chapter_09\DllLifetimeRaceCondition\host>main.cpp
//
static
HRESULT
MainHR(
    __in int argc,
    __in_ecount(argc) WCHAR* argv[]
    )
{
    HMODULE hModule = NULL;
    PFN_AsynchronousCall pfnAsynchronousCall;

    ChkProlog();
...
    hModule = ::LoadLibraryW(argv[1]);
    ChkWin32(hModule);

    pfnAsynchronousCall = (PFN_AsynchronousCall) GetProcAddress(
        hModule, "AsynchronousCall");
    ChkBool(pfnAsynchronousCall, E_FAIL);

    ChkHr(pfnAsynchronousCall());

    ChkCleanup();

    if (hModule)
    {
        FreeLibrary(hModule);
    }

    ChkEpilog();
}
```

Unfortunately, because the *FreeLibrary* API call in the previous program can unload the DLL hosting the API while the worker threads are still executing, this program results in an access violation except in rare cases where the worker-thread callbacks finish their work before the *MainHR* function unloads the DLL in its cleanup section.

```
0:000> vercommand
command line: '"c:\Program Files\Debugging Tools for Windows (x86)\windbg.exe"
C:\book\code\chapter_09\DllLifetimeRaceCondition\host\objfre_win7_x86\i386\host.exe
C:\book\code\chapter_09\DllLifetimeRaceCondition\bug\objfre_win7_x86\i386\test.dll'
0:000> .symfix
0:000> .reload
0:000> g
<Unloaded_test.dll>+0x1369:
71fa1369 ??              ???
0:007> .lastevent
Last event: 3d8.13f4: Access violation - code c0000005 (first chance)
```

Debugging Unloaded Code

When you're faced with situations involving unloaded code, the call stack that the debugger displays by default won't be all that helpful. In this case, notice that the *k* command shows meaningless frames from a module called *unloaded_test.dll* at the top of the call stack. This is because the access violation is from an attempt to execute code from the *test.dll* module after it was unloaded, which you're able to confirm by using the *lm* ("list modules") command. As a result, the debugger isn't able to resolve those code addresses to valid symbols.

```
0:007> k
ChildEBP RetAddr
0087fc8c 71fa1160 <Unloaded_test.dll>+0x1369
0087fc98 7590ed6c <Unloaded_test.dll>+0x1160
0087fca4 774737f5 kernel32!BaseThreadInitThunk+0xe
0087fce4 774737c8 ntdll!__RtlUserThreadStart+0x70
0087fcfc 00000000 ntdll!_RtlUserThreadStart+0x1b
0:007> lm
start    end        module name
00070000 00075000   host       (deferred)
75660000 756aa000   KERNELBASE   (deferred)
...
Unloaded modules:
72d90000 72d95000   test.dll
```

It's not clear yet what code was being executed when the access violation was raised. To see the proper call stack, you can reload the symbols corresponding to the unloaded *test.dll* module using the */unl* switch of the regular *.reload* command ("reload unloaded symbols"), as shown in the following listing. Notice that you're then able to see the precise call stack at the time of the exception, which indicates that the crash occurred while executing the *WorkerThread* callback routine.

```
0:007> .sympath+ C:\book\code\chapter_09\DllLifetimeRaceCondition\bug\objfre_win7_x86\i386
0:007> .reload /unl test.dll
0:007> k
ChildEBP RetAddr
0087fc98 7590ed6c test!CMainApp::WorkerThread+0x15
```

```
[c:\book\code\chapter_09\dlllifetimeracecondition\bug\test.cpp @ 48]
0087fca4 774737f5 kernel32!BaseThreadInitThunk+0xe
0087fce4 774737c8 ntdll!__RtlUserThreadStart+0x70
0087fcfc 00000000 ntdll!_RtlUserThreadStart+0x1b
```

Note that because the *test.dll* module was unloaded, the debugger doesn't know the base directory of the image (which it usually is able to extract automatically for the loaded modules) or where to automatically find its corresponding PDB symbol file. This is why the first command in the previous listing added the location of the symbol file to the symbols search path so that the debugger could successfully locate it when resolving addresses on the call stack.

Notice that the *lpParameter* local variable in the *WorkerThread* callback also points to invalid memory. The *ln* command, which lists the nearest symbol to a raw virtual address and is often useful when debugging unloaded code, is able to map that address (exactly) to the *g_params* global variable. Given that the DLL was already unloaded, its global variables are also invalid and reside in de-committed memory.

```
0:007> $ Display the local variables in scope
0:007> dv
    lpParameter = 0x72d93038
0:007> db 0x72d93038
72d93038  ?? ?? ?? ?? ?? ?? ?? ??-?? ?? ?? ?? ?? ?? ?? ??  ????????????????
0:007> $ List the nearest symbol to the (unloaded) address in question
0:007> ln 0x72d93038
(72d93038)   test!CMainApp::g_params   |  (72d9303c)   test!__proc_attached
Exact matches:
    test!CMainApp::g_params = class CThreadParams
0:007> $ Terminate this debugging session now...
0:007> q
```

DLL Module Lifetime-Management Bugs: A Few Suggested Fixes

The best way to handle the problem described in this section is probably to avoid hiding the asynchronous nature of your APIs behind synchronous-looking signatures. If your API does asynchronous processing by starting background threads, it's best to reflect that in your API design so that your callers have an idea of what to expect when they use your framework.

That being said, there is a way to fix the problem even if you were really bent on keeping the API signature unchanged. The idea behind this fix, again, is to use reference counting—only this time, you keep track of references to the DLL module itself. You increment the reference count of the DLL module by calling *LoadLibrary* every time a new background thread is created by your API, and you then have the worker-thread callback routine decrement it upon its exit by using the atomic *FreeLibraryAndExitThread* Win32 API call. It's critical that you use this atomic call to free the library and exit the thread as part of the same transaction, as opposed to calling *FreeLibrary* followed by *ExitThread*. This way, control is never returned to the callback even if the backing DLL module gets unloaded from memory as its reference count drops down to 0 from the *FreeLibrary* call!

There are a few additional considerations you should also remember when using this scheme:

- No code after the call to *FreeLibraryAndExitThread* in the callbacks ever gets to run. In particular, this includes C++ destructors for smart-pointer variables destroyed at the end of the thread callback function. So, you need to ensure that the necessary cleanup occurs before you issue the call to unload the library and exit the thread.
- It's important to *pin* the DLL module synchronously before your API call returns to the caller. This means incrementing the DLL reference count cannot happen inside the worker-thread callbacks. That would be too late, and the caller could unload the DLL before the module is pinned in memory, again leading to an access violation inside the callbacks.
- This scheme should be used only if you're creating the threads manually. If you're posting your work into one of the threads in the NT thread pool, the threads aren't yours to exit! This is why the Win32 thread-pool API gives you an easy way of asking the system to pin the DLL module for your callbacks as long as they're executing. To do so, you can simply call the *SetThreadPoolCallbackLibrary* API. The thread pool implementation inside the *ntdll.dll* system module then automatically takes care of managing the references to the DLL library hosting your callbacks.

The companion source code contains an implementation of this idea. Notice that this new version of the API is now immune to the caller freeing the backing DLL module handle while the worker threads are still in progress.

```
C:\book\code\chapter_09\DllLifetimeRaceCondition>host\objfre_win7_x86\i386\host.exe
Fix\objfre_win7_x86\i386\test.dll
Test message... Hello World!
Test message... Hello World!
Test message... Hello World!
Test message... Hello World!
Test message... Hello World!
Success.
```

Debugging Deadlocks

One solution for fixing state-consistency race conditions is to establish exclusive access to the affected shared state by using *locks*. If used incorrectly, though, locks can also introduce a new set of programming bugs, most prominently *deadlock* conditions. This section contains examples to introduce you to this category of bugs and also shows you how to effectively debug these conditions so that you can eliminate them in the software you ship.

A *deadlock* is a condition in which two or more threads of execution get stalled waiting to unblock each other. Deadlock bugs can also be race conditions that happen only under the right lock-acquisition and thread-scheduling order, which sometimes makes them hard to reproduce. The good news, however, is that once you get a reproducible case, debuggers are usually the perfect tool to inspect the threads involved in the deadlock and discover how they might have reached the deadlock condition.

Lock-Ordering Deadlocks

A basic deadlock scenario is when two threads mistakenly acquire locks in reverse order, and then wait on each other to release the lock that the other thread is already holding. This case is demonstrated in the following C++ program from the companion source code, which starts two worker threads that then proceed to acquire two critical sections in reverse order.

```
//
// C:\book\code\chapter_09\Deadlocks\MultiLockDeadlock>main.cpp
//
static
DWORD
WINAPI
WorkerThread(
    __in LPVOID lpParameter
    )
{
    CThreadParams* pParameter;
    CWin32CriticalSectionHolder autoLockOne, autoLockTwo;

    pParameter = reinterpret_cast<CThreadParams*>(lpParameter);
    InterlockedIncrement(&(pParameter->m_nThreadsStarted));
    wprintf(L"Thread #%d Callback.\n", pParameter->m_nThreadsStarted);

    if (pParameter->m_nThreadsStarted % 2 == 0)
    {
        autoLockOne.Lock(pParameter->m_csOne);
        wprintf(L"One-Two locking order...\n");
        Sleep(1000);
        autoLockTwo.Lock(pParameter->m_csTwo);
    }
    else
    {
        autoLockTwo.Lock(pParameter->m_csTwo);
        wprintf(L"Two-One locking order...\n");
        Sleep(1000);
        autoLockOne.Lock(pParameter->m_csOne);
    }
    return EXIT_SUCCESS;
}
```

You'll notice that the program seems to run to completion in certain tries but sometimes also hangs indefinitely.

```
C:\book\code\chapter_09\Deadlocks\MultiLockDeadlock>objfre_win7_x86\i386\bug.exe
Thread #1 Callback.
Two-One locking order...
Thread #2 Callback.
One-Two locking order...
^C
```

Debugging the Deadlock Condition

To debug the hang condition, you can either run the process directly under the debugger or attach a debugger after running the program in standalone mode and notice that its progress appears to stall indefinitely. In both cases, you'll see three total threads in the process (plus the *break-in* thread if you're trying the attach case). The main thread (thread #0) will be waiting on the other two worker threads to exit their callback routines, but those two threads (thread #1 and thread #2) both seem to be waiting (seemingly forever) to acquire a critical section, as shown in the following listing.

```
0:003> .symfix
0:003> .reload
0:003> ~*k
   0  Id: 4dc.b58 Suspend: 1 Teb: 7ffde000 Unfrozen
ChildEBP RetAddr
000bfcf0 77456a04 ntdll!KiFastSystemCallRet
000bfcf4 75666a36 ntdll!ZwWaitForMultipleObjects+0xc
000bfd90 7590bd1e KERNELBASE!WaitForMultipleObjectsEx+0x100
000bfdd8 7590bd8c kernel32!WaitForMultipleObjectsExImplementation+0xe0
000bfdf4 0005185d kernel32!WaitForMultipleObjects+0x18
000bfe5c 000518b7 bug!CMainApp::MainHR+0x65
000bfe60 00051a41 bug!wmain+0x5
...
   1  Id: 4dc.1ddc Suspend: 1 Teb: 7ffdd000 Unfrozen
ChildEBP RetAddr
004bfc9c 77456a24 ntdll!KiFastSystemCallRet
004bfca0 77442264 ntdll!NtWaitForSingleObject+0xc
004bfd04 77442148 ntdll!RtlpWaitOnCriticalSection+0x13e
004bfd2c 00051491 ntdll!RtlEnterCriticalSection+0x150
004bfd3c 000516a2 bug!CWin32CriticalSectionHolder::Lock+0x1f
004bfd64 7590ed6c bug!CMainApp::WorkerThread+0x9d
...
   2  Id: 4dc.1f04 Suspend: 1 Teb: 7ffdc000 Unfrozen
ChildEBP RetAddr
002cf88c 77456a24 ntdll!KiFastSystemCallRet
002cf890 77442264 ntdll!NtWaitForSingleObject+0xc
002cf8f4 77442148 ntdll!RtlpWaitOnCriticalSection+0x13e
002cf91c 00051491 ntdll!RtlEnterCriticalSection+0x150
002cf92c 000516a2 bug!CWin32CriticalSectionHolder::Lock+0x1f
002cf954 7590ed6c bug!CMainApp::WorkerThread+0x9d
...
#  3  Id: 4dc.1bc4 Suspend: 1 Teb: 7ffdb000 Unfrozen
ChildEBP RetAddr
0046f9b4 774af161 ntdll!DbgBreakPoint
0046f9e4 7590ed6c ntdll!DbgUiRemoteBreakin+0x3c
...
```

The *!cs* Debugger Extension Command

You can use the *!cs* debugger command to dump the critical sections that threads #1 and #2 are waiting on in the previous listing. The address of the two critical sections can be found by following the frame pointers for the *RtlEnterCriticalSection* call frames, respectively. The first parameter to that function is the critical section that the thread is trying to acquire (enter). For thread #1, for instance, you'll see that the critical section that it's trying to enter is already held (LOCKED) by thread #2. Notice in the following listing that, indeed, the owning thread given by the *!cs* extension command matches the client ID (Cid) of thread #2, which you can find by using the ~ debugger command that lists the active threads in the process.

```
0:003> $ Saved EBP, followed by the return address and then the first argument
0:003> dd 004bfd2c
004bfd2c  004bfd3c 00051491 000bfe18 000bfe50
0:003> !cs 000bfe18
Critical section   = 0x000bfe18 (+0xBFE18)
DebugInfo          = 0x0013b2a0
LOCKED
LockCount          = 0x1
WaiterWoken        = No
OwningThread       = 0x00001f04
RecursionCount     = 0x1
LockSemaphore      = 0x3C
SpinCount          = 0x00000000
0:003> $ ~ lists all the threads in the process, along with their respective client ID (CID)
0:003> ~
   0  Id: 4dc.b58 Suspend: 1 Teb: 7ffde000 Unfrozen
   1  Id: 4dc.1ddc Suspend: 1 Teb: 7ffdd000 Unfrozen
   2  Id: 4dc.1f04 Suspend: 1 Teb: 7ffdc000 Unfrozen
.  3  Id: 4dc.1bc4 Suspend: 1 Teb: 7ffdb000 Unfrozen
```

Similarly, you can verify that the owning thread field of the critical section that thread #2 is waiting on corresponds to the thread client ID (Cid) of thread #1 in the process. This fully explains the reason for the deadlock. It also suggests why it doesn't happen consistently because the condition that leads to it requires both threads to be preempted right after entering the first critical section but before entering the second one.

You can also look at the fields from the _RTL_CRITICAL_SECTION structure directly by using the *dt* ("dump type") debugger command, given that type is included in the symbols shipped by Microsoft for the *ntdll.dll* system module.

```
0:003> dt ntdll!_RTL_CRITICAL_SECTION 000bfe18
   +0x000 DebugInfo        : 0x0013b2a0 _RTL_CRITICAL_SECTION_DEBUG
   +0x004 LockCount        : 0n-6
   +0x008 RecursionCount   : 0n1
   +0x00c OwningThread     : 0x00001f04 Void
   +0x010 LockSemaphore    : 0x0000003c Void
   +0x014 SpinCount        : 0
0:003> $ The LockSemaphore field is in fact an event, not a semaphore
0:003> !handle 3c f
Handle 3c
  Type             Event
...
  Name             <none>
  Object Specific Information
    Event Type Auto Reset
    Event is Waiting
```

As you've probably already guessed, the *!cs* command is simply a helper command that parses the critical section structure and conveniently interprets the meaning of its fields, just as you were able to do manually in the previous listing.

```
0:003> $ Terminate this debugging session now...
0:003> q
```

Because of how they're internally built, critical sections have excellent user-mode debugging support. Unlike mutexes, which are pure kernel dispatcher objects, critical sections can be used only within the boundaries of the same user-mode process. Notice also that they're internally constructed on top of the event kernel-dispatcher object, which is precisely how true waiting for locked critical sections is implemented. When a thread tries to enter a critical section, the *LockCount* field is checked in user mode (*ntdll.dll*) to see if it is free. If it is, the lock count is updated atomically to indicate the critical section is now locked and the thread is given ownership of the critical section. If not, the thread might first enter a busy-spin loop in user mode (if you provided a non-zero *dwSpinCount* argument when you initialized the critical section using the *InitializeCriticalSectionAndSpinCount* Win32 API) before finally deciding to transition to kernel mode and wait on the event dispatcher object if the critical section is still locked.

Avoiding Lock-Ordering Deadlocks

One of the common techniques for preventing the type of deadlock shown in this section is the *lock-ordering* scheme. The idea is to assign an arbitrary level (1, 2, ... , *n*) for every lock in your program and enforce the invariant that locks can be acquired only in ascending order. If *m_csOne* and *m_csTwo* were ordered that way in the previous example, the sequence of lock acquisition where *m_csOne* is acquired after *m_csTwo* would've been illegal.

This technique can be implemented by having a global data structure tracking all the threads in the process (identified by thread ID, for instance) and associating every thread with a stack representing the locks that they happen to be holding. By checking the requested lock level against the level of the lock at the top of the (per-thread) stack during lock acquisitions, lock-ordering deadlock bugs can be caught immediately. This idea is captured in Figure 9-3.

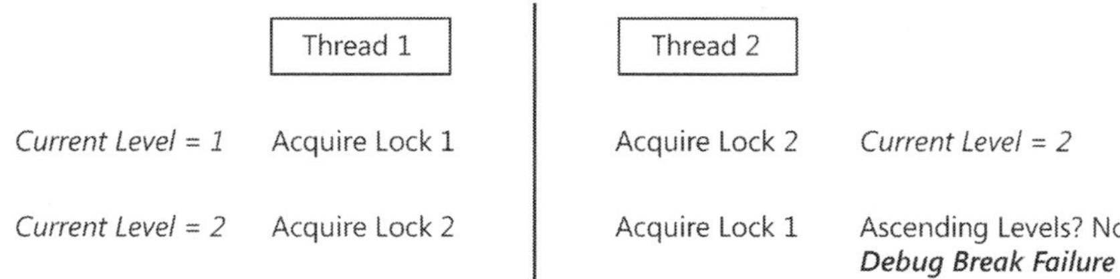

FIGURE 9-3 Deadlock prevention using the lock-ordering technique.

Despite the engineering discipline this approach entails, it's still frequently adopted in low-level system software. For example, the Common Language Runtime (CLR) code base uses this technique internally to prevent deadlock bugs in its execution engine. Microsoft SQL Server also uses this technique to prevent deadlock bugs early during the development cycle. As we all know, this type of bug can be especially nefarious in the case of a database system with a need for a high degree of reliability, and the engineering effort in the case of the SQL Server product is certainly worth the investment.

Logical Deadlocks

Deadlocks can happen even when there is only a single lock or no locks involved at all. This is because threads in Windows don't block only when trying to acquire a lock that's already held by another thread; they can also block when waiting for logical *events* to occur, such as thread/process exit events, asynchronous I/O completions, or the explicit application calls that signal the primitive kernel event objects (*SetEvent* Win32 API).

For a deadlock example that involves a lock construct and a logical wait by the application, consider the following C++ example from the companion source code, where this native DLL tries to create a new thread in response to the DLL_PROCESS_ATTACH notification it receives when it gets loaded into a host process. While still in the *DllMain* routine, the DLL proceeds to also wait on this new thread's callback routine to complete.

```
//
// C:\book\code\chapter_09\Deadlocks\SingleLockDeadlock>test.cpp
//
DWORD
WINAPI
WorkerThread(
    __in LPVOID pParam
    )
{
    wprintf(L"Inside WorkerThread.\n");
    return EXIT_SUCCESS;
}

BOOL
WINAPI
DllMain(
    __in HINSTANCE hInstance,
    __in DWORD dwReason,
    __in PVOID pReserved
    )
{
    CHandle shThread;

    ChkProlog();

    switch (dwReason)
```

```
{
        case DLL_PROCESS_ATTACH:
            ::DisableThreadLibraryCalls(hInstance);

            shThread.Attach(::CreateThread(
                NULL, 0, WorkerThread, NULL, 0, NULL));
            ChkWin32(shThread);
            VERIFY(::WaitForSingleObject(shThread, INFINITE) == WAIT_OBJECT_0);
            break;

        case DLL_THREAD_ATTACH:
        case DLL_THREAD_DETACH:
        case DLL_PROCESS_DETACH:
            break;
    }

    ChkNoCleanupRet(SUCCEEDED(ChkGetHr()));
    UNREFERENCED_PARAMETER(pReserved);
}
```

As soon as you try to load this DLL, you'll notice that the host process seems to hang while loading the DLL and before the new thread callback routine gets a chance to print its message to the console.

Debugging the Deadlock Condition

Unlike the lock-ordering deadlock example shown earlier, this deadlock occurs consistently. Attaching a user-mode debugger once the program hangs shows the following two threads (in addition to the break-in thread injected by the user-mode debugger).

```
C:\book\code\tools\dllhost\objfre_win7_x86\i386\host.exe
C:\book\code\chapter_09\Deadlocks\SingleLockDeadlock\objfre_win7_x86\i386\test.dll
...
0:002> .symfix
0:002> .reload
0:002> ~*k
   0  Id: 5a8.e04 Suspend: 1 Teb: 7ffde000 Unfrozen
ChildEBP RetAddr
0019f6cc 76dd6a24 ntdll!KiFastSystemCallRet
0019f6d0 751d179c ntdll!NtWaitForSingleObject+0xc
0019f73c 76bac2f3 KERNELBASE!WaitForSingleObjectEx+0x98
0019f754 76bac2a2 kernel32!WaitForSingleObjectExImplementation+0x75
0019f768 7297156a kernel32!WaitForSingleObject+0x12
0019f784 72971875 test!DllMain+0x5e
[c:\book\code\chapter_09\deadlocks\singlelockdeadlock\test.cpp @ 45]
0019f7e4 76de89d8 test!__DllMainCRTStartup+0xe1
0019f804 76df5c41 ntdll!LdrpCallInitRoutine+0x14
0019f8f8 76df052e ntdll!LdrpRunInitializeRoutines+0x26f
0019fa64 76df232c ntdll!LdrpLoadDll+0x4d1
0019fa98 751d8b51 ntdll!LdrLoadDll+0x92
0019fad4 76baef53 KERNELBASE!LoadLibraryExW+0x1d3
```

```
0019fae8 00bc155e kernel32!LoadLibraryW+0x11
0019faf8 00bc15b9 host!CMainApp::MainHR+0x14
0019fb0c 00bc1747 host!wmain+0x20
0019fb50 76baed6c host!__wmainCRTStartup+0x102
...
   1  Id: 5a8.f58 Suspend: 1 Teb: 7ffdd000 Unfrozen
ChildEBP RetAddr
0025f604 76dd6a24 ntdll!KiFastSystemCallRet
0025f608 76dc2264 ntdll!NtWaitForSingleObject+0xc
0025f66c 76dc2148 ntdll!RtlpWaitOnCriticalSection+0x13e
0025f694 76df3795 ntdll!RtlEnterCriticalSection+0x150
0025f728 76df3636 ntdll!LdrpInitializeThread+0xc6
0025f774 76df3663 ntdll!_LdrpInitialize+0x1ad
0025f784 00000000 ntdll!LdrInitializeThunk+0x10

#  2  Id: 5a8.fd8 Suspend: 1 Teb: 7ffdd000 Unfrozen
ChildEBP RetAddr
004bfc54 76e2f161 ntdll!DbgBreakPoint
...
```

Thread #0 seems to be waiting on the new thread object created in the *DllMain* routine to become signaled. This is thread #1 in the process, which you can verify by looking at the object handle argument used in the call to *WaitForSingleObject* at the top of thread #0's call stack.

```
0:002> $ First argument to WaitForSingleObject is the object handle
0:002> dd 0019f768
0019f768  0019f784 7297156a 00000030 ffffffff
0:002> !handle 00000030 f
Handle 30
  Type             Thread
...
  Object Specific Information
    Thread Id   5a8.f58
    Start Address 729712c9 test!WorkerThread
0:002> ~
   0  Id: 5a8.e04 Suspend: 1 Teb: 7ffde000 Unfrozen
   1  Id: 5a8.f58 Suspend: 1 Teb: 7ffdd000 Unfrozen
.  2  Id: 5a8.fd8 Suspend: 1 Teb: 7ffdc000 Unfrozen
```

However, thread #1 itself seems to be stuck waiting for another critical section, which you can dump using the *!cs* debugger command and the first argument to the *RtlEnterCriticalSection* call at the top of thread #1's call stack.

```
0:002> $ First argument to RtlEnterCriticalSection is the _RTL_CRITICAL_SECTION structure
0:002> dd 0025f694
0025f694  0025f728 76df3795 76e67340 74f77896
0:002> !cs 76e67340
Critical section   = 0x76e67340 (ntdll!LdrpLoaderLock+0x0)
DebugInfo          = 0x76e67540
LOCKED
LockCount          = 0x1
WaiterWoken        = No
OwningThread       = 0x00000e04
RecursionCount     = 0x1
LockSemaphore      = 0x34
```

```
SpinCount          = 0x00000000
0:002> ~
   0  Id: 5a8.e04 Suspend: 1 Teb: 7ffde000 Unfrozen
   1  Id: 5a8.f58 Suspend: 1 Teb: 7ffdd000 Unfrozen
.  2  Id: 5a8.fd8 Suspend: 1 Teb: 7ffdc000 Unfrozen
```

The owning thread for this critical section is the thread with client ID (Cid) *0xe04*, which refers to thread #0 in the process. This is a cyclic dependency between thread #0 and thread #1, causing both of them to stall indefinitely. This is the root cause of the deadlock condition in this example.

The Loader Lock and *DllMain* Hazards

The critical section (*ntdll!LdrpLoaderLock*) from the previous example is an important system lock and is referred to as the *loader lock*. This lock is used by the operating system's (OS) module loader code in *ntdll.dll* to synchronize calls to the *DllMain* functions for the loaded modules. Although you never explicitly acquired locks of any type in your code, the OS loader did just that before invoking your *DllMain* function. This behavior guarantees that the execution of the *DllMain* region of code is always serialized thanks to this system lock, and it allows you to perform the initialization work required by your DLL module in a thread-safe manner.

When a new thread is created, the OS loader also tries to acquire the same loader lock before calling the *DllMain* routines of the loaded modules (DLL_THREAD_ATTACH notifications) to let them know about the new thread in the process. Even though you declined to receive these particular notifications by calling the *DisableThreadLibraryCalls* Win32 API in your *DllMain* routine, other system DLL modules still expect to receive them and the OS loader will always acquire the loader lock when initializing new threads. This is precisely why thread #1 was blocked waiting for thread #0 to exit *DllMain* and release its exclusive hold on the loader lock global variable.

An important takeaway is that *DllMain* is always called under a lock—the system loader lock. As such, you need to keep the code in your *DllMain* routines short and simple and also understand the underlying work done by any functions you invoke in that code path. Here are a few things to keep in mind:

- It's strictly disallowed to create and wait on new threads inside *DllMain*, or call any functions that might do so. For example, it is illegal to invoke a COM object as part of *DllMain* because that might also require the creation of new threads (by the COM library code in the *ole32.dll* system module) to service the COM activation request.

- Many of the other typical rules you should follow when explicitly acquiring a lock also apply to your *DllMain* code. In particular, you should avoid performing network or other lengthy operations because you will be holding the loader lock for a long period of time. As a general rule, you should limit the work done in *DllMain* to simply initializing the DLL module's global variables.

- C++ static (global) objects in a DLL module will also be initialized by the C runtime under the loader lock before your actual *DllMain* routine is invoked. So, the same rules also apply to the code in the constructors of those C++ global objects.

The Loader Lock and the Debugger Break-in Sequence

If creating a new thread results in acquiring the loader lock, why can the debugger inject its *attach* remote thread (thread #2) despite the lock already being held by the main thread (#0) in the previous example? If you have a Windows XP machine available to run this experiment on, try to break in at the time of the deadlock. You'll see that *windbg.exe* waits for a while (30 seconds, to be exact) before deciding to forcibly suspend the threads in the process and break in anyway.

```
Break-in sent, waiting 30 seconds...
WARNING: Break-in timed out, suspending.
         This is usually caused by another thread holding the loader lock
```

The reason this debugging user experience is improved in Windows 7 is that WinDbg now uses a special system function to inject the remote thread. The unique thing about this function, compared with the regular thread creation API in Win32, is that it asks the kernel to create the thread without performing the usual initialization that requires the loader lock to be acquired. In the thread environment block (TEB) structure for thread #2 in the Windows 7 case (using the *@$teb* pseudo-register as an alias to the current TEB address), you can see that most of its fields are uninitialized.

```
0:002> dt ntdll!_TEB @$teb
...
   +0x02c ThreadLocalStoragePointer : (null) ...
   +0x03c CsrClientThread  : (null)
   +0x040 Win32ThreadInfo  : (null) ...
   +0x1a8 ActivationContextStackPointer : (null)
0:002> q
```

In particular, this thread isn't registered with the Windows Client/Server subsystem process (*csrss.exe*), which means that it can't create UI windows or use thread local storage. However, this is perfectly fine in this case because all the injected debugger break-in thread wants to do is execute a debug break (*int 3*) instruction.

Debugging Access-Check Problems

Security is deeply integrated into the Windows operating system. Resources in Windows can be secured so that only authorized users running with sufficient security rights can access them. Operations such as registry or file access involve a security check, of course, but security is also virtually everywhere in the Windows development landscape. For example, killing user-mode processes, sending UI messages, gaining access to the desktop foreground, attaching to a process debug port as a user-mode debugger, activating or starting remote COM servers are all operations that are subject to access checks. Having at least a cursory knowledge of the way these checks work can save you a lot of time when the programs you write fail due to security restrictions and you need to debug the root cause of those failures.

The Basic NT Security Model

The fundamental security model used since the early days of Windows NT assigns rights to each user during logon. These rights are based on a number of rules, including a set of group memberships and system privileges granted to the user account. This way, administrators can manage these rights more easily by assigning them to security groups instead of individual users. These dynamic rights are computed by the Local Security Authority subsystem process (*lsass.exe*) during the initial user logon and are represented in the OS by an executive object called a user *access token*. This access token is then attached to the first user process (the shell process, in particular) and gets inherited by the child processes that run within that user session.

Every user-mode process in Windows has a token associated with it that represents its security context. Threads inherit their security context from their containing process, but they're also able to temporarily assume the identity of another access token through a controlled system mechanism known as *impersonation*. This can be useful, for example, when a highly privileged server thread wants to perform operations on behalf of its client caller, but it wants to do so in the security context of the client to prevent elevation-of-privilege attacks.

Access checks in Windows involve checking the identity of the caller (represented by access tokens) against the security rules applied to the target executive resource (file, registry key, mutex, thread, process, and so on). These rules are formally represented by a structure called a *security descriptor*, which is tracked as part of the object header in the kernel and represents, among other things, a list of access-control rules to grant (or deny) access for a single user or a group of users. Note that access checks in Windows are also sometimes initiated manually without any kernel-resource access attempt. For example, a Win32 API might check the effective thread token to see if it's a member of the built-in administrators group and fail early in its execution if that's not the case.

Table 9-1 provides a quick summary of the key concepts in the NT security model and how they relate to each other.

TABLE 9-1 Important Windows NT Security Concepts

Concept	Description
Security Identifier (SID)	Pronounced "sid." Security identifiers are used to represent users and groups of users. They're also used to represent other principals in the Windows security subsystem. For example, a logon session also has a logon SID that represents it in the Windows security system.
Privileges	Privileges confer special rights to groups or individual user accounts. Examples include the ability to debug programs from other users (*SeDebugPrivilege*) or shut down the system (*SeShutdownPrivilege*).
Access Control Entry (ACE)	Pronounced "ace." An access control entry is composed primarily of a SID and a bit mask specifying the access rights granted to the SID in question.
Access Control List (ACL)	Pronounced "ack-el." A collection of access control entries used to describe the rules for access to a securable object.

Concept	Description
Security Descriptor	Security descriptors fully describe the authorization rules applied to securable objects. They contain the owner and primary group SIDs of the object, as well as a discretionary ACL (DACL) that governs who can access the object and another system ACL (SACL) that describes when audit events should be generated to log attempts to access the object into the security event log.
Access Token	Access tokens are dynamic objects created during logon to hold the security context of the new user session. They contain the main user SID and privileges, but they also cache other data, such as the user's group memberships and other information about the user session.

Anatomy of an Access Check

When a thread wants to access a resource or perform a privileged operation, an access check is initiated by the system to determine whether the access should be authorized. This is done in kernel mode using the internal *nt!SeAccessCheck* function in the kernel-mode portion of the security subsystem, also referred to as the security reference monitor (SRM). Figure 9-4 illustrates this sequence.

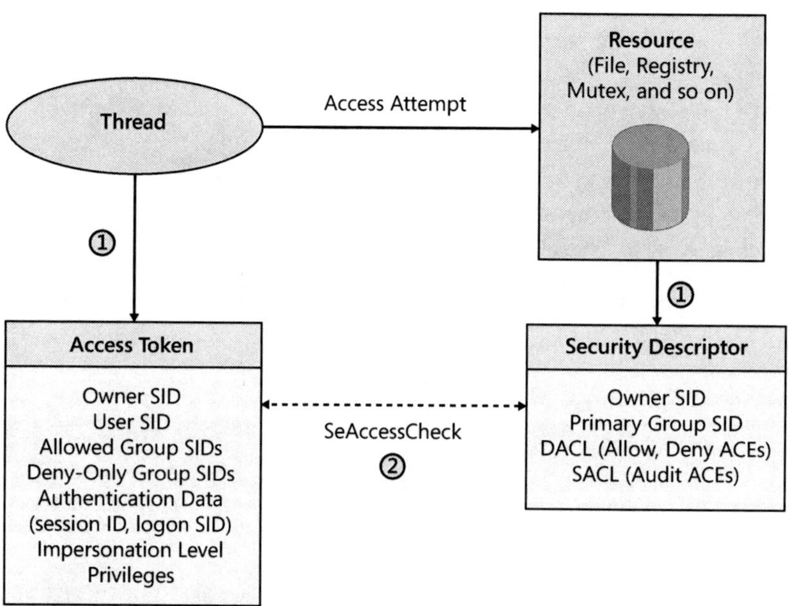

FIGURE 9-4 Access control checks in Windows.

The effective access token for the thread during an access check is either that of the process or the explicit impersonation token if the thread is impersonating a client during the call that triggered the access check. Several authorization rules are applied between the token and the target resource's security descriptor. For example, the user SID from the token is checked against the access control entries from the DACL in the security descriptor. If an entry matches the user SID or a group that the user SID belongs to, the access bit mask from the access control entry (ACE) is considered to be part of the access-check authorization. Based on the access intent (read, write, and so on) expressed by the thread when trying to access the resource, the access is either granted or denied based on the final access bit masks resulting from the authorization logic.

The *!token* Debugger Extension Command

The WinDbg debugger has several useful extension commands to dump the contents of the structures used by the Windows security system for access checks, including the *!token* command. This command, which you've already seen in a few experiments earlier in this book, can be used to display thread and process access tokens. In many access-check failures, you will probably already know the security restrictions applied to the resource your program is trying to access, so looking at the dynamic token context provides you with the other side of the equation and, hopefully, the final clue to figuring out the root cause of the failed access check. With no additional arguments, this command displays the effective access token of the current thread context. Using the *–n* option also resolves the names of the user and group SIDs in the output from the command, which is often useful to make sense of the cryptic SID textual representations. In the following live kernel debugging listing, for example, the *!token* command is used to display the access token of the current thread context, which happens to be the user security context of the live kernel debugger process itself.

```
lkd> .symfix
lkd> .reload
lkd> !process -1 0
PROCESS 84fba470  SessionId: 1  Cid: 1930    Peb: 7ffdf000  ParentCid: 1d4c
    Image: windbg.exe
lkd> !token -n
Thread is not impersonating. Using process token...
TS Session ID: 0x1
User: S-1-5-21-175793949-1629915048-1417430240-1001 (User: tariks-lp03\admin)
Groups:
 01 S-1-1-0 (Well Known Group: localhost\Everyone)
    Attributes - Mandatory Default Enabled
 02 S-1-5-32-544 (Alias: BUILTIN\Administrators)
    Attributes - Mandatory Default Enabled Owner
...
Privs:
 05 0x000000005 SeIncreaseQuotaPrivilege          Attributes -
 08 0x000000008 SeSecurityPrivilege               Attributes -
 09 0x000000009 SeTakeOwnershipPrivilege          Attributes -
 10 0x00000000a SeLoadDriverPrivilege             Attributes -
...
Authentication ID:         (0,53252)
Impersonation Level:       Anonymous
TokenType:                 Primary
Source: User32             TokenFlags: 0x2000 ( Token in use )
Token ID: 18d06a0          ParentToken ID: 0
Modified ID:               (0, 18d070c)
RestrictedSidCount: 0      RestrictedSids: 00000000
OriginatingLogonSession: 3e7
```

Notice that the command displays the primary user SID (my administrator user SID in this case), as well as its group memberships and privileges. The command also dumps other useful information from the token, such as the current session ID, the token type (impersonation or primary), and the token's impersonation level.

You can also use an explicit access token with the command by providing it with an additional argument. In user-mode debugging, you can pass a token handle to dump the content of any token object in the process context. To see this in action, you can use the token-handle leak sample program from the previous chapter. After letting the program run for a few seconds, attach to it using the WinDbg user-mode debugger (using the F6 shortcut, for example), and then use the *!token* command to dump one of the open (leaked) token handles, as illustrated in the following listing.

```
C:\book\code\chapter_08\HandleLeak\adduser.bat
C:\book\code\chapter_08\HandleLeak\HandleLeak.exe
0:007> $ List all the open token handles in the process
0:007> !handle 0 1 Token
...
Handle 3b7c
  Type              Token
Handle 3b80
  Type              Token
3691 handles of type Token
0:007> !token -n 3b80
TS Session ID: 0x3
User: S-1-5-21-3268063145-3624069009-1332808237-1019 (User: tariks-lp03\test_user_hl)
...
Auth ID: 0:3e18311
Impersonation Level: Impersonation
TokenType: Impersonation
Is restricted token: no.
```

In kernel-mode debugging sessions, you're also able to provide an optional token structure address to the *!token* command, which allows you to dump the security context of any thread or process in the system. You typically obtain this address from the executive thread or process structures, or from the output of the *!thread* or *!process* kernel debugger commands. To illustrate this important usage pattern, the following live kernel debugging listing confirms that the *lsass.exe* system process runs under the *LocalSystem* account context, which is the most powerful account in the Windows security model.

```
lkd> !process 0 1 lsass.exe
PROCESS 89ceed40  SessionId: 0  Cid: 0264    Peb: 7ffd6000  ParentCid: 021c
    Image: lsass.exe
    VadRoot 89d60738 Vads 147 Clone 0 Private 1222. Modified 2749. Locked 4.
    DeviceMap 89a08b10
    Token                             9edc55e0
    ElapsedTime                       00:15:29.435
    UserTime                          00:00:01.092
    KernelTime                        00:00:00.530
...
lkd> !token -n 9edc55e0
_TOKEN 9edc55e0
TS Session ID: 0
```

```
User: S-1-5-18 (Well Known Group: NT AUTHORITY\SYSTEM)
Groups:
 00 S-1-5-32-544 (Alias: BUILTIN\Administrators)
    Attributes - Default Enabled Owner
...
```

The *!sd* Debugger Extension Command

After you determine the security context of the calling thread using the *!token* command, you can examine the security descriptor in effect for the target resource you were trying to access. You can do this using the *!sd* debugger extension command. For example, you'll now run an experiment to display the security descriptor of the *lsass.exe* process object. The first step is to find the raw address of the security descriptor, which you can do by using the *!object* kernel-debugger extension command to locate the security descriptor in the object header structure, as shown in the following listing.

```
lkd> !process 0 0 lsass.exe
PROCESS 89ceed40  SessionId: 0  Cid: 0264    Peb: 7ffd6000  ParentCid: 021c
    Image: lsass.exe
lkd> !object 89ceed40
Object: 89ceed40  Type: (84a28490) Process
    ObjectHeader: 89ceed28 (new version)
    HandleCount: 13  PointerCount: 482
lkd> dt nt!_object_header 89ceed28
   +0x000 PointerCount     : 0n480
   +0x004 HandleCount      : 0n13
   +0x004 NextToFree       : 0x0000000d Void
   +0x008 Lock             : _EX_PUSH_LOCK
   +0x00c TypeIndex        : 0x7 ''
   +0x00d TraceFlags       : 0 ''
   +0x00e InfoMask         : 0x8 ''
   +0x00f Flags            : 0 ''
   +0x010 ObjectCreateInfo : 0x82b37a00 _OBJECT_CREATE_INFORMATION
   +0x010 QuotaBlockCharged : 0x82b37a00 Void
   +0x014 SecurityDescriptor : 0x89a0501b Void
   +0x018 Body             : _QUAD
```

One key consideration is that the low-order three bits are internally used by the kernel and aren't part of the security descriptor itself, which is always aligned on 8-byte boundaries. This means that you should mask those bits before you use the *!sd* command with the address stored in the object header. The extra flag (1) used in the following listing at the end of the command is similar to the *–n* option of the *!token* command in that it similarly asks the *!sd* command to display the friendly names of the user and group security identifiers (SIDs) in the security descriptor.

```
lkd> ?? 0x89a0501b & ~7
unsigned int 0x89a05018
lkd> !sd 0x89a05018 1
...
->Owner    : S-1-5-32-544 (Alias: BUILTIN\Administrators)
->Group    : S-1-5-18 (Well Known Group: NT AUTHORITY\SYSTEM)

->Dacl     :
->Dacl     : ->AclRevision: 0x2
->Dacl     : ->Sbz1       : 0x0
```

```
->Dacl      : ->AclSize     : 0x3c
->Dacl      : ->AceCount    : 0x2
->Dacl      : ->Sbz2        : 0x0

->Dacl      : ->Ace[0]: ->AceType: ACCESS_ALLOWED_ACE_TYPE
->Dacl      : ->Ace[0]: ->AceFlags: 0x0
->Dacl      : ->Ace[0]: ->AceSize: 0x14
->Dacl      : ->Ace[0]: ->Mask : 0x001fffff
->Dacl      : ->Ace[0]: ->SID: S-1-5-18 (Well Known Group: NT AUTHORITY\SYSTEM)

->Dacl      : ->Ace[1]: ->AceType: ACCESS_ALLOWED_ACE_TYPE
->Dacl      : ->Ace[1]: ->AceFlags: 0x0
->Dacl      : ->Ace[1]: ->AceSize: 0x18
->Dacl      : ->Ace[1]: ->Mask : 0x00121411
->Dacl      : ->Ace[1]: ->SID: S-1-5-32-544 (Alias: BUILTIN\Administrators)
...
```

Notice that only the *LocalSystem* account and members of the local built-in administrators group on the machine have access to the *lsass.exe* process object. In particular, this explains why this process can't be killed from a nonadministrative user context (including nonelevated command prompts), as illustrated in Figure 9-5.

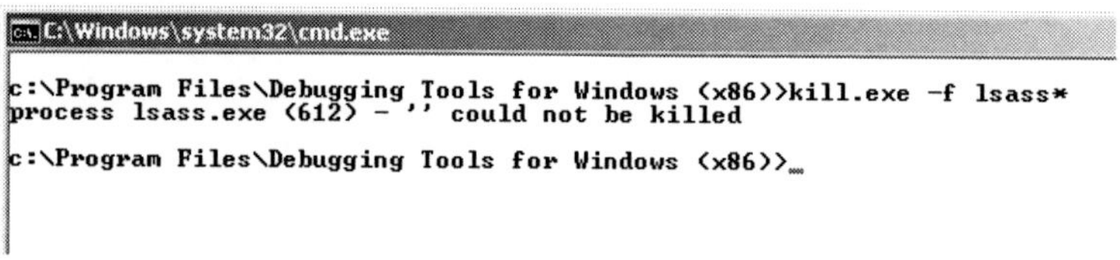

```
C:\Windows\system32\cmd.exe

c:\Program Files\Debugging Tools for Windows (x86)>kill.exe -f lsass*
process lsass.exe (612) - '' could not be killed

c:\Program Files\Debugging Tools for Windows (x86)>_
```

FIGURE 9-5 Failure to kill the LSASS process when running in a regular user context.

Windows Vista Improvements

An important extension to the NT security model that was introduced in the Windows Vista release is the concept of *integrity levels*. This concept enhances the user-based NT security model by enabling processes to run with different trust levels, even when they're started by the same user. One of the most important special-case applications of integrity levels is the *User Account Control* (UAC) feature, and understanding the way it can affect access checks is crucial when debugging security issues in Windows Vista and later releases.

Integrity Levels

The article at *http://msdn.microsoft.com/library/bb625963.aspx* does a good job introducing the high-level design of integrity-level checks in Windows. The good news is that integrity levels and UAC are also implemented using the same building blocks upon which access tokens and security descriptors have been built since the early days of NT security, including SIDs and ACEs.

Each process token is assigned a default *integrity level SID* at the time of its initialization, based on the group membership SIDs of the token. This integrity level SID is also saved in the access token of the corresponding process object. In order of more trusted to less trusted, the levels are as follows: System, High, Medium, Low, and Untrusted. They're represented using special SID values by the security system (all of the form *S-1-16-**) so that the access rules from the basic NT access checks can be extended seamlessly to cover integrity levels too, as illustrated in Figure 9-6.

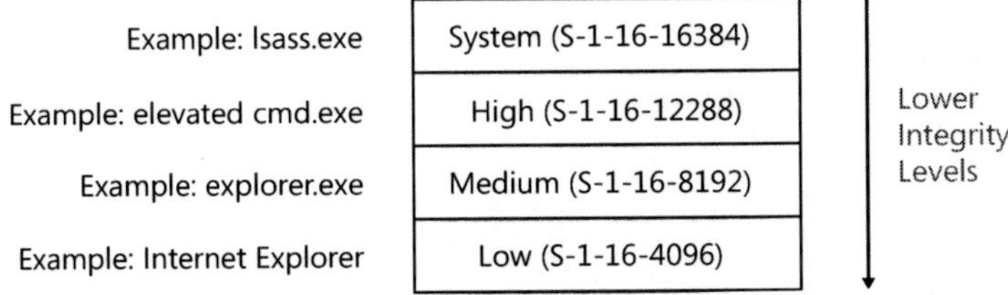

FIGURE 9-6 Integrity levels in the Windows operating system.

To make integrity levels a central part of access checks in Windows, security descriptors were also extended to support rules (access control entries) that can be used to prevent callers with a lower integrity level from accessing a resource labeled with a higher level. These special ACE entries are named *mandatory integrity labels*, and they define policies (read, write, and so on) for access to the resource based on the target integrity level of the thread initiating the access check. To preserve backward compatibility with the previous structure format, mandatory integrity labels are tracked in security descriptors as part of the SACL that was used to describe audit rules. Starting with Windows Vista, this SACL also describes the mandatory integrity label ACE in effect for the object, with the default being the Medium integrity label.

For example, the interactive window station allows access to any process in the user session whose token has at least the Low integrity level, which is why even low-privileged programs can display visible UI elements in Windows! To see this, you first find the address of the interactive window station object (named *winsta0*) by using the *!object* kernel debugger command to traverse the directory structure used by the object manager.

```
lkd> !object \Windows
Object: 8ea0ba00  Type: (84a289a8) Directory
    Hash Address  Type          Name
    ---- -------  ----          ----
     04  87f57728 ALPC Port     SbApiPort
     09  87f57d90 ALPC Port     ApiPort
     14  82213e98 Section       SharedSection
     32  8a762198 Directory     WindowStations
lkd> !object 8a762198
Object: 8a762198  Type: (84a289a8) Directory
    Hash Address  Type          Name
    ---- -------  ----          ----
     01  9fcb8b58 WindowStation Service-0x0-3e4$
     04  865804c8 WindowStation Service-0x0-3e5$
     06  883ffbb0 WindowStation msswindowstation
     11  9423e170 WindowStation Service-0x0-3e7$
     27  94239dd8 WindowStation WinSta0
```

You can now use the *!sd* command to dump the security descriptor of this named window station object using the same steps described earlier in this section.

```
lkd> !object 94239dd8
Object: 94239dd8  Type: (84aa8c58) WindowStation
    ObjectHeader: 94239dc0 (new version)
    HandleCount: 9  PointerCount: 18
    Directory Object: 8a762198  Name: WinSta0
lkd> dt nt!_object_header 94239dc0 SecurityDescriptor
   +0x014 SecurityDescriptor : 0x9a2405ea Void
lkd> ?? 0x9a2405ea & ~7
unsigned int 0x9a2405e8
lkd> !sd 0x9a2405e8 1
...
->Sacl    :
->Sacl    : ->AclRevision: 0x2
->Sacl    : ->Sbz1       : 0x0
->Sacl    : ->AclSize    : 0x1c
->Sacl    : ->AceCount   : 0x1
->Sacl    : ->Sbz2       : 0x0
->Sacl    : ->Ace[0]: ->AceType: SYSTEM_MANDATORY_LABEL_ACE_TYPE
->Sacl    : ->Ace[0]: ->AceFlags: 0x0
->Sacl    : ->Ace[0]: ->AceSize: 0x14
->Sacl    : ->Ace[0]: ->Mask : 0x00000001
->Sacl    : ->Ace[0]: ->SID: S-1-16-4096
```

As you can see, the SACL of this window station object allows access for *S-1-16-4096* (the Low integrity level group SID) and higher integrity levels.

UAC in Action

The User Account Control (UAC) feature uses integrity levels, but there is also more to it. An elevated access token in UAC grants similar rights to the default administrative context in Windows XP. In following the security principles of *defense in depth* and *least required privileges*, the *default* rights of members of the administrative group were lowered in Windows Vista and later by filtering their access token to include only a subset of groups and privileges of the local built-in Administrators group. In addition, a nonelevated access token is also sandboxed to the Medium integrity level, as opposed to the High integrity level that's assigned to elevated UAC tokens.

To observe UAC in action, you can use the *whoami.exe* command-line utility to dump the access tokens for an elevated and a nonelevated *cmd.exe* command prompt side by side. This tool allows you to see the same token information displayed by the *!token* debugger command, though it's less generic because it dumps only the current *cmd.exe* process token. However, it often proves convenient because it allows you to quickly determine the security context of your command-prompt window. Another way to also figure out whether your command prompt is elevated or not is to check its title bar: if the title says "Administrator: Command Prompt," it's an elevated window.

Using the *whoami.exe* command, you'll see that elevated command prompts have many more privileges than nonelevated command prompts. They also have a group membership for the High integrity level group SID.

----Elevated CMD.exe----

```
C:\windows\system32\whoami.exe /all
Group Name                             Type             SID
====================================== ================ ===================
...
Mandatory Label\High Mandatory Level Label              S-1-16-12288

Privilege Name                  Description                               State
=============================== ========================================= ========
SeIncreaseQuotaPrivilege        Adjust memory quotas for a process        Disabled
SeSecurityPrivilege             Manage auditing and security log          Disabled
SeTakeOwnershipPrivilege        Take ownership of files or other objects  Disabled
SeLoadDriverPrivilege           Load and unload device drivers            Disabled
SeSystemProfilePrivilege        Profile system performance                Disabled
SeSystemtimePrivilege           Change the system time                    Disabled
...
```

----Nonelevated CMD.exe----

```
C:\windows\system32\whoami.exe /all
Group Name                             Type             SID
====================================== ================ ===================
...
Mandatory Label\Medium Mandatory Level Label              S-1-16-8192

Privilege Name                Description                          State
============================= ==================================== ========
SeShutdownPrivilege           Shut down the system                 Disabled
SeChangeNotifyPrivilege       Bypass traverse checking             Enabled
SeUndockPrivilege             Remove computer from docking station Disabled
SeIncreaseWorkingSetPrivilege Increase a process working set       Disabled
SeTimeZonePrivilege           Change the time zone                 Disabled
```

To see the other side of UAC in access checks, you can observe the mandatory integrity labels in the SACL part of security descriptors using the *!sd* debugger command, or (in the case of files or directories) by using the *icacls.exe* command-line utility, which can be used to read and also modify the security descriptors of files and directory objects. Most file objects don't have an explicit SACL and get the default Medium integrity label. That being said, some files that need to override this default carry an explicit mandatory integrity label in their SACL. An example is files under the volume root, which have a High integrity label, preventing regular users and nonelevated administrative UAC tokens from accessing them. This explains why the resource access attempt shown in Figure 9-7, which tries to delete *autoexec.bat* at the volume root, is denied—it's because the *del* command is executed from within a nonelevated command prompt (Medium integrity level). The integrity-level check for the Medium integrity-level command prompt against the High mandatory integrity label in the file security descriptor fails in this case, as demonstrated in Figure 9-7.

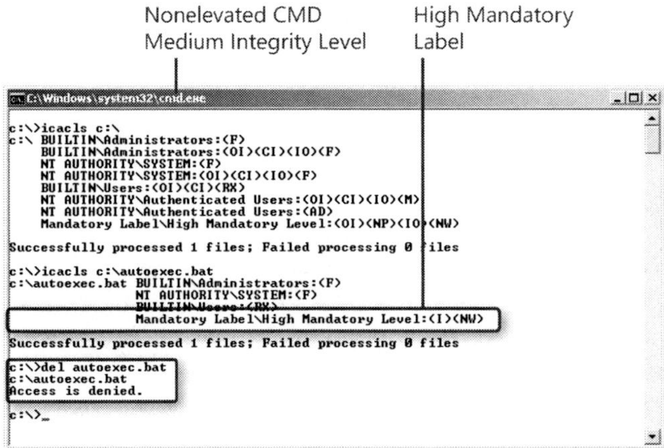

FIGURE 9-7 Access denied when a Medium integrity-level access token tries to access an object with a High mandatory integrity label SACL.

Wrapping Up

UAC and integrity levels play an important role in access checks because they extend the DACL and privilege checks that have been at the heart of the NT security model since its early inception. The following considerations are usually worth verifying when you're faced with access-check failures:

- The effective access token of the thread initiating the access check must have a user SID and group memberships that satisfy the requirements expressed by the DACL part of the resource security descriptor. Alternatively, the "owner" SID of the resource, as described in its security descriptor, is allowed access to the resource regardless of the DACL.
- Note that some access checks bypass the DACL requirements if the effective access token of the calling thread possesses special user privileges. For example, the *SeDebugPrivilege* user privilege allows a user-mode program to open a handle to any thread in the target process because the *OpenThread* Win32 API checks that privilege first before running through the DACL rules of the thread object's security descriptor.
- The integrity level group SID in the effective access token of the calling thread must be higher than the mandatory integrity label of the resource. If the SACL part of the resource security descriptor is missing an explicit mandatory integrity label, the default is the Medium integrity label. Finally, the access intent (read, write, and so on) that's expressed by the caller must also be allowed by the access masks in the mandatory integrity label ACE.

Summary

This chapter presented several common debugging scenarios in the concurrency and security areas. It also distilled a few generic techniques for recognizing and investigating related issues in your software. In particular, the following high-level points are worth reiterating:

- Race conditions are often hard to reproduce without stress testing. Once you get a reproducible case, you should use the debuggers to extract as much information as you can from the state of the target so that you can form hypotheses on how the race condition came to be. You'll only be able to eradicate these conditions from your code if you take them seriously when you're lucky enough to get a reproducible case.
- Deadlock bugs are equally serious and can have negative effects on the reliability of your software. Strategies for deadlock avoidance, such as lock ordering in your code base, are sometimes worth the engineering effort they require, especially in complex, low-level software. The debuggers are an excellent tool for debugging deadlock conditions because they allow you to break in and inspect the state of the threads in the process at the time of the deadlock. Depending on whether the deadlock is contained within the same process or involves more than one process, you might find it useful to switch from user-mode debugging to live kernel debugging so that you can examine the state of other processes on the system.
- Access-denied failures are another common debugging scenario. Often, you can understand these conditions by looking at the security requirements of the APIs you call, which you can usually find in the MSDN documentation. You'll also often find the *!token* and *!sd* debugger extension commands—as well as the *whoami.exe* and *icacls.exe* command-line utilities—useful when debugging and testing hypotheses for fixing access-check failures.

CHAPTER 10

Debugging System Internals

In this chapter

Debuggers can be more than just tools for investigating code defects because you also can apply them to validate and extend your understanding of the components and technologies you use to build your software. I've seen this learning strategy diligently used by many of the best engineers I've worked with in my career. What makes it particularly appealing is how it encourages the mindset that software behavior can always be traced and debugged, so you don't have to treat the components you use as complete black boxes, at least when it comes to having a sense of their high-level operations.

In this chapter, you'll apply this approach to dissect two familiar system mechanisms: printing text to the console and writing data to a local file on disk. You'll see how several of the generic tricks and techniques covered in earlier chapters will again prove their worth when using the debuggers in this manner. The strategies applied in these two case studies will also lay out a set of common guiding principles you can use and extend when you need to explore other system internals on your own.

The Windows Console Subsystem

Most of us started our college programming courses with a "Hello World!" example. As it turns out, quite a bit of work goes on behind the scenes in the system to display a string to the console. Knowing these internal details is also useful to better understand such mechanisms as handling a Ctrl+C keypress combination in console applications. This section illustrates the importance of acquiring a feel for what happens when you call third-party APIs in your code. In fact, this topic is becoming even more important as higher-level development platforms (.NET, HTML5/JavaScript, and so on) take center stage because even the simplest API calls might sometimes have unintended effects on the scalability and performance of your software—especially when they're used to solve the wrong set of problems in the name of expedience.

The Magic Behind *printf*

A basic question worth asking is how the C runtime library (CRT) code, which implements the *printf* function call, is able to render the text provided to that API on the screen. Surely, a standalone library such as the CRT wouldn't have any preconceptions about the coordinates of the text on the screen or the size of the console window, for example. Other layers *must* be involved to enable the C runtime library to access that functionality.

The Console Host Process in Windows 7

To discover the various layers involved in the *printf* sequence, you need to find a way to slow down the execution of this API so that you can inspect its internal behavior. A useful first step when studying new unfamiliar areas is to find all the new processes that get started as a result of running your experiment.

There are two common ways to accomplish this goal. The first will be covered in the next part of this book, when you'll learn how to use Event Tracing for Windows (ETW) to log a variety of system events, including new process creation events. The second approach uses the kernel-debugging trick shown in Chapter 7, "Expert Debugging Tricks," which introduced the *nt!PspInsertProcess* kernel breakpoint as a way to break into the debugger whenever a new process is created on the target machine of a kernel-debugging session. This is the method you'll use here to start dissecting the *printf* sequence.

This experiment requires a Windows 7 target operating system (OS), in which you'll open a standard command prompt, using the host kernel debugger at the same time to watch any new processes started as a result of that action. First, though, you need to add the process-creation breakpoint in the host kernel debugger, as shown in the following listing.

```
kd> vertarget
Windows 7 Kernel Version 7600 MP (1 procs) Free x86 compatible
Built by: 7600.16481.x86fre.win7_gdr.091207-1941
kd> .symfix
kd> .reload
kd> bp nt!PspInsertProcess
kd> g
```

Now that you have this breakpoint set up, you can open a new standard (nonelevated) command prompt on the target machine of this kernel-debugging session. Before you even get a chance to run the program that calls *printf* within that command-prompt window, you'll see the previous breakpoint hit twice: once for the *cmd.exe* command-prompt process and a second time for another process named *conhost.exe*, as shown in the following listing.

```
Breakpoint 0 hit
nt!PspInsertProcess:
kd> dt nt!_EPROCESS @eax ImageFileName
   +0x16c ImageFileName : [15]  "cmd.exe"
kd> g
Breakpoint 0 hit
```

```
nt!PspInsertProcess:
kd> dt nt!_EPROCESS @eax ImageFileName
   +0x16c ImageFileName : [15]  "conhost.exe"
```

The *conhost.exe* process plays an important role in the UI processing of Windows console applications—including *cmd.exe*—in Windows 7. This process is central to the workings of *printf* as well. The Windows Client/Server subsystem process (*csrss.exe*)—with which every new user-mode process gets registered—creates a new instance of *conhost.exe* whenever a new top-level console application is started. Notice, indeed, that the creator of the new *conhost.exe* process is the *csrss.exe* instance from the current user session (session #1 in this case), as shown by the *k* command in the following listing.

```
kd> !process -1 0
PROCESS 88b0bd40  SessionId: 1  Cid: 01bc    Peb: 7ffd7000  ParentCid: 01ac
    Image: csrss.exe
kd> .reload /user
kd> k
ChildEBP RetAddr
8d879604 828a44df nt!PspInsertProcess
8d879d00 8269147a nt!NtCreateUserProcess+0x6fe
...
00b3fb2c 75d12018 winsrv!CreateConsoleHostProcess+0x155
00b3fb60 75d532c1 winsrv!ConsoleClientConnectRoutine+0xbc
00b3fb80 75d54d55 CSRSRV!CsrSrvClientConnect+0x60
00b3fcf4 77ba5d0b CSRSRV!CsrApiRequestThread+0x3bb
00b3fd34 77bfb3c8 ntdll!__RtlUserThreadStart+0x28
00b3fd4c 00000000 ntdll!_RtlUserThreadStart+0x1b
kd> $ Disable the previous breakpoint now
kd> bd *
kd> g
```

Because console applications don't implement their own UI message loop, the system uses the console host process (*conhost.exe*) to manage the drawing area represented by the common window, which is shared by all the console processes started from that top-level *cmd.exe* process. This allows the UI message-loop handling in these console processes to be shared as well.

Note Prior to the release of Windows 7, the UI message-loop handling for console applications was carried out directly by the *csrss.exe* Windows subsystem process itself. Although this also met the goal of code sharing, it wasn't following the "least required privileges" secure design principle—both because *LocalSystem* privileges aren't required for UI processing and because any instability in the *csrss.exe* process is fatal to the entire system. So, the *conhost.exe* worker process was introduced to provide better security isolation.

After *csrss.exe* creates the new *conhost.exe* instance, all the console processes started from the same top-level command window can also use it to carry out tasks that require UI processing. This communication takes place using the advanced local procedure call (ALPC) interprocess communication (IPC) mechanism, which was described in a high level of detail back in Chapter 1, "Software Development in Windows." Figure 10-1 depicts this mechanism, summarizing the key components in the console subsystem architecture in Windows 7 and later.

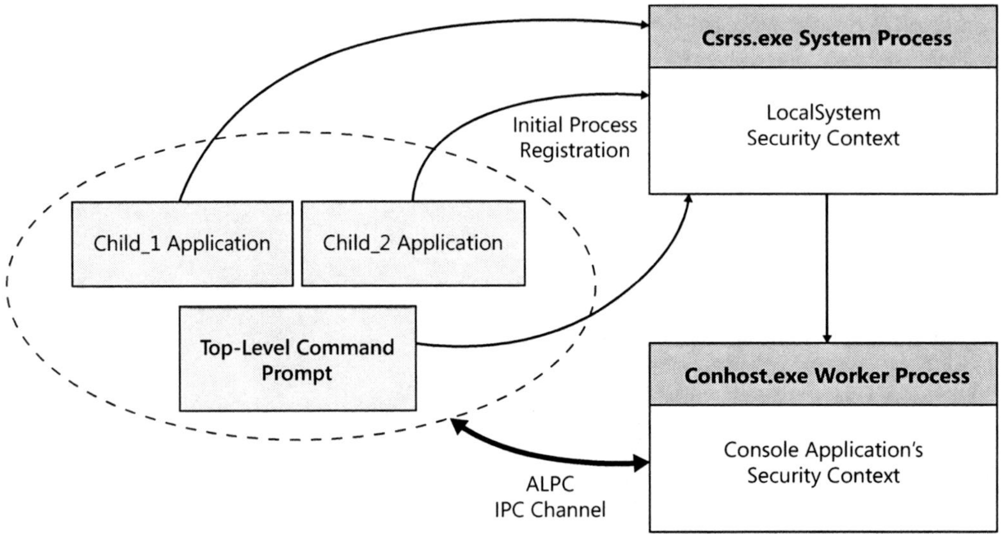

FIGURE 10-1 Console subsystem components in Windows 7.

In addition to handling the regular UI events on behalf of its associated console processes, the *conhost.exe* worker process provides a set of services that are central to the operations of the console I/O functions, including the *printf* call from the C runtime library. This is why you'll see two threads in the *conhost.exe* process: the ALPC server thread that receives and handles calls from all the associated console processes, and a second thread that implements the standard Windows UI message loop on behalf of those processes.

You can see these two threads in the following debugger listing, where WinDbg is used to attach as a user-mode debugger to a running instance of *conhost.exe* and the *~*k* debugger command is then used to list all the threads in the process. At the end of this session, be sure to use the *qd* command to detach from *conhost.exe* without terminating it. If you use the *q* command instead, you not only kill *conhost.exe*, but you also kill its associated console processes because they can't survive without their *conhost.exe* worker process!

```
0:002> .symfix
0:002> .reload
0:002> ~*k
   0  Id: 1fb0.12b4 Suspend: 1 Teb: 7ffde000 Unfrozen
ChildEBP RetAddr
00a7fa60 776e6424 ntdll!KiFastSystemCallRet
00a7fa64 00e61632 ntdll!NtReplyWaitReceivePort+0xc
00a7fb38 76daed6c conhost!ConsoleLpcThread+0xc9
00a7fb44 777037f5 kernel32!BaseThreadInitThunk+0xe
00a7fb84 777037c8 ntdll!__RtlUserThreadStart+0x70
00a7fb9c 00000000 ntdll!_RtlUserThreadStart+0x1b

   1  Id: 1fb0.358 Suspend: 1 Teb: 7ffdf000 Unfrozen
ChildEBP RetAddr
008cfa04 76e6cde0 ntdll!KiFastSystemCallRet
008cfa08 76e6ce13 USER32!NtUserGetMessage+0xc
008cfa24 00e63131 USER32!GetMessageW+0x33
008cfa68 76daed6c conhost!ConsoleInputThread+0xed
008cfa74 777037f5 kernel32!BaseThreadInitThunk+0xe
008cfab4 777037c8 ntdll!__RtlUserThreadStart+0x70
008cfacc 00000000 ntdll!_RtlUserThreadStart+0x1b
...
0:002> $ Detach from conhost.exe and quit the user-mode debugging session...
0:002> qd
```

The C Runtime Library's I/O Functions

After using a kernel-mode debugging session earlier to discover the role (and existence!) of the *conhost.exe* worker process, you're in position to switch back to user-mode debugging now that you suspect that the *printf* CRT call would end up invoking the ALPC server thread (thread #0) in the *conhost.exe* instance of the target console application. To see this in action, you can use the following C++ program from the companion source code, which you can compile using the procedure described in the Introduction to this book.

```
//
// C:\book\code\chapter_10\ConsoleApp>main.cpp
//
int
__cdecl
wmain()
{
    fwprintf(stdout, L"%s\n", L"This is an output sent to stdout.");
    return 0;
}
```

Start by running this process in a user-mode debugging session, and step through it until you reach the source line of the *fwprintf* call, as illustrated in the following listing. This will be called *Debugger Session A* in this experiment and is shown in Figure 10-2.

```
0:000> vercommand
command line: '"c:\Program Files\Debugging Tools for Windows (x86)\windbg.exe"
c:\book\code\chapter_10\ConsoleApp\objfre_win7_x86\i386\consoleapp.exe'
0:000> .symfix
0:000> .reload
0:000> bp ConsoleApp!wmain
0:000> g
Breakpoint 0 hit
consoleapp!wmain:
0:000> p
consoleapp!wmain+0x5:
```

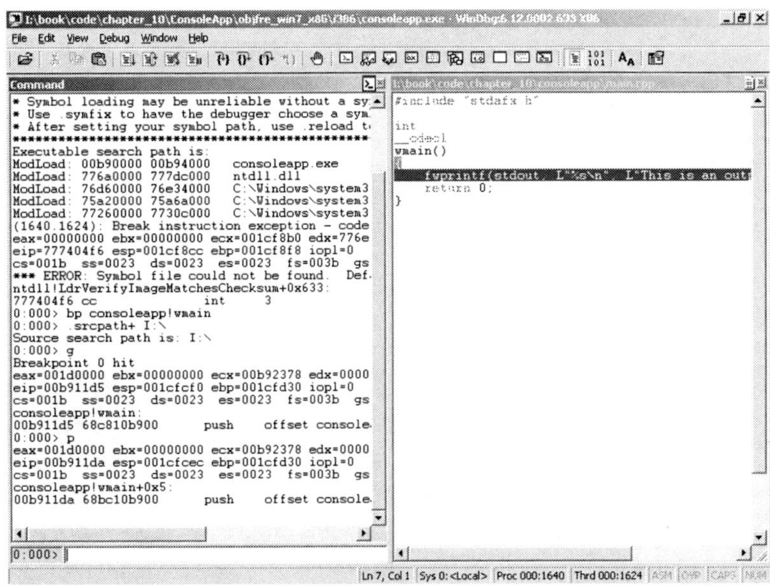

FIGURE 10-2 Debugger Session A: debugging the console application using WinDbg.

By now, the system would've already created the associated *conhost.exe* process. So, you can now attach a second user-mode debugger to that instance. You might find multiple running *conhost.exe* instances on your system (each corresponding to a different top-level command-prompt window), but the interesting one will likely be at the bottom of the list of processes, given it's the most recent one, as shown in Figure 10-3. This will be called *Debugger Session B* in this experiment.

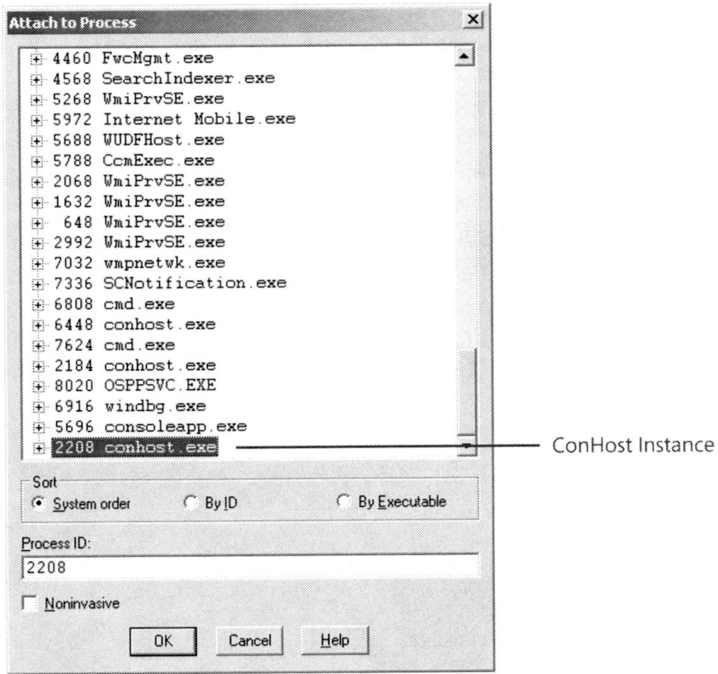

FIGURE 10-3 Debugger Session B: attaching to the *conhost.exe* process instance associated with the target console application.

The ALPC server thread in the *conhost.exe* process offers a good breakpoint to slow down the execution of the *fprintf* call so that you can inspect the steps it involves more closely. In particular, you can set a breakpoint in Debugger Session B using the return address from the wait on ALPC messages in the ALPC server thread, as illustrated in the following listing.

```
0:002> $ Debugger Session B
0:002> .symfix
0:002> .reload
0:002> ~*k
   0  Id: 140c.f08 Suspend: 1 Teb: 7ffde000 Unfrozen
ChildEBP RetAddr
0062f6d4 779a6424 ntdll!KiFastSystemCallRet
0062f6d8 00c61632 ntdll!NtReplyWaitReceivePort+0xc
0062f7ac 76f9ed6c conhost!ConsoleLpcThread+0xc9
0062f7b8 779c377b kernel32!BaseThreadInitThunk+0xe
0062f7f8 779c374e ntdll!__RtlUserThreadStart+0x70
0062f810 00000000 ntdll!_RtlUserThreadStart+0x1b
...
0:002> bp 00c61632
0:002> g
```

You're now ready to step through the *fprintf* call. If you go back to Debugger Session A and press F10 to step over the call to *fprintf*, you'll hit the breakpoint you just inserted in the *conhost.exe* process in Debugger Session B.

At this point in time, the target console application will be blocked waiting on the ALPC call it issued to its associated *conhost.exe* process to return. To inspect the call stack of the client side of this ALPC call, break into Debugger Session A using the Debug\Break menu action. After doing so, switch to the main thread using the *~0s* command and look at the current call stack using the *k* command, as shown in the following listing. Note that the main thread (thread #0) indeed issued an ALPC call that is yet to be completed. At this stage, the *fprintf* call is deep inside the C runtime code trying to get the input mode of the current console window from the *conhost.exe* process that manages it.

```
(1260.1c90): Break instruction exception - code 80000003 (first chance)
ntdll!DbgBreakPoint:
7799410c cc              int     3
0:001> $ This is the break-in thread in Debugger Session A -> Switch over to thread #0
0:001> ~0s
0:000> k
ChildEBP RetAddr
0017f6a0 779a6464 ntdll!KiFastSystemCallRet
0017f6a4 76fa4b6e ntdll!ZwRequestWaitReplyPort+0xc
0017f6c4 76fac141 kernel32!ConsoleClientCallServer+0x88
0017f784 75fc4483 kernel32!GetConsoleMode+0x31
0017fd34 75fc40eb msvcrt!_write_nolock+0x128
0017fd78 75fbf15e msvcrt!_write+0x9f
0017fd98 75fd5f07 msvcrt!_flush+0x3b
0017fda8 75fd6f54 msvcrt!_ftbuf+0x1e
0017fdf8 009d11ef msvcrt!fwprintf+0x72
0017fe08 009d135d consoleapp!wmain+0x1a [c:\book\code\chapter_10\consoleapp\main.cpp @ 7]
...
```

If you let both debuggers continue by typing the *g* command in each of them, you'll see the ALPC thread hit the breakpoint again. The *fprintf* call will still be in progress at the time, which you can verify by breaking into Debugger Session A once again using the Debug\Break menu action. Using the same steps you executed in the previous listing, you'll now see the following call stack.

```
(1260.1c90): Break instruction exception - code 80000003 (first chance)
0:001> ~0s
0:000> k
ChildEBP RetAddr
0017f634 779a6464 ntdll!KiFastSystemCallRet
0017f638 76fa4b6e ntdll!ZwRequestWaitReplyPort+0xc
0017f658 76f9be7c kernel32!ConsoleClientCallServer+0x88
0017f740 76f9bf35 kernel32!WriteConsoleInternal+0xb3
0017f75c 76f9bf49 kernel32!WriteConsoleA+0x18
0017f778 75fc4236 kernel32!WriteFileImplementation+0x6f
0017fd34 75fc40eb msvcrt!_write_nolock+0x3fb
0017fd78 75fbf15e msvcrt!_write+0x9f
0017fd98 75fd5f07 msvcrt!_flush+0x3b
0017fda8 75fd6f54 msvcrt!_ftbuf+0x1e
0017fdf8 009d11ef msvcrt!fwprintf+0x72
0017fe08 009d135d consoleapp!wmain+0x1a [c:\book\code\chapter_10\consoleapp\main.cpp @ 7]
...
```

This is the client side of the ALPC call that ultimately causes the message to be displayed on the screen. You can see how the *fprintf* call in the C runtime library layer is built on top of the *kernel32!WriteConsoleA* Win32 API, which in turn communicates with the *conhost.exe* process internally using the ALPC interprocess communication mechanism. The *conhost.exe* process, which keeps all the information about the console window's drawing area (such as cursor position, size of the screen, and so on), then completes the ALPC request by finally printing the message to the UI window. This sequence is summarized in Figure 10-4.

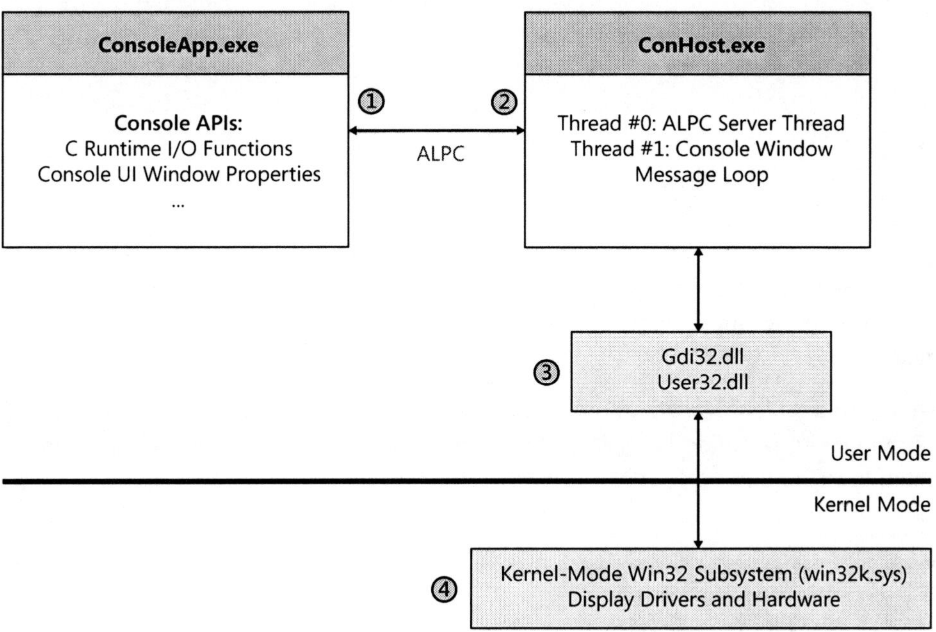

FIGURE 10-4 Printing text to the screen in console applications (Windows 7 architecture).

Handling of Windows UI Events

It's easy to continue the experiment conducted in the previous section and confirm that *conhost .exe* also processes the UI events received by the console window. When you look at a Windows GUI process inside a debugger, you can quickly recognize the main UI thread in the process by dumping the call stacks of all the threads in that process and looking for a thread that's in a continuous *USER32!GetMessageW* loop. In the case of *conhost.exe*, this is thread #1, as shown in the following listing from Debugger Session B.

```
0:002> $ Debugger Session B
0:002> ~*k
...
   1  Id: 1990.180c Suspend: 1 Teb: 7ffdf000 Unfrozen
ChildEBP RetAddr
00c3f950 76e6cde0 ntdll!KiFastSystemCallRet
```

```
00c3f954 76e6ce13 USER32!NtUserGetMessage+0xc
00c3f970 00e63131 USER32!GetMessageW+0x33
00c3f9b4 76daed6c conhost!ConsoleInputThread+0xed
00c3f9c0 777037f5 kernel32!BaseThreadInitThunk+0xe
00c3fa00 777037c8 ntdll!__RtlUserThreadStart+0x70
00c3fa18 00000000 ntdll!_RtlUserThreadStart+0x1b
...
```

By setting a breakpoint in the return address from *USER32!GetMessageW*, which you're able to obtain from the call stack in the previous listing, you can now witness firsthand the GUI message handling for the target console window.

```
0:002> $ Debugger Session B
0:002> bp 00e63131
0:002> g
Breakpoint 1 hit
conhost!ConsoleInputThread+0xed:
```

Notice that any interaction with the console window now causes this breakpoint to be hit to handle the repaint and other UI events sent by the system to that window. This proves that *conhost.exe* does receive those messages and handles them on behalf of its associated console applications.

Remember to disable the previous breakpoints at the end of this experiment so that the target process continues its execution normally without the *conhost.exe* process breaking back continuously into the debugger.

```
0:001> $ Debugger Session B
0:001> bd *
0:001> g
```

This section concludes the *printf* system debugging example, so you can terminate both debugger sessions A and B once you're done observing this experiment. The following section examines the handling of other *asynchronous* UI events in console applications and the Ctrl+C signal, in particular.

Handling of the Ctrl+C Signal

When the Ctrl+C signal is received by a console window, it's reasonable to assume that the GUI message-loop thread in *conhost.exe* handles that special event too. What happens next and causes the process to exit is less obvious, however, and this is precisely what this section will describe.

This experiment will use the following C# program from the companion source code, which subscribes to the *CancelKeyPress* event by using the += operator to add a C# delegate (defined inline for simplicity) to the list of handlers that should be invoked when Ctrl+C or Ctrl+Break is received by the console window.

```
//
// C:\book\code\chapter_10\CtrlC>test.cs
//
public class Test
{
    public static void Main()
    {
        Console.CancelKeyPress += delegate
        {
            Console.WriteLine("Stopping...");
        };
        Console.WriteLine("Starting...");
        Thread.Sleep(300000);
    }
}
```

Console Termination Handlers in .NET/Win32

The *System.Console* .NET class uses the *kernel32!SetConsoleCtrlHandler* Win32 API in its implementation of the *CancelKeyPress* event. This Win32 API adds termination handlers (function pointers) to a global list of console event handlers maintained by the *kernel32.dll* module implementing it. To see how this program works, run it from a command prompt, and then press the Ctrl+C keyboard combination. You'll notice that the delegate you added gets executed before the program is terminated.

```
C:\book\code\chapter_10\CtrlC>test.exe
Starting...
Stopping...
^C
```

If you run this program again, but this time under the control of a user-mode debugger, you'll notice a new thread gets inserted into the target process in response to the Ctrl+C signal.

```
0:000> vercommand
command line: '"c:\Program Files\Debugging Tools for Windows (x86)\windbg.exe"  c:\book\code\
chapter_10\CtrlC\test.exe'
0:000> .symfix
0:000> .reload
0:000> g
(4e8.10b0): Control-C exception - code 40010005 (first chance)
First chance exceptions are reported before any exception handling.
This exception may be expected and handled.
KERNEL32!CtrlRoutine+0xcb:
76dde37d c745fcfeffffff  mov     dword ptr [ebp-4],0FFFFFFFEh ss:0023:0433fecc=00000000
0:004> k
```

```
ChildEBP RetAddr
0433fed0 76daed6c KERNEL32!CtrlRoutine+0xcb
0433fedc 777037f5 KERNEL32!BaseThreadInitThunk+0xe
0433ff1c 777037c8 ntdll!__RtlUserThreadStart+0x70
0433ff34 00000000 ntdll!_RtlUserThreadStart+0x1b
```

By letting the target continue from this point *without* handling the first-chance *Control-C* exception notification in the debugger (by using *gn* instead of *g*), you can progress in the program's execution and break into the debugger as your delegate handler is being executed. You can then use the SOS debugger command to display the managed call stack at the moment of the breakpoint, as illustrated in the following listing.

```
0:004> bp kernel32!WriteConsoleA
0:004> gn
Breakpoint 0 hit
KERNEL32!WriteConsoleA:
0:005> .loadby sos clr
0:005> !clrstack
OS Thread Id: 0x1594 (5)
Child SP IP       Call Site
...
042fef20 5a2a77fb System.IO.__ConsoleStream.WriteFileNative(Microsoft.Win32.SafeHandles.
SafeFileHandle,
Byte[], Int32, Int32, Int32, Int32 ByRef)
042fef4c 5a2a7774 System.IO.__ConsoleStream.Write(Byte[], Int32, Int32)
042fef6c 5a29bc8b System.IO.StreamWriter.Flush(Boolean, Boolean)
042fef84 5a2a7959 System.IO.StreamWriter.Write(Char[], Int32, Int32)
042fefa4 5a2a833c System.IO.TextWriter.WriteLine(System.String)
042fefc0 5a2a7841 System.IO.TextWriter+SyncTextWriter.WriteLine(System.String)
042fefd0 5a2a70c3 System.Console.WriteLine(System.String)
042fefdc 001f0126 Test.<Main>b__0(System.Object, System.ConsoleCancelEventArgs)
[c:\book\code\chapter_10\CtrlC\test.cs @ 10]
042fefec 5a87b78c System.Console.ControlCDelegate(System.Object)
...
```

As it turns out, the event handlers (delegates) defined in .NET are not directly registered with the Win32 API and instead are maintained inside the *System.Console* .NET class, which registers a single managed delegate with the *kernel32!SetConsoleCtrlHandler* Win32 API. (This is the *Console.BreakEvent* method you see in the following listing.) When invoked by the *kernel32!CtrlRoutine* thread (thread #4 in this experiment), this single handler delegate, in turn, executes all the managed event handlers associated with the *Console.CancelKeyPress* event property using a new .NET thread-pool thread (which is thread #5, whose call stack you already saw in the previous listing).

```
0:005> ~4s
0:004> k
...
0422fed4 76dde3d8 mscorlib_ni+0x8fbbda
0422ff60 76daed6c KERNEL32!CtrlRoutine+0x126
0422ff6c 777037f5 KERNEL32!BaseThreadInitThunk+0xe
0422ffac 777037c8 ntdll!__RtlUserThreadStart+0x70
0422ffc4 00000000 ntdll!_RtlUserThreadStart+0x1b
0:004> !clrstack
OS Thread Id: 0x1b70 (4)
```

```
Child SP IP       Call Site
System.Threading.WaitHandle.WaitOneNative(System.Runtime.InteropServices.SafeHandle, UInt32,
Boolean, Boolean)
0422fe2c 5a2fb5ef System.Threading.WaitHandle.InternalWaitOne(System.Runtime.InteropServices.
SafeHandle,
Int64, Boolean, Boolean)
0422fe48 5a2db1ee System.Threading.WaitHandle.WaitOne(System.TimeSpan, Boolean)
0422fe68 5a87b8a0 System.Console.BreakEvent(Int32)
0422fe7c 5a94bbda DomainNeutralILStubClass.IL_STUB_ReversePInvoke(Int32)
0:004> $ Quit this debugging session once you're done inspecting the target...
0:004> q
```

By default, there is only one Ctrl+C handler at the *kernel32.dll* level, which simply terminates the console process. In this case, however, you also added another handler. These user-defined handlers get executed before the default handler is finally run to terminate the process. Adding a custom cancel event handler can be useful when a console application needs to dispose of its open resources (database connections, file handles, and so on) before gracefully shutting down.

Console Termination Handlers at the System Level

The only remaining issue now is to figure out how the new *kernel32!CtrlRoutine* thread that got injected in response to the Ctrl+C signal came into existence. Knowing what you do now about the console subsystem in Windows, it is reasonable to suspect that either the *conhost.exe* worker process or, more likely, the higher-privilege *csrss.exe* Windows subsystem process does that.

To confirm this hunch, you can run the scenario again with breakpoints at the low-level *ntdll!NtCreateThread** functions, which are used (indirectly through the Win32 API layer) in user-mode applications to create new threads. Because you're interested in debugging the *csrss.exe* subsystem process, you need to switch to using a kernel-debugging session. This is because using a user-mode debugger to control the *csrss.exe* process might cause deadlocks or temporary hangs in the system if the rest of the OS is left free to continue running. This could happen because other processes might stop and wait for *csrss.exe* to respond (to an ALPC call, for example) while it's frozen inside the user-mode debugger.

For this experiment, you need to start a new instance of the *test.exe* process. While the program is still running (and blocked) on the target machine, break into the host kernel debugger and insert the aforementioned breakpoints, as demonstrated in the following listing. Because the thread-creation functions are called quite frequently, you can improve your debugging experience by also restricting the scope of the breakpoints to the *csrss.exe* process for the user session. Notice the use of the *$proc* kernel debugger pseudo-register to conveniently reference the address of the current *csrss.exe* process context in the kernel debugger when adding the breakpoints.

```
0: kd> vertarget
Windows 7 Kernel Version 7600 MP (2 procs) Free x86 compatible
Built by: 7600.16695.x86fre.win7_gdr.101026-1503
0: kd> !process 0 0 csrss.exe
PROCESS 86af3650  SessionId: 0  Cid: 01a4    Peb: 7ffde000  ParentCid: 019c
    Image: csrss.exe
PROCESS 86af3110  SessionId: 1  Cid: 01e4    Peb: 7ffde000  ParentCid: 01cc
    Image: csrss.exe
```

```
0: kd> $ Switch the current process context to the target (session 1) csrss.exe process
0: kd> .process /i 86af3110
0: kd> g
Break instruction exception - code 80000003 (first chance)
0: kd> .reload /user
0: kd> x ntdll!*NtCreateThread*
77ae49c0          ntdll!NtCreateThread = <no type information>
77ae49d0          ntdll!NtCreateThreadEx = <no type information>
0: kd> bp /p @$proc ntdll!NtCreateThread
0: kd> bp /p @$proc ntdll!NtCreateThreadEx
0: kd> g
```

Notice that as soon as you issue the Ctrl+C key combination inside the *test.exe* console window on the target machine, you immediately break back into the host kernel debugger with the following call stack.

```
Breakpoint 1 hit
ntdll!ZwCreateThreadEx:
0: kd> .reload /user
0: kd> k
ChildEBP RetAddr
0191f914 75d943e2 ntdll!ZwCreateThreadEx
0191f994 75d945fd winsrv!InternalCreateCallbackThread+0xcc
0191f9fc 75d94541 winsrv!CreateCtrlThread+0xa0
0191fc64 75dd4d65 winsrv!SrvEndTask+0x109
0191fddc 77be5e7a CSRSRV!CsrApiRequestThread+0x3cb
0191fe1c 77c437c8 ntdll!__RtlUserThreadStart+0x28
0191fe34 00000000 ntdll!_RtlUserThreadStart+0x1b
```

This is the *csrss.exe* process attempting to inject (by using the *winsrv!CreateCtrlThread* function from the previous call stack) the new *kernel32!CtrlRoutine* thread into the target console process, which confirms the initial stipulation. At this point, the *conhost.exe* process instance associated with the *test.exe* console process (which you're able to find in the *ConsoleHostProcess* field of the executive console process structure) is deep inside the message handler routine for the Ctrl+C signal and is waiting for the ALPC call it issued to the *csrss.exe* process to inject the *CtrlRoutine* thread into the target process and return. This sequence is confirmed in the following listing.

```
0: kd> !process 0 0 test.exe
PROCESS 85b3f030  SessionId: 1  Cid: 155c    Peb: 7ffdf000  ParentCid: 11d4
    Image: test.exe
0: kd> dt nt!_EPROCESS 85b3f030 ConsoleHostProcess
   +0x14c ConsoleHostProcess : 0xd34
0: kd> !process 0xd34 0
Searching for Process with Cid == d34
PROCESS 85fd9488  SessionId: 1  Cid: 0d34    Peb: 7ffdd000  ParentCid: 01e4
    Image: conhost.exe
0: kd> .process /r /p 85fd9488
0: kd> !process 85fd9488 7
```

```
PROCESS 85fd9488  SessionId: 1  Cid: 0d34    Peb: 7ffdd000  ParentCid: 01e4
    Image: conhost.exe
...
THREAD 85797468  Cid 0d34.1360  Teb: 7ffdf000 Win32Thread: fe7d1360 WAIT: (WrLpcReply) UserMode
Non-Alertable
    Waiting for reply to ALPC Message a7f0b610 : queued at port 86af7c08 : owned by process
86af3110
...
        0163f778 77c3c7ee 00000014 0163f7bc 0163f7bc ntdll!NtRequestWaitReplyPort+0xc
        0163f798 76f4611e 0163f7bc 00000000 00030401 ntdll!CsrClientCallServer+0xc3
        0163f82c 0031a7dc 00000008 0163f864 00000010 USER32!ConsoleControl+0x120
        0163f898 00311568 000a0be0 0163f8a4 0163f8a4 conhost!ProcessCtrlEvents+0x208
        0163f8ac 00313067 0163f9b8 00000102 00000000 conhost!UnlockConsole+0x41
        0163f93c 76f3c4e7 000300ca 00000102 00000003 conhost!ConsoleWindowProc+0xe5e
        0163f968 76f3c5e7 00312f9b 000300ca 00000102 USER32!InternalCallWinProc+0x23
        0163f9e0 76f3cc19 00000000 00312f9b 000300ca USER32!UserCallWinProcCheckWow+0x14b
        0163fa40 76f3cc70 00312f9b 00000000 0163fa88 USER32!DispatchMessageWorker+0x35e
        0163fa50 00313128 0163fa68 00000000 00000000 USER32!DispatchMessageW+0xf
        0163fa88 77d7ed6c 00000000 0163fad4 77c437f5 conhost!ConsoleInputThread+0xe4
        0163fa94 77c437f5 00000000 7424a445 00000000 kernel32!BaseThreadInitThunk+0xe
        0163fad4 77c437c8 00313080 00000000 00000000 ntdll!__RtlUserThreadStart+0x70
        0163faec 00000000 00313080 00000000 00000000 ntdll!_RtlUserThreadStart+0x1b
```

By using the *!alpc* kernel debugger extension and */m* option with the address displayed in the previous kernel-debugger command, you can dump the ALPC message structure and verify that it's a message sent to an ALPC port that's owned by the *csrss.exe* process.

```
0: kd> !alpc /m a7f0b610
...
  OwnerPort              : 857bf8b8 [ALPC_CLIENT_COMMUNICATION_PORT]
  WaitingThread          : 85797468
  QueueType              : ALPC_MSGQUEUE_PENDING
  QueuePort              : 86af7c08 [ALPC_CONNECTION_PORT]
  QueuePortOwnerProcess : 86af3110 (csrss.exe)
  ServerThread           : 86dc74d0
...
```

One useful observation that follows immediately from this experiment is that the user-defined cancel event handlers get executed on a new thread that's injected into the console process on the fly by *csrss.exe*, when other threads in the process are still alive. As such, you need to synchronize any access to shared variables from the code that runs in those handlers with the rest of the threads in the console process.

Figure 10-5 summarizes the Ctrl+C signal handling sequence in console applications, which you were able to dissect using the WinDbg debugger in this section.

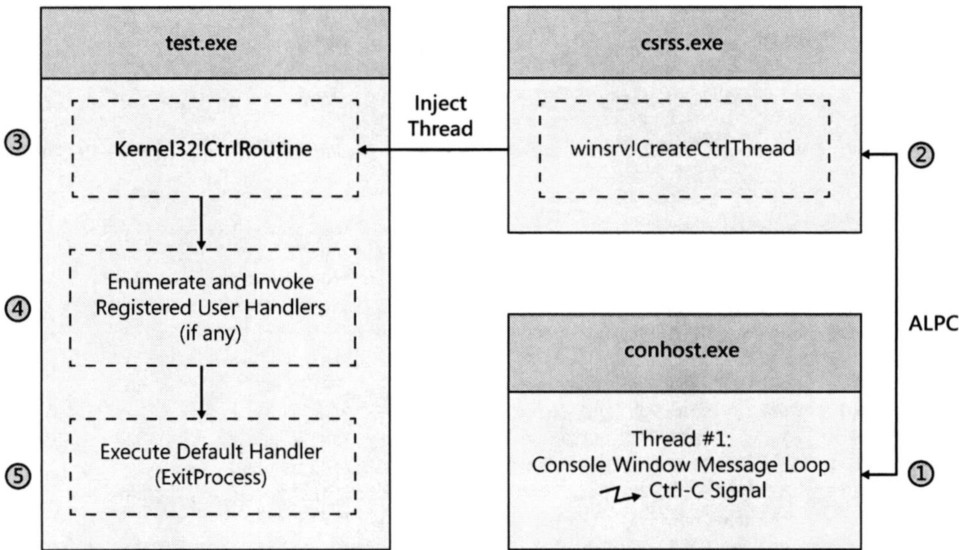

FIGURE 10-5 Ctrl+C signal handling in Windows console applications.

Anatomy of System Calls

When certain functions in the Win32 API are invoked from user mode, a transition to kernel mode is sometimes needed to perform privileged operations. This is important because user-mode code runs in a sandbox enforced by the CPU, where it's not allowed to directly access I/O ports or other privileged virtual memory pages, such as those assigned to the kernel. Naturally, it would be a security hole if user-mode code could directly execute arbitrary kernel code, so a CPU-controlled mechanism is needed for getting in and out of the kernel of the operating system.

This section digs a little deeper into how the OS and CPU collaborate to implement this critical capability on behalf of code running in user mode. On the CPU side, modern processors expose a fast instruction to transition into the kernel and another one to return control to the code that initiated the system call in user mode. On *x86*, the *sysenter* and *sysexit* instructions provide this functionality while on *x64*, the *syscall* and *sysret* instructions implement this facility. These instructions act as an indirect way for user-mode code to pass control (that is, change the instruction pointer register) over to kernel code by instructing the CPU and kernel to do so in a secure way.

Many Win32 APIs pass through the *ntdll.dll* layer when they need to perform the system call transition into the kernel. This DLL is mapped into every user-mode process and contains, among other things, the user-mode side of the NT executive services that perform the actual CPU instruction to transition to kernel mode. The sequence of calls from a user-mode process into one of the system services exported by the executive layer is illustrated in Figure 10-6.

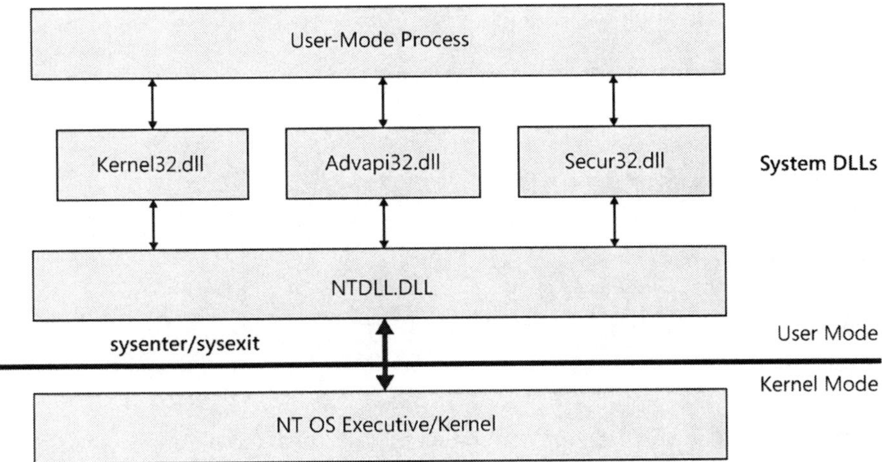

FIGURE 10-6 System calls in the Windows architectural stack.

A key component in the OS implementation of the system call mechanism is a hard-coded, kernel-mode table of exposed system service routines, such as creating a mutex, waiting on a synchronization handle, writing into a file, and so on. This table is called the *System Service Dispatch Table (SSDT)*.

Note Though this table was never officially documented by Microsoft, its details are widely known in the developer community because it was used in the past by antivirus products to hook system service calls on the kernel side rather than on the Win32 user-mode side, where there are many more calls to hook. Unfortunately, the SSDT also became a target for malware trying to hide its existence on the system. With the introduction of the Kernel Patch Protection (also known as PatchGuard) feature in 64-bit versions of Windows to specifically protect the integrity of the OS kernel and prevent tampering of important data structures such as the SSDT, this approach is no longer widely used in antivirus products, even though it's still possible to use it on *x86* versions of Windows.

The User-Mode Side of System Calls

Before issuing the system-call CPU instruction, the index of the requested service routine in the SSDT is loaded into a well-known register so that it can be shared with the kernel side of the system call. To see this in action, you can use the following C# program to observe the system-call sequence involved when writing data to a local file on disk. This experiment is conducted on 32-bit Windows, with the *x86*-specific system-call instructions, but the same concepts are also applicable on *x64* Windows.

```
//
// C:\book\code\chapter_10\SystemCall>systemcall.cs
//
public class Test
{
    public static void Main()
    {
        Console.ReadLine();
        File.WriteAllText(@"c:\temp\abc.txt", "abc");
        Console.WriteLine("Success.");
    }
}
```

Just as you did earlier when you used the debuggers to learn the internals of the console subsystem in Windows, you'll again use WinDbg to dissect the system-call mechanism. To that end, you can run the previous program on the target of a kernel-debugging session and set a breakpoint at *ntdll!NtWriteFile* while the program waits for user input on the target machine. Notice the use of the *$proc* kernel debugger pseudo-register in the *bp* command so that the scope of this common breakpoint is restricted to the current process context.

```
kd> vertarget
Windows 7 Kernel Version 7600 MP (1 procs) Free x86 compatible
kd> .symfix
kd> .reload
kd> !process 0 0 SystemCall.exe
PROCESS 865e7340  SessionId: 1  Cid: 1b4c    Peb: 7ffde000  ParentCid: 047c
    Image: systemcall.exe
kd> .process /i 865e7340
kd> g
Break instruction exception - code 80000003 (first chance)
kd> .reload /user
kd> bp /p @$proc ntdll!NtWriteFile
kd> g
```

Once you let the program continue its execution by pressing **Enter** inside the target command window, you'll see the following host kernel debugger breakpoint on the user-mode side of the system call. Using the *uf* ("unassemble function") command, you can obtain the disassembly of this function call.

```
Breakpoint 0 hit
ntdll!NtWriteFile:
kd> $ "." is an alias for the current instruction pointer
kd> uf .
ntdll!NtWriteFile
001b:77185eb0 b88c010000      mov     eax,18Ch
001b:77185eb5 ba0003fe7f      mov     edx,offset SharedUserData!SystemCallStub (7ffe0300)
001b:77185eba ff12            call    dword ptr [edx]
001b:77185ebc c22400          ret     24h
```

Because the SSDT is considered an internal implementation detail by Microsoft, there is no debugger extension command to display its contents, at least not in the Windows debuggers package. However, you can clearly see from the previous listing that the *eax* register is used to store the index of the requested service routine during the system call (*0x18C* in the case of *nt!NtWriteFile*). After loading this value into *eax*, the code in *ntdll.dll* calls into a stub located in a common virtual memory page that includes the actual transition code into the kernel, as you can see in the following listing.

```
kd> uf .
ntdll!NtWriteFile
001b:77185eb0 b88c010000      mov     eax,18Ch
001b:77185eb5 ba0003fe7f      mov     edx,offset SharedUserData!SystemCallStub (7ffe0300)
001b:77185eba ff12            call    dword ptr [edx]
001b:77185ebc c22400          ret     24h
kd> dd 7ffe0300
7ffe0300  776e70b0 776e70b4 00000000 00000000
...
kd> uf 776e70b0
ntdll!KiFastSystemCall:
776e70b0 8bd4            mov     edx,esp
776e70b2 0f34            sysenter
776e70b4 c3              ret
```

The benefit of calling through this common stub is that the kernel will know exactly where to go back to when returning into user mode without having to save the user-mode instruction pointer. The following listing follows the next few instructions in the debugger to the point of the system call CPU instruction.

```
kd> $ Step over (F10) a few instructions
kd> p
ntdll!NtWriteFile+0x5:
001b:77185eb5 ba0003fe7f      mov     edx,offset SharedUserData!SystemCallStub (7ffe0300)
kd> p
ntdll!NtWriteFile+0xa:
001b:77185eba ff12            call    dword ptr [edx]
kd> $ Now step into (F11) the function call whose address is stored in the edx register
kd> t
ntdll!KiFastSystemCall
kd> uf .
ntdll!KiFastSystemCall
001b:776e70b0 8bd4            mov     edx,esp
001b:776e70b2 0f34            sysenter
001b:776e70b4 c3              ret
```

The Transition into Kernel Mode

The API call is now about to enter kernel mode. As shown in the previous listing, the only thing that the *ntdll!KiFastSystemCall* function does before issuing the *sysenter* instruction is save the user-mode stack pointer (*esp*) in the *edx* register so that it can be restored when returning back to user mode. Remember that every thread has a kernel-mode and a user-mode stack, so the stack pointer must be restored when returning to user mode. Given the disassembly of the common stub, you can reasonably stipulate that the *sysenter* CPU instruction is responsible for changing the stack pointer register to point to the kernel-mode stack and also set the instruction pointer register to the virtual address of the entry point in kernel-mode memory.

The interesting question, though, is how the CPU is able to figure out these locations. The answer to this lies within Intel's Model-Specific Registers (MSR). As part of the Fast System Call facility introduced in the Intel Pentium II family of processors, the following registers were reserved for use by the operating system to configure the values it expects the CPU to set during a *sysenter* call:

- **SYSENTER_CS_MSR (0x174)** Contains the value of the segment selector to load into the *cs* register when transitioning into kernel mode
- **SYSENTER_ESP_MSR (0x175)** Contains the value of the kernel-mode stack pointer to set after the transition
- **SYSENTER_EIP_MSR (0x176)** Contains the value of the kernel-mode instruction pointer to execute once the transition is complete

You can use the kernel-mode debugger once again to confirm this bit of theory. By setting a breakpoint at the target entry point after the transition to kernel mode (which you can obtain using the *rdmsr* command in the kernel debugger), you'll see that breakpoint hit as soon as you let the target machine execute the *sysenter* instruction. You can also verify that the value of the *esp* register after the transition is the same value held in SYSENTER_ESP_MSR, as shown in the following listing.

```
kd> $ read the value of SYSENTER_CS_MSR
kd> rdmsr 174
msr[174] = 00000000'00000008
kd> $ read the value of SYSENTER_ESP_MSR
kd> rdmsr 175
msr[175] = 00000000'80790000
kd> $ read the value of SYSENTER_EIP_MSR
kd> rdmsr 176
msr[176] = 00000000'8265d320
kd> $ set a breakpoint using the address stored in SYSENTER_EIP_MSR (176)
kd> !process -1 0
PROCESS 865e7340  SessionId: 1  Cid: 1b4c    Peb: 7ffde000  ParentCid: 047c
    Image: systemcall.exe
kd> bp /p @$proc 8265d320
kd> g
Breakpoint 1 hit
nt!KiFastCallEntry:
8265d320 b923000000      mov     ecx,23h
kd> r
eax=000011b4 ebx=0000005c ecx=00150578 edx=0069fb6c esi=76494fda edi=815c0001
eip=8265d320 esp=80790000 ebp=0069fb78 iopl=0         nv up di ng nz na po cy
cs=0008  ss=0010  ds=0023  es=0023  fs=0030  gs=0000             efl=00000083
```

The Kernel-Mode Side of System Calls

Once in kernel mode, the service routine reads the value passed in the *eax* register to figure out the index of the requested service in the SSDT before calling the handler corresponding to that entry. In this case, it's the *nt!NtWriteFile* executive service routine, which you can verify by setting another breakpoint at that code address, as demonstrated in the following listing.

```
kd> bl
 0 e 77c26a68     0001 (0001) ntdll!NtWriteFile
     Match process data 862924c8
 1 e 828560f0     0001 (0001) nt!KiFastCallEntry
     Match process data 862924c8
kd> $ clear the previous breakpoints...
kd> bc *
kd> $ set a new per-process breakpoint at nt!NtWriteFile
kd> !process -1 0
PROCESS 865e7340  SessionId: 1  Cid: 1b4c    Peb: 7ffde000  ParentCid: 047c
    Image: systemcall.exe
kd> bp /p @$proc nt!NtWriteFile
kd> g
Breakpoint 0 hit
nt!NtWriteFile:
kd> $ execute a few instructions in the service routine so user-mode frames are set up...
kd> pc 2
kd> .reload /user
kd> $ you're now at the system service routine for WriteFile
kd> k
ChildEBP RetAddr
87d97d08 8285621a nt!NtWriteFile+0x3a
97927d08 77c270b4 nt!KiFastCallEntry+0x12a
002fed20 77c26a74 ntdll!KiFastSystemCallRet
002fed24 75ee75d4 ntdll!NtWriteFile+0xc
002fed88 77d8543c KERNELBASE!WriteFile+0x113
002feda4 65071c8b KERNEL32!WriteFileImplementation+0x76
...
```

The executive finally constructs an I/O Request Packet (IRP) and delegates the completion of the I/O request to the driver or drivers associated with the file handle, as was discussed in Chapter 1. Figure 10-7 recaps the steps involved in executing the single line of C# code from the sample program shown earlier in this section, which simply writes a string buffer to a local file on disk. As you can see, quite a bit of work is performed by the OS and its various layers on your application's behalf to service that seemingly trivial line of code.

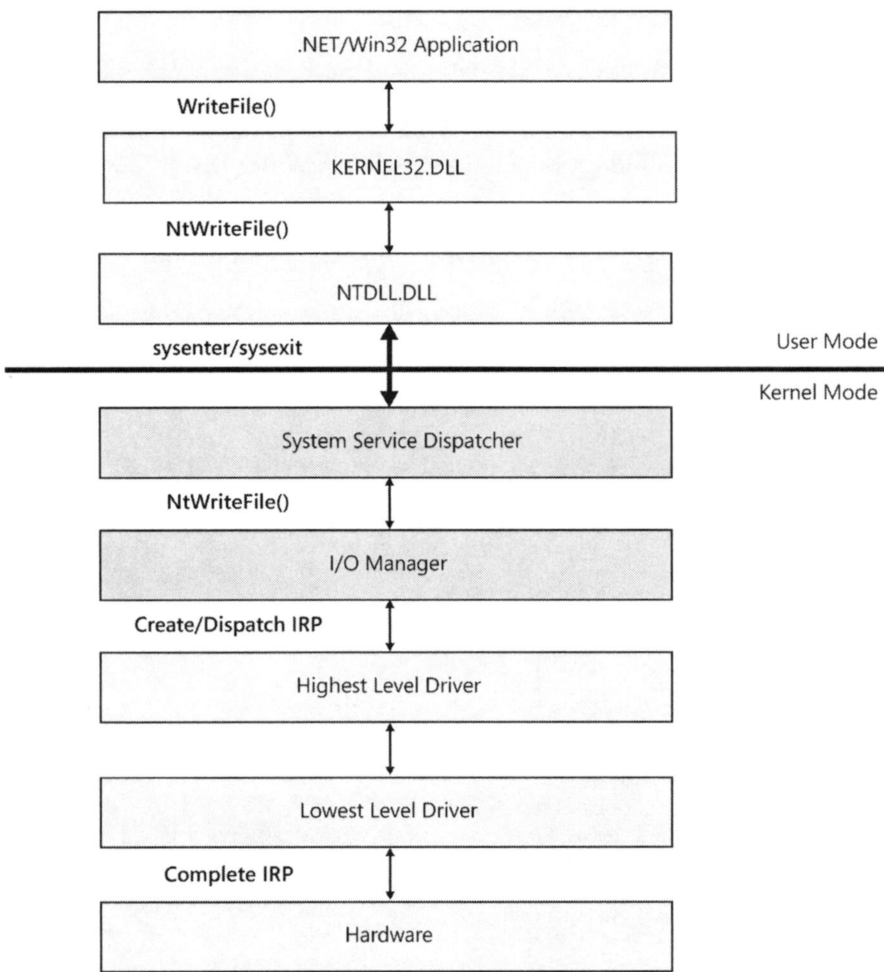

FIGURE 10-7 I/O processing in the Windows operating system.

Summary

This chapter closes the second part in this book with the introduction of a learning strategy in which the debuggers are used as an integral part of the software-development process—before they're needed to investigate bugs in the new code that you write. It also presented practical case studies to illustrate the capabilities of the debuggers as useful tools to observe and study the behavior of software. Several useful strategies emerged from those experiments:

- The *printf* example demonstrated a key strategy in studying unfamiliar components when it used the *nt!PspInsertProcess* kernel-mode breakpoint to discover the processes that get started when executing your scenario. This is usually an effective first step when you know little about the internal operations of your scenario because it can alert you to the interprocess interactions involved in your experiment, which is very important when trying to draw a high-level architecture diagram for the mechanisms underlying your scenario.
- Once you've drawn the process boundaries in your scenario, it's often more efficient to transition to user-mode debugging when trying to zoom in on the local operations of each process in the conceptual diagram you developed in the previous step. This is what you did in the *printf* example too, where you were able to debug the operations of the console host process (*conhost.exe*) using a user-mode debugger after you discovered its existence using a host kernel debugger.
- When deciding between user-mode and kernel-mode debugging, consider the potential of deadlocks when you need to debug system processes that might be necessary for the operations of the user-mode debugger itself. In those cases, you'll need to use kernel-mode debugging to avoid causing the target machine to freeze or deadlock. This was highlighted in your study of the Ctrl+C signal handling in console applications, when you used a host kernel debugger to trace the thread injection of the user control handler back to the *csrss.exe* Windows Client/Server subsystem process.

The next part in this book will demonstrate, among other useful applications of tracing, how you can extend the system-debugging strategies introduced in this chapter through the use of tracing and profiling tools in Windows.

PART 3

Observing and Analyzing Software Behavior

Event Tracing for Windows (ETW) is a logging framework for analyzing application behavior that's used extensively throughout the Microsoft Windows operating system. When I started studying ETW a few years ago, I was mostly interested in the technology as it pertained to profiling and performance analysis in Windows and this part of the book will certainly cover that important angle. However, as the technology evolved in recent Windows releases to support capturing stack traces for the events it logs, and as more convenient GUI front-end tools were also built around it, I came to realize that there was much more to it and also started employing it as a troubleshooting aid. While the debuggers provide discrete snapshot views of a given target, ETW and the tracing tools that leverage it can be used to develop a timeline of events to complement those snapshots. The combination of these two approaches is often a great way to trace the root causes of the anomalies or bugs you observe when running your software.

The previous part of this book demonstrated the use of debuggers not only for investigating bugs, but also as great tools for learning system internals. The problem with that approach, however, is that you often need to know a few key breakpoints before you can start digging deeper, not to mention the need for hooking a debugger, which can sometimes affect the normal flow of execution. To make matters worse, an extra reboot might also be required to enable kernel-mode debugging if it wasn't already. Fortunately, ETW can be used to obtain a quick, first-order approximation of how programs work at a macro level. It also often proves to be a great way for getting the breakpoints needed in a more thorough analysis under a user-mode or kernel-mode debugger. As it turns out, though, you'll find that it's often possible to carry out full investigations using tracing tools exclusively, without ever needing to invasively attach a user-mode debugger or hook a kernel-mode debugger.

Chapter 11, "Introducing Xperf," provides you with the information you need to acquire the Windows Performance Toolkit (WPT) and start using it for basic tracing investigations. Chapter 12, "Inside ETW," then delves into the design tenets of ETW. Without at least a cursory knowledge of the architectural foundations of ETW, you'll find it more difficult to master the use patterns of the ETW-based tools covered in Chapter 13, "Common Tracing Scenarios," which presents several real-world examples to illustrate the importance of tracing as an investigative technique in Windows.

CHAPTER 11

Introducing Xperf

In this chapter

The Event Tracing for Windows (ETW) framework, which ships as an integral part of the Microsoft Windows operating system, provides a uniform way to instrument your code by logging trace events with very little overhead to your application's run-time performance. What makes this framework particularly useful to learn is that any software you develop in Windows is already using it—either directly or indirectly—because several components in the operating system (OS) are already heavily instrumented using ETW. Even without explicit instrumentation on your part, you can still take advantage of the plethora of events logged by the system (process and thread creation events, disk I/O events, context switch events, sample profiling events, and so on) for analyzing the behavior of your software.

Even the shortest ETW trace sessions typically generate thousands of events. Without a good front-end UI tool to group and analyze this data, you would quickly get overwhelmed by the sheer number of events in the resulting log file. Fortunately, the Windows 7 Software Development Kit (SDK) contains a powerful tool, called Xperf, which can serve both as a controller for the settings used during ETW trace collections, as well as a visualizer for the events in the collected log files. This chapter will show you how you can install this tool and start using it for basic tracing investigations.

Acquiring Xperf

Just like the Windows debuggers, Xperf is free. It is also backward-compatible, meaning that you can use a new Xperf with an older version of Windows (but the reverse isn't always true), so the Xperf version targeting Windows 7 will be used throughout. However, you can also use that version of the tool to collect and view traces on Windows Vista too.

Xperf comes with the Windows Performance Toolkit (WPT), which is included as part of the Windows 7 SDK. It is available both in SDK version 7.0 (labeled "Windows SDK for Windows 7 and Microsoft .NET Framework 3.5" at the Microsoft Download Center) and also in SDK version 7.1 (labeled "Windows SDK for Windows 7 and Microsoft .NET Framework 4.0" at the Microsoft Download Center). Version 7.1, which maps to the Windows 7 SP1 release, is the version that will be used throughout this part of this book because its version of Xperf contains several new additions compared to the one included in SDK version 7.0, which shipped earlier at Windows 7 RTM.

The good news is you don't need to download yet another large file if you already saved the Windows SDK 7.1 ISO from *http://www.microsoft.com/download/en/details.aspx?id=8279* to your local hard drive, as was suggested back in Chapter 2, "Getting Started." The following procedure will walk you through the steps needed to install the WPT binaries to your system.

Installing the Windows Performance Toolkit

1. Mount the Windows SDK 7.1 ISO file to a drive letter on your machine. You can again use the Virtual Clone Drive freeware to mount this SDK ISO file, just as you did back in Chapter 2 when you installed the Windows debuggers from the Windows 7 SDK. When that freeware is installed, you should be able to right-click the ISO file and mount it, as shown in the following screen shot:

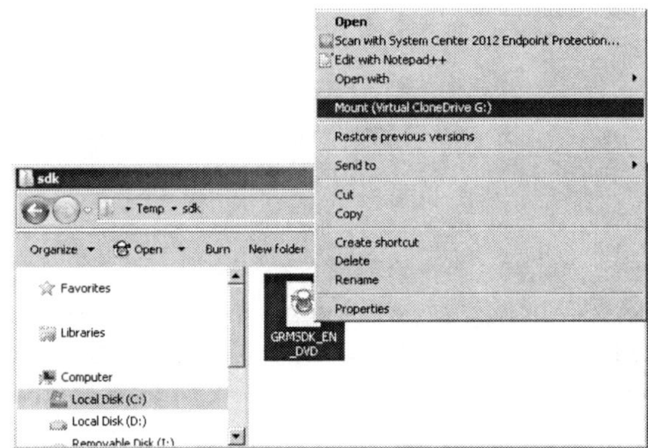

2. Right-click the newly mounted drive letter, and open its root directory. You should see the following files under that directory:

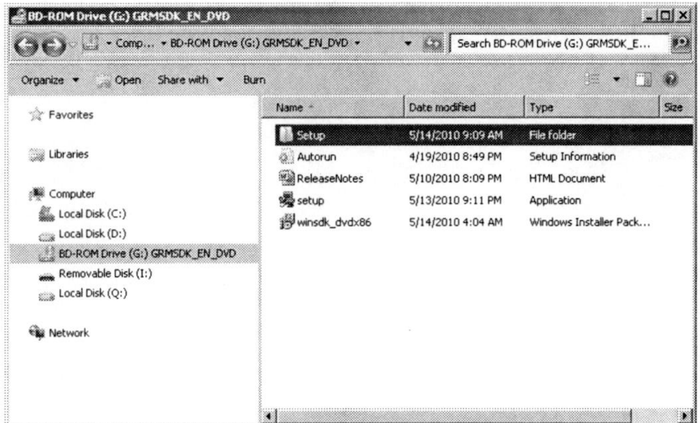

3. Under the Setup subdirectory, you'll find the *x86*, *x64* (*amd64*), and *ia64* setup installers for the WPT, which carry the architecture-specific *xperf.exe* tool.

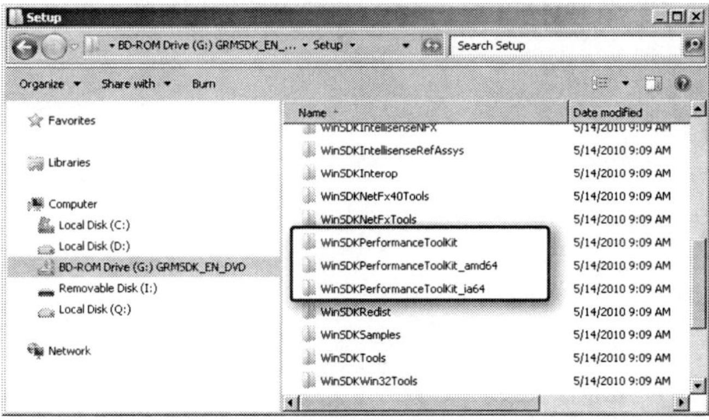

You should always install and use the version of WPT that's native to your system during trace collections; otherwise, you'll fail to decode the symbols when analyzing the traces. Parsing and visualizing the captured traces, on the other hand, can be done using any flavor of the tool.

In particular, you'll need to use the *x64* toolkit under the WinSDKPerformanceToolkit_amd64 folder to collect traces on *x64* Windows, even if you're interested in profiling an *x86* program running in the WOW64 environment. If you're running on *x86* Windows, use the wpt_x86.msi file under the WinSDKPerformanceToolkit folder to install the *x86* version of Xperf, as shown in the following screen shot:

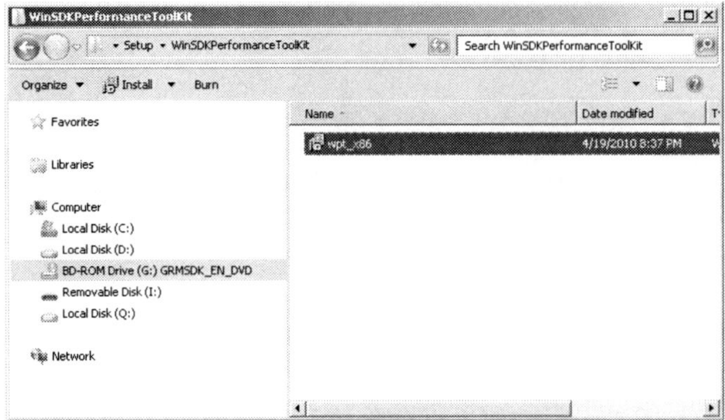

4. Double-click the WPT setup file for your target CPU architecture, and then follow the step-by-step installation instructions. The installation process takes only a few seconds to complete.

Once the installation is complete, you'll find the *xperf.exe* tool in the following default location:

```
C:\Program Files\Microsoft Windows Performance Toolkit>xperf.exe
    Microsoft (R) Windows (R) Performance Analyzer Version 4.8.7701
    Performance Analyzer Command Line
    Copyright (c) Microsoft Corporation. All rights reserved.

    Usage: xperf options ...
        xperf -help view            for xperfview, the graphical user interface
        xperf -help start           for logger start options
        xperf -help providers       for known tracing flags
...
```

The setup program also automatically places *xperf.exe* on your search path. For brevity's sake, the commands used in this book will refer to the tool without its full path. In addition, the WPT package also comes with a nice Help file that describes the command-line options and features exposed in the Xperf tool, so be sure to also consult it when you need help with particular commands or topics. This help isn't integrated with the Xperf visualizer using the standard F1 shortcut, however, so you'll need to start it from the Start menu, where the WPT setup program has already inserted an entry for it, as shown in Figure 11-1.

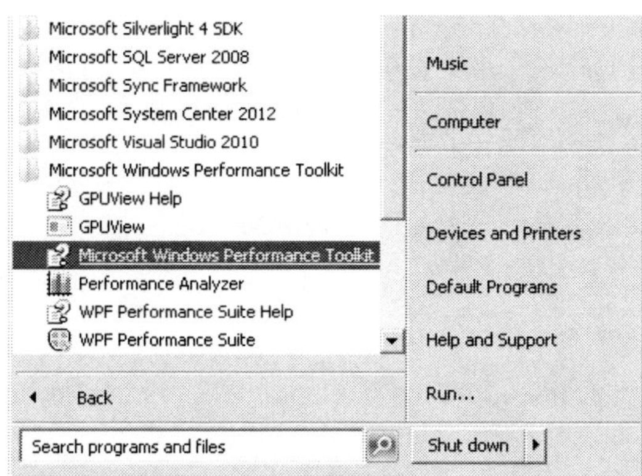

FIGURE 11-1 Starting the WPT Help from the Start menu.

Important Microsoft unveiled a new version of the Windows Performance Toolkit with its preview of the Windows 8 release. Several improvements were introduced, including new controller and viewer UI tools, called *Windows Performance Recorder* (WPR) and *Windows Performance Analyzer* (WPA), respectively. WPR and WPA have a convenient user interface for capturing and analyzing ETW traces and are meant to replace the functionality that Xperf used to provide. That being said, the transition to WPR/WPA is going to be easy for you once you've learned how to use Xperf and understand the ETW foundations that support it.

The examples shown in this part of the book are conducted using the Windows 7 version of WPT, so they'll be using Xperf, but the majority of the concepts you'll learn will remain applicable. If you're interested in learning more about WPA/WPR, though, you can download the Windows 8 consumer preview's WPT package from *http://www.microsoft.com/download/en/details.aspx?displaylang=en&id=28997*, where WPT is included as part of the Windows 8 Assessment and Deployment Kit (ADK). As stated earlier in this chapter, WPT is backward-compatible, so WPA/WPR can also be used for tracing experiments on Windows 7.

Your First Xperf Investigation

To illustrate the power of the Xperf tool when coupled with the rich ETW instrumentation in the Windows operating system, you'll now use it in a real-world investigation to determine why the *notepad.exe* text editor takes a long time to open large files.

You can create a test file for use in this case study by using the *fsutil.exe* utility, for example, which is available as part of Windows under the *system32* directory. The following command creates a file that's about 500 MB in size, which should be sufficient for the purpose of this experiment. You need to execute this step from an elevated administrative command prompt because the *fsutil.exe* tool requires full administrative privileges. For a reminder of how to start an elevated command prompt, refer back to the Introduction of this book.

```
C:\book\code\chapter_11\NotepadDelay>create_large_file.cmd -size 500000000
INFO: Invoking fsutil to create a 500000000-byte file...
CmdLine: (fsutil.exe file createnew c:\temp\test.dat 500000000)
File c:\temp\test.dat is created
```

If you try opening this file using *notepad.exe*, you'll see that the operation takes a long time (about a minute or so on my 2-GHz, dual-processor machine) to complete. If you have a slow machine and find that it is taking *notepad.exe* even longer to open the file, try providing a smaller size to the script used in the previous command when creating the large test file. The precise size of the file isn't important in this experiment, as long as it is large enough to cause *notepad.exe* to take several seconds to load the file.

```
notepad.exe c:\temp\test.dat
```

While *notepad.exe* is struggling to open the large file, you'll see that the application UI becomes unresponsive to user input, as illustrated in Figure 11-2. This is the telltale sign of a GUI application in Windows that's not promptly fetching and processing the messages arriving on its UI message queue, which is most often due to a bug whereby a long, synchronous operation gets erroneously scheduled directly on the main UI thread, stalling its ability to process incoming UI messages.

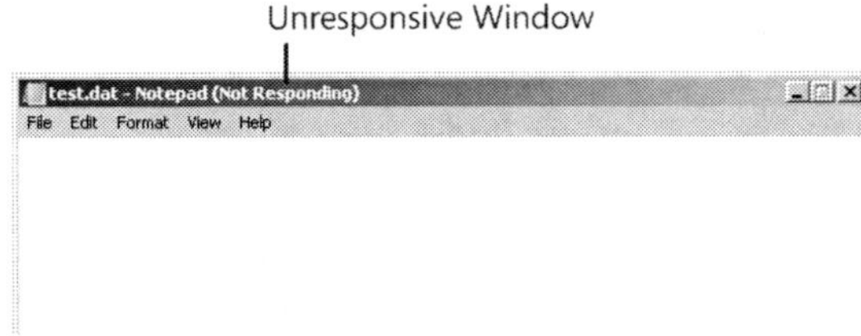

FIGURE 11-2 Unresponsive *notepad.exe* user interface while opening large files.

Devising an Investigation Strategy

The first step in any profiling or tracing investigation using Xperf is to figure out the set of ETW events most relevant to the scenario you're dealing with. Performance issues such as the one at hand in this experiment often come down to excessive time spent executing a certain operation, though the reasons behind such delays vary, as do the ways you go about tracing those root causes.

You might be dealing, for instance, with a program that's overtaxing the CPU resources on the machine with expensive computations, or with a program where threads have logical waits that cause them to stall waiting on each other. You might also be dealing with an overindulgent program that uses too much memory and causes CPU cache misses or, worse yet, excessive paging to disk, in turn degrading the observed execution time.

Because performance issues don't come labeled with what is causing them, a two-step procedure is often needed:

1. First, you need to narrow the list of potential causes for the delay in execution time. This can be done either by using high-level tools such as the Resource Monitor (*resmon.exe*) tool or simply by capturing an Xperf trace with a large-enough set of events.

2. Once the high-level cause (CPU contention, disk contention, and so on) becomes clear, you can get down to the source-code level of the *hot spot* by capturing ETW stack-walk events to describe where the overtaxed resource is being used. This might require a second trace capture, this time with additional stack-trace events. The ability to capture this stack-walk information (in the form of associated ETW events) for the logged events is one of the great features of the ETW framework because it allows you to tie high-level behaviors back to the call sites that cause them at the source-code level.

The Xperf viewer UI is also designed to enable you to effectively control the scope of your analysis and zoom in on subsets of the trace timeline so that you can adapt your analysis to the phase you happen to be at in your understanding of the behavior you're studying. This two-phase approach will be demonstrated in this section as part of the *notepad.exe* soft hang investigation.

Collecting an ETW Trace for the Scenario

Because it isn't yet clear whether the delay in this case is CPU-bound, disk-bound, or something else, a good starting point is to collect an ETW trace containing a basic set of events, grouped under the predefined *Base* group. This group includes many useful events logged from the kernel, including several events related to performance characteristics of the traced scenario. In particular, this group covers events logged when disk I/O is performed, as well as the periodic (every 1 millisecond, by default) events logged by the CPU sampling profile object in the kernel, which help explain where the CPU time was spent during the trace session. To obtain the call sites of any potential CPU bottlenecks, this trace session also uses the *Profile* stack-walk switch to request stack-trace data for the CPU sampling profile events.

Note ETW traces are global system traces, which means that the events you elect to capture are logged regardless of the process context. It's only during the analysis step that you'll be able to filter the events by process. ETW tracing can also be enabled dynamically, so trace sessions can be started and stopped at any time without a need for a process restart or system reboot.

Starting and stopping ETW trace sessions using Xperf is a common task that involves the same set of command-line switches (namely, a set of kernel events, or *flags*, and an optional set of stack-walk switches), so it's useful to have scripts to automate those steps. To that end, the companion source code of this book contains two simple scripts that do just that. You need to run these scripts from within an elevated command prompt because starting and stopping ETW sessions requires full administrative privileges. Also, if you're trying this experiment on 64-bit Windows, the following command, which starts the tracing session, will give you a warning about a missing registry key. You can ignore this warning for now. This particular experiment will work even without setting that additional registry key and the extra reboot, though you're free to do so. You'll see more on that registry setting in the next chapter.

```
C:\book\code\common\scripts>start_kernel_trace.cmd -kf Base -ks Profile
INFO: Invoking xperf to start the session...
CmdLine: (xperf.exe -on PROC_THREAD+LOADER+Base -stackwalk Profile)
SUCCESS.
```

Once the trace session is started, you can go ahead and run the scenario you're interested in tracing, which in this case takes a minute or so to complete.

```
C:\book\code\common\scripts>notepad c:\temp\test.dat
```

After this file load operation is finished, close the new *notepad.exe* instance and then stop the tracing session using the following command.

```
C:\book\code\common\scripts>stop_kernel_trace.cmd
INFO: Invoking xperf to stop the session...
CmdLine: (xperf.exe -stop -d c:\temp\merged.etl)
Merged Etl: c:\temp\merged.etl
```

This stops the session and saves the final trace file under the c:\temp\merged.etl location that's hard-coded in the script. This trace file location will be used to hold the most recently captured trace throughout the experiments from this part of this book. When a previous file with the same name exists under that directory location, it will automatically get overwritten when the new trace is saved. If you elect to change this script to save the traces elsewhere, you should remember to periodically delete the old traces you no longer need because ETW trace files tend to be relatively large.

Analyzing the Collected ETW Trace

ETW traces captured using Xperf can be copied and analyzed on any machine. Merged trace files saved using the *–d* command-line option of *xperf.exe* (such as the previous ETW trace file) contain all the information needed to be self-sufficient and support this important "capture anywhere/process anywhere" paradigm.

Unlike starting or stopping trace sessions, you can view ETW traces from any user context, without administrative privileges. The companion source code also contains a script to automate the process of viewing a trace file using Xperf. This script sets two important environment variables used by Xperf to locate the symbols to use when decoding ETW stack-trace events. It then loads the trace file previously saved in the c:\temp\merged.etl location in the Xperf viewer UI, as shown in Figure 11-3. Keep in mind that symbols are needed only when the trace contains ETW stack-walk events, and only when viewing the trace. In particular, symbol files aren't required at all when capturing ETW traces.

```
C:\book\code\common\scripts>view_trace.cmd
set _NT_SYMBOL_PATH=srv*c:\localsymbolcache*http://msdl.microsoft.com/download/symbols
set _NT_SYMCACHE_PATH=c:\symcache

INFO: Invoking xperf to view the trace...
CmdLine: (xperf.exe c:\temp\merged.etl)
SUCCESS.
```

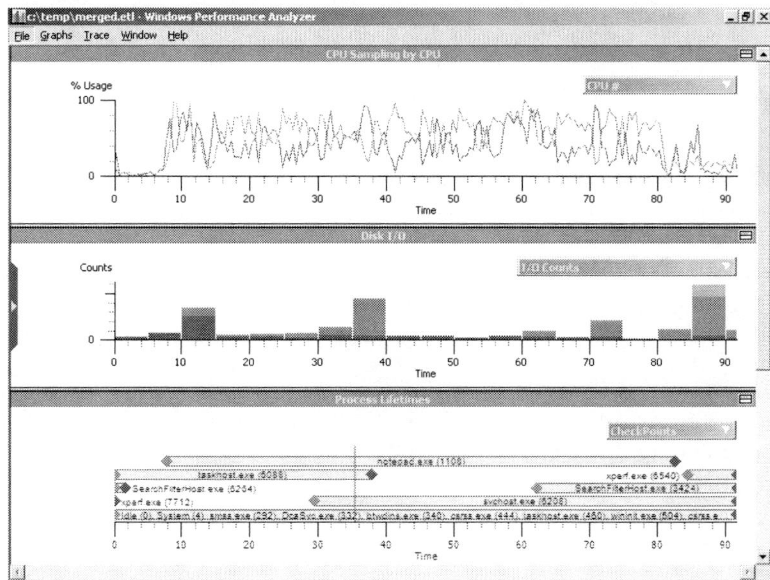

FIGURE 11-3 Xperf viewer's main UI window.

The main UI window comprises several graphs, each depicting a set of logged events from the trace file. One of the standard graphs is the Process Lifetimes graph, which shows all the processes that were running at any point during the trace session, including their start and end times, which is possible thanks to the rich ETW instrumentation in the OS that also logs process creation and termination events as part of the Base kernel group. Those times can be deduced either from the graphic itself or by right-clicking the graph and selecting the Process Summary Table option, as shown in Figure 11-4.

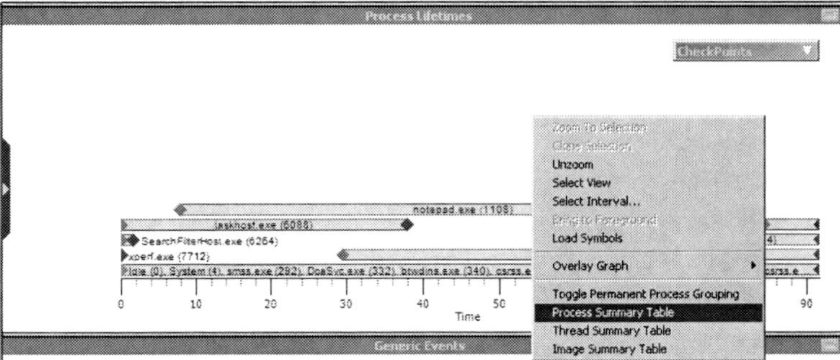

FIGURE 11-4 Right-clicking to select the Process Summary Table.

As you right-click the graph, make sure you don't select a time interval (using the left mouse button) at the same time. If you do that, you see only the process creation and deletion events from that interval in the summary table. Although this is useful when you want to focus on a smaller time interval during your analysis, you want to view the events from the entire lifetime of the trace in this case. A quick way to confirm that you've done this right is to check the summary table's title bar and ensure that it starts at 0 seconds (the beginning of the trace session), as demonstrated in Figure 11-5.

Processes Summary Table - c:\temp\merged.etl - [0 s - 91.606234209 s] - 91.606234209 s - Windows Performance A...

File Columns View Trace Window Help

Line	Process Name	Command Line	Start Time (s)
32	msseces.exe	"C:\Program Files\Microsoft Security Client\msseces.exe" -hide -runkey	0.000 000 000
33	NisSrv.exe	"c:\Program Files\Microsoft Security Client\Antimalware\NisSrv.exe"	0.000 000 000
34	notepad.exe	notepad c:\temp\test.dat	7.811 224 443
35	nvvsvc.exe		0.000 000 000
36	OSPPSVC.EXE	"C:\Program Files\Common Files\Microsoft Shared\OfficeSoftwarePr...	0.000 000 000
37	ouc.exe	"C:\ProgramData\Internet Mobile\OnlineUpdate\ouc.exe" "C:/Progr...	0.000 000 000
38	PMBDeviceInfoProvider.exe	"C:\Program Files\Sony\PMB\PMBDeviceInfoProvider.exe"	0.000 000 000
39	PMBVolumeWatcher.exe	"C:\Program Files\Sony\PMB\PMBVolumeWatcher.exe"	0.000 000 000
40	PwdMgmtProxy.exe	"C:\Program Files\Microsoft Forefront Identity Manager\2010\Passw...	0.000 000 000

FIGURE 11-5 Process Summary Table window.

The title bar in the previous view shows that the trace session ran for about 91 seconds and that *notepad.exe* was started around 7.8 seconds into the trace. Your ETW trace, of course, will have different start and end times, but you can use the same process to derive this information for your particular experiment. You can also see the command lines of all the other active processes during the trace, with processes that were already running when the ETW trace session started showing with a start time of 0 seconds, and those that were still running when it ended being marked with an end time that's equal to that of the trace session itself.

Note The Process Summary Table graph also includes, in particular, the *xperf.exe* command lines that were used to start and end the trace session. These can be useful when you need to figure out the types of ETW events that were collected during the tracing session, especially if you no longer remember when or how the trace file was captured.

You can also find more information about the system where the trace file was generated by clicking the Trace menu item in the main UI and selecting System Configuration (as shown in Figure 11-6). In particular, you can use this view to find the OS version and build information, the number of processors on the machine where the trace was collected, the Windows services that were running during the trace session, and so on, as illustrated in Figure 11-7.

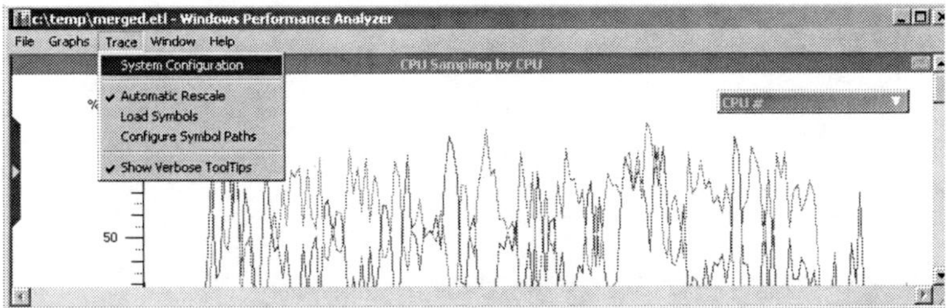

FIGURE 11-6 Selecting the System Configuration view.

System Configuration - c:\temp\merged.etl

General | Traces | Storage | Display | Network | Services | IRQ | PnP

Line	Configuration	Value
1	Computer Name	TARIKS-LP03
2	Domain Name	redmond.corp.microsoft.com
3	Product Name	Windows 7 Enterprise
4	Build Lab	7601.17713.x86fre.win7sp1_gdr.111025-1505
5	OS Version	6.1
6	Build	7601
7	Number of Processors	2
8	Processor Speed	2261 MHz
9	Hyper-Threading Enabled Processors	0x00000000
10	Memory Size	2036 MB
11	Page Size	4096 Bytes
12	Allocation Granularity	65536 Bytes
13	Supported Power States	S3 S4 S5
14	Boot Drive	Disk 0 - Drive C - NTFS
15	ETW Internal Version	25

FIGURE 11-7 System Configuration window, with detailed information about the system.

Phase 1: Narrowing the List of Bottlenecks

Picking the right graphs—and, by extension, data views—in the Xperf UI is one of the main challenges facing developers and performance analysts who are new to Xperf. You should spend some time looking at the graphs available in Xperf for the trace you're analyzing (which depends on the type of events contained within your trace) so that you can familiarize yourself with the data views they offer. These graphs can be selected using the frame list flyout located in the middle of the left side of the main window, as indicated by the arrow in Figure 11-8.

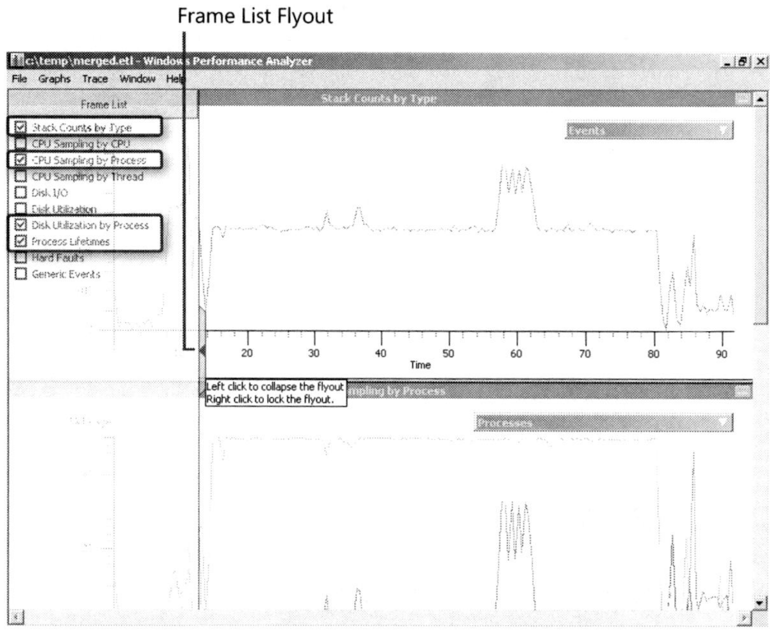

FIGURE 11-8 Selecting graphs using the frame list flyout.

Given the nature of this experiment, it's reasonable to suspect that the problem is either disk-bound (due to the large file being loaded) or CPU-bound (due to expensive processing of the file by *notepad.exe*).

The Disk Utilization graph, which measures the percentage of time in which an I/O request is outstanding to disk, doesn't suggest sustained disk activity. In fact, the Summary Table view of that graph, which you can invoke by using the shortcut menu anywhere within the area of the graph (as shown in Figure 11-9), shows no actual disk read for the large file used in this experiment. This is shown in Figure 11-10, where the Path Name column shows no such file reads.

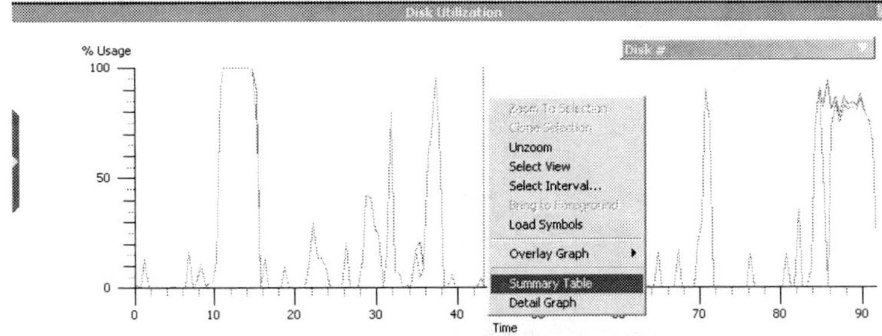

FIGURE 11-9 Right-clicking to select the Summary Table view.

More on Disk I/O Analysis

When analyzing disk activity, you should be mindful of the effects of the caching done at the I/O manager layer in the Windows operating system's kernel. The first time you load a file, a read I/O is issued to retrieve the data from disk. However, once this data is retrieved, the I/O manager tries to cache it in memory so that the next attempt to read the file returns this cached data without incurring another I/O access to disk. Remember that disk access is several orders of magnitude slower than memory access, so this is a critical performance optimization in the system.

The system has another important performance optimization called the *read-ahead* optimization, where the I/O manager can have system threads running in the context of the operating system's kernel read more data from the file than requested by the application, in anticipation of further read attempts. This means that when an application issues a request to read a file in chunks, it's quite possible the disk I/O reported in Xperf will be spread between the application's user-mode process context and the OS kernel context, which is identified in the Xperf UI as the *system process*, though it isn't really a true user-mode process. In the current case study, you'll find that no read disk access for the large file was performed, neither in the context of *notepad.exe* nor in the context of the OS kernel.

Similarly, the I/O manager has another optimization for disk writes, called the *write-behind* optimization. Instead of writing to disk right away, the I/O manager acts as a buffer between the application and disk, and it groups write attempts together to amortize the cost of accessing the disk resource. This means that the write attempts by user-mode applications can be buffered in memory and might only get committed later (asynchronously), again in the context of the system process.

Disk Summary Table - c:\temp\merged.etl - [0 s - 91.6382414 s] - 91.6382414 s - Window...

File Columns View Trace Window Help

Line	Process	Path Name	Size
1	⊞ CcmExec.exe (4752)		151,552
2	⊞ cmd.exe (5076)		162,304
3	DcaSvc.exe (332)	C:\pagefile.sys	4,096
4	⊞ dwm.exe (4432)		425,984
5	⊞ explorer.exe (4488)		202,240
6	⊞ FwcAgent.exe (2088)		169,472
7	lsass.exe (576)	C:\pagefile.sys	4,096
8	msitcertsvc.exe (2348)	C:\pagefile.sys	8,192
9	⊞ MsMpEng.exe (872)		3,597.312
10	⊟ notepad.exe (1108)		820.736
11		C:\Windows\winsxs\x86_microsoft.window...	393,216
12		⊞ C:\Windows\Fonts\StaticCache.dat	262,144
13		⊞ C:\pagefile.sys	24,576
14		C:\Windows\system32\lpk.dll	4,096
15		⊞ C:\Windows\system32\user32.dll	65,536
16		C:\Windows\Fonts\marlett.ttf	27,136
17		⊞ C:\Windows\system32\notepad.exe	44,032
18	⊞ ouc.exe (2292)		14,336
19	⊞ SCNotification.exe (5556)		208,896

FIGURE 11-10 Disk Summary Table window.

The absence of disk I/O reads is expected in this case because the *fsutil.exe* tool produces what is called a *sparse* file, which has no actual data clusters. The read attempts from the file are simply simulated by the OS in a transparent manner to the application, and no actual disk I/O is incurred to retrieve the data.

It's now time to turn your attention to the processor utilization reported by Xperf. The CPU sampling profile graph shown by default in the Xperf viewer UI is the CPU Sampling By CPU graph depicted in Figure 11-11. Unfortunately, this graph isn't too useful in this case—specifically, because it offers a global view of the CPU utilization on the system (two processors in the case of this trace), when you're actually interested in what happens at the *notepad.exe* process level.

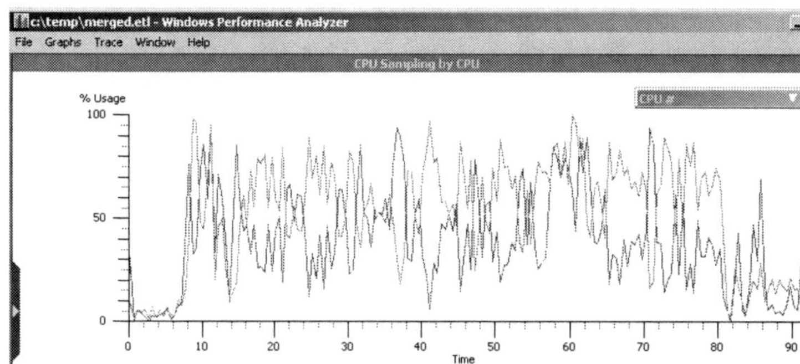

FIGURE 11-11 Inconclusive CPU Sampling By CPU data view.

In this case study example, it's better to look at the per-process CPU utilization graph so that you can focus on what is happening at the *notepad.exe* process level. To do so, select the CPU Sampling By Process graph using the frame list flyout. In that graph, you can filter the view to include only the CPU utilization by the *notepad.exe* process, as illustrated in Figure 11-12.

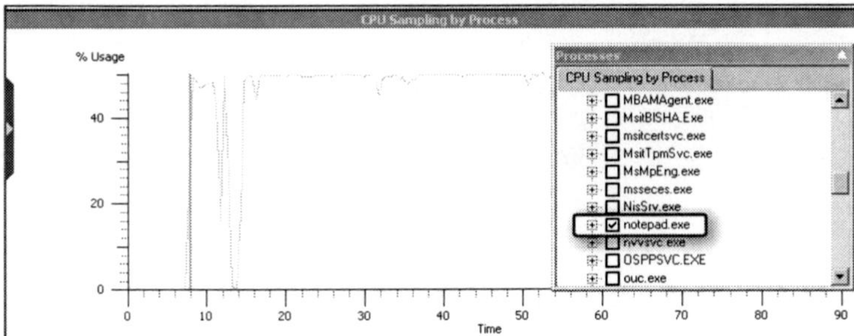

FIGURE 11-12 CPU utilization by the *notepad.exe* process.

This data view clearly shows that *notepad.exe* was consistently using 50 percent of the processor resources, which is the equivalent of one full processor resource in the dual-processor system where the trace was captured. It also indicates that the majority of the time (as shown by the time axis in the graph) when opening the large file was spent in this CPU-bound state. This confirms that the processor resource was the primary bottleneck in this experiment and that the observed delay was CPU-bound!

Phase 2: Getting Stack Traces for the Hot Spots

Now that you know the delay is caused by excessive CPU processing, your next step is to determine which code paths are contributing the most to that heavy utilization. These call sites are often referred to as *hot spots* in performance analysis. By reviewing these hot spots, you can determine whether the software is behaving as designed, or if there are potential improvements that can help alleviate the performance problems exhibited by the scenario.

As mentioned earlier in this section, getting down to the source-code level requires special ETW events called *stack-walk events*, so it's often the case that you might need to capture a new trace of the scenario for this second phase of your investigation. Fortunately, though, the trace you captured earlier already included stack-walk events for every CPU sampling event logged by the kernel profiler object. These ETW events are logged at regular intervals (1 millisecond, by default) and interrupt the normal execution on the CPU, which means that they will have the call stack of every running thread at each profiler timer occurrence. Those events are perfect for figuring out hot spots in CPU-bound scenarios because they provide you (when grouped by call stack) with a statistical view of where the CPU time was spent.

To see this in practice, first right-click anywhere within the main viewer window and select Load Symbols, as illustrated in Figure 11-13. By default, Xperf doesn't try to resolve symbols for the ETW stack-trace events contained within the target trace file. You should remember to select this option whenever you start a new instance of the Xperf viewer if you care about decoding stack traces and seeing proper function names in the UI.

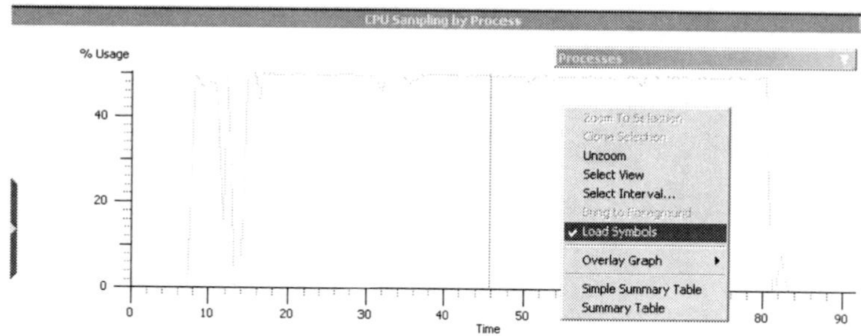

FIGURE 11-13 Selecting the Load Symbols option for proper stack-trace resolution in the Xperf viewer.

You're now ready to look at the CPU sample profiling events and their corresponding stack traces. To do so, open the Summary Table window for the CPU Sampling By Process graph, as demonstrated in Figure 11-14.

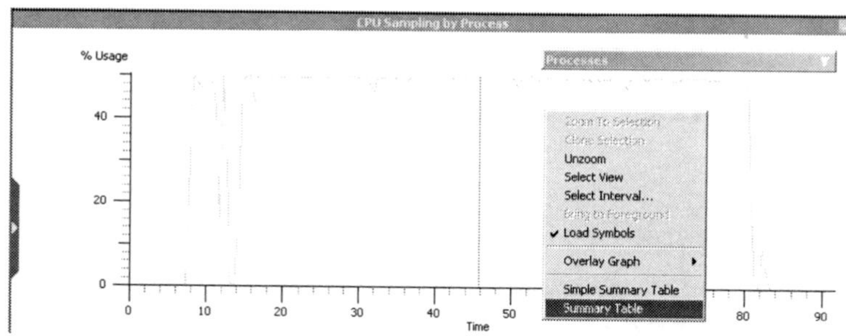

FIGURE 11-14 Invoking the CPU Sampling Summary Table window, with stack-trace symbols resolution.

You'll immediately be presented with a dialog box asking you to agree to the terms of use for the Microsoft public symbols, as shown in Figure 11-15. Xperf then proceeds to download the required symbols off the network, but note it will take Xperf a while to download the symbols and display the Summary Table window. Even on a fast Internet connection, the Xperf viewer UI might get stuck for several minutes while Xperf downloads the symbols. This is expected and happens only the first time you download the symbols off the network. Once the symbols are retrieved and saved by the tool to the local cache, this step won't take nearly as long the next time you analyze the trace in the Xperf viewer UI.

After Xperf is done building its optimized symbols cache store for the trace file, you can finally interact with the CPU Sampling Summary Table window. The Stack column in that view contains the stack traces associated with the CPU sampling profile events from the target trace file. Unfortunately, it isn't shown by default, so you need to add it (as well as any other columns you're interested in but that are absent from the default Summary Table view). You can do this by using the Column Chooser flyout located in the middle of the left side of the window, as shown in Figure 11-16.

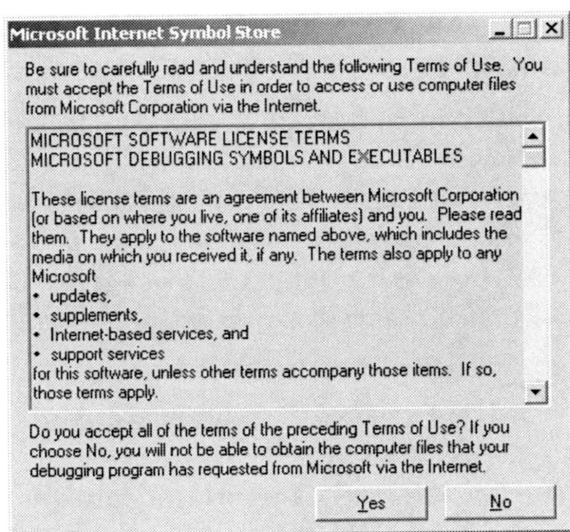

FIGURE 11-15 Terms of use dialog box.

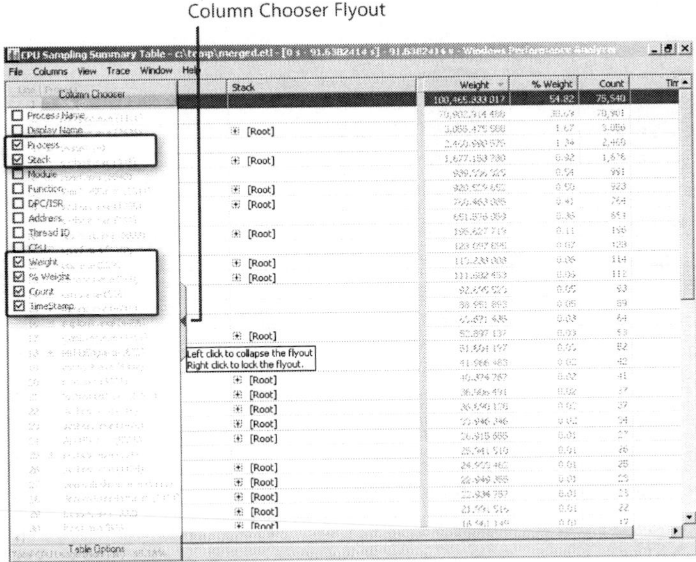

FIGURE 11-16 Selecting columns in Summary Table windows.

If you progressively expand the stack-trace tree nodes corresponding to the *notepad.exe* process in the Stack column and ensure that the Weight column is also added to the view and moved to the left of the *gold bar* (indicated with an arrow in Figure 11-17), you'll get the stack traces ordered by their relative CPU utilizations. If the function names are shown as "*module_name!?*" when you expand the stack traces in the summary table, it's likely because you missed the first step described at the top of this section and did not select the Load Symbols option in the main UI window. To fix that, you can go back to the main Xperf viewer window, select that option, and open the Summary Table window again. Notice also that stack traces in Xperf are displayed with the deeper call frames at the bottom, in the opposite direction that WinDbg uses when listing call stacks.

Caching Trace Symbols from the Command Line

The _NT_SYMBOL_PATH environment variable, which is set by the *view_trace.cmd* helper script to automatically include the Microsoft public symbols server URL, is used by Xperf to determine where to download the symbols from, as well as the directory path to cache the symbols locally after they are downloaded. In addition to this environment variable, which can also be used in the Windows debuggers and other NT tools (such as the UMDH tool that was covered in Chapter 8, "Common Debugging Scenarios, Part 1"), the same script sets an environment variable called _NT_SYMCACHE_PATH.

```
set _NT_SYMBOL_PATH=SRV*c:\LocalSymbolCache*http://msdl.microsoft.com/download/symbols
set _NT_SYMCACHE_PATH=c:\SymCache
```

Unlike _NT_SYMBOL_PATH, however, the _NT_SYMCACHE_PATH environment variable is specific to Xperf. This second variable should point to a different local path than the local symbols cache path specified in between the * signs in _NT_SYMBOL_PATH. Xperf defines its own proprietary format to compress the cached symbol files and strip them of all superfluous data that's not relevant to Xperf operations. This allows Xperf to speed up its access to symbols once this local optimized cache repository (specified by the _NT_SYMCACHE_PATH environment variable) has been built.

Unlike the Windows debuggers, Xperf won't automatically locate the symbols for the binaries you build even when analyzing the trace on the same build machine. So, you need to include all the symbol search paths in the _NT_SYMBOL_PATH variable. Also important to realize is that only the symbols in the Xperf optimized cache directory are ultimately used when resolving trace symbols in the Xperf UI.

One way to verify that Xperf is downloading symbols while its UI looks to be hung in the previous step is to observe the local symbols cache path (C:\LocalSymbolCache in this example) or the optimized Xperf symbols cache path (C:\SymCache) and make sure that new files are progressively appearing under those directories. Alternatively, the companion source code has a convenient wrapper script that allows you to cache the symbols for an ETW trace from the command line by using the *symcache* processing action in *xperf.exe*.

```
C:\book\code\common\scripts>cache_trace_symbols.cmd
...
INFO: Invoking xperf to cache trace symbols locally...
CmdLine: (xperf -i c:\temp\merged.etl -symbols -a symcache -build)
```

Although this *xperf.exe* command downloads symbols for the entire set of binaries used in the ETW trace and can take longer to complete than simply opening a Summary Table window with stack traces in the Xperf UI, it has the distinct advantage of showing you progress information for the operation.

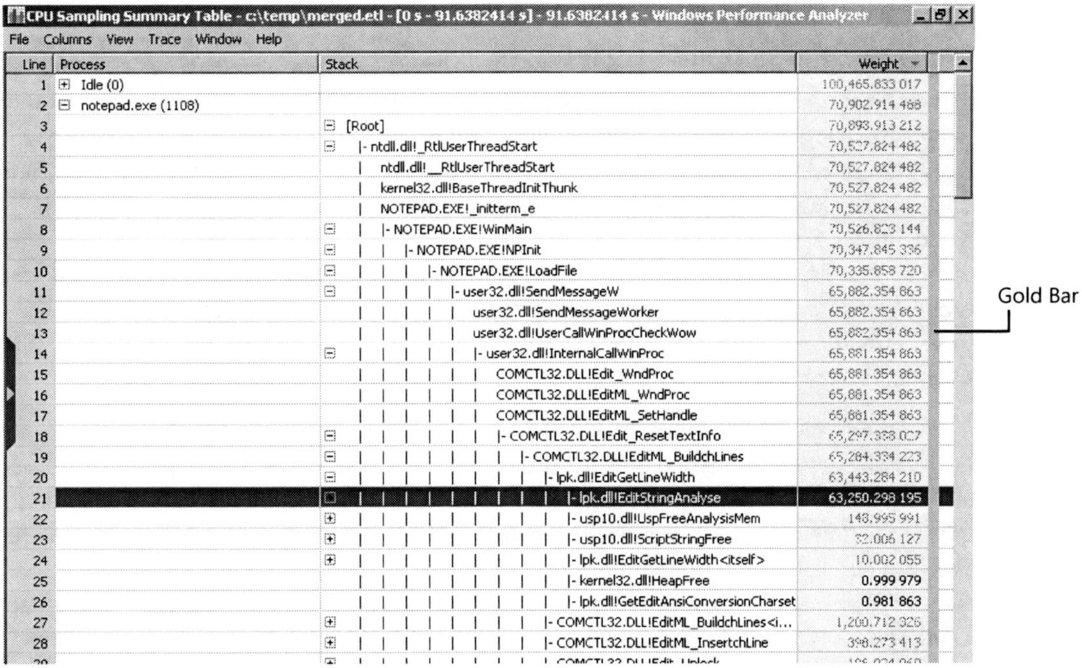

CPU Sampling Summary Table - c:\temp\merged.etl - [0 s - 91.6382414 s] - 91.6382414 s - Windows Performance Analyzer

File Columns View Trace Window Help

Line	Process	Stack	Weight
1	Idle (0)		100,465.833 017
2	notepad.exe (1108)		70,902.914 468
3		[Root]	70,893.913 212
4		ntdll.dll!_RtlUserThreadStart	70,527.824 482
5		ntdll.dll!__RtlUserThreadStart	70,527.824 482
6		kernel32.dll!BaseThreadInitThunk	70,527.824 482
7		NOTEPAD.EXE!_initterm_e	70,527.824 482
8		NOTEPAD.EXE!WinMain	70,526.823 144
9		NOTEPAD.EXE!NPInit	70,347.845 336
10		NOTEPAD.EXE!LoadFile	70,335.858 720
11		user32.dll!SendMessageW	65,882.354 863
12		user32.dll!SendMessageWorker	65,882.354 863
13		user32.dll!UserCallWinProcCheckWow	65,882.354 863
14		user32.dll!InternalCallWinProc	65,881.354 863
15		COMCTL32.DLL!Edit_WndProc	65,881.354 863
16		COMCTL32.DLL!EditML_WndProc	65,881.354 863
17		COMCTL32.DLL!EditML_SetHandle	65,881.354 863
18		COMCTL32.DLL!Edit_ResetTextInfo	65,297.338 027
19		COMCTL32.DLL!EditML_BuildchLines	65,284.334 223
20		lpk.dll!EditGetLineWidth	63,443.284 210
21		lpk.dll!EditStringAnalyse	63,250.298 195
22		usp10.dll!UspFreeAnalysisMem	148.995 991
23		usp10.dll!ScriptStringFree	32.006 127
24		lpk.dll!EditGetLineWidth<itself>	10.002 055
25		kernel32.dll!HeapFree	0.999 979
26		lpk.dll!GetEditAnsiConversionCharset	0.981 863
27		COMCTL32.DLL!EditML_BuildchLines<i...	1,200.712 326
28		COMCTL32.DLL!EditML_InsertchLine	398.273 413

FIGURE 11-17 Stack traces of CPU sample profiling events.

The gold bar in Xperf summary tables plays an important role in how the data gets sorted: columns located on the left of the gold bar are used as sort columns. So, you can change how the data is sorted by moving columns to the left of the gold bar, which you can easily do in the UI by clicking the column title in the Summary Table window and sliding it all the way to its intended position.

As you can see in Figure 11-17, a large percentage of the processor time was consumed in *NOTEPAD!LoadFile*. By following the call tree and expanding the functions with the highest weight, you can see that the bulk of the time in that call, in turn, was spent inside a function called *COMCTL32!EditML_BuildcchLines*. You have now identified the main hot spot in your scenario! The UI thread in *notepad.exe* was trying to read the data from the file and display it in a multiline edit control, which eagerly proceeds to parse it line by line to figure out the width of each line and show the appropriate document width in the status bar. This is an expensive CPU-bound operation, especially with large files such as the one used in this experiment. The fact it's performed synchronously on the main UI thread (as you can see from the thread call stack) explains why the main *notepad.exe* window seemed to hang for such a long time while loading the large file.

More on CPU Sample Profiling

As demonstrated in the experiment from this section, the ETW Profile events are a great way to analyze delays that are due to high CPU utilization, but you should not read more into them than they describe. You need to understand, in particular, that CPU sample profiling accounts only for time spent actively on the CPU. As such, logical delays, such as waits on kernel dispatcher objects aren't captured by those ETW events because the blocked threads get switched out while they're waiting. Another set of ETW events, called *CSwitch*, can be used instead to examine such logical waits. These important context switch events are logged from the OS thread-scheduler component in the kernel and will be covered in more detail later in Chapter 13, "Common Tracing Scenarios."

A second aspect to be aware of is that sample profiling is a statistical analysis of where the instruction pointer is recorded on each profiling timer tick, which only works well with enough collected samples. Charging the full sampling interval to the function that is executing on the CPU at the time of sample recording is not entirely fair because many other functions might have run on the CPU during that time interval. However, sampling theory also predicts that the statistical margin of error decreases (roughly) proportionally to the square root of the total number of samples—that is, *margin of error ≈ 1/sqrt(n)*, where *n* is the number of samples. So, the longer you run an experiment with CPU sample profiling turned on, the more accurate results you're likely to get.

As a general rule, you should run a scenario for at least 1 second and preferably for 10 seconds or more for the sample profiling results to be meaningful. If you capture CPU sample profiling events for more than 10 seconds, for instance, you get over 10,000 samples (in the case of the default 1-ms profiling interval) and less than a 1 percent margin of error. Conversely, you should eye with suspicion any observations for a region of time that has less than 10 samples (less than 10 ms).

Also, because CPU sample profiling is a statistical approach, it can't provide the exact number of times a function has been called, nor the precise time spent executing a certain routine—only its relative contribution to the overall CPU utilization compared to other routines in the program. To be able to ascertain a small performance variation in the running time of a particular function using Xperf and ETW, you need to insert code to explicitly log custom ETW events at the beginning and end of the target routine. This allows you to measure the time spent in that function by using the timestamps that get automatically logged with every ETW event payload. This generic Start/End event-pair instrumentation approach is very useful in ETW-based performance analysis because it allows you to measure the time spent executing any arbitrary operation using ETW and the Xperf tool. Chapter 12, "Inside ETW," will show a practical example of how to add this custom instrumentation to your software.

Xperf's Strengths and Limitations

The Windows Vista release saw a lot of OS components (both in user mode and kernel mode) get instrumented with more ETW events. It also saw many important improvements to the ETW framework, with the ability to capture stack traces for kernel events being a momentous addition during that release. This combination propelled ETW to its current status as the de facto tracing standard in Windows, with the Windows 7 release bringing more improvements to the ETW framework in the OS. WPT (Xperf) is the premier front-end tool to control and analyze ETW instrumentation, and it derives many of its advantages directly from the architecture of ETW, including its low CPU overhead tracing and the ability to observe systemwide behavior dynamically without the need to restart processes or reboot the OS.

Xperf also supports the "capture anywhere/process anywhere" paradigm. When you use the *–d* command-line option to stop tracing and generate a log file for the session, Xperf adds important rundown information about the environment where the ETW trace session was captured to the saved trace file, making it self-sufficient for analysis on any other machine. This important capability is why this book focuses primarily on WPT (Xperf) when it comes to ETW-based tracing and profiling tools in Windows.

As you were able to see in the *notepad.exe* case study, ETW tracing has systemwide scope, which is great for getting a complete picture of all the aspects related to your scenario. Even though you're able to filter the events by process during the analysis step in the Xperf viewer, the events generated by other processes can sometimes be distracting when all you want is to quickly determine the cause of an issue that you know is local to your own code. Just like in the case of the Windows debuggers, Xperf is great for investigations in live production environments because it's lightweight and also allows you to look beyond the boundaries of your immediate application. However, when you're already writing, compiling, and running your code inside a development environment such as Microsoft Visual Studio, where you have the source code and symbols already set up, it's usually more productive to use the integrated profiler to focus on what is happening inside your target application.

The Ultimate and Premium editions of Visual Studio 2010 come with a set of profiling tools that you can access in the Analyze menu. In addition to being particularly convenient for analyzing the native programs you build in Visual Studio, the Visual Studio profiler can analyze .NET code too. Though Xperf can also be used to trace and profile .NET applications, it isn't able to resolve the function names correctly when displaying the dynamic call frames generated by the Common Language Runtime's (CLR) Just-in-Time compiler—at least not in the Windows 7 SDK version of the tool, which lacked the necessary integration with the CLR to be able to resolve managed frames when displaying ETW stack-trace events. Note that the Windows 8 consumer preview version of the Windows Performance Toolkit, which includes the new WPR/WPA tools, closed this gap by adding this feature as one of its new capabilities.

Summary

In this chapter, you used the Xperf tool in a real-life performance investigation. By taking advantage of the existing ETW instrumentation in kernel components, you were able to observe several aspects of the scenario, including its likely resource bottlenecks (the disk and CPU), and you were eventually able to trace the call site causing the hung UI and long delay by using the Profile stack-trace events and taking advantage of Xperf's ability to decode and group those stack traces in the UI.

There are two important takeaways from that experiment that are worth reiterating:

- Devising a deliberate investigation strategy should always be your first step in tracing investigations. A common approach is to capture a trace with Xperf using the Base group of kernel events and get a first-order understanding of the behavior you're studying. Even this basic trace will give you a wealth of information about the scenario, including several hardware characteristics of the machine (number of processors, RAM size, and so on), the processes that got started or were already running during the trace, the disk I/O attempts, the CPU resource utilization, and much more. Once the observed behavior is understood at a high level, ETW stack-trace events can also be collected to get down to the source code call sites responsible for the observed behavior.
- It's important that you not rely on guesswork in performance investigations. You saw that in action in the *notepad.exe* experiment, where the Xperf tool left no doubt that the scenario wasn't disk-bound. The only sure way to draw solid conclusions is to measure early and often. This is why a lightweight tool such as Xperf, which can also be run directly from a USB drive or a network share without any additional installation steps on the target machine, can be especially useful in tracing investigations.

As part of running the *notepad.exe* case study, you also got a hands-on introduction to Xperf and its trace viewer UI. At the risk of leaving useful concepts that you learned in this chapter out, the following points are certainly worth remembering when using the Xperf tool:

- You should use scripts to automate the most common Xperf tasks so that you don't end up typing the same long commands every time. This book's companion source code has convenient scripts for starting, stopping, and viewing ETW traces. You should use them as a starting point and feel free to expand them to fit your needs, as appropriate.
- Always use the *–d* command-line option when stopping your ETW kernel trace sessions using Xperf or, better yet, have a script that always does that when you stop your ETW sessions. This option adds important rundown information to the saved kernel trace, which is necessary for proper symbol decoding in ETW stack-trace events and, more generally, for making the trace self-sufficient so that it can be analyzed on any machine.

- Symbols for ETW stack-trace events are needed only when viewing the target trace, but not during trace collection. This means you don't need access to any online symbol servers on the machine where the trace is being captured. Also, remember to select Load Symbols in the UI if you want Xperf to decode symbols in its summary tables and display the proper call stacks. It won't try to resolve symbols otherwise.
- Graphs and summary tables are Xperf's way of compiling the data described by the ETW events from the target trace into a visual representation that's easy to use for analysis. In addition, the gold bar allows you to customize the Summary Table views for each graph by adding sort columns. For example, you group by call stack to view the common function calls, group by process to focus on just your code, or group by path to observe the disk accesses corresponding to a certain file. Picking the right sort columns can often be the difference between a quick, efficient investigation and a series of futile searches, so you should spend some time familiarizing yourself with this important feature in the Xperf UI.
- By default, the Xperf viewer shows only a subset of graphs and summary table columns that it deems most relevant to the trace being analyzed. It's often useful to explore the unselected graphs and columns (by using the flyout buttons located in the middle of the left side of Xperf windows) at the beginning of your analysis and consider whether you need any of them to be added to the Xperf views.

The next chapter will delve deeper into the foundations of ETW so that you can maximize the value you get out of your Xperf investigations, whether you decide to add your own custom ETW logging to your applications or simply use the existing instrumentation in the OS.

CHAPTER 12

Inside ETW

In this chapter

This chapter delves into how the Event Tracing for Windows (ETW) framework is designed, and it explains important concepts that will help you understand how to best use Xperf and other ETW-based tools in your profiling and tracing investigations.

After a brief introduction to the basic components that drive the operations of ETW, this chapter covers the existing instrumentation in the operating system (OS). Although ETW has been around since the Microsoft Windows 2000 release, it wasn't until Windows Vista that important parts of the operating system got heavily instrumented. Knowing the events that are already logged in the system allows you to make an informed decision as to whether you need to add custom ETW events to your code to investigate the specific behaviors you're studying.

After covering these essential concepts, the chapter discusses the way ETW supports stack-trace capture for kernel and user events. This understanding is useful when diagnosing the common decoding issues you're likely to run into when you use stack-trace events in your tracing investigations. This section culminates with detailed steps for how to diagnose these stack-walking problems in practice.

This chapter concludes with a section describing how to enable ETW logging automatically when Windows starts up so that you can trace any boot activity that occurs before you get an opportunity to log in and start issuing commands on the desktop. Though this isn't a need most developers would ever have, this type of analysis is primordial whenever drivers or auto-start applications are added to the boot path so that this critical performance path doesn't get negatively affected by such activity.

ETW Architecture

ETW was born from a desire to provide a generic tracing platform for user-mode and kernel-mode code that could also be enabled with minimal impact to the performance of the software being traced. These key requirements drive the fundamental tenets of ETW in the operating system.

ETW Design Principles

A naïve approach to code instrumentation is to use *fprintf* statements to log messages to the console or into a dedicated log file. Though this simple approach might sound appealing, it also suffers from several flaws. In fact, understanding those flaws is a great way to introduce many of the fundamental design decisions underlying the ETW framework in the OS:

- As you saw in Chapter 10, "Debugging System Internals," a *printf* function call is not really as simple as it sounds because it involves quite a bit of work behind the scenes by the operating system, including interprocess communication calls by the C runtime library to the components of the Windows console subsystem to finally get the message printed on the computer screen. This also means that any components in this chain of function calls will suffer reentrancy issues if they ever use *printf* as a tracing mechanism. For these reasons, ETW tracing is implemented in kernel mode (though it has wrapper Win32 APIs for use by user-mode software too), without taking dependencies on components that are higher in the OS architecture stack.
- It would also be difficult to create tools to parse and view the freeform events logged by a scheme such as the *fprintf* tracing approach suggested here. By standardizing the logging framework and introducing a well-defined schema for the events, ETW makes it possible to build sophisticated viewer tools in a version-resilient way.
- An even more serious drawback is that writing to a file or to a console window every time a trace request is made comes with a significant performance impact (particularly in high-rate tracing). So, this type of logging generally needs to be disabled on release builds, rendering it of no value for investigating issues that happen in live production environments. This is one of the primary benefits of ETW tracing, given that the cost of the ETW event logging calls is nearly insignificant (in the order of a conditional flag check) until tracing actually gets enabled. Even when tracing is turned on, ETW is designed to be very lightweight. To give you a rough approximation, ETW introduces less than 2.5 percent CPU overhead on a 2-GHz processor for a sustained rate of 10,000 events per second.
- An improvement over the previous idea is to save the events to an in-memory data structure and have a worker thread periodically flush the data to a file on disk. This design addresses the performance penalty associated with writing to disk for each trace message but has another major drawback: if the process crashes unexpectedly, the trace messages that haven't yet been persisted to disk are lost permanently. This again limits the usefulness of such a tracing scheme, given that tracing is often used for debugging such crashes. Even worse, I've seen

several naïve implementations of the previous idea where locks are used to synchronize access to the buffers, and the custom logging framework ends up being the bottleneck in the application it's trying to profile!

ETW builds on top of this last idea of logging events to in-memory buffers and writing them to disk asynchronously, but instead of using a data structure that's local to the user-mode process address space, it delegates that responsibility to built-in support in the kernel of the Windows operating system. Trace-event messages are logged in *lock-free* fashion to buffers maintained by the kernel, which then periodically flushes them to disk so that those buffers that are full can get reused for holding other new events. This disk I/O access happens in the context of dedicated system (kernel) threads with little visible impact to the performance of the logging application, though the fact it will still be competing for the shared disk resources with other applications has to be taken into consideration.

ETW Components

ETW gives special names to the components underlying the aforementioned design:

- **ETW sessions** The main engine behind the ETW tracing model. Sessions represent the kernel environment managing the in-memory buffers and the system threads that periodically flush them to disk. ETW logging sessions are also simply called *loggers* in Xperf.
- **ETW providers** The conceptual components in user mode and kernel mode that *provide* the events. Each category of events usually defines its own provider. For example, the TCP/IP driver defines its own ETW provider, as does the Windows Logon subsystem in user mode. Also, the events from one provider don't have to come from a single binary source because they can be logged from more than one executable, dynamic-link library (DLL), or driver module.

  The relationship between providers and sessions is a *many-to-many* relationship, meaning that an ETW session can receive events from multiple providers and that an ETW provider can also log its events to multiple sessions, though this second scenario is rare in practice.
- **ETW consumers** The tools used to parse and view the event traces generated from ETW logging sessions. Xperf and the Windows Performance Analyzer (WPA) that succeeds it in Windows 8 are ETW consumers. The Microsoft Network Monitor and the Windows event viewer are two more examples.
- **ETW controllers** The utilities used to start logging sessions and associate providers with those sessions. Once a provider is enabled within a session, that session will start receiving the events logged by the provider (component) regardless of the application context in which they occur. ETW exposes Win32 APIs to help controllers start sessions and associate providers with those sessions (*StartTrace* and *EnableTraceEx2*, respectively). As you saw in the previous chapter, Xperf also operates as an ETW controller, as does the Windows Performance Recorder (WPR) that succeeds it in Windows 8.

Figure 12-1 recaps the ETW architecture described so far, with these four main components represented by the white boxes.

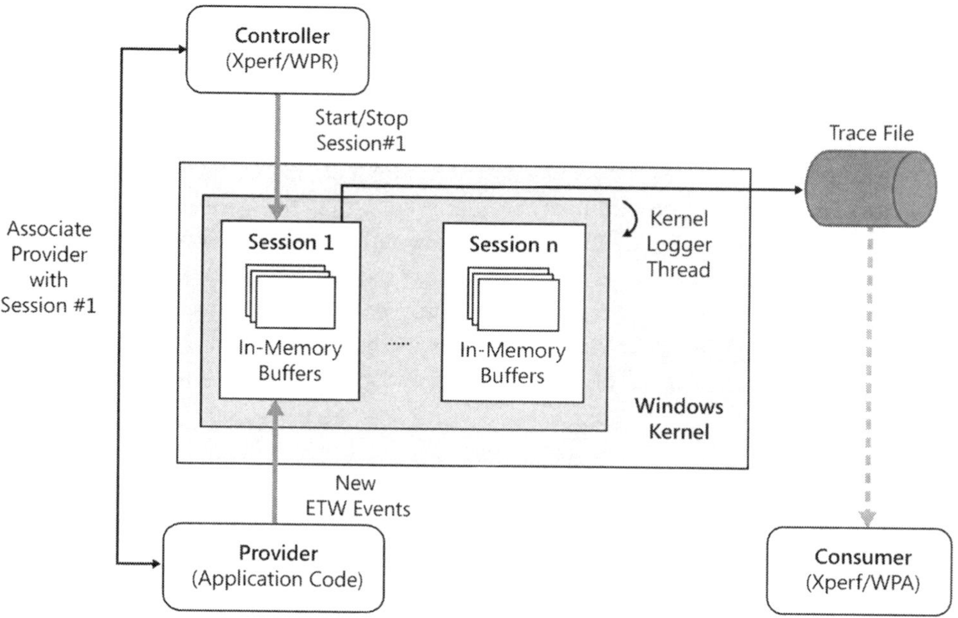

FIGURE 12-1 ETW architecture overview.

The Special NT Kernel Logger Session

New ETW logging sessions can be started in Xperf by using the *–start* command-line option, which expects an optional session name. This operation also expects the set of ETW providers to be enabled in the new session at start time, which you specify by using the *–on* command-line option and a union of provider identifiers (represented by the + sign convention on the Xperf command line). You can repeat this sequence for as many sessions as you would like to start concurrently. This basic syntax can be summarized as follows.

```
xperf.exe -start [<Session_Name_1>] -on <Provider_1+Provider_2+...+Provider_n>
          -start [<Session_Name_2>] -on <ProviderPrime_1+ProviderPrime_2+...+ProviderPrime_m>
...
```

To stop the previously started sessions and merge the events collected from all of them into the same trace file, you can use the *–stop* command-line option in Xperf. As mentioned in the previous chapter, you should also always use the *–d* option when stopping ETW trace sessions so that important kernel rundown information is also added into the saved trace at this time, making it self-sufficient for analysis on any other machine. This syntax can be summarized as follows.

```
xperf.exe -stop [<Session_Name_1>] -stop [<Session_Name_2>] ... -d merged_trace_file.etl
```

When you omit the session name parameter in the previous commands, Xperf defaults to starting and stopping a special logging session, called the *NT Kernel Logger* session. This session can be used only for the events logged by providers in the kernel itself (such as the built-in providers included in the Base kernel group that you used in the previous chapter for analyzing why *notepad.exe* took a long time to load a large file), but not for other events logged from user code.

In *xperf.exe*, the following commands are all equivalent. Notice that the last variation skips the *–start* command-line option completely. That last form is often used for brevity when dealing with the built-in kernel provider events, which is precisely what the *start_kernel_trace.cmd* script that was introduced earlier in the previous chapter did.

```
xperf.exe -start "NT Kernel Logger" -on Base
xperf.exe -start -on Base
xperf.exe -on Base
```

Remember to run the previous commands from an elevated administrative command prompt because controlling ETW sessions requires full administrative privileges. For a reminder of how to start an elevated command prompt, refer back to the Introduction of this book.

Also, you won't be able to start the NT Kernel Logger session twice, so you need to stop the previous session first before you're able to try another command variation. You can also omit the session name when stopping the NT Kernel Logger session, so the following Xperf commands are also equivalent.

```
xperf.exe -stop "NT Kernel Logger" -d c:\temp\merged.etl
xperf.exe -stop -d c:\temp\merged.etl
```

Configuring ETW Sessions Using Xperf

As you saw in the previous section, there are two types of ETW sessions:

- **The NT Kernel Logger session** Used by all the built-in kernel providers for logging their events. It's special in that it can't be used by other user providers.
- **Other user sessions** Must be used by all the ETW providers that can't log to the NT Kernel Logger session, though the same session can be shared by more than one user provider. User providers include your own custom providers, but also anything in the operating system that's not considered to be a part of the *core* kernel. For example, TCP/IP events are considered *user* events, even though they are logged by the network driver stack in kernel mode.

Though the basic syntax detailed in the previous section will be sufficient for the vast majority of tracing and profiling scenarios you conduct using Xperf, other command-line options are also supported when starting new ETW sessions. If you type **xperf.exe –help start** inside a command prompt, you'll see a list of all the session configuration options exposed in Xperf. To understand why you would ever need to override the default settings, it's useful to look at some common scenarios that might call for doing just that.

Filled Buffers and Lost ETW Events

Scenarios that log events at an unusually high rate into a given ETW session can cause the in-memory buffers in that session to fill up faster than the writes to disk that flush the events to the trace file are able to be processed. This can result in *lost events* during tracing. Whether a scenario runs into the "lost events" problem, though, depends not only on its intrinsic nature but also on the specific hardware in use, including the hard drive's throughput.

The Xperf tool will alert you to this situation when you stop the trace session, and it will display a warning message that indicates, among other things, the number of events that were lost over the lifetime of the session, as shown in the following example.

```
xperf.exe -on Base -start UserSession -on Microsoft-Windows-TCPIP
```

Run a scenario that logs TCP/IP network events at a very high rate, and then stop both sessions and merge their events along with the kernel rundown information, as illustrated by the following Xperf command.

```
xperf.exe -stop UserSession -stop -d c:\temp\merged.etl
xperf: warning: Session "UserSession" lost 918336 events.
...
```

To allow the ETW session to keep up with the rate of incoming events, you can try one of the following solutions:

- Increase the size of the in-memory buffers, or adjust the range used by the kernel when determining how many buffers should be allocated for the trace session. In Xperf, these settings can be controlled using the *–BufferSize*, *–MinBuffers*, and *–MaxBuffers* command-line options, with the default values being 64 KB, 64 KB, and 320 KB, respectively. Increasing the buffer size in the ETW session should typically be your first reaction to the "lost events" scenario.
- Simplify the test scenario to reduce the incoming rate of events into the session. One way to do so is to enable fewer event providers. Another way is to split the providers across multiple sessions. If you decide to use more than one user session, however, you need to also change the file location used by ETW to store the events from those sessions. By default, user sessions flush their buffers to .\user.etl (the NT Kernel Logger events go to .\kernel.etl), but because sessions can't share the same trace file, you need to also use the *–f* option of Xperf to pick a different file location for each user session and eliminate the conflict.

The following Xperf command, which increases the size of the buffers in the previous user session to 1,024 KB (1 MB), illustrates the first approach.

```
xperf.exe -on Base -start UserSession -on Microsoft-Windows-TCPIP -BufferSize 1024
```

Note that the NT Kernel Logger session also started by the previous command will still be using the default 64-KB buffer size because the *–BufferSize* command-line option is session-specific and can appear more than once on the command line if you want to change the default size in multiple sessions. You can confirm this by using the *–loggers* command-line option in Xperf, which allows you to view all the active ETW logging sessions on the machine. Remember to run this command from an elevated administrative command prompt because enumerating ETW sessions also requires full administrative privileges.

```
xperf.exe -loggers
Logger Name           : NT Kernel Logger
Logger Id             : ffff
Logger Thread Id      : 00001608
Buffer Size           : 64
...
Log Filename          : C:\kernel.etl
Trace Flags           : PROC_THREAD+LOADER+DISK_IO+HARD_FAULTS+FILENAME+PROFILE+MEMINFO+CPU_
CONFIG
PoolTagFilter         : *
...
Logger Name           : UserSession
Logger Id             : e
Logger Thread Id      : 00001314
Buffer Size           : 1024
...
Log Filename          : C:\user.etl
Trace Flags           : "Microsoft-Windows-TCPIP":0xffffffffffffffff:0xff
...
```

You can now stop the logging sessions again. If increasing the buffer size to 1 MB for the ETW session that was exhibiting the lost events still doesn't solve the problem, you can try to adjust it even higher and run the scenario again until the issue is fixed.

```
xperf.exe -stop UserSession -stop -d c:\temp\merged.etl
```

Using Circular ETW Logging

Circular-mode sessions are useful when you want to continuously monitor the behavior of a component because they allow you to record the latest events logged by your scenario, with the most recent events overwriting the oldest when necessary. With this mode, tracing can be enabled for a long period of time in production environments (much like a *flight recorder* on an airplane) without having to worry about consuming too much disk space, given that the events wrap around after hitting the predefined maximum size on disk. When a rare behavioral anomaly (such as UI sluggishness) is observed, you can stop the circular-mode session shortly thereafter and analyze the recent ETW events in the trace file to help you track down the root cause of the problem.

You can start a circular logging session in Xperf by using the *–FileMode* option, which also requires you to specify a maximum size (by using the *–MaxSize* option) for the trace file used to record the sliding window of events. The following command, for instance, starts a new user session in circular mode and limits the size of its trace file to 50 MB.

```
xperf.exe -start UserSession -on Microsoft-Windows-TCPIP -FileMode Circular -MaxFile 50
-f c:\CircularUserSession.etl
xperf.exe -stop UserSession
```

To conclude this section, Table 12-1 recaps the ETW session configuration settings described so far in this chapter, along with the Xperf command-line options you can use to control them.

TABLE 12-1 Common ETW Session Settings

Xperf Option	Description	Default Value
–f FileLocation	Intermediate trace location where the session events are flushed during logging	\kernel.etl for the NT Kernel Logger. \user.etl for other user sessions.
–BufferSize Size	The size of the kernel in-memory buffers used by the session	64 KB.
–MinBuffers n	The minimum number of buffers in the session	64 buffers.
–MaxBuffers n	The maximum number of buffers in the session	320 buffers.
–MaxFile Size	Maximum log-file size in megabytes	This option is required for circular ETW sessions. Otherwise, the trace size is unlimited by default.
–FileMode Mode	Commonly used modes are as follows: ■ **Sequential** Data is persisted in sequential order to the trace log file until its maximum file size (if any) is reached. ■ **Circular** Data is persisted to disk, with newer buffers replacing the oldest ones once the maximum file size is reached. ■ **NewFile** Data is written to log files in sequential order, but a new log file is created when the maximum size is reached for the file currently in use.	Sequential mode.

Existing ETW Instrumentation in Windows

Several Windows components (both kernel-mode and user-mode) are already heavily instrumented using ETW. This includes critical parts of the operating system, such as the module loader, the process subsystem, the thread scheduler, the networking stack, the I/O manager, the registry configuration manager, and many other components. In addition, an increasing number of applications and development frameworks are also now instrumented using ETW events. In particular, the Common Language Runtime (CLR), which is the core engine that manages the execution of .NET applications, also defines its own ETW events, emitting useful debugging information related to the operations of many of its internal components (such as the garbage collector, Just-in-Time compiler, and so on), which can prove particularly helpful when analyzing the behavior of .NET applications.

Instrumentation in the Windows Kernel

The kernel of the Windows operating system defines a number of ETW providers, represented by discrete *flags* in the ETW framework. For convenience, the Xperf tool also defines a set of useful kernel flag combinations, or *groups*. The amount of information you're able to derive from these providers is very wide in range, and you can, in fact, conduct several tracing and profiling investigations using only these kernel flags, without any additional user providers.

The PROC_THREAD and LOADER Kernel Flags

Two kernel flags you should always enable when starting the NT Kernel Logger session are the PROC_THREAD and LOADER flags. The PROC_THREAD flag captures all the new process and thread creation and deletion events on the system, and the LOADER flag logs any module load and unload events that happen during the tracing session's lifetime.

The reason these two flags are so important is two-fold:

- These flags are required for proper symbol decoding when your trace contains stack-trace events.
- These flags provide the data displayed by Xperf in the important Process Lifetimes graph, as you saw in the previous chapter. Without these events, you won't know which processes got started during the trace or what modules got loaded by the scenario you're studying. Even when you're primarily interested in the events logged by custom user providers, you'll usually also want to have important kernel events (PROC_THREAD and LOADER flags, in particular) merged with your user session events so that you can make sense of the entire picture that ETW is describing.

Because these two flags are special, Xperf conveniently adds them to all of its predefined kernel groups, including the Base group you used in the previous chapter. This is also the reason that the helper *start_kernel_trace.cmd* script from this book's companion source code automatically includes these two flags regardless of which other kernel flags (the *–kf* option) you provide when starting the NT Kernel Logger session using that script.

Other Kernel Flags and Groups

You can view all the ETW flags supported by the Xperf tool using the following command, where the *KF* filter is used to restrict the scope of the output from the *–providers* option of *xperf.exe* to only show the available kernel flags.

```
xperf.exe -providers KF
  PROC_THREAD     : Process and Thread create/delete
  LOADER          : Kernel and user mode Image Load/Unload events
  PROFILE         : CPU Sample profile
  CSWITCH         : Context Switch
...
```

Similarly, you can also enumerate the predefined kernel groups in Xperf by using the *KG* filter with the same *–providers* option, as shown in the following command.

```
xperf.exe -providers KG
  Base        : PROC_THREAD+LOADER+DISK_IO+HARD_FAULTS+PROFILE+MEMINFO
  Diag        : PROC_THREAD+LOADER+DISK_IO+HARD_FAULTS+DPC+INTERRUPT+CSWITCH+PERF_
COUNTER+COMPACT_CSWITCH
  DiagEasy    : PROC_THREAD+LOADER+DISK_IO+HARD_FAULTS+DPC+INTERRUPT+CSWITCH+PERF_COUNTER
  Latency     : PROC_THREAD+LOADER+DISK_IO+HARD_FAULTS+DPC+INTERRUPT+CSWITCH+PROFILE
  FileIO      : PROC_THREAD+LOADER+DISK_IO+HARD_FAULTS+FILE_IO+FILE_IO_INIT
  IOTrace     : PROC_THREAD+LOADER+DISK_IO+HARD_FAULTS+CSWITCH
  ResumeTrace : PROC_THREAD+LOADER+DISK_IO+HARD_FAULTS+PROFILE+POWER
```

```
SysProf     : PROC_THREAD+LOADER+PROFILE
Network     : PROC_THREAD+LOADER+NETWORKTRACE
```

Note that groups are a mere convenience, so the following two Xperf commands are, in fact, equivalent:

```
xperf.exe -on Base
xperf.exe -on PROC_THREAD+LOADER+DISK_IO+HARD_FAULTS+PROFILE+MEMINFO
```

By pure convention, the kernel flags are capitalized when displayed by Xperf, while the kernel groups are not. That being said, *xperf.exe* is case-insensitive, so either capitalization works when you enter the flags and groups on the command line. You can also use the plus sign (+) to request any combination of flags and groups. The following command, for example, starts the NT Kernel Logger session with all the flags from the Base kernel group, as well as the CSWITCH kernel flag, which logs every context-switch event during the trace session.

```
xperf.exe -on Base+CSWITCH
xperf.exe -stop -d c:\temp\merged.etl
```

You can also combine multiple groups: Xperf won't complain if you list the same flag multiple times on the command line.

```
xperf.exe -on Base+FileIO
xperf.exe -stop -d c:\temp\merged.etl
```

Table 12-2 provides an overview of a few important kernel flags and some scenarios where you might want to enable them.

TABLE 12-2 Important Kernel Flags and Their Practical Applications

Kernel Flag	Event Volume	Description	Additional Considerations
PROC_THREAD	Light	Process and thread start/exit events.	Required for ETW stack-walk support. It's also useful for observing process lifetimes.
LOADER	Light	Image load/unload events.	Also required for stack-walk support. It can be useful when debugging performance issues in which new code paths start loading additional DLLs into a process.
PROFILE	Heavy	The profile flag causes an event to be logged with each sampling of the CPU (every 1 millisecond, by default).	Useful for analyzing high-CPU-utilization issues.
CSWITCH DISPATCHER	Heavy	The context-switch events are logged whenever a thread is switched in for execution on one of the CPUs on the machine. The dispatcher events are logged whenever a blocked thread is moved to the ready state (awoken by another thread), but before it actually gets switched in.	Useful for analyzing logical delays and building causality chains for why a thread might be spending a long time before getting unblocked.

Kernel Flag	Event Volume	Description	Additional Considerations
REGISTRY	Moderate	This flag enables a set of events that track registry operations (create, delete, read, write, and so on).	Can be used for reverse-engineering the behavior of software. It's also useful in performance analysis.
FILE_IO_*	Moderate	The FILE_IO_* flags enable monitoring of operations performed over executive file objects (create, delete, read, write, and so on).	Useful for reverse-engineering the behavior of software and performance analysis. These events also require the kernel rundown metadata (the *–d* option in Xperf) so that Xperf is able to display the friendly file names associated with each file object.
DISK_IO_*	Moderate	The DISK_IO_* flags monitor lower level activity at the disk level.	Useful in performance analysis.
SYSCALL	Heavy	This flag causes an ETW event to be logged at the entry and exit of every system call.	The exit event contains the error code returned by the system call, so it can be useful when debugging low-level failures (such as access denied or file-not-found issues).

Chapter 13, "Common Tracing Scenarios," will also provide several hands-on examples for how to use these flags in practical tracing investigations.

Viewing Kernel Provider Events in Xperf

Several kernel provider events have dedicated graphs and summary tables in Xperf. Xperf also conveniently determines the kernel providers used in the logging sessions from the trace file and offers only the relevant graphs and summary tables as choices in the Frame List flyout in the viewer UI. Figure 12-2 shows some of these graphs, obtained using a simple Xperf tracing experiment where a number of kernel flags were enabled. Again, remember to start and stop this session from an elevated administrative command prompt.

```
C:\book\code\common\scripts>start_kernel_trace.cmd -kf
Base+CSWITCH+DISPATCHER+REGISTRY+FILENAME+FILE_IO+FILE_IO_INIT+POWER+SYSCALL+ALPC
INFO: Invoking xperf to start the session...
CmdLine: (xperf.exe -on
PROC_THREAD+LOADER+Base+CSWITCH+DISPATCHER+REGISTRY+FILENAME+FILE_IO+FILE_IO_
INIT+POWER+SYSCALL+ALPC )

C:\book\code\common\scripts>stop_kernel_trace.cmd
INFO: Invoking xperf to stop the session...
CmdLine: (xperf.exe -stop -d c:\temp\merged.etl)
Merged Etl: c:\temp\merged.etl

C:\book\code\common\scripts>view_trace.cmd
...
INFO: Invoking xperf to view the trace...
CmdLine: (xperf.exe c:\temp\merged.etl)
```

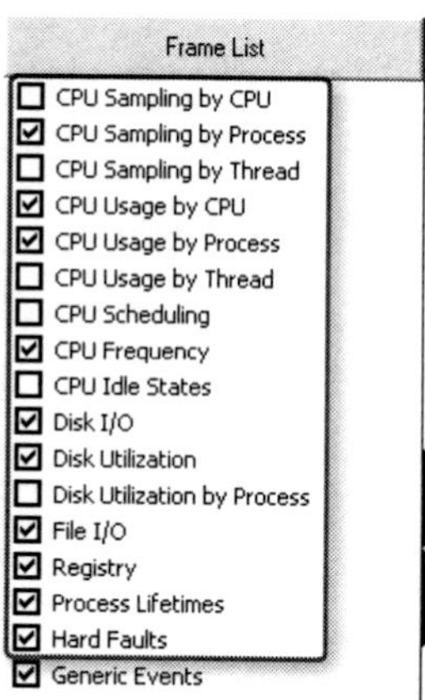

FIGURE 12-2 Dedicated kernel provider graphs in the Xperf viewer UI.

Not every kernel flag has a dedicated graph in Xperf. The SYSCALL ("system calls") and ALPC ("Advanced Local Procedure Calls") kernel flags from the previous experiment, for example, aren't used frequently in tracing investigations and so have no such graphs. However, you can still view these events in the Generic Events graph, which lumps together all the ETW event types that haven't been claimed by another dedicated graph in Xperf.

Instrumentation in Other Windows Components

ETW instrumentation is also prevalent in other components of the Windows operating system that fall outside the core kernel. This includes areas such as the TCP/IP networking stack, the Remote Procedure Call (RPC) runtime, the Win32 heap, the NT thread pool, and much more.

Note that even though Xperf refers to these as *user-mode providers*, this description is not strictly accurate. The Microsoft-Windows-TCPIP user provider, for instance, logs its events from the *tcpip.sys* kernel-mode driver. To avoid any confusion and still keep in line with the Xperf terminology, the term "user providers" will be used in this book to describe any providers that can't log to the NT Kernel Logger session. These user providers are identified using globally unique identifiers (GUIDs), as opposed to the flags used to describe the kernel providers.

Manifest-Based User Providers

In Windows Vista, ETW introduced an extensible model where new ETW user providers can be defined to log event payloads of any shape but still get recognized by existing ETW viewers. To support this idea, a declarative XML schema is used to describe the data types logged by each event from the provider, along with the order in which this data appears in the event payload. Because the vast majority of user providers in Windows Vista and Windows 7 are manifest-based, this book deals only with this particular type of user provider.

Manifest-based user providers require a one-time installation step on the target machine in order for ETW consumers to be able to retrieve this information when parsing their events. For Windows components, this is already done as part of the Windows setup process. Other applications usually also perform this step for their custom user providers at installation time. This provider installation is done by using the *wevtutil.exe* tool, as described in the MSDN web page at the following URL: *http://msdn.microsoft.com/library/windows/desktop/dd996919.aspx*.

In addition to publishing the location of the instrumentation manifest, this installation step also publishes other useful metadata, including a friendly name to go along with the mandatory GUID used internally in ETW to identify the user provider. As an implementation detail, this metadata is currently stored as part of the Windows registry under the key shown in Figure 12-3, where each log channel is associated with an *OwningPublisher* GUID that represents the owning user provider.

```
[HKEY_LOCAL_MACHINE\SOFTWARE\Microsoft\Windows\CurrentVersion\WINEVT]
```

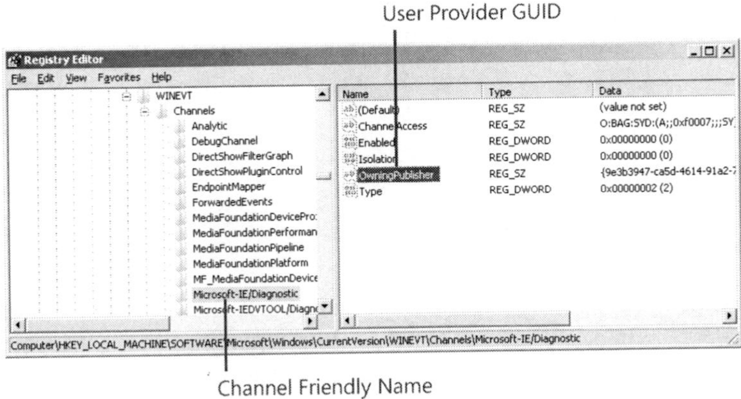

FIGURE 12-3 Manifest-based user provider's registration information.

Discovering User Providers

Xperf allows you to enumerate the installed user providers by using the *I* filter with the *–providers* command-line option. A user provider doesn't need to be installed to be usable on the machine, but this installation step allows ETW consumers to recognize the events logged by the provider, so most OS user providers will have their manifests installed on the system.

```
xperf.exe -providers I
  0063715b-eeda-4007-9429-ad526f62696e          : Microsoft-Windows-Services
  6ad52b32-d609-4be9-ae07-ce8dae937e39          : Microsoft-Windows-RPC
  c861d0e2-a2c1-4d36-9f9c-970bab943a12          : Thread Pool
  222962ab-6180-4b88-a825-346b75f2a24a          : Heap Trace Provider
  3ac66736-cc59-4cff-8115-8df50e39816b          : Critical Section Trace Provider
  2f07e2ee-15db-40f1-90ef-9d7ba282188a          : Microsoft-Windows-TCPIP
  7d44233d-3055-4b9c-ba64-0d47ca40a232          : Microsoft-Windows-WinHttp
  43d1a55c-76d6-4f7e-995c-64c711e5cafe          : Microsoft-Windows-WinINet
...
```

The first column in the previous command's output shows the user provider GUID, while the second column displays the corresponding friendly names, which by convention often have the following format: *CompanyName–ProductName–ComponentName*.

Just because a provider has been installed on the machine doesn't mean that it's currently logging events. ETW mandates that user-mode applications call the *advapi32!EventRegister* API to register any user providers they plan to use before calling the *advapi32!EventWrite* Win32 API to log ETW events from that provider. As a result, the kernel-mode side of the ETW framework has knowledge of all the registered user providers that are currently in use by active processes on the system. This dynamic list can be obtained from the ETW framework by using the *advapi32!EnumerateTraceGuidsEx* Win32 API, which Xperf internally uses to display the registered user providers on the system shown by the *R* filter in the *–providers* option. A registered provider is essentially ready to emit events in the context of the process that registered it, but until the provider gets dynamically enabled into a session using an ETW controller tool (such as Xperf), no events from that provider are actually logged.

```
xperf.exe -providers R

...
  Microsoft-Windows-ParentalControls
  e27950eb-1768-451f-96ac-cc4e14f6d3d0
  Microsoft-Windows-AIT
  Microsoft-Windows-Kernel-EventTracing
```

Even though the *EnumerateTraceGuidsEx* Win32 API also returns the ID of the process (PID) that registered each user provider, Xperf doesn't allow you to filter the list of registered providers on the system and scope it down to the process level. Fortunately, however, the *logman.exe* tool, which ships as part of Windows under the *system32* directory, can be used to work around this current limitation. This essentially gives you an idea beforehand whether the user providers you're thinking of enabling in an ETW session would actually collect any events from the user-mode process you're looking to trace.

As an illustration, you'll now discover the user providers that the Local Security Authority Subsystem (LSASS) process uses to log ETW events. (This, of course, is in addition to the events logged by the kernel components on its behalf.) First, you can use the *tlist.exe* command to find the PID of the *lsass.exe* process.

```
"C:\Program Files\Debugging Tools for Windows (x86)\tlist.exe" -p lsass.exe
580
```

The actual PID you'll see on your machine will likely be different, but you can take the value you obtain in the previous step and use it with the *logman.exe* tool to query the registered user providers in the target process, as illustrated in the following command.

```
logman.exe query providers -pid 580
Provider                                   GUID
-------------------------------------------------------------------------------
Active Directory Domain Services: SAM      {8E598056-8993-11D2-819E-0000F875A064}
Active Directory: Kerberos Client          {BBA3ADD2-C229-4CDB-AE2B-57EB6966B0C4}
Active Directory: NetLogon                 {F33959B4-DBEC-11D2-895B-00C04F79AB69}
FWPUCLNT Trace Provider                    {5A1600D2-68E5-4DE7-BCF4-1C2D215FE0FE}
Local Security Authority (LSA)             {CC85922F-DB41-11D2-9244-006008269001}
LsaSrv                                     {199FE037-2B82-40A9-82AC-E1D46C792B99}
Microsoft-Windows-AIT                      {6ADDABF4-8C54-4EAB-BF4F-FBEF61B62EB0}
Microsoft-Windows-CAPI2                    {5BBCA4A8-B209-48DC-A8C7-B23D3E5216FB}
Microsoft-Windows-CertPolEng               {AF9CC194-E9A8-42BD-B0D1-834E9CFAB799}
Microsoft-Windows-DCLocator                {CFAA5446-C6C4-4F5C-866F-31C9B55B962D}
Microsoft-Windows-Diagnosis-PCW            {AABF8B86-7936-4FA2-ACB0-63127F879DBF}
Microsoft-Windows-DNS-Client               {1C95126E-7EEA-49A9-A3FE-A378B03DDB4D}
Microsoft-Windows-EFS                      {3663A992-84BE-40EA-BBA9-90C7ED544222}
Microsoft-Windows-LDAP-Client              {099614A5-5DD7-4788-8BC9-E29F43DB28FC}
Microsoft-Windows-Networking-Correlation {83ED54F0-4D48-4E45-B16E-726FFD1FA4AF}
Microsoft-Windows-RPC                      {6AD52B32-D609-4BE9-AE07-CE8DAE937E39}
Microsoft-Windows-Shell-Core               {30336ED4-E327-447C-9DE0-51B652C86108}
...
```

What this tells you is that *lsass.exe* (or one of its loaded DLL modules) is likely logging events from these ETW user providers at one point or another during its lifetime. In addition, any user providers outside of that list are probably not going to matter when tracing this process. This is very valuable information when you're devising your tracing strategy and deciding which flags and user providers to enable before starting your ETW trace session.

Viewing User Provider Events in Xperf

With the exception of a few special user providers (such as the Win32 heap provider), custom user provider events won't have dedicated graphs. As a result, the events from those providers will usually end up in the Generic Events graph, which tends to be near the bottom of the main window in the Xperf viewer UI. This catch-all graph is depicted in Figure 12-4. Notice that you can filter the output of the graph to show only events from a subset of providers.

```
C:\book\code\common\scripts>start_user_trace.cmd -kf Base -up
Microsoft-Windows-RPC+Microsoft-Windows-TCPIP
INFO: Invoking xperf to start the kernel and user sessions...
CmdLine: (xperf.exe -on PROC_THREAD+LOADER+Base
-start UserSession -on Microsoft-Windows-RPC+Microsoft-Windows-TCPIP)

C:\book\code\common\scripts>stop_user_trace.cmd
INFO: Invoking xperf to stop the kernel and user sessions...
CmdLine: (xperf.exe -stop -stop UserSession -d c:\temp\merged.etl)

C:\book\code\common\scripts>view_trace.cmd
...
INFO: Invoking xperf to view the trace...
CmdLine: (xperf.exe c:\temp\merged.etl)
```

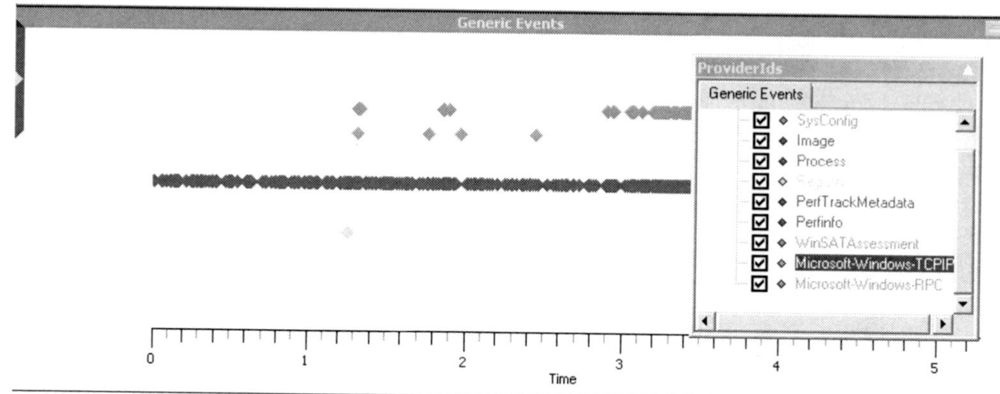

FIGURE 12-4 Generic Events graph in the Xperf viewer UI.

You can use the Summary Table view of the graph to visualize the data using the powerful sort capabilities of the Xperf viewer. Alternatively, you can also point to any dot in the graph with the mouse to get more information on the ETW event payload that it represents. For user providers that log events at a high rate (such as the RPC user provider), however, there will be too many dots over the trace timeline, making it difficult to conduct an efficient search of the logged events. That being said, you can achieve a better resolution of the events in the UI by picking a time interval using the left mouse button, right-clicking anywhere in the graph's drawing area to open the shortcut menu, and then clicking the Select View action to zoom in on the events logged during the selected timeline.

A useful trick to make selecting relevant intervals easier is to log *marks* during the lifetime of your scenario. This technique works for any graph in Xperf, but it's especially useful in the case of high-volume user providers and the Generic Events graph. These marks you log are added to the trace as special ETW events, with the label description that you provide also injected as part of their payload. The following sequence illustrates how you can use the *–m* command-line option in Xperf to insert mark events.

```
C:\book\code\common\scripts\start_user_trace.cmd -kf Base -up Microsoft-Windows-RPC
INFO: Invoking xperf to start the kernel and user sessions...
CmdLine: (xperf.exe -on PROC_THREAD+LOADER+Base  -start UserSession -on Microsoft-Windows-RPC)

---- Mark the start of an important phase in the scenario ----
xperf.exe -m "First Mark"
---- Mark the end of the previous phase ----
xperf.exe -m "Second Mark"

C:\book\code\common\scripts\stop_user_trace.cmd
INFO: Invoking xperf to stop the kernel and user sessions...
CmdLine: (xperf.exe -stop -stop UserSession -d c:\temp\merged.etl)
```

When viewing the collected trace, you can see marks in the special Marks graph, as illustrated in Figure 12-5.

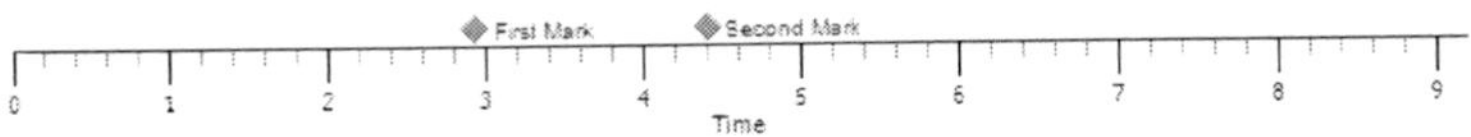

FIGURE 12-5 Marks graph in the Xperf viewer UI.

You can also use the convenient capability in Xperf to overlay graphs and have the marks appear alongside the other user events in the Generic Events graph, as demonstrated in Figure 12-6.

```
C:\book\code\common\scripts\view_trace.cmd
...
INFO: Invoking xperf to view the trace...
CmdLine: (xperf.exe c:\temp\merged.etl)
```

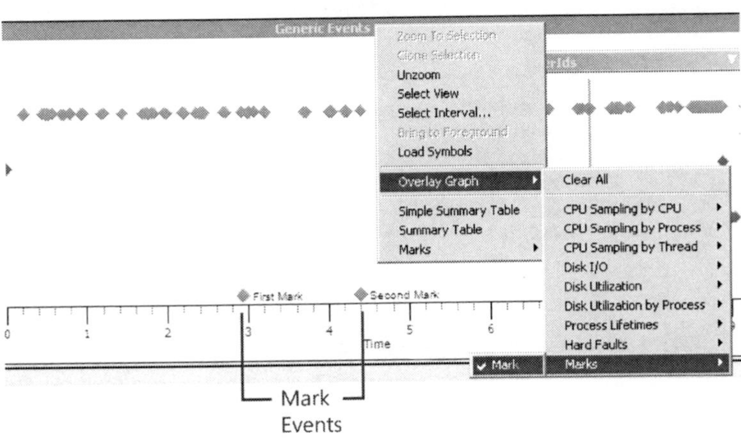

FIGURE 12-6 Overlaying marks into the Generic Events graph in the Xperf viewer UI.

This way, you can establish clear marks for the boundaries of the time interval you would like to zoom in on during the analysis of the trace.

Understanding ETW Stack-Walk Events

ETW allows you to also capture the call stacks where the events in your session get logged. You already saw this capability in action in the previous chapter, where you were able to capture the stack traces of every sample profiling event occurrence. Since its introduction in Windows Vista, this powerful feature continues to see improvements with each new release of the Windows operating system.

In particular, support for this feature was also added to the 64-bit versions of Windows during the Windows Vista SP1 release. Later in Windows 7, the ability to collect call stacks for user events was also introduced, complementing the support that already existed for kernel events. Other improvements included support for deeper call stacks.

ETW does this magic by logging a special stack-walk event for each event from the providers for which stack-walk capture is enabled during the trace session—with the event payload being the addresses of the frames on the call stack. This stack-walk event shares the same timestamp with its associated ETW event, even though the two events get logged at different times, so that ETW consumers can correlate them to each other when parsing the target trace file. Note the payload of the ETW stack-walk events captures only the hexadecimal virtual addresses for the frames on the call stack, so symbols are required to resolve the function addresses to their friendly names during trace analysis, though they're not needed at collection time.

Enabling and Viewing Stack Traces for Kernel Provider Events

You can enable stack trace collection for kernel events by using the *–stackwalk* command-line option in Xperf when starting the NT Kernel Logger session. You can list the available stack-walking flags by typing **xperf.exe –help stackwalk** in a command-prompt window, as shown in the following listing.

```
xperf.exe -help stackwalk
  NT Kernel Logger provider:
    ProcessCreate                    PagefaultTransition
    ProcessDelete                    PagefaultDemandZero
    ImageLoad                        PagefaultCopyOnWrite
    ImageUnload                      PagefaultGuard
    ThreadCreate                     PagefaultHard
    ThreadDelete                     PagefaultAV
    CSwitch                          VirtualAlloc
    ReadyThread                      VirtualFree
...
```

Note that each kernel flag might have several associated stack-walk events. The PROC_THREAD kernel flag, for example, has four different stack-walking events (ProcessCreate, ProcessDelete, ThreadCreate, and ThreadDelete), each corresponding to a separate ETW event logged by that event provider flag. Table 12-3 lists a few more kernel providers and their respective stack-walking flags.

TABLE 12-3 Kernel Flags and Their Associated Stack-Walk Events

Kernel Flag	Stack-Walk Events
PROC_THREAD	ProcessCreate, ProcessDelete, ThreadCreate, ThreadDelete
LOADER	ImageLoad, ImageUnload
PROFILE	Profile
CSWITCH	CSwitch
DISPATCHER	ReadyThread
REGISTRY	RegQueryKey, RegEnumerateKey, RegDeleteKey, RegCreateKey, RegOpenKey, RegSetValue, RegDeleteValue, RegQueryValue

Kernel Flag	Stack-Walk Events
FILE_IO_*	FileCreate, FileRead, FileWrite, FileDelete, FileRename
DISK_IO_*	DiskReadInit, DiskWriteInit, DiskFlushInit
SYSCALL	SyscallEnter, SyscallExit

The following example shows how to enable stack-trace collection for all the SyscallExit events from the SYSCALL kernel flag, which get logged when system calls return from kernel mode to the user-mode code that invoked them. As mentioned earlier in this chapter, you must always enable the PROC_THREAD and LOADER flags whenever you want to include stack-walk events in your ETW trace, which the Xperf wrapper scripts from the companion source code already do.

```
C:\book\code\common\scripts>start_kernel_trace.cmd -kf SYSCALL -ks SysCallExit
INFO: Invoking xperf to start the session...
CmdLine: (xperf.exe -on PROC_THREAD+LOADER+SYSCALL -stackwalk SysCallExit)

C:\book\code\common\scripts>stop_kernel_trace.cmd
INFO: Invoking xperf to stop the session...
CmdLine: (xperf.exe -stop -d c:\temp\merged.etl)
```

You should also be aware that *xperf.exe* won't warn you if you try to enable a stack-walk event without also enabling its corresponding kernel flag. If you fail to add the proper provider flag, the associated stack-trace events won't be emitted into the trace file, either.

When analyzing a trace using the Xperf viewer, you can find the stack traces you enabled when you started the session in one of two places:

- The Stack Counts By Type graph contains all the stack-walk events from the trace file. The summary table for this special graph groups these events together in a single view.
- You can also find the stack traces in the graph representing their associated events. In the previous case, because the SYSCALL kernel flag doesn't have a dedicated graph, its events (and their call stacks) will be in the Generic Events graph summary table, where the Stack column contains the associated stack-trace events (when present in the trace).

You'll now see how to use the Stack Counts By Type graph to view the ETW stack-trace events from the previous session, and the following section will demonstrate the second approach, where you can use the summary table of the target event type. Choosing between these two approaches is usually a matter of preference.

You should keep in mind that Xperf doesn't resolve symbols by default, so you need to enable that option in the UI (by right-clicking and selecting Load Symbols, as shown in Figure 12-7) before you can see the proper call stacks, which are shown in Figure 12-8.

```
C:\book\code\common\scripts>view_trace.cmd
...
INFO: Invoking xperf to view the trace...
CmdLine: (xperf.exe c:\temp\merged.etl)
```

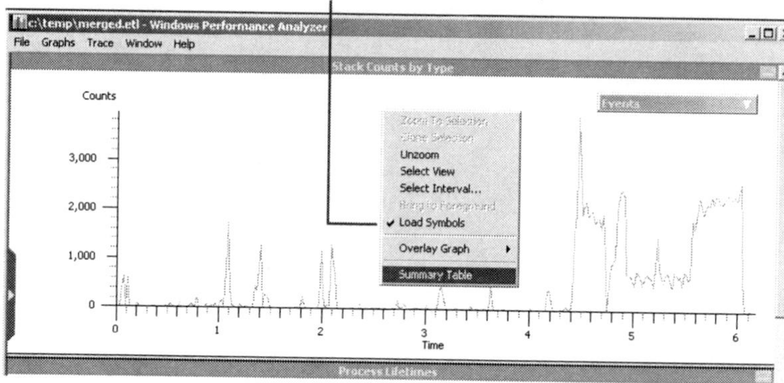

FIGURE 12-7 Selecting Load Symbols to enable stack-trace symbol decoding in the Xperf viewer UI.

Stack Counts Summary Table - c:\temp\merged.etl - [0 s - 6.1663527 s] - 6.1663527 s - Windows Performance

File Columns View Trace Window Help

Line	Process	Stack	Count
1	xperf.exe (5828)	⊟ [Root]	45,730
2		⊟ |- ntdll.dll!_RtlUserThreadStart	45,302
3		| ntdll.dll!__RtlUserThreadStart	45,302
4		⊞ | |- kernel32.dll!BaseThreadInitThunk	45,301
5		⊟ | |- xperf.exe!wmainCRTStartup	1
6		| | xperf.exe!__security_init_cookie	1
7		| | ntdll.dll!RtlQueryPerformanceCounter	1
8		| | ntdll.dll!ZwQueryPerformanceCounter	1
9		| | ntkrpamp.exe!KiServiceExit2	1
10		| |	1
11		⊞ |- ntdll.dll!LdrInitializeThunk	428
12	svchost.exe (712)	⊞ [Root]	35,276
13	services.exe (564)	⊞ [Root]	24,072
14	svchost.exe (1012)	⊞ [Root]	12,964
15	WmiPrvSE.exe (3636)	⊞ [Root]	8,219
16	notepad.exe (6300)	⊞ [Root]	2,074
17	explorer.exe (4604)	⊞ [Root]	1,755

FIGURE 12-8 Stack Counts By Type summary table.

Notice that you're able to see all the system calls that are performed during the lifetime of the previous trace session, along with their call stacks, including those made by *xperf.exe* itself!

Enabling and Viewing Stack Traces for User Provider Events

Enabling stack-walk events for user providers uses a different syntax in Xperf than the one previously shown for kernel stack-walk events. More specifically, the *–stackwalk* option is applicable only to kernel events. For user providers, you need to append the :::'stack' string to the provider GUID or friendly name on the Xperf command line. You'll see a full explanation of this seemingly cryptic syntax later in the "Adding ETW Logging to Your Code" section, where the level and keyword filters will be introduced. Note also that, as mentioned earlier in this chapter, ETW and Xperf didn't support stack-walk capture for user provider events until the Windows 7 release.

As an illustration for how to request stack traces of user events, the following command starts a new user session for the events from the Microsoft-Windows-TCPIP and Microsoft-Windows-RPC providers, and it requests stack-walk events for the RPC provider but not for the TCP/IP user provider.

```
C:\book\code\common\scripts>start_user_trace.cmd -kf Base -up
Microsoft-Windows-RPC:::'stack'+Microsoft-Windows-TCPIP
INFO: Invoking xperf to start the kernel and user sessions...
CmdLine: (xperf.exe -on PROC_THREAD+LOADER+Base
-start UserSession -on Microsoft-Windows-RPC:::'stack'+Microsoft-Windows-TCPIP)

C:\book\code\common\scripts>stop_user_trace.cmd
INFO: Invoking xperf to stop the kernel and user sessions...
CmdLine: (xperf.exe -stop -stop UserSession -d c:\temp\merged.etl)
```

When viewing the trace file in Xperf, you can find the call stacks where the RPC events were logged in the summary table describing those events, which in this case is the Generic Events graph summary table. You again need to first enable stack-trace symbol decoding in the Xperf viewer UI by selecting the corresponding option, as shown in Figure 12-9.

```
C:\book\code\common\scripts>view_trace.cmd
...
INFO: Invoking xperf to view the trace...
CmdLine: (xperf.exe c:\temp\merged.etl)
```

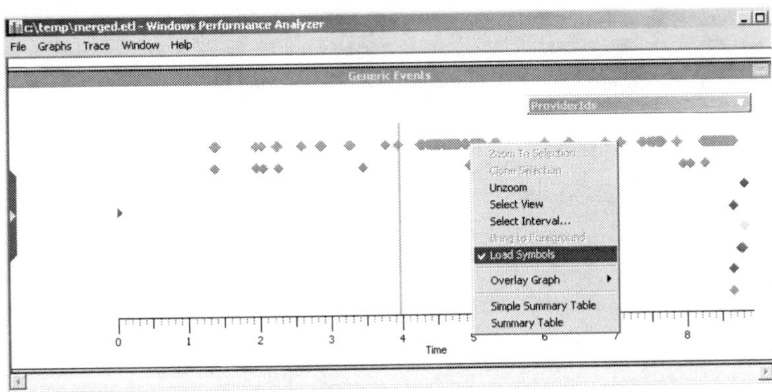

FIGURE 12-9 Enabling stack-trace symbol decoding in the Xperf viewer UI.

Once you've done that, you can invoke the summary table for this graph and organize its columns, for example, with the Process Name, Provider Name, Task Name, and Stack columns to the left of the gold bar, as shown in Figure 12-10. This allows you to view the data in the summary table sorted by those columns. Remember that some columns (most notably the Stack column) might be missing from the default Summary Table view, so you need to explicitly select them using the flyout menu in the middle of the left side of the Summary Table window. Notice that by expanding the call-stack nodes included in the Stack column, you're able to see the (many) RPC client and server calls that were performed on the system during the tracing session.

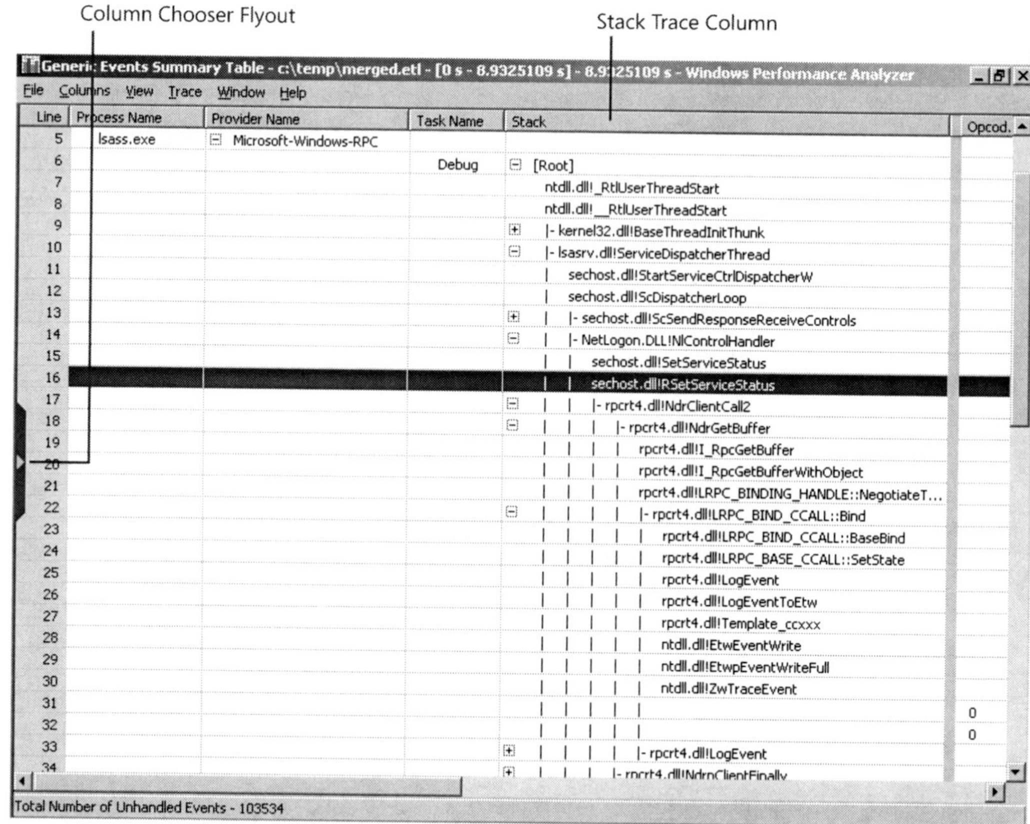

FIGURE 12-10 Viewing call stacks of user events in the Generic Events summary table.

Diagnosing ETW Stack-Trace Issues

There are three categories of symptoms you'll see when you find yourself unable to get the proper call stacks in the Xperf viewer UI:

- Missing call stack events from the trace
- Unresolved call stacks, where Xperf displays the frames from the stack trace but is unable to map them to their symbolic function names
- Incomplete call stacks, where Xperf displays the frames from the stack but the stack trace seems to stop prematurely before hitting the bottom frames in user mode

Diagnosing Missing Call Stacks

The telltale sign of this condition is if your stacks are showing as *?* in the Xperf viewer UI, as illustrated in Figure 12-11, where the trace was captured with the PROC_THREAD kernel flag but without the ProcessCreate stack-walk flag. Notice how the Creation Stack column in the Process Lifetimes summary table shows no call stacks because the events were missing from the trace.

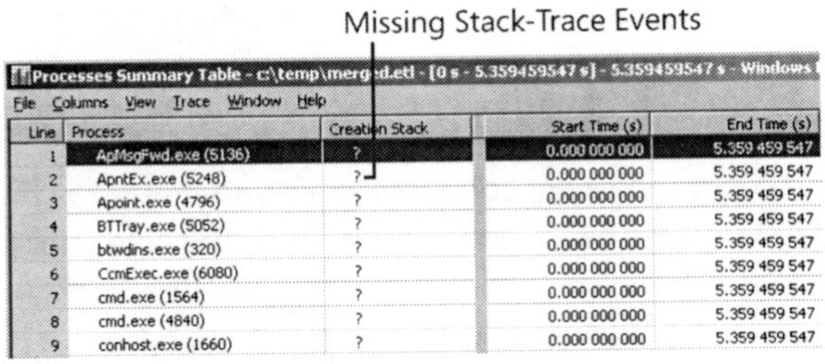

Missing Stack-Trace Events

Line	Process	Creation Stack	Start Time (s)	End Time (s)
1	ApMsgFwd.exe (5136)	?	0.000 000 000	5.359 459 547
2	ApntEx.exe (5248)	?	0.000 000 000	5.359 459 547
3	Apoint.exe (4796)	?	0.000 000 000	5.359 459 547
4	BTTray.exe (5052)	?	0.000 000 000	5.359 459 547
5	btwdins.exe (320)	?	0.000 000 000	5.359 459 547
6	CcmExec.exe (6080)	?	0.000 000 000	5.359 459 547
7	cmd.exe (1564)	?	0.000 000 000	5.359 459 547
8	cmd.exe (4840)	?	0.000 000 000	5.359 459 547
9	conhost.exe (1660)	?	0.000 000 000	5.359 459 547

FIGURE 12-11 Missing stack-trace events.

The following steps will help you figure out the reason why the stack-trace events are missing from the trace:

- Make sure you've requested stack-trace capture for the target providers when you started your session by using the correct *–stackwalk* flag for kernel events or the :::'stack' suffix in the case of user events.
- In the case of kernel events, make sure that the associated kernel flag was also enabled during trace collection. Xperf won't warn you or generate an error if you specify a stack-walk flag (for example, SysCallExit) but fail to enable its corresponding kernel flag (for example, SYSCALL).

If you determine that you must have the missing stacks for your analysis, unfortunately your only solution is to recapture the trace after enabling the correct flags.

Diagnosing Unresolved Call Stacks

This is the most common case when dealing with stack-trace issues in Xperf, and it can be due to a number of reasons. The common pattern, however, is that you'll see frames marked as *?!?* or *module!?*. Figure 12-12, for example, shows a scenario where a summary table with stack-trace events was invoked without first enabling symbol lookup in the Xperf UI.

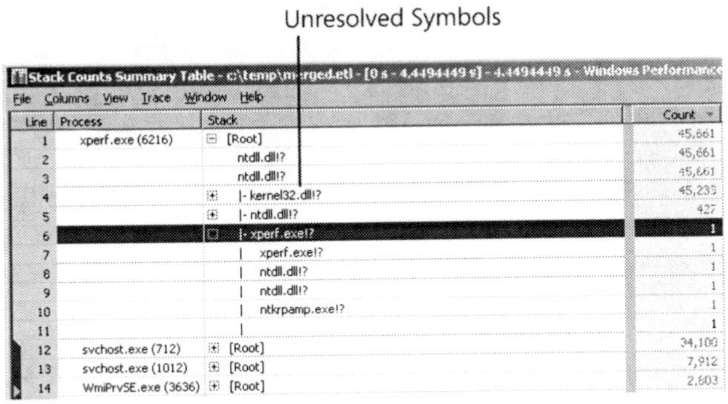

Unresolved Symbols

Line	Process	Stack	Count
1	xperf.exe (6216)	[Root]	45,661
2		ntdll.dll!?	45,661
3		ntdll.dll!?	45,661
4		|- kernel32.dll!?	45,233
5		|- ntdll.dll!?	427
6		|- xperf.exe!?	1
7		| xperf.exe!?	1
8		| ntdll.dll!?	1
9		| ntdll.dll!?	1
10		| ntkrpamp.exe!?	1
11		|	1
12	svchost.exe (712)	[Root]	34,109
13	svchost.exe (1012)	[Root]	7,912
14	WmiPrvSE.exe (3636)	[Root]	2,603

FIGURE 12-12 Unresolved stack-trace events.

The following steps will help you figure out why the frames in your trace weren't properly mapped to their symbolic function names:

- Verify that you set _NT_SYMBOL_PATH and _NT_SYMCACHE_PATH correctly before you started the Xperf viewer or directly in its symbols path configuration UI. This step can be automated using a script, such as the *view_trace.cmd* script included with the companion source code. If you're tracing your own code, the _NT_SYMBOL_PATH variable should also explicitly include the paths to the symbols for your binaries in addition to the Microsoft public symbols server.

  If this is the root cause of your problem, you'll see frames displayed as *module!?*. It's easy to fix this issue, though, because you can do so on the viewer side and you don't need to recapture a new trace. That's assuming, of course, that you're able to point Xperf to the correct symbol files for the target modules on the call stacks. The *xperf.exe* module, for example, doesn't have its symbols posted on the Microsoft public symbols server, so its frames will still show up as *xperf.exe!?* even if your symbols paths are set correctly.

- Similarly, verify that you also enabled symbol lookup by selecting the Load Symbols shortcut menu option in the Xperf viewer UI.

  If you miss this step, you'll again see *module!?* frames, which you can easily rectify in the UI without a need to restart the Xperf viewer.

- Make sure that you enabled the PROC_THREAD and LOADER kernel flags when you started your trace capture, even if you're collecting user events. Better yet, use a helper script (such as the *start_kernel_trace.cmd* and *start_user_trace.cmd* scripts provided in the companion source code) that does that automatically for you.

  If you miss this step, the frames in your stack-trace events will all be shown as *?!?*, given that Xperf wouldn't have the necessary information to decode the modules in the trace file. To fix this issue, unfortunately you need to recapture a new trace for the scenario.

- The next thing to check is that you merged the events from your trace session with the kernel rundown information on the machine where the ETW trace capture was performed (by using the *–d* command-line option of Xperf). It's again a good idea to use a helper script that always does that when you stop your ETW trace sessions.

  Without this kernel rundown information, symbol decoding doesn't work in Xperf, and you'll again end up with unresolved frames, with the module information but without the function names (*module!?*). To fix this issue, unfortunately you also need to recapture a new trace for the scenario.

- Finally, the Windows 7 version of Xperf isn't able to decode the managed frames in the case of dynamically generated .NET code (it shows *module!?*), even when you have the correct symbols for those .NET modules. On 64-bit Windows 7, the situation gets even worse when *x64* managed modules are present because the call stack stops at the first 64-bit managed frame, preventing you from even getting to the native frames above that managed frame. You move from simply unresolved symbols on the stack to incomplete stacks in that case!

Diagnosing Incomplete Call Stacks

Another common problem when using ETW stack-walk events is call stacks that stop prematurely before all of their frames have been captured, which usually happens when the ETW code in the OS fails to walk the stack of the logging call site at trace-collection time. Figure 12-13 demonstrates this situation in a 64-bit, sample profiling kernel trace without the *DisablePagingExecutive* value having been set to 1. Notice in particular how the *ntdll!ZwMapViewOfSection* frame is never shown to call *nt!NtMapViewOfSection* in this call stack, suggesting an incomplete kernel stack scenario.

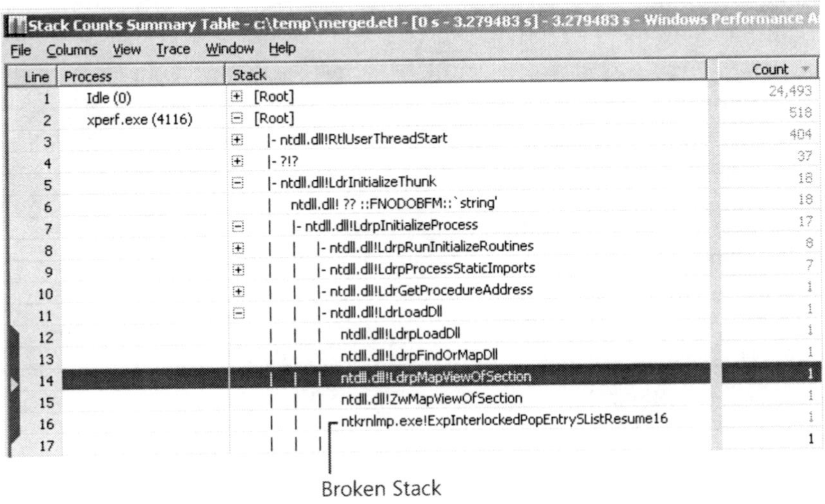

Stack Counts Summary Table - c:\temp\merged.etl - [0 s - 3.279483 s] - 3.279483 s - Windows Performance A

File Columns View Trace Window Help

Line	Process	Stack	Count
1	Idle (0)	[Root]	24,493
2	xperf.exe (4116)	[Root]	518
3		|- ntdll.dll!RtlUserThreadStart	404
4		|- ?!?	37
5		|- ntdll.dll!LdrInitializeThunk	18
6		| ntdll.dll! ?? ::FNODOBFM::`string'	18
7		| |- ntdll.dll!LdrpInitializeProcess	17
8		| | |- ntdll.dll!LdrpRunInitializeRoutines	8
9		| | |- ntdll.dll!LdrpProcessStaticImports	7
10		| | |- ntdll.dll!LdrGetProcedureAddress	1
11		| | |- ntdll.dll!LdrLoadDll	1
12		| | | ntdll.dll!LdrpLoadDll	1
13		| | | ntdll.dll!LdrpFindOrMapDll	1
14		| | | ntdll.dll!LdrpMapViewOfSection	1
15		| | | ntdll.dll!ZwMapViewOfSection	1
16		| | | ntkrnlmp.exe!ExpInterlockedPopEntrySListResume16	1
17		| | |	1

Broken Stack

FIGURE 12-13 Incomplete stack-trace events.

Because the way the system performs stack walking is different between 32-bit (*x86*) and 64-bit (*x64*) versions of Windows, the root causes that lead to this condition are also different.

Incomplete call stacks on 32-bit (*x86*) Windows On *x86* Windows, the OS walks backward from the call site where the associated event is logged and uses the chain of frame pointers saved on the stack to reconstruct the call stack. This is done both for the user-mode and kernel-mode stacks of the logging thread. One case where this scheme runs into problems is when the frame pointers aren't saved on the stack—an optimization referred to as the *Frame Pointer Omission (FPO)*.

When FPO is enabled for functions on the call stack, you'll see incomplete ETW stack traces. The solution to this problem is to make sure FPO is disabled (by using the */Oy–* compiler option in C++) for your project. Fortunately, this is now the default setting when you compile your code using Visual Studio. In a world where CPU models in the GHz range are commonplace, the performance benefits gained from this optimization (less than 2 percent, and typically much less than that) are not worth the debugging and tracing problems they introduce.

History of the Frame Pointer Omission Optimization

A typical function prologue on *x86* saves a pointer to the start of the current function frame (held by the stack pointer register at the beginning of each function) in the special *ebp* register so that local variables can be easily referenced in the disassembly of the function by their displacement from this base location.

```
00fd1407 55              push    ebp
00fd1408 8bec            mov     ebp,esp
```

Back in the early days of *x86*, the number of registers was limited. So, the compiler engineers came up with an elaborate optimization where the *ebp* register isn't used to save the stack location at the start of each function and locals are instead referenced directly by their displacement from the current stack pointer location (*esp*). This freed up the *ebp* register for other use within the functions that had this optimization. In so doing, however, a very useful artifact was lost because it was no longer easy to traverse the chain of functions on the call stack by easily finding the return addresses relative to the frame pointers. Because this chain was no longer readily available in the binary's address space itself, this call chain information was moved to the symbol file (PDB) of the binary so that debugger programs could access it from there.

Because ETW can't use symbol files at collection time, however, FPO essentially breaks ETW stack walking. Fortunately, all of the Windows source code is now compiled without this optimization so that this problem won't affect your ability to view stack traces for system components in Xperf. Unfortunately, there are still third-party drivers and applications that get compiled with the FPO optimization, so you'll see broken stacks on occasion when those frames are encountered during ETW tracing.

Incomplete call stacks on 64-bit (*x64*) Windows On 64-bit Windows, stack walking is implemented differently than on *x86* Windows because the metadata used to walk the call chain is saved outside of the stack. This introduces another problem: when ETW tries to construct the kernel-mode call stack of the logging thread, the corresponding metadata can sometimes require a page-in from disk to memory. In the case of ETW kernel events logged at elevated Interrupt Request Levels (IRQLs), such as the sample profiling events, paging from disk to memory wouldn't be allowed. So, in that case, the kernel portion of the stack cannot be traversed.

Another scenario of incomplete stacks on 64-bit Windows occurs in the presence of .NET call frames in the call stack. The Windows 7 kernel code that constructs ETW stack traces doesn't handle the dynamic code generated by the 64-bit Just-in-Time (JIT) compiler correctly. You can easily tell these two scenarios apart by their respective symptoms:

- If the stacks are broken on the kernel side, the solution is to set the *DisablePagingExecutive* registry value to *1* and reboot. You then need to recapture a new trace. Note this setting affects stack walking only for kernel-mode events. User-mode events are not affected, nor are the user-mode call frames of kernel provider stack-trace events. If you run into this situation and determine that you really must see the complete stacks, including the kernel-mode frames, you can set this registry value *reactively*, as demonstrated by the following command:

```
reg add "HKLM\System\CurrentControlSet\Control\Session Manager\Memory Management"
-v DisablePagingExecutive -d 0x1 -t REG_DWORD -f
```

This is the approach I usually take in my tracing experiments on *x64* Windows, especially if I am debugging a live scenario and don't want to reboot the machine. Note that Xperf displays a warning on 64-bit Windows when it detects that you're starting a session with kernel stack-walk flags and this registry value isn't set. You're free to ignore the warning, however, just as you did in the *notepad.exe* CPU profiling experiment from the previous chapter, where the kernel part of the sample profiling events didn't matter much, given that the CPU consumption was exclusively on the user-mode side in that case.

It's also a good idea to restore this registry key to its default (where paging is enabled) after you're done collecting your trace even if you're not concerned about its memory impact. This is particularly true if you're using the machine to develop and test drivers because disabling paging in the executive can mask serious kernel-mode development bugs.

- When the call stack contains code from a 64-bit .NET module, the ETW stack trace stops at the first such managed frame in user mode and does not show any further frames (even native ones!). You can work around this bug by recompiling your .NET application as a 32-bit, platform-specific Microsoft Intermediate Language (MSIL) application and using that version instead when tracing your scenario on the target 64-bit OS. Fortunately, this problem is fixed in Windows 8, where the ETW framework in the kernel was changed to recognize 64-bit JIT frames and traverse them without issues.

Adding ETW Logging to Your Code

This section delves deeper into the structure of ETW events and the Win32 APIs exposed for developers to add custom ETW instrumentation to their user-mode applications.

Anatomy of ETW Events

An ETW event comprises a descriptor header structure followed by a variable-size array of data descriptors. These data descriptors are optional and represent a user-defined payload that differs from one user event template to another. An example of such a payload is a string log message or an integer property value. The *evntprov.h* Windows Software Development Kit (SDK) header file contains the definitions of these two structures.

```
//
// C:\DDK\7600.16385.1\inc>evntprov.h
//
typedef struct _EVENT_DESCRIPTOR {
    USHORT      Id;
    UCHAR       Version;
```

```
    UCHAR       Channel;
    UCHAR       Level;
    UCHAR       Opcode;
    USHORT      Task;
    ULONGLONG   Keyword;
} EVENT_DESCRIPTOR, *PEVENT_DESCRIPTOR;

typedef struct _EVENT_DATA_DESCRIPTOR {
    ULONGLONG   Ptr;        // Pointer to data
    ULONG       Size;       // Size of data in bytes
    ULONG       Reserved;
} EVENT_DATA_DESCRIPTOR, *PEVENT_DATA_DESCRIPTOR;
```

In addition to these user-defined fields, the ETW framework also automatically adds a few standard fields to each logged event. In particular, the current timestamp (displayed in nanoseconds when using the default performance counters resolution), the current processor number, and the process and thread IDs (PID and TID) are automatically added to every event.

The event descriptor header is required in every logged ETW event, and its fields deserve more explanation. The Id and Version fields uniquely identify the type of event within the user provider, while the other fields (channel, level, task, opcode, and keyword) are all aimed at providing a more granular organization of the events logged within the same provider. The meaning of these fields is described in more detail in Table 12-4.

TABLE 12-4 ETW Event Descriptor Header Fields

Field	Description	Remarks
Id	16-bit integer identifier for the event within the provider	The Version and Id fields uniquely identify the ETW event type within the provider.
Version	8-bit version field to support versioning of events	The Version and Id fields uniquely identify the ETW event type within the provider.
Channel	Defines the event log location into which the ETW event should be channeled	Enables filtering during analysis based on the target audience for the event. System, Application, and Security are built-in channels that cannot be deleted.
Task	Identifies the subcomponent that was responsible for raising the event	Enables filtering during analysis based on the logical components in the provider. Multiple tasks can be defined within the same user provider.
Opcode	A numeric identifier for the activity (or a phase within an activity) that the application was performing when the event was raised	Enables filtering during analysis based on a specific suboperation. Several standard opcodes are defined in the ETW framework, including the Start and End opcodes representing the start and end of an activity.
Level	Indicates the severity of the event	Enables filtering during analysis, and during trace collection too. Several standard values are defined in the ETW framework, including error, warning, and informational-level values.
Keyword	Bit masks in a 64-bit value used to group similar events	Enables filtering during analysis, and during trace collection too.

As mentioned in Table 12-4, channel, task, opcode, level, and keyword are all used to help produce a structured hierarchy for the logged events. While all of these fields can be used for filtering during trace analysis, only the level and keyword fields can be used for filtering during trace capture, resulting in potentially smaller trace files. Xperf supports this capability and allows you to provide level filters, keyword filters, or both when you enable each user provider. The full syntax for enabling user providers can be summarized as follows:

```
-on ProviderName:Keyword:Level:'stack|[,]sid|[,]tsid'
Example: -on Microsoft-Windows-TCPIP:0x0001000000000000:0x4:'stack'
```

This also fully explains the cryptic :::'stack' syntax you used earlier in this chapter when enabling stack-walk capture for user provider events. In that case, because the level and keyword flags were left empty, all the events from the user provider were emitted into the trace, with no additional filtering. The syntax also allows you to optionally request ETW to inject the security identifier (SID) and terminal session ID (TSID) of the logging thread to every event payload from the user provider you're enabling, which can sometimes be useful to troubleshoot access-check failures or to differentiate between events that can be logged from multiple user sessions.

Note When you enable a user provider in an ETW trace session, you need to decide at that point if you also want to capture stack traces for all the events from that provider. ETW doesn't currently provide a way to collect stack traces for only a subset of user provider events within the same session. You can, however, work around this limitation by taking advantage of keyword filtering. You first need to segregate the two subsets of events by keyword bit masks when you author your instrumentation manifest. When you start your trace using Xperf, you also need to create two user sessions: one to enable the subset of user provider events that should have associated stack traces (filtered by keyword), and another session to host the other subset of provider events that shouldn't have any (again filtered by keyword).

A natural question is whether you can discover the meaning of the keyword bit masks in a user provider without going back to the XML instrumentation manifest in the target binary where it's stored as a compiled resource. Though Xperf doesn't have a command that helps you do that, the *logman.exe* tool again comes to the rescue and allows you to query this information for each user provider, as illustrated here.

```
logman.exe query providers Microsoft-Windows-RPC
Provider                                 GUID
-------------------------------------------------------------------------------
Microsoft-Windows-RPC                    {6AD52B32-D609-4BE9-AE07-CE8DAE937E39}

Value               Keyword              Description
-------------------------------------------------------------------------------
0x8000000000000000  Microsoft-Windows-RPC/EEInfo EEInfo
0x4000000000000000  Microsoft-Windows-RPC/Debug  Debug

Value               Level                Description
```

```
--------------------------------------------------------------------------------
0x02                  win:Error                   Error
0x04                  win:Informational           Information
0x05                  win:Verbose                 Verbose
```

You can then use this information to start a session with only a subset of keyword flags or levels, as illustrated in the following listing, where only informational events from the RPC user provider that are also logged with the Debug keyword are injected into the ETW trace session.

```
C:\book\code\common\scripts>start_user_trace.cmd -kf Base -up
"Microsoft-Windows-RPC:0x4000000000000000:4:'stack,sid,tsid'"
INFO: Invoking xperf to start the kernel and user sessions...
CmdLine: (xperf.exe -on PROC_THREAD+LOADER+Base
-start UserSession -on "Microsoft-Windows-RPC:0x4000000000000000:4:'stack,sid,tsid'")

C:\book\code\common\scripts>stop_user_trace.cmd
INFO: Invoking xperf to stop the kernel and user sessions...
CmdLine: (xperf.exe -stop -stop UserSession -d c:\temp\merged.etl)
```

Dumping Raw ETW Events Using Xperf

Xperf supports a number of actions (invoked using the –*a* command-line option) that allow you to process ETW trace files and extract useful information from them. You've already seen one such action in the previous chapter, where the *symcache* action was used to process the modules in the trace file and cache their symbols locally. Another useful Xperf action is the *dumper* action, which parses a trace file and outputs the ETW events it contains into a comma-separated (CSV) text file, where the events are sorted in chronological order by their respective timestamp. This can sometimes allow you to more efficiently search the events for known patterns, but it is also useful if you simply want to view the events in their raw format. The companion source code contains a helper script around that Xperf command.

```
C:\book\code\common\scripts>dump_trace_to_csv.cmd
...
INFO: Invoking xperf to dump trace file to text...
CmdLine: (xperf -i c:\temp\merged.etl -o c:\temp\merged.txt -symbols -a dumper)
```

The text file produced by this transformation is usually quite large, especially when the trace also contains stack-walk information, so you won't be able to search it efficiently using *notepad.exe*. You instead need a viewer that is more adept at parsing and viewing large files. One such viewer is the Large Text File Viewer freeware, which you can download from *http://www.swiftgear.com/ltfviewer/features.html*. In Figure 12-14, this viewer is used to load the text file produced by the *dumper* action from the previous step.

```
LTFViewr5u.exe c:\temp\merged.txt
```

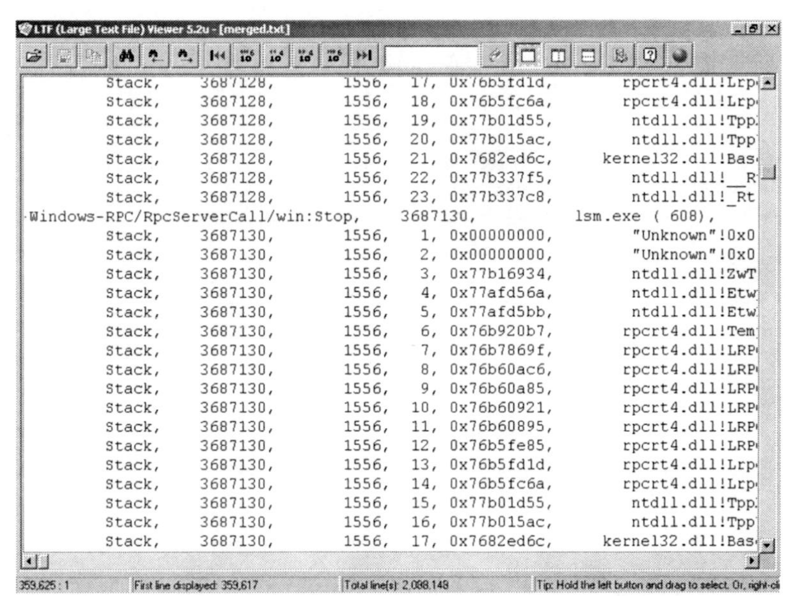

FIGURE 12-14 Viewing raw ETW events using Large Text File Viewer.

When you're done with this experiment, don't forget to delete the raw text file from your hard drive if you no longer need it.

```
C:\book\code\common\scripts>del c:\temp\merged.txt
```

Logging Events Using the ETW Win32 APIs

A common need in performance investigations is to measure the amount of time spent executing a certain task. As was explained in the previous chapter, the existing ETW sample profiling instrumentation in the OS can't help you do this (being that it's a statistical approach), but you can add explicit Start and End events to your code to answer this need. Because this is such a common scenario, ETW, in fact, has built-in opcodes to describe these Start and End points in an activity.

As it turns out, you don't even need custom payloads for these two events because the ETW framework already includes timestamp information with each logged event. This also means you won't need to define a template for the events or build an instrumentation manifest to view the payload of these events in Xperf. To provide a practical illustration, the companion source code contains a simple C++ application you can compile using the procedure described in the Introduction to this book. This program logs a Start and End ETW event pair to measure the time it spends in its main routine. The ETW provider GUID used for this event pair is generated randomly and will also be used later when enabling the user provider in Xperf.

```
//
// C:\book\code\chapter_12\LoggingApp>main.cpp
//

//
// ETW Provider GUID (use uuidgen.exe from the Windows 7 SDK, for example, to
// generate a random value, or simply use this one)
// GUID_AppEtwProvider = 35f7872e-9b6d-4a9b-a674-66f1edd66d5c
//
const GUID GUID_AppEtwProvider =
{ 0x35f7872e, 0x9b6d, 0x4a9b, { 0xa6, 0x74, 0x66, 0xf1, 0xed, 0xd6, 0x6d, 0x5c }
};

class CMainApp
{
private:
    static
    VOID
    LogEvent(
        __in USHORT EventId,
        __in UCHAR Opcode,
        __in UCHAR Level,
        __in ULONGLONG Keyword,
        __in USHORT Task
        )
    {
        EVENT_DESCRIPTOR eventDesc = {0};
        eventDesc.Id = EventId;
        eventDesc.Version = 1;
        eventDesc.Task = Task;
        eventDesc.Opcode = Opcode;
        eventDesc.Level = Level;
        eventDesc.Keyword = Keyword;

        g_AppEtwProvider.Write(eventDesc);
    }

public:
    static
    HRESULT
    MainHR()
    {
        ChkProlog();

        LogEvent(1, WINEVENT_OPCODE_START,
            WINEVENT_LEVEL_INFO, WINEVT_KEYWORD_ANY, WINEVENT_TASK_NONE);

        Sleep(5000);

        LogEvent(2, WINEVENT_OPCODE_STOP,
            WINEVENT_LEVEL_INFO, WINEVT_KEYWORD_ANY, WINEVENT_TASK_NONE);
```

```
        ChkNoCleanup();
    }

private:
    static CEtwProvider g_AppEtwProvider;
};

CEtwProvider
CMainApp::g_AppEtwProvider(GUID_AppEtwProvider);

//
// C:\book\code\chapter_12\LoggingApp>etwtrace.h
//
class CEtwProvider
{
    CEtwProvider(
        __in REFGUID ProviderId
        )
    {
        (VOID) Register(ProviderId);
    }

    HRESULT
    Register(
        __in REFGUID ProviderId
        )
    {
        Unregister();
        return HRESULT_FROM_WIN32(
            EventRegister(&ProviderId, 0, 0, &m_hProviderHandle));
    }

    COREDEFS_INLINE
    VOID
    Write(
        __in const EVENT_DESCRIPTOR& eventDesc
    {
        (VOID) EventWrite(m_hProviderHandle, &eventDesc, 0, NULL);
    }
...
  REGHANDLE m_hProviderHandle;
};
```

Table 12-5 summarizes the key Win32 APIs used in the previous code listing to log ETW events. The *EventRegister* API signals intent by the user-mode process to log events from that user provider GUID, which gives the ETW code in the kernel knowledge of the full list of user providers that are currently registered in each running process. This, in turn, allows ETW to dynamically enable tracing for processes that have registered a user provider as soon as it gets enabled in a new trace session, without the need for any process restarts.

TABLE 12-5 Basic ETW User-Mode Win32 APIs

Win32 API (*advapi32.dll*)	Description
EventRegister	Register a provider GUID in the process. This function must be called before events from the user provider are logged because the handle it returns is required when writing those events.
EventUnregister	Unregister the user provider from the process.
EventEnabled	Determine if an event is enabled in an ETW session. Calling this API is optional, and it can be used by the application to bypass doing more work when it knows there is no need to call the EventWrite API for the event in question.
EventWrite	Log an ETW event. This API takes the event-provider handle obtained from the provider registration call (*EventRegister*), the event-descriptor header structure, and an optional list of data descriptors (representing the custom user payload). An actual event is generated only if the target provider was independently enabled using an ETW controller.

To view the previous Start/End event pair in Xperf, you can start a user session and enable the custom provider GUID used in the previous C++ application, as illustrated in the following command.

```
C:\book\code\common\scripts>start_user_trace.cmd -kf Base -up
35f7872e-9b6d-4a9b-a674-66f1edd66d5c
INFO: Invoking xperf to start the kernel and user sessions...
CmdLine: (xperf.exe -on PROC_THREAD+LOADER+Base
-start UserSession -on 35f7872e-9b6d-4a9b-a674-66f1edd66d5c)
```

After starting this session, run the test application and wait for it to exit. This should log the Start and End events around the main routine's ends in the application. Once the program exits, stop and merge the user and kernel trace sessions, as demonstrated in the following commands.

```
C:\book\code\chapter_12\LoggingApp\objfre_win7_x86\i386\LoggingApp.exe
Success.

C:\book\code\common\scripts>stop_user_trace.cmd
INFO: Invoking xperf to stop the kernel and user sessions...
CmdLine: (xperf.exe -stop -stop UserSession -d c:\temp\merged.etl)
```

In the Xperf viewer UI, the two custom events will be listed in the Generic Events graph, as demonstrated in Figure 12-15, which shows the summary table for that graph. Notice that the Start and End ETW events were logged at 3.47 seconds and 8.47 seconds from the start of the trace session, respectively, exactly 5 seconds apart from each other. This is as you would expect, given that all the function you were measuring did was call a *Sleep* for 5 seconds.

```
C:\book\code\common\scripts>view_trace.cmd
...
INFO: Invoking xperf to view the trace...
CmdLine: (xperf.exe c:\temp\merged.etl)
```

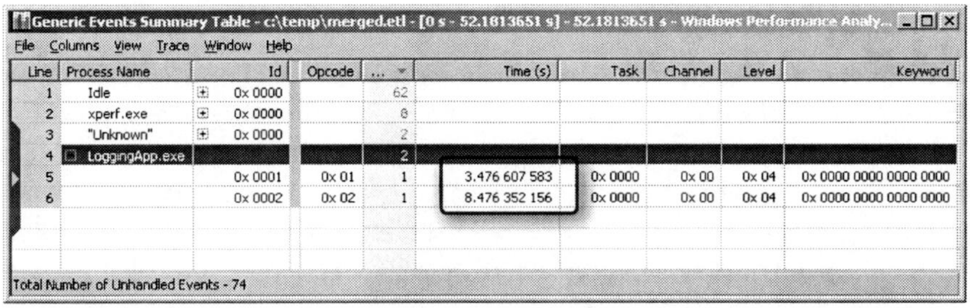

Generic Events Summary Table - c:\temp\merged.etl - [0 s - 52.1813651 s] - 52.1813651 s - Windows Performance Analy...

File Columns View Trace Window Help

Line	Process Name	Id	Opcode	...	Time (s)	Task	Channel	Level	Keyword
1	Idle	0x 0000		62					
2	xperf.exe	0x 0000		8					
3	"Unknown"	0x 0000		2					
4	LoggingApp.exe			2					
5		0x 0001	0x 01	1	3.476 607 583	0x 0000	0x 00	0x 04	0x 0000 0000 0000 0000
6		0x 0002	0x 02	1	8.476 352 156	0x 0000	0x 00	0x 04	0x 0000 0000 0000 0000

Total Number of Unhandled Events - 74

FIGURE 12-15 Timestamps of the explicit Start and End ETW events.

Note that in a more complete solution, these event pairs might need to be logged for more than one routine, which is where the task field can be used to identify the exact operation corresponding to each Start and Stop ETW event pair that gets logged in the session. You can also define a custom event payload as part of an instrumentation manifest to distinguish the event pairs more easily. The MSDN website has more information on how to build and install a user provider with a custom instrumentation manifest at the following URL: *http://msdn.microsoft.com/library/dd996930.aspx*. You might also find the following blog entry useful as a complement to the relatively terse MSDN documentation: *http://blogs.microsoft.co.il/blogs/roadan/archive/2011/02/13/creating-and-publishing-events-using-etw-manifest-based-provider.aspx*.

Boot Tracing in ETW

Xperf works fairly well as an interactive ETW controller that allows you to enable and disable sessions and providers from the command line. When you're interested in tracing the activity of code that runs early during the boot sequence, however, a different way to enable tracing automatically when the machine starts up is required. Fortunately, ETW supports boot tracing natively and allows you to specify the sessions and providers that you want to enable at boot time by using predefined locations in the system registry. During each boot, the ETW code in the kernel enumerates those registry keys and automatically starts the requested sessions and providers on your behalf.

There are two registry keys that the ETW framework in the kernel consults when the OS starts up. The first one is the *GlobalLogger* registry key, which is used to automatically kick off the special NT Kernel Logger session and enable events from kernel-mode providers at system startup. The second hierarchy of keys resides under the *AutoLogger* registry key, which can be used to start additional sessions at startup and enable events from user providers into those sessions. The combination of these two mechanisms (the global and auto-logging sessions) allows you to capture events from any kernel or user provider during the boot sequence, just as you're able to do when using the Xperf command-line ETW control options. Once the boot completes and you get to the interactive desktop, the rest of the steps are similar to regular tracing scenarios: you can pick any time to stop the boot tracing sessions and merge their events with the kernel rundown information using Xperf, producing the final boot trace file that you can then analyze using the Xperf viewer UI, as usual.

Logging Kernel Provider Events During Boot

One way to safely edit the values under the *GlobalLogger* registry key mentioned earlier and capture kernel provider events during the boot process is to use the convenient *–BootTrace* option of Xperf. To see a practical illustration, you'll now use ETW boot tracing to list the processes that get started as part of the Windows 7 boot sequence. Note that this is a more natural way to approach this problem than is the solution you used back in Chapter 7, "Expert Debugging Tricks," where you used the *nt!PspInsertProcess* breakpoint to log the process names into the debugger. As you'll also shortly see, the approach described in this section even allows you to answer more similar questions, such as discovering the list of all the startup applications (from the *Run* and *RunOnce* registry keys) that get automatically started during user logon.

The companion source code includes another helper script that conveniently wraps the boot trace Xperf functionality. You can also enable the ProcessCreate stack-walking flag so that your trace also includes the creation call stacks for every new process. This configuration is demonstrated in the following command, which you need to execute from an elevated administrative command prompt.

```
C:\book\code\common\scripts>edit_global_logger.cmd -kf Base -ks ProcessCreate
INFO: Invoking xperf to edit the global logger settings...
CmdLine: (xperf.exe -boottrace PROC_THREAD+LOADER+Base -stackwalk ProcessCreate)
```

You can run this script with different kernel flags and stack-walking options and see how that gets reflected in the values under the *GlobalLogger* registry key. With the previous command, the values should be in line with those shown in Figure 12-16.

```
[HKEY_LOCAL_MACHINE\SYSTEM\CurrentControlSet\Control\WMI\GlobalLogger]
```

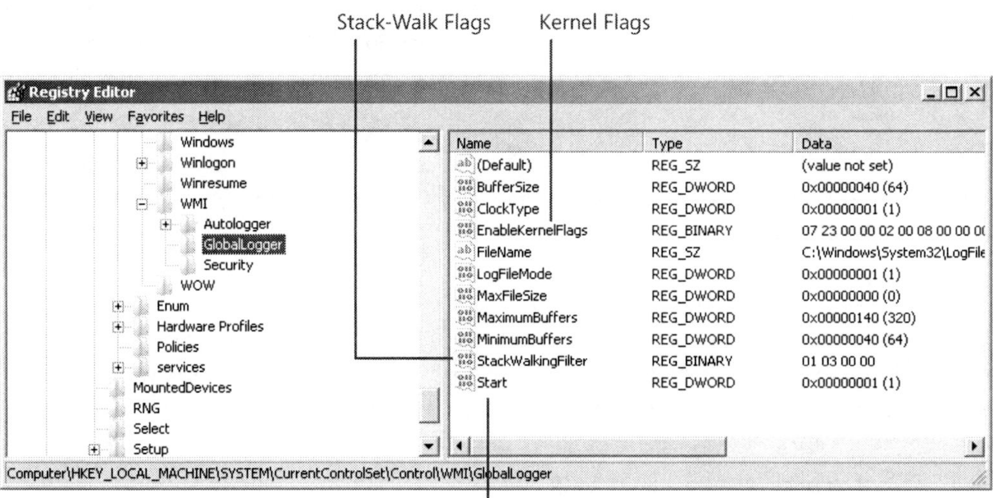

FIGURE 12-16 Kernel boot trace settings under the *GlobalLogger* registry key.

At this point, you can reboot the machine. When you log in after the reboot, you'll find that the special NT Kernel Logger session is already running. You can stop it and merge its events with the kernel rundown information from an elevated administrative command prompt, as usual.

```
---- After reboot ----
C:\book\code\common\scripts>stop_kernel_trace.cmd
INFO: Invoking xperf to stop the session...
CmdLine: (xperf.exe -stop -d c:\temp\merged.etl)
```

You can now open this merged trace in the Xperf viewer UI. The list of processes that got started from the beginning of the boot sequence till the moment you decided to stop the trace session should be easily accessible in the Processes Summary Table of the Process Lifetimes graph, as shown in Figure 12-17.

```
C:\book\code\common\scripts>view_trace.cmd
...
INFO: Invoking xperf to view the trace...
CmdLine: (xperf.exe c:\temp\merged.etl)
```

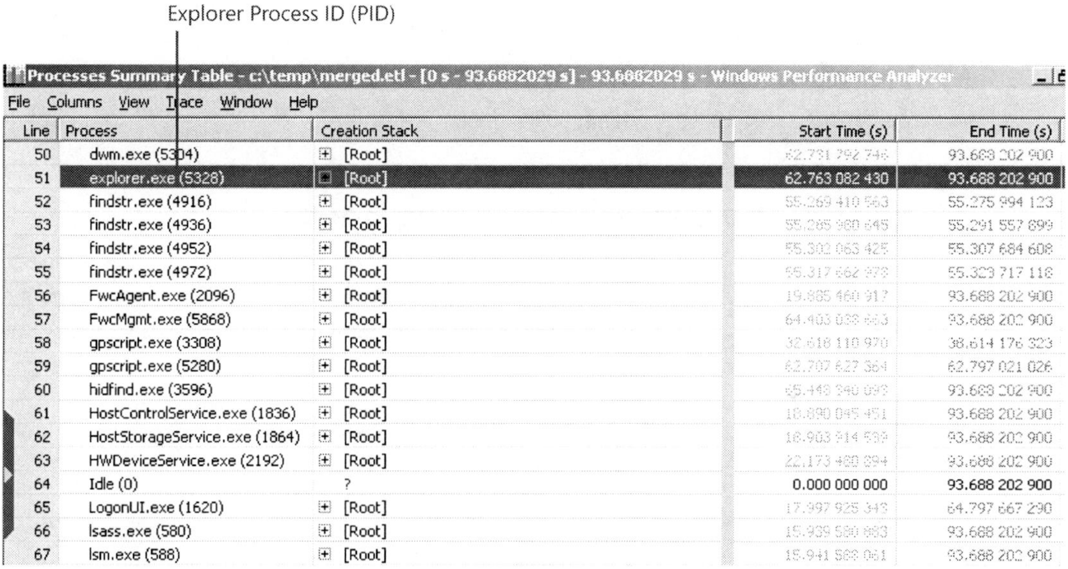

Line	Process	Creation Stack	Start Time (s)	End Time (s)
50	dwm.exe (5304)	[Root]	62.731 292 746	93.688 202 900
51	explorer.exe (5328)	[Root]	62.763 082 430	93.688 202 900
52	findstr.exe (4916)	[Root]	55.269 410 563	55.275 994 123
53	findstr.exe (4936)	[Root]	55.285 980 645	55.291 557 699
54	findstr.exe (4952)	[Root]	55.302 063 425	55.307 684 608
55	findstr.exe (4972)	[Root]	55.317 662 970	55.323 717 116
56	FwcAgent.exe (2096)	[Root]	19.885 460 917	93.688 202 900
57	FwcMgmt.exe (5868)	[Root]	64.403 038 663	93.688 202 900
58	gpscript.exe (3308)	[Root]	32.618 110 970	38.614 176 323
59	gpscript.exe (5280)	[Root]	62.707 627 364	62.797 021 026
60	hidfind.exe (3596)	[Root]	65.449 940 092	93.688 202 900
61	HostControlService.exe (1836)	[Root]	18.890 045 451	93.688 202 900
62	HostStorageService.exe (1864)	[Root]	18.903 914 599	93.688 202 900
63	HWDeviceService.exe (2192)	[Root]	22.173 480 094	93.688 202 900
64	Idle (0)	?	0.000 000 000	93.688 202 900
65	LogonUI.exe (1620)	[Root]	17.997 925 343	64.797 667 290
66	lsass.exe (580)	[Root]	15.939 580 883	93.688 202 900
67	lsm.exe (588)	[Root]	15.941 588 061	93.688 202 900

FIGURE 12-17 Processes Summary Table from the boot trace.

You can also group the data in the boot trace so that you can extract other useful information, such as all the *Run* (and *RunOnce*) applications that get automatically started by the *explorer.exe* process during user logon. To do so, you can add the Parent Process ID column to the Processes Summary Table view and look at all the child processes of the *explorer.exe* PID, which you can obtain from the previous Summary Table view. You can even see the creation call stacks for all of those startup applications by using the Creation Stack column, thanks to the ProcessCreate stack-walking option you originally included in your kernel boot trace, as shown in Figure 12-18.

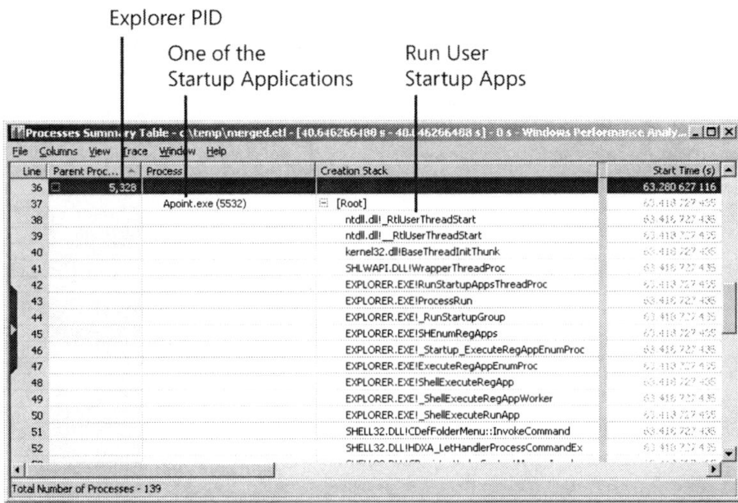

FIGURE 12-18 List of applications started automatically during user logon.

At the end of this experiment, don't forget to delete the *GlobalLogger* registry key so that you disable ETW tracing in future boots of your machine, as shown in the following command.

```
C:\book\code\common\scripts>edit_global_logger.cmd -disable
```

Logging User Provider Events During Boot

Though adding user provider events to your boot trace is conceptually similar to adding the built-in ETW kernel events in the OS, it's not as easy in practice because Xperf doesn't have support for editing the *AutoLogger* registry key hierarchy that the ETW framework consults when deciding what user sessions to start during the boot process. That being said, the companion source code contains a helper script that tries to mimic how the *–boottrace* option of Xperf works and helps you edit the correct registry values in those rare cases when you find yourself needing to automatically enable user providers during the boot sequence.

As an illustration for how to use that script, the following command enables the Microsoft-Windows-Services user provider, which as its name indicates logs events related to the operations of the NT service control manager (SCM) subsystem process (*services.exe*). The script expects the raw provider GUID, which you can discover by looking at the output from the *xperf.exe –providers* command, for example. Note that just like in regular tracing scenarios, you need to enable the NT Kernel Logger session in addition to the user session so that you can correlate the user events with other important kernel events over the trace lifetime (and also so that you can resolve user call stacks correctly).

```
C:\book\code\common\scripts>xperf.exe -providers
    0063715b-eeda-4007-9429-ad526f62696e    : Microsoft-Windows-Services
...
```

```
C:\book\code\common\scripts>edit_global_logger.cmd -kf Base
INFO: Invoking xperf to edit the global logger settings...
CmdLine: (xperf.exe -boottrace PROC_THREAD+LOADER+Base )

C:\book\code\common\scripts>edit_auto_logger.cmd -enable 0063715b-eeda-4007-9429-ad526f62696e
-stack
```

Note that you can also run the *edit_auto_logger.cmd* script multiple times if you need to enable more than one user provider. In the case of this experiment, only one user provider is enabled, and Figure 12-19 depicts the registry modifications made by the previous run of the script under the *AutoLogger* registry key.

```
[HKEY_LOCAL_MACHINE\SYSTEM\CurrentControlSet\Control\WMI\AutoLogger\UserSession]
```

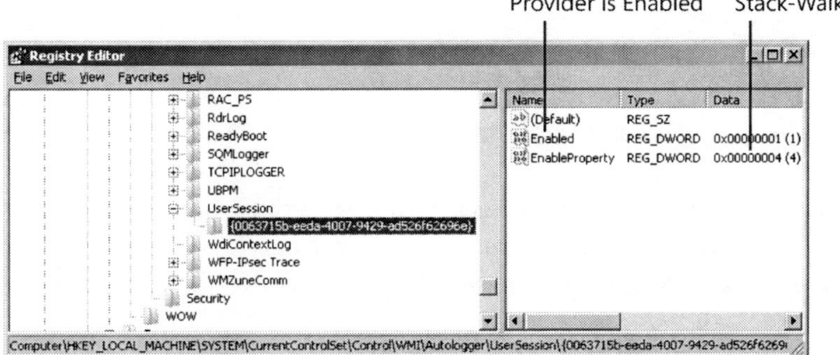

FIGURE 12-19 Enabling user providers under the *AutoLogger* registry key.

The *EnableProperty* registry value you see in Figure 12-19 is a bit mask, where bit *0x4* represents whether stack traces should be collected for the user events from the provider, as you can see in the *evntcons.h* SDK header file.

```
//
// C:\Program Files\Microsoft SDKs\Windows\v7.1\Include>evntcons.h
//
#define EVENT_ENABLE_PROPERTY_SID                    0x00000001
#define EVENT_ENABLE_PROPERTY_TS_ID                  0x00000002
#define EVENT_ENABLE_PROPERTY_STACK_TRACE            0x00000004
```

After you reboot the machine, the special NT Kernel Logger session and the user logging session you enabled under the *AutoLogger* key should already be running by the time you log in and get to the interactive desktop. You can then stop both sessions and merge their events with the kernel rundown information just as if this were a regular user session started from the Xperf command line.

```
C:\book\code\common\scripts>stop_user_trace.cmd
INFO: Invoking xperf to stop the kernel and user sessions...
CmdLine: (xperf.exe -stop -stop UserSession -d c:\temp\merged.etl)
```

The events from the Microsoft-Windows-Services user provider have a dedicated graph in the Xperf viewer UI, which in this case contains a variety of events related to the Windows services started during the boot of the machine, as illustrated in Figure 12-20.

```
C:\book\code\common\scripts>view_trace.cmd
INFO: Invoking xperf to view the trace...
CmdLine: (xperf.exe c:\temp\merged.etl)
```

Line	Service	Container	Started At (s)	Ended At (s)
21	EapHost	netsvcs svchost (1168)	21.701 248 212	21.715 540 545
22	EFS	lsass.exe (620)	24.772 387 419	24.842 254 002
23	eventlog	LocalServiceNetworkRestricted svchost (1108)	21.140 787 495	21.180 445 345
24	EventSystem	LocalService svchost (1444)	21.488 649 420	21.518 979 980
25	FDResPub	LocalServiceAndNoImpersonation svchost (1404)	24.772 637 415	25.050 337 924
26	FIMPasswordReset	PwdMgmtProxy.exe" (1792)	24.785 199 704	27.746 947 628
27	FontCache	LocalServiceAndNoImpersonation svchost (1404)	68.108 357 785	68.852 458 088
28	FwcAgent	FwcAgent.exe" (2152)	25.326 038 920	25.374 658 123
29	gpsvc	netsvcs svchost (1168)	21.435 730 017	21.485 580 631
30	hidserv	LocalSystemNetworkRestricted svchost (1144)	44.320 937 556	44.335 747 091
31	hkmsvc	netsvcs svchost (1168)	44.041 669 591	44.098 223 444

Total Number of Service Transitions - 96

FIGURE 12-20 Services Summary Table in the Xperf viewer UI.

The call stacks for the user events from the previous provider can also be seen in the Stack Counts Summary Table in Xperf. You'll notice that they're all logged from the context of the *services.exe* SCM process, as shown in Figure 12-21.

Line	Process	Stack
1	services.exe (604)	[Root]
2		ntdll.dll!_RtlUserThreadStart
3		ntdll.dll!__RtlUserThreadStart
4		kernel32.dll!BaseThreadInitThunk
5		|- ntdll.dll!TppWorkerThread
6		|- services.exe!_initterm_e
7		| services.exe!main
8		| services.exe!SvcctrlMain
9		| services.exe!ScAutoStartServices
10		| |- services.exe!ScStartServiceAndDependencies
11		| | |- services.exe!ScStartMarkedServices
12		| | | services.exe!ScStartService
13		| | | |- services.exe!ScActivateServiceRecord
14		| | | |- services.exe!ScDeactivateServiceRecord
15		| | |- services.exe!ScLogStatusChange
16		| |- services.exe!ScStartServiceByName
17		| |- services.exe!ScLogStatusChange

Total Number of Events with Stacks - 523

FIGURE 12-21 Stack-walk events from the Microsoft-Windows-Services user provider.

Once you're done analyzing the merged trace, be sure to delete the global and auto loggers from the registry so that future boots won't start them automatically, as shown in the following commands.

```
C:\book\code\common\scripts>edit_auto_logger.cmd -disable
C:\book\code\common\scripts>edit_global_logger.cmd -disable
```

Summary

In this chapter, you were able to gain practical insights into how ETW works in the Windows operating system, and also how its concepts are exposed in the Xperf tool. With this solid knowledge base, you should now have the necessary background to take full advantage of the power of ETW in your profiling and tracing investigations.

Before moving to the next chapter, which will present several case studies illustrating the use of tracing techniques to observe and troubleshoot unexpected behaviors, it's useful to take a moment to reflect on a few important concepts you learned in this chapter:

- Sessions are the main engine that drives ETW logging, supplying the kernel workspace environment where *provider* components from both user mode and kernel mode are able to log events with very low overhead to their performance.
- There are two categories of events in ETW: kernel and user events. The kernel events are logged by components that are considered to be part of the core kernel, such as the process subsystem, thread scheduler, and registry configuration manager. Any other events (including those logged by kernel-mode drivers) are called *user* events.
- Kernel and user events go into different ETW sessions: kernel events are logged into a special session called the NT Kernel Logger, while user events require a separate user-defined session. Xperf allows you to merge events from multiple sessions, however. So, even though this requirement is important to understand when starting sessions and enabling providers, it doesn't really restrict your ability to correlate user and kernel events from the same tracing experiment.
- The kernel providers are represented using fixed flags. User providers, on the other hand, are represented using GUIDs and friendly names. They are also a dynamic set that can change depending on the software you have installed on your machine.
- You can also define custom user providers for your ETW instrumentation. In addition, providing and installing an XML instrumentation manifest for your ETW user provider allows viewer tools such as Xperf to recognize the templates used by your events if they happen to carry nonstandard fields.
- Many kernel event types have dedicated graphs in the Xperf viewer, as do a few user providers. Events that aren't handled by any first-class graphs in the Xperf viewer end up in the Generic Events graph, which makes this last graph particularly important in the case of custom user providers.

- ETW can collect stack traces for any kernel (in Windows Vista and later) or user (in Windows 7 and later) event, though the syntax in Xperf to enable stack walking is different between user and kernel providers. There are several pitfalls you might run into when trying to view call stacks in the Xperf viewer. The "Diagnosing ETW Stack-Trace Issues" section in this chapter gives you a good starting point, however, for troubleshooting those problems.
- Boot tracing is supported natively by the ETW framework. This allows you to start the NT Kernel Logger session or any other user session automatically when the OS starts up, making it possible to trace activities that take place during the boot sequence in the same logical way that you conduct other interactive ETW tracing investigations.

CHAPTER 13

Common Tracing Scenarios

In this chapter

This chapter presents a few practical case studies that illustrate the power of tracing as an investigative technique for discovering the cause of performance bottlenecks, studying system internals, and debugging code bugs. You already saw the power of Event Tracing for Windows (ETW) and Xperf in action when you used that combination in Chapter 11, "Introducing Xperf," to determine why *notepad.exe* was freezing for a long time when opening very large files. In that case, you used the operating system's (OS) ability to capture sample CPU profiling ETW events to track down the call site of the performance bottleneck. This chapter presents more scenarios illustrating the use of ETW instrumentation in performance analysis, starting with the fairly common case of measuring blocked time and building *causality chains* for unexpectedly long thread waits.

Another common area of concern in performance analysis is memory usage because it tends to be the next cause of latency once you optimize CPU-bound computations and I/O activities. This is even truer in execution environments with automatic memory management, such as the .NET Common Language Runtime (CLR)—where the more memory a program consumes, the more work the CLR ends up doing to manage it.

This chapter concludes with a few case studies illustrating the use of tracing as an efficient and noninvasive debugging technique, both for debugging failures in your programs as well as for exploring system internals.

Analyzing Blocked Time

When you need to analyze unexpected performance delays, two issues must be considered. If the observed problem has to do with CPU activity, CPU sample profiling is sufficient and enables you to track down the hot spots responsible for any wasteful processor usage. Many delays, though, are not manifested by *high* CPU activity but rather by *stalled* execution. This can be due to lock contention, disk or network I/O bottlenecks, and other logical interthread dependencies.

In this section, you'll see two methods for approaching these investigations, and they're both based on ETW and the CPU scheduling instrumentation in the OS. The first tool showcased in this section will be the *Parallel Performance Analyzer (PPA)*, which was introduced during the Microsoft Visual Studio 2010 release. Just like Xperf, the PPA is both an ETW controller and consumer, though its usage is simplified so that you don't have to deal with sessions and providers directly. The user interface is also relatively easy to learn because it's tailored to the specific scenario of "blocked time" analysis. Finally, the PPA can also show .NET call stacks, which Xperf doesn't support (at least in its Microsoft Windows 7 SDK version).

You can also use the PPA to monitor standalone applications that were built outside of the Visual Studio Integrated Development Environment (IDE). However, the main focus in the PPA user interface is placed on the application and its immediate threads of execution, even though global ETW sessions are used behind the scenes. This is a conscious (and general) design decision in Visual Studio so that its user interface would be simple enough to suit the needs of the majority of users from the developer community. By contrast, you can use the Xperf viewer to observe what happens outside the boundaries of an application and understand interthread dependencies that involve multiple processes too. To illustrate these advantages and drawbacks, this section will use the following Microsoft Visual Basic script.

```
//
// C:\book\code\chapter_13\BlockedTime>RemoteWmi.vbs
//
Option Explicit

Dim objLocator, objServer

Set objLocator = CreateObject("WbemScripting.SWbemLocator")
Set objServer = objLocator.ConnectServer("MissingComputer", "\root\cimv2",
"UserName", "Password")
```

If you run this script after unplugging your network cable, you'll notice that it fails within less than one second. This is expected because the script tries to connect to a Windows Management Instrumentation (WMI) namespace on a nonexistent machine.

```
C:\book\code\chapter_13\BlockedTime>cscript RemoteWmi.vbs
C:\book\code\chapter_13\BlockedTime\RemoteWmi.vbs(6, 1) SWbemLocator: The RPC server is
unavailable.
```

When running the same script while having an Internet connection, however, you'll see that it takes several seconds before displaying the previous error message. The goal in the rest of this section will be to figure out the reasons behind this delay. Before doing that, though, you'll need to understand a few basic concepts related to thread and CPU scheduling in Windows, and also be aware of the available ETW instrumentation in that space.

The CSwitch and ReadyThread ETW Events

Context switches in Windows can happen in a number of conditions and have a direct and measurable impact on execution delays in the threads of your application. These conditions include the following, for instance:

- A thread explicitly waiting on a kernel synchronization (dispatcher) object, such as an event, a semaphore, or a process object
- A thread performing an I/O request and waiting on its completion
- A thread's quantum expiring and the OS deciding to schedule another thread to run in its place

The OS kernel is instrumented to log ETW events every time a thread is switched-in to run on a CPU core. These events are controlled using the context switch (CSWITCH) kernel flag in Xperf. When you couple these ETW events with the ability to capture their associated call stacks (using the CSwitch stack-walk option in Xperf), you get a complete picture of the scheduling sequence on every CPU core during the timeline of the trace session, as illustrated in Figure 13-1. Note that there is no causal relationship between any two consecutive threads in this diagram and that it's entirely up to the OS scheduler to determine which thread to run next on each CPU core. In particular, thread T1 has no relationship to threads T0, T2, or T5 in the scheduling example illustrated by Figure 13-1.

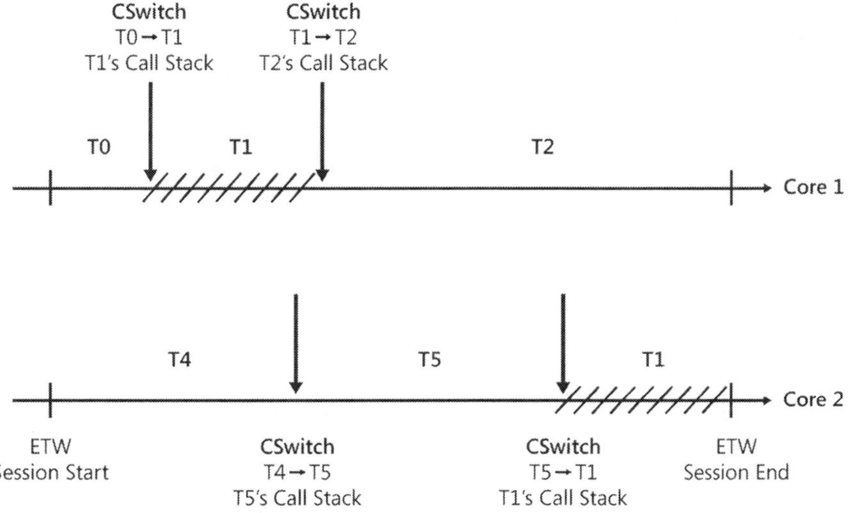

FIGURE 13-1 Context-switch ETW events.

The previous timelines are a treasure trove for performance analysts because they tell exactly when any given thread got to run its code. What that data doesn't indicate, however, is what each thread was waiting on when it was blocked, and what later caused it to wake up and become ready to run again. This information is captured with a second category of events that was added to the OS during the Windows 7 release timeframe. These events can be turned on using the DISPATCHER kernel flag, and their associated ReadyThread stack-walk option also allows you to capture the call stack of the *readying* thread, as illustrated in Figure 13-2. Notice in that figure there is a time gap (represented by the *ReadyTime* interval) between when the thread is signaled and becomes ready to run and the time it gets to execute on the CPU (the new switch-in time). This time span is not always insignificant. For example, when a thread is running with low priority and is also competing for CPU resources with other higher-priority tasks, the OS scheduler might not schedule the thread to run right away even though it's ready to run.

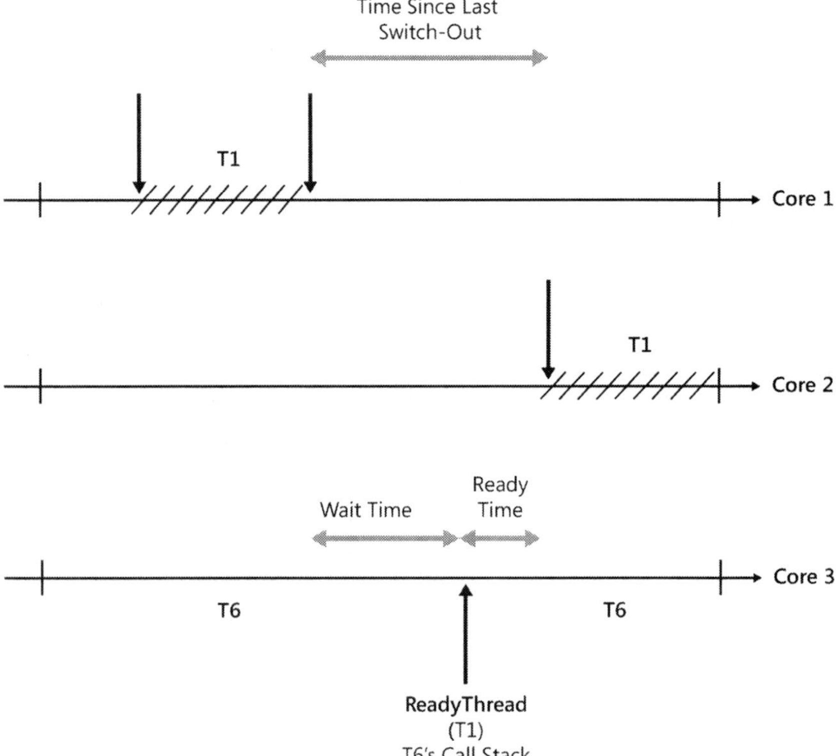

FIGURE 13-2 ReadyThread ETW events.

It's important to understand that one thread can ready multiple threads at the same time. In addition, the ReadyThread events provide only a partial (though very valuable) picture because they capture only the last event that caused a thread to become ready ("runnable"). This means that if a thread waits on multiple conditions, only the last condition will be captured by a ReadyThread event, though the other conditions might be important contributors to the long wait too. The last condition is said to be on the *critical path* of the performance delay. If that interthread dependency can be optimized, the next condition might appear next on the critical path of the scenario. So, optimizing CPU waits often involves tracking down these interthread dependencies through an iterative process that gradually shortens the critical paths in the overall scenario.

Wait Analysis Using Visual Studio 2010

As mentioned earlier, one of the highlights of the Visual Studio 2010 release was the addition of the Parallel Performance Analyzer (PPA)—also called the *Concurrency Analyzer*—to the set of profiling options under the Analyze menu, though you need either the Premium or Ultimate edition of Visual Studio to use these profiling capabilities. This section will provide a practical introduction to the wait-analysis capabilities in the PPA, and you can complement it by reading the MSDN website documentation, which offers several good articles on the PPA. For example, the article at *http://msdn.microsoft.com/magazine/ee336027.aspx* is a good place to start.

You can use the PPA for tracing an existing process or, alternatively, start a new instance of the process and a corresponding PPA profiling session at the same time. This second approach is detailed in the following procedure, which will allow you to observe the thread waits in the Visual Basic script listed at the top of this section.

Starting a Parallel Performance Analyzer Tracing Session

1. Right-click the Microsoft Visual Studio 2010 Start menu item, choose Run As Administrator as demonstrated in the following screen shot, and complete the UAC (User Account Control) elevation request. The PPA internally starts ETW sessions to perform its tracing, so full administrative privileges are required.

2. Configure the symbols search path in Visual Studio 2010 to include the Microsoft public symbols server. Those symbols are required so that the PPA can decode the ETW stack-trace events it collects while profiling the target application. To complete this step, open the Debug\Options And Settings dialog box; then, on the Debugging\Symbols page, select the built-in

Microsoft Symbol Servers option and provide a path (C:\LocalSymbolCache in this example) to cache the symbols locally, as shown in the following screen shot:

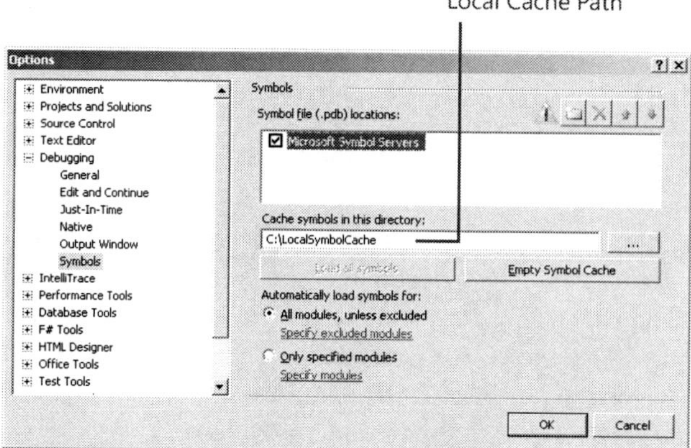

Note that this is a one-time configuration step and doesn't need to be repeated the next time you start a new PPA profiling session.

3. In the Analyze menu, click Launch Performance Wizard.

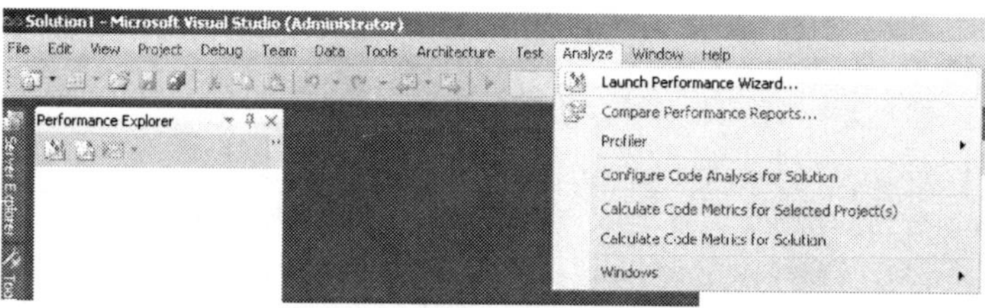

4. On the first page of the new wizard, choose the Concurrency option and select Visualize The Behavior Of A Multithreaded Application, as illustrated in the following screen shot:

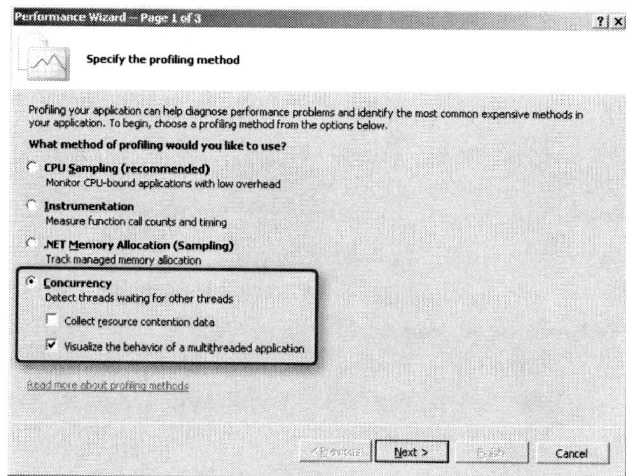

5. When asked to enter the executable to profile, specify the full path to the *cscript.exe* host process, which comes with Windows under the *system32* directory, and provide the path to the Visual Basic script as a command-line parameter, as demonstrated in the following screen shot:

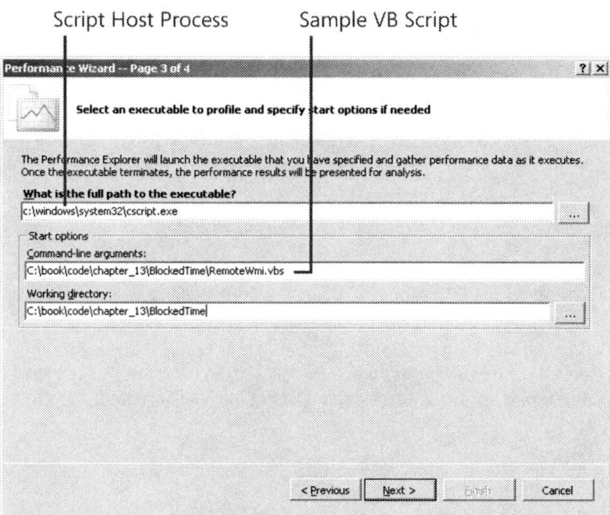

Use the script's folder path in the Working Directory text box and click Next to move to the final page of the wizard.

6. On the final page of the wizard, leave the Launch Profiling After The Wizard Finishes option at its default selected state and click Finish.

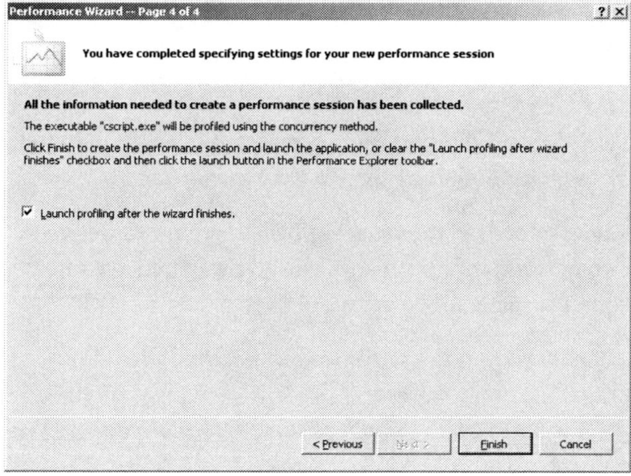

On 64-bit Windows, you'll also get a dialog box at the end of the previous steps warning you to set the *DisablePagingExecutive* registry value to *1* and reboot if you haven't done so already. You can ignore that warning and follow this experiment even without that setting, just as you did in the *notepad.exe* experiment from Chapter 11, given that the kernel-mode portion of the ETW call stacks isn't critical in this tracing scenario.

The reason you get this warning dialog box is because the PPA internally starts the NT Kernel Logger session (and an additional user session) to conduct its tracing, and it also enables stack-trace capture for a few kernel flags. You can confirm this, for example, by running the *xperf.exe –loggers* command inside an administrative command prompt while the previous PPA profiling session is in progress. As you saw in Chapter 12, "Inside ETW," this command-line option allows you to enumerate the active ETW sessions on the system.

```
xperf.exe -loggers
Logger Name        : NT Kernel Logger
...
Maximum File Size : 0
Log Filename       : C:\Users\tariks\Documents\Visual Studio 2010\Projects\cscript120208.krn.ctl
Trace Flags        : PROC_THREAD+LOADER+DISK_IO+DISK_IO_INIT+FILENAME+PROFILE+CSWITCH+DISPATCHER

Logger Name        : VSPerfMon Logger
...
Maximum File Size : 0
Log Filename       : C:\Users\tariks\Documents\Visual Studio 2010\Projects\cscript120208.app.ctl
Trace Flags        :
...
```

You'll recognize several familiar kernel flags in the NT Kernel Logger session started by the PPA tool, including the PROFILE (CPU sample profiling) flag and, more important, the CSWITCH and DISPATCHER kernel flags that control the CSwitch and ReadyThread stack-walk events used in blocked time analysis, respectively. The PPA automatically stops these sessions after it's done profiling the target application and displays the collected ETW traces in three views, which are highlighted in Figure 13-3:

- **CPU Utilization** This view displays the CPU sample profiling usage during the PPA trace session, as reflected by the events logged by the PROFILE kernel flag.
- **Cores** This view shows how threads in the target application bounce between CPU cores, and it provides insight into performance problems caused by excessive context switching between cores and missed CPU cache hits.
- **Threads** This view lists the threads in the target application and provides a convenient view of the waits they entered during their execution. This view relies on the CSWITCH and DISPATCHER events in the trace session to show how long each wait took, as well as the readying call stack for every thread.

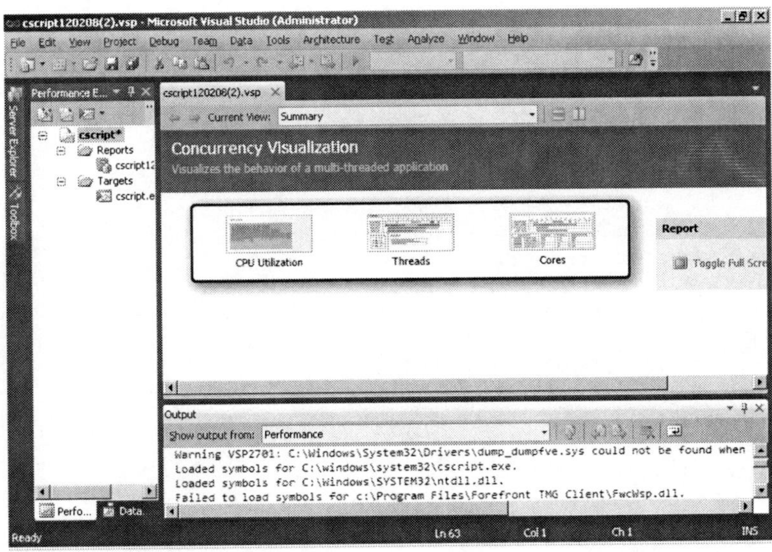

FIGURE 13-3 The Summary view in the PPA.

In the case of the previous Visual Basic script, the CPU Utilization view indicates very little active CPU usage by the *cscript.exe* process over its lifetime. The Threads view, however, shows two particularly long waits, as shown in Figure 13-4. The call stacks of these two waits are displayed next. Notice the PPA also provides the duration of each wait. In my particular run of the experiment, the first wait lasted for about 2.24 seconds and the second wait was just over 2.98 seconds, as highlighted in bold text in the following call stacks:

```
---- Call Stack 1 ----
Category = Synchronization
API = WaitForMultipleObjects
Delay = 2240.1454 ms
kernel32.dll!_WaitForMultipleObjectsExImplementation@20
mswsock.dll!_Nbt_WaitForResponse@8
mswsock.dll!_Nbt_ResolveName@16
mswsock.dll!_Rnr_NbtResolveName@8
mswsock.dll!_Rnr_DoDnsLookup@4
mswsock.dll!_Dns_NSPLookupServiceNext@16
ws2_32.dll!NSPROVIDER::NSPLookupServiceNext
ws2_32.dll!NSPROVIDERSTATE::LookupServiceNext
ws2_32.dll!NSQUERY::LookupServiceNext
ws2_32.dll!_WSALookupServiceNextW@16
ws2_32.dll!_WSALookupServiceNextA@16
ws2_32.dll!getxyDataEnt
ws2_32.dll!_gethostbyname@4
wbemcomn.dll!GetFQDN_Ipv4
wbemprox.dll!GetPrincipal
wbemprox.dll!CDCOMTrans::DoActualConnection
wbemprox.dll!CDCOMTrans::DoConnection
wbemprox.dll!CLocator::ConnectServer
wbemdisp.dll!CSWbemLocator::ConnectServer
...
```

```
cscript.exe!CHost::Execute
cscript.exe!CHost::Main
cscript.exe!_main

---- Call Stack 2 ----
Category = UI Processing
API = Message Processing
Delay = 2982.9184 ms
Unblocked by thread 7424; click 'Unblocking Stack' for details.
user32.dll!_RealMsgWaitForMultipleObjectsEx@20
ole32.dll!CCliModalLoop::BlockFn
ole32.dll!ModalLoop
ole32.dll!ThreadSendReceive
ole32.dll!CRpcChannelBuffer::SwitchAptAndDispatchCall
...
ole32.dll!_CoCreateInstanceEx@24
wbemprox.dll!CDCOMTrans::DoActualCCI
wbemprox.dll!CDCOMTrans::DoCCI
wbemprox.dll!CDCOMTrans::DoActualConnection
wbemprox.dll!CDCOMTrans::DoConnection
wbemprox.dll!CLocator::ConnectServer
wbemdisp.dll!CSWbemLocator::ConnectServer
...
cscript.exe!CHost::Execute
cscript.exe!CHost::Main
cscript.exe!_main
```

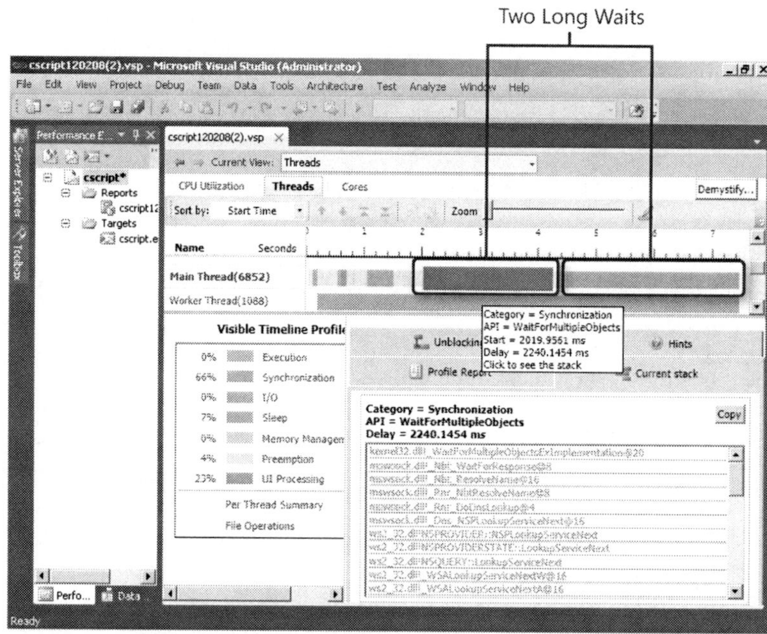

FIGURE 13-4 The Threads view in the PPA.

The call stack of the first wait shows an attempt to resolve the machine name to an IPv4 address using the NetBIOS-over-TCP/IP networking protocol (*mswsock.dll!Nbt_ResolveName*). The second call stack indicates a subsequent COM activation attempt. Because the PPA starts the NT Kernel Logger ETW session with the DISPATCHER kernel flag too, you can also get the ReadyThread call stacks for every satisfied wait during the trace. However, because the readying thread that unblocked the first wait comes from outside the *cscript.exe* process, the PPA doesn't display that call stack, as shown in Figure 13-5.

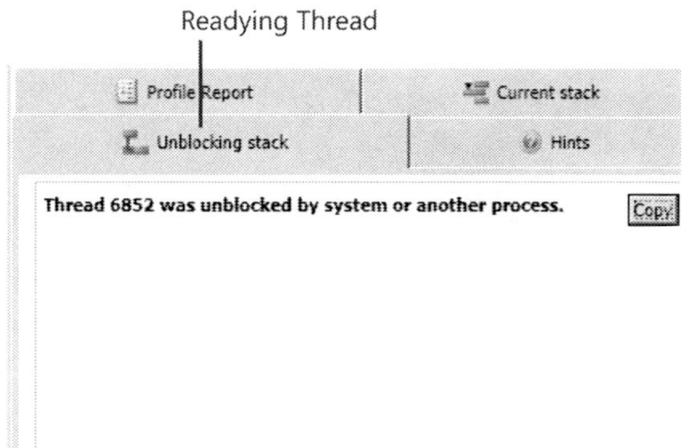

FIGURE 13-5 Unblocking (ReadyThread) stack trace in the PPA.

In this case, you can form an educated guess as to why the two significant waits took over 2 seconds each before getting unblocked because you can reasonably assume it was a network delay in both cases. However, you can also follow the chain of waits across multiple process boundaries without having to take this leap of faith by using the Xperf viewer UI and its CPU Scheduling graph, as will be demonstrated in the next section.

Wait Analysis Using Xperf

To see an illustration of blocked-time analysis using Xperf, you can capture a new trace for the same sample Visual Basic script that was used earlier to demonstrate wait analysis using the Parallel Performance Analyzer (PPA) from Visual Studio 2010. Note the CSWITCH and DISPATCHER kernel flags are not included in the Base kernel group, so you'll need to add them explicitly to the other flags from the Base group when you start the NT Kernel Logger session, as shown in the following sequence of commands.

```
C:\book\code\common\scripts\start_kernel_trace.cmd -kf Base+CSWITCH+DISPATCHER -ks
Profile+CSwitch+ReadyThread
INFO: Invoking xperf to start the session...
CmdLine: (xperf.exe -on PROC_THREAD+LOADER+Base+CSWITCH+DISPATCHER -stackwalk
Profile+CSwitch+ReadyThread)

---- Execute the Visual Basic script ----
cscript.exe C:\book\code\chapter_13\BlockedTime\RemoteWmi.vbs
C:\book\code\chapter_13\BlockedTime\RemoteWmi.vbs(6, 1) SWbemLocator: The RPC server is
unavailable.

C:\book\code\common\scripts\stop_kernel_trace.cmd
INFO: Invoking xperf to stop the session...
CmdLine: (xperf.exe -stop -d c:\temp\merged.etl)
```

The CSwitch and ReadyThread events have their own dedicated graph in the Xperf viewer UI, called the *CPU Scheduling graph*, which is shown in Figure 13-6. As usual, make sure you select this graph and add it to your view using the Frame List flyout if it's not included by default.

```
C:\book\code\common\scripts\view_trace.cmd
...
INFO: Invoking xperf to view the trace...
CmdLine: (xperf.exe c:\temp\merged.etl)
```

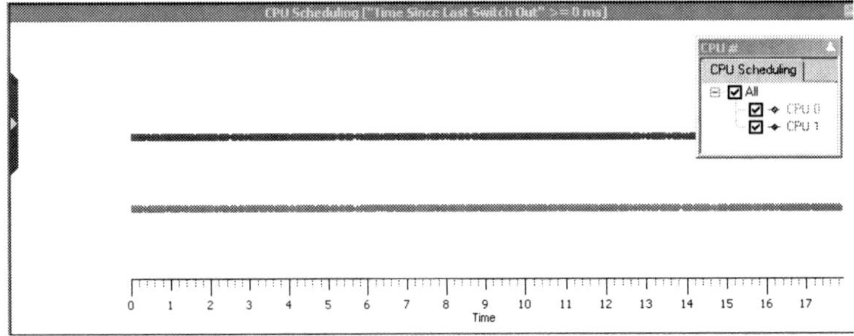

FIGURE 13-6 CPU Scheduling graph in Xperf.

Notice the very high rate of CSwitch events, highlighted by the number of dots shown in the previous graph over the trace timeline. Not all waits, of course, are bad. Even long waits can sometimes be expected, such as when a GUI application blocks and waits on user input.

In this experiment, the wait you're trying to analyze was several seconds long, so you can also use the shortcut menu and filter down the events in the graph to only those CSwitch events where the Time Since Last Switch Out is above a certain threshold. This allows you to ignore benign waits and focus on longer waits that are more likely to explain the delay you observed in this experiment. In Figure 13-7, for instance, the wait threshold is set to 1,000 milliseconds, meaning that only waits of more than one full second will be displayed in the graph.

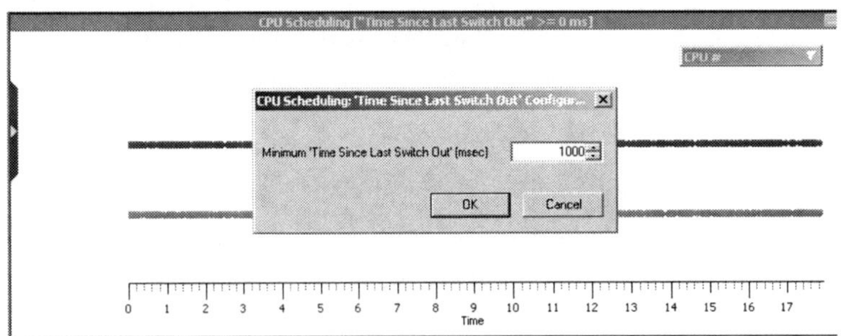

FIGURE 13-7 Setting the wait threshold in the CPU Scheduling graph.

To analyze the context switches in this scenario along with their corresponding ReadyThread events, you can choose the Summary Table With Ready Thread option in the shortcut menu, as illustrated in Figure 13-8. Also, remember to select the Load Symbols option too so that Xperf resolves symbols for the call stacks in the summary table.

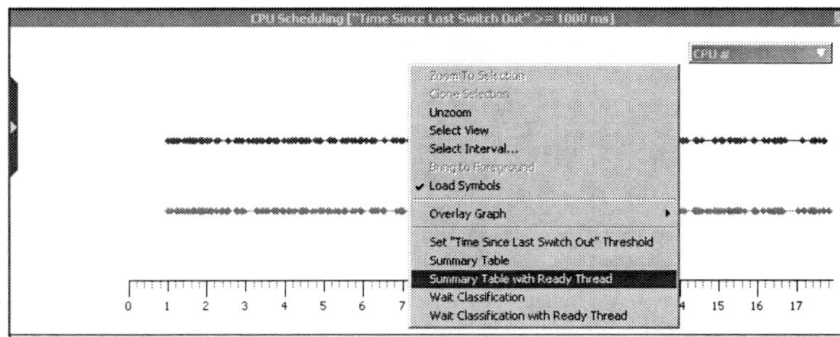

FIGURE 13-8 CPU Scheduling summary table with ready thread information.

Unlike other summary tables in Xperf, where the column names generally tend to be self-explanatory, this particular summary table contains an unusually large number of columns and deserves further explanation. Table 13-1 introduces the most useful columns when performing wait analysis, along with their respective meanings.

TABLE 13-1 Important Columns in the CPU Scheduling Summary Table in Xperf

Column Name	Description
NewProcess	The process containing the new thread in a CSwitch event.
NewThreadStack	The call stack of the thread switched in (the stack-trace event associated with a CSwitch event).
ReadyingProcess	The process containing the readying thread in a ReadyThread event.
ReadyThreadStack	The call stack of the thread that readied a thread (the stack-trace event associated with a ReadyThread event).
Max:Waits (us) Sum:Waits (us)	The longest wait and sum of all waits (in microseconds) under the current selection, respectively. Waits are computed by correlating the ReadyThread and CSwitch events from the trace.
Max:Ready (us) Sum:Ready (us)	The longest ready time and sum of all ready times (in microseconds) under the current selection, respectively. Ready times represent the time spent by a thread in the ready ("runnable") state before it gets scheduled to run on one of the cores.
Max:TimeSinceLast (us) Sum:TimeSinceLast (us)	TimeSinceLast is the duration (in microseconds) separating the current CSwitch event and the time the thread was previously switched out. In other words: TimeSinceLast = WaitTime + ReadyTime. However, the TimeSinceLast duration is computed from the CSwitch events only, so this column is available even when the trace doesn't contain ReadyThread events. The Max column represents the longest TimeSinceLast under the current selection. The Sum column represents the summation of all TimeSinceLast under the current selection.

If you organize the summary table in the current experiment to have the NewProcess and NewThreadStack columns on the left of the gold bar, with the Max:Waits and Sum:Waits columns just to the right of it, you'll be able to view the call stacks with the highest wait durations over the lifetime of the *cscript.exe* process. By expanding the call stack nodes, you again see the same two "long" waits that you were able to observe by using the PPA profiling option in Visual Studio 2010. In Figure 13-9, notice the *wbemprox!GetPrincipal* function call that ultimately invokes the NetBIOS name-resolution routine, which blocked for about 2.24 seconds, and the *wbemprox!CDCOMTrans::DoCCI* COM activation attempt, which waited for about 2.61 seconds.

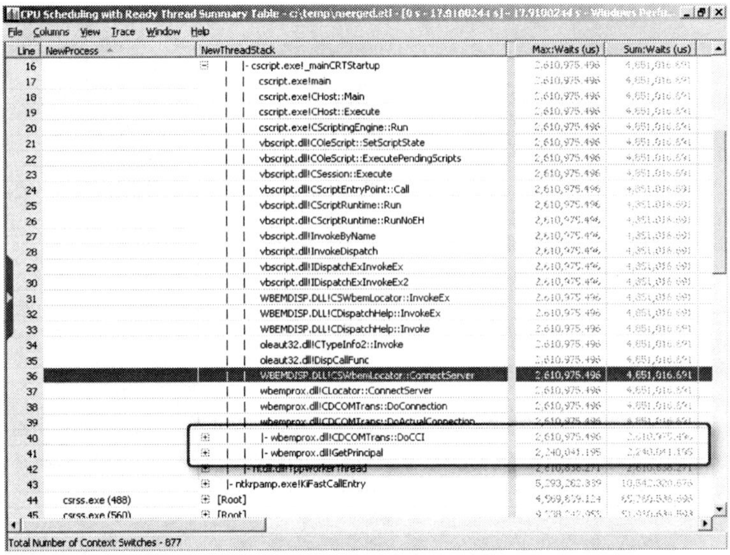

Line	NewProcess	NewThreadStack	Max:Waits (us)	Sum:Waits (us)
16		⊟ | |- cscript.exe!_mainCRTStartup	2,610,975.496	4,651,016.691
17		| | cscript.exe!main	2,610,975.496	4,651,016.691
18		| | cscript.exe!CHost::Main	2,610,975.496	4,651,016.691
19		| | cscript.exe!CHost::Execute	2,610,975.496	4,651,016.691
20		| | cscript.exe!CScriptingEngine::Run	2,610,975.496	4,651,016.691
21		| | vbscript.dll!COleScript::SetScriptState	2,610,975.496	4,651,016.691
22		| | vbscript.dll!COleScript::ExecutePendingScripts	2,610,975.496	4,651,016.691
23		| | vbscript.dll!CSession::Execute	2,610,975.496	4,651,016.691
24		| | vbscript.dll!CScriptEntryPoint::Call	2,610,975.496	4,651,016.691
25		| | vbscript.dll!CScriptRuntime::Run	2,610,975.496	4,351,016.691
26		| | vbscript.dll!CScriptRuntime::RunNoEH	2,610,975.496	4,351,016.691
27		| | vbscript.dll!InvokeByName	2,610,975.496	4,351,016.691
28		| | vbscript.dll!InvokeDispatch	2,610,975.496	4,351,016.691
29		| | vbscript.dll!IDispatchExInvokeEx	2,610,975.496	4,351,016.691
30		| | vbscript.dll!IDispatchExInvokeEx2	2,610,975.496	4,351,016.691
31		| | WBEMDISP.DLL!CSWbemLocator::InvokeEx	2,610,975.496	4,351,016.691
32		| | WBEMDISP.DLL!CDispatchHelp::InvokeEx	2,610,975.496	4,651,016.691
33		| | WBEMDISP.DLL!CDispatchHelp::Invoke	2,610,975.496	4,651,016.691
34		| | oleaut32.dll!CTypeInfo2::Invoke	2,610,975.496	4,651,016.691
35		| | oleaut32.dll!DispCallFunc	2,610,975.496	4,651,016.691
36		| | WBEMDISP.DLL!CSWbemLocator::ConnectServer	2,610,975.496	4,651,016.691
37		| | wbemprox.dll!CLocator::ConnectServer	2,610,975.496	4,651,016.691
38		| | wbemprox.dll!CDCOMTrans::DoConnection	2,610,975.496	4,651,016.691
39		| | wbemprox.dll!CDCOMTrans::DoActualConnection	2,610,975.496	4,651,016.691
40		⊞ | | |- wbemprox.dll!CDCOMTrans::DoCCI	2,610,975.496	2,610,975.496
41		⊞ | | |- wbemprox.dll!GetPrincipal	2,240,041.195	2,240,041.195
42		⊞ | |- ntdll.dll!TppWorkerThread	2,610,938.271	2,610,938.271
43		⊞ |- ntkrpamp.exe!KiFastCallEntry	5,293,282.339	10,542,320.676
44	csrss.exe (488)	⊞ [Root]	4,969,619.124	[illegible]
45	csrss.exe (560)	⊞ [Root]	[illegible]	[illegible]

Total Number of Context Switches - 877

FIGURE 13-9 Observing the longest waits in the *cscript.exe* process.

You can also display the readying thread information for these two waits by adding the ReadyingProcess and ReadyThreadStack columns to the left of the gold bar. In Figure 13-10, the readying thread's call stack of the name resolution call shows the wait is unblocked by the NetBIOS over TCP/IP driver (*netbt.sys*) in kernel mode.

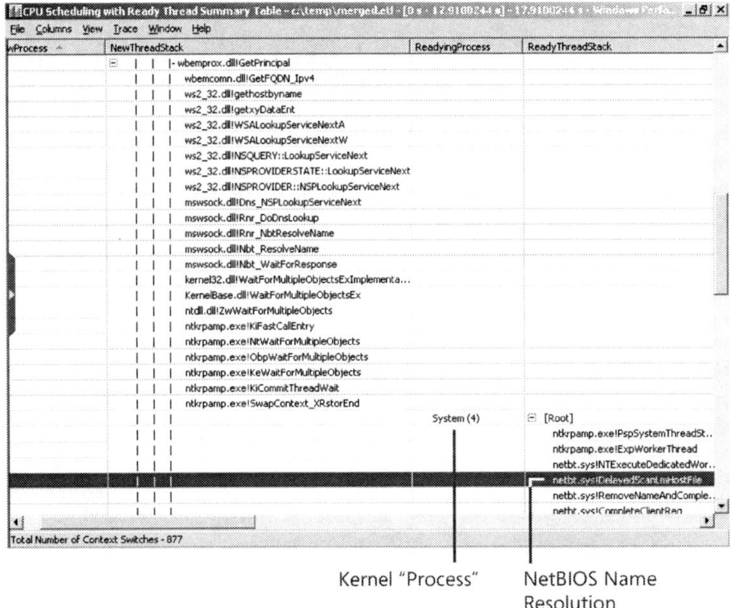

FIGURE 13-10 Readying-thread call stack for the first (*mswsock!Nbt_ResolveName*) "long" wait.

Similarly, you can also find the readying thread for the second "long" wait. However, that won't tell you much in this case because the wait is unblocked by a thread-pool callback routine in the same process (*cscript.exe*), as shown in Figure 13-11.

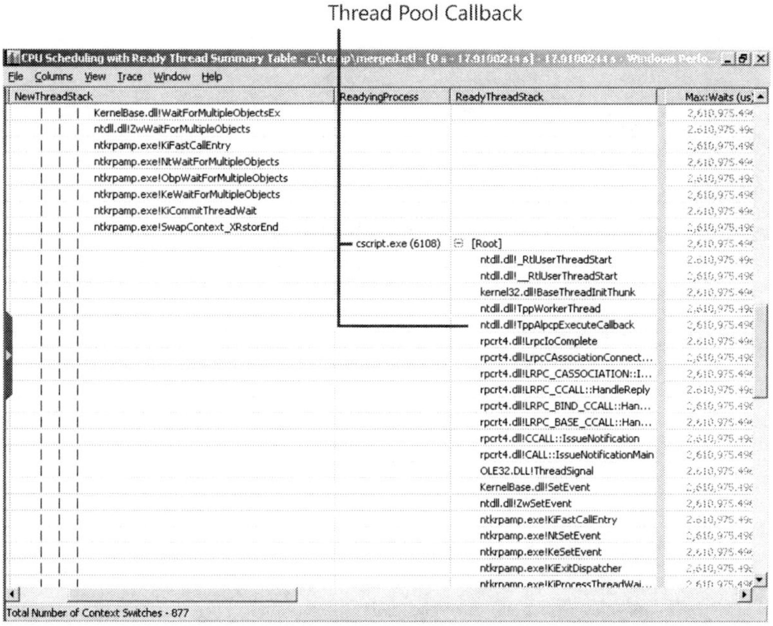

FIGURE 13-11 Readying-thread call stack for the second (*ole32!CoCreateInstance*) "long" wait.

To find the thread that resulted in the previous callback getting invoked, you need to look at the thread pool waits within *cscript.exe* (specifically, the *WaitForWorkViaWorkerFactory* calls). This reveals a readying thread from a service host (*svchost.exe*) process instance, as demonstrated in Figure 13-12.

Using the list of Windows services from the Trace\System Configuration dialog box, you can map the process ID (PID) of this *svchost.exe* instance to the *RpcSs* COM activator service. In my run of the experiment, the decimal PID of the readying *svchost.exe* process in Figure 13-12 was 904, which as shown in Figure 13-13 is used to host the *RpcSs* and *RpcEptMapper* services.

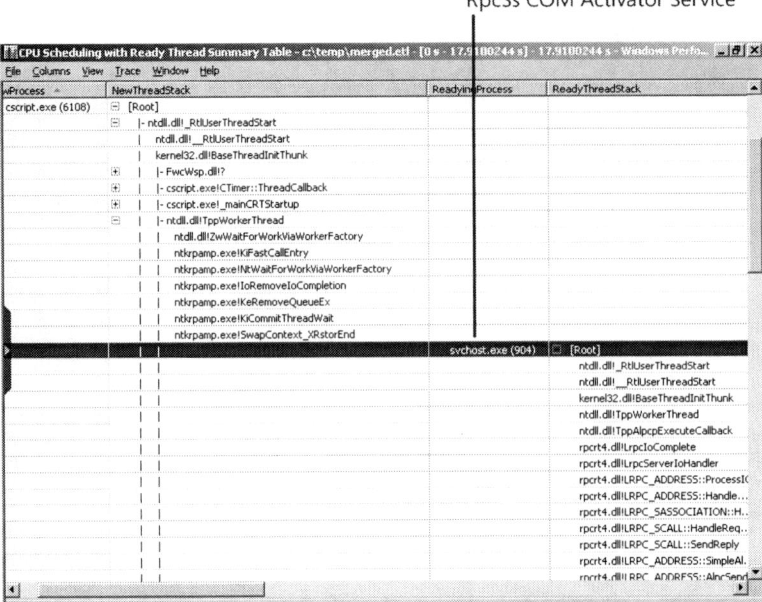

FIGURE 13-12 Moving one step back in the blocking COM activation call's causality chain.

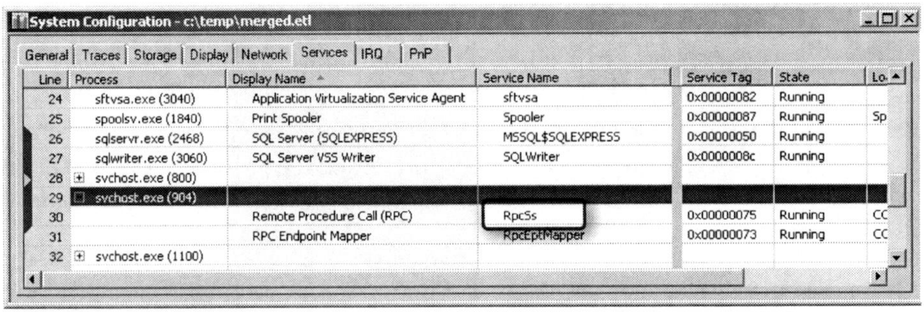

System Configuration - c:\temp\merged.etl

General | Traces | Storage | Display | Network | Services | IRQ | PnP

Line	Process	Display Name	Service Name	Service Tag	State	Lo
24	sftvsa.exe (3040)	Application Virtualization Service Agent	sftvsa	0x00000082	Running	
25	spoolsv.exe (1840)	Print Spooler	Spooler	0x00000087	Running	Sp
26	sqlservr.exe (2468)	SQL Server (SQLEXPRESS)	MSSQL$SQLEXPRESS	0x00000050	Running	
27	sqlwriter.exe (3060)	SQL Server VSS Writer	SQLWriter	0x0000008c	Running	
28	svchost.exe (800)					
29	svchost.exe (904)					
30		Remote Procedure Call (RPC)	RpcSs	0x00000075	Running	CC
31		RPC Endpoint Mapper	RpcEptMapper	0x00000073	Running	CC
32	svchost.exe (1100)					

FIGURE 13-13 Identifying the readying *svchost.exe* instance using the System Configuration dialog box in Xperf.

You now know the identity of the thread that the COM activation attempt was (indirectly) waiting on. All that's left for you to do is switch to the *svchost.exe* process in the summary table and expand the call-stack nodes under that thread. You'll see a wait duration of about 2.596 seconds that closely maps to the second (COM activation attempt) blocked time in the *cscript.exe* process, as shown in Figure 13-14. Notice the call to *RpcSs.dll!RemoteActivationCall* on the call stack taking the full 2.596 seconds, indicating that the delay is caused entirely by the failed remote COM activation operation.

The process of reconstructing causality chains as you just did for this second wait is common in blocked-time analysis, where you often need to go several steps backward until you determine the operation that was truly responsible for the observed execution delay.

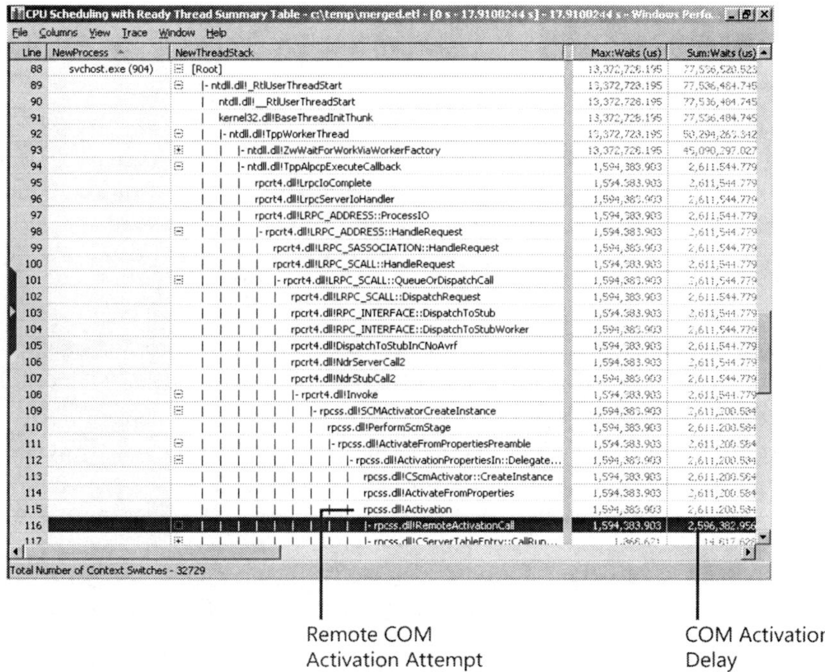

FIGURE 13-14 Remote activation call stack in the COM activator service (*RpcSs*).

Analyzing Memory Usage

Wasteful memory usage is a common cause of performance problems in live production environments. Most developers understand that long waits or aggressive CPU computations will make their applications run slower, but few also realize the importance of building lean programs that consume as little memory as possible. Memory usage can equally have a direct impact on how fast an application runs, though, for several compelling reasons:

- Programs that consume too much memory (hundreds of megabytes) can suffer greatly when the OS needs to reclaim physical RAM space for other applications to run on the system. When the OS then switches the program back in, the memory pages previously saved to disk must be brought back into main memory. The more memory that program consumes, the slower this process becomes and the more sluggish the application appears to the user. You should always keep in mind that, generally speaking, disk I/O is several orders of magnitude slower than accessing memory, and that accessing memory is itself several orders of magnitude slower than fetching data directly from the CPU caches.
- This last point brings up another consideration. When a program performs heavy CPU operations that depend on data stored in memory, the cost of transferring the data from main memory into the CPU can outweigh the cost of performing the actual computations inside the CPU and become the main bottleneck. In that case, it might sometimes be far better to store

the data *compressed* (such as by using a bit-map data structure instead of a byte array) so that it occupies less memory. Sure, it might take a few extra CPU instructions to *decompress* that data, but that's a beneficial tradeoff if it allows the processor to keep the smaller data in its cache lines, saving the cost of a roundtrip to main memory. This memory locality effect is also the reason that the vector data structure from the C++ Standard Template Library (STL), which is represented by a contiguous block of memory, can perform better for many algorithms than the noncontiguous STL list data structure. This is despite the cost involved in copying the contents of a vector when it becomes full and it needs to be expanded to make room for more elements.

- Finally, .NET programs that use too much memory can create more work for the garbage collector (GC) to mark and sweep the managed objects graph. The more objects the GC has to traverse, the longer the managed program stalls during the garbage collections performed periodically by the CLR execution engine. These chronic stalls can become a serious performance problem in any .NET application, but particularly in those with a need for a high degree of responsiveness (such as game applications).

This section will illustrate a few techniques for observing memory-consumption patterns, covering the two most common cases of user-mode memory investigations: native (NT heap) and managed (GC heap) memory analysis.

Analyzing High-Level Memory Usage in a Target Process

Both the managed and native heap allocations are reported as *private bytes* for the application when measuring its memory usage. Before digging into the details of those dynamic allocations, however, it's usually wise to look at a high-level memory breakdown so that you know where to focus your attention. If the GC heap allocations, for example, represent only a small portion of the overall heap allocations in your application, it makes more sense to analyze native allocations first before you spend time looking at the GC heap.

There are several high-level tools you can use for this preliminary memory-usage inspection. The Resource Monitor (*resmon.exe*) and the performance monitor (*perfmon.exe*) tools are both relatively easy to use and can help you observe general memory-usage trends in your application. The tool I like to use in this step, however, is the VMMap tool from the Sysinternals suite, which as described in the Introduction of this book can be found at *http://technet.microsoft.com/en-us/sysinternals/bb842062*. This tool has a convenient user interface that offers a detailed breakdown of the virtual memory in the target process, including dynamic (GC and native) allocations, stack memory usage, and the amount of memory consumed by the code (images) loaded into the virtual address space of the target process.

VMMap can dump a snapshot of the memory usage in a running process. You can also use the F5 shortcut in the main VMMap window to trigger a refresh and capture updated statistics over the lifetime of the target process. Figure 13-15 shows the main user interface you see when using VMMap to observe memory consumption in a target process. In the case of this screen shot, the tool was used to observe a memory snapshot from the *LoadXml.exe* example you'll study later in this section.

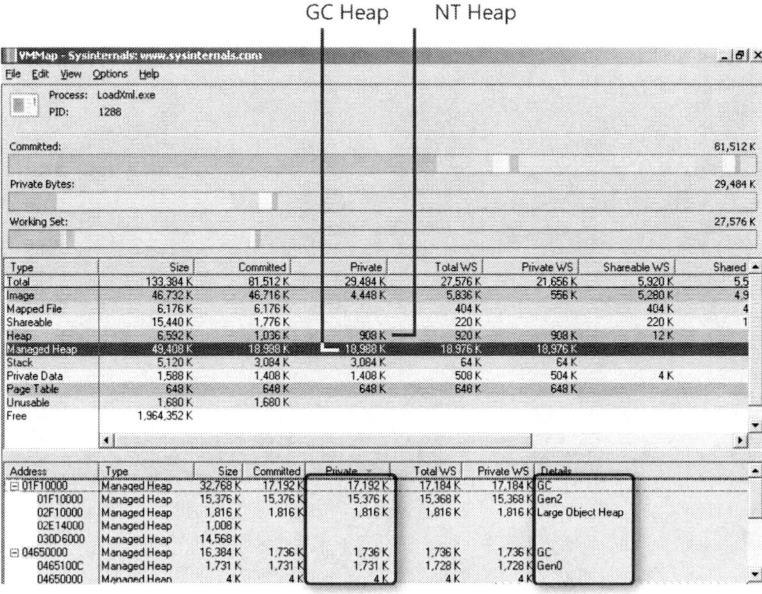

FIGURE 13-15 VMMap breakdown of memory usage for a process.

Notice that the tool provides a convenient breakdown of all allocation types in the target process. It also provides a granular breakdown of the managed (GC) heap, including the size of each GC generation (*gen0*, *gen1*, or *gen2*) and the size of the large object heap (LOH) too. This high-level breakdown is useful so that you know whether there are any memory-usage anomalies that need further analysis. It also helps you determine the next area to target in your investigation, including the NT heap or GC heap areas of the process virtual address space.

Analyzing NT Heap Memory Usage

Chapter 8, "Common Debugging Scenarios, Part 1," covered a few memory-management basics in Windows. It also explained the relationships among several common user-mode allocators in its "Debugging Heap Corruptions" section. One particularly important point made there was that many allocators are built on top of the NT heap allocator implemented by the system in the *ntdll.dll* layer. Fortunately, this allocator is also instrumented using ETW events, allowing you to analyze the heap memory consumption in your applications.

Though the NT heap ETW provider existed in Windows Vista too, it wasn't until Windows 7 that the ETW framework in the OS started supporting the capture of stack-trace events for user providers. Without stack traces, heap analysis becomes more difficult because you can't tie observed memory usage back to the source code of the application.

The following C++ code sample from the companion source code, which you can compile by following the procedure described in the Introduction of this book, will be used in this section to illustrate an interesting application of Xperf and ETW for tracking down the call site of a heap memory leak. As you'll see, leaks are just an extreme case of the *wasteful* memory-usage patterns that you can also analyze using the same technique.

```
//
// C:\book\code\chapter_13\NTHeapMemory>main.cpp
//
static
HRESULT
LeakOneBuffer()
{
    LPBYTE pMem = NULL;
    DWORD n;

    ChkProlog();

    wprintf(L"Leaking the last buffer in %d allocations.\n", NUM_BUFFERS);
    for (n = 0; n < NUM_BUFFERS; n++)
    {
        if (pMem != NULL)
        {
            delete[] pMem;
        }
        pMem = new BYTE[SIZE_OF_EACH_BUFFER];
        ChkAlloc(pMem);
    }

    ChkNoCleanup();
}
```

Capturing ETW Heap Traces Using Xperf

Fundamentally, the ETW heap trace provider is just another user provider (named *Heap Trace Provider*). However, it's also special in two ways:

- It must be explicitly enabled for the target process you want to analyze, and it doesn't get enabled systemwide like all the other user providers.
- Xperf has intimate support of the heap trace provider and exposes a special syntax for enabling it within a new user session. Instead of using the *–on* command-line option to enable the provider when you start a new user session, you instead use the dedicated *–heap* option.

The syntax for starting a heap tracing session in Xperf can take one of the following two forms:

```
xperf.exe [NT Kernel Logger] -start UserSession -heap -pids PID_1 PID_2 ... PID_n
                             [-stackwalk HeapAlloc+HeapRealloc+...]
OR
xperf.exe [NT Kernel Logger] -start UserSession -heap -pidnewprocess CommandLine
                             [-stackwalk HeapAlloc+HeapRealloc+...]
```

The former syntax allows you to trace heap allocations in programs that are already running on the system (identified by their process IDs), while the latter starts a new instance of the target process and enables heap tracing at the same time. The flaw in this second approach, however, is that the new process instance is started as a child of the *xperf.exe* process, so it will also be started with full administrative privileges, given that you need to start *xperf.exe* with those privileges when you use it to control ETW and start sessions. Another limitation of that approach is that some processes, such as Windows service processes or COM servers, cannot be started directly in this standalone fashion.

Fortunately, there is a better way (at least in Windows 7 and later) to enable heap tracing automatically when new instances of your target process start up. You can do that by setting the *TracingFlags* registry value under the *Image File Execution Options* (IFEO) key for the target image. Xperf allows you to pass *0* for the PID value (which is never a valid process ID) to indicate that you'll enable heap tracing using this alternative approach. This is the method used in this experiment to track down the source of the heap memory leak in the sample C++ program shown earlier.

The GFLAGS tool doesn't support setting this value, but the companion source code has a simple script to help you do so without manually editing the registry, as illustrated in the following command, which you need to run from an elevated administrative command prompt.

```
C:\book\code\common\scripts>configure_heap_tracing.cmd -enable leak.exe
```

Once this command runs successfully, the *TracingFlags* value for this executable image should be set to *1*, as shown in Figure 13-16.

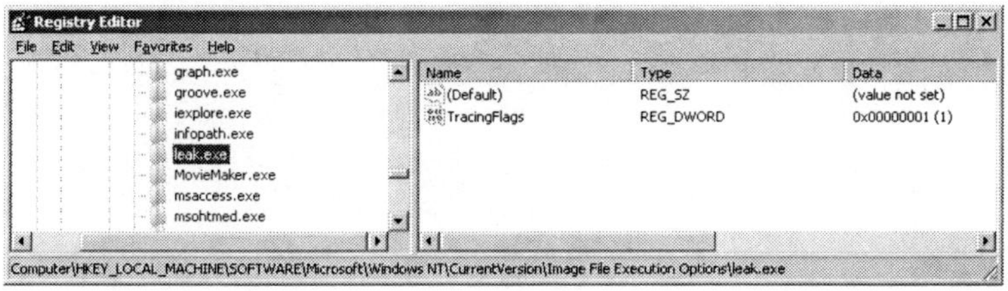

FIGURE 13-16 Enabling ETW heap tracing for an image.

You can now monitor heap allocations in the target process by setting the PID value to *0* on the Xperf command line. The companion source code contains another wrapper script to automate the process of starting heap tracing sessions in this manner, as demonstrated in the following sequence of commands.

```
C:\book\code\common\scripts\start_w32heap_user_trace.cmd -hs HeapAlloc+HeapRealloc
INFO: Invoking xperf to start the heap user sessions...
CmdLine: (xperf.exe -on PROC_THREAD+LOADER  -start UserSession -heap -pids 0 -stackwalk
HeapAlloc+HeapRealloc)

---- Execute the test application ----
C:\book\code\chapter_13\NTHeapMemory\objfre_win7_x86\i386\leak.exe

C:\book\code\common\scripts\stop_user_trace.cmd
INFO: Invoking xperf to stop the kernel and user sessions...
CmdLine: (xperf.exe -stop -stop UserSession -d c:\temp\merged.etl)
```

The captured ETW trace file contains events logged by the heap calls made in the context of the target process. It also contains stack-trace events for all *HeapAlloc* and *HeapRealloc* operations, which allows you to observe the call sites for all NT heap allocations from the target process.

At this stage, you can also disable heap tracing again for the target process because the *TracingFlags* IFEO hook isn't needed for analyzing the heap trace; it is needed only when the trace is being captured.

```
C:\book\code\common\scripts\configure_heap_tracing.cmd -disable leak.exe
```

Analyzing ETW Heap Traces Using Xperf

Xperf also has dedicated graphs for visualizing the events logged by the heap provider. One of these graphs is Heap Total Allocation Size, which shows the amount of allocations in the target process. Figure 13-17 shows the pattern you'll see when analyzing the previous trace file. Notice the additional *–sympath* argument used with the helper *view_trace.cmd* script, which appends the path you provide for your symbols to the Microsoft public symbols server path in the _NT_SYMBOL_PATH environment variable, allowing Xperf to also resolve the function names from your application when displaying the stack-trace events in the trace.

```
C:\book\code\common\scripts\view_trace.cmd -sympath C:\book\code\chapter_13\NTHeapMemory\objfre_
win7_x86\i386
...
INFO: Invoking xperf to view the trace...
CmdLine: (xperf.exe c:\temp\merged.etl)
```

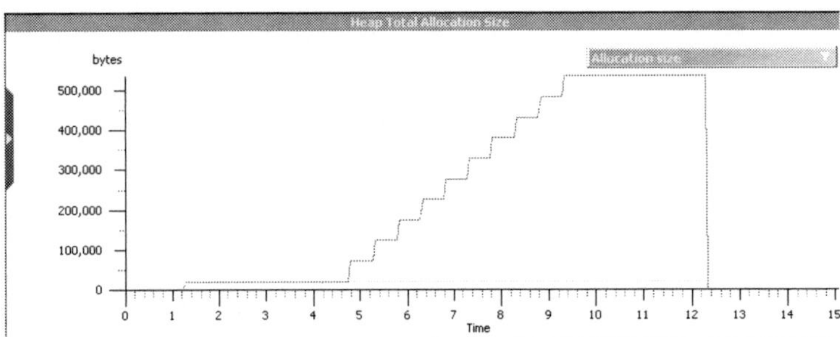

FIGURE 13-17 Total NT heap allocations in the target process.

This tells you that the traced application consumed about 500 KB of NT heap memory, which appears consistent with the fact it had 10 iterations, each allocating 50 buffers 1 KB in size. Of course, the exact size will be slightly larger than 500 KB because other system code that runs in your process (such as the module loader, for instance) also allocates dynamic memory on the heap for its own operations.

The previous graph doesn't consider freed memory (49 out of the 50 buffers allocated in each iteration were freed) and only provides the cumulative NT heap size. When you're trying to debug a suspected NT heap memory leak, you need to instead look at the Heap Outstanding Allocation Size graph, which also shows an increasing amount of "outstanding" allocations (allocations that haven't been freed yet) in the target application. This is the telltale sign of a *potential* memory leak. Remember that just like when you used the UMDH tool in Chapter 8 to investigate memory leaks, the allocations might be freed at a later point during the process lifetime. In this case, however, there was no such calls to release the heap memory until the target process exited, resulting in a steep drop to 0 bytes, as shown in Figure 13-18. This is a strong indication that this might in fact be a legitimate memory leak.

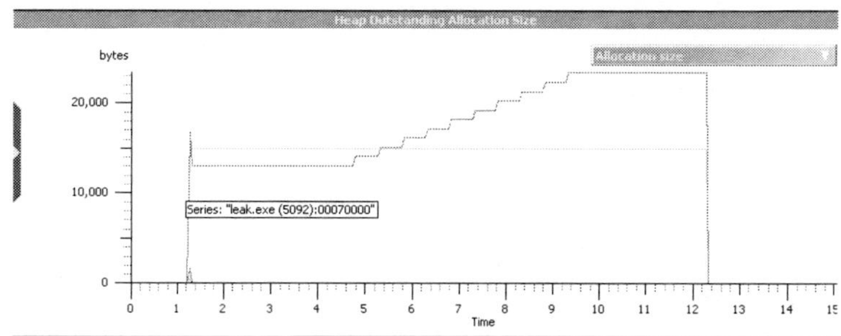

FIGURE 13-18 Outstanding NT heap allocations in the target process.

To find the allocation call sites of these potential memory leaks, you can select the region of the graph that shows the periodic spikes and invoke the heap summary table for that time interval by right-clicking the graph and selecting Summary Table, as illustrated in Figure 13-19.

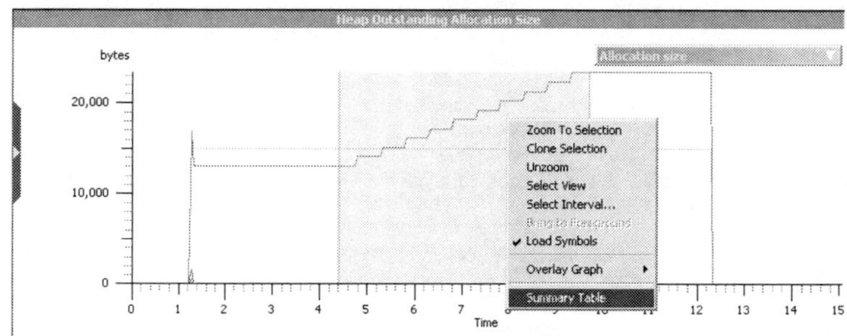

FIGURE 13-19 Invoking the Heap Outstanding Allocation Size summary table.

In the heap Summary Table view, which is shown in Figure 13-20, you can see that the stack traces are segregated by type. An allocation in the AIFO ("Allocated Inside the selection, Freed Outside the selection") indicates a potential leak call site, though as indicated earlier this is not definitive proof that there is a memory leak.

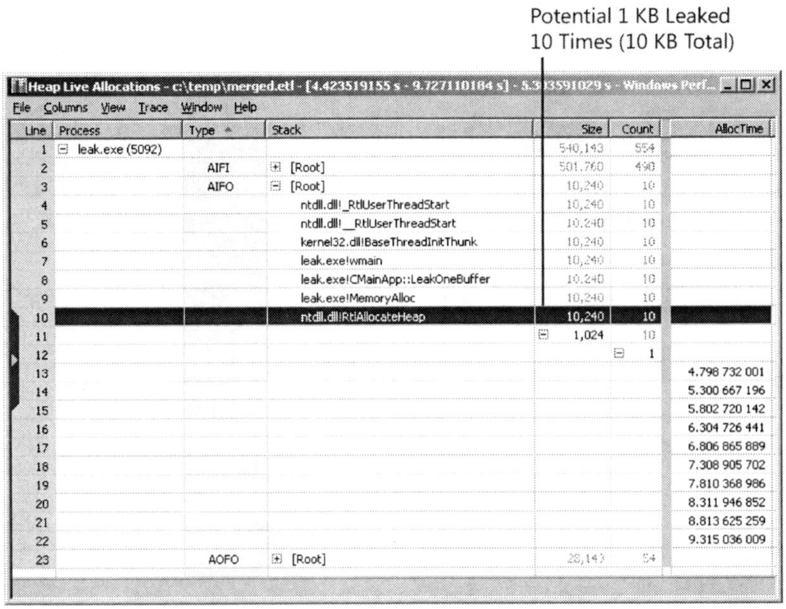

Potential 1 KB Leaked
10 Times (10 KB Total)

Line	Process	Type	Stack	Size	Count	AllocTime
1	⊟ leak.exe (5092)			540,143	554	
2		AIFI	⊞ [Root]	501,760	490	
3		AIFO	⊟ [Root]	10,240	10	
4			ntdll.dll!_RtlUserThreadStart	10,240	10	
5			ntdll.dll!__RtlUserThreadStart	10,240	10	
6			kernel32.dll!BaseThreadInitThunk	10,240	10	
7			leak.exe!wmain	10,240	10	
8			leak.exe!CMainApp::LeakOneBuffer	10,240	10	
9			leak.exe!MemoryAlloc	10,240	10	
10			ntdll.dll!RtlAllocateHeap	10,240	10	
11				⊟ 1,024	10	
12					⊟ 1	
13						4.798 732 001
14						5.300 667 196
15						5.802 720 142
16						6.304 726 441
17						6.806 865 889
18						7.308 905 702
19						7.810 368 986
20						8.311 946 852
21						8.813 625 259
22						9.315 036 009
23		AOFO	⊞ [Root]	28,143	54	

FIGURE 13-20 Heap Live Allocations summary table window.

The four allocation categories you'll encounter when performing heap analysis using the Xperf tool are summarized in Table 13-2.

TABLE 13-2 Allocation Types in Xperf's Heap Summary Table

Type	Stands For	Description
AIFO	Allocated In, Freed Out	Allocations in the selected time interval with no corresponding free in the selection. The "freed out" part is only assumed in this case. This category of allocations is important when debugging NT heap memory leaks.
AIFI	Allocated In, Freed In	Allocations in the selection that also have a corresponding free in the same selected time interval.
AOFI	Allocated Out, Freed In	Allocations that occurred outside the selection but were freed in the selected time interval.
AOFO	Allocated Out, Freed Out	Both allocation and free occurred outside the selection.

In this case, there were 10 allocations (per the Count column) in the AIFO category that all have the same call stack. Notice also that each allocation was 1 KB (1,024 bytes) in size (per the Size column). You can even see the timestamps of each allocation by adding the AllocTime column to the columns in your Summary Table view.

All that is left for you to do is review the application's source code and inspect the code in the *leak!CMainApp::LeakOneBuffer* function that was flagged in the previous call stack. The last 1-KB buffer is being leaked in each call to this function, just as the heap analysis performed in Xperf suggested.

Analyzing GC Heap (.NET) Memory Usage

GC heap memory allocations aren't built on top of the NT heap layer, so the previous ETW instrumentation isn't useful when you need to analyze .NET memory-usage patterns. Because the CLR makes direct virtual allocation calls to the OS and manages its heap internally, only it knows about the internal structure of the GC heap. Though the CLR is also instrumented using ETW, the Windows 7 SDK version of Xperf has no special support for those events. Luckily, there is another tool, called *PerfView*, which does a commendable job filling the gaps that exist in the Windows 7 SDK version of Xperf as it pertains to managed code tracing using ETW.

In this section, you'll study the GC heap consumption in the following C# program from the companion source code, which uses the *XmlDocument* .NET class to open an XML file and display the name of the very first element in the document.

```
//
// C:\book\code\chapter_13\GCHeapMemory>LoadXml.cs
//
public static void Main(
    string[] args
    )
{
    XmlDocument document;
    int ticks;

    if (args.Length != 1)
    {
        Console.WriteLine("USAGE: loadxml.exe InputFile");
        return;
    }
    ticks = Environment.TickCount;
    document = new XmlDocument();
    document.Load(args[0]);
    Console.WriteLine("XmlDocument load took {0} milliseconds",
        (Environment.TickCount - ticks));

    Console.WriteLine("Enter any key to continue...");
    Console.ReadLine();

    Console.WriteLine("Name of the first element in the input document is: {0}",
        document.DocumentElement.ChildNodes[0].Name);
}
```

To follow this experiment, a simple tool is provided with the companion source code to create large XML files for testing. For example, the following command generates an XML file with 100,000 elements for use with the previous program, which should result in a file larger than 3 MB in size.

```
C:\book\code\chapter_13\GCHeapMemory>CreateLargeXml.exe C:\temp\test.xml 100000
```

The goal of this section will be to figure out how much memory the previous program ends up using to merely display the name of the first element in a 3-MB XML file. Note the time it will take for this program to execute will also be shorter after the first run, given that the file will be cached in memory by the I/O manager when it's first fetched from disk in the first *cold* run of the application. This section will focus on the subsequent *warm* runs, where disk I/O access won't be a factor and only the run-time behavior of the .NET program (including its dynamic memory consumption) is in play.

```
C:\book\code\chapter_13\GCHeapMemory>LoadXml.exe C:\temp\test.xml
Xml document load took 234 milliseconds
Enter any key to continue...
Name of the first element in the input document is: name0
```

Analyzing GC Heap Memory Using PerfView

Like Xperf, PerfView is also free and acts as an ETW controller and consumer; however, it also has intimate knowledge of the ETW instrumentation in the CLR. You can download this tool from *http://www.microsoft.com/download/en/details.aspx?id=28567*. It's also easy to install and is packaged as a single executable that can be used without any additional registration requirements on the target machine, making it particularly convenient for performance investigations in live production environments—just like Xperf.

Though PerfView will be used in this section for analyzing the GC heap memory usage in a .NET application, it can also be used for CPU sample profiling (Profile ETW events), blocked-time analysis (CSwitch and ReadyThread events), and many other ETW-based investigations of both native and managed code. PerfView's user interface isn't polished to the level of Visual Studio and the Windows Performance Toolkit (WPT), but it's probably the most complete tool you'll find today for ETW-based tracing investigations of managed (.NET) applications.

Starting ETW tracing using PerfView is easy, as the following procedure shows.

Collecting ETW Traces Using PerfView

1. Start PerfView from an elevated administrative command prompt. PerfView is smart enough to recognize when it needs elevation and will conveniently restart itself with elevated privileges after prompting for administrative credentials (or consent to elevate if you're already a member of the built-in Administrators group).
2. Use the Alt+C UI shortcut (or the Collect item in the Collect menu) in the tool, and click the Start Collection button, as shown in the following screen shot. This starts ETW logging globally on the system, just as Xperf does. You can also expand the Advanced Options at the bottom of the dialog box to view the providers enabled by PerfView and confirm that the CLR (.NET) provider events are enabled by default.

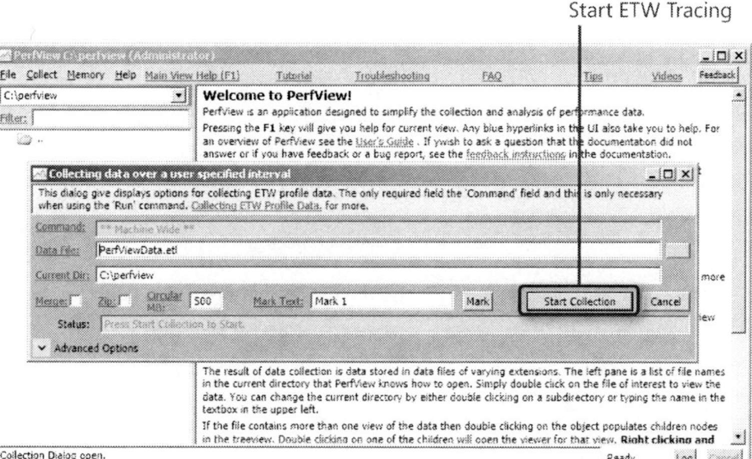

3. Run your scenario in standalone mode. In this experiment, this is the C# program shown at the top of this section:

```
C:\book\code\chapter_13\GCHeapMemory>LoadXml.exe C:\temp\test.xml
```

4. When you want to stop tracing, click the Stop Collection button in the same dialog box used during step 2. This will take a few seconds while the rundown information is collected from the CLR ETW provider. The status bar at the bottom of the main PerfView window will print messages indicating the current progress.

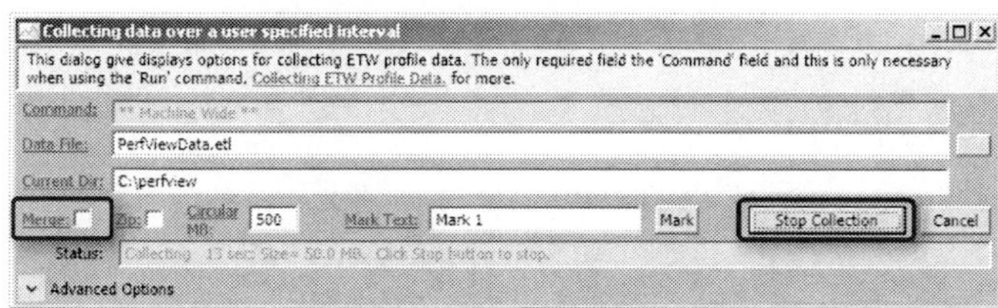

5. If you plan to analyze the saved trace file on a different machine, you should also select the Merge check box in the previous dialog box before stopping the trace collection. By default, PerfView doesn't merge the traces it collects with the kernel rundown information.

After ETW tracing is stopped, PerfView displays a summary table of all the processes that ran during the trace session. Double-clicking one of the rows takes you to a CPU usage view for the selected process—not the memory usage view you are interested in! To look at the memory views from the previous trace collection, dismiss this dialog box and return to the main window, where you need to expand the node representing the new trace file, as shown in Figure 13-21.

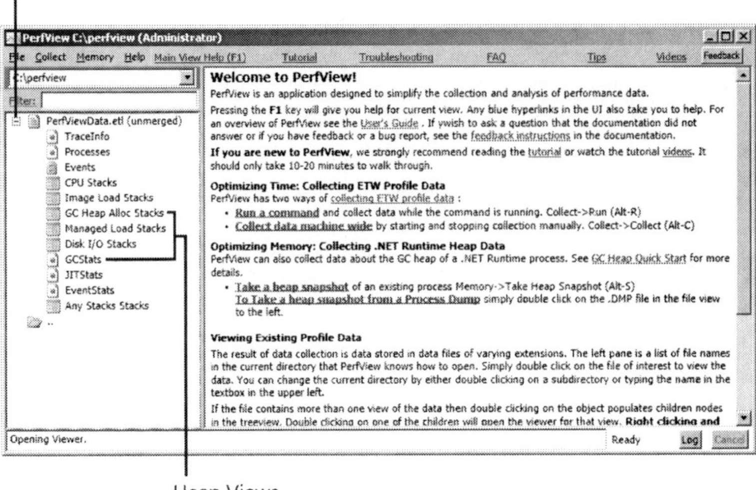

FIGURE 13-21 Expanding the collected trace node in PerfView.

A good place to start your GC memory analysis is the GCStats view, which displays a summary of GC heap statistics from all the managed code processes that were present during the trace session. The *LoadXml.exe* process from this experiment should show almost 20 MB of total GC heap allocations, as shown in Figure 13-22. This is surprising given that the size of the input XML file was only 3 MB and all you wanted to do was display the name of the first element in that document.

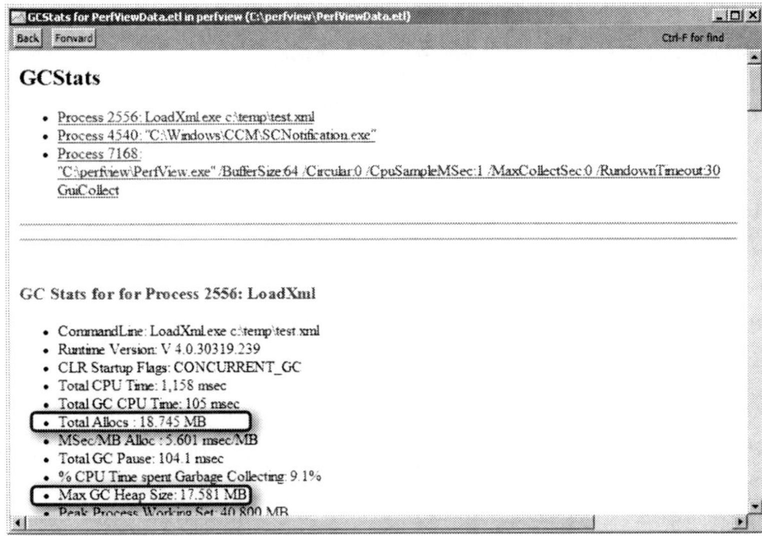

FIGURE 13-22 GC heap usage statistics by process in the GCStats view.

Farther down in the same GCStats view, you'll find the GC Events By Time table, which details every GC occurrence in the target process during the trace lifetime, with a wealth of useful information that gets emitted by the CLR ETW provider when garbage collections occur. This table is depicted in Figure 13-23, which shows that my run of the experiment in this section saw four generational GC occurrences: two *gen0* collections, one *gen1* collection, and one even more extensive *gen2* collection. The table also displays the size of the heap after each collection and shows the increase in GC heap size over the lifetime of the trace until it peaked at almost 18 MB.

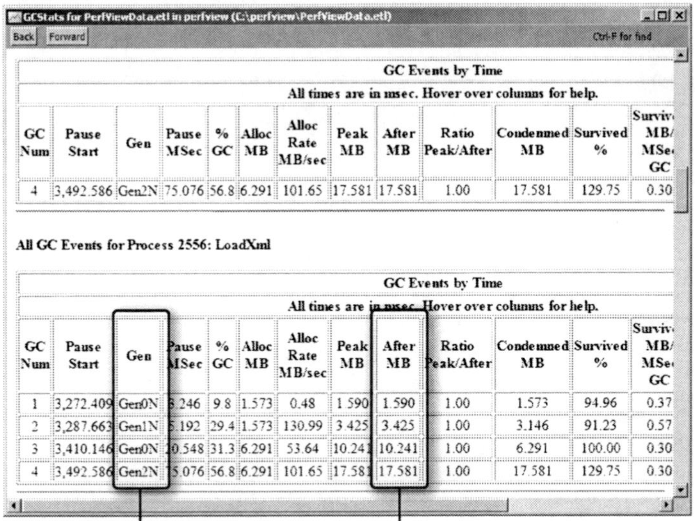

GCStats for PerfViewData.etl in perfview (C:\perfview\PerfViewData.etl)

Back Forward Ctrl-F for find

GC Events by Time

All times are in msec. Hover over columns for help.

GC Num	Pause Start	Gen	Pause MSec	% GC	Alloc MB	Alloc Rate MB/sec	Peak MB	After MB	Ratio Peak/After	Condemned MB	Survived %	Surviv MB/ MSe GC
4	3,492.586	Gen2N	75.076	56.8	6.291	101.65	17.581	17.581	1.00	17.581	129.75	0.30

All GC Events for Process 2556: LoadXml

GC Events by Time

All times are in msec. Hover over columns for help.

GC Num	Pause Start	Gen	Pause MSec	% GC	Alloc MB	Alloc Rate MB/sec	Peak MB	After MB	Ratio Peak/After	Condemned MB	Survived %	Surviv MB/ MSe GC
1	3,272.409	Gen0N	3.246	9.8	1.573	0.48	1.590	1.590	1.00	1.573	94.96	0.37
2	3,287.663	Gen1N	5.192	29.4	1.573	130.99	3.425	3.425	1.00	3.146	91.23	0.57
3	3,410.146	Gen0N	10.548	31.3	6.291	53.64	10.241	10.241	1.00	6.291	100.00	0.30
4	3,492.586	Gen2N	75.076	56.8	6.291	101.65	17.581	17.581	1.00	17.581	129.75	0.30

Type of GC

Heap Memory After Each GC

FIGURE 13-23 Garbage collection events by time in the GCStats view.

Now that you know you have unexpectedly large GC heap memory usage, the next step is to narrow the list of functions in your code that are most responsible for these allocations. PerfView helps you do that too by providing another heap usage view called GC Heap Alloc Stacks. When you double-click that view under the collected trace node in the main window, you'll see a dialog box with a list of processes, as shown in Figure 13-24.

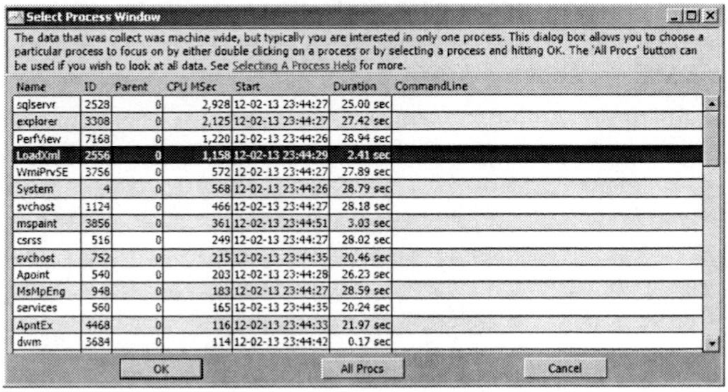

Select Process Window

The data that was collect was machine wide, but typically you are interested in only one process. This dialog box allows you to choose a particular process to focus on by either double clicking on a process or by selecting a process and hitting OK. The 'All Procs' button can be used if you wish to look at all data. See Selecting A Process Help for more.

Name	ID	Parent	CPU MSec	Start	Duration	CommandLine
sqlservr	2528	0	2,928	12-02-13 23:44:27	25.00 sec	
explorer	3308	0	2,125	12-02-13 23:44:27	27.42 sec	
PerfView	7168	0	1,220	12-02-13 23:44:26	28.94 sec	
LoadXml	2556	0	1,158	12-02-13 23:44:29	2.41 sec	
WmiPrvSE	3756	0	572	12-02-13 23:44:27	27.89 sec	
System	4	0	568	12-02-13 23:44:26	28.79 sec	
svchost	1124	0	466	12-02-13 23:44:27	28.18 sec	
mspaint	3856	0	361	12-02-13 23:44:51	3.03 sec	
csrss	516	0	249	12-02-13 23:44:27	28.02 sec	
svchost	752	0	215	12-02-13 23:44:35	20.46 sec	
Apoint	540	0	203	12-02-13 23:44:28	26.23 sec	
MsMpEng	948	0	183	12-02-13 23:44:27	28.59 sec	
services	560	0	165	12-02-13 23:44:35	20.24 sec	
ApntEx	4468	0	116	12-02-13 23:44:33	21.97 sec	
dwm	3684	0	114	12-02-13 23:44:42	0.17 sec	

OK All Procs Cancel

FIGURE 13-24 Process selection window in PerfView.

After you choose the row corresponding to the target process (*LoadXml*) and double-click it, you'll see a summary table of the heap allocations by call stack. Note also that PerfView doesn't resolve unmanaged (native) module symbols by default (just like Xperf!) because of the cost involved in doing so, but you can easily select one or multiple rows (functions) and use the Alt+S keyboard shortcut to download symbols for the target modules. PerfView conveniently adds the Microsoft public symbols URL to its search path automatically, so you need to configure only the paths to your own native code when using PerfView. Figure 13-25 shows how you can explicitly force PerfView to resolve the symbols for a single row by using the right-click context menu, though you'll find the Alt+S keyboard shortcut much more convenient in practice.

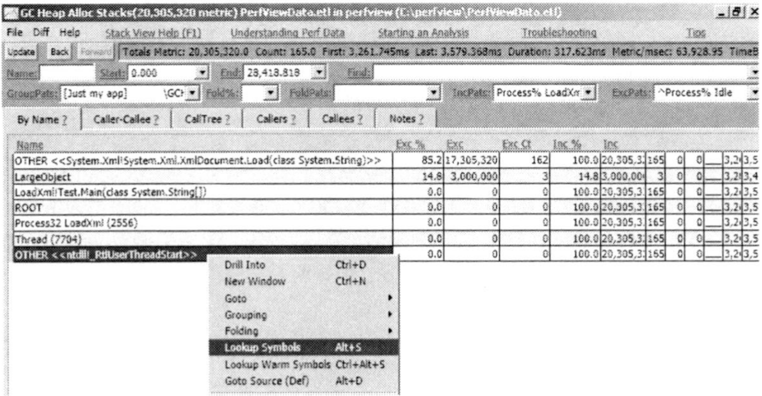

FIGURE 13-25 Resolving symbols for native modules in PerfView.

By default, PerfView shows you only the subset of call stacks that it thinks are from your own code (the *[Just my app]* filter). In this case, your call to *XmlDocument.Load* is responsible for the bulk of GC heap allocations. If you need to drill down farther into allocations under that call, you should first clear the *GroupPats* and *IncPats* filters and double-click the function row. You'll then see a hierarchical view of where allocations occurred, as demonstrated in Figure 13-26.

You now have a detailed breakdown of the exact functions in the *System.Xml.dll* .NET assembly that contributed to the high GC heap memory usage. By following the call stacks all the way to the bottom (by selecting the corresponding function rows), you'll see that your one-line call to *XmlDocument.Load* resulted in parsing the entire document and creating a Document Object Model (DOM) tree for all the name and string value nodes. That's certainly a lot of overhead if all you need to do is display the string name of the first element! It is also a reminder that it's important to understand how the APIs and framework functions you use implement their features so that you can be sure you're applying the right tools to the problems your software is solving.

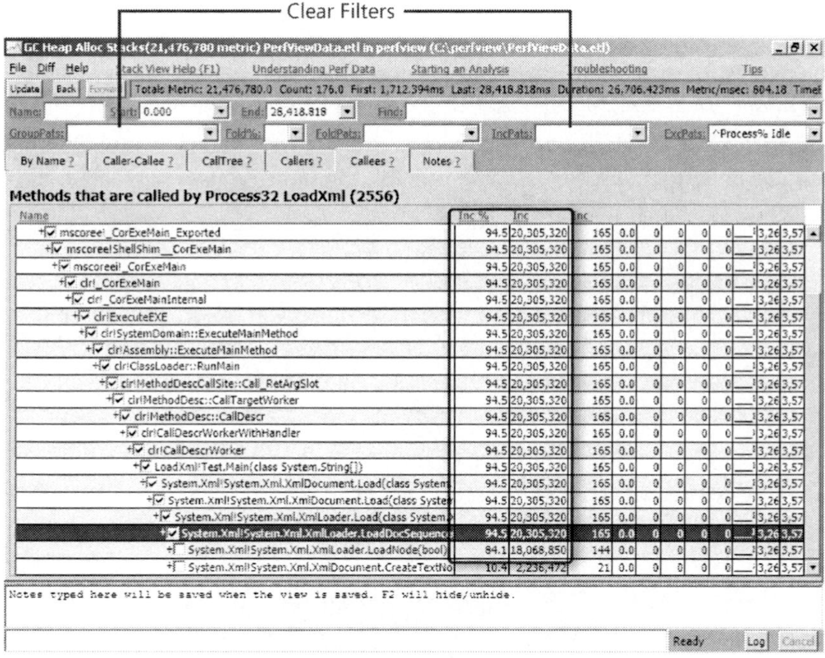

FIGURE 13-26 GC allocations by call stack in PerfView.

In this case, the companion source code contains an alternative implementation based on the *XmlTextReader* class, which is a pure XML reader. Unlike *XmlDocument*, which also supports insertions and deletions from the target XML, *XmlTextReader* doesn't need to build the DOM structure for the target file. This version of the program uses almost no GC heap memory, as shown in Figure 13-27, where PerfView was used again to capture the GCStats information. As a result, no garbage collections were needed, either! Compare this with the four collections (and the several millisecond pauses) in the first version of the program.

```
C:\book\code\chapter_13\GCHeapMemory>LoadXmlWithReader.exe c:\temp\test.xml
```

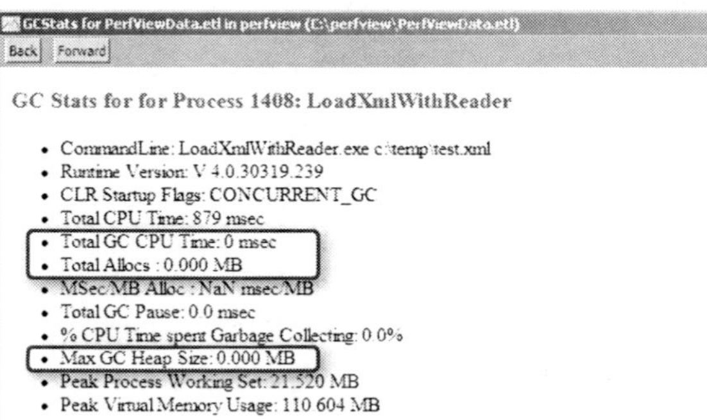

FIGURE 13-27 GC allocations in the alternative implementation based on *XmlTextReader*.

The analysis in this section relied on the GCStats and GC Heap Alloc Stacks views, which show the total allocations over the course of the trace capture. In the previous case, this was enough to diagnose the problem because the size of collected (freed) objects was only a small percentage of the total size of allocations. When you need to look at a stable snapshot of GC heap memory, you can choose the Take Heap Snapshot item from the Memory menu in the PerfView tool. Alternatively, you can also use the SOS debugging extension to accomplish the same goal, as detailed in the next section.

Analyzing GC Heap Memory Using SOS

If you don't mind freezing the target process for inspection, you can attach a debugger and use the SOS extension to inspect the objects in the GC heap. For example, you can start by running the sample C# program used earlier, which loads the XML document and blocks while waiting for additional user input.

```
c:\book\code\chapter_13\GCHeapMemory>LoadXml.exe c:\temp\test.xml
XML document load took 218 milliseconds
Enter any key to continue...
```

While the program is still stopped, you can attach the WinDbg debugger (using the F6 shortcut) and use the *!eeheap* command to dump general statistics for the GC heap in the target process, as illustrated in the following listing.

```
0:004> .symfix
0:004> .reload
0:004> .loadby sos clr
0:004> !eeheap -gc
Number of GC Heaps: 1
generation 0 starts at 0x0402100c
generation 1 starts at 0x04021000
generation 2 starts at 0x01a71000
ephemeral segment allocation context: none
 segment     begin allocated  size
01a70000  01a71000  02971054  0xf00054(15728724)
04020000  04021000  041d1ff4  0x1b0ff4(1773556)
Large object heap starts at 0x02a71000
 segment     begin allocated  size
02a70000  02a71000  02c35300  0x1c4300(1852160)
...
GC Heap Size:              Size: 0x1275348 (19354440) bytes.
```

Notice that the previous command shows where each generation on the GC heap starts as well as the total size of the GC heap at the time of the break-in. You can also obtain a summary view of all the object types on the GC heap by using the *!dumpheap* command with the *–stat* option, as shown in the following listing. Note this command is rarely useful without the *–stat* option because the output from it is too verbose otherwise and lists every object on the GC heap.

```
0:004> !dumpheap -stat
total 0 objects
Statistics:
      MT    Count    TotalSize Class Name
```

```
5c1b6524        1          12 System.Nullable'1[[System.Boolean, mscorlib]]
5c1b5938        1          1
System.Collections.Generic.ObjectEqualityComparer'1[[System.Type, mscorlib]]
...
5c166ba8       38     1075004 System.Object[]
597304fc   100000     2000000 System.Xml.XmlText
59730cfc   100022     2000440 System.Xml.NameTable+Entry
59729b44   100001     2800028 System.Xml.XmlElement
597303f0   100001     3600036 System.Xml.XmlName
5claf92c   200606     6772820 System.String
Total 600936 objects
```

Notice, in particular, the large size (over 3 MB) occupied by objects of type *XmlName* (element names), as well as an inordinate number of string objects (over 200,000!). That high number, however, is consistent with the number of name/value pairs that were emitted to the large XML file created at the beginning of this experiment (100,000 name/value rows).

Like other debugger-based techniques, this provides only a snapshot of the GC memory usage in the process as opposed to the aggregate views provided by tracing tools. However, this can be useful when you've already used a tracing method to locate the memory-usage anomalies—in which case, the use of a debugger can give you control over the target for a more thorough investigation of the live objects on the GC heap. Using this method, you can also find the references (roots) that are keeping those objects alive. This can be particularly useful when tracking down GC heap "leak" scenarios, where objects aren't truly leaked as can happen in native programs, but they are instead kept away from the reach of garbage collections due to long-lived roots.

As an illustration, you can use the *!gcroot* command to verify that most of the objects on the GC heap in this case are kept alive by the *XmlDocument* instance in the *Main* method of the program, which in turn is alive due to its use after the *Console.ReadLine* line when displaying the string name of the first element. If you run *!dumpheap* without the *–stat* option, the command gives you all the objects on the GC heap. In the following listing, the command is interrupted using Debug\Break and a root for one of the displayed objects is tracked back to the *XmlDocument* object created in the *Main* function of the program using the *!gcroot* command.

```
0:004> !dumpheap
...
01df6f98 597304fc       20
01df6fac 5claf92c       32
01df6fcc 59730cfc       20
Command cancelled at the user's request.
0:004> !do 01df6fcc
Name:        System.Xml.NameTable+Entry
MethodTable: 59730cfc
...
0:004> !gcroot 01df6fcc
Scan Thread 0 OSTHread 1080
ESP:1bed88:Root:
  01a78710(System.Xml.XmlDocument)->
  01a78a14(System.Xml.DomNameTable)->
  01a787b8(System.Xml.NameTable)->
  02b352d0(System.Object[])->
  01df6fcc(System.Xml.NameTable+Entry)
```

Table 13-3 recaps the useful SOS GC heap inspection commands described in this section.

TABLE 13-3 GC Heap Memory Inspection Commands in the SOS Extension

Command	Description
!eeheap –gc	Dump high-level GC heap memory statistics, including the start and end of each generation segment on the heap and the total size of the GC heap.
!dumpheap –stat	Dump a summary of the type of objects that are currently present on the GC heap and the number of objects from each type.
!gcroot <object_address>	Look up the list of roots for an object on the GC heap. This command is useful in managed memory "leak" investigations where objects are kept alive on the GC heap by other roots, unnecessarily increasing the overall size of the GC heap.

Tracing as a Debugging Aid

In addition to being a critical component in performance analysis, tracing can also be used to complement the debuggers when investigating program anomalies or studying system internals. Although the debuggers allow you to zoom in and accurately analyze snapshots of the state of the system (when using kernel-mode debugging) or of a given user-mode process (when using user-mode debugging), they don't give you a temporal view of what led to the state described in the snapshot. A common problem while developing interactive applications, for example, is perceived sluggishness when the main UI thread appears to freeze sporadically, only to snap back to life before you have a chance to attach a debugger. This is a great example of when the timelines provided by tracing prove more effective than the static views offered by the debuggers.

The second issue with using the debuggers is that you might not know which code paths and function calls are invoked when running the scenario you're interested in. Without that preliminary knowledge, it can be difficult to set effective breakpoints and analyze the behavior under a debugger. In those cases, it's useful to start by capturing an ETW trace to get a first-order approximation of where the time is spent (for example, by using the CSWITCH or PROFILE events, along with the corresponding stack traces) before running the experiment again under the control of a debugger so that you can more invasively inspect snapshots of the scenario over its lifetime.

Finally, there are also bugs that don't reproduce when the same scenario is executed under the control of a debugger. Tracing is less invasive by nature and can sometimes allow you to investigate these issues more efficiently. The first example in this section provides a practical illustration of this situation.

Tracing Error Code Failures

In theory, you could trace the call site of any failure if you instrument the exit of every function in your code base with a custom ETW event that logs its return code. Fortunately, though, you won't need to go that far to take advantage of ETW in your debugging investigations because you can often use the existing ETW instrumentation in the OS.

For example, you can use the CSWITCH and PROFILE events (and their corresponding stack-trace events) to get a detailed account of the threads that ran during the trace session, which can allow you to narrow down the code paths that the traced program took during its execution and derive the call site where the scenario might have failed. In the case of Win32 APIs, you can also use the SYSCALL events, which get logged whenever a system call is made on the system, to help you pinpoint failures that happen on the kernel side of Win32 API calls without using a debugger. You should remember, however, that the SYSCALL kernel provider generates events at a very high rate, so you should not enable it for more than a few seconds at most or your trace will become very large.

Why Trace When You Can Debug?

Chapter 7, "Expert Debugging Tricks," showed a neat trick for debugging low-level failures in Win32 APIs by using the internal *ntdll!g_dwLastErrorToBreakOn* variable. However, that technique requires you to have a debugger attached to the failing process so that you can edit the value of that global variable in memory. In some cases, though, the mere presence of a user-mode debugger can alter the execution environment of the target process, leading up to different results from when the scenario is run outside of the debugger.

An example of this situation was provided back in Chapter 5, "Beyond the Basics," where the NT global flag value was automatically adjusted by the system for processes started under a user-mode debugger to enable the debug heap settings, making memory corruption bugs more likely to happen when running under the control of a user-mode debugger. In that particular case, the debugger changes the behavior for the better, so to speak, and helps surface bugs that might otherwise be harder to reproduce outside of it. The reverse situation is also possible, though, and bugs that happen outside of the debugger might sometimes (only in rare cases, fortunately!) stop reproducing as soon as you run the target with a debugger attached.

To provide a concrete example, consider the following C++ program from the companion source code, which tries to emulate the functionality of the *kill.exe* utility from the Windows debuggers package and forcibly terminate running processes on the system (identified by their process ID).

```
//
// C:\book\code\chapter_13\Kill>kill.cpp
//
static
HRESULT
KillProcess(
    __in DWORD dwProcessId
    )
{
    CHandle shProcess;

    ChkProlog();
```

```
    shProcess.Attach(::OpenProcess(
        PROCESS_TERMINATE,
        FALSE,
        dwProcessId
        ));
    ChkWin32(shProcess);

    ChkWin32(::TerminateProcess(shProcess, 0));

    ChkNoCleanup();
}
```

You can use the previous C++ program to terminate any process that's running under the same user identity, but you'll also notice that you can't kill Windows service processes using the same program, even when executed from an elevated administrative command prompt. To see this in action, use an elevated administrative command prompt and start the trusted installer service, for example, which is used when delivering Microsoft Windows updates to your machine and runs as a *LocalSystem* service (highest privileges on the system).

```
net start trustedinstaller
tlist.exe -p trustedinstaller
708
```

Trying to kill this new instance of the trusted installer service fails when you use the sample C++ program shown earlier, as demonstrated in the following command, which uses the PID obtained in the previous listing.

Warning The process ID (PID) you'll see will be different in each run of the experiment, so make sure you use the one you obtain in the previous step so that you don't end up killing a critical process on your system.

```
C:\book\code\chapter_13\Kill\objfre_win7_x86\i386\kill.exe 708
HRESULT: 0x80070005
```

The returned HRESULT (*0x8007005*) is the Win32 "access denied" error code, which usually indicates a failed access check. If you run the program under a user-mode debugger to try to debug the failure's call site, however, you'll see that the behavior no longer reproduces and that the trusted installer service process is now terminated without errors!

```
0:000> vercommand
command line: '"c:\Program Files\Debugging Tools for Windows (x86)\windbg.exe"
c:\book\code\chapter_13\Kill\objfre_win7_x86\i386\kill.exe 708'
0:000> $ Run the target process to completion
0:000> g
0:000> $ Terminate the session
0:000> q
```

You can confirm that the trusted installer process has vanished after this run, as indicated by the *tlist.exe* tool, which displays a process ID (PID) value of *–1* when no instances of the specified process name are found on the system.

```
tlist.exe -p trustedinstaller
-1
```

The reason behind this surprising behavior is that terminating a service process requires the *SeDebugPrivilege* security privilege. Though members of the built-in Administrators group possess this privilege, it's not enabled in their access tokens by default. As mentioned in Chapter 3, "How Windows Debuggers Work," the Windows user-mode debuggers enable that privilege (when available in the user security context) so that they can freely open and debug processes running with different user identities. As an unintended side effect, however, the target process in the previous experiment, which was started as a child of the debugger process, inherited the same access token, including the enabled debug privilege! This explains why the observed behavior couldn't be reproduced under the control of the user-mode debugger.

One way to avoid this interference is to attach the user-mode debugger after the target has been started. Another approach to obtain the call stack of the failure is to use ETW tracing to noninvasively trace the behavior of the program, as shown in the next section.

Note If you use the *Process* class of the *System.Diagnostics* .NET namespace to try to kill a process running under a different user identity from an elevated administrative command prompt, you'll be pleasantly surprised to see that the code succeeds in that case:

```
C:\book\code\chapter_13\KillManaged>net start trustedinstaller
C:\book\code\chapter_13\KillManaged>kill.exe trustedinstaller
```

The reason is this .NET class automatically takes care of enabling the *SeDebugPrivilege* privilege for the current process (when the user possesses that privilege). So, an administrator running with full elevated privileges is able to use the previous program to terminate processes belonging to any user on the machine, just like when using the native *kill.exe* utility that comes with the Windows debuggers package.

Tracing System Call Failures

Given their noninvasive nature, you can also use ETW and Xperf to debug the previous example once you find that attaching a user-mode debugger alters the observed behavior. To do so, you can start a tracing session and enable the SYSCALL kernel flag and the SyscallExit stack-walk option so that a stack-trace event is logged at the exit (return) from each system call made during the trace session. The following listing, which you need to execute from an elevated administrative command prompt, illustrates this sequence of commands.

```
net start trustedinstaller
tlist.exe -p trustedinstaller
4328
```

```
C:\book\code\common\scripts\start_kernel_trace.cmd -kf SYSCALL -ks SyscallExit
INFO: Invoking xperf to start the session...
CmdLine: (xperf.exe -on PROC_THREAD+LOADER+SYSCALL -stackwalk SyscallExit)

---- Execute the kill.exe test program ----
C:\book\code\chapter_13\Kill\objfre_win7_x86\i386\kill.exe 4328
HRESULT: 0x80070005

C:\book\code\common\scripts\stop_kernel_trace.cmd
INFO: Invoking xperf to stop the session...
CmdLine: (xperf.exe -stop -d c:\temp\merged.etl)
```

You can now view the resulting ETW trace log file using the Xperf viewer UI. The SYSCALL provider is not used frequently and doesn't have a dedicated graph, so its associated stack traces will only be in the Stack Counts By Type graph. The summary table for that graph shows you all the system calls made in every process during the trace session.

When you expand the call stacks from the *kill.exe* process context, you'll notice that the system call for the *TerminateProcess* Win32 API was never attempted by *MainHR*. You also see that *OpenProcess* was invoked by the *MainHR* function, as shown in Figure 13-28. This essentially tracks the source of the "access denied" failure back to the *OpenProcess* Win32 API, which must have returned that error.

```
C:\book\code\common\scripts\view_trace.cmd -sympath
C:\book\code\chapter_13\kill\objfre_win7_x86\i386
...
INFO: Invoking xperf to view the trace...
CmdLine: (xperf.exe c:\temp\merged.etl)
```

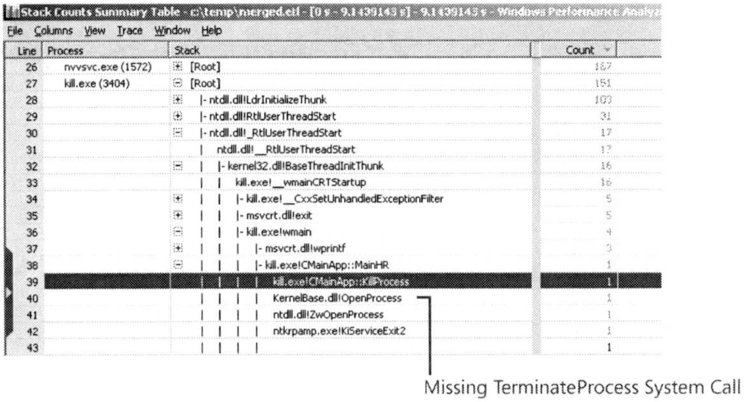

Missing TerminateProcess System Call

FIGURE 13-28 System call stack traces in the Xperf viewer UI.

Tracing System Internals

ETW tracing can also be used as an effective complement to debuggers when it comes to studying the internals of system features and components. The process and loader kernel events, in particular, are invaluable when studying system internals because they allow you to gain a macro-level understanding of the components involved in the scenario you're tracing. This section demonstrates this approach by showing a practical application of ETW tracing for dissecting the internals of the UAC elevation sequence in Windows Vista and later.

Devising an Exploration Strategy

In Windows Vista, Microsoft introduced UAC to solve the problem of users too often running with full administrative privileges even when performing mundane tasks, such as browsing the Internet, which did not require those powerful privileges. This is in line with the overall security philosophy Microsoft has been diligently following and recommending to the industry in the past decade or so, which preaches among other things the concepts of "defense-in-depth" and running with the "least privileges" possible.

UAC enables users to run as administrators or, better yet, regular users and elevate to a full administrative access token only when an application needs to perform administrative tasks. One of the main benefits of UAC is that it forces all Windows developers to think about security when designing, writing, and testing their applications. Too often in the past (Windows XP and earlier), sloppy applications were released without proper testing in "regular user" scenarios, forcing their end users to run as administrators and putting them at higher risk of Internet viruses that could take advantage of those administrative privileges to cause greater damage.

You can reasonably suspect that a process with high-enough privileges needs to be involved at some point during the UAC elevation sequence to securely *broker* the transition from the lower integrity level (Medium) of the Windows shell process (*explorer.exe*) to the greater integrity level (High) of the new elevated *cmd.exe* command-prompt process. Chapter 9, "Common Debugging Scenarios, Part 2," had a good introduction to integrity levels and their role in the Windows security model, so be sure to read it if you want a reminder of how UAC and integrity levels relate to each other.

Fortunately, the system has built-in ETW instrumentation (enabled using the PROC_THREAD kernel flag) that allows you to see the creation call stack for every new process that gets started during the trace session. This is generally the first step in all system-tracing explorations. A common strategy for observing system internals is to enable providers progressively as you gain more knowledge of the internals of the scenario and need more events to confirm the hypotheses you form about how the scenario works. The following approach is fairly common:

- Enable the PROC_THREAD and LOADER kernel flags so that you can observe process, thread, and image load information during the trace capture.
- Enable the CSWITCH and PROFILE kernel flags so that you can observe the threads that ran on each core on the system during the trace session, as well as a sampling of what they spent their CPU time doing.
- The previous two steps provide you with a good approximation of what code paths were taken by each process in the trace session. You can also choose to observe the scenario while enabling more providers. For example, you can enable the Remote Procedure Call (RPC) or TCP/IP user providers if you want to observe communication patterns in your scenario. You can also use the REGISTRY and FILE_IO_* kernel flags if you want to more closely observe registry and file I/O accesses, and so on.

Observing the Scenario Using Kernel ETW Events

By following the aforementioned strategy, you can start an ETW trace session and enable the PROC_THREAD, LOADER, PROFILE, and CSWITCH kernel providers, as shown in the following command. Several stack-walk options are also enabled so that key stack traces from the scenario are also logged into the trace.

```
C:\book\code\common\scripts\start_kernel_trace.cmd -kf CSWITCH+PROFILE -ks
ProcessCreate+CSwitch+Profile
INFO: Invoking xperf to start the session...
CmdLine: (xperf.exe -on PROC_THREAD+LOADER+CSWITCH+PROFILE -stackwalk
ProcessCreate+CSwitch+Profile)
```

After starting the previous session, request UAC elevation by right-clicking the command-prompt Start menu item and selecting Run As Administrator, as illustrated in Figure 13-29.

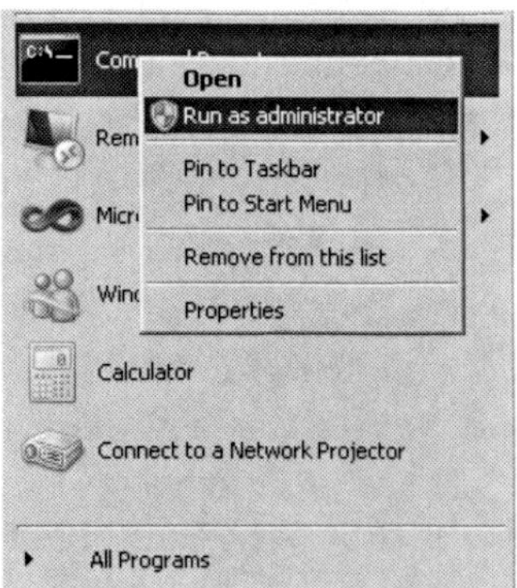

FIGURE 13-29 Starting the UAC elevation sequence for *cmd.exe*.

After you consent to the elevation request and the new *cmd.exe* process is finally created, you can stop the ETW trace session and merge the trace, as usual.

```
C:\book\code\common\scripts\stop_kernel_trace.cmd
INFO: Invoking xperf to stop the session...
CmdLine: (xperf.exe -stop -d c:\temp\merged.etl)
```

You can now analyze the events captured in the previous trace using the Xperf viewer UI. You'll notice under the Process Lifetimes graph an interesting process, named *consent.exe*, that seems to run for a few seconds and exit just before the new *cmd.exe* process instance is created, as shown in Figure 13-30. This is the owner of the UI dialog box that asks you to consent to the UAC elevation request before creating the elevated instance of the target process.

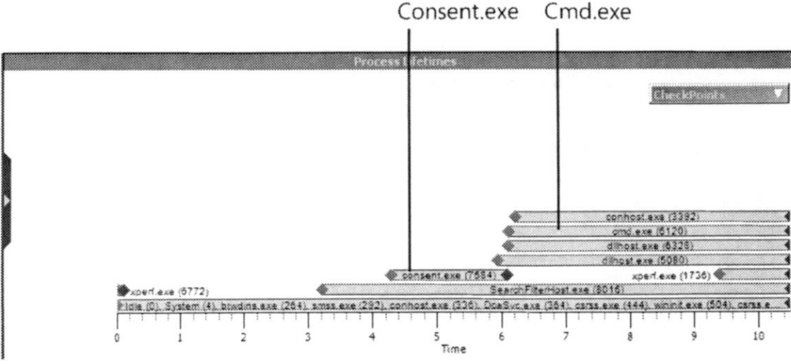

FIGURE 13-30 Process lifetimes during the trace session.

The creation call stack for the *consent.exe* process instance, captured in the trace thanks to the ProcessCreate stack-walk option that was used when the NT Kernel Logger session was started, represents an interesting checkpoint during the UAC elevation sequence. Specifically, it reveals that the *consent.exe* process is created by a service called *AppInfo* (*AppInfo!RAiLaunchAdminProcess*). This is shown in Figure 13-31, which depicts the summary table of the previous Process Lifetimes graph.

AppInfo Service

Processes Summary Table - c:\temp\merged.etl - [0 s - 10.4960495 s] - 10.4960495 s - Windows Performance Analyzer

File Columns View Trace Window Help

Line	Process	Parent Process ID	Creation Stack	Start Time (s)
17	consent.exe (7584)	1,124	[Root]	4.286 785 955
18			ntdll.dll!_RtlUserThreadStart	4.286 785 955
19			ntdll.dll!__RtlUserThreadStart	4.286 785 955
20			kernel32.dll!BaseThreadInitThunk	4.286 785 955
21			ntdll.dll!TppWorkerThread	4.286 785 955
22			ntdll.dll!TppAlpcpExecuteCallback	4.286 785 955
23			rpcrt4.dll!LrpcIoComplete	4.286 785 955
24			rpcrt4.dll!LrpcServerIoHandler	4.286 785 955
25			rpcrt4.dll!LRPC_ADDRESS::ProcessIO	4.286 785 955
26			rpcrt4.dll!LRPC_ADDRESS::HandleRequest	4.286 785 955
27			rpcrt4.dll!LRPC_SASSOCIATION::HandleRequest	4.286 785 955
28			rpcrt4.dll!LRPC_SCALL::HandleRequest	4.286 785 955
29			rpcrt4.dll!LRPC_SCALL::QueueOrDispatchCall	4.286 785 955
30			rpcrt4.dll!LRPC_SCALL::DispatchRequest	4.286 785 955
31			rpcrt4.dll!RPC_INTERFACE::DispatchToStubWithObj...	4.286 785 955
32			rpcrt4.dll!RPC_INTERFACE::DispatchToStub	4.286 785 955
33			rpcrt4.dll!RPC_INTERFACE::DispatchToStubWorker	4.286 785 955
34			rpcrt4.dll!DispatchToStubInCNoAvrf	4.286 785 955
35			rpcrt4.dll!NdrAsyncServerCall	4.286 785 955
36			rpcrt4.dll!Invoke	4.286 785 955
37			appinfo.dll!RAiLaunchAdminProcess	4.286 785 955
38			appinfo.dll!AiCheckLUA	4.286 785 955
39			appinfo.dll!AiLaunchConsentUI	4.286 785 955
40			appinfo.dll!AiLaunchProcess	4.286 785 955
41			kernel32.dll!CreateProcessAsUserW	4.286 785 955
42			kernel32.dll!CreateProcessInternalW	4.286 785 955
43			ntdll.dll!ZwCreateUserProcess	4.286 785 955

Total Number of Processes - 101

FIGURE 13-31 Creation call stack for *consent.exe* in the Process Lifetimes Xperf summary table.

The previous call stack was logged in the context of the creator (parent) process, whose process ID (PID) is also included in the ProcessCreate ETW event payload. In the case of this experiment, the value of that PID was 1,124. Looking at the Services tab from the System Configuration dialog box, this PID can be tracked back to a *svchost.exe* instance hosting the shared *AppInfo* service, as illustrated in Figure 13-32. This explains the call frames from the *appinfo.dll* DLL in the call stack observed in Figure 13-31.

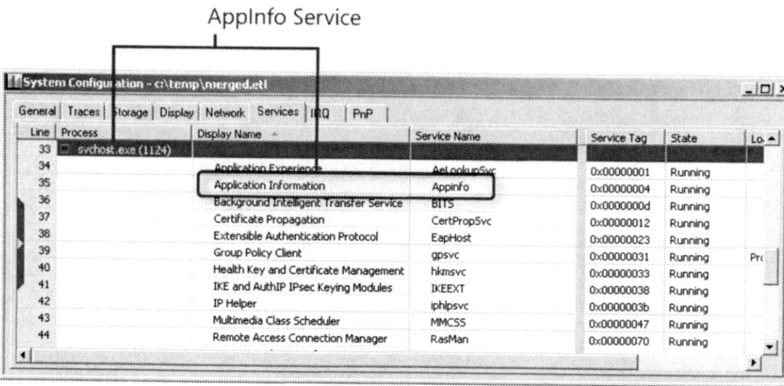

FIGURE 13-32 The *AppInfo* (application information) Windows service.

The *AppInfo* service runs under the powerful *LocalSystem* account and is the *broker* agent in the UAC elevation sequence. Because of its *LocalSystem* privileges, this service can start processes with any integrity level, provided of course that the user consents to the elevation request. As it turns out, this service not only creates *consent.exe* but also the elevated *cmd.exe* process at the end of the UAC elevation sequence.

Now that you have this high-level understanding, you can expand your analysis by using the CSWITCH and PROFILE events logged in the previous session and determine what the *AppInfo!RAiLaunchAdminProcess* function did in between the call to create *consent.exe* and the call it made later to create *cmd.exe*. These stack-trace events are shown in the Stack Counts By Type summary table, as illustrated in Figure 13-33.

Stack Counts Summary Table - c:\temp\merged.etl - [0 s - 10.4960495 s] - 10.4960495 s - Windows Performance Analyzer

File Columns View Trace Window Help

Line	Process	Stack	Count
62	svchost.exe (1124)	[Root]	1,875
63		|- ntdll.dll!_RtlUserThreadStart	1,819
64		ntdll.dll!__RtlUserThreadStart	1,819
65		kernel32.dll!BaseThreadInitThunk	1,819
66		|- ntdll.dll!TppWorkerThread	1,393
67		|- ntdll.dll!TppAlpcpExecuteCallback	660
68		|- rpcrt4.dll!LrpcIoComplete	659
69		|- rpcrt4.dll!LrpcServerIoHandler	604
70		rpcrt4.dll!LRPC_ADDRESS::ProcessIO	604
71		|- rpcrt4.dll!LRPC_ADDRESS::HandleRequest	594
72		rpcrt4.dll!LRPC_SASSOCIATION::HandleRequest	594
73		rpcrt4.dll!LRPC_SCALL::HandleRequest	594
74		|- rpcrt4.dll!LRPC_SCALL::SendReply	444
75		|- rpcrt4.dll!LRPC_SCALL::QueueOrDispatchCall	137
76		rpcrt4.dll!LRPC_SCALL::DispatchRequest	137
77		|- rpcrt4.dll!RPC_INTERFACE::DispatchToStubWithObject	91
78		rpcrt4.dll!RPC_INTERFACE::DispatchToStub	91
79		rpcrt4.dll!RPC_INTERFACE::DispatchToStubWorker	91
80		rpcrt4.dll!DispatchToStubInCNoAvrf	91
81		|- rpcrt4.dll!NdrAsyncServerCall	52
82		rpcrt4.dll!Invoke	52
83		|- appinfo.dll!RAiLaunchAdminProcess	51
84		|- appinfo.dll!AiLaunchProcess	24
85		|- appinfo.dll!AiCheckLUA	12
86		|- appinfo.dll!AiIsEXESafeToAutoApprove	8
87		|- kernel32.dll!CheckElevation	4
88		|- appinfo.dll!AiCheckSecureApplicationDirectory	2

Total Number of Events with Stacks - 45195

FIGURE 13-33 CSwitch and Profile stack-walk events logged during the trace session.

First, *AppInfo!AiIsEXESafeToAutoApprove* is invoked to determine whether the process has asked for auto-approval without a consent UI, as shown in the following call stack.

```
---- stack traces going from caller to callee, per the Xperf convention ----
...
appinfo.dll!RAiLaunchAdminProcess
appinfo.dll!AiIsEXESafeToAutoApprove
appinfo.dll!AipCheckFusion
kernel32.dll!CreateActCtxW
KernelBase.dll!MapViewOfFile
...
```

One of the important UAC changes in Windows 7 was the introduction of a list of safe Microsoft-signed system binaries that are able to auto-elevate without an additional UAC consent prompt. The number of UAC prompts that users (including administrators!) were seeing was painfully high in Windows Vista and auto-elevation was introduced to help address this issue for administrators. (Standard users, naturally, still see the elevation dialog box when required.) Several Microsoft-signed processes in the *system32* directory, such as the task manager (*taskmgr.exe*) process, request auto-elevation in their manifest (the RT_MANIFEST resource stored as a resource in the binary's image), but not *cmd.exe*, so the previous check fails.

The *AppInfo!RAiLaunchAdminProcess* function then proceeds to create the consent UI process, as seen in the following call stack, which is also obtained from the previous Stack Counts By Type summary table.

```
---- stack traces going from caller to callee, per the Xperf convention ----
...
appinfo.dll!RAiLaunchAdminProcess
appinfo.dll!AiCheckLUA
appinfo.dll!AiLaunchConsentUI
appinfo.dll!AiLaunchProcess
kernel32.dll!CreateProcessAsUserW
...
```

After the user consents to the elevation, *AppInfo!RAiLaunchAdminProcess* finally creates the elevated *cmd.exe*.

Observing the Scenario Using User ETW Events

The *AppInfo!RAiLaunchAdminProcess* process-creation call stack shown in the previous section seems to be the result (server side) of a Remote Procedure Call (RPC).

```
---- stack traces going from caller to callee, per the Xperf convention ----
...
ntdll.dll!TppWorkerThread
ntdll.dll!TppAlpcpExecuteCallback
rpcrt4.dll!LrpcIoComplete
rpcrt4.dll!LrpcServerIoHandler
rpcrt4.dll!LRPC_ADDRESS::ProcessIO
rpcrt4.dll!LRPC_ADDRESS::HandleRequest...
rpcrt4.dll!NdrAsyncServerCall
rpcrt4.dll!Invoke
```

```
appinfo.dll!RAiLaunchAdminProcess
appinfo.dll!AiLaunchProcess
kernel32.dll!CreateProcessAsUserW
kernel32.dll!CreateProcessInternalW
ntdll.dll!ZwCreateUserProcess
...
```

Using the previous ETW trace session, you were able to determine the key function calls that were made after this checkpoint and before the new elevated command prompt process was finally created. The only remaining piece of the puzzle is to determine what happened prior to this checkpoint and, more specifically, the client side of this RPC communication. One way to do so is to capture another ETW trace for the UAC elevation sequence, but this time also enable the RPC user provider, as illustrated in the following sequence of commands.

```
C:\book\code\common\scripts>start_user_trace.cmd -kf CSWITCH+PROFILE -ks
ProcessCreate+CSwitch+Profile -up Microsoft-Windows-RPC:::'stack'

---- Launch a new elevated cmd.exe process instance ----

C:\book\code\common\scripts>stop_user_trace.cmd
```

By looking at the RPC events logged in the time interval around the creation time of the *consent.exe* process, you can discover the client side of the RPC communication. This is demonstrated in Figure 13-34, which selects the RPC client calls in the Generic Events graph using a time interval centered on the *consent.exe* process creation event.

```
C:\book\code\common\scripts>view_trace.cmd
```

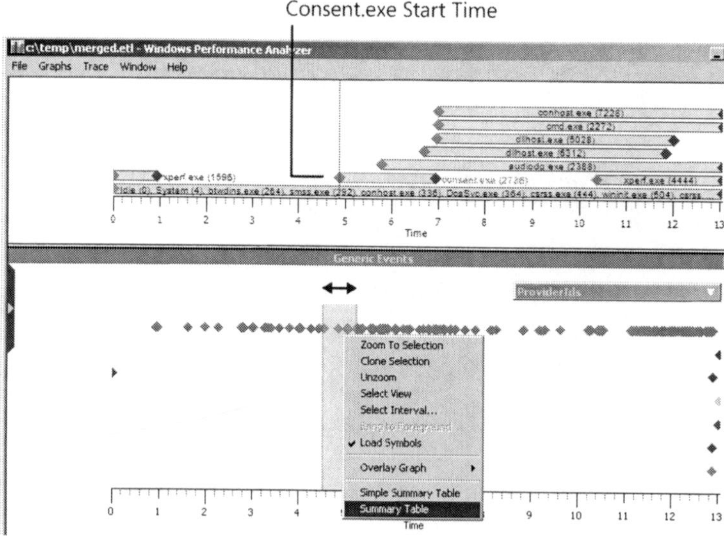

FIGURE 13-34 Viewing the RPC events using the Generic Events graph and its summary table.

As you see in Figure 13-35, which shows the summary table opened in the previous step, the RPC request to the *AppInfo* service is initiated from the Windows shell process (*explorer.exe*), which is as expected given that's where the UAC elevation operation is started.

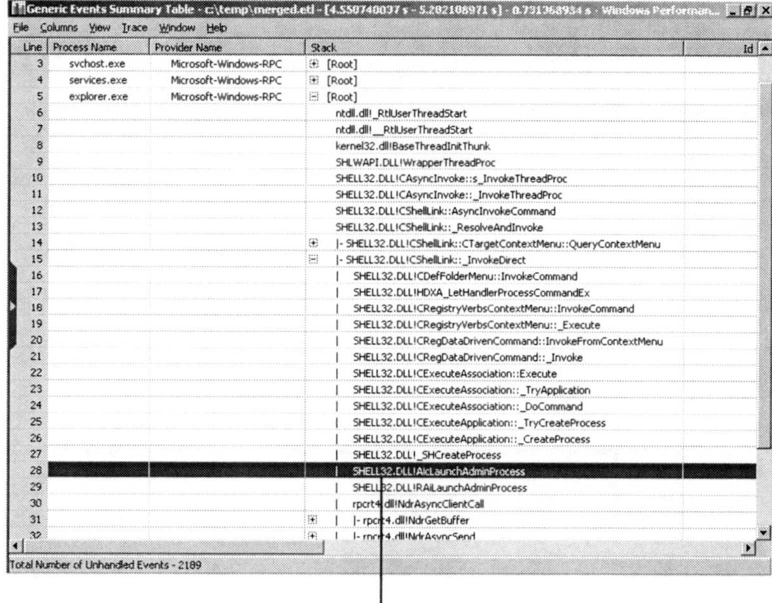

FIGURE 13-35 The RPC client call from *explorer.exe* to the *AppInfo* service.

The *shell32!AicLaunchAdminProcess* function is invoked by the *explorer.exe* process as the client side of the *appinfo!RAiLaunchAdminProcess* remote procedure call. This thread, in turn, is created to complete the *shell32!ShellExecuteW* function call that the Windows shell process invokes when you right-click the Run As Administrator menu action and initiate a UAC elevation sequence.

Figure 13-36 summarizes the architecture described in this case study example, from the time *ShellExecute* is invoked in the shell explorer process (step 1 in this diagram) to when the new command-prompt process instance is created by the *AppInfo* broker service with the High integrity level (step 4), after asking the user to consent to the UAC elevation request (steps 2 and 3).

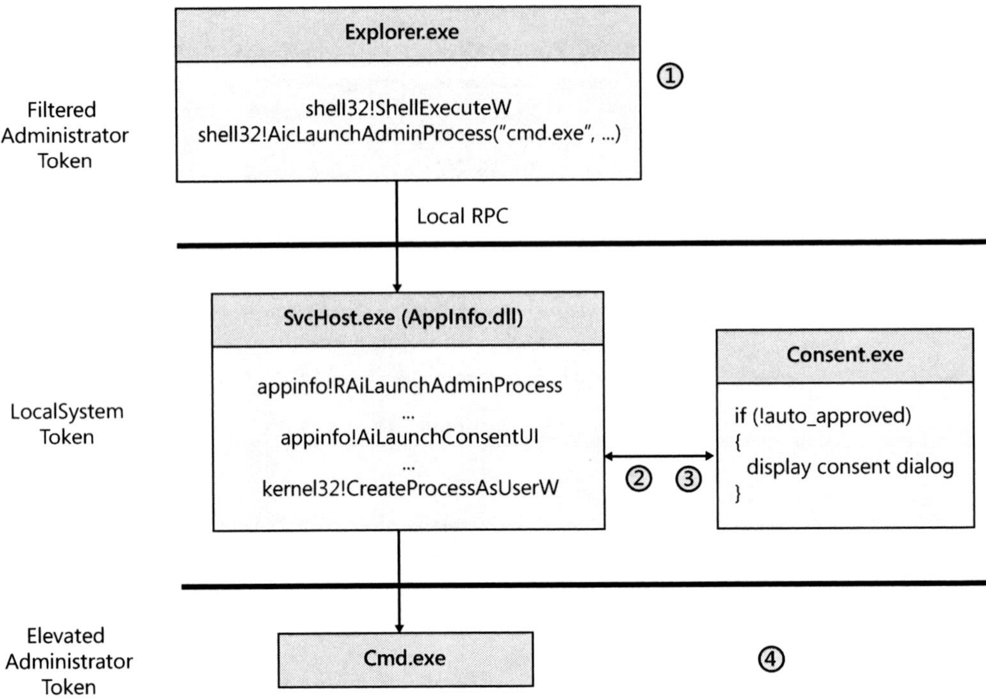

FIGURE 13-36 UAC elevation sequence in Windows Vista and later.

Summary

This chapter covered several common tracing needs and demonstrated a few techniques to investigate them. Using the most appropriate tool for the task you want to accomplish is often a key ingredient to efficient and successful investigations, which is why the list of tools presented in this chapter was kept deliberately short, with only the best tools for each task making the cut. As it turns out, the tracing tools used in this chapter were all ETW-based (except VMMap), with each trying to strike a balance between ease of use and the ability to still support advanced tracing needs.

Before closing this chapter, I would like to leave you with a few recommendations to help you pick the right tool or tools for each scenario:

- Performance delays don't come labeled with what caused them, so you need to start your investigation by looking at resource (CPU and disk, generally speaking) utilization. Xperf gets the nod for disk I/O investigations because it has dedicated graphs that allow you to see both file-level and disk-level activity with a high degree of accuracy.
- If it turns out that your scenario is CPU-bound, CPU sample profiling will help you pinpoint the call sites of the bottlenecks. This is supported well by both the Xperf and PerfView tools, though you should use PerfView if you're tracing managed (.NET) code.

- If the execution delay is due to interthread dependencies instead of active CPU usage, you must then conduct a "blocked time" investigation. The Parallel Performance Analyzer (PPA) in Visual Studio 2010 probably has the most convenient visualization user interface to help you see when threads get blocked and what they were waiting on. However, the PPA is really targeted at concurrency analysis within the same process. It also requires Visual Studio, which virtually excludes it from consideration in live server investigations. For cross-process dependencies or in-production tracing, you can use either Xperf or PerfView, with PerfView again getting the nod for .NET investigations.
- Memory analysis is one of the less-understood areas of performance analysis, which also means it often gets neglected by developers until serious performance problems surface under heavy load. VMMap has a unique ability that other tools don't, which allows you to easily see the breakdown of memory usage (by heaps, stacks, and images) within a process. Once you've used VMMap to narrow down the memory usage problem to being a native or managed heap problem, for example, you can then use Xperf for NT heap analysis and PerfView for GC heap analysis. PerfView has no support for NT heap analysis as of the writing of this book, and Xperf in the Windows 7 SDK has no managed code integration, either.
- Xperf can also be used to help you track down NT heap memory leaks, which are just extreme cases of wasteful NT heap memory usage. The graphs provided in Xperf often make this method more convenient to use than the command-line UMDH tool covered in Chapter 8.
- PerfView can also be used for GC heap "leak" investigations, where you can use its ability to capture a dump of the GC heap from a target (running) process for analyzing the managed objects on the heap. Though managed memory doesn't get leaked per se, a common problem in long-lived .NET programs is objects that are kept alive on the GC heap due to references from other live roots. The SOS debugger extension can also be used for this purpose and works very well for this particular task, though it lacks the visualization and grouping features of the PerfView UI.
- Finally, Xperf—and the Windows Performance Recorder (WPR) and Windows Performance Analyzer (WPA) tools that succeed it in Windows 8—remains the tool of choice for system-level tracing. Like the Windows debuggers package, the Windows Performance Toolkit is also used internally by the Windows group at Microsoft during the development of the OS, so it often takes advantage of the most recent additions to the ETW framework. Similarly, PerfView is used internally by the .NET group at Microsoft, so it's likely to remain the tracing tool of choice for managed code in production environments.

APPENDIX A

WinDbg User-Mode Debugging Quick Start

This appendix provides a basic overview of the most common user-mode debugging tasks and how to accomplish them using the WinDbg debugger. Note that this isn't meant to be an exhaustive list of debugger commands, but rather a task-centric summary you can use as a reference for jump-starting your user-mode debugging investigations.

Starting a User-Mode Debugging Session

To start a user-mode process directly under the WinDbg debugger, you can provide its path as a parameter on the command line, as shown in the following listing, which starts a new instance of the *notepad.exe* text editor under *windbg.exe*.

```
windbg.exe notepad.exe
...
0:000> $ Display the command line of the windbg.exe debugging session
0:000> vercommand
command line: 'windbg.exe  notepad.exe'
```

Alternatively, you can start debugging an existing user-mode process while it's running by using the F6 shortcut in WinDbg. This operation is known as *attaching* the debugger to the target process.

Fixing the Symbols Path

The fastest way to add the Microsoft public symbols server path to your debugger symbols search path is to use the *.symfix* debugger command. Once you've done so, you can ask the debugger to look up the symbols using the new path and reload them by using the *.reload* command, as shown in the following listing.

```
0:000> .symfix
0:000> $ The current symbols search path now contains the Microsoft public symbols server
0:000> .sympath
Expanded Symbol search path is: cache*;SRV*http://msdl.microsoft.com/download/symbols
0:000> .reload
Reloading current modules....................
```

You can also add other paths to help the debugger locate additional symbols, such as those corresponding to your own binaries, by using the *.sympath+* command.

```
0:000> .sympath+ F:\book\code\chapter_02\HelloWorld\objfre_win7_x86\i386
Expanded Symbol search path is:
cache*;SRV*http://msdl.microsoft.com/download/symbols;F:\book\code\chapter_02\HelloWorld\objfre_
win7_x86\i386
```

Fixing the Sources Path

Although WinDbg will automatically locate the source files from the PDB symbols file if you run your application on the same machine it was compiled on, there are other situations in which the source code will be hosted on a remote machine. In these cases, you need to help the debugger find the source files you are interested in stepping through.

For example, if you build a C++ program that uses the Standard Template Library (STL), you need to explicitly set the source path in the debugger if you want to perform source-level debugging and the program (and STL) sources are saved on a different server. Remember that STL (being a C++ template library) is shipped as a set of implementation headers that get pulled into your binary at compile time, so its source code is readily available for you to step through, provided the debugger knows where to locate it.

```
0:000> vercommand
command line: '"c:\Program Files\Debugging Tools for Windows (x86)\windbg.exe"
c:\book\code\chapter_05\StlSample\objfre_win7_x86\i386\stlsample.exe'
0:000> .srcpath
Source search path is: <empty>
0:000> $ Add the paths to the program and STL code locations to the WinDbg search path
0:000> .srcpath+ \\SourceServer\book\code\chapter_05\stlsample
0:000> .srcpath+ \\SourceServer\ddk\7600.16385.1\inc\api\crt\stl70
...
```

Assuming the sources search path was set up correctly, you can list the source lines when viewing call stacks (*k*), the current source file line (*lsc*), or the code around the address held in the current instruction pointer (*lsa*), as illustrated in the following listing.

```
0:000> k
ChildEBP RetAddr
000df8a0 00ed192c
stlsample!std::basic_string<char,std::char_traits<char>,std::allocator<char>,_STL70>::end
[\\SourceServer\ddk\7600.16385.1\inc\api\crt\stl70\xstring @ 1187]
000df8d8 00ed1982 stlsample!CMainApp::MainHR+0x2c
[\\SourceServer\book\code\chapter_05\stlsample\main.cpp @ 16]
000df8dc 00ed1de0 stlsample!wmain+0x5
[\\SourceServer\book\code\chapter_05\stlsample\main.cpp @ 32]
...
```

```
0:000> lsa .
  1183:         return (_STRING_CONST_ITERATOR(_Myptr()));
  1184:         }
  1185:
  1186:     iterator __CLR_OR_THIS_CALL end()
> 1187:         {    // return iterator for end of mutable sequence
  1188:         return (_STRING_ITERATOR(_Myptr() + _Mysize));
  1189:         }
  1190:
  1191:     const_iterator __CLR_OR_THIS_CALL end() const
  1192:         {    // return iterator for end of nonmutable sequence
0:000> lsc
Current: \\SourceServer\ddk\7600.16385.1\inc\api\crt\stl70\xstring(1193)
```

Displaying the Command Line of the Target Process

The process environment block (PEB) of a user-mode process contains, among other things, its startup command line. As such, the *!peb* debugger extension command can be used to find the command line of the target process in a user-mode debugging session.

```
0:000> vercommand
command line: '"c:\Program Files\Debugging Tools for Windows (x86)\windbg.exe"  notepad.exe'
0:000> .symfix
0:000> .reload
0:000> !peb
PEB at 7ffd5000
    InheritedAddressSpace:    No
    ReadImageFileExecOptions: No
    BeingDebugged:            Yes
    ImageBaseAddress:         00150000
...
    ProcessParameters: 00221710
    WindowTitle:  'C:\Windows\system32\notepad.exe'
    ImageFile:    'C:\Windows\system32\notepad.exe'
    CommandLine:  'notepad.exe'
...
```

Control Flow Commands

You can control the execution of the target process, deciding each time how many instructions you would like the debugger to step over before breaking back. Table A-1 summarizes the most useful ways to do so.

TABLE A-1 Control Flow Commands

Debugger Command	WinDbg Shortcut	Description
p	F10	Step over function calls (source-mode debugging) or instructions (assembly-mode debugging).
pc	None	Step over until the next function call.
t	F11	Step into (trace) function calls (source-mode debugging) or assembly instructions (assembly-mode debugging).
gu	Shift+F11	Step out of (go up) the current function, and return to its caller.
g	F5	Continue execution of the target—let the target g(o).
g [address]	None	A useful variation of the g(o) debugger command that lets the target execute until the instruction at [*address*] is executed.

Listing Loaded Modules and Their Version

It is often useful to list the DLLs loaded by the user-mode target process being debugged. This can be done using the *lm* ("list modules") command.

```
0:000> lm
start    end        module name
00150000 00180000   notepad    (deferred)
73c70000 73cc1000   WINSPOOL   (deferred)
743b0000 7454e000   COMCTL32   (deferred)
74ba0000 74ba9000   VERSION    (deferred)
75ac0000 75b0a000   KERNELBASE   (deferred)
75b60000 75c01000   RPCRT4     (deferred)
75c60000 75dbc000   ole32      (deferred)
75ed0000 75fa4000   kernel32   (deferred)
...
776c0000 777fc000   ntdll      (pdb symbols)          c:\Program Files\Debugging Tools
for Windows (x86)\sym\ntdll.pdb\120028FA453F4CD5A6A404EC37396A582\ntdll.pdb
...
```

To find extended information about a specific module, you can use the *m* option to specify an additional module parameter to the command. Note this module name shouldn't include the *.dll* extension. The correct usage is illustrated in the following listing (the *v* appended to the *lm* command is to request verbose output).

```
0:000> $ Do not include the extension in the module name used with the lm command!
0:000> lmv m ntdll.dll
start    end        module name
0:000> lmv m ntdll
start    end        module name
776c0000 777fc000   ntdll      (pdb symbols)          c:\Program Files\Debugging Tools
for Windows (x86)\sym\ntdll.pdb\120028FA453F4CD5A6A404EC37396A582\ntdll.pdb
    Loaded symbol image file: C:\Windows\SYSTEM32\ntdll.dll
    Image path: ntdll.dll...
    File version:     6.1.7601.17514...
    CompanyName:      Microsoft Corporation
    ProductName:      Microsoft® Windows® Operating System...
```

```
FileVersion:       6.1.7601.17514 (win7sp1_rtm.101119-1850)
FileDescription:   NT Layer DLL
LegalCopyright:    © Microsoft Corporation. All rights reserved.
```

Resolving Function Addresses

When you need to find the address at which a known function or a global variable resides, you can use the *x* command of the *windbg.exe* debugger. This translation is often useful when trying to set code or data breakpoints. For this to work, naturally, the module (DLL or main EXE) that contains the function or global symbol should've already been loaded by the target process. Note that this command also supports the wildcard character (*), which is often convenient for discovering the available symbol (function or global variable) names that match a given pattern.

```
0:000> x notepad!*main*
00151320 notepad!_imp____getmainargs = <no type information>
00151405 notepad!WinMain = <no type information>
00153689 notepad!WinMainCRTStartup = <no type information>
0:000> x notepad!g_*
0015c00c notepad!g_ftOpenedAs = <no type information>
0015e040 notepad!g_ftSaveAs = <no type information>
0015c100 notepad!g_wpOrig = <no type information>
```

Setting Code (Software) Breakpoints

You can set a code breakpoint with the *bp* command, using either the symbolic name or the direct hexadecimal virtual memory address of a function. The *bl* and *bd* commands can subsequently be used to list and disable active code breakpoints, respectively. Disabled breakpoints can be resurrected using the *be* command. When a breakpoint is no longer needed, the *bc* command can be used to remove it permanently from the list of breakpoints maintained by WinDbg.

```
0:000> x notepad!*main*
00581320 notepad!_imp____getmainargs = <no type information>
00581405 notepad!WinMain = <no type information>
00583689 notepad!WinMainCRTStartup = <no type information>
0:000> $ Set a breakpoint using the address of the WinMain function
0:000> bp 0x00581405
0:000> $ Set the same breakpoint using the symbolic name (notepad!WinMain) of the function
0:000> bp notepad!WinMain
breakpoint 0 redefined
0:000> $ Breakpoint #0 (first one) is enabled ("e")
0:000> bl
 0 e 00581405     0001 (0001)  0:**** notepad!WinMain
0:000> bd 0
0:000> $ Breakpoint #0 is now disabled ("d")
0:000> bl
 0 d 00581405     0001 (0001)  0:**** notepad!WinMain
0:000> $ Clear the breakpoint (remove it permanently)
0:000> bc 0
0:000> $ No registered breakpoints exist in the debugging session now
0:000> bl
```

You can also set unresolved breakpoints using the *bu* command. This command can be used if you are trying to set a breakpoint at a function residing in a module that has yet to be loaded or that might get unloaded and later reloaded. With the *bp* command, the breakpoint is lost once the current module is unloaded. With the *bu* command, the breakpoint shifts to an *unresolved* state when the module unloads and automatically becomes active again when the module is reloaded. Even when using the *bu* command, however, it's recommended that you use the *x* command at least once (after the module is loaded) to verify that you're providing the right symbol name for the breakpoint.

A third alternative (*bm*) exists for setting code breakpoints. Unlike *bp* and *bu*, the *bm* command sets breakpoints that match the symbolic name used with the command, so you can use it to set breakpoints in all the overloads of a particular function in one shot. Also, the *bm* command supports regular expressions. This allows you to use the wildcard character, for example, to set multiple breakpoints at once. However, the *bm* command requires private symbols, which means you cannot use it to set breakpoints in system code—only in your own code.

Setting Data (Hardware) Breakpoints

You can set a breakpoint whenever a virtual address is fetched, written to, or executed by the CPU. These types of breakpoints are called *data breakpoints*, and they can be inserted using the *ba* ("break on access") debugger command. For example, the following listing shows how you can set a read data breakpoint ("r") to stop in the debugger whenever the target process reads the NT global flag (4-byte integer) from its PEB. In this example, the *$peb* pseudo-register is used to reference the address of the PEB structure of the current process. For more on pseudo-registers and data breakpoints, see Chapter 5, "Beyond the Basics."

```
0:000> vercommand
command line: '"c:\Program Files\Debugging Tools for Windows (x86)\windbg.exe"  notepad.exe'
0:000> .symfix
0:000> .reload
0:000> $ The NT global flag field is a 4-byte integer at offset +0x068 from the start of the PEB
0:000> dt ntdll!_PEB @$peb NtGlobalFlag
   +0x068 NtGlobalFlag : 0x40470
0:000> ba r4 @$peb+0x068
0:000> g
Breakpoint 0 hit
ntdll!RtlGetNtGlobalFlags+0xc:
0:000> k
ChildEBP RetAddr
0017edf4 778ceb45 ntdll!RtlGetNtGlobalFlags+0xc
0017eecc 778f5ae0 ntdll!RtlpAllocateHeap+0xbec
0017ef50 77965eab ntdll!RtlAllocateHeap+0x23a
0017ef9c 7792a376 ntdll!RtlDebugAllocateHeap+0xb5
0017f080 778f5ae0 ntdll!RtlpAllocateHeap+0xc4
0017f104 779007eb ntdll!RtlAllocateHeap+0x23a
...
```

Notice that this breakpoint is hit a lot of times, mostly in components within the *ntdll.dll* system module, such as the NT heap manager routines. Once you no longer need the data breakpoint, you can disable it in the exact same way that you disable regular code breakpoints by using the *bd* command with the breakpoint number (0, in this case).

```
0:000> bd 0
0:000> g
```

Switching Between Threads

Issuing the ~ command in the user-mode debugger with no additional parameters displays the available threads that are running within the target process.

```
0:001> $ List current threads in the process
0:001> ~
   0  Id: d30.20c Suspend: 1 Teb: 7ffde000 Unfrozen
.  1  Id: d30.17c0 Suspend: 1 Teb: 7ffdd000 Unfrozen
```

You can then switch the current context over to any thread by using its thread number and the *s* suffix of the ~ command, as illustrated in the following listing:

```
0:001> ~0s
0:000> $ Notice the debugger prompt now indicates thread #0 (0:000 instead of 0:001)
```

Displaying Call Stacks

The *k* command can be used to display the call stack of any thread in the target process. By default, the command displays the stack trace of the current thread. You can append the *n* suffix to also get the command to display the frame numbers next to each function on the call stack. For example, the following command shows the call stack (and frame numbers) of the break-in thread after attaching to a running instance of the *notepad.exe* process.

```
0:001> kn
 # ChildEBP RetAddr
00 00ebf924 7775f161 ntdll!DbgBreakPoint
01 00ebf954 75f1ed6c ntdll!DbgUiRemoteBreakin+0x3c
02 00ebf960 777237f5 kernel32!BaseThreadInitThunk+0xe
03 00ebf9a0 777237c8 ntdll!__RtlUserThreadStart+0x70
04 00ebf9b8 00000000 ntdll!_RtlUserThreadStart+0x1b
```

You can also display the stack trace of any thread in the process without having to first switch over to its context. You can do that by prefixing the *k* command with the ~ character and the target thread number.

```
0:001> ~
   0  Id: 7d0.12c0 Suspend: 1 Teb: 7ffdf000 Unfrozen
.  1  Id: 7d0.744 Suspend: 1 Teb: 7ffde000 Unfrozen
0:001> $ Current thread is thread #1. Display the stack trace for thread #0
0:001> ~0k
ChildEBP RetAddr
```

```
000ef8b4 7600cde0 ntdll!KiFastSystemCallRet
000ef8b8 7600ce13 USER32!NtUserGetMessage+0xc
000ef8d4 00fe148a USER32!GetMessageW+0x33
000ef914 00fe16ec notepad!WinMain+0xe6
...
```

You can also use the wildcard character (*) to dump the stack traces of all the threads within the target process at once.

```
0:000> ~*k
.  0  Id: d30.20c Suspend: 1 Teb: 7ffde000 Unfrozen
0013f860 758acde0 ntdll!KiFastSystemCallRet
0013f864 758ace13 USER32!NtUserGetMessage+0xc
0013f880 00ab148a USER32!GetMessageW+0x33
0013f8c0 00ab16ec notepad!WinMain+0xe6
...
#  1  Id: d30.17c0 Suspend: 1 Teb: 7ffdd000 Unfrozen
01a4ff18 7709f161 ntdll!DbgBreakPoint
01a4ff48 757eed6c ntdll!DbgUiRemoteBreakin+0x3c
01a4ff54 770637f5 kernel32!BaseThreadInitThunk+0xe
01a4ff94 770637c8 ntdll!__RtlUserThreadStart+0x70
01a4ffac 00000000 ntdll!_RtlUserThreadStart+0x1b
```

When you have very deep call stacks such as those commonly found in .NET applications, you might need to also explicitly provide a frame count with the *k* command to see the complete call stack if its depth happens to exceed the default size displayed by the WinDbg debugger (20 frames). This use pattern is illustrated in the following listing:

```
0:001> $ Display up to 50 frames from thread #0's call stack
0:001> ~0k 50
ChildEBP RetAddr
000ef8b4 7600cde0 ntdll!KiFastSystemCallRet
000ef8b8 7600ce13 USER32!NtUserGetMessage+0xc
000ef8d4 00fe148a USER32!GetMessageW+0x33
000ef914 00fe16ec notepad!WinMain+0xe6
...
```

Displaying Function Parameters

When debugging your own code, displaying the parameters of functions on the call stack can be done by using the *kP* command. The *P* suffix tells the debugger to also print the values of the parameters to the functions on the call stack.

```
0:000> vercommand
command line: '"c:\Program Files\Debugging Tools for Windows (x86)\windbg.exe"
c:\book\code\chapter_08\RefCountDB\objfre_win7_x86\i386\RefCountDB.exe'
0:000> .symfix
0:000> .reload
0:000> bp RefCountDB!CRefCountDatabase::AddRef
0:000> g
Breakpoint 0 hit
0:000> kP
```

```
ChildEBP RetAddr
0014f718 00c0211a RefCountDB!CRefCountDatabase::AddRef(
    void * pObj = 0x00225478) [c:\book\code\chapter_08\refcountdb\reftracker.h @ 174]
0014f724 00c021a0 RefCountDB!CRefCountDatabase_AddRef(
    void * pObj = 0x00225478)+0x14 [c:\book\code\chapter_08\refcountdb\reftracker.h @ 359]
0014f730 00c02217 RefCountDB!CIUnknownImplT<1>::CIUnknownImplT<1>(void)+0x11
[c:\book\code\chapter_08\refcountdb\reftracker.h @ 39]
0014f738 00c02290 RefCountDB!CRefCountObject::CRefCountObject(void)+0xa
0014f74c 00c022de RefCountDB!CMainApp::MainHR(void)+0x1f
[c:\book\code\chapter_08\refcountdb\main.cpp @ 44]
0014f754 00c0246f RefCountDB!wmain(void)+0x14 [c:\book\code\chapter_08\refcountdb\main.cpp @ 70]
...
```

When debugging system code using only public symbols, finding the parameters to the functions in the call stack is slightly more involved because it requires you to understand the calling conventions used by each function. For a description of calling conventions and how to find function parameters when using the public symbols for Microsoft binaries, refer to the "Listing Parameters and Locals for System Code" section of Chapter 2, "Getting Started."

Displaying Local Variables

The *dv* command (or the View\Locals menu action in WinDbg) can be used to display local variables, though this command works only when you have private symbols for the modules you are debugging. In the example from the previous section, this command shows the following output when the target is stopped at the *AddRef* function:

```
0:000> dv
           this = 0x00c04020
           pObj = 0x00225478
       spObjRef = class ATL::CComPtr<CRefCountDatabase::CObjRef> { 00000000 }
```

Displaying Data Members of Native Types

One of the most important debugger commands is the *dt* ("dump type") command, which allows you to display the fields of C/C++ structures and classes and whose functionality can also be accessed in the View\Watch UI window. In the example from the previous section, for instance, you're able to use the debugger's knowledge of the type described by the symbols of the binary to automatically display the internal fields of the current class instance (the *this* object pointer). You can also use the *–r* option of the *dt* command to display the subtypes of each field recursively, as shown in the following debugger listing.

```
0:000> dt this
Local var @ ecx Type CRefCountDatabase*
   +0x000 m_objs           : ATL::CAtlMap<unsigned
long,ATL::CComPtr<CRefCountDatabase::CObjRef>,ATL::CElementTraits<unsigned
long>,ATL::CElementTraits<ATL::CComPtr<CRefCountDatabase::CObjRef> > >
   +0x030 m_cs             : _RTL_CRITICAL_SECTION
   +0x048 m_bInited        : 0n1
```

```
   =00c00000 MAX_CAPTURED_STACK_DEPTH : 0n9460301
0:000> dt -r this
Local var @ ecx Type CRefCountDatabase*
   +0x000 m_objs           : ATL::CAtlMap<unsigned
long,ATL::CComPtr<CRefCountDatabase::CObjRef>,ATL::CElementTraits<unsigned
long>,ATL::CElementTraits<ATL::CComPtr<CRefCountDatabase::CObjRef> > >
      +0x000 m_ppBins          : (null)
      +0x004 m_nElements       : 0
      +0x008 m_nBins           : 0x11
      +0x00c m_fOptimalLoad    : 0.75
      +0x010 m_fLoThreshold    : 0.25
      +0x014 m_fHiThreshold    : 2.25
      +0x018 m_nHiRehashThreshold : 0x26
      +0x01c m_nLoRehashThreshold : 0
      +0x020 m_nLockCount      : 0
      +0x024 m_nBlockSize      : 0xa
      +0x028 m_pBlocks         : (null)
      +0x02c m_pFree           : (null)
   +0x030 m_cs             : _RTL_CRITICAL_SECTION
...
```

When debugging system code in which the debugger isn't able to deduce the type information from the symbols, the *dt* command can also take an explicit type. For example, the following listing shows how you can display the PEB structure of the target process using the *$peb* pseudo-register as an alias to the virtual address where the structure is stored.

```
0:000> r @$peb
$peb=7ffd5000
0:000> dt ntdll!_PEB 7ffd5000
   +0x000 InheritedAddressSpace : 0 ''
   +0x001 ReadImageFileExecOptions : 0 ''
   +0x002 BeingDebugged    : 0x1 ''
...
   +0x010 ProcessParameters : 0x003d2ad8 _RTL_USER_PROCESS_PARAMETERS
```

The memory address of the type used in the *dt* command can appear either before or after the type itself. For example, the following commands are equivalent:

```
0:000> dt 0x003d2ad8 _RTL_USER_PROCESS_PARAMETERS
0:000> dt _RTL_USER_PROCESS_PARAMETERS 0x003d2ad8
```

Navigating Between Call Frames

You can navigate between call frames in a thread's call stack by using the View\Call Stack window in WinDbg and double-clicking on the frame you want to navigate to. Alternatively, you can get the frame number using the *kn* command and then use the *.frame* command to easily jump to the context (source code, local variables, and so on) of that frame, as illustrated in the following debugger listing.

```
0:000> kn
 # ChildEBP RetAddr
```

```
00 0014f718 00c0211a RefCountDB!CRefCountDatabase::AddRef
[c:\book\code\chapter_08\refcountdb\reftracker.h @ 174]
01 0014f724 00c021a0 RefCountDB!CRefCountDatabase_AddRef+0x14
[c:\book\code\chapter_08\refcountdb\reftracker.h @ 359]
02 0014f730 00c02217 RefCountDB!CIUnknownImplT<1>::CIUnknownImplT<1>+0x11
[c:\book\code\chapter_08\refcountdb\reftracker.h @ 39]
03 0014f738 00c02290 RefCountDB!CRefCountObject::CRefCountObject+0xa
04 0014f74c 00c022de RefCountDB!CMainApp::MainHR+0x1f
[c:\book\code\chapter_08\refcountdb\main.cpp @ 44]
05 0014f754 00c0246f RefCountDB!wmain+0x14 [c:\book\code\chapter_08\refcountdb\main.cpp @ 70]
...
0:000> $ Switch from frame #0 to the context of frame #2 in the call stack
0:000> .frame 2
02 0014f730 00c02217 RefCountDB!CIUnknownImplT<1>::CIUnknownImplT<1>+0x11
[c:\book\code\chapter_08\refcountdb\reftracker.h @ 39]
```

Notice how typing this last command also automatically changes the source code location in the WinDbg debugger to point to the function from frame #2 in the call stack (assuming that you set the source search path correctly in the debugger or that you're debugging the program on the same machine you compiled it on). This gives you an easy way to quickly navigate the source code of functions on the call stack. You can also use the *dv* command to display the locals of that call frame. Be aware, however, that the *dv* command might display incorrect values for the locals because the debugger might not be able to automatically derive those values from the stack for you. Chapter 2 has a detailed description of calling conventions and how they affect where locals and parameters are stored on different CPU architectures.

Listing Function Disassembly

You can view the full disassembly of a function using the *uf* command. This command works regardless of whether you have symbols or not for the containing binary, though you need to use the raw hexadecimal virtual address of the function in the absence of symbols.

```
0:000> vercommand
command line: '"c:\Program Files\Debugging Tools for Windows (x86)\windbg.exe"  notepad.exe'
0:000> uf notepad!WinMain
notepad!WinMain:
00051405 8bff            mov     edi,edi
00051407 55              push    ebp
00051408 8bec            mov     ebp,esp
...
```

You can also decode the immediate disassembly that follows a given memory location using the *u* command. The special "." parameter can be used as an alias to the memory location held by the current instruction pointer register.

```
0:000> k
ChildEBP RetAddr
001df93c 77740dc0 ntdll!LdrpDoDebuggerBreak+0x2c
001dfa9c 77726077 ntdll!LdrpInitializeProcess+0x11a9
001dfaec 77723663 ntdll!_LdrpInitialize+0x78
```

```
001dfafc 00000000 ntdll!LdrInitializeThunk+0x10
0:000> u .
ntdll!LdrpDoDebuggerBreak+0x2c:
777604f6 cc              int     3
777604f7 8975fc          mov     dword ptr [ebp-4],esi
...
```

Although the *u* command allows you to decode the disassembly immediately following a memory location, you might sometimes need to find the disassembly instructions before a given location in memory, in a sense decoding the disassembly backward. The debugger allows you to do that by using the *ub* variation of the command, which you will find handy when investigating debugger breaks. In those cases, this command allows you to quickly see what instructions were executed leading up to the break-in, though the decoding can sometimes be ambiguous because the stream of bytes can have different interpretations on several CPU architectures when walking backward. The debugger might end up picking the wrong interpretation, so you'll still need to use the *uf* command to verify the validity of the output from the *ub* command if you suspect it might be wrong.

```
0:000> ub .
ntdll!LdrpDoDebuggerBreak+0x19:
77d704e3 5e              pop     esi
77d704e4 56              push    esi
77d704e5 e87e5bfaff      call    ntdll!NtQueryInformationThread (77d16068)
77d704ea 3bc3            cmp     eax,ebx
77d704ec 7c1c            jl      ntdll!LdrpDoDebuggerBreak+0x40 (77d7050a)
...
0:000> $ Notice that the "uf" output matches the decoding from "ub" in this case
0:000> uf ntdll!LdrpDoDebuggerBreak
...
77d704e3 5e              pop     esi
77d704e4 56              push    esi
77d704e5 e87e5bfaff      call    ntdll!NtQueryInformationThread (77d16068)
77d704ea 3bc3            cmp     eax,ebx
77d704ec 7c1c            jl      ntdll!LdrpDoDebuggerBreak+0x40 (77d7050a)
...
```

Displaying and Modifying Memory and Register Values

You can view the memory and register values using the View\Memory and View\Registers windows in the WinDbg UI. Alternatively, you can use the *r* command to view the current values stored in the CPU registers and the *d** ("dump") commands to dump the values stored in memory. The most common suffixes used with the *d* command are listed in Table A-2.

TABLE A-2 Memory Display Suffixes

Suffix	Debugger Command	Description
d	*dd [address]*	Dump the memory after *[address]* as an array of DWORD (4-byte) values.
b	*db [address]*	Dump the memory after *[address]* as an array of bytes.

Suffix	Debugger Command	Description
p	*dp [address]*	Dump the memory after *[address]* as an array of pointer-sized values (4 bytes or 8 bytes, depending on the target CPU architecture).
u	*du [address]*	Display the memory following *[address]* as a Unicode string.
a	*da [address]*	Display the memory following *[address]* as an ASCII string.

In the following example, the *$peb* pseudo-register is used to reference the memory location of the current PEB structure, which is then displayed using the *dd* and *db* commands.

```
0:000> $ Dump the memory location where the PEB is stored as a series of DWORD values
0:000> dd @$peb
7ffd3000  08010000 ffffffff 00320000 770d7880
0:000> $ Dump the memory location where the PEB is stored as a series of bytes
0:000> db @$peb
7ffd3000  00 00 01 08 ff ff ff ff-00 00 32 00 80 78 0d 77  ..........2..x.w
```

You can also overwrite memory values directly in the WinDbg debugger by using one of the *e** ("edit") commands, with the same suffixes as the *d** commands. This is often useful when you want to alter the behavior of the program inside the debugger. The following example forcibly overwrites the *BeingDebugged* byte in the PEB structure of the target process, making it behave as if it wasn't being debugged by a user-mode debugger anymore. For more details on the *BeingDebugged* field of the PEB and its relevance in debugging situations, see Chapter 7, "Expert Debugging Tricks."

```
0:000> $ Overwrite the ntdll!_PEB.BeingDebugged field and set it to 0
0:000> $ Edit the byte at offset 2 from where the PEB structure starts in memory
0:000> eb @$peb+2 0
0:000> $ Ctrl-Break (Debug\Break) to break-in after 'g'...
0:000> $ Notice how the break-in gets delayed as if the app isn't being debugged anymore!
0:000> g
Break-in sent, waiting 30 seconds...
WARNING: Break-in timed out, suspending.
         This is usually caused by another thread holding the loader lock
```

Similarly, you can use the *f* command to fill a range of memory with values of your choice. (Note that this command is not related in any way to the *~[thread_num]f* command that's used to freeze threads in the user-mode debugger.) This can be useful when you need to edit more than just a few bytes. A practical example is when you need to disable a sequence of instructions in the debugger. The following listing shows how to insert NOP instructions (*0x90* in the *x86* and *x64* instruction sets) in place of a function call using the *f* command. Notice how the program in this listing never displays the "Hello World!" string it was meant to write to the console before exiting.

```
0:000> vercommand
command line: '"c:\Program Files\Debugging Tools for Windows (x86)\windbg.exe"
c:\book\code\chapter_02\HelloWorld\objfre_win7_x86\i386\HelloWorld.exe'
0:000> .symfix
0:000> .reload
0:000> bp HelloWorld!wmain
0:000> g
Breakpoint 0 hit
0:000> uf .
...
```

```
    28 004611b8 8b356c104600     mov     esi,dword ptr [HelloWorld!_imp__wprintf (0046106c)]
    28 004611be 68bc104600       push    offset HelloWorld!'string' (004610bc)
    28 004611c3 ffd6             call    esi
    35 004611c5 c70424d8104600   mov     dword ptr [esp],offset HelloWorld!'string' (004610d8)
...
0:000> du 004610bc
004610bc  "Hello World!."
0:000> f 0x004611c3 0x004611c4 0x90
Filled 0x2 bytes
0:000> uf .
HelloWorld!wmain [c:\book\code\chapter_02\helloworld\main.cpp @ 24]:
    24 004611b5 8bff             mov     edi,edi
    24 004611b7 56               push    esi
    28 004611b8 8b356c104600     mov     esi,dword ptr [HelloWorld!_imp__wprintf (0046106c)]
    28 004611be 68bc104600       push    offset HelloWorld!'string' (004610bc)
    28 004611c3 90               nop
    28 004611c4 90               nop
    35 004611c5 c70424d8104600   mov     dword ptr [esp],offset HelloWorld!'string' (004610d8)
    35 004611cc ffd6             call    esi
    35 004611ce 59               pop     ecx
    37 004611cf 33c0             xor     eax,eax
    37 004611d1 5e               pop     esi
    38 004611d2 c3               ret
0:000> $ Notice that "Hello World!" is not displayed on the console before the program exits!
0:000> g
```

Finally, you can also overwrite register values using the *r* debugger command. The following example modifies the return code (stored in the *eax* register on *x86*) from a Win32 API call to force a failure in the application code path that invokes that function.

```
0:000> bp kernel32!CreateFileW
0:000> g
Breakpoint 1 hit
kernel32!CreateFileW:
0:000> $ Shift-F11 to step-out and return to the caller (or 'gu')
0:000> gu
eax=00000001 ebx=757efed4 ecx=0025f32c edx=770470b4 esi=00000104 edi=75866620
0:000> $ eax is 1 (indicating TRUE was returned by the API); overwrite with FALSE (0)
0:000> r eax=0
0:000> r
eax=00000000 ebx=757efed4 ecx=0025f32c edx=770470b4 esi=00000104 edi=75866620
```

Ending a User-Mode Debugging Session

You can end a user-mode debugging session at any time using either the *q* command (if you intend to also terminate the target process at the same time) or, more often, using the *qd* command (which simply detaches the debugger and lets the target continue its execution without an active debugger).

```
0:000> $ Exit the debugging session, but let the target process continue running
0:000> qd
```

APPENDIX B

WinDbg Kernel-Mode Debugging Quick Start

This appendix presents an overview of the most common kernel-mode debugging tasks and how to accomplish them using the WinDbg debugger. Like Appendix A, which was a user-mode debugging reference, this appendix isn't meant to be an exhaustive list of all the kernel-mode debugger commands. Instead, it is written as a short summary you can use for jump-starting your kernel-mode debugging experiments without the complex details.

All the user-mode debugger commands from the previous appendix also work in the kernel-mode debugger, so you can apply them in exactly the same way, though the ~ and *lm* commands have different semantics when used during kernel debugging. There are also new commands that work only in the kernel debugger, as you'll shortly see.

Starting a Kernel-Mode Debugging Session

Refer to Chapter 2, "Getting Started," which has comprehensive coverage of the different ways to set up a kernel-mode debugging environment.

Switching Between CPU Contexts

When the target machine in a kernel-mode debugging session has more than one processor, you can change the processor context in the host kernel debugger using the ~ command. Unlike the user-mode debugger case where this command controls the current thread context within the target process, this command controls the current processor context in the kernel-mode debugger.

```
1: kd> $ Switch to processor #0 (first CPU)
1: kd> ~0
0: kd> $ Switch back to processor #1 (second CPU)
0: kd> ~1
1: kd> $ This machine has 2 processors only
1: kd> ~2
2 is not a valid processor number
```

Displaying Process Information

The *!process* extension command is one of the most important kernel-mode debugging commands. It's used to list processes on the system and display the information relevant to their associated executive process object. In its most common usage pattern, this command takes two arguments. The first argument is a process identifier, and the second argument is a bit mask used to control the level of detail in the command output.

```
1: kd> !process <Process> <Flags> [<Image Name>]
```

The output from this command returns important details about the process, such as its name, session ID, and process client ID (Cid), which is the same as the process ID (PID) displayed by the Microsoft Windows task manager. Depending on the flags used with the command, more detailed process information can also be obtained, such as the security access token of the process, its uptime, and the stack traces for the threads contained within the process.

When the first argument to the command is set to 0, the command conveniently displays the list of all the processes on the system, including the system "process," which represents the OS kernel/executive and isn't really a true user-mode process. (The Cid of this special "process" is always 4.)

```
1: kd> !process 0 0
**** NT ACTIVE PROCESS DUMP ****
PROCESS 88e92ae8  SessionId: none  Cid: 0004    Peb: 00000000  ParentCid: 0000
    DirBase: 00185000  ObjectTable: 8c801cb8  HandleCount: 608.
    Image: System
PROCESS 89fd9af0  SessionId: none  Cid: 0150    Peb: 7ffdd000  ParentCid: 0004
    DirBase: 3eec5020  ObjectTable: 90896e60  HandleCount:  30.
    Image: smss.exe
...
PROCESS 892958b0  SessionId: 1  Cid: 08d8    Peb: 7ffdd000  ParentCid: 0c80
    DirBase: 3eec56c0  ObjectTable: 8d84d758  HandleCount: 741.
    Image: explorer.exe
PROCESS 89165030  SessionId: 1  Cid: 1204    Peb: 7ffdf000  ParentCid: 10f0
    DirBase: 3eec5700  ObjectTable: b55676d8  HandleCount:   8.
    Image: HighCpuUsage.exe
```

You can also use *–1* as a convenient shortcut to the current process that was running on the processor at the time of the break-in.

```
1: kd> !process -1 0
PROCESS 89165030  SessionId: 1  Cid: 1204    Peb: 7ffdf000  ParentCid: 10f0
    Image: HighCpuUsage.exe
```

To find all instances of a given process name on the system, you can also append the name of the process to the command. The following listing, for instance, lists all the instances of the Windows Client/Server subsystem (*csrss.exe*) process.

```
1: kd> $ Each session (session 0, session 1, and so on) has its own csrss.exe process
1: kd> !process 0 0 csrss.exe
PROCESS 8a44f308  SessionId: 0  Cid: 01a4    Peb: 7ffdb000  ParentCid: 019c
    Image: csrss.exe
```

```
PROCESS 8a32ec78  SessionId: 1  Cid: 01e0    Peb: 7ffdf000  ParentCid: 01cc
    Image: csrss.exe
```

If you already know the process ID or the address of the process kernel object (*nt!_EPROCESS* structure), you can use those values to restrict the search to that particular process.

```
1: kd> !process 0x01e0 0
Searching for Process with Cid == 1e0
Cid handle table at 8c801238 with 917 entries in use
PROCESS 8a32ec78  SessionId: 1  Cid: 01e0    Peb: 7ffdf000  ParentCid: 01cc
    Image: csrss.exe
1: kd> $ Try the same command, except using the address of the executive object this time...
1: kd> !process 8a32ec78 0
PROCESS 8a32ec78  SessionId: 1  Cid: 01e0    Peb: 7ffdf000  ParentCid: 01cc
    Image: csrss.exe
```

The second argument of the command is particularly important because it allows you to control the level of detail displayed by the command. Using *0* (all bits clear) indicates the minimal detail level. Using *7*, on the other hand, indicates to the command that extended information about the process, including the stack traces for all of the threads that it contains, should be displayed. This last form is one of the most common ways of using the *!process* extension command in practice.

```
1: kd> !process 8a32ec78 7
PROCESS 8a32ec78  SessionId: 1  Cid: 01e0    Peb: 7ffdf000  ParentCid: 01cc
    Image: csrss.exe
    VadRoot 8a43a268 Vads 83 Clone 0 Private 322. Modified 844. Locked 0.
    DeviceMap 8c8050a0
    Token                             9899d268
    ElapsedTime                       2 Days 19:52:57.552
    UserTime                          00:00:00.000
    KernelTime                        00:00:00.046
...
        THREAD 8a57b8c8  Cid 01e0.01ec  Teb: 7ffdd000 ...
        ChildEBP RetAddr  Args to Child
        8dadbae8 828a7c25 8a57b8c8 807c9308 807c6120 nt!KiSwapContext+0x26
        8dadbb20 828a6523 8a57b988 8a57b8c8 8a57bafc nt!KiSwapThread+0x266
        8dadbb48 828a040f 8a57b8c8 8a57b988 00000000 nt!KiCommitThreadWait+0x1df
        8dadbbc0 828efc66 8a57bafc 00000011 8a57b801 nt!KeWaitForSingleObject+0x393
        8dadbbe8 82aaf0ce 8a57bafc 8a57b801 00000000 nt!AlpcpSignalAndWait+0x7b
...
```

Displaying Thread Information

As you just saw, the *!process* command can be used to get the virtual address of the kernel objects for each thread in the process. Once you have those addresses in hand, you can also use them with the *!thread* kernel-mode debugger command to directly display the thread information. As you see in the following listing, the *!thread* command outputs the same information displayed with the *!process* extension command when the second parameter has its extended information bits set (*7*), except that it displays only a single thread instead of all the threads in the process, so its output is usually easier to browse than that of the more verbose *!process [Process] 7* command.

```
1: kd> !thread 8a57b8c8
THREAD 8a57b8c8  Cid 01e0.01ec  Teb: 7ffdd000 Win32Thread: ffb21978 WAIT: (WrLpcReply) UserMode
Non-Alertable
    8a57bafc  Semaphore Limit 0x1
Waiting for reply to ALPC Message 9ddaae78 : queued at port 8a3486b0 : owned by process 8a5f0d40
Not impersonating
DeviceMap                 8c8050a0
Owning Process            8a32ec78       Image:         csrss.exe
Attached Process          N/A            Image:         N/A
Wait Start TickCount      15379785       Ticks: 2170 (0:00:00:33.906)
Context Switch Count      306            IdealProcessor: 0
UserTime                  00:00:00.000
KernelTime                00:00:00.000
Win32 Start Address 0x75c63ee1
Stack Init 8dadbfd0 Current 8dadbad0 Base 8dadc000 Limit 8dad9000 Call 0
Priority 15 BasePriority 15 UnusualBoost 0 ForegroundBoost 0 IoPriority 2 PagePriority 5
ChildEBP RetAddr  Args to Child
8dadbae8 828a7c25 8a57b8c8 807c9308 807c6120 nt!KiSwapContext+0x26 (FPO: [Uses EBP] [0,0,4])
8dadbb20 828a6523 8a57b988 8a57b8c8 8a57bafc nt!KiSwapThread+0x266
8dadbb48 828a040f 8a57b8c8 8a57b988 00000000 nt!KiCommitThreadWait+0x1df
8dadbbc0 828efc66 8a57bafc 00000011 8a57b801 nt!KeWaitForSingleObject+0x393
8dadbbe8 82aaf0ce 8a57bafc 8a57b801 00000000 nt!AlpcpSignalAndWait+0x7b
8dadbc0c 82aa514f 8a57b801 8dadbc78 00000000 nt!AlpcpReceiveSynchronousReply+0x27
...
```

The thread's Cid displayed by the debugger is again a unique identifier for the thread object. It's displayed by the debugger prefixed with the PID, followed by a dot and then the actual thread identifier relative to that process. (In the previous listing, the displayed thread has thread ID *0x1ec* in the process with PID *0x1e0*.)

Switching Process and Thread Contexts

You can switch the implicit thread context in the kernel-mode debugger using the *.thread* command (a close parallel to the *~[thread_number]s* command in the user-mode debugger). This allows you to also use the *k* command to dump the stack trace of the thread in question instead of the *!thread* extension command.

```
1: kd> .thread 8a57b8c8
Implicit thread is now 8a57b8c8
1: kd> k
  *** Stack trace for last set context - .thread/.cxr resets it
ChildEBP RetAddr
8dadbae8 828a7c25 nt!KiSwapContext+0x26
8dadbb20 828a6523 nt!KiSwapThread+0x266
8dadbb48 828a040f nt!KiCommitThreadWait+0x1df
8dadbbc0 828efc66 nt!KeWaitForSingleObject+0x393 ...
```

Similarly, you can use the *.process* command to set the implicit process context. The command takes the address of a kernel process object (the */p* option), and it can be useful when you need to inspect the state of other processes on the system. It also allows you to reload the user-mode symbols (the */r* option) for the target process used in the command.

```
1: kd> !process 0 0 csrss.exe
PROCESS 8a44f308  SessionId: 0  Cid: 01a4    Peb: 7ffdb000  ParentCid: 019c
    Image: csrss.exe
PROCESS 8a32ec78  SessionId: 1  Cid: 01e0    Peb: 7ffdf000  ParentCid: 01cc
    Image: csrss.exe
1: kd> .process /r /p 0x8a32ec78
Implicit process is now 8a32ec78
.cache forcedecodeuser done
Loading User Symbols
..................
1: kd> !process 0x8a32ec78 7
```

Finally, the */i* option of the *.process* command can be used to cause an *intrusive* process switch and change the default process context in the debugger. This command requires the target to run before immediately breaking back into the host kernel debugger with the default process context changed to the process specified in the *.process /i* command.

```
1: kd> !process -1 0
PROCESS 89165030  SessionId: 1  Cid: 1204    Peb: 7ffdf000  ParentCid: 10f0
    Image: HighCpuUsage.exe
1: kd> $ Switch over to the context of session #1's csrss.exe instance
1: kd> .process /i 0x8a32ec78
You need to continue execution (press 'g' <enter>) for the context
to be switched. When the debugger breaks in again, you will be in
the new process context.
1: kd> g
Break instruction exception - code 80000003 (first chance)
1: kd> $ Verify that the current process context is indeed that of csrss.exe after the break-in
1: kd> !process -1 0
PROCESS 8a32ec78  SessionId: 1  Cid: 01e0    Peb: 7ffdf000  ParentCid: 01cc
    Image: csrss.exe
```

Listing Loaded Modules and Their Version

The *lm* ("list modules") command can be used to display information about the modules on the system, including drivers as well as user-mode executable and dynamic-link library (DLL) images. To list the information about a user-mode process or DLL, however, you might first need to reload the user-mode symbols for their target process:

```
0: kd> !process 0 0 explorer.exe
PROCESS 892958b0  SessionId: 1  Cid: 08d8    Peb: 7ffdd000  ParentCid: 0c80
    Image: explorer.exe
0: kd> .process /r /p 892958b0
Implicit process is now 892958b0
Loading User Symbols..................
0: kd> lmv m explorer
start    end        module name
00350000 005d0000   Explorer   (deferred)
    Image path: C:\Windows\Explorer.EXE
...
    FileDescription:  Windows Explorer
    LegalCopyright:   © Microsoft Corporation. All rights reserved.
```

Alternatively, you can use the */i* switch of the *.process* debugger command to perform an intrusive switch, and then use the *.reload* command with the */user* switch to reload the user-mode symbols in the default process context after the machine switches over to the target process.

```
0: kd> .process /i 892958b0
0: kd> g
Break instruction exception - code 80000003 (first chance)
0: kd> .reload /user
Loading User Symbols................
0: kd> lmv m explorer
start    end        module name
00350000 005d0000   Explorer   (deferred)
    Image path: C:\Windows\Explorer.EXE
...
```

Finally, note that there is also a command in the kernel-mode debugger you can use if you want to obtain the list of DLLs loaded by a given user-mode process. This is the closest equivalent to what the *lm* command actually does in the user-mode debugger. The command in question is the *!dlls* debugger extension command, which is demonstrated in the following listing.

```
1: kd> !process 0 0 explorer.exe
PROCESS 892958b0  SessionId: 1  Cid: 08d8    Peb: 7ffdd000  ParentCid: 0c80
    Image: explorer.exe
1: kd> .process /p 892958b0
Implicit process is now 892958b0
.cache forcedecodeuser done
1: kd> !dlls
0x001a1d90: C:\Windows\Explorer.EXE
      Base   0x00350000  EntryPoint  0x0037a8df  Size        0x00280000
      Flags  0x00004000  LoadCount   0x0000ffff  TlsIndex    0x00000000
             LDRP_ENTRY_PROCESSED
0x001a1e10: C:\Windows\SYSTEM32\ntdll.dll
      Base   0x77aa0000  EntryPoint  0x00000000  Size        0x0013d000
      Flags  0x80004004  LoadCount   0x0000ffff  TlsIndex    0x00000000
             LDRP_IMAGE_DLL
             LDRP_ENTRY_PROCESSED
...
```

Setting Code (Software) Breakpoints Inside Kernel-Mode Code

Setting a breakpoint in kernel-mode code is straightforward and can be done in the same way that you set breakpoints under the user-mode debugger.

```
1: kd> x nt!*insertprocess*
82abca67          nt!PspInsertProcess = <no type information>
0: kd> bp nt!PspInsertProcess
0: kd> g
Breakpoint 0 hit
0: kd> $ Disable the new breakpoint (breakpoint #0)
0: kd> bd 0
0: kd> g
```

Setting Code (Software) Breakpoints Inside User-Mode Code

Setting breakpoints in user-mode code from the kernel-mode debugger is slightly more involved because user-mode virtual addresses are interpreted relative to the process that was active at the time of the debugger break-in. To set a breakpoint in user-mode code from a different process, you need to first transition over to that process context by using the */i* switch of the *.process* command. Once you break back into the debugger, you can then use the *bp* command to set the desired breakpoint. The following example shows how to set a breakpoint in the system code inside the service control manager (SCM) process and break into the debugger every time a new Windows service is started on the target machine.

```
0: kd> x services!*
                 ^ Couldn't resolve 'x services'
0: kd> !process 0 0 services.exe
PROCESS 8a59ed40  SessionId: 0  Cid: 0248    Peb: 7ffd4000  ParentCid: 01d4
    Image: services.exe
0: kd> .process /i 8a59ed40
0: kd> g
Break instruction exception - code 80000003 (first chance)
0: kd> .reload /user
Loading User Symbols..............
0: kd> x services!*startservice*
004388ac          services!ScStartService = <no type information>
...
0: kd> $ Break into the debugger each time a new Windows service is started
0: kd> bp services!ScStartService
0: kd> g
```

Setting Data (Hardware) Breakpoints

You can set all three types of data breakpoints (execution, read, and write) during your kernel-mode debugging sessions by using the *ba* command and the same syntax as in the user-mode debugging case. The only difference is that you can set global breakpoints that would be hit in any process on the target machine. Chapter 5, "Beyond the Basics," shows several practical illustrations for how to use this technique in kernel-debugging investigations. As a simple application, the following listing shows how you can set a read data breakpoint so that you can trace all the kernel code paths on the system that access the NT global flag value.

```
0: kd> x nt!NtGlobalFlag
829bd928          nt!NtGlobalFlag = 0x40400
0: kd> ba r4 nt!NtGlobalFlag
0: kd> g
Breakpoint 0 hit
1: kd> !process -1 0
PROCESS 86abd030  SessionId: 0  Cid: 06ac    Peb: 7ffd6000  ParentCid: 0248
    Image: vmicsvc.exe
1: kd> .reload /user
1: kd> k
ChildEBP RetAddr
```

```
92b85aa8 82a78c66 nt!ObpInitializeHandleTableEntry+0x1c
92b85b00 82a79288 nt!ObpCreateHandle+0x29c
92b85ca0 82a791af nt!ObInsertObjectEx+0xd0
92b85cbc 82a967d1 nt!ObInsertObject+0x1e
92b85d18 828931fa nt!NtCreateEvent+0xba
92b85d18 770170b4 nt!KiFastCallEntry+0x12a
00c3fd14 770155b4 ntdll!KiFastSystemCallRet
00c3fd18 751f78c6 ntdll!ZwCreateEvent+0xc
00c3fd58 751f7916 KERNELBASE!CreateEventExW+0x6e
00c3fd70 00d5b5d8 KERNELBASE!CreateEventW+0x27
...
```

Notice that this breakpoint is hit a lot as the various system components with NT global flag debugging hooks try to read that global value and determine if their corresponding bits were set. Once you no longer need this breakpoint, you can use the *bd* or *bc* command to disable or clear (delete) it, respectively.

```
1: kd> bd 0
1: kd> g
```

Ending a Kernel-Mode Debugging Session

You can end the kernel-mode debugging session at any point by simply exiting the debugger process on the host machine. Note, however, that you should first let the target machine continue running (using the *g* command) before you do that; otherwise, the target will remain frozen and can be unblocked only by re-attaching the host kernel debugger and issuing the *g* command.

Index

Symbols and Numbers

A

B

C

D

E

F

G

H

I

J

K

L

N

O

P

Q

R

S

T

U

V

W

X

Y

Z

About the Author

TARIK SOULAMI, a principal development lead on the Windows Fundamentals Team, has more than 10 years of experience designing and developing system-level software at Microsoft. Before joining the Windows team, Tarik spent several years on the Common Language Runtime (CLR) Team, where he helped shape early releases of the Microsoft .NET framework.